DECISIONS
ON THE RULES OF GOLF
2012–2013

The USGA conducts the U.S. Open, U.S. Women's Open and U.S. Senior Open, as well as 10 national amateur championships, two state team championships and international matches. Together with The R&A, the USGA governs the game worldwide, jointly administering the Rules of Golf, Rules of Amateur Status, Equipment Standards and World Amateur Golf Rankings. The USGA's working jurisdiction comprises the United States, its territories and Mexico.

The USGA is a global leader in the development and support of sustainable golf course management practices. It serves as a primary steward for the game's history and funds an ongoing "For the Good of the Game" grants program. Additionally, the USGA's Course Rating and Handicap systems are used on six continents in more than 50 countries.

For more information about the USGA, visit www.usga.org.

DECISIONS
ON THE RULES OF GOLF
2012–2013

THE
UNITED STATES
GOLF ASSOCIATION
AND
THE R&A

GENDER

In the Rules of Golf and the Decisions on the Rules of Golf, the gender used in relation to any person is understood to include both genders.

For more information on the USGA®, contact:
United States Golf Association®
Golf House
Far Hills, New Jersey 07931
T 908.234.2300

Printed in the United States of America

FSC

MIX
Paper from
responsible sources
FSC® C021247
www.fsc.org

A GUIDE TO DECISIONS ON THE RULES OF GOLF

Each year, the United States Golf Association (USGA) and the R&A receive thousands of inquiries regarding clarification of the Rules of Golf. In order to help millions of golfers around the world better understand how these detailed Rules are applied and interpreted, the USGA and the R&A develop the comprehensive Decisions on the Rules of Golf. The format is geared towards questions and answers and is designed to be used as a reference for golf administrators and those with an interest in the Rules of the game.

Since 1951, the USGA and the R&A have been meeting regularly in order to establish a uniform code of Rules. However, each year brings about new questions that are not specifically addressed in the Rules of Golf, requiring Committees from both organizations to meet to discuss these new questions and arrive at a decision with which both the USGA and the R&A agree. Many of these agreed positions then find their way into the Decisions on the Rules of Golf, which is amended every two years in order to keep up with the ever evolving game of golf.

The purpose of the Decisions on the Rules of Golf is to clarify matters that may not be entirely clear from the Rules of Golf. The Rules of Golf should be consulted in the first instance, but if a question cannot be answered by reference to the Rules, the solution may be found in the "Decisions book."

The Decisions book also contains the full text of the Rules of Golf. The Rules of Golf are amended every four years and the latest edition of the Rules became effective on January 1, 2012.

In the Decisions book, Decisions are listed under the Rule number and sub section that is considered most pertinent to the facts of the case. For example, if a Decision relates to the removal of a loose impediment in a hazard, it will be listed under Rule 13-4 (Ball in Hazard; Prohibited Actions) as 13-4/#.

Decisions that apply generally to an entire Rule may simply be listed by the Rule number, followed by a number. For example, if a Decision relates to whether a ball at rest is deemed to have moved, it will be listed under Rule 18 (Ball at Rest Moved) as 18/#.

If a Decision has been introduced for the first time to the latest edition of the book, the word "New" is contained in parenthesis at the end of the Decision. If an existing Decision has been amended in the latest edition of the book, the word "Revised" is contained in parenthesis at the end of the Decision. In addition, Decisions are sometimes withdrawn because they are no longer necessary, or re-numbered so that they can be more easily accessed by the reader. For ease of reference, all the amendments to the previous edition of the book are contained in the section entitled "Amendments to the 2010–2011 Edition."

Where a Decision number is listed as "Reserved" this means that this Decision has been withdrawn at some point in the past but, rather than re-number the Decisions following it, the number is held in reserve until a new Decision is introduced and given the vacant number.

The best method for consistently and efficiently locating Decisions that are relevant to the query that has arisen is through use of the Decisions book Index. For guidance on how best to utilize the Index please refer to the "Introduction to the Index" on page 582.

GENERAL

The USGA and R&A have agreed to a two-year revision cycle for the "Decisions on the Rules of Golf." Therefore, no existing Decisions will be revised or withdrawn and no new Decisions will be added to the book until the next edition is published in 2014. The Rules of Golf will not be amended until 2016.

PRINCIPAL CHANGES INTRODUCED IN THE 2012 CODE
Definitions

Addressing the Ball
The Definition is amended so that a player has addressed the ball simply by grounding his club immediately in front of or behind the ball, regardless of whether or not he has taken his stance. Therefore, the Rules generally no longer provide for a player addressing the ball in a hazard. (See also related change to Rule 18-2b)

Rules

Rule 1-2.   Exerting Influence on Movement of Ball or Altering Physical Conditions
The Rule is amended to establish more clearly that, if a player intentionally takes an action to influence the movement of a ball or to alter physical conditions affecting the playing of a hole in a way that is not permitted by the Rules, Rule 1-2 applies only when the action is not already covered in another Rule. For example, a player improving the lie of his ball is in breach of Rule 13-2 and therefore that Rule would apply, whereas a player intentionally improving the lie of a fellow-competitor's ball is not a situation covered by Rule 13-2 and, therefore, is governed by Rule 1-2.

Rule 6-3a.   Time of Starting
Rule 6-3a is amended to provide that the penalty for starting late, but within five minutes of the starting time, is reduced from disqualification to loss of the first hole in match play or two strokes at the first hole in stroke play. Previously this penalty reduction could be introduced as a condition of competition.

Rule 12-1.   Seeing Ball; Searching for Ball
Rule 12-1 is reformatted for clarity. In addition, it is amended to (i) permit a player to search for his ball anywhere on the course when it may be covered by sand and to clarify that there is no penalty if the ball is moved in these circumstances, and (ii) apply a penalty of one stroke under Rule 18-2a if a player moves his ball in a hazard when searching for it when it is believed to be covered by loose impediments.

Rule 13-4.   Ball in Hazard; Prohibited Actions
Exception 2 to Rule 13-4 is amended to permit a player to smooth sand or soil in a hazard at any time, including before playing from that hazard, provided it is for the sole purpose of caring for the course and Rule 13-2 is not breached.

Rule 18-2b. Ball Moving After Address
A new Exception is added that exonerates the player from penalty if his ball moves after it has been addressed when it is known or virtually certain that he did not cause the ball to move. For example, if it is a gust of wind that moves the ball after it has been addressed, there is no penalty and the ball is played from its new position.

Rule 19-1.   Ball in Motion Deflected or Stopped; By Outside Agency
The note is expanded to prescribe the various outcomes when a ball in motion has been deliberately deflected or stopped by an outside agency.

Rule 20-7c. Playing from Wrong Place; Stroke Play
Note 3 is amended so that if a player is to be penalized for playing from a wrong place, in most cases the penalty will be limited to two strokes, even if another Rule has been breached prior to his making the stroke.

Appendix IV
A new Appendix is added to prescribe general regulations for the design of devices and other equipment, such as tees, gloves and distance measuring devices.

NEW DECISIONS

1-2/0.7   Meaning of "Sole Purpose of Caring for the Course"

1-2/3   Breaking Bush in Area into Which Ball May Roll After Drop

5-1/1.7   Status of Ball to Be Removed from List of Conforming Golf Balls

6-3a/5   Players Start Early

13-2/0.5   Meaning of "Improve" in Rule 13-2

13-4/9   Player Creates and Smoothes Footprints in Bunker Prior to Making Stroke

13-4/9.5   Loose Impediment in Bunker Moved When Player Smoothes Sand in Bunker for Sole Purpose of Caring for Course

14-3/0.7   Player Obtains Distance Information Measured with Electronic Device

14-3/17   Player Listens to Music or Broadcast During Round

14-5/2   Making Stroke at Oscillating Ball

16-1b/4   Ball Lifted from Putting Green by Opponent or Fellow-Competitor While Player's Ball in Motion

18-2b/2   Ball Addressed in Hazard

18-2b/5   Ball Moves When Club Rested on Grass Immediately Behind Ball

26-1/1.3   When is it Necessary to Go Forward to Establish "Virtual Certainty"

33-8/37.5   Local Rule for Water Hazard with Bunker Adjacent

33-8/39.5   Local Rule Deeming Partially Grass-Covered Wall of Bunker to Be Part of Bunker

34-3/1.3   Competitor Incorrectly Advised to Cancel Stroke

REVISED DECISIONS

1-3/2   Agreement to Concede Short Putts
Answer expanded to clarify that players must be aware that they are agreeing to waive a Rule in order to be in breach of Rule 1-3.

1-4/12   Player Breaches Rules More Than Once; Whether Multiple Penalties Should Be Applied
Principles amended for clarity and additional examples added.

4-1/1   Groove and Punch Mark Specifications Effective January 1, 2010 Including Condition of Competition
New first paragraph added for clarity.

4-3/2   Meaning of "Repair"
Expanded to clarify that the term "repair" contemplates the club being comprised of the same grip, shaft and clubhead after the repair as it had prior to the damage occurring.

4-4a/5   Competitor Inadvertently Uses and Thereafter Carries Fellow-Competitor's Club
Expanded to address the case where the competitor continues to carry his fellow-competitor's club after using it in error.

4-4a/6   Excess Club Put in Player's Golf Bag
Amended to provide clarification on when a player is penalized after a club is added to his bag by mistake by another player prior to starting the round.

4-4a/15   Assembly of Club Components During Stipulated Round
Expanded for clarity.

8-1/2   Exchanging Distance Information
Second paragraph deleted in view of the introduction of new Decision 14-3/0.7.

9-3/1   Competitor in Hole-by-Hole Play-Off Gives Wrong Information
Amended so that a competitor does not incur a penalty for lifting his ball as a result of being provided wrong information by his fellow-competitor during a stroke-play hole-by-hole play-off.

13-2/32   Improving Line of Play by Removing Stone from Wall
Expanded to clarify why individual stones may not be removed from a stone wall.

15-3b/2   Play of Two Different Wrong Balls Between Strokes with Ball in Play
Amended to provide for a penalty of four strokes and to reference Decisions 1-4/12 and 1-4/13.

17-2/2   Flagstick Attended by Opponent or Fellow-Competitor Without Authority While Player's Ball in Motion
Expanded to clarify when it is deemed that removing the flagstick "might have influenced the movement of the ball" in breach of Rule 17-2.

19-2/10   Ball Stopped or Deflected by Rake Held by Player's Caddie
Amended to provide that the player is penalized under Rule 19-2.

20-2b/2   Measuring Club-Lengths
Expanded to clarify that a player may not measure through a natural undulation of the ground.

20-3b/8   Loose Impediment Affecting Lie of Ball Moved
Answer expanded to clarify that, although loose impediments may affect the lie of the ball, they are not part of the lie.

20-7c/3   Ball Believed to Be Lost in Bunker; Competitor Drops Another Ball in Bunker and Plays It; Original Ball Then Found Outside Bunker
Answer amended to clarify that the ball was in play when it was dropped.

21/1   Removing Paint from Ball
Amended to refer to paint rather than lime.

26-1/1   Meaning of "Known or Virtually Certain"
Expanded to further clarify the term "virtual certainty."

27/17   Competitor Plays Out of Turn Other Than from Teeing Ground and Puts Another Ball into Play at Spot of Previous Stroke
Answer amended to refer to the Definition of "Lost Ball."

30-2/1   Player Plays Out of Turn from Tee in Three-Ball Match
Amended for clarity.

33-7/4.5   Competitor Unaware of Penalty Returns Wrong Score; Whether Waiving or Modifying Disqualification Penalty Justified
Amended to provide for exceptional circumstances where a Committee would be justified in waiving the penalty of disqualification under Rule 6-6d for returning a score lower than that actually taken due to failure to include a penalty that the competitor did not know he had incurred.

33-8/27   Local Rule Providing Relief Without Penalty from Bunker Filled with Casual Water
Expanded to provide recommended wording for the Local Rule.

RE-NUMBERED DECISIONS

1-2/9   Player Presses Ball into Surface of Putting Green (Formerly 18-2a/6)

1-2/10   Player Wraps Towel Around Self or Places Towel on Cactus Before Taking Stance (Formerly 1-4/11.5)

10-1a/3   Players Agree Not to Tee Off in Prescribed Order to Save Time (Formerly 1-3/1)

DECISIONS REVISED DUE TO RULES CHANGES AND DECISIONS WITH MINOR REVISIONS

1-2/0.5   Serious Breach of Rule 1-2

1-2/1.5   Competitor Alters Line of Play of Fellow-Competitor

1-2/2   Shielding Line of Putt from Wind

1-2/3.5   Player Repairs Hole After Holing Out But Before Opponent, Fellow-Competitor or Partner Holes Out

1-2/4   Player Jumps Close to Hole to Cause Ball to Fall into Hole

1-2/5.5   Player Purposely Stops or Deflects Ball; Where Next Stroke Must Be Played from

1-2/7   Player Purposely Deflects Partner's Ball in Motion on Putting Green

1-2/8   Player Presses Down Turf as Ball Is Rolling Towards Area

1-4/9   Bird's Nest Interfering with Stroke

1-4/10   Dangerous Situation; Rattlesnake or Bees Interfere with Play

2-4/15   Player Concedes Match After Winning It When Opponent Lodges Invalid Claim Regarding Strokes Taken

2-4/16   Valid Timely Claim Made After Concession of Match

2-5/2   Procedure for a Valid Claim

2-5/3   Player Lifts Ball Before Holing Out; Opponent Then Picks Up His Ball Claiming Player Loses Hole

3-3/2   Second Ball Played Despite Adverse Ruling

3-3/9   Second Ball Played in Match Play

5-3/3   Ball Not Unfit for Play Deemed Unfit

5-3/8   Opponent or Fellow-Competitor Disputes Player's Claim That Ball Is Unfit for Play

6-3a/1.5   Exceptional Circumstances Which Warrant Waiving of Disqualification Penalty Under Rule 6-3a

6-3a/2   Time of Starting; All Competitors Must Be Present

6-3a/2.5   Meaning of "Time of Starting"

6-3a/3   Time of Starting; Both Players in Match are Late

6-8a/6   Match Discontinued by Agreement Due to Rain; One Player Subsequently Wishes to Resume; Opponent Refuses on Ground Course Unplayable

10-2c/2   Competitors in Stroke Play Agree to Play Out of Turn But Not for Purpose of Giving One of Them an Advantage

12-1/3   Top of Ball in Hazard Covered by Leaves But Part of Ball Visible from Another Angle

12-1/5   Player Kicks Ball While Probing for It in Water in Water Hazard

13-2/14.5   Branch Broken on Backswing and Swing Discontinued

13-2/16   Stake Supporting Tree Broken in Attempt to Remove It

13-2/29   Worsening and Then Restoring Line of Play

13-2/35   Removal of Dew or Frost

13-4/7   Touching Casual Water in Bunker with Club

13-4/10   Referee Enters Bunker; Whether Player May Smooth Footprints

13-4/11   Smoothing Footprints Made in Search for Ball in Bunker Before Playing Stroke from Bunker

13-4/12   Ball Touched Accidentally with Club in Hazard But Not Moved

13-4/16   Removal of Loose Impediment in Water Hazard Covering Wrong Ball

13-4/19   Condition of Bunker Altered by First Player to Play from It

13-4/35.8   Player Deems Ball Unplayable in Bunker, Announces His Intention to Proceed Under Rule 28a Outside Bunker and Then Rakes Bunker on New Line of Play

14-2/2   Player Holds Umbrella Over Own Head When Playing Stroke

14-2/2.5   Player Positions Bag for Purpose of Providing Shade for Ball

14-2/3   Caddie Shields Player from Sun During Stroke

14-3/14   Electronic Instrument Used to Find Ball

14-6/1   Ball Moves in Water in Water Hazard After Stance Taken

16/4   Hole-Liner Not Sunk Deep Enough

16-1a/6   Damaged Hole; Procedure for Player

16-1a/10   Loose Impediments Brushed Along Line of Putt Rather Than to Side

16-1a/13	Line of Putt Damaged Accidentally by Opponent, Fellow-Competitor or Their Caddies
16-1a/17	Ball Lifted on Putting Green Placed Ahead of Ball-Marker and Then Moved Back to Original Position
16-1b/1	Ball on Putting Green Lifted Because Player Feared Ball Might Move
16-1b/2	Ball Lifted from Putting Green; Ball Replaced While Another Ball in Motion But Then Lifted Because Moving Ball Might Strike It
16-1b/3	Ball Lifted from Putting Green; Ball Replaced While Another Ball in Motion Subsequently Deflects Ball
17/4	Adjustment of Flagstick; Player's Rights
17-3/2	Opponent or Fellow-Competitor Attending Flagstick for Player Fails to Remove It; Player's Ball Strikes Flagstick
18-2a/9	Ball Lifted Without Authority Dropped Instead of Being Replaced
18-2b/3	Ball Moves After Player Has Taken Stance in Bunker
18-2b/4	Ball Moves After Player Grounds Club Short Distance Behind Ball But Before Grounding Club Immediately Behind Ball
18-2b/5.5	Placing Clubhead on Ground in Front of Ball When Addressing
18-2b/5.7	When Player Who Putts "Side-Saddle" Has Addressed Ball
18-2b/7	Ball Moves After Player Addresses It and Then Steps Away
18-2b/11	Ball Moved by Another Agency After Address
18-2b/12	Ball Moves After Address and Is Stopped by Player's Club
19-1/4.1	Ball Deliberately Deflected or Stopped Through the Green by Spectator
19-1/5	Ball Deliberately Deflected or Stopped on Putting Green by Fellow-Competitor
19-2/1	Ball Stopped by Player's Foot Moves When Foot Removed
19-2/1.5	Ball Moves Prior to Address and Is Accidentally Stopped by Player's Club; Player Removes Club and Ball Moves Away
20-1/19	Placing Object Marking Position of Ball Other Than Behind Ball
20-2a/3	Ball Dropped in Improper Manner and in Wrong Place
20-2a/5	Caddie Holds Back Tree Branch to Prevent Branch from Deflecting Dropped Ball
20-2c/2	Ball Dropped Third Time When Placement Required After Second Drop

20-2c/4   Caddie Stops Dropped Ball Before It Comes to Rest; When Penalty Incurred

20-3a/0.5   Whether Player Himself Must Place or Replace Ball

20-3b/4   Lie of Ball Through the Green Altered; Original Lie of Ball Known But Spot Where Ball Lay Not Determinable

20-3b/5   Lie of Ball in Rough Altered by Outside Agency; Original Lie of Ball Not Known and Spot Where Ball Lay Not Determinable

20-3b/6   Lie of Ball in Bunker Altered; Original Lie of Ball Known But Spot Where Ball Lay Not Determinable

20-4/2   Ball Lifted from Putting Green and Placed by Caddie Behind Marker

22/7   Ball Assisting Fellow-Competitor on Putting Green; Procedure for Referee If Competitor Does Not Lift Ball

23-1/10   Removal of Loose Impediments Affecting Player's Play

24-2b/17   Obstruction Interferes with Abnormal Stroke; Abnormal Stroke Reasonable in Circumstances

24-2b/18   Obstruction Interferes with Abnormal Stroke; Abnormal Stroke Not Reasonable in Circumstances

24-2b/19   Stroke at Ball Impracticable Due to Interference by Immovable Obstruction and Casual Water

25-1b/19   Ball Lies on Mound Made by Burrowing Animal; Impracticable to Make Stroke Due to Bush

25-1b/20   Stance Interfered with by Burrowing Animal Hole; Impracticable to Make Stroke Because of Other Condition

25-1b/25.5   Application of Exception to Rule 25-1b When Ball Lies Underground in Burrowing Animal Hole

26/6   Ball Assumed to Be in Water Hazard Found Outside Hazard After Another Ball Played Under Stroke-and-Distance Procedure

26-1/4   Ball Played Under Water Hazard Rule Without Knowledge or Virtual Certainty That Original Ball in Hazard; Original Ball Then Found in Hazard

30-3f/4   Wrong Information Given by Player Out of Contention in Four-Ball Match

30-3f/13   Partner Stands on Extension of Player's Line of Play Behind Ball

31-2/1   Absent Player Joins Partner After Fellow-Competitor Plays from Teeing Ground But Before Partner Plays

33-7/5   Play of Wrong Ball Not Rectified on Advice of Referee

33-8/4   Local Rule for Events in Which Motorized Golf Carts Permitted

34-3/1.5   Committee Error and Scoring in Stroke Play

34-3/2   Committee Does Not Penalize Player in Breach of Pace of Play
            Condition Believing Player Had Already Lost Hole

34-3/3   Player in Match Makes Stroke from Wrong Place Due
            to Incorrect Ruling; Procedure for Player When Error is
            Discovered

34-3/3.3   Competitor in Stroke Play Makes Stroke from Wrong Place
            Due to Incorrect Ruling; Procedure for Competitor When
            Error is Discovered

34-3/3.5   Player Lifts Ball Without Authority Due to Misunderstanding
            Referee's Instructions

34-3/3.7   Player Incorrectly Advised to Continue with Provisional Ball

34-3/7   Player Proceeds on Basis of Ruling; Subsequent Facts Prove
            Ruling to Be Incorrect

34-3/8   Player Proceeds on Basis of Ruling; Player's Version of Facts
            Subsequently Found to Be Incorrect

34-3/9   Resolution of Questions of Fact; Referee and Committee
            Responsibility

WITHDRAWN DECISIONS

1-2/3.8   Player Jumps Close to Hole to Cause Ball to Drop; Ball Does
            Not Move

1-2/4.5   Player Leaves Putt Short and Instinctively Throws Putter at Ball

1-2/6   Player Removes Loose Impediment Affecting Lie of Opponent
            or Fellow-Competitor in Hazard

2-4/18   Defaulting Player Plays Informal Match with Opponent and Wins

2-5/1   Player's Obligation Re Lodging Claim

3-2/3   Competitor in Error Does Not Hole Out; Error Corrected
            Before Playing from Next Tee

4-4a/3   Competitor Withdraws During Round and Puts His Clubs in
            Fellow-Competitor's Bag

8-1/1   Seeking Information About Length of Hole

12-1/1   Searching with Clubhead for Ball Covered by Sand in Bunker

12-1/2   Ball Covered by Sand in Bunker Removed from Buried Lie
            During Search

13-2/22   Knocking Down Leaves with Practice Swing

13-2/32.5   Improving Line of Play by Removing Part of Fence

13-4/0.7	Player Rakes Bunker When Ball Lies in Another Bunker
13-4/23	When Stance Taken in Bunker
13-4/32	Club Touches Partially Embedded Pine Needle on Backswing in Bunker
14/6	Ball Popped Up Swung at in Disgust
14-2/4	Caddie Inadvertently Stands on Extension of Line of Play Behind Ball
16-1e/2	Player Plays from Stance Astride Extension of Line of Putt Behind Ball
16-2/3	Casting Shadow on Ball Overhanging Hole
17-1/6	Attended Flagstick Placed on Ground Subsequently Lifted
17-1/8	Removed Flagstick Being Held by Opponent or Fellow-Competitor Subsequently Moved
18-1/11	Ball Moved by Wind or Casual Water While Play Suspended
18-2a/5	Ball in Hazard Moves After Loose Impediment Outside Hazard Moved
18-2b/2	Ball Moves After Stance Taken in Hazard Without Club (Note: Replaced by New Decision)
18-2b/5	When Club Grounded in Grass (Note: Replaced by New Decision)
18-2b/6	Ball Perched on Heather Moves When Club Rested on Heather
19-1/4	Ball Played from Putting Green Deliberately Deflected or Stopped by Spectator
19-1/10	Ball in Motion After Stroke on Putting Green Deflected by Ball Played at Another Hole
19-5/3	Competitor's Ball Played on Putting Green Deflected by Balls of Two Fellow-Competitors
20-1/10	Ball-Marker Moved Off Green by Wind or Casual Water While Play Suspended
24/10	Paved Area
24/16	Opponent or Fellow-Competitor Removes Movable Obstruction Affecting Player's Play
26/4	Man-Made Reservoir
29/5.5	Raking Sand in Bunker After Partner Fails to Extricate Ball but Before Stroke; Foursome Match
33/5	Distance Markers

CONTENTS

SECTION

I	ETIQUETTE	3
II	DEFINITIONS	6
III	THE RULES OF PLAY	17

THE GAME

Rule 1	The Game	17
Rule 2	Match Play	37
Rule 3	Stroke Play	57

CLUBS AND THE BALL

Rule 4	Clubs	68
Rule 5	The Ball	86

PLAYER'S RESPONSIBILITIES

Rule 6	The Player	93
Rule 7	Practice	127
Rule 8	Advice; Indicating Line of Play	135
Rule 9	Information as to Strokes Taken	144

ORDER OF PLAY

Rule 10	Order of Play	153

TEEING GROUND

Rule 11	Teeing Ground	160

PLAYING THE BALL

Rule 12	Searching for and Identifying Ball	167
Rule 13	Ball Played as it Lies	171
Rule 14	Striking the Ball	207
Rule 15	Substituted Ball; Wrong Ball	224

THE PUTTING GREEN

Rule 16	The Putting Green	237
Rule 17	The Flagstick	255

BALL MOVED, DEFLECTED OR STOPPED

Rule 18	Ball at Rest Moved	265
Rule 19	Ball in Motion Deflected or Stopped	297

RELIEF SITUATIONS AND PROCEDURE

Rule 20 Lifting, Dropping and Placing; Playing from
Wrong Place   310
Rule 21 Cleaning Ball   349
Rule 22 Ball Assisting or Interfering with Play   351
Rule 23 Loose Impediments   354
Rule 24 Obstructions   363
Rule 25 Abnormal Ground Conditions, Embedded Ball and
Wrong Putting Green   382
Rule 26 Water Hazards (Including Lateral Water Hazards)   410
Rule 27 Ball Lost or Out of Bounds; Provisional Ball   428
Rule 28 Ball Unplayable   449

OTHER FORMS OF PLAY

Rule 29 Threesomes and Foursomes   457
Rule 30 Three-Ball, Best-Ball and Four-Ball Match Play   464
Rule 31 Four-Ball Stroke Play   480
Rule 32 Bogey, Par and Stableford Competitions   486

ADMINISTRATION

Rule 33 The Committee   491
Rule 34 Disputes and Decisions   534

APPENDIX I

Part A Local Rules   551
Part B Specimen Local Rules   553
Part C Conditions of the Competition   563

APPENDIX II

Design of Clubs   570

APPENDIX III

The Ball   579

APPENDIX IV

Devices and Other Equipment   580

Introduction to Index   582
Contents of Index   C-1
Index   I-1

SECTION I

ETIQUETTE; BEHAVIOR ON THE COURSE

INTRODUCTION
This section provides guidelines on the manner in which the game of golf should be played. If they are followed, all players will gain maximum enjoyment from the game. The overriding principle is that consideration should be shown to others on the course at all times.

THE SPIRIT OF THE GAME
Golf is played, for the most part, without the supervision of a referee or umpire. The game relies on the integrity of the individual to show consideration for other players and to abide by the Rules. All players should conduct themselves in a disciplined manner, demonstrating courtesy and sportsmanship at all times, irrespective of how competitive they may be. This is the spirit of the game of golf.

SAFETY
Players should ensure that no one is standing close by or in a position to be hit by the club, the ball or any stones, pebbles, twigs or the like when they make a stroke or practice swing.

Players should not play until the players in front are out of range.

Players should always alert greenstaff nearby or ahead when they are about to make a stroke that might endanger them.

If a player plays a ball in a direction where there is a danger of hitting someone, he should immediately shout a warning. The traditional word of warning in such situations is "fore."

CONSIDERATION FOR OTHER PLAYERS
No Disturbance or Distraction
Players should always show consideration for other players on the course and should not disturb their play by moving, talking or making unnecessary noise.

Players should ensure that any electronic device taken onto the course does not distract other players.

On the teeing ground, a player should not tee his ball until it is his turn to play.

Players should not stand close to or directly behind the ball, or directly behind the hole, when a player is about to play.

On the Putting Green
On the putting green, players should not stand on another player's line of putt or, when he is making a stroke, cast a shadow over his line of putt.

Players should remain on or close to the putting green until all other players in the group have holed out.

Scoring

In stroke play, a player who is acting as a marker should, if necessary, on the way to the next tee, check the score with the player concerned and record it.

PACE OF PLAY

Play at Good Pace and Keep Up

Players should play at a good pace. The Committee may establish pace of play guidelines that all players should follow.

It is a group's responsibility to keep up with the group in front. If it loses a clear hole and it is delaying the group behind, it should invite the group behind to play through, irrespective of the number of players in that group. Where a group has not lost a clear hole, but it is apparent that the group behind can play faster, it should invite the faster moving group to play through.

Be Ready to Play

Players should be ready to play as soon as it is their turn to play. When playing on or near the putting green, they should leave their bags or carts in such a position as will enable quick movement off the green and towards the next tee. When the play of a hole has been completed, players should immediately leave the putting green.

Lost Ball

If a player believes his ball may be lost outside a water hazard or is out of bounds, to save time, he should play a provisional ball.

Players searching for a ball should signal the players in the group behind them to play through as soon as it becomes apparent that the ball will not easily be found. They should not search for five minutes before doing so. Having allowed the group behind to play through, they should not continue play until that group has passed and is out of range.

PRIORITY ON THE COURSE

Unless otherwise determined by the Committee, priority on the course is determined by a group's pace of play. Any group playing a whole round is entitled to pass a group playing a shorter round. The term "group" includes a single player.

CARE OF THE COURSE

Bunkers

Before leaving a bunker, players should carefully fill up and smooth over all holes and footprints made by them and any nearby made by others. If a rake is within reasonable proximity of the bunker, the rake should be used for this purpose.

Repair of Divots, Ball-Marks and Damage by Shoes

Players should carefully repair any divot holes made by them and any damage to the putting green made by the impact of a ball (whether or not made by the player himself). On completion of the hole by all players in the group, damage to the putting green caused by golf shoes should be repaired.

Preventing Unnecessary Damage

Players should avoid causing damage to the course by removing divots when taking practice swings or by hitting the head of a club into the ground, whether in anger or for any other reason.

Players should ensure that no damage is done to the putting green when putting down bags or the flagstick.

In order to avoid damaging the hole, players and caddies should not stand too close to the hole and should take care during the handling of the flagstick and the removal of a ball from the hole. The head of a club should not be used to remove a ball from the hole.

Players should not lean on their clubs when on the putting green, particularly when removing the ball from the hole.

The flagstick should be properly replaced in the hole before the players leave the putting green.

Local notices regulating the movement of golf carts should be strictly observed.

CONCLUSION; PENALTIES FOR BREACH

If players follow the guidelines in this section, it will make the game more enjoyable for everyone.

If a player consistently disregards these guidelines during a round or over a period of time to the detriment of others, it is recommended that the Committee considers taking appropriate disciplinary action against the offending player. Such action may, for example, include prohibiting play for a limited time on the course or in a certain number of competitions. This is considered to be justifiable in terms of protecting the interest of the majority of golfers who wish to play in accordance with these guidelines.

In the case of a serious breach of etiquette, the Committee may disqualify a player under Rule 33-7.

SECTION II

DEFINITIONS

The Definitions are listed alphabetically and, in the Rules themselves, defined terms are in *italics*.

ABNORMAL GROUND CONDITIONS

An *"abnormal ground condition"* is any *casual water*, *ground under repair* or *hole, cast or runway* on the *course* made by a *burrowing animal*, a reptile or a bird.

ADDRESSING THE BALL

A player has *"addressed the ball"* when he has grounded his club immediately in front of or immediately behind the ball, whether or not he has taken his stance.

ADVICE

"Advice" is any counsel or suggestion that could influence a player in determining his play, the choice of a club or the method of making a *stroke*.

Information on the *Rules*, distance or matters of public information, such as the position of *hazards* or the *flagstick* on the *putting green*, is not *advice*.

BALL DEEMED TO MOVE

See *"Move or Moved."*

BALL HOLED

See *"Holed."*

BALL LOST

See *"Lost Ball."*

BALL IN PLAY

A ball is *"in play"* as soon as the player has made a *stroke* on the *teeing ground*. It remains *in play* until it is *holed*, except when it is *lost*, *out of bounds* or lifted, or another ball has been *substituted*, whether or not the substitution is permitted; a ball so *substituted* becomes the *ball in play*.

If a ball is played from outside the *teeing ground* when the player is starting play of a hole, or when attempting to correct this mistake, the ball is not *in play* and Rule 11-4 or 11-5 applies. Otherwise, *ball in play* includes a ball played from outside the *teeing ground* when the player elects or is required to play his next *stroke* from the *teeing ground*.

Exception in match play: *Ball in play* includes a ball played by the player from outside the *teeing ground* when starting play of a hole if the *opponent* does not require the *stroke* to be canceled in accordance with Rule 11-4a.

BEST-BALL
See *"Forms of Match Play."*

BUNKER
A *"bunker"* is a *hazard* consisting of a prepared area of ground, often a hollow, from which turf or soil has been removed and replaced with sand or the like.

Grass-covered ground bordering or within a *bunker*, including a stacked turf face (whether grass-covered or earthen), is not part of the *bunker*. A wall or lip of the *bunker* not covered with grass is part of the *bunker*. The margin of a *bunker* extends vertically downwards, but not upwards.

A ball is in a *bunker* when it lies in or any part of it touches the *bunker*.

BURROWING ANIMAL
A *"burrowing animal"* is an animal (other than a worm, insect or the like) that makes a hole for habitation or shelter, such as a rabbit, mole, groundhog, gopher or salamander.

Note: A hole made by a non-burrowing animal, such as a dog, is not an *abnormal ground condition* unless marked or declared as *ground under repair*.

CADDIE
A *"caddie"* is one who assists the player in accordance with the *Rules*, which may include carrying or handling the player's clubs during play.

When one *caddie* is employed by more than one player, he is always deemed to be the *caddie* of the player sharing the *caddie* whose ball (or whose *partner*'s ball) is involved, and *equipment* carried by him is deemed to be that player's *equipment*, except when the *caddie* acts upon specific directions of another player (or the *partner* of another player) sharing the *caddie*, in which case he is considered to be that other player's *caddie*.

CASUAL WATER
"Casual water" is any temporary accumulation of water on the *course* that is not in a *water hazard* and is visible before or after the player takes his stance. Snow and natural ice, other than frost, are either *casual water* or *loose impediments*, at the option of the player. Manufactured ice is an *obstruction*. Dew and frost are not *casual water*.

A ball is in *casual water* when it lies in or any part of it touches the *casual water*.

COMMITTEE
The *"Committee"* is the committee in charge of the competition or, if the matter does not arise in a competition, the committee in charge of the *course*.

COMPETITOR

A *"competitor"* is a player in a stroke-play competition. A *"fellow-competitor"* is any person with whom the *competitor* plays. Neither is *partner* of the other.

In stroke-play *foursome* and *four-ball* competitions, where the context so admits, the word *"competitor"* or *"fellow-competitor"* includes his *partner*.

COURSE

The *"course"* is the whole area within any boundaries established by the *Committee* (see Rule 33-2).

EQUIPMENT

"Equipment" is anything used, worn or carried by the player or anything carried for the player by his *partner* or either of their *caddies*, except any ball he has played at the hole being played and any small object, such as a coin or a tee, when used to mark the position of a ball or the extent of an area in which a ball is to be dropped. *Equipment* includes a golf cart, whether or not motorized.

Note 1: A ball played at the hole being played is *equipment* when it has been lifted and not put back into play.

Note 2: When a golf cart is shared by two or more players, the cart and everything in it are deemed to be the *equipment* of one of the players sharing the cart.

If the cart is being moved by one of the players (or the *partner* of one of the players) sharing it, the cart and everything in it are deemed to be that player's *equipment*. Otherwise, the cart and everything in it are deemed to be the *equipment* of the player sharing the cart whose ball (or whose *partner's* ball) is involved.

FELLOW-COMPETITOR

See *"Competitor."*

FLAGSTICK

The *"flagstick"* is a movable straight indicator, with or without bunting or other material attached, centered in the *hole* to show its position. It must be circular in cross-section. Padding or shock absorbent material that might unduly influence the movement of the ball is prohibited.

FORECADDIE

A *"forecaddie"* is one who is employed by the *Committee* to indicate to players the position of balls during play. He is an *outside agency*.

FORMS OF MATCH PLAY

Single: A match in which one player plays against another player.
Threesome: A match in which one player plays against two other players, and each *side* plays one ball.

Foursome: A match in which two players play against two other players, and each *side* plays one ball.

Three-Ball: Three players play a match against one another, each playing his own ball. Each player is playing two distinct matches.

Best-Ball: A match in which one player plays against the better ball of two other players or the best ball of three other players.

Four-Ball: A match in which two players play their better ball against the better ball of two other players.

FORMS OF STROKE PLAY

Individual: A competition in which each *competitor* plays as an individual.

Foursome: A competition in which two *competitors* play as *partners* and play one ball.

Four-Ball: A competition in which two *competitors* play as *partners*, each playing his own ball. The lower score of the *partners* is the score for the hole. If one *partner* fails to complete the play of a hole, there is no penalty.

Note: For bogey, par and Stableford competitions, see Rule 32-1.

FOUR-BALL

See "*Forms of Match Play*" and "*Forms of Stroke Play.*"

FOURSOME

See "*Forms of Match Play*" and "*Forms of Stroke Play.*"

GROUND UNDER REPAIR

"*Ground under repair*" is any part of the *course* so marked by order of the *Committee* or so declared by its authorized representative. All ground and any grass, bush, tree or other growing thing within the *ground under repair* are part of the *ground under repair*. *Ground under repair* includes material piled for removal and a hole made by a greenkeeper, even if not so marked. Grass cuttings and other material left on the *course* that have been abandoned and are not intended to be removed are not *ground under repair* unless so marked.

When the margin of *ground under repair* is defined by stakes, the stakes are inside the *ground under repair*, and the margin of the *ground under repair* is defined by the nearest outside points of the stakes at ground level. When both stakes and lines are used to indicate *ground under repair*, the stakes identify the *ground under repair* and the lines define the margin of the *ground under repair*. When the margin of *ground under repair* is defined by a line on the ground, the line itself is in the *ground under repair*. The margin of *ground under repair* extends vertically downwards but not upwards.

A ball is in *ground under repair* when it lies in or any part of it touches the *ground under repair*.

Stakes used to define the margin of or identify *ground under repair* are *obstructions*.

Note: The *Committee* may make a Local Rule prohibiting play from *ground under repair* or an environmentally-sensitive area defined as *ground under repair*.

HAZARDS

A "*hazard*" is any *bunker* or *water hazard*.

HOLE

The "*hole*" must be 4¼ inches (108 mm) in diameter and at least 4 inches (101.6 mm) deep. If a lining is used, it must be sunk at least 1 inch (25.4 mm) below the *putting green* surface, unless the nature of the soil makes it impracticable to do so; its outer diameter must not exceed 4¼ inches (108 mm).

HOLED

A ball is "*holed*" when it is at rest within the circumference of the *hole* and all of it is below the level of the lip of the *hole*.

HONOR

The player who is to play first from the *teeing ground* is said to have the "*honor.*"

LATERAL WATER HAZARD

A "*lateral water hazard*" is a *water hazard* or that part of a *water hazard* so situated that it is not possible, or is deemed by the *Committee* to be impracticable, to drop a ball behind the *water hazard* in accordance with Rule 26-1b. All ground and water within the margin of a *lateral water hazard* are part of the *lateral water hazard*.

When the margin of a *lateral water hazard* is defined by stakes, the stakes are inside the *lateral water hazard*, and the margin of the *hazard* is defined by the nearest outside points of the stakes at ground level. When both stakes and lines are used to indicate a *lateral water hazard*, the stakes identify the *hazard* and the lines define the *hazard* margin. When the margin of a *lateral water hazard* is defined by a line on the ground, the line itself is in the *lateral water hazard*. The margin of a *lateral water hazard* extends vertically upwards and downwards.

A ball is in a *lateral water hazard* when it lies in or any part of it touches the *lateral water hazard*.

Stakes used to define the margin of or identify a *lateral water hazard* are *obstructions*.

Note 1: That part of a *water hazard* to be played as a *lateral water hazard* must be distinctively marked. Stakes or lines used to define the margin of or identify a *lateral water hazard* must be red.

Note 2: The *Committee* may make a Local Rule prohibiting play from an environmentally-sensitive area defined as a *lateral water hazard*.

Note 3: The *Committee* may define a *lateral water hazard* as a *water hazard*.

LINE OF PLAY

The *"line of play"* is the direction that the player wishes his ball to take after a *stroke*, plus a reasonable distance on either side of the intended direction. The *line of play* extends vertically upwards from the ground, but does not extend beyond the *hole*.

LINE OF PUTT

The *"line of putt"* is the line that the player wishes his ball to take after a *stroke* on the *putting green*. Except with respect to Rule 16-1e, the *line of putt* includes a reasonable distance on either side of the intended line. The *line of putt* does not extend beyond the *hole*.

LOOSE IMPEDIMENTS

"Loose impediments" are natural objects, including:
• stones, leaves, twigs, branches and the like,
• dung, and
• worms, insects and the like, and the casts and heaps made by them,
provided they are not:
• fixed or growing,
• solidly embedded, or
• adhering to the ball.
Sand and loose soil are *loose impediments* on the *putting green*, but not elsewhere.

Snow and natural ice, other than frost, are either *casual water* or *loose impediments*, at the option of the player.

Dew and frost are not *loose impediments*.

LOST BALL

A ball is deemed *"lost"* if:
a. It is not found or identified as his by the player within five minutes after the player's *side* or his or their *caddies* have begun to search for it; or
b. The player has made a stroke at a *provisional ball* from the place where the original ball is likely to be or from a point nearer the *hole* than that place (see Rule 27-2b); or
c. The player has put another *ball into play* under penalty of stroke and distance under Rule 26-1a, 27-1 or 28a; or
d. The player has put another *ball into play* because it is known or virtually certain that the ball, which has not been found, has been *moved* by an *outside agency* (see Rule 18-1), is in an *obstruction* (see Rule 24-3), is in an *abnormal ground condition* (see Rule 25-1c) or is in a *water hazard* (see Rule 26-1b or c); or
e. The player has made a *stroke* at a *substituted ball*.
Time spent in playing a *wrong ball* is not counted in the five-minute period allowed for search.

MARKER

A *"marker"* is one who is appointed by the *Committee* to record a *competitor's* score in stroke play. He may be a *fellow-competitor*. He is not a *referee*.

MOVE OR MOVED

A ball is deemed to have *"moved"* if it leaves its position and comes to rest in any other place.

NEAREST POINT OF RELIEF

The *"nearest point of relief"* is the reference point for taking relief without penalty from interference by an immovable *obstruction* (Rule 24-2), an *abnormal ground condition* (Rule 25-1) or a *wrong putting green* (Rule 25-3).

It is the point on the *course* nearest to where the ball lies:
(i) that is not nearer the *hole*, and
(ii) where, if the ball were so positioned, no interference by the condition from which relief is sought would exist for the stroke the player would have made from the original position if the condition were not there.

Note: In order to determine the *nearest point of relief* accurately, the player should use the club with which he would have made his next *stroke* if the condition were not there to simulate the *address* position, direction of play and swing for such a *stroke*.

OBSERVER

An *"observer"* is one who is appointed by the *Committee* to assist a *referee* to decide questions of fact and to report to him any breach of a *Rule*. An *observer* should not attend the *flagstick*, stand at or mark the position of the *hole*, or lift the ball or mark its position.

OBSTRUCTIONS

An *"obstruction"* is anything artificial, including the artificial surfaces and sides of roads and paths and manufactured ice, except:
a. Objects defining *out of bounds*, such as walls, fences, stakes and railings;
b. Any part of an immovable artificial object that is *out of bounds*; and
c. Any construction declared by the *Committee* to be an integral part of the *course*.

An *obstruction* is a movable *obstruction* if it may be moved without unreasonable effort, without unduly delaying play and without causing damage. Otherwise it is an immovable *obstruction*.

Note: The *Committee* may make a Local Rule declaring a movable *obstruction* to be an immovable *obstruction*.

OPPONENT

An *"opponent"* is a member of a *side* against whom the player's *side* is competing in match play.

OUT OF BOUNDS

"*Out of bounds*" is beyond the boundaries of the *course* or any part of the *course* so marked by the *Committee*.

When *out of bounds* is defined by reference to stakes or a fence or as being beyond stakes or a fence, the *out of bounds* line is determined by the nearest inside points at ground level of the stakes or fence posts (excluding angled supports). When both stakes and lines are used to indicate *out of bounds*, the stakes identify *out of bounds* and the lines define *out of bounds*. When *out of bounds* is defined by a line on the ground, the line itself is *out of bounds*. The *out of bounds* line extends vertically upwards and downwards.

A ball is *out of bounds* when all of it lies *out of bounds*. A player may stand *out of bounds* to play a ball lying within bounds.

Objects defining *out of bounds* such as walls, fences, stakes and railings are not *obstructions* and are deemed to be fixed. Stakes identifying *out of bounds* are not *obstructions* and are deemed to be fixed.

Note 1: Stakes or lines used to define *out of bounds* should be white.

Note 2: A *Committee* may make a Local Rule declaring stakes identifying but not defining *out of bounds* to be *obstructions*.

OUTSIDE AGENCY

In match play, an "*outside agency*" is any agency other than either the player's or *opponent's* side, any *caddie* of either *side*, any ball played by either *side* at the hole being played or any *equipment* of either *side*.

In stroke play, an *outside agency* is any agency other than the *competitor's* side, any *caddie* of the *side*, any ball played by the *side* at the hole being played or any *equipment* of the *side*.

An *outside agency* includes a *referee*, a *marker*, an *observer* and a *forecaddie*. Neither wind nor water is an *outside agency*.

PARTNER

A "*partner*" is a player associated with another player on the same *side*.

In *threesome*, *foursome*, *best-ball* or *four-ball* play, where the context so admits, the word "player" includes his *partner* or *partners*.

PENALTY STROKE

A "*penalty stroke*" is one added to the score of a player or *side* under certain *Rules*. In a *threesome* or *foursome*, *penalty strokes* do not affect the order of play.

PROVISIONAL BALL

A "*provisional ball*" is a ball played under Rule 27-2 for a ball that may be *lost* outside a *water hazard* or may be *out of bounds*.

PUTTING GREEN

The "*putting green*" is all ground of the hole being played that is specially prepared for putting or otherwise defined as such by the *Committee*. A ball is on the *putting green* when any part of it touches the *putting green*.

REFEREE

A *"referee"* is one who is appointed by the *Committee* to decide questions of fact and apply the *Rules*. He must act on any breach of a *Rule* that he observes or is reported to him.

A *referee* should not attend the *flagstick*, stand at or mark the position of the *hole*, or lift the ball or mark its position.

Exception in match play: Unless a *referee* is assigned to accompany the players throughout a match, he has no authority to intervene in a match other than in relation to Rule 1-3, 6-7 or 33-7.

RUB OF THE GREEN

A *"rub of the green"* occurs when a ball in motion is accidentally deflected or stopped by any *outside agency* (see Rule 19-1).

RULE OR RULES

The term *"Rule"* includes:

a. The Rules of Golf and their interpretations as contained in "Decisions on the Rules of Golf";

b. Any Condition of Competition established by the *Committee* under Rule 33-1 and Appendix I;

c. Any Local Rules established by the *Committee* under Rule 33-8a and Appendix I; and

d. The specifications on:

    (i) clubs and the ball in Appendices II and III and their interpretations as contained in "A Guide to the Rules on Clubs and Balls"; and

    (ii) devices and other equipment in Appendix IV.

SIDE

A *"side"* is a player, or two or more players who are *partners*. In match play, each member of the opposing *side* is an *opponent*. In stroke play, members of all *sides* are *competitors* and members of different *sides* playing together are *fellow-competitors*.

SINGLE

See *"Forms of Match Play"* and *"Forms of Stroke Play."*

STANCE

Taking the *"stance"* consists in a player placing his feet in position for and preparatory to making a *stroke*.

STIPULATED ROUND

The *"stipulated round"* consists of playing the holes of the *course* in their correct sequence unless otherwise authorized by the *Committee*.

The number of holes in a *stipulated round* is 18 unless a smaller number is authorized by the *Committee*. As to extension of *stipulated round* in match play, see Rule 2-3.

STROKE

A "*stroke*" is the forward movement of the club made with the intention of striking at and moving the ball, but if a player checks his downswing voluntarily before the clubhead reaches the ball he has not made a *stroke*.

SUBSTITUTED BALL

A "*substituted ball*" is a ball put into play for the original ball that was either *in play, lost, out of bounds* or lifted.

TEEING GROUND

The "*teeing ground*" is the starting place for the hole to be played. It is a rectangular area two club-lengths in depth, the front and the sides of which are defined by the outside limits of two tee-markers. A ball is outside the *teeing ground* when all of it lies outside the *teeing ground*.

THREE-BALL

See "*Forms of Match Play.*"

THREESOMES

See "*Forms of Match Play.*"

THROUGH THE GREEN

"*Through the green*" is the whole area of the *course* except:

a. The teeing ground and putting green of the hole being played; and
b. All *hazards* on the *course*.

WATER HAZARD

A "*water hazard*" is any sea, lake, pond, river, ditch, surface drainage ditch or other open water course (whether or not containing water) and anything of a similar nature on the course. All ground and water within the margin of a *water hazard* are part of the *water hazard*.

When the margin of a *water hazard* is defined by stakes, the stakes are inside the *water hazard*, and the margin of the *hazard* is defined by the nearest outside points of the stakes at ground level. When both stakes and lines are used to indicate a *water hazard*, the stakes identify the *hazard* and the lines define the *hazard* margin. When the margin of a *water hazard* is defined by a line on the ground, the line itself is in the *water hazard*. The margin of a *water hazard* extends vertically upwards and downwards.

A ball is in a *water hazard* when it lies in or any part of it touches the *water hazard*.

Stakes used to define the margin of or identify a *water hazard* are *obstructions*.

Note 1: Stakes or lines used to define the margin of or identify a *water hazard* must be yellow.

Note 2: The *Committee* may make a Local Rule prohibiting play from an environmentally-sensitive area defined as a *water hazard*.

WRONG BALL

A "*wrong ball*" is any ball other than the player's:
• *ball in play*;
• *provisional ball*; or
• second ball played under Rule 3-3 or Rule 20-7c in stroke play;
and includes:
• another player's ball;
• an abandoned ball; and
• the player's original ball when it is no longer *in play*.
Note: *Ball in play* includes a ball *substituted* for the *ball in play*, whether or not the substitution is permitted.

WRONG PUTTING GREEN

A "*wrong putting green*" is any *putting green* other than that of the hole being played. Unless otherwise prescribed by the *Committee*, this term includes a practice *putting green* or pitching green on the *course*.

SECTION III

THE RULES OF PLAY

RULE I

THE GAME

DEFINITIONS
All defined terms are in *italics* and are listed alphabetically in the Definitions section – see pages 6–16.

I-1. GENERAL
The Game of Golf consists of playing a ball with a club from the *teeing ground* into the *hole* by a *stroke* or successive *strokes* in accordance with the *Rules*.

I-2. EXERTING INFLUENCE ON MOVEMENT OF BALL OR ALTERING PHYSICAL CONDITIONS
A player must not (i) take an action with the intent to influence the movement of a *ball in play* or (ii) alter physical conditions with the intent of affecting the playing of a hole.

Exceptions:
1. An action expressly permitted or expressly prohibited by another *Rule* is subject to that other *Rule*, not Rule 1-2.
2. An action taken for the sole purpose of caring for the *course* is not a breach of Rule 1-2.

*PENALTY FOR BREACH OF RULE I-2:
<u>Match play</u> – Loss of hole; <u>Stroke play</u> – Two strokes.

*In the case of a serious breach of Rule 1-2, the *Committee* may impose a penalty of disqualification.

Note I: A player is deemed to have committed a serious breach of Rule 1-2 if the *Committee* considers that the action taken in breach of this Rule has allowed him or another player to gain a significant advantage or has placed another player, other than his *partner*, at a significant disadvantage.
Note 2: In stroke play, except where a serious breach resulting in disqualification is involved, a player in breach of Rule 1-2 in relation to the movement of his own ball must play the ball from where it was stopped, or, if the ball was deflected, from where it came to rest. If the movement of a player's ball has been intentionally influenced by a *fellow-competitor* or other *outside agency*, Rule 1-4 applies to the player (see Note to Rule 19-1).

1-3. AGREEMENT TO WAIVE RULES

Players must not agree to exclude the operation of any *Rule* or to waive any penalty incurred.

PENALTY FOR BREACH OF RULE 1-3:

Match play – Disqualification of both *sides*;
Stroke play – Disqualification of *competitors* concerned.

(Agreeing to play out of turn in stroke play – see Rule 10-2c)

1-4. POINTS NOT COVERED BY RULES

If any point in dispute is not covered by the *Rules*, the decision should be made in accordance with equity.

THE GAME OF GOLF: GENERAL

1-1/1
Two Balls in Play Simultaneously at Different Holes

Q. Two players on the 8th hole play their approach shots to the 8th green. They agree to tee off at the 9th hole and then putt out on the 8th green. This is to avoid having to walk back up a hill to the 9th tee and to save time. What is the ruling?

A. In match play, the players are disqualified under Rule 1-3 for excluding the operation of Rule 2-1 by failing to play the stipulated round.

In stroke play, the competitors are disqualified under Rule 3-2 for failing to hole out on the 8th hole before making a stroke from the 9th tee.

1-1/2
Player Unaware He has Holed Out Puts Another Ball into Play

Q. A player, unable to find his ball, puts another ball into play. He then discovers that his original ball is in the hole. What is the ruling?

A. The score with the original ball counts. The play of the hole was completed when the player holed that ball.

1-1/3
Player Discovers Original Ball in Hole after Searching Five Minutes And then Continuing Play with Provisional Ball

Q. At a par-3 hole, a player, believing his original ball may be lost, plays a provisional ball. He searches five minutes for the original ball and then plays the provisional ball onto the green. At that point, the original ball is found in the hole. What is the ruling?

A. The player's score is 1. The play of the hole was completed when the player holed the original ball (Rule 1-1).

1-1/4
Player Discovers Own Ball Is in Hole After Playing Wrong Ball

Q. A player played to a blind green and putted what he thought was his ball. He then discovered that his own ball was in the hole and that the ball he had putted was a wrong ball. What is the ruling?

A. Since the play of the hole was completed when the original ball was holed (Rule 1-1), the player was not in breach of Rule 15-3 for subsequently playing a wrong ball.

Related Decisions:
• 2-4/9 Player Concedes Hole After Which It Is Discovered Opponent Had Played Wrong Ball.
• 2-4/10 Player Concedes Hole After Which Opponent Plays Wrong Ball.
• 2-4/11 Player with Lost Ball Concedes Hole; Ball Then Found in Hole.

EXERTING INFLUENCE ON MOVEMENT OF BALL OR ALTERING PHYSICAL CONDITIONS

1-2/0.5
Serious Breach of Rule 1-2

Q. Should the standard for determining whether a serious breach of Rule 1-2 has occurred be the same in match play and stroke play?

A. In deciding whether a player has committed a serious breach of Rule 1-2, the Committee should consider all aspects of the incident. Given the different impact on players in match play and stroke play, it is possible for the same act to constitute a serious breach of Rule 1-2 in stroke play but not in match play. In many cases in match play (e.g., a player who intentionally stops his ball from entering a water hazard), a penalty of loss of hole is sufficient while in stroke play the player should be disqualified for a serious breach. In some cases (e.g., the purposeful act of damaging the line of putt referred to in Decision 1-2/1), a penalty of disqualification in match play may be appropriate. (Revised)

1-2/0.7
Meaning of "Sole Purpose of Caring for the Course"

Q. What is the meaning of the phrase "sole purpose of caring for the course" in Exception 2 to Rule 1-2?

A. The phrase "sole purpose of caring for the course" in the Exception refers to the performance of acts that are encouraged in the Etiquette Section of the Rules of Golf provided they are taken at the appropriate time and in a manner permitted by the Rules. The provisions of Rule 1-2 do not prevent a player from taking acts that conform with the Etiquette Section, so long as the player does so for the sole purpose of caring for the course and without intentionally influencing the movement of a ball, or the physical conditions affecting play, of a player in the player's group or match. For example, while a player may not smooth the ragged edge of a hole or tap down spike marks in order to influence the movement of a ball of an opponent, fellow-competitor or partner, the player may generally smooth the ragged edge of a hole or tap down spike marks as a courtesy to players in following groups or matches, or for care of the course (see Decision 1-2/3.5). Similarly, while a player may not press down a piece of turf in the area in which a ball in motion may come to rest or in the area in which a ball is to be dropped or placed with the intention of influencing the movement of the ball, a player generally may attempt to tidy up the course by repairing divot holes and/or replacing divots that do not affect play of the hole by a player in the player's group or match (see Decision 1-2/8). (New)

1-2/1
Line of Putt Altered Purposely by Opponent or Fellow-Competitor by Stepping on It

Q. An opponent or a fellow-competitor purposely steps on the player's line of putt with the intention either of improving the line (e.g., by pressing down a raised tuft of grass) or of damaging it (e.g., by making spike marks). What is the ruling?

A. In either case, the opponent or the fellow-competitor was in breach of Rule 1-2. The penalty is loss of hole in match play or two strokes in stroke play, unless the Committee decides to impose a penalty of disqualification – see the penalty statement of Rule 1-2.

In stroke play if the line of putt has been damaged, the player, in equity (Rule 1-4), may restore the line of putt to its previous condition. A player is entitled to the lie and line of putt he had when his ball came to rest. The line of putt may be restored by anyone.

Decisions related to 1-2/0.5 and 1-2/1:
- 13-2/36 Competitor Sanctions Repair of Spike Damage on His Line of Putt by Fellow-Competitor.
- 16-1a/13 Line of Putt Damaged Accidentally by Opponent, Fellow-Competitor or Their Caddies.
- 17-3/2 Opponent or Fellow-Competitor Attending Flagstick for Player Fails to Remove It; Player's Ball Strikes Flagstick.
- 19-1/5 Ball Deliberately Deflected or Stopped on Putting Green by Fellow-Competitor.
- See also "Equity: player entitled to lie, line of play and stance when ball comes to rest after stroke" in the Index.

1-2/1.5
Competitor Alters Line of Play of Fellow-Competitor

Q. In stroke play, A's ball is under a partially detached tree branch from which he believes he is entitled to relief without penalty. A calls for a ruling. B, A's fellow-competitor, argues A's case to a referee and, during the conversation, lifts the branch and improves or worsens A's line of play. What is the ruling?

A. As B did not alter physical conditions with the intent of affecting A's playing of the hole, B is not in breach of Rule 1-2. A incurs no penalty. A may replace the branch, but he is not required to do so. (Revised)

1-2/2
Shielding Line of Putt from Wind

Q. May a player lay his golf bag parallel to the line of putt to shield the line from the wind?

A. No. Such an action taken with the intent to influence the movement of the ball would be a breach of Rule 1-2, even if the golf bag were removed prior to the stroke being made. (Revised)

1-2/3
Breaking Bush in Area into Which Ball May Roll After Drop

Q. A player elects to take relief from an area of ground under repair through the green. He correctly determines his nearest point of relief and the one club-length area in which the ball must be dropped under Rule 25-1b(i). The player is aware that there is a small bush located outside the dropping area. Fearing that his ball could come to rest close to the bush when dropped, without a re-drop being required under Rule 20-2c, the player intentionally breaks off and removes part of the bush. What is the ruling?

A. As the player has not improved the area in which a ball is to be dropped, (i.e., the area in which the ball must first strike a part of the course when dropped under Rule 25-1b(i)), Rule 13-2 does not apply. However, the player is in breach of Rule 1-2 for taking an action with the intent to affect the playing of the hole by altering the physical conditions.

The same principles apply to a situation where a player's ball is at rest, but he fears that it might move. For example, if a player's ball is at rest on a steep slope through the green and he breaks an attached tree branch that might interfere with his swing if the ball were to roll ten feet down the slope, the player is in breach of Rule 1-2 for taking an action with the intent to affect the playing of the hole by altering the physical conditions. (New)

1-2/3.5
Player Repairs Hole After Holing Out But Before Opponent, Fellow-Competitor or Partner Holes Out

Q. After holing out, a player observes that the edge of the hole is ragged. He pats the ragged edge with his hand and smoothes it. Does the player incur a penalty under Rule 1-2 if his opponent, fellow-competitor or partner has not holed out?

A. If the player smoothed the edge of the hole solely for the purpose of caring for the course, he was not in breach of Rule 1-2. However, if the smoothing of the ragged edge was in any way intended to influence the movement of his opponent's, fellow-competitor's or partner's ball, or alter physical conditions with the intent of affecting the playing of the hole, he was in breach of Rule 1-2. It is recommended that a player should only smooth the ragged edge of a hole after all players in the group or match have completed play of the hole.

As the player had holed out, he is not subject to penalty under Rule 16-1a or Rule 13-2.

In a four-ball competition, if the player's partner had not completed play of the hole, the partner incurs the penalty for a breach of Rule 16-1a – see Definition of "Partner." (Revised)

Related Decisions:
- 16-1a/6 Damaged Hole; Procedure for Player.
- 33-2b/2 Relocating Hole After Ball Already Positioned Nearby on Putting Green.

1-2/4
Player Jumps Close to Hole to Cause Ball to Fall into Hole

Q. A player whose ball overhangs the lip of the hole jumps close to the hole in the hope of jarring the ground and causing the ball to fall into the hole. Is the player penalized under Rule 1-2 for trying to exert influence on the movement of his ball in play?

A. If the player's ball was at rest (or deemed to be at rest under Rule 16-2) and does not move, Rule 1-2 does not apply because the player was attempting to move a ball at rest and this is specifically covered by Rule 18-2a (see Exception 1 to Rule 1-2). As the ball did not move, there was no penalty under Rule 18-2a.

If the player's ball was at rest (or deemed to be at rest under Rule 16-2) and the ball moves, Rule 1-2 does not apply because Rule 18-2a specifically covers a ball at rest moved by the player – see Exception 1 to Rule 1-2. The player is deemed to have caused his ball to move and incurs a penalty of one stroke in both match play and stroke play under Rule 18-2a and the ball must be replaced.

If the player's ball was still moving when the player jumped, Rule 1-2 was the applicable Rule because the player took an action with the intent to influence the movement of the ball. In match play, he lost the hole. In stroke play, he incurred a penalty of two strokes and must play the ball from where it came to rest; if the ball was holed, the player completed play of the hole with his last stroke and must apply the two-stroke penalty under Rule 1-2. (Revised)

Related Decisions:
- 2-4/2 Ball Falls into Hole After Concession of Next Stroke.
- 16-2/2 Ball Overhanging Hole Knocked Away by Opponent Before Player Determines Status.
- 18-2a/23 Ball Knocked from Lip of Hole in Disgust.
- 18-2b/10 Ball Falls into Hole After Being Addressed.

1-2/5
Player Putts with One Hand and Catches Ball in Hole with Other Hand

Q. A player whose ball is on the lip of the hole putts with one hand and catches the ball with his other hand after the ball is below the level of the lip of the hole. What is the ruling?

A. The player purposely stopped his moving ball.

In match play, he lost the hole – Rule 1-2.

In stroke play, he incurred a penalty of two strokes and was required to place his ball on the lip of the hole and hole out – Rule 1-2. If he did not do so, he was disqualified under Rule 3-2 for failing to hole out.

In order for a ball to be holed (see Definition of "Holed"), it must be at rest within the circumference of the hole.

Related Decision:
• 16/5.5 Player Holes Short Putt and Allegedly Removes Ball from Hole Before It Is at Rest.

1-2/5.5
Player Purposely Stops or Deflects Ball; Where Next Stroke Must Be Played from

Q. A player's ball lies through the green. After playing a pitch shot up a slope, the player sees his ball start to roll back towards him. He places his club in front of the ball and stops it. The ball would have rolled only a few yards more and remained through the green. What is the ruling?

A. Since the player purposely stopped the ball, he is in breach of Rule 1-2. As the breach was not serious, the player incurs a penalty of loss of hole in match play or two strokes in stroke play. In stroke play, he must play the ball from the point where he stopped it with his club – see Note 2 to Rule 1-2.

If the player had purposely deflected the ball but not stopped it, in match play, he would lose the hole. In stroke play, if a serious breach has not occurred, he would incur a two-stroke penalty and must then play the ball from its new position – see Note 2 to Rule 1-2. In stroke play, if a serious breach has occurred, the player is disqualified.

Rule 19-2 is not applicable since it only covers situations when a player accidentally deflects or stops his ball. (Revised)

Related Decision:
• 20-2c/4 Caddie Stops Dropped Ball Before It Comes to Rest; When Penalty Incurred.

1-2/6 (Reserved)

1-2/7
Player Purposely Deflects Partner's Ball in Motion on Putting Green

Q. In four-ball match play, A and B are playing C and D. All four balls lie on the putting green in five strokes. A lies four feet from the hole and B lies 30 feet from the hole. Player A is standing near and behind the hole with respect to B's line of putt while B putts. B's ball goes past the hole and is rolling towards where A is standing. Without waiting for B's ball to come to rest, A knocks B's ball back to B. What is the ruling?

A. A's intentional interference with the movement of B's ball is a breach of Rule 1-2. However, the penalty for that breach is incurred by B – the partner whose ball was in motion – and results in disqualification from the hole for B. A may continue to represent the side without penalty as the breach of Rule 1-2 did not assist him. (Revised)

1-2/8
Player Presses Down Turf as Ball Is Rolling Towards Area

Q. A player's ball lies through the green at the bottom of a slope. The player makes a stroke and sees that his ball is rolling back down the slope towards the spot from which he just played. Before the ball reaches that spot, the player presses down a raised piece of turf in that area with the intent of ensuring that his ball will not come to rest against the raised piece of turf or in the divot hole. Is the player in breach of Rule 1-2?

A. Yes, as he acted with the intent to influence the movement of his ball in play and with the intent to alter the physical conditions affecting playing of the hole. As the pressing down of the raised piece of turf was not for the sole purpose of caring for the course, Exception 2 to Rule 1-2 does not apply.

If the player had not realized his ball was returning to the area, there would be no breach of Rule 1-2. (Revised)

1-2/9
Player Presses Ball into Surface of Putting Green

Q. In replacing his ball but before putting it back into play, a player firmly presses the ball into the surface of the putting green in order to prevent it from being moved by the wind or gravity. What is the ruling?

A. In altering the surface of the putting green, the player has breached Rule 1-2 by intentionally taking action to influence the movement of a ball in play and to alter physical conditions that affect the playing of the hole.

In match play, the player loses the hole – Rule 1-2.

In stroke play, the player incurs a penalty of two strokes and must play the ball as it lies – Rule 1-2. (Revised – Formerly 18-2a/6)

Related Decisions:
- 14-5/2 Making Stroke at Oscillating Ball.
- 18/2 Ball Oscillating During Address.
- 20-3d/2 Ball in Bunker Moves Closer to Hole When Obstruction Removed and Ball Will Not Remain at Rest When Replaced; All Other Parts of Bunker Are Nearer Hole.

1-2/10
Player Wraps Towel Around Self or Places Towel on Cactus Before Taking Stance

Q. A player's ball lies near a cactus, and to play the ball, the player would have to stand with his legs touching the cactus. To protect himself from the cactus needles, the player wraps a towel around his legs before taking his stance. He then plays the ball. What is the ruling?

A. Provided the player does not breach Rule 13-2 (i.e., he takes his stance fairly), there is no breach of the Rules. However, if the player were to place the towel on the cactus, the player would be in breach of Rule 1-2 for altering physical conditions with the intent of affecting the playing of the hole; as a result, he would lose the hole in match play or incur a penalty of two strokes in stroke play. (Revised – Formerly 1-4/11.5)

Related Decision:
- 13-3/2 Making Stroke While Kneeling on Towel.

Other Decisions related to Rule 1-2: See "Exerting Influence on Ball" in the Index.

AGREEMENT TO WAIVE RULES

1-3/0.5
When Breach of Rule 1-3 Occurs

Q. While walking to the 1st green, A and B agree that for a ball that is out of bounds they will drop a ball at the spot where the ball went out of bounds under penalty of one stroke, even though they know the penalty is stroke and distance. Someone overhears this conversation and advises A and B that they may not make such an arrangement. Neither player has yet hit a ball out of bounds. What is the ruling?

A. A and B are disqualified under Rule 1-3 for agreeing to waive Rule 27-1b.

Even though A and B had not yet acted on the agreement, they were in breach of Rule 1-3 as soon as the agreement was reached during the stipulated round.

In match play, if the players in a match agree to waive the Rules before their stipulated round, they are in breach of Rule 1-3 if either of them starts the stipulated round without having canceled the agreement.

In stroke play, if competitors agree to waive the Rules before their stipulated round, each competitor is in breach of Rule 1-3 if one competitor who was part of the agreement starts his stipulated round without having canceled the agreement.

1-3/1 (Reserved)

1-3/2
Agreement to Concede Short Putts

Q. In a match, the two players agree in advance to concede all putts within a specified length. Is this agreement contrary to Rule 1-3?

A. In order to be in breach of Rule 1-3 for agreeing to waive a Rule, players must be aware that they are doing so. Therefore, the answer depends on whether the players knew that Rule 2-4 only allows the concession of the "next stroke" and does not permit them to agree in advance to concede putts within a specified length.

If the players were unaware that the Rules prevented them from agreeing to concede putts in this manner, there is no penalty under Rule 1-3.

If the players were aware that they were excluding the operation of a Rule then they are disqualified under Rule 1-3. (Revised)

1-3/3
Player and Opponent or Fellow-Competitor Agree to Repair Spike Marks on One Another's Line of Putt

Q. A player and his opponent or fellow-competitor agree that they will repair spike marks on one another's line of putt. Is this a breach of Rule 1-3?

A. Yes. Both would be subject to disqualification for agreeing to waive Rule 16-1a (Touching Line of Putt).

1-3/4
Failure of Players to Apply Known Penalty

Q. In a match, a player discovers at the 2nd hole that he has 15 clubs in his bag contrary to Rule 4-4a, but his opponent refuses to apply the penalty. The extra club is declared out of play and the match continues. The Committee disqualifies both players. Is this correct?

A. Yes. Since the players agreed to waive the penalty, they should be disqualified under Rule 1-3.

1-3/5
Players Unaware Penalty Incurred

Q. In a match, A incurred a penalty stroke under Rule 12-2 for lifting his ball for identification without announcing his intention to B, his opponent.

A did not penalize himself and B did not make a claim because neither A nor B was aware a penalty had been incurred. Should the Committee disqualify A and B under Rule 1-3 for agreeing to waive a penalty?

A. No. Since the players were not aware a penalty had been incurred, there could have been no agreement between them to waive the penalty.

Related Decisions:
- 2-1/1 Players Unable to Resolve Rules Problem Agree to Consider Hole Halved.
- 2-5/8.5 Player and Opponent Agree on Incorrect Procedure; Whether Valid Claim May Be Made After Procedure Followed.

1-3/6
Marker Attests Wrong Score Knowingly and Competitor Aware Score Wrong

Q. In stroke play, B failed to hole out at a hole. A few holes later he realized he had erred. A, B's marker and fellow-competitor, was aware both that B had infringed the Rules and that B knew this, but nevertheless he signed B's card. B was disqualified under Rule 3-2 (Failure to Hole Out). Should A, who knowingly overlooked the breach, be penalized?

A. A should have been disqualified for a breach of Rule 1-3.

Related Decisions:
- 6-6a/5 Marker Attests Wrong Score Knowingly But Competitor Unaware Score Wrong.
- 33-7/9 Competitor Who Knows Player Has Breached Rules Does Not Inform Player or Committee in Timely Manner.

1-3/7
Agreement That Side Losing After 18 Holes of 36-Hole Match Will Concede Match

Q. Prior to a 36-hole match, the players agree that they will play only 18 holes and whoever is behind at that point will concede the match. Is this permissible?

A. No. Both players should be disqualified under Rule 1-3 for agreeing to exclude the operation of a condition of the competition (Rule 33-1).

Related Decisions:
- 2-4/21 Wrong Form of Play Used to Decide Which Side Concedes Match.
- 6-1/1 Wrong Form of Play Used in Match-Play Event.
- 33-1/4 Match Decided by Wrong Form of Play by Agreement of Players.

Other Decisions related to Rule 1-3: See "Agreement to Waive Rules" in the Index.

1-4/1
Player Distracted by Ball Dropped by Another Player Mis-Hits Ball

Q. As A was making his backswing, B accidentally dropped a ball, which rolled within six inches of A's ball. The appearance of the dropped ball startled A, causing him to top his shot. In equity, should A be permitted to replay his stroke?

A. No. Distractions are a common occurrence which players must accept.

1-4/2
Ball Adhering to Face of Club After Stroke

Q. A player plays a stroke from wet sand or soil and the ball adheres to the face of the club. What is the ruling?

A. In equity (Rule 1-4), the ball should be dropped, without penalty, as near as possible to the spot where the club was when the ball stuck to it. But see also Decision 14-4/1.

1-4/3
Flagstick Stuck into Green Some Distance from Hole by Practical Joker

Q. A practical joker removes the flagstick from the hole and sticks it into the putting green some distance from the hole. The players approaching the green are unaware of this action and they play towards the flagstick and not the hole. Do the players have the option to replay?

A. No. In equity (Rule 1-4), the players must accept the resultant advantage or disadvantage.

1-4/4
In Anger Player Strikes Ball Played by Player in Following Group

Q. A is nearly struck by a ball played by a player in the following group. In anger, A hits the ball back towards the group. Has A played a practice stroke or a wrong ball?

A. No. However, in equity (Rule 1-4), A should incur the general penalty of loss of hole in match play or two strokes in stroke play.

Related Decision:
• 7-2/5.5 Player Finds Ball and Hits It to Player Who Lost It.

1-4/5
Removal of Obstruction in Hazard Would Move Loose Impediment

Q. In a hazard, a player's ball lies against a movable obstruction. A loose impediment lies on top of the obstruction in such a position that the player cannot remove the obstruction without also moving the loose impediment. The player is entitled to move the movable obstruction under Rule 24-1 but is not entitled to move the loose impediment under Rule 23. What is the procedure?

A. The player may remove the obstruction as authorized by Rule 24-1. As the loose impediment will be moved in the process, in equity (Rule 1-4), the player incurs no penalty and must place the loose impediment as near as possible to the spot where it originally lay. If the player fails to place the loose impediment as required, in equity (Rule 1-4) and in view of the purpose of Rule 13-4, he would lose the hole in match play or incur a penalty of two strokes in stroke play.

Related Decisions:
• 13-4/16 Removal of Loose Impediment in Water Hazard Covering Wrong Ball.
• 13-4/35.7 Player Deems Ball Unplayable in Bunker, Lifts Ball and Then Removes Loose Impediment from Bunker.
• 23-1/6.5 Removal of Loose Impediments from Spot on Which Ball to Be Placed.
• 23-1/7 Loose Impediment Affecting Lie Moved When Ball Lifted.
• 23-1/8 Loose Impediments Affecting Lie Removed While Ball Lifted.

1-4/6 (Reserved)

1-4/7
Ball Lost in Either Water Hazard or Casual Water Overflowing Hazard

Q. A ball is lost. It is either in a water hazard or in casual water overflowing the hazard. What is the proper procedure?

A. In equity (Rule 1-4), the player must proceed under the water hazard Rule.

Related Decision:
• 25/2 Overflow from Water Hazard.

1-4/8
Nearest Point of Relief from Cart Path Is in Casual Water; Nearest Point of Relief from Casual Water Is Back on Cart Path

Q. A player's ball lies on a paved cart path from which he wishes to take relief under Rule 24-2b(i). It appears that the nearest point of relief will be in a large area of casual water which adjoins the cart path and the nearest point of relief from the casual water under Rule 25-1b(i) would be back on the cart path. What are the player's options?

A. The player may proceed in accordance with Rule 24-2 and then, if applicable, Rule 25-1. He is not entitled to take relief from both the immovable obstruction and the casual water in a single procedure, unless after proceeding under these Rules, the player is essentially back where he started and it is evident that such a procedure is necessary to obtain relief from both conditions.

Therefore, the player should proceed as follows:

1. He may lift and drop the ball in accordance with Rule 24-2b(i) in the casual water.
2. He may play the ball as it lies or take relief from the casual water, in which case he would lift and drop the ball in accordance with Rule 25-1b(i).
3. If the ball when dropped comes to rest in such a position that there is interference by the cart path, he may play the ball as it lies or proceed in accordance with Rule 24-2b(i). If the nearest point of relief is in the casual water, as an additional option, the player may, in equity (Rule 1-4) obtain relief without penalty as follows: Using the new position of the ball on the cart path, the nearest point of relief from both the cart path and the casual water shall be determined which is not in a hazard or on a putting green. The player shall lift the ball and drop it within one club-length of and not nearer the hole than the nearest point of relief, on a part of the course which avoids interference by the cart path and the casual water and is not in a hazard or on a putting green.

If the dropped ball rolls into a position where there is interference by either the cart path or the casual water, Rule 20-2c applies.

The same principle would apply if there was interference from any two conditions, i.e., casual water, a hole made by a burrowing animal, an immovable obstruction, from which relief without penalty was available and in taking relief from one condition it resulted in interference from the second condition.

Related Decision:
• 25-1b/11.5 Ball in Casual Water Within Ground Under Repair; Whether Player Entitled to Take Relief from Both Conditions in Single Procedure.

1-4/8.5
Nearest Point of Relief from Cart Path Is in Casual Water,
Nearest Point of Relief from Casual Water Is Back on Cart Path;
Impracticable for Player to Drop Ball Into Area of Casual Water

Q. In the circumstances described in Decision 1-4/8, if the nature of the area of casual water were such that it was impracticable or impossible for the player to drop the ball, when taking relief from the cart path, into the area of casual water, how may the player proceed?

A. If it is impracticable for the player to proceed under one of the two Rules, he may, in equity (Rule 1-4), obtain relief without penalty as follows: Using the position of the ball on the cart path, the nearest point of relief from both the cart path and the casual water must be determined that is not in a hazard or on a putting green. The player must lift the ball and drop it within one club-length of and not nearer the hole than the nearest point of relief, on a part of the course that avoids interference by the cart path and the casual water and is not in a hazard or on a putting green.

It would be considered impracticable for the player to drop the ball in the area of casual water if the casual water were so deep that unreasonable effort would be required to retrieve a ball lying in this area of casual water – see Decision 25-1/1.

Other examples of conditions into which it would be considered impracticable for the player to drop the ball would include:
- in or under an immovable obstruction such that it would be extremely difficult or impossible to drop the ball (e.g., inside a locked building or beneath a rain-shelter that is raised off the ground).
- within a large hole made by a greenkeeper or similar area of ground under repair from which the player could not reasonably be expected to play a ball.

1-4/9
Bird's Nest Interfering with Stroke

Q. A player's ball comes to rest in a bird's nest or so close to the nest that he could not make a stroke without damaging it. In equity (Rule 1-4), does the player have any options in addition to playing the ball as it lies or, if applicable, proceeding under Rule 26 or 28?

A. Yes. It is unreasonable to expect the player to play from such a situation and unfair to require the player to incur a penalty stroke under Rule 26 (Water Hazards) or Rule 28 (Ball Unplayable).

If the ball lay through the green, the player may, without penalty, drop a ball within one club-length of and not nearer the hole than the nearest spot not nearer the hole that would allow him to make his stroke without damaging the nest and that is not in a hazard and not on a putting green. The ball when dropped must first strike a part of the course through the green.

If the ball lay in a hazard, the player may drop a ball, without penalty, within one club-length of and not nearer the hole than the nearest spot not nearer the hole that would allow him to make his stroke without damaging the nest. If possible, the ball must be dropped in the same hazard and, if not possible, in a similar nearby hazard, but in either case not nearer the hole. If it is not possible for the player to drop the ball in a hazard, he may drop it, under penalty of one stroke, outside the hazard, keeping the point where the original ball lay between the hole and the spot on which the ball is dropped.

If the ball lay on the putting green, the player may, without penalty, place a ball at the nearest spot not nearer the hole and not in a hazard that would allow him to make his stroke without damaging the nest.

If interference by anything other than the bird's nest makes the stroke clearly impracticable or if damage to the bird's nest would occur only through the use of a clearly unreasonable stroke or an unnecessarily abnormal stance, swing, or direction of play, the player may not take relief as prescribed above, but he is not precluded from proceeding under Rule 26 or 28 if applicable. (Revised)

1-4/10
Dangerous Situation; Rattlesnake or Bees Interfere with Play

Q. A player's ball comes to rest in a situation dangerous to the player, e.g., near a live rattlesnake or a bees' nest. In equity (Rule 1-4), does the player have any options in addition to playing the ball as it lies or, if applicable, proceeding under Rule 26 or 28?

A. Yes. It is unreasonable to expect the player to play from such a dangerous situation and unfair to require the player to incur a penalty under Rule 26 (Water Hazards) or Rule 28 (Ball Unplayable).

If the ball lay through the green, the player may, without penalty, drop a ball within one club-length of and not nearer the hole than the nearest spot not nearer the hole that is not dangerous and is not in a hazard and not on a putting green.

If the ball lay in a hazard, the player may drop a ball, without penalty, within one club-length of and not nearer the hole than the nearest spot not nearer the hole that is not dangerous. If possible, the ball must be dropped in the same hazard and, if not possible, in a similar nearby hazard, but in either case not nearer the hole. If it is not possible for the player to drop the ball in a hazard, he may drop it, under penalty of one stroke, outside the hazard, keeping the point where the original ball lay between the hole and the spot on which the ball is dropped.

If the ball lay on the putting green, the player may, without penalty, place a ball at the nearest spot not nearer the hole that is not dangerous and that is not in a hazard.

If interference by anything other than the dangerous situation makes the stroke clearly impracticable or if the situation would be dangerous only through the use of a clearly unreasonable stroke or an unnecessarily abnormal stance, swing, or direction of play, the player may not take relief as prescribed above, but he is not precluded from proceeding under Rule 26 or 28 if applicable. (Revised)

Related Decision:
• 33-8/22 Local Rule Treating Ant Hills as Ground Under Repair.

1-4/11
Meaning of "Dangerous Situation"

Q. According to Decision 1-4/10, a ball lying near a live rattlesnake or a bees' nest is a "dangerous situation" and relief should be granted in equity.

If a player's ball comes to rest in or near an area of plants such as poison ivy, cacti or stinging nettles, should the provisions of Decision 1-4/10 apply?

A. No. The player must either play the ball as it lies or, if applicable, proceed under Rule 26 (Water Hazards) or Rule 28 (Ball Unplayable).

Decision 1-4/10 contemplates a situation which is unrelated to conditions normally encountered on the course. Unpleasant lies are a common occurrence which players must accept.

1-4/12
Player Breaches Rules More Than Once; Whether Multiple Penalties Should Be Applied

Situations arise prior to or as a result of a stroke in which a player breaches a single Rule more than once, or breaches separate Rules, in a single act or in different but sequential acts. The question arises whether it is appropriate to apply a penalty to each separate breach.

The Rules expressly provide that multiple penalties are not to be applied in certain situations (e.g., Rules 15-2, 18, 20-7 and 21). However, there are many other situations where multiple breaches of the Rules may occur and the Rules themselves do not expressly specify whether a penalty should be applied to each separate breach. In such cases, equity (Rule 1-4) applies, and the following principles should be used:

1. **One Act Results in One Rule Being Breached More Than Once – Single Penalty Applied**
   Example: In stroke play, a competitor's ball on the putting green strikes a fellow-competitor's ball in breach of Rule 19-5a and then strikes another fellow-competitor's ball, also in breach of Rule 19-5a. The ruling would be a single two-stroke penalty.

2. **One Act Results in Two Rules Being Breached – Single Penalty Applied**
   Example: In stroke play, a competitor is considering putting his ball from a bunker and rakes a footprint in the bunker on his line of play. Both Rule 13-2 and Rule 13-4a have been breached. The ruling would be a single two-stroke penalty.

3. **Related Acts Result in One Rule Being Breached More Than Once – Single Penalty Applied**
   Example 1: In stroke play, a competitor takes several practice swings in a hazard, touching the ground each time. The practice swings are related acts breaching a single Rule. The ruling would be a single two-stroke

penalty under Rule 13-4b (see Decision 13-4/3 but also see Principle 6 Example 3).

Example 2: A and B are fellow-competitors playing a par three hole. B is to play first and A asks B whether it is best to play for the center of the green or to play for the flagstick and B advises that it is best to play for the center of the green. A then asks what club B is going to use. B says he will hit a six iron. After B's stroke, which fell short of the green, A asks B if he had hit it well and B confirms that he did. A then hit his shot. The ruling is that both competitors incur a single two-stroke penalty under Rule 8-1 for seeking or giving three related pieces of information all of which might assist A in his choice of club for his next stroke and the way to play it (But see also Principle 6 Example 2).

4. **Related Acts Result in Two Rules Being Breached – Single Penalty Applied**

Example 1: In stroke play, a competitor is considering putting his ball from a bunker and rakes several footprints in the bunker on his line of play. Both Rule 13-2 and Rule 13-4a have been breached multiple times by related acts. The ruling would be a single two-stroke penalty.

Example 2: In stroke play, a competitor's ball moves prior to address and, while it is in motion, it is accidentally stopped by the competitor's club in breach of Rule 19-2 and comes to rest against it. The competitor then moves the club, as a result of which his ball moves – a breach of Rule 18-2a. These related acts would result in a single one-stroke penalty (see Decision 19-2/1.5).

5. **Unrelated Acts Result in Two Rules Being Breached – Multiple Penalties Applied**

Example 1: In stroke play, a competitor (1) touches the ground in a hazard with his club while taking practice swings in a hazard and (2) improves his line of play by bending a shrub with his hand. The ruling would be a two-stroke penalty under Rule 13-4 (touching the ground in a hazard with his club) and a further penalty of two strokes under Rule 13-2 (for the unrelated act of improving his line of play by moving something growing), giving a total penalty of four strokes (see Decision 13-4/28).

Example 2: Under Example 2 in Principle 4 above, if the ball is not replaced before the competitor makes his next stroke, the failure to replace the ball is an unrelated act and the competitor incurs an additional penalty of two strokes under Rule 18-2a.

6. **Unrelated Acts Result in One Rule Being Breached More Than Once – Multiple Penalties Applied**

Example 1: In stroke play, a competitor (1) purposely steps on another player's line of putt with the intention of improving the line, and then (2) purposely stops his own ball in motion after it began moving without apparent cause before address. As the two acts were unrelated, the ruling would be two separate penalties, each of two strokes, for breaches of Rule 1-2, giving a total penalty of four strokes.

Example 2: A and B are fellow-competitors waiting for the green to clear at a par three hole. A, who has been hitting all his iron shots right of target, asks B if his (A's) alignment has been wrong. B confirms that A's alignment has been wrong. After the green clears A asks B what club B is going to play. B does not answer. The ruling would be that A and B both incur a two-stroke penalty for asking for and giving advice about A's alignment (advice on the method of making a stroke). A incurs an additional two-stroke penalty for asking for information from B, which might assist A with his choice of club. Although both requests by A are breaches of the same Rule (Rule 8-1) their character is sufficiently different to warrant two separate penalties.

Example 3: Under Example I in Principle 3 above, the competitor then makes a stroke and fails to get the ball out of the hazard. He makes two more practice swings in the hazard, again touching the ground each time. The ruling would be two separate two-stroke penalties under Rule 13-4b. The link between the acts was broken by the competitor's intervening stroke (see also Decision 1-4/14).

For the purposes of this Decision:
- in making the judgment whether two acts are related or unrelated, the Committee should consider, among other things, the similarity of the acts, how close to one another they are in terms of time and location and whether there were any intervening events;
- each principal subsection of a Rule is considered a separate Rule (e.g., Rules 1-2, 1-3 and 1-4 are considered separate Rules); and
- the following sub-subsections (but only these ones) are also considered separate Rules: 4-3a, 4-3b, 13-4a, 13-4b, 13-4c, 14-2a, 14-2b, 16-1a, 16-1b, 16-1c, 16-1d, 16-1e, 16-1f, 17-3a, 17-3b, 17-3c, 18-2a and 18-2b. (Revised)

1-4/13
Player Advised of Breach of Rule; Player Breaches Same Rule Prior to Stroke

Q. In stroke play, a competitor, whose ball lies in a bunker, makes a practice swing and touches the ground in the bunker with his club. His fellow-competitor advises him that his action may be a breach of the Rules. The competitor disagrees and makes several more practice swings prior to making his stroke, touching the sand each time. What is the penalty?

A. As the competitor was correctly advised that touching the ground in the bunker with his club during a practice swing was a breach of the Rules (Rule 13-4b), the third principle in Decision 1-4/12 is not applicable. Therefore, the competitor is penalized four strokes – two strokes for the initial breach and two strokes for all subsequent breaches when the additional practice swings were made.

Related Decisions:
- 13-4/3 Touching Ground in Hazard with Several Practice Swings.
- 13-4/28 Grounding Club, Moving Loose Impediments and Improving Area of Intended Swing in Hazard.

1-4/14
Player Breaches Same Rule Before and After Stroke

Q. In stroke play, a competitor whose ball lies in a bunker makes a practice swing, touching the ground in the bunker with his club in breach of Rule 13-4. He makes the stroke, but the ball remains in the bunker. Before his next stroke, he makes another practice swing, again touching the ground in the bunker. What is the penalty?

A. The competitor incurs two separate penalties, each of two strokes, for breaches of Rule 13-4, giving a total penalty of four strokes. The third principle in Decision 1-4/12 does not apply in this case as the player made a stroke between the two breaches.

1-4/15
Player Breaches Two Rules with Different Penalties; More Severe Penalty Applied

Q. In stroke play, a competitor is searching for his ball under a tree. He accidentally moves his ball with his foot in breach of Rule 18-2a and, at the same time, breaks a branch, improving the area of his intended swing in breach of Rule 13-2. What is the ruling?

A. The competitor has breached two Rules as a result of a single act. In accordance with the second principle in Decision 1-4/12, the competitor only incurs a single penalty. However, in this case, the Rules that have been breached by the competitor give different penalties (i.e., Rule 18-2a carries a one stroke penalty and Rule 13-2 carries a two stroke penalty). In such circumstances, in equity (Rule 1-4), the more severe of the two penalties must be applied and, therefore, the competitor is penalized two strokes under Rule 13-2.

If the same circumstances arose in match play, the player would lose the hole for the breach of Rule 13-2.

Decisions related to Decisions 1-4/12 through 1-4/15, whether multiple penalties apply: See "Multiple Penalty Situations" in the Index.

Other Decisions related to Rule 1-4: See "Equity" in the Index.

RULE 2

MATCH PLAY

DEFINITIONS
All defined terms are in *italics* and are listed alphabetically in the Definitions section – see pages 6–16.

2-1. GENERAL
A match consists of one *side* playing against another over a *stipulated round* unless otherwise decreed by the *Committee*.

In match play the game is played by holes.

Except as otherwise provided in the *Rules*, a hole is won by the *side* that *holes* its ball in the fewer *strokes*. In a handicap match, the lower net score wins the hole.

The state of the match is expressed by the terms: so many "holes up" or "all square," and so many "to play."

A *side* is "dormie" when it is as many holes up as there are holes remaining to be played.

2-2. HALVED HOLE
A hole is halved if each *side holes* out in the same number of *strokes*.

When a player has *holed* out and his *opponent* has been left with a *stroke* for the half, if the player subsequently incurs a penalty, the hole is halved.

2-3. WINNER OF MATCH
A match is won when one *side* leads by a number of holes greater than the number remaining to be played.

If there is a tie, the *Committee* may extend the *stipulated round* by as many holes as are required for a match to be won.

2-4. CONCESSION OF MATCH, HOLE OR NEXT STROKE
A player may concede a match at any time prior to the start or conclusion of that match.

A player may concede a hole at any time prior to the start or conclusion of that hole.

A player may concede his *opponent's* next *stroke* at any time, provided the *opponent's* ball is at rest. The *opponent* is considered to have *holed* out with his next *stroke*, and the ball may be removed by either *side*.

A concession may not be declined or withdrawn.

(Ball overhanging hole – see Rule 16-2)

2-5. DOUBT AS TO PROCEDURE; DISPUTES AND CLAIMS
In match play, if a doubt or dispute arises between the players, a player may make a claim. If no duly authorized representative of the *Committee* is available within a reasonable time, the players must continue the match

without delay. The *Committee* may consider a claim only if it has been made in a timely manner and if the player making the claim has notified his *opponent* at the time (i) that he is making a claim or wants a ruling and (ii) of the facts upon which the claim or ruling is to be based.

A claim is considered to have been made in a timely manner if, upon discovery of circumstances giving rise to a claim, the player makes his claim (i) before any player in the match plays from the next *teeing ground*, or (ii) in the case of the last hole of the match, before all players in the match leave the *putting green*, or (iii) when the circumstances giving rise to the claim are discovered after all the players in the match have left the *putting green* of the final hole, before the result of the match has been officially announced.

A claim relating to a prior hole in the match may only be considered by the *Committee* if it is based on facts previously unknown to the player making the claim and he had been given wrong information (Rules 6-2a or 9) by an *opponent*. Such a claim must be made in a timely manner.

Once the result of the match has been officially announced, a claim may not be considered by the *Committee*, unless it is satisfied that (i) the claim is based on facts which were previously unknown to the player making the claim at the time the result was officially announced, (ii) the player making the claim had been given wrong information by an *opponent* and (iii) the *opponent* knew he was giving wrong information. There is no time limit on considering such a claim.

Note 1: A player may disregard a breach of the *Rules* by his *opponent* provided there is no agreement by the *sides* to waive a *Rule* (Rule 1-3).

Note 2: In match play, if a player is doubtful of his rights or the correct procedure, he may not complete the play of the hole with two balls.

2-6. GENERAL PENALTY

The penalty for a breach of a *Rule* in match play is loss of hole except when otherwise provided.

MATCHES: GENERAL

2/1
Players in Singles Match Accompanied by Third Party

Q. Prior to a singles match between A and B, A stated to B that a third player, C, would be playing with them. B played the match under protest and lost. What ruling should the Committee give?

A. A single is a match in which one plays against another. Since B made a timely claim, the Committee should have awarded the match to B. If B had not protested, i.e., had agreed that C accompany the match, the result of the match would stand as played.

2/2
Stipulated Round in Match Play

In all forms of match play other than threesomes and foursomes, a player has begun his stipulated round when he makes his first stroke in that round. In threesomes and foursomes match play, the side has begun its stipulated round when it makes its first stroke in that round.

The stipulated round has ended in match play when all of the players in the match have completed the final hole of the match (although a player may lodge a subsequent claim under Rule 2-5 or correct wrong information under Rule 9-2b(iii)). With the first round of a 36-hole match, the stipulated round has ended when all the players in the match have completed the final hole of that stipulated round.

2/3
Refusal to Comply with Rule in Match Play

Q. In a match, A requests B to lift B's ball that is on A's line of play. B refuses to do so. What is the ruling?

A. In equity (Rule 1-4), B loses the hole for failing to comply with A's request to lift his ball under Rule 22-2.

Related Decisions: See "Refusal to Comply with Rule" in the Index.

MATCH PLAY: GENERAL

2-1/1
Players Unable to Resolve Rules Problem Agree to Consider Hole Halved

Q. In a match, A putted to within three inches of the hole and then knocked his ball away. B, the opponent, objected. He stated that he wanted A's ball left by the hole. A and B were uncertain how to resolve the matter, so they agreed to consider the hole halved. Should A and B be disqualified under Rule 1-3?

A. No. There was no agreement to waive the Rules. Rather, the players were ignorant of the Rules.

Related Decisions:
- 1-3/5 Players Unaware Penalty Incurred.
- 2-5/8.5 Player and Opponent Agree on Incorrect Procedure; Whether Valid Claim May Be Made After Procedure Followed.

2-1/1.5
Players Agree to Consider Hole Halved During Play of Hole

Q. In a match, a player and his opponent play their second shots on a par 5 hole. Unexpectedly, neither ball can be found. Rather than proceeding under Rule 27-1, both players agree to a half. Is this permitted?

A. Yes. An agreement to halve a hole being played does not of itself constitute an agreement to waive the Rules.

However, if the players agree to consider a hole halved without either player making a stroke, they should be disqualified under Rule 1-3 for agreeing to exclude the operation of Rule 2-1 by failing to play the stipulated round.

2-1/2
Minus or Zero Net Score

Q. In a handicap match, a player entitled to two handicap strokes at a par-3 hole scores a 2 or a hole-in-one. What would be his net score in each case?

A. The player's net score would be zero (0) if he scored a 2 or minus 1 (-1) if he had a hole-in-one.

The same would be true in a four-ball stroke-play or Stableford competition since scores are calculated on a hole-by-hole basis.

2-1/3
Hole Inadvertently Omitted in Match; Error Discovered After Match Concluded

Q. The players in a match inadvertently omitted playing a hole. The error was discovered after the match had been played to a conclusion. What is the ruling?

A. The result should stand.

2-1/4
Two Holes Purposely Omitted in Match

Q. The players in a match agreed to omit two holes, i.e., agreed to settle the match over 16 holes. Is this permitted?

A. No. The players are disqualified under Rule 1-3 for excluding the operation of Rule 2-1 by failing to play the stipulated round.

2-1/5
Three Holes Played Out of Sequence in Match

Q. In a match, the players by mistake play three holes out of sequence. The error is discovered before the match concludes. What is the ruling?

A. There is no penalty, and those three holes stand as played. If the players were to replay the three holes in the proper sequence, there would be no penalty, and the three holes would stand as replayed.

2-1/6
Replaying Match When Play Discontinued Instead of Resuming from Where Play Stopped

Q. A match which was all square after 16 holes was discontinued by agreement due to darkness. The match should have been resumed at the 17th hole. However, the players, thinking it was in accordance with the Rules, replayed the match starting at the 1st tee. The result was posted. At that point the Committee became aware of the improper procedure. What is the ruling?

A. The result of the match as replayed should stand. The players were not subject to disqualification under Rule 1-3 because they were unaware that their procedure was contrary to the Rules.

HALVED HOLE

2-2/1
Player Putting for Half Is Given Advice by Opponent

The following is an example of the application of the second paragraph of Rule 2-2: In a match, A has holed out. As B, A's opponent, is preparing to putt for a half, A gives B advice as to his line of putt. A would normally lose the hole for a breach of Rule 8-1, but Rule 2-2 becomes operative in these circumstances and the hole is halved.

Related Decision:
• 30-3/3 Application of Rule 2-2 in Four-Ball Match Play.

Other Decisions related to Rule 2-2: See "Halved Hole" in the Index.

WINNER OF MATCH

2-3/1
Players Under Impression Match Is Over Later Realize It Was All Square

Q. In a match, A and B left the 18th green under the impression that A had won. They later realized that in fact the match was all square. The matter was referred to the Committee. What is the ruling?

A. Since there was no indication that wrong information had been given, the match stands as played, with A the winner.

2-3/2
Result of Match When Player Dormie and Opponent Concedes

Q. In a match between A and B, A is one up playing the last hole. In the following situations and considering B's actions, does A win by one hole or two holes?

(i) B is on the green in three strokes but a long way from the hole. A plays his third stroke from the edge of the green and it comes to rest about one foot from the hole. B goes over and shakes hands with A.

(ii) B is on the green in two strokes. A holes his third stroke and B shakes hands with A.

(iii) A plays his second shot from the fairway on to the green. B's second shot misses the green and plugs in a bunker. B immediately walks over to A and shakes his hand.

(iv) B is on the green in six strokes but a long way from the hole. A plays his third stroke from the edge of the green and it comes to rest about one foot from the hole. B goes over and shakes hands with A.

(v) A is on the green in two strokes. B plays his third stroke from the fairway onto the green and the ball comes to rest about one foot from the hole. B goes over and shakes hands with A.

A. The handshake between the players is deemed to represent an agreement to concede each player's next stroke. Accordingly, in situations (i)–(iii), A wins the match by one hole. In situations (iv) and (v), A has won the final hole and wins the match by two holes.

CONCESSION OF MATCH, HOLE OR NEXT STROKE

2-4/1
Player Concedes Opponent's Next Stroke and Then Knocks Opponent's Ball into Hole

Q. A player conceded his opponent's next stroke and then, in attempting to knock the opponent's ball back to him, he inadvertently knocked the ball into the hole. The opponent, who had played three strokes prior to the concession, claimed a 3 for the hole. Was the claim valid?

A. No. The player conceded the opponent a 4 for the hole and, at that point, the opponent had completed the hole. It is irrelevant that the player subsequently knocked the opponent's ball into the hole, whether he did so inadvertently or otherwise.

2-4/2
Ball Falls into Hole After Concession of Next Stroke

Q. A player's ball overhung the edge of the hole. After elapse of the time allowed in Rule 16-2, the opponent conceded the player's next stroke for a 5, after which the player's ball fell into the hole. What was the player's score for the hole?

A. The player's score was 5. It is immaterial that the player's ball fell into the hole after the opponent had conceded the player's next stroke. If the opponent had not conceded the next stroke, the player's score would also be 5 because in those circumstances the player would be deemed to have holed out with his last stroke and he would incur a penalty stroke – Rule 16-2.

Related Decisions:
- 1-2/4 Player Jumps Close to Hole to Cause Ball to Drop; Ball Moves.
- 16-2/2 Ball Overhanging Hole Knocked Away by Opponent Before Player Determines Status.
- 18-2b/10 Ball Falls into Hole After Being Addressed.

2-4/3
Player Lifts Ball in Mistaken Belief That Next Stroke Conceded

Q. In a match between A and B, B made a statement which A interpreted to mean that his (A's) next stroke was conceded. Accordingly, A lifted his ball. B then said that he had not conceded A's next stroke. What is the ruling?

A. If B's statement could reasonably have led A to think his next stroke had been conceded, in equity (Rule 1-4), A should replace his ball as near as possible to where it lay, without penalty.

Otherwise, A would incur a penalty stroke for lifting his ball without marking its position – Rule 20-1 – and he must replace his ball as near as possible to where it lay.

2-4/3.5
Stroke Conceded by Caddie

Q. In a match between A and B, B's caddie purports to concede A's next stroke, whereupon A lifts his ball. What is the ruling?

A. As a player's caddie does not have the authority to make a concession, the purported concession is invalid. As A had reasonably believed his next stroke had been conceded, in equity (Rule 1-4), A incurs no penalty and must replace the ball. B incurs no penalty; however, had B's caddie lifted A's ball, B would have incurred a one-stroke penalty under Rule 18-3b.

Decisions related to 2-4/3 and 2-4/3.5:
- 9-2/5 Incorrect Information Causes Opponent to Lift His Ball-Marker.
- 20-1/8 Ball-Marker Lifted by Player Who Mistakenly Believes He Has Won Hole.
- 26-1/9 Caddie Lifts Ball in Water Hazard Without Player's Authority.

2-4/4
Whether Picking Up Opponent's Ball Is Concession of Next Stroke

Q. In match play, A holes a putt and, thinking he has won the match, picks up B's ball. B then advises A that he (B) had a putt to win the hole. Did A concede B's next stroke when he picked up B's ball?

A. No. A incurred a penalty stroke under Rule 18-3b; B must replace his ball and now has two putts to win the hole.

2-4/5
Whether Lifting Opponent's Ball-Marker Is Concession of Next Stroke

Q. In a match, A believing he has won a hole picks up the coin marking the position of his opponent B's ball. In fact B had a putt to halve the hole. Should the picking up of B's ball-marker be considered a concession of B's next stroke?

A. No. In equity (Rule 1-4), A should be penalized one stroke. Therefore, under the second paragraph of Rule 2-2 the hole is automatically halved.

Decisions related to 2-4/4 and 2-4/5:
• 2-4/17 Player in Erroneous Belief Match Is Over Shakes Opponent's Hand and Picks Up Opponent's Ball.
• 30/5 In Four-Ball Match Player with Putt for Half Picks Up in Error at Suggestion of Opponent Based on Misunderstanding.

2-4/6
Putting Out After Concession of Stroke

Rule 2-4 does not cover the question of whether a player may putt out after his next stroke has been conceded. A player incurs no penalty for holing out in such circumstances. However, if the act would be of assistance to a partner in a four-ball or best-ball match, the partner is, in equity (Rule 1-4), disqualified for the hole.

2-4/7
Concession of Stroke Refused by Player and Withdrawn by Opponent; Player Then Putts and Misses

Q. In a match between A and B, A putts and his ball comes to rest near the hole. B concedes A's next stroke. A says: "No. I haven't holed out yet." B says: "OK. Go ahead and putt." A putts and misses. In such circumstances, is the concession invalidated?

A. No. When B conceded A's next stroke, A had completed the hole. Concession of a stroke may not be declined or withdrawn – see Rule 2-4.

2-4/8
Player Concedes Opponent's Next Stroke and Plays Before Opponent Has Opportunity to Lift Ball

Q. In a match between A and B, A chips and his ball comes to rest about one foot from the hole. B concedes A's next stroke. A states that he wishes to lift his ball. However, B proceeds to play his next stroke before A has an opportunity to lift his ball and B's ball strikes A's ball. What is the ruling?

A. B deprived A of his right to lift his ball after his next stroke was conceded. In equity (Rule 1-4), B lost the hole, whether or not his ball struck A's ball.

Related Decisions:
- 2/3 Refusal to Comply with Rule in Match Play.
- 3-4/1 Competitor Not Given Opportunity to Lift Ball Assisting Fellow-Competitor.
- 16-2/4 Ball Overhanging Lip of Hole Moves When Flagstick Removed.
- 17-4/2 Ball Resting Against Flagstick; Putt Conceded and Ball Removed Before Player Can Remove Flagstick.
- 22/6 Competitor Requests That Ball in Position to Assist Him Not Be Lifted.
- 30-3f/11 Request to Lift Ball That Might Assist Partner Not Honored.

2-4/9
Player Concedes Hole After Which It Is Discovered Opponent Had Played Wrong Ball

Q. In a match between A and B, A has made two strokes and the ball with which he made his second stroke out of the rough is on the green. B, having played five, concedes the hole to A. A then discovers that he has played a wrong ball to the green. What is the ruling?

A. A lost the hole (Rule 15-3a) before B conceded it to him. Therefore, B's concession was irrelevant.

2-4/10
Player Concedes Hole After Which Opponent Plays Wrong Ball

Q. In a three-ball match, A loses his ball and concedes the hole to B and C. Subsequently, B plays a wrong ball. Is A's concession to B binding?

A. Yes.

2-4/11
Player with Lost Ball Concedes Hole; Ball Then Found in Hole

Q. In a match, A played his second shot towards the green but he could not find his ball. He conceded the hole to B, whose second shot was on the green. The following players then found A's ball in the hole. What is the ruling?

A. Since a player may not concede a hole after conclusion of the hole (Rule 2-4) A holed out in two strokes and won the hole if he made a claim before B played from the next teeing ground (Rule 2-5). If A did not do so, he lost the hole.

Decisions related to 2-4/10 and 2-4/11:
• 1-1/4 Player Discovers Own Ball Is in Hole After Playing Wrong Ball.
• 2-5/5 Invalid Claim Not Disputed.
• 9-2/11 Opponent's Misreading of Number on Player's Ball Results in Agreement That Player Lost Hole.

2-4/12
Player Concedes Hole on Basis of Invalid Claim

Q. In a match between A and B, A putts out of turn. B incorrectly claims that A loses the hole for putting out of turn. A protests but concedes the hole. Later, A, having consulted the Rule book, lodges an official protest with the Committee. How should the Committee rule?

A. Although B's claim was invalid – see Rule 10-1c – A lost the hole when he conceded it (Rule 2-4).

2-4/13
Implied Concession of Hole Withdrawn

Q. A, unable to find his ball after a two-minute search, suggests to B, his opponent, that they move on to the next hole. A's ball is then found. A withdraws his suggestion to move on to the next hole and play is resumed. Before A plays his ball, B plays a stroke with a wrong ball. What is the ruling?

A. A's suggestion amounted to a concession of the hole and B won the hole. Concession of a hole may not be withdrawn (Rule 2-4). B's actions after A's concession could not deprive him of a hole already won.

2-4/14
Player Concedes Match Due to Misconception as to Opponent's Score at Last Hole

Q. In a match, A and B were all square playing the last hole. A had a short putt for a 4. B holed a putt for a 4. A, mistakenly believing that B had holed out in three strokes, shook hands with B, conceded the match and lifted his ball. At that point B told A that he (B) had scored a 4. What is the ruling?

A. A conceded the match. Even if A had not conceded the match, he lost it when he lifted his ball without marking its position and thereby incurred a penalty stroke under Rule 20-1.

2-4/15
Player Concedes Match After Winning It When Opponent Lodges Invalid Claim Regarding Strokes Taken

Q. In a match, A and B were all square playing the last hole. A incurred a penalty without knowing it, and accordingly did not advise B of the penalty. B was aware of what had happened but did not realize it was a breach of the Rules either.

A won the hole and the match, and the result was posted.

Subsequently, a spectator informed B that A had incurred a penalty at the 18th hole. B then claimed the hole and the match, and A conceded the match to B.

Who was the rightful winner?

A. A won the match because a match can only be conceded prior to its conclusion (Rule 2-4).

A gave wrong information when he did not advise B that he had incurred a penalty and would have lost the hole had a claim been made in a timely manner – Rule 9-2b(i). However, a belated claim by B was not valid for two reasons:

(1) it was not based on facts previously unknown to B, and

(2) the claim was made after the result of the match was announced – see Rule 2-5. (Revised)

2-4/16
Valid Timely Claim Made After Concession of Match

Q. In a match, A and B are playing the last hole. B is 1 up. A holes out for a 4. B putts from a wrong place and holes the putt for a 4. A congratulates B and concedes the match. Before leaving the putting green, A asks B if he (B) had putted from a wrong place. B acknowledges that he did so. A claims that B loses the hole under Rule 20-7b. Is the claim valid?

A. Yes. Concession of a match is not binding if subsequently a valid claim is made in a timely manner. A's valid claim was made within the time limit in Rule 2-5. (Revised)

Related Decision:
• 9-2/10 Player Omits Penalty Stroke When Advising Opponent as to Score for Hole; Error Discovered After Match Conceded by Opponent.

2-4/17
Player in Erroneous Belief Match Is Over Shakes Opponent's Hand and Picks Up Opponent's Ball

Q. In match play, A holes a putt and, thinking he has won the match, shakes hands with B and picks up B's ball. The referee advises B that he had a putt to win the hole and keep the match alive. Has B conceded the match by his acquiescence in A's action of shaking hands and picking up B's ball?

A. No. B was entitled to replace his ball and hole out. Since A incurred a one-stroke penalty under Rule 18-3b, B now had two putts to win the hole.

Related Decisions:
- 2-4/4 Whether Picking Up Opponent's Ball Is Concession of Next Stroke.
- 2-4/5 Whether Lifting Opponent's Ball-Marker Is Concession of Next Stroke.
- 30/5 In Four-Ball Match Player with Putt for Half Picks Up in Error at Suggestion of Opponent Based on Misunderstanding.

2-4/18 (Reserved)

2-4/19
Winner of Match Wishes to Default to Beaten Opponent

Q. In match play, A defeats B and then concedes the match to B because he (A) cannot continue in the competition. Is this permissible?

A. No. A won the match. A beaten player may not be reinstated in such circumstances. A should be posted as the winner and, since A cannot continue, A's opponent in the next round would win by default.

Under Rule 2-4, a side may concede a match at any time prior to conclusion of the match, but not thereafter.

2-4/20
Player Unable to Meet Match-Play Schedule Defaults; Schedule Then Changed and Player Requests Reinstatement

Q. The final matches in a competition were to be played on a Saturday. A was to play B in one match. On Thursday, A defaulted to B, saying that he would be out of town on Saturday.

On Saturday, the course was unplayable and the matches were postponed until the following Saturday.

On Monday, A requested that he be reinstated. Should the Committee reinstate A?

A. No. A conceded the match as provided for in Rule 2-4. In the circumstances, concession is irrevocable.

Related Decision:
- 6-8b/4 Player Unable to Resume Suspended Match at Scheduled Time.

2-4/21
Wrong Form of Play Used to Decide Which Side Concedes Match

Q. In a foursome match, the players are unable to arrange a date to play their match within the prescribed time limit for the round. As a result, the players agree to play a singles match between one player from each side in order to decide which side would concede the match in accordance with Rule 2-4. Is this permissible?

A. There is nothing in the Rules of Golf to prohibit players from agreeing to a method of determining which side will concede a match. However, in view of the intention of Rule 1-3 (Agreement to Waive Rules), if players agree to play a match other than in the form prescribed in the conditions of the competition in order to decide which side will concede, both sides should be disqualified under Rule 1-3 for agreeing to exclude the operation of a condition of competition (Rule 33-1).

If the players agree to use some other method which does not involve playing a match to determine which side will concede, such as a putting competition, tossing a coin, etc., they are not considered to be in breach of Rule 1-3.

Related Decisions:
- 1-3/7 Agreement That Side Losing After 18 Holes of 36-Hole Match Will Concede Match.
- 6-1/1 Wrong Form of Play Used in Match-Play Event.
- 33-1/4 Match Decided by Wrong Form of Play by Agreement of Players.

2-4/22
Players Agree to Concede Holes to Each Other

Q. Before or during a match, A and B agree to concede one or more holes to each other, thereby enabling them, in effect, to play a shorter match. If A and B know that such an arrangement is not permissible, are they subject to disqualification under Rule 1-3?

A. Yes. Although Rule 2-4 allows a player to concede a hole before playing it, an agreement between players to concede holes to each other exceeds this authority as it undermines the principle in Rule 2-1 of playing a stipulated round. Therefore, such an agreement constitutes an agreement to waive the Rules.

Other Decisions related to Rule 2-4: See "Concession" and "Default" in the Index

DOUBT AS TO PROCEDURE: DISPUTES AND CLAIMS

2-5/1 (Reserved)

2-5/2
Procedure for a Valid Claim

For a claim to be valid, the claimant must notify his opponent (i) that he is making a claim or wants a ruling and, (ii) the facts of the situation. He must do so within the time required by Rule 2-5. For example, Rule 16-1e prohibits putting from a stance astride an extension of the line of putt behind the ball. In a match between A and B, if A putts from a stance astride an extension of the line and B states "that is not allowed, you are penalized" or

"I'm making a claim because of that stroke," the Committee should consider the claim.

Statements by B such as "I'm not sure that's allowed" or "I don't think you can do that" do not by themselves constitute a valid claim because each statement does not contain the notice of a claim or that he wants a ruling and the facts of the situation. (Revised)

2-5/3
Player Lifts Ball Before Holing Out; Opponent Then Picks Up His Ball Claiming Player Loses Hole

Q. In match play, A's ball was resting against the flagstick but it was not holed. A, believing he had holed out, lifted his ball without first marking its position. In doing so, A incurred a penalty stroke under Rule 20-1. Since A was not aware that he had incurred a penalty, he did not inform B. B, who had not witnessed A's actions, made his next stroke. A's actions were then brought to the attention of B and he picked up his ball, claiming that A's lifting of his ball entailed a penalty of loss of hole. A and B agreed to continue the match and refer B's claim to the Committee later. How should the Committee have ruled?

A. The Committee should have ruled that B won the hole. B's claim was valid since he notified his opponent that he was making a claim or wanted a ruling (A and B agreed to refer B's claim to the Committee), and the facts that gave rise to the claim (A's lifting of the ball). Although the penalty for A's lifting of the ball without first marking its position is one stroke, he lost the hole for giving wrong information (Rule 9-2b) when he failed to inform B before he (B) made his next stroke that he (A) had incurred the penalty stroke.(Revised)

Related Decisions:
- 9-2/6 Player Reporting Wrong Score Causes Opponent with Chance for Half to Pick Up Ball.
- 30/5 In Four-Ball Match Player with Putt for Half Picks Up in Error at Suggestion of Opponent Based on Misunderstanding.
- 30-3f/3 Player's Ball Resting Against Flagstick Lifted Before Being Holed; Others in Match Pick Up Mistakenly Believing Player Won Hole.

2-5/4
Player Wins Hole with Own Ball After Playing Wrong Ball; Opponent Lodges Belated Claim

Q. In a match, A and B are all square playing the last hole. A plays a wrong ball in the rough and discovers the error before his next stroke. A and B go back to look for A's ball without any question being raised as to whether A had incurred a penalty. A's ball is found. A plays out the hole with his original ball and wins the hole and the match.

Several days later B claims the last hole and the match by virtue of the fact that A played a wrong ball.

Is the claim valid?

A. No. A gave wrong information when he did not advise B that he (A) had incurred a penalty – Rule 9-2b(i). However, a belated claim by B was not valid for two reasons:

(1) it was not based on facts previously unknown to B, and

(2) the claim was made after the result of the match was announced – see Rule 2-5.

Related Decisions:
- 9-2/8 Player Wins Hole with Wrong Ball; Error Discovered at Next Hole; Opponent Claims Previous Hole.
- 30-3c/2 Player Wins Hole with Wrong Ball and Partner Picks Up; Error Discovered at Next Hole.
- 30-3c/3 Players on Opposite Sides Exchange Balls During Play of Hole and Their Partners Pick Up; Error Discovered at Next Hole.
- 30-3c/4 Player Plays Partner's Ball; Error Discovered After Opponents Have Played Next Strokes.

2-5/5
Invalid Claim Not Disputed

Q. In a match, A played a wrong ball to a green and then found his own ball in the hole. His own ball had been holed in three strokes, which was fewer strokes than B had taken. However, B claimed the hole on the grounds that A had played a wrong ball. A did not dispute the claim. A lost the match.

Later, A learned that, because he had completed the hole when his own ball was holed and before play of a wrong ball, the play of the wrong ball was irrelevant and he was the rightful winner of the hole in question. A then lodged a claim with the Committee. Was the claim valid?

A. No. Since A did not dispute B's invalid claim before B played from the next teeing ground, B's claim stands and B won the hole in question (Rule 2-5).

Related Decisions:
- 2-4/10 Player Concedes Hole After Which Opponent Plays Wrong Ball.
- 2-4/11 Player with Lost Ball Concedes Hole; Ball Then Found in Hole.
- 9-2/11 Opponent's Misreading of Number on Player's Ball Results in Agreement That Player Lost Hole.

2-5/5.5
Breach of 14-Club Rule Discovered After Match Concluded But Before Result Officially Announced

Q. On completion of the 14th hole in a match between A and B, A wins by 5 and 4. The players continue the round. After the 16th hole, it is discovered by the players that A has 15 clubs in his bag.

Before the result of the match has been officially announced, B reports the facts to the Committee and asks for a ruling. Is the claim valid?

A. Yes. Although the players had left the putting green of the last hole of the match, B's claim is based on facts previously unknown to him and he is deemed to have been given wrong information by A (Rule 9-2b(i)). The players must return to the 15th hole and resume the match. A is penalized under Rule 4-4a and is three up with four holes to play.

2-5/6
Players Mistakenly Believe Match Is All Square After 18 Holes and Play Extra Hole Without Claim Being Made

Q. In a match between A and B, A is 1 up after the prescribed 18 holes. However, both A and B believe the match is all square. So they play extra holes and B wins at the 20th hole. The error is then discovered. What is the ruling?

A. Since A did not make a claim before either player played from the tee at the 19th hole, the match must be considered all square at that point. Thus, B was the winner.

2-5/7
Rightful Winner of Match Makes No Claim and Agrees to Play Extra Holes

Q. In a match, A and B are all square going to the 18th hole. On completion of the 18th hole, B states that he has scored 7; A states that he (A) has scored 6. A and B go into the clubhouse under the impression that A has won the match. At that point B tells A that, on reflection, he (B) believes A scored 7 at the 18th hole. On recounting, A acknowledges that he had a 7.

By agreement, A and B resume the match; A wins it at the 20th hole and the result is posted.

That night, B discovers that, because A gave wrong information after completion of the 18th hole, under Rule 9-2b(iii) he (B) was rightfully the winner of the 18th hole and the match. B reports the matter to the Committee and claims the match. What is the ruling?

A. The match stands as played, with A the winner.

B's claim was not made within the time limit in Rule 2-5. B's claim would have been valid if he had refused to play extra holes or had played the extra holes under protest.

2-5/8
Status of Valid Claim If Players Accept Wrong Ruling from Someone Not on Committee and Continue Match

Q. In an 18-hole match between A and B, A's ball strikes the flagstick which was attended by B. A and B believe that a loss-of-hole penalty is incurred but they are in doubt as to which one of them incurs the penalty. Accordingly, before teeing off at the next hole, they agree to refer the matter to the Committee later.

At the conclusion of 18 holes, A and B agree that if B incurred a loss-of-hole penalty at the hole in question, the match is all square; if A incurred it,

B has won the match by two holes. A and B seek a ruling from X, who is not on the Committee. X incorrectly advises A and B that B incurred the penalty and that the match is therefore all square.

A and B accept X's ruling, play extra holes and A wins.

Subsequently, the incident was brought to the attention of the Committee. What should the Committee do?

A. When A and B accepted X's incorrect ruling, they, in effect, settled the doubt themselves and, after A and B began playing extra holes, the Committee was no longer entitled to consider a claim. The match stands as played, with A the winner.

2-5/8.5
Player and Opponent Agree on Incorrect Procedure; Whether Valid Claim May Be Made After Procedure Followed

Q. In a match, a player's ball comes to rest on an artificially-surfaced road. He is uncertain if the road is to be treated as an immovable obstruction or an integral part of the course. He asks his opponent and they agree that the player should treat the road as an immovable obstruction. The player drops the ball in accordance with the procedure under Rule 24-2b and plays it. Prior to playing from the next tee, the opponent discovers that he and the player were wrong as the Committee had introduced a Local Rule declaring the road to be an integral part of the course and, therefore, the player was not entitled to take relief under Rule 24-2b. The player should have incurred a loss of hole penalty under Rule 18 for lifting his ball without authority and failing to replace it. May the opponent claim the hole?

A. No. The claim must not be considered by the Committee because the opponent and the player agreed that the player was entitled to relief under Rule 24-2b. When this agreement was reached, there was no longer a doubtful or disputed point and there was no basis under Rule 2-5 for making a claim.

The players were not in breach of Rule 1-3 as they believed at the time they were proceeding properly.

Related Decisions:
- 1-3/5 Players Unaware Penalty Incurred.
- 2-1/1 Players Unable to Resolve Rules Problem Agree to Consider Hole Halved.

2-5/9
Player Agreeing with Opponent That Hole Was Halved Later Realizes He Has Won Hole; Player Then Makes Claim

Q. In a match between A and B, at the 16th hole A scored 6 and B scored 5. When leaving the putting green, B commented to A: "A half?" and A replied: "Yes."

A won the match at the 20th hole and the result was posted. Later, B realized that he had won the 16th hole and, if the mistake had not been made, he would have won the match 1 up.

A admitted that he had made a mistake. B reported the matter to the Committee and claimed the match. Is the claim valid?

A. No. The match stands as played, with A the winner. After the result of the match was posted, the claim by B could have been considered only if A had knowingly given wrong information as to the number of strokes he (A) had taken at the 16th hole – see Rule 2-5.

Related Decision:
• 9-2/12 Conscious Failure to Correct Opponent's Misunderstanding of State of Match; What Constitutes Wrong Information.

2-5/10
Player Accepting Erroneous Claim Disputes It After Result Announced

Q. In a match, A was in breach of a Rule. Although the penalty for a breach of the Rule in question was only one stroke, B, his opponent, claimed that A lost the hole. A did not dispute the claim. B won the match and the result was posted. Three days later, A protested to the Committee that B had misinformed him with respect to the Rules. What is the ruling?

A. The match stands as played. Under Rule 2-5, no claim may be considered after the result of a match has been announced unless the opponent knowingly gave wrong information. Incorrect information on the Rules is not wrong information. It is up to each player to know the Rules.

Related Decision:
• 9/1 Incorrect Information on Rules.

2-5/11
Wrong Information Given After Play of Last Hole; Claim Made After Result Announced

Q. In a match, A and B came to the last hole all square. After completion of the hole, A stated that he had scored 9 and B stated that he (B) had scored 8, making B the winner, 1 up. The result was recorded by the Committee.

A few minutes later, a spectator told A that B had scored 9 at the last hole. B reviewed the hole and acknowledged that he had made a mistake and that his actual score was 9. What is the ruling?

A. The match stands as played, with B the winner. Under Rule 2-5 no claim may be considered after the result of a match is announced unless wrong information has been given knowingly.

2-5/12
Imposition of Penalty by Referee After Any Player in Match Has Played from Next Tee

Q. In match play, may a referee penalize a player for a breach of a Rule at a hole if he does not become aware of the breach until someone in the match has played from the next teeing ground?

A. Yes, unless the facts giving rise to the penalty were known to the opponent.

2-5/13
Extra Stroke Taken by Mistake in Handicap Match; Status of Late Claim

Q. Prior to the start of a handicap match, the two players correctly advised one another as to the handicaps to which they were entitled. However, during the match, A, by mistake, took a stroke to which he was not entitled at a certain hole. The error was discovered several holes later. Could B, the opponent, then claim the hole in question?

A. No. A late claim would not be valid unless it was based on facts previously unknown to B and B had been given wrong information by A. In this case A did not give B wrong information as to the number of strokes to which he was entitled during the round, and it was B's responsibility to know the holes at which handicap strokes were to be given (see Note under Rule 6-2). The hole in question stands as played.

Related Decision:
• 6-2a/3 Handicap Stroke Wrongly Claimed at Hole; Error Discovered Before Hole Completed.

2-5/14
When Match Result "Officially Announced"

Q. Rule 2-5 prohibits a Committee from considering a claim after the result of a match has been "officially announced," except in cases where a player knowingly gave wrong information. When is the result of a match "officially announced"?

A. It is a matter for the Committee to decide when the result of the match has been "officially announced" and it will vary depending on the nature of the competition. When an official scoreboard exists, Rule 2-5 should be interpreted so that the recording of the winner of the match on the official scoreboard is the official announcement of the result of the match. In such cases where a referee has been assigned by the Committee to accompany a match, any announcement of the result of the match by the referee on the final putting green is not the official announcement. However, there may be cases where an official scoreboard is not used, in which case the Committee must clarify when it considers the results "officially announced."

In some cases the official scoreboard will be a prominent structure and in other cases it might be a sheet of paper in the golf shop or locker room. The Committee is generally responsible for recording the winner's name on the scoreboard, but there may be times when the Committee charges the players with this responsibility.

Other Decisions related to Rule 2-5: See "Claims and Disputes" in the Index.

RULE 3

STROKE PLAY

DEFINITIONS

All defined terms are in *italics* and are listed alphabetically in the Definitions section – see pages 6–16.

3-1. GENERAL; WINNER

A stroke-play competition consists of *competitors* completing each hole of a *stipulated round* or rounds and, for each round, returning a score card on which there is a gross score for each hole. Each *competitor* is playing against every other *competitor* in the competition.

The *competitor* who plays the *stipulated round* or rounds in the fewest *strokes* is the winner.

In a handicap competition, the *competitor* with the lowest net score for the *stipulated round* or rounds is the winner.

3-2. FAILURE TO HOLE OUT

If a *competitor* fails to hole out at any hole and does not correct his mistake before he makes a *stroke* on the next *teeing ground* or, in the case of the last hole of the round, before he leaves the *putting green*, he is disqualified.

3-3. DOUBT AS TO PROCEDURE

a. Procedure

In stroke play, if a *competitor* is doubtful of his rights or the correct procedure during the play of a hole, he may, without penalty, complete the hole with two balls.

After the doubtful situation has arisen and before taking further action, the *competitor* must announce to his *marker* or *fellow-competitor* that he intends to play two balls and which ball he wishes to count if the *Rules* permit.

The *competitor* must report the facts of the situation to the *Committee* before returning his score card. If he fails to do so, he is disqualified.

Note: If the *competitor* takes further action before dealing with the doubtful situation, Rule 3-3 is not applicable. The score with the original ball counts or, if the original ball is not one of the balls being played, the score with the first ball put into play counts, even if the *Rules* do not allow the procedure adopted for that ball. However, the *competitor* incurs no penalty for having played a second ball, and any *penalty strokes* incurred solely by playing that ball do not count in his score.

b. Determination of Score for Hole

(i) If the ball that the *competitor* selected in advance to count has been played in accordance with the *Rules*, the score with that ball is the *competitor's* score for the hole. Otherwise, the score with the other ball counts if the *Rules* allow the procedure adopted for that ball.

(ii) If the *competitor* fails to announce in advance his decision to complete the hole with two balls, or which ball he wishes to count, the score with the original ball counts, provided it has been played in accordance with the *Rules*. If the original ball is not one of the balls being played, the first ball put into play counts, provided it has been played in accordance with the *Rules*. Otherwise, the score with the other ball counts if the *Rules* allow the procedure adopted for that ball.

Note 1: If a *competitor* plays a second ball under Rule 3-3, the *strokes* made after this Rule has been invoked with the ball ruled not to count and *penalty strokes* incurred solely by playing that ball are disregarded.

Note 2: A second ball played under Rule 3-3 is not a *provisional ball* under Rule 27-2.

3-4. REFUSAL TO COMPLY WITH A RULE

If a *competitor* refuses to comply with a *Rule* affecting the rights of another *competitor*, he is disqualified.

3-5. GENERAL PENALTY

The penalty for a breach of a *Rule* in stroke play is two strokes except when otherwise provided.

STROKE PLAY: GENERAL

3/1
Disqualification in Play-Off

Q. A competitor in a stroke-play play-off incurs a penalty of disqualification. Does the disqualification apply to the play-off only or to the entire competition?

A. The disqualification applies only to the play-off.

3/2
Competitors Play Two Holes Not Included in Stipulated Round

Q. In stroke play, the stipulated round was 16 holes, i.e., the 13th and 14th holes were omitted. After play of the 12th hole, one group elected to play the 13th and 14th holes without counting their scores for those holes. They then completed the round. What is the ruling?

A. The stipulated round consists of playing the holes of the course in the sequence prescribed by the Committee – see Definition of "Stipulated Round." These competitors were in breach of the conditions of the competition and the Committee should in this case impose a penalty of disqualification under Rule 33-7.

3/3
Stipulated Round in Stroke Play

In all forms of stroke play other than foursomes, a competitor has begun his stipulated round when he makes his first stroke in that round. In foursomes stroke play, the side has begun its stipulated round when it makes its first stroke in that round.

In individual stroke play, the competitor's stipulated round has ended when he has completed play of the final hole of that round (including correction of an error under a Rule, e.g., Rule 15-3b or Rule 20-7c). In foursomes or four-ball stroke play, the stipulated round has ended when the side has completed play of the final hole of that round (including correction of an error under a Rule).

STROKE PLAY: FAILURE TO HOLE OUT

3-2/1
Fellow-Competitor's Ball Knocked from Lip of Hole by Competitor Not Replaced

Q. In stroke play, a competitor concedes his fellow-competitor a short putt and knocks the ball away. The fellow-competitor lifts his ball, does not replace it as required by Rule 18-4 and plays from the next tee. What is the ruling?

A. The fellow-competitor is disqualified (Rule 3-2).

3-2/2
Ball Blown into Hole by Competitor Not Replaced and Holed Out

Q. In stroke play, a competitor's ball stopped on the lip of the hole and on impulse he blew the ball into the hole. He did not replace the ball, as required by Rule 18-2a, and hole out. He played from the next tee. Is the competitor disqualified under Rule 3-2 for failing to hole out?

A. Yes.

Other Decisions related to Rule 3-2: See "Failure to Hole Out" and "Holed and Holing Out" in the Index.

STROKE PLAY: DOUBT AS TO PROCEDURE

3-3/0.5
Guidelines for Determining Which Ball Counts When Player Proceeds Under Rule 3-3

The purpose of Rule 3-3 is to allow a competitor to avoid a penalty when he is in doubt as to the proper procedure. The following are guidelines for determining the ball with which the competitor scores in various situations:

1. If both balls are played in accordance with the Rules, the ball selected counts if the competitor announces in advance his decision to invoke

this Rule and announces in advance the ball with which he wishes to score. If the competitor does not announce or select in advance, the score with the original ball counts if played in accordance with the Rules. Otherwise the score with the second ball counts if played in accordance with the Rules.

2. If the procedure with the ball selected in advance is not in accordance with the Rules, the other ball must count if it was played in accordance with the Rules (see Decision 3-3/5).

3. If neither ball is played in accordance with the Rules, the following applies:
   a. In a case where the competitor plays both balls from a wrong place but is not guilty of a serious breach with either ball, the score with the original ball counts, with an additional penalty under the applicable Rule (see Rule 20-7c).
   b. In a case where the competitor is guilty of a serious breach with one ball and not guilty of a serious breach with the other ball, the score with the other ball counts, with an additional penalty under the applicable Rule (see Rule 20-7c).
   c. In a case where the competitor is guilty of a serious breach with both balls, the competitor is disqualified.

4. If the original ball is played and then Rule 3-3 is invoked, the score with the original ball must count, even if the Rules do not allow the procedure adopted for that ball, i.e., Rule 3-3 is not applicable in such circumstances (Note to Rule 3-3a).

3-3/1
Provisional Ball Used as Second Ball When Not Determinable Whether Original Ball Is Out of Bounds

Q. In stroke play, a player is in doubt as to whether his drive may be out of bounds. He plays a provisional ball under Rule 27-2. He finds the original ball and cannot determine whether it is out of bounds or not. The player wishes to consider the provisional ball as his second ball under Rule 3-3 and complete the play of the hole with both balls. Is this permissible?

A. Yes. In invoking Rule 3-3 after playing a provisional ball, the player must treat the provisional ball as a second ball. Although Note 2 to Rule 3-3 provides: "A second ball played under Rule 3-3 is not a provisional ball under Rule 27-2," the reverse is not true in the present case.

3-3/2
Second Ball Played Despite Adverse Ruling

Q. In stroke play, a competitor believes he is entitled to relief under a Rule, but a referee disagrees. In spite of the ruling by the referee, the competitor invokes Rule 3-3 and opts to score with the second ball. He plays his original ball as it lies and the second ball under the Rule he believes is applicable.

May a competitor invoke Rule 3-3 in such circumstances?

A. The answer depends upon whether or not the Committee has given authority to make final decisions to its individual referees.

If the referee concerned has not been given authority to make final decisions, the competitor is entitled to invoke Rule 3-3.

If, on the other hand, the referee has been given authority to make final decisions, he may, despite his own view that the competitor is not entitled to relief, permit the competitor to invoke Rule 3-3. However, if the referee exercises his authority and gives the competitor a final decision that he is not entitled to the relief he claims, there is then no justification for the competitor invoking Rule 3-3, and he will incur a penalty of two strokes for undue delay (Rule 6-7) if he, nevertheless, goes ahead and invokes Rule 3-3. The score with his original ball, including this two-stroke penalty, must count. (Revised)

3-3/3
Ball Dropped in Wrong Place and Played; Rule 3-3 Then Invoked and Second Ball Dropped in Right Place; Both Balls Played Out

Q. In stroke play, a competitor's ball comes to rest through the green on a paved path. He lifts the ball, drops it off the path at a point almost two club-lengths from the nearest point of relief (i.e., he drops in a wrong place) and plays it. The competitor's marker advises the competitor that he (the marker) believes the ball must be dropped within one club-length of the nearest point of relief. The competitor, in doubt, invokes Rule 3-3, drops a second ball within one club-length of the nearest point of relief and otherwise in accordance with Rule 24-2b(i) and opts to score with the second ball. The competitor holes out with both balls. What is the ruling?

A. Rule 20-7c states in part: "If a competitor makes a stroke from a wrong place, he incurs a penalty of two strokes under the applicable Rule. He must play out the hole with the ball played from the wrong place ...." Thus, the competitor's score with the original ball, with a penalty of two strokes added, must count.

Rule 20-7c does not permit the second ball to count. However, the competitor incurs no penalty for having played the second ball.

3-3/4
Ball Dropped in Wrong Place But Not Played; Rule 3-3 Then Invoked and Second Ball Dropped in Right Place; Both Balls Played Out

Q. With reference to Decision 3-3/3, what would have been the ruling if the marker had advised the competitor of his possible error before the ball dropped in a wrong place was played and the competitor had invoked Rule 3-3 at that point?

A. Rule 20-7c would not have applied because Rule 3-3 was invoked before the ball dropped in a wrong place was played.

The score with the second ball would have counted and no penalty would have been incurred.

The competitor, had he not been in doubt, could have lifted the ball dropped in the wrong place, without penalty (Rule 20-6).

3-3/5
Whether Score with Second Ball Counts If Ball Dropped in Wrong Place and Played

Q. In stroke play, a competitor's ball came to rest on an artificially-surfaced road which had not been declared an integral part of the course. The competitor, not sure whether the road was an obstruction or an integral part of the course, invoked Rule 3-3 and announced that he wished his score with the second ball to count. He played his original ball as it lay and dropped and played a second ball under Rule 24-2b(i). He met all the requirements of that Rule, except that he dropped the second ball almost two club-lengths from the nearest point of relief instead of within one club-length. Does the score with the second ball count?

A. No. Rule 3-3b(i) states in part: "If the ball that the competitor selected in advance to count has been played in accordance with the Rules, the score with that ball is the competitor's score for the hole." In this case, the ball selected in advance to count (i.e., the second ball) was not played in accordance with the Rules since it was dropped almost two club-lengths from the nearest point of relief. Accordingly, the score with the original ball counts.

3-3/6
Competitor Plays Original Ball After Doubtful Situation Has Arisen and Then Invokes Rule 3-3

Q. In stroke play, a competitor's ball lies in a water hazard. A movable stake defining the margin of the hazard interferes with the area of his intended swing. He makes his next stroke, avoiding the stake. It then occurs to him that he may have been entitled to remove the stake. The competitor informs his marker that he is invoking Rule 3-3 and elects to score with a second ball. He removes the stake and drops a second ball at the spot from which his original ball was played. He holes out with both balls. What is the ruling?

A. The situation that caused the doubt arose when the competitor's ball lay in the water hazard and the stake interfered with his swing. Since the competitor took further action, i.e., played the original ball, after the situation that caused the doubt had arisen, the score with the original ball must count – see the Note to Rule 3-3a.

However, the competitor incurs no penalty for having played the second ball.

Related Decision:
• 26-1/5 Ball Dropped and Played Under Water Hazard Rule; Original Ball Then Found in Hazard and Holed Out as Second Ball.

3-3/6.5
Competitor Plays Second Ball Without Announcing Intention to Invoke Rule 3-3 and Fails to Report Facts to Committee

Q. In stroke play, a competitor's ball came to rest on an artificially-surfaced road which had not been declared an integral part of the course. Without announcing his decision to invoke Rule 3-3 or the ball with which he would score if the Rules permitted, the competitor dropped and played a second ball in accordance with Rule 24-2b. The competitor then played the original ball as it lay and completed play of the hole with both balls, scoring 4 with the original ball and 5 with the dropped ball.

The competitor returned his score card to the Committee with a score of 4 on the hole in question and failed to report the facts to the Committee.

What is the ruling?

A. Although the competitor did not announce his decision to invoke Rule 3-3, it is clear from the facts that he intended to invoke such Rule. As the competitor did not report the facts of the situation to the Committee before returning his score card, he is disqualified under Rule 3-3a.

3-3/7
Original Ball Strikes Second Ball or Vice Versa

Q. A competitor invokes Rule 3-3 and plays a second ball. Subsequently, the competitor makes a stroke at one ball and it strikes and moves the other ball. What is the ruling?

A. If both balls lay on the putting green prior to the stroke, the competitor incurs a penalty of two strokes if the score with the striking ball ultimately becomes the competitor's score for the hole – Rule 19-5. Otherwise, there is no penalty. The striking ball must be played as it lies – Rule 19-5. The moved ball must be replaced – Rule 18-5.

Related Decisions:
• 18-5/2 Original Ball Struck by Provisional Ball.
• 19-5/5 Provisional Ball Struck by Original Ball.

3-3/7.5
Competitor Announces Intention to Play Two Balls; Plays Original Ball Before Dropping Second Ball; Elects Not to Play Second Ball

Q. A competitor's ball comes to rest in a rut made by a maintenance vehicle. Believing the Committee might declare the rut to be ground under repair, he announces that he will invoke Rule 3-3 and play a second ball in accordance with Rule 25-1b and that he wishes his score with the second ball to count if the Rules permit. He hits his original ball from the rut to one foot from the hole and then states he will not play a second ball. He completes the hole with his original ball. On completion of the round, the facts are reported to the Committee. What is the ruling?

A. The answer depends on whether the Committee declares the rut to be ground under repair. If the Committee declares the rut to be ground under repair, the competitor is disqualified for failing to hole out (Rule 3-2) since the score with the second ball would have counted – see Rule 3-3 and Decision 3-3/8. Otherwise, the score with the original ball counts.

If a player declares his intention to invoke Rule 3-3, he may change his mind at any time before he takes further action, such as making another stroke at his original ball or putting a second ball into play. Once he invokes the Rule and takes further action, he is bound by the procedures in Rule 3-3.

Related Decisions:
- 18-2a/12.5 Player Entitled to Relief Without Penalty from Condition Lifts Ball; Chooses Not to Take Relief and Wishes to Proceed Under the Unplayable Ball Rule.
- 18-2a/27.5 Player Who States He Will Proceed Under Unplayable Ball Rule Subsequently Assesses Possibility of Playing Ball as It Lies.
- 28/13 After Deeming Ball Unplayable and Lifting It, Player Discovers Ball Was in Ground Under Repair.

3-3/8
Competitor Picks Up Second Ball

Q. In stroke play, a competitor, uncertain whether the road his ball lies on is an obstruction or not, invokes Rule 3-3. He plays his original ball as it lies on the road and a second ball under Rule 24-2b(i), telling his marker he wishes his score with the second ball to count if the Rules permit. Having hit his original ball onto the green and the second ball into a bunker, the competitor picks up the second ball, holes out with the original ball and plays from the next tee. At this point the matter is referred to the Committee, which establishes that the road on which the competitor's ball lay was an obstruction. What is the ruling?

A. Since the road on which the competitor's ball lay was an obstruction and therefore Rule 24-2b(i) allowed the procedure selected by the competitor, the score with the second (or selected) ball would have counted if it had been holed out. However, since the competitor did not hole out with that ball, he is disqualified (Rule 3-2).

If, on the other hand, the road had not been an obstruction, there would have been no penalty. In that case, since the Rules would not have allowed the selected procedure, a score with the second ball would not have counted, and the competitor's score with his original ball would have been his score for the hole. There is no penalty for picking up a ball played under Rule 3-3 if that ball cannot count.

3-3/9
Second Ball Played in Match Play

Q. In a match between A and B, A was unsure of his rights at a hole. Neither A nor B was aware that Rule 3-3 applies only in stroke play, so A played a second ball and holed out with both balls. At the end of the round, the matter was referred to the Committee. What is the ruling?

A. A second ball played in match play is a wrong ball – see Note 2 under Rule 2-5 and Definition of "Wrong Ball." Accordingly, A would have lost the hole had B claimed it under Rule 2-5 before either player had played from the next tee. However, B made no claim. Therefore, the score with A's original ball counts. (Revised)

Related Decision:
• 33-8/3 Local Rule Allowing Play of Second Ball in Match Play.

3-3/10
Competitor Plays Three Balls When Doubtful of Rights

Q. Are there any circumstances under which a competitor in stroke play, who is doubtful of his rights or procedure, may play a third ball under Rule 3-3?

A. No. If a competitor so proceeds, the score with the original ball or, if the original ball is not one of the balls being played, the first ball put into play shall count. If the Rules do not allow the procedure adopted for the original ball or the first ball put into play, the competitor incurs the penalty prescribed for the improper procedure.

3-3/11
Competitor Drops One Ball in Accordance with Two Different Rules Instead of Playing Second Ball

Q. In stroke play, a competitor's ball comes to rest through the green in a deep rut which has not been defined as ground under repair by the Committee. The ball is not playable due to the rut. The competitor believes that the Committee might declare the rutted area to be ground under repair. He announces to his marker or a fellow-competitor that he will drop the ball at a spot which conforms to the procedures prescribed in both Rule 25-1b(i) (Ground Under Repair) and Rule 28c (Ball Unplayable), seek a ruling from the Committee before returning his score card, and accept the penalty stroke in Rule 28 if the Committee does not declare the rutted area to be ground under repair. Is such a procedure permissible?

A. Yes. Although it would have been advisable for the competitor to proceed under Rule 3-3 in this situation, the Rules do not prohibit such a procedure – see also Decision 3-3/12.

Related Decision:
• 25/16 Rut Made by Tractor.

3-3/12
Competitor Drops One Ball in Accordance with Two Different Rules Instead of Playing Second Ball; Dropped Ball Rolls Back into the Condition from Which Relief Taken

Q. In the circumstances described in Decision 3-3/11, what is the ruling if the competitor drops the ball and it rolls and comes to rest where there is still interference from the same rutted area?

A. If this occurred it would be advisable for the competitor to obtain a ruling from the Committee before proceeding further or invoke Rule 3-3.

If the Committee determines that the area is ground under repair, the ball must be re-dropped (Rule 20-2c(v)). Otherwise, the dropped ball is in play and the competitor must either play the ball as it lies or, for a second time, proceed under the unplayable ball Rule (Rule 28) incurring an additional penalty stroke.

Related Decision:
• 20-2c/0.5 Ball Dropped from Ground Under Repair Area Rolls to Position Where Area Interferes with Stance; Whether Re-Drop Required.

3-3/13
Competitor Invokes Rule 3-3; Lifts and Drops Original Ball

Q. A competitor's ball comes to rest in an area that he feels should be marked as ground under repair. Believing the Committee might declare the area to be ground under repair, he announces that he will invoke Rule 3-3 and play a second ball in accordance with Rule 25-1b and that he wishes his score with the ball played under Rule 25-1b to count if the Rules permit. He marks the position of and lifts the original ball, drops it in accordance with Rule 25-1b and plays it. He then places a second ball where the original lay and plays it. Is the competitor's procedure correct?

A. Yes. Rule 3-3 does not require the original ball to be played as it lies and, therefore, the competitor's procedure was acceptable. However, it would also have been correct for the competitor to play his original ball as it lay and play a second ball in accordance with Rule 25-1b.

3-3/14
Competitor Invokes Rule 3-3; Second Ball Played First

Q. A competitor accidentally causes his ball to move after he has addressed it in breach of Rule 18-2b. He is unsure whether the ball must be replaced or played from its new position. He announces that he will invoke Rule 3-3, places a second ball on the spot from which the original ball was moved and states that he wishes the second ball to count if the Rules permit. He plays the second ball first and then plays the original ball. Is the competitor's procedure correct in terms of the order in which the balls were played?

A. Yes. Rule 3-3 does not require the original ball to be played first and, therefore, the competitor's procedure was acceptable.

Other Decisions related to Rule 3-3: See "Doubt as to Procedure" in the Index.

STROKE PLAY: REFUSAL TO COMPLY WITH

3-4/1
Competitor Not Given Opportunity to Lift Ball Assisting Fellow-Competitor

Q. In stroke play, A's ball lies near the hole in a position to assist B, whose ball lies off the putting green. A states his intention to lift his ball under Rule 22-1. B mistakenly believes that A does not have the right to lift his ball and plays before A has an opportunity to lift his ball. What is the ruling?

A. B is disqualified under Rule 3-4 as he intentionally denied A's right to lift his ball. It is irrelevant that B did so in ignorance of the Rules.

Related Decisions:
• 2/3 Refusal to Comply with Rule in Match Play.
• 2-4/8 Player Concedes Opponent's Next Stroke and Plays Before Opponent Has Opportunity to Lift Ball.
• 16-2/4 Ball Overhanging Lip of Hole Moves When Flagstick Removed.
• 17-4/2 Ball Resting Against Flagstick; Putt Conceded and Ball Removed Before Player Can Remove Flagstick.
• 22/6 Competitor Requests That Ball in Position to Assist Him Not Be Lifted.

Other Decisions related to Rule 3-4: See "Refusal to Comply with Rule" in the Index.

CLUBS AND THE BALL

The USGA reserves the right, at any time, to change the *Rules* relating to clubs and balls (see Appendices II and III) and make or change the interpretations relating to these *Rules*.

RULE 4

CLUBS

A player in doubt as to the conformity of a club should consult the USGA.
   A manufacturer should submit to the USGA a sample of a club to be manufactured for a ruling as to whether the club conforms with the *Rules*. The sample becomes the property of the USGA for reference purposes. If a manufacturer fails to submit a sample or, having submitted a sample, fails to await a ruling before manufacturing and/or marketing the club, the manufacturer assumes the risk of a ruling that the club does not conform with the *Rules*.

DEFINITIONS
All defined terms are in *italics* and are listed alphabetically in the Definitions section – see pages 6–16.

4-1. FORM AND MAKE OF CLUBS
a. General
The player's clubs must conform with this Rule and the provisions, specifications and interpretations set forth in Appendix II.
Note: The *Committee* may require, in the conditions of a competition (Rule 33-1), that any driver the player carries must have a clubhead, identified by model and loft, that is named on the current List of Conforming Driver Heads issued by the USGA.

b. Wear and Alteration
A club that conforms with the *Rules* when new is deemed to conform after wear through normal use. Any part of a club that has been purposely altered is regarded as new and must, in its altered state, conform with the *Rules*.

4-2. PLAYING CHARACTERISTICS CHANGED AND FOREIGN MATERIAL

a. Playing Characteristics Changed
During a *stipulated round*, the playing characteristics of a club must not be purposely changed by adjustment or by any other means.

b. Foreign Material
Foreign material must not be applied to the club face for the purpose of influencing the movement of the ball.

*PENALTY FOR CARRYING, BUT NOT MAKING STROKE WITH, CLUB OR CLUBS IN BREACH OF RULE 4-1 or 4-2:

<u>Match play</u> – At the conclusion of the hole at which the breach is discovered, the state of the match is adjusted by deducting one hole for each hole at which a breach occurred; maximum deduction per round – Two holes.

<u>Stroke play</u> – Two strokes for each hole at which any breach occurred; maximum penalty per round – Four strokes (two strokes at each of the first two holes at which any breach occurred).

<u>Match play or stroke play</u> – If a breach is discovered between the play of two holes, it is deemed to have been discovered during play of the next hole, and the penalty must be applied accordingly.

<u>Bogey and par competitions</u> – See Note 1 to Rule 32-1a.

<u>Stableford competitions</u> – See Note 1 to Rule 32-1b.

*Any club or clubs carried in breach of Rule 4-1 or 4–2 must be declared out of play by the player to his *opponent* in match play or his *marker* or a *fellow-competitor* in stroke play immediately upon discovery that a breach has occurred. If the player fails to do so, he is disqualified.

PENALTY FOR MAKING STROKE WITH CLUB IN BREACH OF RULE 4-1 or 4-2:

Disqualification.

4-3. DAMAGED CLUBS: REPAIR AND REPLACEMENT
a. Damage in Normal Course of Play

If, during a *stipulated round*, a player's club is damaged in the normal course of play, he may:

(i)   use the club in its damaged state for the remainder of the *stipulated round*; or

(ii) without unduly delaying play, repair it or have it repaired; or

(iii) as an additional option available only if the club is unfit for play, replace the damaged club with any club. The replacement of a club must not unduly delay play (Rule 6-7) and must not be made by borrowing any club selected for play by any other person playing on the *course* or by assembling components carried by or for the player during the *stipulated round*.

PENALTY FOR BREACH OF RULE 4-3a:

See Penalty Statements for Rule 4-4a or b, and Rule 4-4c.

Note: A club is unfit for play if it is substantially damaged, e.g., the shaft is dented, significantly bent or breaks into pieces; the clubhead becomes loose, detached or significantly deformed; or the grip becomes loose. A club is not unfit for play solely because the club's lie or loft has been altered, or the clubhead is scratched.

b. Damage Other Than in Normal Course of Play

If, during a *stipulated round*, a player's club is damaged other than in the normal course of play rendering it non-conforming or changing its playing characteristics, the club must not subsequently be used or replaced during the round.

PENALTY FOR BREACH OF RULE 4-3b:
Disqualification.

c. Damage Prior to Round

A player may use a club damaged prior to a round, provided the club, in its damaged state, conforms with the *Rules*.

Damage to a club that occurred prior to a round may be repaired during the round, provided the playing characteristics are not changed and play is not unduly delayed.

PENALTY FOR BREACH OF RULE 4-3c:
See Penalty Statement for Rule 4-1 or 4-2.

(Undue delay – see Rule 6-7)

4-4. MAXIMUM OF FOURTEEN CLUBS
a. Selection and Addition of Clubs

The player must not start a *stipulated round* with more than fourteen clubs. He is limited to the clubs thus selected for that round, except that if he started with fewer than fourteen clubs, he may add any number, provided his total number does not exceed fourteen.

The addition of a club or clubs must not unduly delay play (Rule 6-7) and the player must not add or borrow any club selected for play by any other person playing on the *course* or by assembling components carried by or for the player during the *stipulated round*.

b. Partners May Share Clubs

Partners may share clubs, provided that the total number of clubs carried by the *partners* so sharing does not exceed fourteen.

PENALTY FOR BREACH OF RULE 4-4a or b, REGARDLESS OF NUMBER OF EXCESS CLUBS CARRIED:

Match play – At the conclusion of the hole at which the breach is discovered, the state of the match is adjusted by deducting one hole for each hole at which a breach occurred; maximum deduction per round – Two holes.

Stroke play – Two strokes for each hole at which any breach occurred; maximum penalty per round – Four strokes (two strokes at each of the first two holes at which any breach occurred).

Match play or stroke play – If a breach is discovered between the play of two holes, it is deemed to have been discovered during play of the hole just completed, and the penalty for a breach of Rule 4-4a or b does not apply to the next hole.

Bogey and par competitions – See Note 1 to Rule 32-1a.
Stableford competitions – See Note 1 to Rule 32-1b.

c. Excess Club Declared Out of Play

Any club or clubs carried or used in breach of Rule 4-3a(iii) or Rule 4-4 must be declared out of play by the player to his *opponent* in match play or his *marker* or a *fellow-competitor* in stroke play immediately upon discovery that a breach has occurred. The player must not use the club or clubs for the remainder of the *stipulated round*.

PENALTY FOR BREACH OF RULE 4-4c:
Disqualification.

FORM AND MAKE OF CLUBS

4-1/1
Groove and Punch Mark Specifications Effective January 1, 2010 Including Condition of Competition

All new models of clubs manufactured on or after January 1, 2010 must conform to the groove and punch mark specifications described in Appendix II 5c. However, Ping Eye2 irons manufactured before March 31, 1990 with a groove spacing to groove width ratio of 2.3 to 1 are permitted for play under the Rules of Golf, even in certain competitions when the Condition Requiring Clubs Conforming with Groove and Punch Mark Specifications Effective January 1, 2010 is in effect (see below).

A Committee that wishes to limit players to clubs manufactured with grooves and/or punch marks that conform to all aspects of the Rules of Golf, including those that are effective from January 1, 2010, may adopt the condition of competition detailed below.

Between January 1, 2010 and January 1, 2014, it is recommended that this condition of competition be adopted only for competitions involving the highest level of expert player. After January 1, 2014, this condition of competition may be adopted more widely (e.g., at the highest level of amateur golf), but it is recommended only for competitions involving expert players.

"The player's clubs must conform to the groove and punch mark specifications in the Rules of Golf that are effective from January 1, 2010.

*PENALTY FOR CARRYING, BUT NOT MAKING STROKE WITH, CLUB OR CLUBS IN BREACH OF CONDITION:

Match play – At the conclusion of the hole at which the breach is discovered, the state of the match is adjusted by deducting one hole for each hole at which a breach occurred; maximum deduction per round – Two holes.

Stroke play – Two strokes for each hole at which any breach occurred; maximum penalty per round – Four strokes.

Match play or stroke play – If a breach is discovered between the play of two holes, it is deemed to have been discovered during play of the next hole, and the penalty must be applied accordingly.

Bogey and par competitions – See Note 1 to Rule 32-1a.

Stableford competitions – See Note 1 to Rule 32-1b.

*Any club or clubs carried in breach of this condition must be declared out of play by the player to his opponent in match play or his marker or a fellow-competitor in stroke play immediately upon discovery that a breach has occurred. If the player fails to do so, he is disqualified.

PENALTY FOR MAKING STROKE WITH CLUB IN BREACH OF CONDITION:
Disqualification.

Exception: Ping Eye2 irons manufactured before March 31, 1990 with a groove spacing to groove width ratio of 2.3 to 1 are permitted for play under the Rules of Golf, even in certain competitions when the Condition Requiring Clubs Conforming with Groove and Punch Mark Specifications Effective January 1, 2010 is in effect. It is the player's responsibility to refer to the condition of competition posted for the specific competition in which the player is playing to ensure compliance with the above exception and to provide proof of the date on which the club was manufactured. If the player cannot provide such proof, the club must conform with specifications described in Appendix II 5c(i)." (Revised)

4-1/2
Material in Head of Metal Wood Club Broken Away from Shell

Q. A piece of material in the head of a metal wood club, which conformed with the Rules when manufactured, has broken away from the shell due to use, and it rattles around in the head. Appendix II, 1a states in part: "All parts of the club must be fixed so that the club is one unit." Is this metal wood club now non-conforming because of the loose piece of material?

A. No, because Rule 4-1b states in part: "A club that conforms with the Rules when new is deemed to conform after wear through normal use." The piece of material in the metal wood club in question broke loose from the shell due to wear through normal use.

4-1/3
Status of a Chipper

Q. What Rules apply to "chippers"?

A. A "chipper" is an iron club designed primarily for use off the putting green, generally with a loft greater than ten degrees. As most players adopt a "putting stroke" when using a chipper, there can be a tendency to design the club as if it was a putter. To eliminate confusion, the Rules which apply to "chippers" include:

1. The shaft must be attached to the clubhead at the heel (Appendix II, 2c);
2. The grip must be circular in cross-section (Appendix II, 3(i)) and only one grip is permitted (Appendix II, 3(v));
3. The clubhead must be generally plain in shape (Appendix II, 4a) and have only one striking face (Appendix II, 4d); and
4. The face of the club must conform to specifications with regard to hardness, surface roughness, material and markings in the impact area (Appendix II, 5).

4-1/4
Lead Tape Applied to Clubhead or Shaft Before Start of Round

Q. Before the start of a round, may a player attach lead tape to a clubhead or shaft for the purpose of adjusting weight?

A. Yes. The use of lead tape is an exception to Appendix II, 1b(ii).

4-1/5
Adhesive Bandage or Tape Applied to Clubhead to Reduce Glare or for Protection

Q. May a player put an adhesive bandage or tape on the clubhead to reduce glare or to protect the club from being damaged?

A. An adhesive bandage or tape added to the clubhead is considered an external attachment, rendering the club non-conforming (see Appendix II, Rule 1a but see also Decision 4-1/4). However, material attached to the clubhead that does not affect the performance of the club and is semi-permanent, durable, not easily removable and conforms to the shape of the clubhead may be permitted by exception, but an adhesive bandage or tape does not fall under that exception because such items are temporary in nature and easily removable. See "A Guide to the Rules on Clubs and Balls," Section 1a, for detailed criteria regarding permissible external attachments, such as alignment markings, protective coverings or decorative decals.

Additionally, adding such an attachment during the stipulated round would change the club's playing characteristics in breach of Rule 4-2.

Related Decisions:
• 14-2/2.5 Player Positions Bag for Purpose of Providing Shade for Ball.
• 14-2/3 Caddie Shields Player from Sun During Stroke.

Other Decisions related to Rule 4-1: See "Clubs: non-conforming club" in the Index.

CLUBS: PLAYING CHARACTERISTICS

4-2/0.5
Lead Tape Applied to Clubhead or Shaft During Round

Q. With regard to Decision 4-1/4, may a player remove, add or alter lead tape during a round?

A. No. However, lead tape that becomes detached from the club in the normal course of play may be placed back onto the club in the same location. If the lead tape will not remain on the club in the same location, new tape may be used. Every effort should be made to restore the club, as nearly as possible, to its previous condition. Alternatively, the club may be used in its damaged state (without the lead tape) for the remainder of the round (Rule 4-3a).

If the tape is altered or damaged other than in the normal course of play, the club may not be used for the remainder of the round, under penalty of disqualification (see Rules 4-2a and 4-3).

4-2/1 (Reserved)

4-2/2
Playing Characteristics of Club Changed While Play Suspended; Error Discovered Before Play Resumed

Q. While play is suspended, a player changes the lie of four of his clubs. Before play is resumed, he becomes aware that Rule 4-2a prohibits purposely changing the playing characteristics of a club during a round. If the original lie of the four clubs is restored, or if the player discards them before play is resumed, can he avoid the penalty prescribed by Rule 4-2?

A. Rule 4-2a is intended to ensure that, apart from damage sustained in the normal course of play, the playing characteristics of the clubs with which the player starts the stipulated round will not be altered until he has finished it. It would be impossible to restore exactly the original lie of an altered club. Accordingly, although the stipulated round has been suspended and the player did not technically change the playing characteristics during the round, in equity (Rule 1-4):

(1) the player incurs no penalty if he discards the clubs in question or declares them out of play to his opponent in match play or his marker or a fellow-competitor in stroke play before he resumes play and, assuming he started the round with 14 clubs, finishes the round with the remaining ten clubs, or

(2) if the player resumes play carrying one or more of the four clubs without having declared the club or clubs out of play, in view of the purpose of Rule 4-2a, he is deemed to be in breach of Rule 4-2a, whether or not he has attempted to restore the original playing characteristics. The penalty will depend on whether the player uses any of the altered clubs – see penalty statement under Rule 4-2.

Other Decisions related to Rule 4-2: See "Clubs: playing characteristics of club changed" in the Index.

CLUBS: FOREIGN MATERIAL

4-2/3
Applying Chalk to Club Face

Q. During a round, may a player apply chalk to the face of an iron club in order to obtain more backspin?

A. No.

4-2/4
Applying Saliva to Face of Club

Q. A player spat on the face of his club and did not wipe the saliva off before playing his next stroke. Is this permissible?

A. If the purpose of doing this was to influence the movement of the ball, the player was in breach of Rule 4-2b as saliva is "foreign material."

DAMAGED CLUBS: REPAIR AND REPLACEMENT

4-3/1
Meaning of Damage Sustained in "Normal Course of Play"

Q. In Rule 4-3a, what is meant by the term "normal course of play"?

A. The term "normal course of play" is intended to cover all reasonable acts but specifically excludes cases of abuse.

In addition to making a stroke, practice swing or practice stroke, examples of acts that are in the "normal course of play" include the following:
- removing or replacing a club in the bag;
- using a club to search for or retrieve a ball (except by throwing the club);
- leaning on a club while waiting to play, teeing a ball or removing a ball from the hole; or
- accidentally dropping a club.

Examples of acts that are not in the "normal course of play" include the following:
- throwing a club whether in anger, in retrieving a ball, or otherwise;
- "slamming" a club into a bag; or
- intentionally striking something (e.g., the ground or a tree) with the club other than during a stroke, practice swing or practice stroke.

4-3/2
Meaning of "Repair"

Q. During a round, a player may repair a club damaged in the normal course of play, or he may have it repaired by someone else. What does the term "repair" mean within the context of Rule 4-3a(ii)?

A. The term "repair" in Rule 4-3a(ii) means to restore the club, as nearly as possible, to its condition prior to the incident that caused the damage. In doing so, the player is limited to the grip, shaft and clubhead used to comprise the club at the beginning of the stipulated round or, in the case of a club later added, when the club was selected for play.

When a club is damaged to the extent that the grip, shaft or clubhead has to be changed, this change exceeds what is meant by the term "repair." Such action constitutes replacement and is only permitted if the club was "unfit for play" – see Rule 4-3a(iii). (Revised)

4-3/3
Club Damaged in Normal Course of Play Breaks into Pieces When Repaired

Q. The shaft of a player's club is bent in the normal course of play. The player, in attempting to repair the damaged club as permitted by Rule 4-3a(ii), breaks the shaft into pieces. What is the ruling?

A. Since the player was entitled to repair the damaged club, the further damage to the club, which has rendered it unfit for play is also considered to have occurred in the normal course of play. Thus, Rule 4-3a permits the player to use the club in its damaged state, repair it or have it repaired, or replace it with any club.

4-3/4
Modifying Penalty for Holing Short Putt with Club Whose Playing Characteristics Changed Other Than in Normal Course of Play

Q. A player leaves a putt about an inch short of the hole. In disgust, he hits his shoe with the head of his putter. The impact bends the neck of the putter, changing its playing characteristics. The player then holes the one-inch putt with the putter.

Rule 4-3b states in part: "If, during a stipulated round, a player's club is damaged other than in the normal course of play ... changing its playing characteristics, the club must not subsequently be used or replaced during the round." The penalty for breach of Rule 4-3b is disqualification. Would the Committee be justified in waiving or modifying the disqualification penalty in these circumstances, provided the player does not subsequently use the altered putter during the round?

A. No.

4-3/5
Changing Clubs Because of Wet Grips

Q. May a player change clubs during a round if the grips become wet?

A. No. A club is "unfit for play" if it is substantially damaged, but not if the grip becomes slippery – see Note to Rule 4-3a.

4-3/6 (Reserved)

4-3/7
Club Broken While Used as Cane

Q. A player uses one of his clubs as a cane while climbing a hill and the shaft breaks. May he replace the club during the round?

A. Yes. A club broken in such circumstances is considered to have become "damaged in the normal course of play" as its use as a cane is considered a reasonable act – see Decision 4-3/1.

4-3/8
Player Starting with 13 Clubs Breaks Putter in Anger and Replaces It

Q. A player who started a round with 13 clubs broke his putter in anger, i.e., other than in the normal course of play, during the first nine holes. He bought another putter in the pro shop after the first nine holes and used it for the remainder of the round. Rule 4-3a(iii) permits replacing a club only if it becomes unfit for play in the normal course of play. Was the player subject to penalty?

A. No. Since he started with 13 clubs, he was entitled to add another club under Rule 4-4a

4-3/9
Club Broken Due to Habit of Hitting Head of Club on Ground

Q. Rule 4-3a states that a club may be replaced if it becomes "damaged in the normal course of play." A player has a habit of hitting the head of his putter on the ground as he walks to the next tee, especially after missing a putt. On one occasion, after missing a short putt, the player hit the head of his putter on the ground so hard that the putter broke. The player said that he often taps the putter on the ground, and that it was not done in anger or with the intention of breaking the club. Should he be allowed to replace the club?

A. No. A club broken by hitting it hard on the ground or tapping it on the ground is not considered to have become "damaged in the normal course of play" as such actions are not considered reasonable acts – see Decision 4-3/1.

4-3/9.5
Club Rendered Unfit for Play By Outside Agency or Opponent's Side

Q. After reaching the putting green, a player places his clubs near the next tee. A greenkeeper's vehicle or an opponent's golf cart accidentally strikes the player's clubs, breaking several of them. What is the ruling?

A. Rule 4-3 does not contemplate a situation where the player's clubs are damaged by an outside agency or opponent. Therefore, in equity (Rule 1-4), the player may use the clubs in their damaged state, repair them or have them repaired, or replace them in accordance with Rule 4-3a(iii).

4-3/10
Replacement of Club Lost During Round

Q. A player who started a round with 14 clubs lost his putter. May he replace it during the round?

A. No. A lost club is not one which has become unfit for play in the normal course of play – see Rule 4-3.

4-3/11
Replacement of Club Broken on Practice Ground While Play Suspended

Q. Play has been suspended by the Committee. Prior to resuming play, a player is practicing on the practice ground. While hitting a ball, the shaft of his sand wedge breaks. In such circumstances, is the club considered to have become unfit for play in the normal course of play, in which case the player would be entitled to replace the broken club under Rule 4-3a(iii)?

A. Yes.

4-3/12
Replacing Club for Stroke-Play Play-Off

Q. In stroke play, a competitor broke a club in anger, finished the round with 13 clubs and then learned that he would be involved in a hole-by-hole play-off. May the competitor replace his broken club for the play-off?

A. The play-off constitutes a new round – see Definition of "Stipulated Round." The competitor is therefore entitled to replace his broken club.

Other Decisions related to Rule 4-3:
• 4-4a/2 Changing Clubs Between Rounds in 36-Hole Match.
• 4-4c/2 Whether Player May Use Excess Club to Replace Club Damaged in Normal Course of Play.

MAXIMUM OF 14 CLUBS: SELECTION AND ADDITION

4-4a/1
When Club Is Considered Added

Q. A player who started the stipulated round with 14 clubs is putting poorly. Between the play of two holes and without unduly delaying play, the player takes the putter out of his bag and replaces it with another putter that was in his locker. Before he makes a stroke with any club, the player is advised that he is not permitted to add or replace a club. Accordingly, he replaces the second putter with his original putter, leaves the second putter at the clubhouse and continues play. Does he incur a penalty?

A. No. Although the player was not entitled to add or replace a club, he is not considered to be in breach of Rule 4-4a until he makes a stroke with any club while the added putter is in his possession.

The answer would be the same for a player who starts the stipulated round with fewer than 14 clubs and wants to add clubs to bring the total number to 14. This player may select from several clubs that are brought to him, provided that (1) he does not make a stroke with any club before he chooses a club to add, (2) this process does not unduly delay play (Rule 6-7), and (3) none of the clubs he ultimately adds have been selected for play by any other person playing on the course.

4-4a/2
Changing Clubs Between Rounds in 36-Hole Match

Q. In a 36-hole match, may a player who started with 14 clubs change putters after play of the first 18 holes and before the start of the second 18 holes?

A. Yes. Rule 4-4a prohibits such procedure only during a stipulated round. A 36-hole match comprises two stipulated rounds of 18 holes each – see Definition of "Stipulated Round."

4-4a/3 (Reserved)

4-4a/4
Partners' Clubs Carried in One Bag

Q. In a foursome competition, is it permissible for partners to put both sets of clubs in one golf bag, provided each player uses only his own clubs?

A. Yes, provided each player's clubs are clearly identifiable.

4-4a/5
Competitor Inadvertently Uses and Thereafter Carries Fellow-Competitor's Club

Q. In stroke play, A and B both started with 14 clubs. They were using the same model of clubs and similar golf bags. At the 4th hole, B's caddie inadvertently took one of A's clubs from A's bag and gave it to B who made a stroke with it. B's caddie placed the club in B's bag. At the 6th hole, B's caddie discovered the error. What is the ruling?

A. Rule 4-4a states: "The player must start a stipulated round with not more than 14 clubs. He is limited to the clubs thus selected..." B complied with the first sentence of Rule 4-4a. However, when B made a stroke with A's club, he did not comply with the second sentence and was subject to penalty under Rule 4-4a for using a club selected for play by another person playing on the course. Upon discovery of the breach, B was required immediately to declare the club out of play under Rule 4-4c. He incurs a penalty of two strokes for making a stroke with that club on the 4th hole. As B did not intend to add the club to the clubs he had selected for the round, he incurs no additional penalty for having carried it until the breach was discovered on the 6th hole. A may retrieve the club to use during the remainder of the round. (Revised)

4-4a/5.5
Player's Club Put in Another Player's Bag by Mistake During Suspension of Play

Q. A and B both began the stipulated round with 14 clubs. During a suspension of play, one of B's clubs was placed accidentally into A's bag. After play resumed, A noticed B's club in his (A's) bag but he did not play a stroke with B's club. What is the ruling?

A. Both players complied with Rule 4-4a as they began the stipulated round with not more than 14 clubs. Since A did not play a stroke with B's club, there is no penalty to either player and B may have his club returned to him – but see also Decision 4-4a/5.

4-4a/6
Excess Club Put in Player's Golf Bag

Q. A arrives at the 1st tee. After the match or group's starting time while A is preparing to play his tee shot, B, his opponent or fellow-competitor, by mistake places his driver in A's bag, which results in A having 15 clubs. A then drives from the 1st tee. During play of the 1st hole, A discovers that B's club has been put in his (A's) golf bag. Does A incur a penalty for starting the round with more than 14 clubs?

A. No. Although A started the round with more than 14 clubs, A is not considered to have selected B's club for play for the following reasons:
- the additional club was added to his bag by B on the 1st tee,
- the club was added after the match or group's time of starting, and
- the club had already been selected for play by B.

Therefore A incurs no penalty, provided he does not make a stroke with B's club. The club may be returned to B and used by him.

The decision would be different, and A would be penalized under Rule 4-4a, if:
- the additional club had belonged to a player in another match or group,
- the club had been added before A's match or group arrived on the tee, or
- the club had been added before A's match or group's time of starting. (Revised)

4-4a/7
Carrying Weighted Training Club

Q. May a player carry a weighted training club in addition to the 14 clubs selected for the round?

A. No, but a weighted training club may be selected as one of 14 clubs carried by a player, provided it conforms with Rule 4-1 (e.g., an excessively-weighted driver head may breach the limit on Moment of Inertia – see Appendix II).

Related Decision:
- 14-3/10 Use of Training or Swing Aid During Round.

4-4a/8
Retrieving Another Player's Lost Club

Q. A player carrying 14 clubs found another player's club on the course. He picked up the lost club, put it in his bag but did not use it, and handed it in at the pro shop when the round was completed. Was the player in breach of Rule 4-4a for carrying 15 clubs?

A. No.

4-4a/9
Clarification of Match-Play Penalty

Q. Please confirm that the following is a correct interpretation of Rule 4-4a in a match between A and B:

1. After the 1st hole, it is discovered that B has more than 14 clubs:
   a. If B won the hole – The match is all square.
   b. If the hole was halved – A is 1 up.
   c. If A won the hole – A is 2 up.

2. After the 2nd hole, it is discovered that B has more than 14 clubs:
   a. If B won both holes – The match is all square.
   b. If B was 1 up – A is 1 up.
   c. If the match was all square – A is 2 up.
   d. If A was 1 up – A is 3 up.
   e. If A was 2 up – A is 4 up.

3. Later in the match, but before the players leave the last green, it is discovered that B has more than 14 clubs:
   a. If B was more than 2 up – 2 "ups" are deducted.
   b. If B was 2 up – The match is all square.
   c. If B was 1 up – A is 1 up.
   d. If the match was all square – A is 2 up.
   e. If A was 1 up – A is 3 up.
   f. If A was 2 up – A is 4 up.
   g. If A was more than 2 up – 2 "ups" are added to his "ups."

A. As the loss of hole penalty for a breach of Rule 4-4a is not applied to a specific hole, but to the state of the match at the conclusion of the hole at which the breach is discovered, your interpretation is correct.

Related Decision:
• 2-5/5.5 Breach of 14-Club Rule Discovered After Match Concluded But Before Result Officially Announced.

4-4a/10
Breach of 14-Club Rule in Stroke Play Discovered at 8th Hole; Where Penalty Strokes Applied

Q. In stroke play, A discovers during play of the 8th hole that he has 15 clubs in his bag and thus has incurred a penalty of four strokes under Rule 4-4a. How should the four-stroke penalty be applied?

A. A must add penalties of two strokes to his scores for the 1st and 2nd holes.

In four-ball stroke play, both A and his partner would add penalties of two strokes to their scores for the 1st and 2nd holes – see Rule 31-6.

4-4a/11
Excess Club Discovered Before Player Plays from 2nd Tee But After Opponent or Fellow-Competitor Has Played

Q. A player starts a round with 15 clubs. He discovers his error at the 2nd tee after his opponent or a fellow-competitor has played but before he has played. Does the player incur the maximum penalty of (a) deduction of two holes in match play or (b) four strokes in stroke play?

A. No. Since the player has not started play of the 2nd hole, he incurs a penalty of (a) deduction of one hole in match play or (b) two strokes in stroke play.

4-4a/12
Competitor Who Misplaces Putter Borrows Fellow-Competitor's Putter

Q. In stroke play, A, who had mistakenly left his putter at the previous green, borrows a putter from B, a fellow-competitor, and uses it. At the next tee, the Committee is advised of the situation. What is the ruling?

A. A was not entitled to borrow a club selected for play by any other person on the course – Rule 4-4a. A incurs a penalty of two strokes for a breach of Rule 4-4a and must immediately declare B's putter out of play as prescribed in Rule 4-4c. If A recovers his own putter, he may use it.

B may have his putter returned to him and use it for the remainder of the round.

4-4a/13
Player Practices with Another Player's Club

Q. A player starts a round with 14 clubs. Between the play of two holes he borrows another player's putter and makes several practice putts on the putting green of the hole last played. What is the ruling?

A. There is no penalty. Such practice putting is permitted by Rule 7-2. The borrowing of the putter does not breach Rule 4-4a since the putter was not used to make a stroke that counted in the player's score.

Related Decision to 4-4a/12 and 4-4a/13:
• 4-4b/1 Borrowing Partner's Putter.

4-4a/14
Player Carries Pieces of Broken Club

Q. A player starts a round with 14 clubs as well as a club that had been broken into pieces prior to the start of the round, but had not yet been removed from his bag. What is the ruling?

A. The Rules do not contemplate such a situation. In these circumstances, in equity (Rule 1-4), there is no penalty provided the broken club is not used during the stipulated round.

4-4a/15
Assembly of Club Components During Stipulated Round

Q. Rules 4-3a(iii) and 4-4a provide that the replacement or addition of a club must not be made by assembling components carried by or for the player during the stipulated round. What is the ruling in the following situations:
  1. During a stipulated round, a player carries a clubhead and a shaft (i.e., components) that are capable of being assembled into a club, but he does not assemble the components?
  2. During the stipulated round, components from the clubhouse are assembled off the course and then brought to the player, who uses the assembled club as a replacement for a club that has been damaged in the normal course of play or as an additional club when the player started with fewer than 14 clubs?
  3. During the stipulated round, components brought to the player from the clubhouse are assembled on the course, and the assembled club is used as a replacement for a club that has been damaged in the normal course of play or as an additional club when the player started with fewer than 14 clubs?

A. 1. A separate clubhead and shaft do not constitute a club. Therefore, the separate clubhead and shaft do not count towards the number of clubs the player may carry under Rule 4-4a. However, regardless of the number of clubs carried, it is not permissible to assemble a clubhead and shaft carried by or for the player during the stipulated round. Consequently, if the player did replace or add a club by assembling components carried by or for him during the round, the player would be penalized under Rule 4-3a(iii) or Rule 4-4a, as applicable.
  2. As the components were not carried by or for the player on the course (i.e., the components were located and assembled off the course), there is no penalty under Rule 4-3a(iii) or Rule 4-4a.
  3. Provided the components were not being carried by or for the player on the course at the time that the replacement club or additional club was requested by the player, there is no penalty under Rule 4-3a(iii) or Rule 4-4a. (Revised)

4-4a/16
Status of Additional Clubs Being Carried for Player and of Person Carrying Them

Q. A player begins his stipulated round with ten clubs carried by his caddie. The player has also asked another person to walk along with the group and carry eight more clubs. During the round, the player intends to add from the clubs carried by the other person. Is such an arrangement permissible?

A. No. As the player intends to add from such clubs during the round, the eight clubs count towards his total. The player is, therefore, in breach of Rule 4-4a for starting the stipulated round with more than 14 clubs. In addition, the other person is acting as a second caddie in breach of Rule 6-4.

As different acts have resulted in two Rules being breached, multiple penalties would apply (see Principle 5 of Decision 1-4/12).

Other Decisions related to Rule 4-4a: See "Clubs: breach of 14-club Rule" and "Clubs: excess club" in the Index.

PARTNERS MAY SHARE CLUBS

4-4b/1
Borrowing Partner's Putter

Q. Neither A nor B, who were partners in a four-ball match, had 14 clubs, but between them they had more than 14 clubs. Several times during the round A borrowed B's putter. Is this permissible?

A. No. A and B should have had two holes deducted. The penalty would be applied to the state of the match at the conclusion of the hole at which it became known that a breach had occurred.

Related Decisions:
- 4-4a/12 Competitor Who Misplaces Putter Borrows Fellow-Competitor's Putter.
- 4-4a/13 Player Practices with Another Player's Club.
- 5-1/5 Whether Player May Borrow Balls from Another Player.
- 20/2 Borrowing Club for Measuring Purposes.

DECLARING EXCESS CLUB OUT OF PLAY

4-4c/1
Excess Club Declared Out of Play Before Round and Placed on Floor of Golf Cart

Q. Before the start of a round, a player discovers that there are 15 clubs in his golf bag. He declares one of the clubs out of play, removes it from his bag, places it on the floor of his golf cart and begins the round. Is the player subject to penalty?

A. Yes, for starting the round with more than 14 clubs. Rule 4-4c has to do with declaring an excess club out of play on discovery of a breach after a round has started. There is nothing in the Rules to permit carrying, during a round, an excess club declared out of play before the round.

4-4c/2
Whether Player May Use Excess Club to Replace Club Damaged in Normal Course of Play

Q. A player begins a round with 15 clubs. On discovering his error, he applies the appropriate penalty under Rule 4-4a and declares a club out of play in accordance with Rule 4-4c. Later in the round, the player damages one of his remaining clubs in the normal course of play to the extent that it is unfit for play. May the player replace the damaged club with the excess club he declared out of play in accordance with Rule 4-4c?

A. Yes. Rule 4-3a(iii), which states in part that a player may replace a club that is unfit for play as a result of damage that occurred in the normal course of play "with any club" overrides Rule 4-4c, which prohibits the use of a club declared out of play as a result of a breach of Rule 4-4a or b.

Other Decisions related to Rule 4-4c: See "Clubs: breach of 14-club Rule" and "Clubs: excess club" in the Index.

RULE 5

THE BALL

A player in doubt as to the conformity of a ball should consult the USGA. A manufacturer should submit to the USGA samples of a ball to be manufactured for a ruling as to whether the ball conforms with the *Rules*. The samples become the property of the USGA for reference purposes. If a manufacturer fails to submit samples or, having submitted samples, fails to await a ruling before manufacturing and/or marketing the ball, the manufacturer assumes the risk of a ruling that the ball does not conform with the *Rules*.

DEFINITIONS

All defined terms are in *italics* and are listed alphabetically in the Definitions section – see pages 6–16.

5-1. GENERAL

The ball the player plays must conform to the requirements specified in Appendix III.

Note: The *Committee* may require, in the conditions of a competition (Rule 33-1), that the ball the player plays must be named on the current List of Conforming Golf Balls issued by the USGA.

5-2. FOREIGN MATERIAL

The ball the player plays must not have foreign material applied to it for the purpose of changing its playing characteristics.

PENALTY FOR BREACH OF RULE 5-1 or 5-2:

Disqualification.

5-3. BALL UNFIT FOR PLAY

A ball is unfit for play if it is visibly cut, cracked or out of shape. A ball is not unfit for play solely because mud or other materials adhere to it, its surface is scratched or scraped or its paint is damaged or discolored.

If a player has reason to believe his ball has become unfit for play during play of the hole being played, he may lift the ball, without penalty, to determine whether it is unfit.

Before lifting the ball, the player must announce his intention to his *opponent* in match play or his *marker* or a *fellow-competitor* in stroke play and mark the position of the ball. He may then lift and examine it, provided that he gives his *opponent*, *marker* or *fellow-competitor* an opportunity to examine the ball and observe the lifting and replacement. The ball must not be cleaned when lifted under Rule 5-3.

If the player fails to comply with all or any part of this procedure, or if he lifts the ball without having reason to believe that it has become unfit for play during play of the hole being played, he incurs a penalty of one stroke.

If it is determined that the ball has become unfit for play during play of the hole being played, the player may *substitute* another ball, placing it on the spot where the original ball lay. Otherwise, the original ball must be replaced. If a player *substitutes* a ball when not permitted and makes a *stroke* at the wrongly *substituted ball*, he incurs the general penalty for a breach of Rule 5-3, but there is no additional penalty under this Rule or Rule 15-2.

If a ball breaks into pieces as a result of a *stroke*, the *stroke* is canceled and the player must play a ball, without penalty, as nearly as possible at the spot from which the original ball was played (see Rule 20-5).

*PENALTY FOR BREACH OF RULE 5-3:
<u>Match play</u> – Loss of hole; <u>Stroke play</u> – Two strokes.

*If a player incurs the general penalty for a breach of Rule 5-3, there is no additional penalty under this Rule.

Note 1: If the *opponent*, *marker* or *fellow-competitor* wishes to dispute a claim of unfitness, he must do so before the player plays another ball.
Note 2: If the original lie of a ball to be placed or replaced has been altered, see Rule 20-3b.

(Cleaning ball lifted from putting green or under any other Rule – see Rule 21)

THE BALL: GENERAL

5-1/1
Use of Ball Not Conforming with Prescribed Specifications

Q. If a player unwittingly plays one stroke with a ball which does not meet the prescribed specifications, would the Committee be justified, under Rule 33-7, in waiving or modifying the disqualification penalty?

A. No – but see Decision 5-1/3 with regard to a provisional ball.

5-1/1.5
Status of Ball Not on List of Conforming Golf Balls

Q. In a competition in which the Committee has not adopted the condition of competition requiring players to use a brand and model of ball on the current List of Conforming Golf Balls, a player uses a ball that does not appear on the List. What is the status of such a ball?

A. Balls not appearing on the current List of Conforming Golf Balls fall into three categories:
1. Brands and models that have never been tested,
2. Brands and models that appeared on a previous List but that have not been re-submitted for inclusion on the current List, and
3. Brands and models that have been tested and found not to conform to the Rules and specifications set forth in Appendix III.

Balls in categories 1 and 2 are presumed to conform and the onus of proof is on the person alleging that the ball does not.

All balls in category 3 are deemed to be non-conforming.

5-1/1.7
Status of Ball to Be Removed from List of Conforming Golf Balls

Q. A brand of ball included on the current List of Conforming Golf Balls is tested again and found not to conform to the specifications in Appendix III. The brand will therefore be deleted from the next List published. What is the status of the ball in the interim period?

A. Players are entitled to assume that all balls of a brand included on the current List of Conforming Golf Balls conform to the Rules. Therefore, players may continue to use balls of the brand in question until the publication of the next List, unless by a condition of the competition the Committee specifically excludes that brand. This applies whether or not it is a condition of the competition that only brands of golf balls on the List of Conforming Golf Balls may be used. (New)

5-1/2
Condition Requiring Use of Ball on List of Conforming Golf Balls; Penalty for Breach

Q. It is a condition of a competition that players must play a brand and model of ball on the current List of Conforming Golf Balls. May the Committee provide that the penalty for breach of the condition is loss of hole in match play or two strokes in stroke play for each hole at which a breach occurs rather than disqualification?

A. No.

5-1/3
Condition Requiring Use of Ball on List of Conforming Golf Balls; Ball Not on List Played as Provisional Ball

Q. It is a condition of the competition that players must play a brand of ball on the current List of Conforming Golf Balls. A player, believing his ball may be lost or out of bounds, plays a provisional ball. He subsequently finds his original ball and then discovers that the ball he played as his provisional ball was not on the List. What is the ruling?

A. The player incurs no penalty as the provisional ball was never the ball in play.

5-1/4
Status of 'X-out', 'Refurbished' and 'Practice' Balls

Q. What is the status of 'X-out', 'refurbished' and 'practice' balls?

A. 'X-out' is the common name used for a golf ball that a manufacturer considers to be imperfect (usually for aesthetic reasons only, e.g., paint or printing errors) and, therefore, has crossed out the brand name. A 'refurbished' golf ball is a second-hand ball that has been cleaned and stamped as 'refurbished'.

In the absence of strong evidence to suggest that an 'X-out' or 'refurbished' ball does not conform to the Rules, it is permissible for such a ball to be used. However, in a competition where the Committee has adopted the condition that the ball the player plays must be named on the List of Conforming Golf Balls (see Note to Rule 5-1), such a ball may not be used, even if the ball in question (without the X's or without the 'refurbished' stamp) does appear on the List.

In most cases, 'practice' balls are simply listed, conforming golf balls that have been stamped "Practice," in the same way that golf balls often feature a club or company logo. Such balls may be used even where the Committee has adopted the condition that the ball the player plays must be named on the List of Conforming Golf Balls.

5-1/5
Whether Player May Borrow Balls from Another Player

Q. During a stipulated round, a player runs out of balls. May he borrow one or more balls from another player?

A. Yes. Rule 4-4a prohibits a player from borrowing a club from another player playing on the course but the Rules do not prevent a player from borrowing other items of equipment (balls, towels, gloves, tees, etc.) from another player or an outside agency.

If the "One Ball" Condition in Appendix I is in effect, the player would need to obtain the same brand and type of ball as required by that condition.

Other Decisions related to Rule 5-1: See "Ball" in the Index.

BALL UNFIT FOR PLAY

5-3/1
Ball Internally Damaged

Q. A player hit his tee shot and expressed the view that the ball behaved erratically in flight. Before his next shot he examined the ball but he could find no external damage and the ball was not out of shape. He commented that the ball must have been damaged internally by his last stroke and claimed the right to substitute another ball under Rule 5-3. Was the player entitled to invoke Rule 5-3?

A. No.

5-3/2
Ball Declared Unfit for Play Played at Later Hole

Q. A player damaged his ball at a certain hole, declared it unfit for play and substituted another ball. At a subsequent hole he played the damaged ball. What is the ruling?

A. There is no penalty. However, the player may not again declare the ball (in the same condition) unfit for play.

5-3/3
Ball Not Unfit for Play Deemed Unfit

Q. In stroke play, a competitor, after announcing his intention of doing so, lifted his ball to check for damage, showed it to his marker and claimed that it was unfit for play. The marker disputed this claim, but the competitor insisted on substituting and playing another ball. Before completion of the hole, however, a referee was consulted and ruled that the ball taken out of play by the competitor was not, after all, unfit for play. What is the ruling?

A. The competitor should be penalized two strokes for a breach of Rule 5-3 and must hole out with the substituted ball.

In similar circumstances in match play, the player would lose the hole for a breach of Rule 5-3. (Revised)

5-3/3.5
Player Lifts Ball on Putting Green, Throws Ball into Lake and Then Announces That Ball Is Unfit for Play

Q. A player mis-hits his approach shot but the ball comes to rest on the putting green. The player marks the position of his ball, inspects it and throws it into an adjacent lake from which it cannot be retrieved.

The player then announces to his opponent, marker or a fellow-competitor that the ball was unfit for play and that he is substituting another ball. The player did not, as required by Rule 5-3, announce his intention in advance to his opponent in match play or his marker or a fellow-competitor in stroke play and give his opponent, marker or fellow-competitor an opportunity to examine the ball.

What is the ruling?

A. The player was entitled under Rule 16-1b to lift his ball without announcing his intentions. However, when he threw the ball into the lake, he deprived his opponent, marker or fellow-competitor of the opportunity to examine the ball and dispute the claim of unfitness, and he made it impossible to replace the original ball should such a dispute be resolved against him. Accordingly, he incurs a penalty of loss of hole in match play or two strokes in stroke play for a breach of Rule 5-3, but he may substitute another ball to complete the hole.

Related Decisions:
• 15-2/1 Player Substitutes Another Ball on Putting Green Because Original Ball Thrown to Caddie for Cleaning Came to Rest in Lake.
• 18-2a/13.5 Ball Lifted and Thrown into Pond in Anger.

5-3/4
Ball Breaks into Pieces as a Result of Striking Paved Cart Path

Q. A player plays a stroke and the ball strikes a paved cart path. As a result of the impact with the cart path, the ball breaks into pieces. Should the ball be considered to have broken into pieces "as a result of a stroke," in which case the player must replay the stroke without penalty under the last paragraph of Rule 5-3?

A. Yes.

5-3/5
Ball Embedded in Hazard Lifted to Determine Whether Unfit for Play

Q. Under Rule 5-3, a ball in a hazard may be lifted to determine whether it is unfit for play. If a ball embedded in a hazard is lifted to determine whether it is unfit for play and the lie is altered in the lifting process, does Rule 20-3b apply?

A. Yes, see Note 2 to Rule 5-3.
   The same ruling would apply if the lie of a ball in a hazard is altered when the ball is lifted for identification (see the Note to Rule 12-2).

Related Decision:
• 20-3b/7 Whether Original Lie May be "Nearest Lie Most Similar."

5-3/6
Ball Thought to Be Unfit for Play Lifted Under Another Rule and Cleaned; Ball Then Determined to Be Unfit for Play

Q. A player believes that his ball may have become unfit for play as a result of his previous stroke, but he is unable to determine whether the ball is unfit due to a large piece of mud adhering to it. He lifts his ball to take relief from an area of ground under repair. He then cleans the ball as permitted under Rule 25-1b and determines that the ball is unfit for play. Is the player subject to penalty under Rule 5-3 which prohibits cleaning the ball?

A. No. The player is entitled to clean the ball as provided in Rule 25-1b.

5-3/7
Ball Thought to Be Unfit for Play; Committee Involvement

Q. A player wishes to lift his ball to determine if it is unfit for play. May a referee or a member of the Committee fulfill the responsibilities of the opponent, marker or fellow-competitor in the relief procedure under Rule 5-3?

A. Yes.

The same ruling applies if a player wishes to lift his ball for identification (Rule 12-2) or to determine whether he is entitled to relief under a Rule (see Decision 20-1/0.7).

5-3/8
Opponent or Fellow-Competitor Disputes Player's Claim That Ball Is Unfit for Play

Q. A player considers his ball unfit for play. His opponent or fellow-competitor disagrees. There is no referee available for a ruling. In spite of the opponent's or fellow-competitor's disagreement, may the player substitute another ball?

A. Yes, subject to the following considerations:

In match play, if the opponent then makes a claim (Rule 2-5) and the Committee, after examination of the original ball, upholds the opponent's claim, the player would lose the hole. Otherwise, the result of the hole would stand as played.

In stroke play, the player may also play a second ball in accordance with Rule 3-3.

In either form of play, the player must ensure that the condition of the ball he considered unfit for play is preserved until the Committee examines it. Otherwise, the Committee should rule against the player and in match play the player would lose the hole and in stroke play the player incurs a penalty of two strokes. (Revised)

Other Decisions related to Rule 5-3: See "Ball Unfit for Play" in the Index.

THE PLAYER

DEFINITIONS
All defined terms are in *italics* and are listed alphabetically in the Definitions section – see pages 6–16.

6-1. RULES
The player and his *caddie* are responsible for knowing the *Rules*. During a *stipulated round*, for any breach of a *Rule* by his *caddie*, the player incurs the applicable penalty.

6-2. HANDICAP
a. Match Play
Before starting a match in a handicap competition, the players should determine from one another their respective handicaps. If a player begins a match having declared a handicap higher than that to which he is entitled and this affects the number of strokes given or received, he is disqualified; otherwise, the player must play off the declared handicap.

b. Stroke Play
In any round of a handicap competition, the *competitor* must ensure that his handicap is recorded on his score card before it is returned to the *Committee*. If no handicap is recorded on his score card before it is returned (Rule 6-6b), or if the recorded handicap is higher than that to which he is entitled and this affects the number of strokes received, he is disqualified from the handicap competition; otherwise, the score stands.

Note: It is the player's responsibility to know the holes at which handicap strokes are to be given or received.

6-3. TIME OF STARTING AND GROUPS
a. Time of Starting
The player must start at the time established by the *Committee*.

PENALTY FOR BREACH OF RULE 6-3a:
If the player arrives at his starting point, ready to play, within five minutes after his starting time, the penalty for failure to start on time is loss of the first hole in match play or two strokes at the first hole in stroke play. Otherwise, the penalty for breach of this Rule is disqualification.

Bogey and par competitions – See Note 2 to Rule 32-1a.
Stableford competitions – See Note 2 to Rule 32-1b.

Exception: Where the *Committee* determines that exceptional circumstances have prevented a player from starting on time, there is no penalty.

b. Groups

In stroke play, the *competitor* must remain throughout the round in the group arranged by the *Committee*, unless the *Committee* authorizes or ratifies a change.

PENALTY FOR BREACH OF RULE 6-3b:

Disqualification.

(Best-ball and four-ball play – see Rules 30-3a and 31-2)

6-4. CADDIE

The player may be assisted by a *caddie*, but he is limited to only one *caddie* at any one time.

*PENALTY FOR BREACH OF RULE 6-4:

<u>Match play</u> – At the conclusion of the hole at which the breach is discovered, the state of the match is adjusted by deducting one hole for each hole at which a breach occurred; maximum deduction per round – Two holes.

<u>Stroke play</u> – Two strokes for each hole at which any breach occurred; maximum penalty per round – Four strokes (two strokes at each of the first two holes at which any breach occurred).

<u>Match play or stroke play</u> – If a breach is discovered between the play of two holes, it is deemed to have been discovered during play of the next hole, and the penalty must be applied accordingly.

<u>Bogey and par competitions</u> – See Note 1 to Rule 32-1a.

<u>Stableford competitions</u> – See Note 1 to Rule 32-1b.

*A player having more than one *caddie* in breach of this Rule must immediately upon discovery that a breach has occurred ensure that he has no more than one *caddie* at any one time during the remainder of the *stipulated round*. Otherwise, the player is disqualified.

Note: The *Committee* may, in the conditions of a competition (Rule 33-1), prohibit the use of *caddies* or restrict a player in his choice of *caddie*.

6-5. BALL

The responsibility for playing the proper ball rests with the player. Each player should put an identification mark on his ball.

6-6. SCORING IN STROKE PLAY

a. Recording Scores

After each hole the *marker* should check the score with the *competitor* and record it. On completion of the round the *marker* must sign the score card and hand it to the *competitor*. If more than one *marker* records the scores, each must sign for the part for which he is responsible.

b. Signing and Returning Score Card

After completion of the round, the *competitor* should check his score for each hole and settle any doubtful points with the *Committee*. He must ensure that the *marker* or *markers* have signed the score card, sign the score card himself and return it to the *Committee* as soon as possible.

PENALTY FOR BREACH OF RULE 6-6b:
Disqualification.

c. Alteration of Score Card
No alteration may be made on a score card after the *competitor* has returned it to the *Committee*.

d. Wrong Score for Hole
The *competitor* is responsible for the correctness of the score recorded for each hole on his score card. If he returns a score for any hole lower than actually taken, he is disqualified. If he returns a score for any hole higher than actually taken, the score as returned stands.

Note 1: The *Committee* is responsible for the addition of scores and application of the handicap recorded on the score card – see Rule 33-5.

Note 2: In *four-ball* stroke play, see also Rules 31-3 and 31-7a.

6-7. UNDUE DELAY; SLOW PLAY
The player must play without undue delay and in accordance with any pace of play guidelines that the *Committee* may establish. Between completion of a hole and playing from the next *teeing ground*, the player must not unduly delay play.

PENALTY FOR BREACH OF RULE 6-7:
Match play – Loss of hole; Stroke play – Two strokes.
Bogey and par competitions – See Note 2 to Rule 32-1a.
Stableford competitions – See Note 2 to Rule 32-1b.
For subsequent offense – Disqualification.

Note 1: If the player unduly delays play between holes, he is delaying the play of the next hole and, except for bogey, par and Stableford competitions (see Rule 32), the penalty applies to that hole.

Note 2: For the purpose of preventing slow play, the *Committee* may, in the conditions of a competition (Rule 33-1), establish pace of play guidelines including maximum periods of time allowed to complete a *stipulated round*, a hole or a *stroke*.

In match play, the *Committee* may, in such a condition, modify the penalty for a breach of this Rule as follows:
First offense – Loss of hole;
Second offense – Loss of hole;
For subsequent offense – Disqualification.

In stroke play, the *Committee* may, in such a condition, modify the penalty for a breach of this Rule as follows:
First offense – One stroke;
Second offense – Two strokes.
For subsequent offense – Disqualification.

6-8. DISCONTINUANCE OF PLAY; RESUMPTION OF PLAY

a. When Permitted

The player must not discontinue play unless:

(i)   the *Committee* has suspended play;

(ii) he believes there is danger from lightning;

(iii) he is seeking a decision from the *Committee* on a doubtful or disputed point (see Rules 2-5 and 34-3); or

(iv) there is some other good reason such as sudden illness.

Bad weather is not of itself a good reason for discontinuing play.

 If the player discontinues play without specific permission from the *Committee*, he must report to the *Committee* as soon as practicable. If he does so and the *Committee* considers his reason satisfactory, there is no penalty. Otherwise, the player is disqualified.

Exception in match play: Players discontinuing match play by agreement are not subject to disqualification, unless by so doing the competition is delayed.

Note: Leaving the *course* does not of itself constitute discontinuance of play.

b. Procedure When Play Suspended by Committee

When play is suspended by the *Committee*, if the players in a match or group are between the play of two holes, they must not resume play until the *Committee* has ordered a resumption of play. If they have started play of a hole, they may discontinue play immediately or continue play of the hole, provided they do so without delay. If the players choose to continue play of the hole, they are permitted to discontinue play before completing it. In any case, play must be discontinued after the hole is completed.

 The players must resume play when the *Committee* has ordered a resumption of play.

PENALTY FOR BREACH OF RULE 6-8b:

Disqualification.

Note: The *Committee* may provide, in the conditions of a competition (Rule 33-1), that in potentially dangerous situations play must be discontinued immediately following a suspension of play by the *Committee*. If a player fails to discontinue play immediately, he is disqualified, unless circumstances warrant waiving the penalty as provided in Rule 33-7.

c. Lifting Ball When Play Discontinued

When a player discontinues play of a hole under Rule 6-8a, he may lift his ball, without penalty, only if the *Committee* has suspended play or there is a good reason to lift it. Before lifting the ball the player must mark its position. If the player discontinues play and lifts his ball without specific permission from the *Committee*, he must, when reporting to the *Committee* (Rule 6-8a), report the lifting of the ball.

 If the player lifts the ball without a good reason to do so, fails to mark the position of the ball before lifting it or fails to report the lifting of the ball, he incurs a penalty of one stroke.

d. Procedure When Play Resumed

Play must be resumed from where it was discontinued, even if resumption occurs on a subsequent day. The player must, either before or when play is resumed, proceed as follows:

(i)   if the player has lifted the ball, he must, provided he was entitled to lift it under Rule 6-8c, place the original ball or a *substituted ball* on the spot from which the original ball was lifted. Otherwise, the original ball must be replaced;

(ii) if the player has not lifted his ball, he may, provided he was entitled to lift it under Rule 6-8c, lift, clean and replace the ball, or substitute a ball, on the spot from which the original ball was lifted. Before lifting the ball he must mark its position; or

(iii) if the player's ball or ball-marker is moved (including by wind or water) while play is discontinued, a ball or ball-marker must be placed on the spot from which the original ball or ball-marker was moved.

Note: If the spot where the ball is to be placed is impossible to determine, it must be estimated and the ball placed on the estimated spot. The provisions of Rule 20-3c do not apply.

*PENALTY FOR BREACH OF RULE 6-8d:

<u>Match play</u> – Loss of hole; <u>Stroke play</u> – Two strokes.

*If a player incurs the general penalty for a breach of Rule 6-8d, there is no additional penalty under Rule 6-8c.

PLAYER'S RESPONSIBILITIES: RULES

6-1/1
Wrong Form of Play Used in Match-Play Event

Q. In a foursome match-play competition, four players begin their match on a four-ball match-play basis. The error is discovered after play of the 9th hole. What is the ruling?

A. It would be improper to decide any match by a form of play other than the prescribed form.

If the wrong form of play is used as a result of a Committee error, the match should be replayed. If the wrong form of play is used unintentionally by players, the match should be replayed; if, however, this would delay the competition, both sides should be disqualified unless one side concedes the match to the other – see Rules 2-4 and 6-1. If the wrong form of play is used intentionally by players, they should be disqualified – Rule 1-3.

Related Decisions:
• 1-3/7 Agreement That Side Losing After 18 Holes of 36-Hole Match Will Concede Match.
• 2-4/21 Wrong Form of Play Used to Decide Which Side Concedes Match.
• 33-1/4 Match Decided by Wrong Form of Play by Agreement of Players.

HANDICAP: GENERAL

6-2/1
Meaning of "Handicap"

Q. Under a handicapping system where the player has to adjust his handicap in accordance with the rating for the course he is playing, a player's handicap before adjustment is 4.8. After applying the appropriate adjustment for the course and the tees to be used for that competition, the player's handicap is 6. Which is his "handicap" for the purposes of Rule 6-2?

A. 6. In a stroke-play competition the player must ensure that the handicap for the course that he is to play and the tees to be used is recorded on his score card when it is returned to the Committee.

Related Decision:
• 6-2b/0.5 Meaning of "Handicap" When Full Handicap Not Used.

HANDICAP IN MATCH PLAY

6-2a/1
Failure to Determine Handicaps Prior to Start of Match

There is no penalty if players fail to determine one another's handicaps before starting a match. If this results in one of them not receiving a handicap stroke at a hole at which he is entitled to receive one, the hole stands as played.

6-2a/2
Handicap Stroke Given at Incorrect Hole in Error

Q. In a match between A and B, under the Handicap Stroke Table A was to receive a handicap stroke at the 9th hole. However, both A and B mistakenly believed that A should receive a handicap stroke at the 7th hole, and the match was played on this basis. Subsequently, the Committee became aware of the error. What should the Committee do?

A. The Committee should take no action. Since the players did not agree to deviate from the Handicap Stroke Table and did so by mistake, there was no breach of Rule 1-3. The match should stand as played. See Note under Rule 6-2.

6-2a/3
Handicap Stroke Wrongly Claimed at Hole; Error Discovered Before Hole Completed

Q. In match play, on the tee of a hole A states in error that he is to receive a handicap stroke at that hole. When A is preparing to putt, his opponent, B, recalls that A does not receive a handicap stroke. B so advises A and claims the hole on the ground that A gave wrong information. What is the ruling?

A. The hole should have been completed without a stroke being given to A, and with no penalty to either side. A did not give wrong information. It is up to each player to know the holes at which handicap strokes are to be given or received – see Note under Rule 6-2.

Related Decision:
• 2-5/13 Extra Stroke Taken by Mistake in Handicap Match (error discovered several holes later); Status of Late Claim.

6-2a/4
Handicap Stroke Claimed After Hole Conceded

Q. In a handicap match, A holed out in 3. B, having a putt for a gross 4 and forgetting that he was entitled to a handicap stroke at the hole, conceded the hole to A. Before A or B played from the next teeing ground, B remembered that he had a handicap stroke at the last hole. What is the ruling?

A. A won the hole when B conceded it (Rule 2-4). It was B's responsibility to know the holes at which he received handicap strokes – see Note under Rule 6-2. Since B forgot about his handicap stroke, he must suffer the consequences.

6-2a/5
Wrong Handicap Used in Match by Mistake; Error Discovered After Result Officially Announced

Q. In a handicap match between A and B, A stated by mistake before the match began that his handicap was ten strokes, whereas in fact his handicap was nine strokes. The match was played on the basis that A's handicap was ten strokes. A won the match. The error was discovered after the result had been officially announced. What is the ruling?

A. The match stands as played. No claim by B could be considered unless A had known he was giving wrong information about his handicap – see Rules 2-5, 6-2a and 34-1a

6-2a/6
Wrong Handicap Allowance Used in Match

Q. In a handicap match-play competition, the conditions provide that, where handicaps were different, the full difference would be used. In one match, however, the players, unaware of this condition, used ¾ of the difference, and the lower handicapped player won. How should the Committee rule?

A. The Committee should rule that the match stands as played. The players failed to take note of the conditions of the competition (Rule 6-1) and have only themselves to blame.

Decisions related to 6-2a/5 and 6-2a/6:
• 30-3a/3 Determination of Handicap Allowances in Four-Ball Match If One Player Unable to Compete.
• 33-1/12 Wrong Handicap Used Due to Committee Misinformation.

6-2b/0.5
Meaning of "Handicap" When Full Handicap Not Used

Q. It is the condition of a stroke-play competition (e.g., four-ball) that players will not receive their full handicap allowances. Under Rule 6-2b, what is the player responsible for recording on his score card?

A. He must record his full handicap. It is the Committee's responsibility to apply the condition of competition to adjust his handicap.

Related Decision:
• 6-2/1 Meaning of "Handicap."

6-2b/1
Wrong Handicap Used in Stroke Play by Mistake; Error Discovered After Competition Closed

Q. In a stroke-play competition, A believed that his handicap was ten strokes, which he recorded on his score card. In fact his handicap was nine strokes. He won the event because of the error. The result of the competition was announced and the error was then discovered. What is the ruling?

A. The competition should stand as played. Under Rule 34-1b, a penalty under Rule 6-2b may not be imposed after a handicap stroke-play competition has closed unless the competitor has knowingly played off a handicap higher than that to which he was entitled.

6-2b/2
Wrong Handicap Knowingly Used in Stroke Play; Error Discovered After Competition Closed

Q. In late June, A submitted an entry form for a handicap stroke-play competition to be held on 10 July and stated therein that his handicap was seven strokes, which was his correct handicap. On 1 July, A's handicap was reduced to six strokes and he was aware of the reduction.

On 10 July, he played in the stroke-play competition and returned his score card with a handicap of seven strokes recorded thereon, and this affected the number of strokes received. Under the conditions for the event he should have recorded his up-to-date handicap of six strokes. After the competition was closed, it was discovered that A had played off seven, instead of six.

The Committee questioned A, and A stated either that he knew he should have played off his up-to-date handicap or that he was uncertain at the time. What should the Committee do?

A. In either case, he is deemed to have knowingly played off a higher handicap than that to which he was entitled and is disqualified under Rule 34-1b, Exception (ii).

Had A believed players were required to use their handicaps at the time of entry, there would have been no penalty as the competition had closed (Rule 34-1b).

6-2b/2.5
Competitor Records Incorrect Handicap for Partner in Foursome Stroke-Play Competition; Error Discovered After Competition Closed

Q. A and B were partners in a foursome stroke-play competition. At the conclusion of the round, A recorded on the score card that his handicap was eight strokes, but mistakenly and without B's knowledge, recorded B's handicap as ten strokes, whereas B knew that his handicap was nine. The mistake affected the number of strokes received by the side, but was not discovered until after the competition had closed. What is the ruling?

A. The side should be disqualified for returning a score card on which B's recorded handicap was higher than that to which he was entitled and this affected the number of strokes received (Rule 6-2b). Since B knew that his handicap was nine, the fact that the competition had closed makes no difference – see Rule 34-1b(ii).

6-2b/3
Competitor Wins Competition with Handicap Which Was Incorrect Due to Committee Error; Error Discovered Several Days Later

Q. The Committee incorrectly calculated a competitor's handicap and posted it on the notice board as 17 when it should have been 16. The competitor won an 18-hole stroke-play event as a result of the error. May the Committee correct the error several days later and retract the prize?

A. Yes. There is no time limit on correcting such an error. Rule 34-1b is not applicable since it deals with penalties, not with Committee errors.

The competitor should not be disqualified but his net score should be increased by one stroke.

Related Decisions:
• 33-5/2 Wrong Handicap Applied by Committee Results in Player Not Receiving Prize.
• 34-1b/6 Winner's Score Not Posted Due to Committee Error.

6-2b/3.5
Wrong Handicap Recorded on Score Card by Committee; Error Discovered Before Competition Closed

Q. In a stroke-play competition, the Committee issues the score cards containing the competitor's handicap in addition to his name and the date.

The Committee mistakenly records a competitor's handicap as

seven instead of six and this affects the number of strokes received. The error remains unnoticed until after the card is returned, but before the competition has closed. What is the ruling?

A. The competitor should be disqualified under Rule 6-2b. It is the responsibility of the competitor to ensure that his correct handicap is recorded on his score card before it is returned to the Committee.

6-2b/4
Competitors in Foursome Competition Fail to Record Individual Handicaps on Score Card

Q. In a foursome stroke-play competition, partners A and B correctly calculated their combined handicap allowance and recorded it on their score card, rather than their individual handicaps.

A and B were disqualified. Was the ruling correct?

A. Yes. In any round of a handicap stroke-play competition, it is the responsibility of the competitor to ensure that his handicap is recorded on his score card before it is returned to the Committee (Rule 6-2b).

The word "competitor" includes his partner in a stroke-play foursome competition – see Definition of "Competitor." Therefore, the individual handicaps of A and B should have been recorded on the score card. As only the combined handicap allowance was recorded, A and B were correctly disqualified.

6-2b/5
Competition in Which Best Two of Four Scores Used to Determine Winner; Competitor Returns Score Card with Higher Handicap

Q. A handicap competition is based on the best two of four scores. In the first round, a competitor returns his score card with a handicap higher than that to which he is entitled and it affects the number of strokes received. What is the ruling?

A. The competitor is disqualified only from the first round of the competition and now has three rounds in which to determine his best two net scores.

Related Decision:
• 33/8 Application of Disqualification Penalty in Competition in Which Not All Scores Used to Determine Winner.

6-3a/1
Postponement of Final Match Due to Injury of Player

If a player who reaches the final of a match-play event suffers an injury and is unable to play at the time arranged, the Committee may, with the concurrence of the opponent, postpone the match for a reasonable period. This applies in all forms of match play.

Related Decision:
• 6-8a/3 Discontinuing Play Due to Physical Problem.

6-3a/1.5
Exceptional Circumstances Which Warrant Waiving of Disqualification Penalty Under Rule 6-3a

Q. The Exception to Rule 6-3a states that if the Committee determines that exceptional circumstances have prevented a player from starting on time, there is no penalty. With reference to the following examples, what circumstances are considered exceptional such that there would be no penalty if the player failed to start at the time established:
   1. The player gets lost on the way to the course.
   2. Heavy traffic results in the journey to the course taking longer than expected.
   3. A major accident results in the journey to the course taking longer than expected.
   4. The player's car breaks down on the way to the course.
   5. The player was present at the scene of an accident and provided medical assistance or was required to give a statement as a witness and otherwise would not have failed to start on time.

A. There is no hard-and-fast Rule. The proper action depends on the circumstances in each case and must be left to the determination of the Committee.

Generally, only example 5 constitutes an exceptional circumstance under the Exception to Rule 6-3a.

It is the player's responsibility to ensure that he allows enough time to reach the course and he must make allowances for possible delays. (Revised)

6-3a/2
Time of Starting; All Competitors Must Be Present

Q. In a stroke-play competition, A, B and C were drawn by the Committee to play together starting at 9 am. A and B were present at the appointed time. C arrived at 9:02 am after A and B had played from the teeing ground, but just in time to play in the correct order.

What is the ruling?

A. As C arrived and was ready to play within five minutes after his starting time, he incurred a penalty of two strokes for failure to start at the time established by the Committee (Rule 6-3a). If C had arrived more than five minutes after his starting time, the penalty would be disqualification. In either case if the Committee determines that exceptional circumstances had prevented C from starting on time, there is no penalty.

All competitors in a group must be present and ready to play at the time established by the Committee, in this case 9:00 am. The order of play is not relevant. (Revised)

Related Decision:
• 6-8b/9 Resumption of Play; When Players Must Be Present.

6-3a/2.5
Meaning of "Time of Starting"

Q. A player's starting time is listed on the official starting sheet as 9:00 am He does not arrive at the 1st tee until 9:00:45 am and claims that, as it is still 9:00 am, he is not late for his starting time. What is the ruling?

A. When a starting time is listed as 9:00 am, the starting time is deemed to be 9:00 am and the player is subject to penalty under Rule 6-3a if he is not present and ready to play at 9:00:00 am Therefore, the player incurred a penalty of two strokes in stroke play or loss of the first hole in match play unless the Committee determines that exceptional circumstances had prevented him from starting on time (Exception to Rule 6-3). (Revised)

6-3a/3
Time of Starting; Both Players in Match are Late

Q. In a match-play competition, A and B were to start their match at 9 am. A arrives at the 1st tee at 9:01 am, but before B, who arrives at 9:03 am. What is the ruling?

A. If neither player had exceptional circumstances that prevented him from starting on time, each player would incur a penalty of loss of the 1st hole. Therefore, in equity (Rule 1-4), the 1st hole is deemed halved and the match would commence on the 2nd hole. (Revised)

6-3a/4
Time of Starting; Player is Late but Group Unable to Play Due To Delay

Q. A player is assigned by the Committee to a group with a 9:00 am starting time. He arrives at the 1st tee at 9:06 am but for whatever reason (e.g., weather, slow play or a ruling) the starting time has been delayed until after he arrives. What is the ruling?

A. As the group was unable to start at the time originally established by the

Committee and the player arrived before it could do so, the player is not in breach of Rule 6-3a.

Related Decision:
• 33-3/2 Player Not Present at Time of Starting; Course Closed at the Time.

6-3a/5
Players Start Early

Q. In stroke play, A, B and C were scheduled to start at 9:00 am. All players were present at the 1st tee at 8:56 am. Without being given authority to do so by the Committee, A started at 8:58 am, B started at 8:59 am and C started at 9:00 am. What is the ruling?

A. Unless the Committee considers that the players have started early as a result of an error by the Committee or its representative, A and B are subject to a penalty of disqualification for failing to start at the scheduled time (see penalty statement under Rule 6-3a). However, in view of the fact that starting within five minutes after the time of starting results in a penalty of two strokes in stroke play under Rule 6-3a, the penalty for starting early, but within five minutes of the starting time, should be the same. Therefore, under Rule 33-7, the Committee should modify the disqualification penalty to two strokes, unless there is good reason not to do so, e.g., the players ignored a direct instruction from the Committee not to start before 9:00 am.

C incurs no penalty as he did start at 9:00 am, which was the time established by the Committee. (New)

Related Decision:
• 6-8b/6 Play Suspended by Committee; Competitor Does Not Resume Play at Time Ordered by Committee.

Other Decisions related to Rule 6-3a: See "Time of Starting" in the Index.

CADDIE

6-4/1
Meaning of "Specific Directions" in Definition of "Caddie"

Q. A and B are sharing a caddie. A asks the caddie to bring him a club. The caddie removes A's club from his bag, places both bags behind the green and walks towards A to give him his club. At that point B plays and his ball strikes one of the bags. What is the ruling?

A. B incurred a penalty stroke under Rule 19-2 (Ball in Motion Deflected or Stopped by Player's Equipment).

The Definition of "Caddie" (second paragraph) provides that, when a caddie is shared by more than one player, the equipment he carries is deemed to belong to the player whose ball is involved in any incident (in this case, B).

The only exception to the above provision occurs when the shared caddie is acting upon the specific directions of another player (or the partner of another player) sharing the caddie. In this case, although A asked the caddie to bring him a club, he did not instruct the caddie, when complying with his request, to place the two bags in a particular position. In placing the bags where he did, therefore, the caddie was not acting on "specific directions" of A within the meaning of that term in the Definition of "Caddie." Before playing, B could have asked the caddie to move the bags if he thought his ball might strike them.

Related Decision:
- 19-2/8 Player's Ball Strikes Opponent's or Fellow-Competitor's Bag Left Ahead By Shared Caddie.

6-4/2 (Reserved)

6-4/2.5
Status of Individual Who Transports Player's Clubs on Motorized Golf Cart or Trolley

Q. During a round, a player's clubs are transported on a motorized golf cart or trolley by a friend who performs no other functions of a caddie. Is the friend considered to be the player's caddie?

A. Yes. By driving the cart or pulling the trolley the friend is deemed to be carrying the player's clubs – see Definition of "Caddie."

Related Decisions:
- 19/2 Status of Person in Shared Golf Cart.
- 33-1/9.5 Breach of Transportation Condition by Caddie.
- 33-8/4 Local Rule for Events in Which Motorized Golf Carts Permitted.

6-4/3
Player Whose Clubs Are Transported on Motorized Golf Cart Hires Individual to Perform All Other Functions of a Caddie

Q. A player whose clubs are transported on a motorized golf cart hires an individual to perform all the other duties of a caddie. Is this permissible, and is the individual considered to be a caddie?

A. The individual is considered to be a caddie.

This arrangement is permissible provided the player has not engaged someone else to drive the cart. In such a case, the cart driver, since he is transporting the player's clubs, is also a caddie. Rule 6-4 prohibits a player from having two caddies at any one time.

Thus, the arrangement is permissible (a) if the player and an opponent or a fellow-competitor are sharing the cart, even if the player walks and the opponent or fellow-competitor drives the cart, or (b) if the cart is not being shared with an opponent or a fellow-competitor and the player drives the cart.

6-4/4
Caddie Hires Boy to Carry All of Player's Clubs Except Putter

Q. A player's caddie hires a young boy to carry all of the player's clubs except his putter, which the caddie carries. The caddie assists the player in other ways, i.e., attends the flagstick and gives advice. The young boy does not so assist. Is this permissible?

A. No. The player would be considered to have two caddies in contravention of Rule 6-4.

6-4/4.5
Another Caddie or Friend Carries Clubs While Player's Caddie Returns to Tee with Player's Glove

Q. A player walks from the putting green of the previous hole to the next tee with his driver while his caddie walks ahead with the clubs in order to save time. The caddie realizes he has his player's glove and gives the clubs to another player's caddie or friend to be carried while he takes the player his glove.
 Did the player have two caddies in breach of Rule 6-4?

A. No. The casual act of someone assisting the player or his caddie in these circumstances does not constitute a breach of Rule 6-4.

6-4/5
Umbrella Carrier Employed in Addition to Caddie

Q. May a player employ both a caddie and a second person to carry his umbrella and hold it over his head (except when a stroke is being made) to protect him from the sun or rain?

A. Yes. The second person would be an outside agency. However, the Committee may prohibit the employment of an umbrella carrier in the conditions of the competition.

6-4/5.3
Status of Additional Persons and Items Carried by Such Persons for Player

Q. May a player have a caddie carry his clubs and also have additional persons carry items other than clubs (e.g., a rainsuit, umbrella, food and drink) for the player?

A. Yes. The additional persons would be outside agencies, and any items carried by them would also be considered outside agencies while in their possession. However, the Committee may prohibit the use of such persons in the conditions of the competition.

6-4/5.5
Application of Penalty When Player Has Multiple Caddies

Q. A player completes play of the 1st hole using two caddies. While proceeding to the 2nd tee he is advised of his breach of Rule 6-4. What is the ruling?

A. The player is penalized at both the 1st and 2nd holes. Since he did not correct his error prior to holing out at the 1st hole, he was also in breach of Rule 6-4 between the play of the 1st and 2nd holes, which results in a penalty at the 2nd hole. The player must immediately correct his breach and ensure that he has no more than one caddie at any one time for the remainder of the stipulated round.

In match play, the state of the match is adjusted by deducting two holes at the conclusion of the 2nd hole.

In stroke play, the player incurs a penalty of two strokes at both the 1st and 2nd holes, for a total penalty of four strokes.

6-4/6
Status of Carts Pulled by Double Caddie

Q. A and B are sharing a caddie who is pulling A's bag on one cart and B's on another. A makes a stroke and his ball strikes B's cart. With reference to the Definition of "Caddie," since B's cart was not being carried by the caddie, would it be considered B's equipment?

A. No. The cart is considered A's equipment in these circumstances. The word "carrying" in the Definition should not be taken so literally as to exclude the pulling of a cart by a caddie.

6-4/7
Changing Caddies During Round

Q. May a player have more than one caddie during a round? If so, may each caddie give the player advice?

A. A player may have more than one caddie during a round, provided he has only one at a time. He is entitled to receive advice from whoever is his caddie at the time – see Definition of "Caddie."

Related Decision:
• 8-1/26 Player Briefly Changes Caddies for Exchange of Advice.

6-4/8
Player in Competition Caddies for Another Player in Same Event

Q. Two players playing in the same competition at different times on the same day caddie for each other. Is this permissible?

A. Yes.

6-4/9
Competitor Withdraws During Round and Carries Fellow-Competitor's Clubs for Remainder of Round

Q. In stroke play, A, B's fellow-competitor and marker, withdrew during a round and ceased to play. He continued to mark B's card, and also carried B's clubs for the rest of the round. Is this permissible?

A. Yes. A became B's caddie as well as his marker when he started carrying B's clubs.

6-4/10
Acts Which Caddie May Perform

While the Rules do not expressly so state, the following are examples of acts which the caddie may perform for the player without the player's authority:
1. Search for the player's ball as provided in Rule 12-1.
2. Place the player's clubs in a hazard – Exception 1 under Rule 13-4.
3. Repair old hole plugs and ball marks – Rule 16-1a(vi) and 16-1c.
4. Remove loose impediments on the line of putt or elsewhere – Rules 16-1a and 23-1.
5. Mark the position of a ball, without lifting it – Rule 20-1.
6. Clean the player's ball – Rule 21.
7. Remove movable obstructions – Rule 24-1.

Other Decisions related to Rule 6-4: See "Caddie" in the Index.

RECORDING SCORES

6-6a/1
Lone Competitor Appoints Own Marker

Q. In a stroke-play competition, a lone competitor had no marker. No member of the Committee was present to appoint one. So the competitor played with two players playing a friendly game, and one of them served as his marker. Should the Committee accept the card?

A. Yes. Since the Committee failed to provide a marker, the Committee should give retrospective authority to the player who acted as the competitor's marker.

Related Decision:
• 33-1/5 Competitor in Stroke-Play Event Plays with Two Players Engaged in Match.

6-6a/2
Competitor Plays Several Holes Without Marker

Q. A plays three holes by himself while his marker, B, rests. B then resumes play and marks A's scores for the holes he (A) played alone as well as his scores for the remainder of the holes. Should A's card be accepted?

A. No. A should have insisted on B accompanying him or have discontinued play and reported to the Committee. Since A was not accompanied by a marker for three holes, he did not have an acceptable score.

6-6a/3
Hole Scores Entered in Wrong Boxes; Marker Corrects Error by Altering Hole Numbers on Card

Q. In stroke play, a marker recorded some of the competitor's hole scores in the wrong boxes. He altered the hole numbers on the card to correct the error. Should the card be accepted?

A. Yes.

Related Decision:
• 6-6d/3 Hole Scores for First Nine Holes Recorded in Boxes for Second Nine and Vice Versa.

6-6a/4
Marker Refuses to Sign Competitor's Card After Dispute Resolved in Favor of Competitor

Q. In stroke play, B, who was A's fellow-competitor and marker, refused to sign A's score card on the grounds that A had played outside the teeing ground at the 15th hole. A claimed that he played from within the teeing ground.

The Committee decided in favor of A. Despite the Committee's decision, B continued to refuse to sign A's card. Should B be penalized?

A. No. A marker is not obliged to sign a card he believes to be incorrect, notwithstanding the determination of the Committee. However, the marker must report the facts and authenticate those scores which he considers correct.

The Committee should accept certification of A's score at the 15th hole by anyone else who witnessed the play of the hole. If no witness is available, the Committee should accept A's score without certification.

Related Decisions:
• 6-6d/5 Spectators Allege Competitor's Score Incorrect.
• 34-3/4 Dispute as to Whether Competitor Played from Outside Teeing Ground.
• 34-3/9 Resolution of Questions of Fact; Referee and Committee Responsibility.

6-6a/5
Marker Attests Wrong Score Knowingly But Competitor Unaware Score Wrong

Q. In stroke play, a competitor returned a wrong score because his score card did not include a penalty he had incurred. The competitor was unaware that he had incurred the penalty. The competitor's marker (a fellow-competitor) was aware of the penalty but nevertheless signed the card. The facts were discovered before the result of the competition was officially announced.

The competitor is, of course, disqualified (Rule 6-6d). Is the marker also subject to disqualification?

A. Yes. The Committee should disqualify the marker under Rule 33-7.

Related Decisions:
- 1-3/6 Marker Attests Wrong Score Knowingly and Competitor Aware Score Wrong.
- 33-7/9 Competitor Who Knows Player Has Breached Rules Does Not Inform Player or Committee in Timely Manner.

6-6a/6
Requirement That Alteration on Score Card Be Initialled

Q. May a Committee require that alterations made on score cards be initialled?

A. No. Nothing is laid down in the Rules of Golf as to how alterations should be made on a score card.

Related Decisions:
- 6-6b/8 Requirement That Score Be Entered into Computer.
- 33-1/7 Making Competitors Responsible for Adding Scores.

6-6a/7
Different Score Card Returned

Q. At the end of a round in stroke play, a competitor returns to the Committee a score card different from the one issued by the Committee at the start of the round (e.g., because the original score card was lost or illegible due to wet weather). The new score card contained the competitor's name and scores and was signed by both him and his marker. Should the score card be accepted?

A. Yes.

Other Decisions related to Rule 6-6a: See "Scores and Score Cards" in the Index.

6-6b/1
Competitor and Marker Sign Score Card in Wrong Places

There is no penalty if a marker signs the competitor's score card in the space provided for the competitor's signature, and the competitor then signs in the space provided for the marker's signature.

6-6b/2
Competitor Records Initials in Space Reserved for Signature

Q. Instead of recording his usual signature on his score card, a competitor records his initials. Has the competitor met the requirements of Rule 6-6b?

A. Yes.

6-6b/3
Competitor Fails to Sign First-Round Card; Error Discovered on Completion of Last Round

Q. In a 36-hole stroke-play event, it was discovered just before the results were announced that a competitor had omitted to sign his score card at the end of the first round. In all other respects the cards for both rounds were correct. Should he be disqualified?

A. Yes, because he was in breach of Rule 6-6b.

Related Decisions:
- 33-7/3 Competitor's Failure to Countersign Card Blamed on Lack of Time Provided by Committee.
- 34-1b/2 Competitor's Failure to Sign Score Card Discovered After Competition Closed.

6-6b/4
Score Cards Not Returned Promptly Due to Committee Failure to Advise Competitors Where to Return Cards

It is a duty of the Committee to inform competitors where and to whom to return their score cards. If the Committee fails to do so, and as a result some competitors delay in returning cards, a penalty of disqualification under Rule 6-6b or any other Rule would not be justified.

6-6b/5
Marker Not Appointed by Committee Signs Cards

Q. In stroke play, A and B were appointed by the Committee as markers for one another. During the round, C joined them as a spectator; from that point, C marked the cards of both A and B, signed them at the end of the round and returned them to A and B. A and B checked their respective cards, signed them and returned them to the Committee. Before the competition closed, the Committee became aware that A had not signed B's card and vice versa. What is the ruling?

A. Since C had not been appointed as a marker by the Committee and there were no exceptional circumstances, A and B should be disqualified under Rule 6-6b.

6-6b/6
Marker Disappears with Competitor's Score Card

Q. In a stroke-play event, competitors were instructed to return their score cards at the scoreboard. Unbeknownst to a competitor, his marker leaves the course hastily at the end of the round and does not report to the scoreboard. He takes the competitor's score card with him. What should the Committee do?

A. The Committee should make every effort to reach the marker. If unsuccessful, the Committee should accept certification of the score by someone else who witnessed the round, perhaps the marker's caddie or the competitor's caddie. If no one other than the marker witnessed the round, the score should be accepted without attestation by a marker.

6-6b/7
Score Corrected by Competitor After Marker Leaves Area in Which Card Returned

Q. A marker signed a competitor's score card, gave it to the competitor and left the area. The competitor discovered an error in his score for the 14th hole; the marker had recorded a 5 when, in fact, the competitor had scored 4. Without consulting the Committee, the competitor corrected the card, signed it and handed it in to the Committee. Later, the Committee heard what had happened, interviewed the competitor and his marker and established that the competitor did, in fact, score 4 at the 14th hole. Was the competitor in breach of Rule 6-6b and thus disqualified?

A. Yes. When the competitor altered the score card, he invalidated the attestation of his score by the marker. Therefore, he effectively returned a score card which was not signed by the marker.

If the competitor had informed the Committee, before returning his card, that he was correcting the error, he would not have been subject to penalty.

6-6b/8
Requirement That Score Be Entered into Computer

Q. May a Committee, as a condition of competition, provide that a competitor must enter his score into a computer?

A. No. Such a condition would modify Rule 6-6b.

However, while it is not permissible to penalize a player under the Rules of Golf for failing to enter his score into a computer, a Committee may, in order to assist in the administration of the competition, introduce a "club regulation" to this effect and provide disciplinary sanctions (e.g., ineligibility to play in the next club competition(s)) for failure to act in accordance with the regulation.

Related Decision:
• 6-6a/6 Requirement That Alteration on Score Card Be Initialled.
• 33-1/7 Making Competitors Responsible for Adding Scores.

Other Decisions related to Rule 6-6b: See "Scores and Score Cards" in the Index.

ALTERATION OF SCORE CARD

6-6c/1
When Score Card Considered Returned

Q. Rule 6-6c prohibits alterations to the score card "after the competitor has returned it to the Committee." When is a score card considered returned?

A. This is a matter for the Committee to decide and it will vary depending on the nature of the competition. The Committee should designate a "scoring area" where competitors are to return their score cards (e.g., in a tent, a trailer, the golf shop, by the scoreboard, etc.). When it has done so, Rule 6-6c should be interpreted in such a way that a competitor within the "scoring area" is considered to be in the process of returning his score card. Alterations may be made on the score card even if the competitor has handed the score card to a member of the Committee. He is considered to have returned his score card when he has left the scoring area.

Alternatively, the Committee may require a competitor to return his score card by placing it in a box and thus consider it returned when it is dropped into the box, even if he has not left the scoring area.

Other Decisions related to Rule 6-6c: See "Scores and Score Cards: alteration to score card" in the Index.

WRONG SCORE FOR HOLE

6-6d/1
No Score Entered for One Hole But Total Correct

Q. In stroke play, A returned his score card. The Committee discovered that no score had been entered for the 17th hole; however, A's total score for the round as recorded on the card by A or his marker was correct. What is the ruling?

A. A should be disqualified for a breach of Rule 6-6d.

Related Decision:
• 31-3/1 Gross Score of Partner with Better Net Score Omitted from Card.

6-6d/2
Total Score Recorded by Competitor Incorrect

Q. In stroke play, a competitor returns his score card to the Committee. The hole by hole scores are correct, but the competitor records a total score which is one stroke lower than his actual total score. Is the competitor subject to penalty?

A. No. The competitor is responsible only for the correctness of the score recorded for each hole (Rule 6-6d). The Committee is responsible for the addition of scores (Rule 33-5). If the competitor records a wrong total score, the Committee must correct the error, without penalty to the competitor.

6-6d/3
Hole Scores for First Nine Holes Recorded in Boxes for Second Nine and Vice Versa

Q. A competitor who started at the 10th hole returns a card with scores for the first nine holes recorded in the boxes for the second nine holes, and vice versa. Should he be disqualified since the scores for some holes were lower than actually taken?

A. Yes.

Related Decision:
• 6-6a/3 Hole Scores Entered in Wrong Boxes; Marker Corrects Error by Altering Hole Numbers on Card.

6-6d/4
Competitor's Scores Recorded on Score Card with Fellow-Competitor's Name and Vice Versa

Q. A and B are playing together in stroke play. A is B's marker and B is A's marker. A score card is distributed to each player by the starter. When the score cards are returned, the score card with A's name printed on it contains the correct scores of B and vice versa. Each score card contains the signature of the competitor whose scores are recorded together with the signature of his marker.

The mismatch of the competitors' printed names with the reported scores is discovered after the score cards are returned. What is the ruling?

A. Assuming that each competitor himself has signed the score card on which his scores were recorded and that his marker has also signed this score card, the Committee should strike the name printed on the score card, enter the name of the competitor whose scores are recorded on the score card and accept the score card without penalty to either player. Administrative errors of this specific nature are not contemplated by the Rules and the Committee should correct such an error. There is no time limit for correcting such an administrative error. Rule 6-6b implies that the competitor is responsible only for the correctness of the scores recorded for each hole, ensuring that the marker has signed the score card and that the competitor has signed the score card himself.

The same principle would also apply in the case of a score card returned without a name recorded on it.

6-6d/5
Spectators Allege Competitor's Score Incorrect

Q. All strokes played by A at the 18th hole were observed by spectators, but when the card was returned the recorded score for that hole was lower than that which the spectators alleged had been taken. What should the Committee do?

A. If any doubt arises as to the correctness of a card, the Committee should consult with the competitor and marker and also take into account the testimony of other witnesses.

If the evidence indicates that the recorded score for the 18th hole was lower than actually taken, the Committee should disqualify A (Rule 6-6d). Otherwise, no penalty should be applied.

Related Decisions:
- 6-6a/4 Marker Refuses to Sign Competitor's Card After Dispute Resolved in Favor of Competitor.
- 34-3/4 Dispute as to Whether Competitor Played from Outside Teeing Ground.
- 34-3/9 Resolution of Questions of Fact; Referee and Committee Responsibility.

Other Decisions related to Rule 6-6d: See "Scores and Score Cards" in the Index.

UNDUE DELAY

6-7/1
Player Returns to Tee to Retrieve Forgotten Club

Q. A player arrives at a green and discovers that he has left his putter at the tee. He returns to the tee to retrieve the putter. If this delays play, is the player subject to penalty?

A. Yes. Rule 6-7 (Undue Delay) and not Rule 6-8a (Discontinuance of Play) applies in this case.

6-7/2
Searching Ten Minutes for Lost Ball

Q. If a player searches for a lost ball for ten minutes, is he subject to penalty under Rule 6-7 for undue delay?

A. Yes.

Other Decisions related to Rule 6-7: See "Undue Delay" in the Index.

DISCONTINUANCE OF PLAY: WHEN PERMITTED

6-8a/1
Watching Television for 45 Minutes After Nine Holes

Q. In stroke play, a group went into the clubhouse after nine holes and watched the final round of a golf tournament on television for 45 minutes. Then the group resumed play. Should the members of the group be penalized under Rule 6-7 (Undue Delay) or Rule 6-8 (Discontinuance of Play)?

A. The competitors should be disqualified under Rule 6-8a.

6-8a/2
Taking Shelter While Waiting to Play

Q. In stroke play, a group preparing to start a hole is waiting for the group ahead to get out of range. May the group take shelter from the rain in a rain shelter close to the tee?

A. Yes, but the group must leave the shelter and resume play as soon as the group in front is out of range.

6-8a/2.5
Discontinuing Play for Refreshment

The Committee may not permit players to discontinue play for refreshment for an extended period during a stipulated round. Such a condition would modify Rule 6-8a.

The Committee may, however, in the conditions of a competition, permit players to discontinue play for a short period of time (e.g., up to five minutes), if it considers there to be good reason (e.g., a danger of dehydration or heat exhaustion in hot climates or a need to warm up in cold climates).

However, since the Rules make specific provision for players to play without undue delay (Rule 6-7) and continuously (Rule 6-8a), such a condition is not recommended.

6-8a/2.7
Entering Clubhouse or Half-Way House for Refreshment During Round

Q. May a player, between the play of two holes, enter the clubhouse or a "half-way house" to obtain a refreshment if he then proceeds immediately to the next tee and consumes the food and/or drink while continuing his round?

A. Yes. A player may enter the clubhouse or a half-way house without penalty (see Note to Rule 6-8a).

However, the player must not unduly delay either his own play or that of his opponent or any other competitor (Rule 6-7).

6-8a/3
Discontinuing Play Due to Physical Problem

Q. During a round, a player is incapacitated by heat exhaustion, a bee sting or because he has been struck by a golf ball. The player reports his problem to the Committee and requests the Committee to allow him some time to recuperate. Should the Committee comply with the request?

A. The matter is up to the Committee. Rule 6-8a(iv) permits a player to discontinue play because of sudden illness and the player incurs no penalty if he reports to the Committee as soon as practicable and the Committee considers his reason satisfactory. It would seem reasonable for a Committee to allow a player 10 or 15 minutes to recuperate from such a physical problem but ordinarily allowing more time than that would be inadvisable.

Related Decision:
• 6-3a/1 Postponement of Final Match Due to Injury of Player.

6-8a/4
Discontinuing Play Due to Inoperable Motorized Cart

Q. In stroke play, two competitors are sharing a motorized golf cart. During the round the cart becomes inoperable. The competitors discontinue play and return to the clubhouse to obtain another cart. Should the competitors be penalized for discontinuing play?

A. If the competitors reported to the Committee as soon as practicable after discontinuing play (as required by Rule 6-8a), it is recommended that, since it may not always be reasonable to expect players to carry their own bags, the Committee may consider the reason for discontinuance satisfactory, in which case there would be no penalty provided the competitors resume play when directed to do so by the Committee.

6-8a/5
Match Discontinued by Agreement Due to Rain; One Player Subsequently Wishes to Resume; Opponent Refuses Although Course Playable

Q. In accordance with the Exception under Rule 6-8a, A and B discontinue a match due to rain. Subsequently, although the rain continues to fall, A wishes to resume play. B refuses because he does not want to play in the rain, not because he considers the course unplayable. What is the ruling?

A. B is disqualified (Rule 6-8a). The Exception to Rule 6-8a permits discontinuance of a match by mutual agreement. However, when A decided that he wanted to resume play, there was no longer an agreement and B was obliged to resume play.

6-8a/6
Match Discontinued by Agreement Due to Rain; One Player Subsequently Wishes to Resume; Opponent Refuses on Ground Course Unplayable

Q. In accordance with the Exception under Rule 6-8a, A and B discontinue a match due to rain. Subsequently, A wishes to resume play. B refuses on the ground that the course is unplayable. What is the ruling?

A. B is entitled to refer the dispute to a member of the Committee if one is available within a reasonable time. If a member of the Committee is not available within a reasonable time, B is obliged to continue the match without delay – Rule 2-5. If B does not do so, he is disqualified under Rule 6-8a, which allows a player to discontinue play for a decision on a disputed point, but only within the limits prescribed in Rule 2-5.

However, before continuing the match B is entitled to make a claim that the course is unplayable – Rule 2-5. If B does so, (a) the match should be resumed at the spot at which it was discontinued if the Committee subsequently upholds B's claim, or (b) the match should stand as played if the Committee subsequently rejects B's claim. (Revised)

Other Decisions related to Rule 6-8a: See "Discontinuance and Resumption of Play" in the Index.

SUSPENSION OF PLAY: PROCEDURE

6-8b/1
Competitors Playing Hole When Play Suspended Discontinue Play Immediately But Then Complete Hole Before Committee Orders Resumption of Play

Q. In stroke play, a group was playing a hole when it was announced that play was suspended. The group discontinued play for 10 to 15 minutes and then decided to complete the hole, even though the Committee had not yet announced resumption of play. Is this permissible?

A. No. Competitors playing a hole when play is suspended may only continue play of that hole if they do so without delay (Rule 6-8b). The group in question was in breach of Rule 6-8b. The penalty is disqualification.

6-8b/2
Options If Play Suspended After One Competitor in Group Has Played from Tee

Q. In stroke play, A plays a stroke from the teeing ground and the competition is at that point suspended. May B, A's fellow-competitor, also play from the teeing ground, even though play has been suspended?

A. Yes. When A played from the teeing ground, play had commenced for that hole and thus A and B may continue play of the hole provided they do so without delay and then discontinue play either before or immediately after completing it.

6-8b/3
Completion of Hole by One Competitor in Group After Play Suspended During Play of Hole

Q. In stroke play, A plays a stroke from the teeing ground and play is at that point suspended. B, A's marker and fellow-competitor, decides not to play the hole until play is officially resumed. May A play alone and complete the hole?

A. Yes, provided B accompanies A until the hole is completed. Otherwise, A would have no marker for the hole and thus would not have an acceptable score for the round.

6-8b/3.5
Player Plays Out of Turn in Match Play After Play Suspended by Committee and After Opponent Discontinues Play

Q. In match play, A and B are opponents. They are in the process of playing a hole when play is suspended by the Committee due to darkness. A states that he does not wish to continue, but B wants to complete the hole being played. What is the ruling?

A. Although Rule 6-8b suggests that one of the players in the match may complete the hole (see analogous Decision 6-8b/3), the Rules contemplate that opponents will play together and have the opportunity to observe each other's play.

Therefore, when A states that he does not wish to continue the match after play has been suspended by the Committee, the players must discontinue play.

When play is discontinued in this manner, if either player continues play, Rule 6-8b prescribes a penalty of disqualification. However, in the exceptional circumstances described, if B were to continue play of the hole, a penalty of disqualification would be too severe. Accordingly, the Committee should modify the disqualification penalty to loss of the hole concerned (Rule 33-7).

6-8b/4
Player Unable to Resume Suspended Match at Scheduled Time

Q. During a match-play competition, the course becomes unplayable and play is suspended. The Committee announces that the suspended matches will be completed the next day. One player states that he is unable to play the next day. What is the ruling?

A. The player is disqualified under Rule 6-8b.

Related Decision:
• 2-4/20 Player Unable to Meet Match-Play Schedule Defaults; Schedule Then Changed and Player Requests Reinstatement.

6-8b/5
Player Claiming Danger from Lightning Refuses to Resume Play When Resumption Ordered by Committee

Q. In a stroke-play competition, the Committee, after having suspended play because of lightning, orders play to be resumed. Must a player resume play if he considers that there is still danger from lightning?

A. Rule 6-8a authorizes a player to discontinue play if he considers that there is danger from lightning. This is one of the rare occasions on which the player is virtually the final judge. The safety of players is paramount, especially as there is a common natural fear of lightning. Committees should not risk exposing players to danger.

However, if the Committee has used all reasonable means to ascertain the weather prospects and has concluded that no danger from lightning exists, it has the power to order resumption of play and to disqualify under Rule 6-8b any player who refuses to comply.

Related Decisions:
• 6-8b/8 Player Drops Ball After Play Suspended for Dangerous Situation.
• 30-3e/1 Partners Fail to Discontinue Play Immediately Contrary to Condition of Competition.
• 33-2d/3 Competitor Refuses to Start or Picks Up Because of Weather Conditions; Round Subsequently Canceled.

6-8b/6
Play Suspended by Committee; Competitor Does Not Resume Play at Time Ordered by Committee

Q. In stroke play, the Committee suspends play. Subsequently, the Committee advises all competitors that a siren will signify resumption of play at a specified time.

A competitor in one group resumed play about two minutes before the siren sounded, because he saw a group of competitors walking down an adjacent fairway. Should the competitor be disqualified under Rule 6-8b?

A. No. Due to the exceptional nature of resumption of play, such minor errors are inevitable, and a penalty of disqualification is too severe. Accordingly, if the Committee has ordered a resumption of play and a competitor is no more than five minutes late (or five minutes early) in resuming play, the Committee would be justified in modifying the disqualification penalty to two strokes or, if circumstances warrant, waiving it entirely under Rule 33-7.

In this case, modifying the penalty to two strokes would be appropriate.

Related Decision:
• 6-3a/5 Player Starts Early.

6-8b/7
Condition Requiring Immediate Discontinuance of Play; Guidelines for Waiving or Modifying Disqualification Penalty for Failure to Discontinue Play Immediately

Q. It is a condition of the competition (Note under Rule 6-8b) that players must discontinue play immediately following a suspension of play by the Committee in a potentially dangerous situation. In what circumstances should the Committee consider waiving or modifying the disqualification penalty under Rule 33-7?

A. The intent of the condition is to enable the course to be cleared as quickly as possible when a potentially dangerous situation, such as lightning, exists. A player who breaches this condition may place others at serious risk by creating the impression that no danger exists. Therefore, it is generally recommended that the penalty of disqualification should not be waived or modified and that any doubt on this matter should be resolved against the player.

However, if a player plays a stroke after play has been suspended by the sounding of a siren, the Committee must consider all of the relevant facts in determining if the player should be disqualified or if the penalty should be waived or modified.

The following are examples of Committee decisions that are justified in light of the circumstances:

After the siren has sounded

(a) a player finishes assessing his shot, selects a club and plays his stroke, taking approximately 30 seconds to do so – disqualification.
(b) a player approaches the ball and taps in a short putt, all within a few seconds – disqualification.
(c) a player, having addressed the ball, steps away momentarily, addresses the ball again and then completes his stroke within a few seconds – disqualification.
(d) a player, having addressed the ball, completes his stroke without hesitation – no penalty.

6-8b/8
Player Drops Ball After Play Suspended for Dangerous Situation

Q. It is a condition of the competition (Note under Rule 6-8b) that players must discontinue play immediately following a suspension of play by the Committee in a potentially dangerous situation. After such a suspension is signalled by the Committee, may a player proceed under a Rule by dropping a ball or determining an appropriate reference point, e.g., the nearest point of relief?

A. In view of the purpose of this type of suspension of play, it is recommended that all players take shelter immediately without taking such further actions. However, discontinuing play in the context of this condition means making no further strokes and, therefore, there is no penalty for taking actions such as those described.

Related Decisions:
• 6-8b/5 Player Claiming Danger from Lightning Refuses to Resume Play When Resumption Ordered by Committee.
• 30-3e/1 Partners Fail to Discontinue Play Immediately Contrary to Condition of Competition.
• 33-2d/3 Competitor Refuses to Start or Picks Up Because of Weather Conditions; Round Subsequently Canceled.

6-8b/9
Resumption of Play; When Players Must Be Present

Q. In a stroke-play competition, A, B and C are fellow-competitors. When the group is on the 3rd fairway, the Committee suspends play. The group elects to complete play of the 3rd hole. The Committee schedules the resumption of play for 8 am on the following day and the group will be the third group to play from the 4th tee when play is resumed. When is the group required to be at the 4th tee?

A. The group must be present at the 4th tee and ready to play when it becomes possible for the group to play. Any player not present at that time is disqualified under Rule 6-8b.

Related Decision:
• 6-3a/2 Time of Starting; All Competitors Must Be Present.

Other Decisions related to Rule 6-8b: See "Discontinuance and Resumption of Play" in Index.

LIFTING BALL WHEN PLAY DISCONTINUED

6-8c/1
Explanation of "Good Reason to Lift"

When play has been suspended by the Committee under Rule 6-8a(i) and a player discontinues play of a hole, he is entitled to lift his ball without penalty. If a player discontinues play of a hole under Rule 6-8a(ii), (iii) or (iv) he is not entitled to lift his ball unless there is a "good reason" to lift it (Rule 6-8c). It is a matter for the Committee to decide in each case whether a "good reason" exists.

Generally, the ball should not be lifted unless the player is required to leave the area where his ball is located and it is likely that the ball may be moved or taken by an outside agency in his absence.

If the player lifts his ball without a "good reason" to do so, the player is penalized one stroke under Rule 6-8c, unless he was proceeding under another Rule which entitled him to lift the ball, such as Rule 16-1b.

PROCEDURE WHEN PLAY RESUMED

6-8d/1
Resuming Play from Where It Was Discontinued; Lie Altered by Natural Causes

Q. Rule 6-8d states that following a discontinuance of play under Rule 6-8d, play must be resumed "from where it was discontinued" and a ball must be placed on the spot where it lay prior to the discontinuance. Does this requirement mean the player is always entitled to the lie he had prior to discontinuance?

A. No. The original lie or the conditions around the ball may be altered through natural causes (e.g., wind, rain and water) and the player must accept those conditions, whether they worsen or improve the lie of the ball, area of intended stance or swing or the line of play.

6-8d/2
Lie in Bunker Altered Prior to Resumption of Play

Q. After play is suspended by the Committee, a player marks the position of and lifts his ball from a bunker as permitted by Rule 6-8c. When play is resumed and the ball is to be replaced, what is the correct procedure given that the lie of the ball may have been altered by the greenkeeping staff?

A. If the bunker has been prepared by the greenkeeping staff, regardless of whether the ball-marker has been moved, the original lie must be recreated as nearly as possible and a ball must be placed in that lie (Rule 20-3b). The obligation to re-create the original lie is limited to what is practical in the circumstances. For example, a buried lie or footprints around the ball must be re-created whereas the player is not required to replace loose impediments or restore conditions such as washed out areas or casual water that have been eliminated by the greenkeeping staff or have changed naturally.

However, if the bunker has not been prepared by the greenkeeping staff, the player is not necessarily entitled to the lie he had prior to the discontinuance of play (see Decision 6-8d/1). The player must place a ball on the spot from which the original ball was lifted (Rule 6-8d). If the ball-marker is missing when play is resumed (e.g., moved by wind or water), and the spot where the ball is to be placed is impossible to determine, it must be estimated and the ball placed on the estimated spot – see Note to Rule 6-8d(iii) and Exception to Rule 20-3c.

Related Decisions:
- 20-3b/5 Lie of Ball in Rough Altered by Outside Agency; Original Lie of Ball Not Known and Spot Where Ball Lay Not Determinable.
- 20-3b/6 Lie of Ball in Bunker Altered; Original Lie of Ball Known but Spot Where Ball Lay Not Determinable.

6-8d/3
Player Who Drops Ball Immediately After Committee Has Ordered Resumption of Play Subsequently Lifts Ball Under Rule 6-8d(ii)

Q. A player's ball lies on an immovable obstruction when play is suspended by the Committee. After the Committee orders a resumption of play and before the player makes a stroke, he takes relief from the obstruction under Rule 24-2b. Prior to playing the dropped ball, may he lift it under Rule 6-8d(ii) and either clean and replace the ball or substitute another ball?

A. Yes. When the player discontinued play under Rule 6-8a, he was entitled to lift his ball without penalty under Rule 6-8c. When he resumed play under Rule 6-8d, he was entitled to follow the provisions of that Rule, despite the fact that he initially proceeded under Rule 24-2b after the Committee ordered a resumption of play. Resuming play in the context of Rule 6-8d means making a stroke and, therefore, Rule 6-8d(ii) applies to the player's situation. It is not the intent of the Rules to limit the player's options under Rule 6-8d(ii) simply because he did not take relief until the Committee ordered a resumption of play (see analogous Decision 6-8b/8).

6-8d/4
Ball Visible from Tee Disappears While Play Suspended

Q. A player's tee shot came to rest and was visible from the tee by all players in the match or group. At that point play was suspended. The player took cover and did not lift the ball. When play was resumed, the player's ball was missing or was found some distance from where it was seen to come to rest. What is the procedure?

A. As the player's ball was moved while play was suspended, the player must place a ball on the spot from which his ball was moved, without penalty (Rule 6-8d(iii)). If this spot is not determinable, it must be estimated and a ball placed on the estimated spot – see Note to Rule 6-8d(iii) and the Exception to Rule 20-3c.

Related Decision:
- 18-2a/25 Ball Moved Accidentally by Player During Suspension of Play.

6-8d/5
Ball in Bad Lie in Rough Moved by Outside Agency During Suspension of Play; Player Fails to Estimate Position Sufficiently

Q. A player finds his ball in deep rough and the ball is barely visible. Before the player makes a stroke, the Committee suspends play, and the player discontinues play immediately without lifting his ball. During the suspension of play, an outside agency moves the player's ball. The player is made aware of the outside agency's actions and, on the resumption of play, the player estimates the spot where the ball originally lay and places a ball on that spot. However, the ball is placed on top of the grass in a much better lie than prior to the suspension of play. What is the ruling?

A. The Note to Rule 6-8d requires the player to estimate the spot where the ball is to be placed and to place the ball on the estimated spot. If the player places his ball in a lie that is significantly different from the original lie, the player has not estimated the position of the ball with sufficient accuracy. By placing the ball on top of the grass, the player placed the ball in the wrong place. If he makes a stroke from that spot without first correcting his error under Rule 20-6, he would be subject to penalty under Rule 20-7 for playing from a wrong place.

Other Decisions related to Rule 6-8d: See "Discontinuance and Resumption of Play" in the Index.

RULE 7

PRACTICE

DEFINITIONS
All defined terms are in *italics* and are listed alphabetically in the Definitions section – see pages 6–16.

7-1. BEFORE OR BETWEEN ROUNDS
a. Match Play
On any day of a match-play competition, a player may practice on the competition *course* before a round.

b. Stroke Play
Before a round or play-off on any day of a stroke-play competition, a *competitor* must not practice on the competition *course* or test the surface of any *putting green* on the *course* by rolling a ball or roughening or scraping the surface.

   When two or more rounds of a stroke-play competition are to be played over consecutive days, a *competitor* must not practice between those rounds on any competition *course* remaining to be played, or test the surface of any *putting green* on such *course* by rolling a ball or roughening or scraping the surface.

Exception: Practice putting or chipping on or near the first *teeing ground* or any practice area before starting a round or play-off is permitted.

PENALTY FOR BREACH OF RULE 7-1b:
Disqualification.

Note: The *Committee* may, in the conditions of a competition (Rule 33-1), prohibit practice on the competition *course* on any day of a match-play competition or permit practice on the competition *course* or part of the *course* (Rule 33-2c) on any day of or between rounds of a stroke-play competition.

7-2. DURING ROUND
A player must not make a practice *stroke* during play of a hole.

   Between the play of two holes a player must not make a practice *stroke*, except that he may practice putting or chipping on or near:

a. the *putting green* of the hole last played,

b. any practice *putting green*, or

c. the *teeing ground* of the next hole to be played in the round, provided a practice *stroke* is not made from a *hazard* and does not unduly delay play (Rule 6-7).

   Strokes made in continuing the play of a hole, the result of which has been decided, are not practice *strokes*.

Exception: When play has been suspended by the *Committee*, a player may, prior to resumption of play, practice (a) as provided in this Rule,

(b) anywhere other than on the competition *course* and (c) as otherwise permitted by the *Committee*.

PENALTY FOR BREACH OF RULE 7-2:

Match play – Loss of hole; Stroke play – Two strokes.

In the event of a breach between the play of two holes, the penalty applies to the next hole.

Note 1: A practice swing is not a practice *stroke* and may be taken at any place, provided the player does not breach the *Rules*.

Note 2: The *Committee* may, in the conditions of a competition (Rule 33-1), prohibit:

(a) practice on or near the *putting green* of the hole last played, and

(b) rolling a ball on the *putting green* of the hole last played.

PRACTICE BEFORE OR BETWEEN ROUNDS IN STROKE PLAY

7-1b/1
One Practice Stroke Played on Course Before Stroke-Play Round

Q. On the day of a stroke-play competition, a competitor, before starting his round, played one practice stroke from a forward tee at the first hole into an out-of-bounds area. What is the ruling?

A. The competitor infringed Rule 7-1b and was subject to disqualification. However, the Committee would be justified, in the circumstances, in modifying the penalty to two strokes under Rule 33-7. If the competitor played more than one such stroke, modification of the disqualification penalty would not be appropriate.

7-1b/2
Waiving Penalty for Practice on Course

Q. A 36-hole stroke-play competition was scheduled over consecutive days. After completing his first round, a competitor who was a member of the club at which the event was being held played several more holes and thus was subject to disqualification under Rule 7-1b.

Would the Committee be justified in waiving or modifying the penalty?

A. No.

7-1b/3
Competitor Who Practices on Competition Course After Qualifying Round Subsequently Is in Play-Off on Same Day

Q. Having completed his play in a stroke-play qualifying round for a match-play event, a competitor practiced on the competition course after the last group in the competition had teed off. After the conclusion of play, the competitor was tied for the last qualifying place for the match-play event. Such a tie was to be decided by a hole-by-hole play-off, which was scheduled to be played immediately. Was the competitor subject to disqualification from the play-off under Rule 7-1b? If so, would the Committee have been justified in waiving the penalty under Rule 33-7?

A. The competitor was subject to disqualification. Waiving the penalty is not warranted in such circumstances.

7-1b/4
Stroke Play Over 36 Holes on Two Courses; Player Completes First Round, Practices on Same Course and Is Later in Play-Off on That Course

Q. Stroke play to determine the qualifiers for match play was scheduled over 36 holes on consecutive days. Eighteen holes were to be played on the East Course and 18 on the North Course. Any play-off was to be held on the East Course.

Several competitors who played their first qualifying round on the East Course wanted to play more golf. They knew that they would be in breach of Rule 7-1b if they played the North Course, so they played the East Course again.

After the second qualifying round, one of the competitors was tied for the last qualifier's place. Should he be disqualified from the play-off on the East Course under Rule 7-1b?

A. Yes.

7-1b/5
Competitor's Caddie Practices on or Tests Putting Green Surfaces of the Course Before Stroke-Play Round

Q. In stroke play, a competitor's caddie practices on or tests the putting green surfaces of the course before the competitor tees off. Is the competitor disqualified under Rule 7-1b?

A. No. A competitor is responsible for the actions of his caddie only during a stipulated round (Rule 6-1).

7-1b/6
Stroke Play Over 54 Holes on Consecutive Days; Second Round Canceled and Competitor Practices on Course Following Cancellation

Q. A 54-hole stroke-play competition was scheduled to be played on consecutive days. The second round was canceled when the course became unplayable, and the competition was reduced to 36 holes. A competitor practiced on the course on the day of the second round after that round was canceled. Was the competitor subject to disqualification for a breach of Rule 7-1b?

A. Yes, because the competition was scheduled to be played over consecutive days. It is irrelevant that at the time the competitor practiced the competition was no longer to be played over consecutive days.

However, the Committee may in such circumstances permit practice on the course between rounds – see Note under Rule 7-1b.

7-1b/7
Competitor Practices Putting on 3rd Green After Finishing Hole During First Round of 36-Hole Stroke-Play Competition

Q. A 36-hole stroke-play competition was scheduled to be played on one day. During the first round a competitor, having holed out at the 3rd hole, plays a practice putt on the 3rd green. Is the competitor disqualified under Rule 7-1b for practicing on the course before his second round?

A. No. A competitor is entitled to do anything which the Rules permit him to do during a stipulated round. Rule 7-2 permits a player between the play of two holes to practice putting or chipping on or near the putting green of the hole last played, any practice putting green or the teeing ground of the next hole to be played in the round, provided such practice stroke is not played from a hazard and does not unduly delay play (Rule 6-7).

Related Decisions:
- 7-2/8 Competitor Practices Putting on 18th Green Immediately After Finishing First Round of Stroke-Play Competition Played Over Consecutive Days.
- 7-2/9 Competitor Practices Putting on 3rd Green of 9-Hole Course During 18-Hole Stroke-Play Competition.

Other Decisions related to Rule 7-1: See "Practice" in the Index

PRACTICE DURING ROUND

7-2/1
When Practice Between Holes Permitted

Q. When is play of a hole completed by a player so that he may practice as permitted in Rule 7-2?

A. *Match play:*

Single	When he has holed out, his next stroke has been conceded, or the hole has been conceded by either player.
Four-ball	When both he and his partner have holed out, their next strokes have been conceded, or either side has conceded the hole.

Stroke play:

Individual	When he has holed out.
Four-ball	When both he and his partner have holed out or picked up.
Bogey, Par and Stableford	When he has holed out or picked up.

Related Decision:
• 30/6 Player Plays Practice Putt After He and Partner Have Holed Out But Before Opponents Hole Out.

7-2/1.5
Continuing Play of Hole in Match Play After Result of Hole Decided

Q. In a match between A and B, A holes out for a 4. B has played four strokes and his ball lies in a bunker. Thus, the hole has been decided. If B plays from the bunker, would the stroke be considered a practice stroke?

A. No. Strokes played in continuing play of a hole, the result of which has been decided, are not practice strokes – see Rule 7-2.

7-2/1.7
Explanation of "Strokes Played in Continuing the Play of a Hole"

Q. Rule 7-2 states that strokes played in continuing the play of a hole, the result of which has been decided, are not practice strokes. What is meant by "continuing the play of a hole"?

A. This phrase covers situations in which a player plays the remainder of the hole with one ball in play. Its interpretation is not restricted to continuing the play of the hole in accordance with the Rules and includes, for example, situations where a player plays a ball from a spot close to where his original ball went out of bounds or in the area where it was lost.

7-2/2
Putting on Fairway While Waiting to Play to Green

Q. While waiting to play to the putting green, a player dropped a ball on the fairway and struck it several times with his putter. When questioned, he stated that he was not practicing but was "killing time." What is the ruling?

A. The player was in breach of Rule 7-2.

7-2/3
Player Practices Putting Off Green While Waiting to Putt

Q. A player lifted his ball on the putting green and, while waiting for his opponent or a fellow-competitor to play, dropped his ball off the green and played a few practice putts. What is the penalty?

A. Under Rule 7-2 the player lost the hole in match play or incurred a penalty of two strokes in stroke play.

7-2/4
Hitting Plastic Ball Before Playing Ball in Play

Q. During play of a hole, a player plays a stroke with a plastic ball before playing his ball in play. Is he in breach of Rule 7-2?

A. Yes.

Related Decision:
• 14-3/10 Use of Training or Swing Aid During Round.

7-2/5
Hitting Practice Range Ball Back to Range

Q. During play of a hole, a player saw some balls from the adjoining practice range lying on the course and flicked one back to the range with his club. Is there a penalty under Rule 7-2?

A. In some circumstances the hitting of a practice range ball back towards the range during the play of a hole would be a breach of Rule 7-2, but the casual flicking of a range ball, apparently only for the purpose of tidying up the course, is not a breach.

7-2/5.5
Player Finds Ball and Hits It to Player Who Lost It

Q. As A was playing the 13th hole, X, who was playing the adjoining 14th, was searching for his ball on the 13th fairway. X could not find his ball and walked off down the 14th. A then found X's ball plugged in the 13th fairway and called to him. X requested that the ball be returned to him. As X was out of throwing range, A hit the ball to him with a short iron.

In doing so, should A be considered to have played a practice stroke in contravention of Rule 7-2?

A. No. Since A was acting out of courtesy, there is no penalty.

Related Decision:
• 1-4/4 In Anger Player Strikes Ball Played by Player in Following Group.

7-2/6 (Reserved)

7-2/7
Practice Swing Dislodges Concealed Ball

Q. A player makes a practice swing in the rough and dislodges a concealed ball. Is there any penalty?

A. No. Since the player had no intention of striking the concealed ball, his swing remained a practice swing and was not a stroke. Consequently, there is no question of his having played either a practice stroke (Rule 7-2) or a stroke with a wrong ball (Rule 15-3).

Related Decisions:
- 15/2 Player's Stroke at Own Ball Dislodges Concealed Ball.
- 18-2a/19 Ball Moved Accidentally by Practice Swing Prior to Tee Shot.
- 18-2a/20 Ball in Play Moved Accidentally by Practice Swing.

7-2/8
Competitor Practices Putting on 18th Green Immediately After Finishing First Round of Stroke-Play Competition Played Over Consecutive Days

Q. In a 72-hole stroke-play competition held over four consecutive days, a competitor, immediately after holing out at the 18th hole of the first round, plays a practice putt on the 18th green. Is the competitor disqualified under Rule 7-1b for practicing on the course between rounds?

A. No. Rule 7-2 permits practice putting or chipping on or near the putting green of the hole last played between the play of two holes. It follows that the same privilege applies immediately after completion of the last hole of the round, even though technically such practice would be between rounds, not during a round.

Rule 7-1b would apply if a competitor, after holing out at the 18th hole, left the course and later returned and played a practice putt on the 18th green.

7-2/9
Competitor Practices Putting on 3rd Green of 9-Hole Course During 18-Hole Stroke-Play Competition

Q. An 18-hole stroke-play competition is played on a 9-hole course. A competitor, having holed out at the 3rd hole, plays a practice putt on the 3rd green. Since the stipulated round requires that the competitor play the 3rd hole as the 12th hole later in the round, is the competitor penalized for practicing?

A. No. Rule 7-2 permits a player between the play of two holes to practice putting or chipping on or near the putting green of the hole last played.

Related Decision to 7-2/8 and 7-2/9:
- 7-1b/7 Competitor Practices Putting on 3rd Green After Finishing Hole During First Round of 36-Hole Stroke-Play Competition.

7-2/10
Match Discontinued by Agreement Cannot be Resumed Until Three Days Later; One Player Wishes to Play on Competition Course Prior to Resumption

Q. In accordance with the Exception under Rule 6-8a, a match is discontinued due to fading light. The players establish that the only mutually convenient time for play to be resumed, which will not delay the competition, is three days later.

They agree to resume play at that time, but one of them wishes to take part in another competition on the course the following day. What is the ruling?

A. Rule 7-2 does not contemplate such a case and as it is unreasonable to prohibit a player from playing on the competition course in such circumstances, in equity (Rule 1-4), either player may play on the course at any time prior to the resumption of play.

7-2/11
Match Discontinued by Agreement on 13th Tee Cannot be Resumed Until Following Day; May Players Play First Twelve Holes Prior to Resuming Match

Q. In accordance with the Exception under Rule 6-8a, a match is discontinued at the 13th tee due to fading light. The players agree to resume the match the following afternoon. However, the next day, it is not possible for the players to resume play on the competition course at the 13th tee, due to heavy play on the course.

The players wish to play the first twelve holes and resume the match at the 13th tee. What is the ruling?

A. Rule 7-2 does not contemplate such a case. In equity (Rule 1-4), the players may play the first twelve holes and resume the match at the 13th tee.

7-2/12
Play Suspended by Committee; Player Wishes to Practice After Resumption

Q. In a stroke-play competition, the Committee suspends play and schedules the resumption for 8:00 am on the following day. A player, whose group will be the third group to play from a particular tee, wishes to continue practicing on the designated practice area after play has been resumed at 8:00 am because his group will not be able to play at that time. What is the ruling?

A. When play is resumed at 8:00 am, the Exception to Rule 7-2 no longer applies. Accordingly, the player is restricted to practicing in accordance with Rule 7-2.

Other Decisions related to Rule 7-2: See "Practice" in the Index.

RULE 8

ADVICE; INDICATING LINE OF PLAY

DEFINITIONS
All defined terms are in *italics* and are listed alphabetically in the Definitions section – see pages 6–16.

8-1. ADVICE
During a *stipulated round*, a player must not:

a. give *advice* to anyone in the competition playing on the *course* other than his *partner*, or

b. ask for *advice* from anyone other than his *partner* or either of their *caddies*.

8-2. INDICATING LINE OF PLAY
a. Other Than on Putting Green
Except on the *putting green*, a player may have the *line of play* indicated to him by anyone, but no one may be positioned by the player on or close to the line or an extension of the line beyond the *hole* while the *stroke* is being made. Any mark placed by the player or with his knowledge to indicate the line must be removed before the *stroke* is made.

Exception: *Flagstick* attended or held up – see Rule 17-1.

b. On the Putting Green
When the player's ball is on the *putting green*, the player, his *partner* or either of their *caddies* may, before but not during the *stroke*, point out a line for putting, but in so doing the *putting green* must not be touched. A mark must not be placed anywhere to indicate a line for putting.

PENALTY FOR BREACH OF RULE:
<u>Match play</u> – Loss of hole; <u>Stroke play</u> – Two strokes.

Note: The *Committee* may, in the conditions of a team competition (Rule 33-1), permit each team to appoint one person who may give *advice* (including pointing out a line for putting) to members of that team. The *Committee* may establish conditions relating to the appointment and permitted conduct of that person, who must be identified to the *Committee* before giving *advice*.

ADVICE

8/1
Conditions of Team Competition Stipulate Who Is Authorized to Give Advice

Q. A condition of a team competition stipulates that only the Team Captain may give advice or that the person to be appointed by each team to give advice must be an amateur. Is this permitted?

A. Yes – see Note to Rule 8.

8/2
Team Captain Gives Advice While Playing

Q. If the Committee has adopted the Note to Rule 8 as a condition of the competition, may a Team Captain, while playing in the competition, give advice to a team mate other than his partner?

A. No.

Decisions related to 8/1 and 8/2: See "Team Competition" in the Index.

8-1/1 (Reserved)

8-1/2
Exchanging Distance Information

Information regarding the distance between two objects is public information and not advice. It is therefore permissible for players to exchange information relating to the distance between two objects. For example, a player may ask anyone, including his opponent, fellow-competitor or either of their caddies, the distance between his ball and the hole. (Revised)

Related Decisions:
- 14-3/0.5 Local Rule Permitting Use of Distance-Measuring Device.
- 14-3/0.7 Player Obtains Distance Information Measured with Electronic Device

8-1/3
Asking If Distance Marker Accurate

Q. A player inquires of another player as to the accuracy of a 150-yard marker. Was the player in breach of Rule 8-1?

A. No.

8-1/4 (Reserved)

8-1/5
Seeking Information on Whereabouts of Another Player's Ball

Q. A player preparing to play to a putting green asks a spectator to advise him how far his opponent's or fellow-competitor's ball, which is on the green, lies from the flagstick. Was the player in breach of Rule 8-1?

A. No.

Related Decision:
• 9-2/16 Ascertaining Whereabouts of Opponent's Ball Before Playing.

8-1/6
Asking Opponent or Fellow-Competitor What Club He Used at Previous Hole

Q. During play of the 6th hole, A asked B what club he (B) had used on the 4th hole, which is a par-3 of a similar length. Was A in breach of Rule 8-1?

A. No.

8-1/7
After Player Has Played to Green He Asks Opponent or Fellow-Competitor What Club He Used in Playing to Green

Q. A plays his second shot which lands on the green. B does likewise. A then asks B what club he used for his second shot. Was A in breach of Rule 8-1?

A. No.

8-1/8
Comment About Club Selection After Stroke

Q. After playing a stroke, a player says: "I should have used a 5-iron." Was the player in breach of Rule 8-1?

A. If the statement was made casually, there was no breach. If the statement was made to another player who had a shot to play from about the same position, there was a breach.

8-1/9
Misleading Statement About Club Selection

Q. A made a statement regarding his club selection which was purposely misleading and was obviously intended to be overheard by B, who had a similar shot. What is the ruling?

A. A was in breach of Rule 8-1 and lost the hole in match play or incurred a two-stroke penalty in stroke play.

8-1/10
Looking into Another Player's Bag to Determine Club Used

Q. A looks into B's bag to determine which club B used for his last stroke. Is this the equivalent of asking for advice?

A. No. Information obtained by observation is not advice. But see also Decision 8-1/11.

8-1/11
Removing Towel Covering Another Player's Clubs to Determine Club Used

Q. Decision 8-1/10 states that it is not a breach of Rule 8-1 for A to look into B's golf bag to determine which club B used for his last stroke. Suppose a towel was covering B's clubs and A removed the towel in order to determine which club B had used, would that be a breach of Rule 8-1?

A. Yes. A player is prohibited from obtaining such information through a physical act.

8-1/12
Double Caddie Informs One Employer About Club Used by Another

Q. When one caddie is employed by two players, A and B, who are not partners, is it permissible for A, who is about to play, to ask the caddie which club B used for a stroke from a nearby position?

A. Yes. A is entitled to seek from the caddie any information the caddie might possess.

8-1/13
Player Giving Opponent or Fellow-Competitor Instruction During Round

Q. During a round a player tells an opponent or a fellow-competitor that he is overswinging. Is this giving advice in breach of Rule 8-1?

A. Yes.

8-1/14
Competitor, After Finishing Hole, Demonstrates to Fellow-Competitor How to Play Shot

Q. In individual stroke play, A, who had just holed out on the 7th hole, demonstrated to B, whose ball was just off the putting green, how he should play his chip shot. What is the ruling?

A. B incurred no penalty as he did not seek advice. A incurred a penalty of two strokes for giving advice to B. As one of the competitors involved (B) had not completed the hole, the penalty would be applied at the 7th hole.

Had both A and B completed the 7th hole, A's penalty would be applied at the 8th hole.

Related Decision:
• 8-1/23 Player's Team Mate in Gallery Hits Ball to Green to Show Player Whether Green Will Hold.

8-1/15
Caddie Swings Club to Show Player How to Play Shot

Q. A player's caddie takes one of his clubs and swings it to show him how to play a certain shot. Is this permissible?

A. Yes, provided there is no undue delay. A player may always seek and accept advice from his caddie (Rule 8-1).

8-1/16
Suggesting to Competitor That He Deem His Ball Unplayable

Q. B's ball was lying badly. B was deliberating what action to take when A, his fellow-competitor, said: "You have no shot at all. If I were you, I would deem the ball unplayable." Was A giving advice, contrary to Rule 8-1?

A. Yes. A's suggestion could have influenced B "in determining his play." Thus, it constituted advice – see Definition of "Advice." It did not constitute "information on the Rules," which is not advice.

8-1/17
Request for Advice Made in Error to Opponent's Caddie Withdrawn Before Advice Given

Q. While surveying his putt, A sought advice from B's caddie whom he mistook for his own caddie. A immediately realized his mistake and told B's caddie not to answer. The caddie said nothing. What is the ruling?

A. There should be no penalty.

Related Decision:
• 16-1d/6 Caddie Roughens Surface of Putting Green But Player Does Not Benefit.

8-1/18
Player Who Has Not Yet Played Seeks Advice from Player Who Has Finished Round

Q. May a player about to start his round seek advice as to clubs used at various holes from a player who has just finished?

A. Yes. Rule 8-1 applies only during the play of a round.

8-1/19
Advice Between Rounds in 36-Hole Match

Q. May a player seek advice, other than from his partner or caddie, after 18 holes in a 36-hole match?

A. Yes. Rule 8-1 applies only during a stipulated round. A 36-hole match consists of two 18-hole stipulated rounds – see Definition of "Stipulated Round."

8-1/20
Asking Advice When Play Suspended

Q. A is about to play the 6th hole, a par-3, when play is suspended by the Committee. Prior to the resumption of play, A asks X, who had already played the 6th, what club he used for his tee shot. Is A penalized under Rule 8-1?

A. No. The prohibition against giving or asking for advice applies only during a stipulated round. In this case, the stipulated round had been suspended.

8-1/21
Advice Given by Team Mate in Another Group in Stroke Play

Q. Individual and team competitions are being played concurrently in stroke play. A competitor is given advice by a team mate who is playing in another group. What is the ruling?

A. The team mate would be penalized two strokes.

8-1/22
Team Mates Playing as Fellow-Competitors Exchange Advice

Q. The format for a competition between two teams is as follows: Individual stroke play, with the winner being the team with the lowest aggregate score. Play is in groups of four, with two players from each team in each group.

In such an event, may two team members playing in the same group give each other advice?

A. No. The team mates are fellow-competitors and not partners in this type of event, which is not the same as four-ball stroke play (Rule 31-1), and they would be penalized for each breach of Rule 8-1.

8-1/23
Player's Team Mate in Gallery Hits Ball to Green to Show Player Whether Green Will Hold

Q. In a team competition, A, a member of one team, is playing against B, a member of the opposing team. X, a team mate of A, is in the gallery. X drops a ball close to A's ball and hits it to the green to show A whether or not the green will hold. What is the ruling?

A. In equity (Rule 1-4), if A did nothing to stop X's irregular action, he should lose the hole in view of the purpose of Rule 8-1.

8-1/24
Advice Given by Team Coach or Captain

Q. A team competition is being played, and in the conditions the Committee has not authorized captains or coaches to give advice under the Note to

Rule 8. A non-playing coach or captain gives advice during a round to one of the members of his team. What is the ruling?

A. There is no penalty. However, the player should take action to stop this irregular procedure. If he does not do so, he should, in equity (Rule 1-4), incur a penalty of loss of hole in match play or two strokes in stroke play in view of the purpose of Rule 8-1.

Decisions related to 8-1/21 through 8-1/24: See "Team Competition" in the Index.

8-1/25
Advice Given on Request; Penalties in Various Forms of Play

In singles match play, if A asks for advice from B, it is irrelevant whether B gives advice because A lost the hole as soon as he asked.

In a four-ball match, A and B versus C and D, if A asks for advice from C and C gives advice, A and C are disqualified for the hole. The penalties do not apply to their partners (Rule 30-3f).

In stroke play, if A asks for advice from B, a fellow-competitor, A incurs a penalty of two strokes. If B gives advice, he also incurs a penalty of two strokes.

Related Decision:
• 30-3a/2 Absent Partner Gives Advice Before Joining Match.

8-1/26
Player Briefly Changes Caddies for Exchange of Advice

Q. In view of the fact that a player may change caddies during his stipulated round, may a player briefly change caddies for the purpose of receiving advice from the new caddie?

A. No. It would be contrary to the purpose and spirit of the Rules for a player to change caddies briefly for the purpose of circumventing Rule 8-1 (Advice). Therefore, in equity (Rule 1-4), the player would incur a penalty of loss of hole in match play or two strokes in stroke play for each hole at which the action occurred.

Related Decision:
• 6-4/7 Changing Caddies During Round.

Other Decisions related to Rule 8-1: See "Advice" in the Index.

INDICATING LINE OF PLAY OTHER THAN ON PUTTING GREEN

8-2a/1
Club Placed on Ground to Align Feet

Q. A player places a club on the ground parallel to the line of play to assist him in aligning his feet properly. Is this permissible?

A. Yes, provided the player removes the club before playing his stroke. Otherwise, a breach of Rule 8-2a would occur.

Related Decision:
• 14-3/10.3 Use of Rod During Round for Alignment or as Swing Aid.

8-2a/2
Object Placed Beside or Behind Ball to Indicate Line of Play

Q. May a player place his pipe or a club beside his ball, or an object behind his ball, to indicate the line of play and leave the object there while playing a stroke?

A. No. Such action would be a breach of Rule 8-2a.

8-2a/3
Player Places Mark to Indicate Distance for Pitch Shot

Q. A player who has a pitch shot places a club on the ground off his line of play to indicate the distance he would like his ball to carry and leaves the club there during the stroke. What is the ruling?

A. In view of the purpose of Rule 8-2a, in equity (Rule 1-4), the player incurs the general penalty of loss of hole in match play or two strokes in stroke play.

Other Decisions related to Rule 8-2a: See "Indicating Line of Play" and "Line of Play" in the Index.

INDICATING LINE OF PUTT

8-2b/1
Caddie Casts Shadow to Indicate Line for Putting

Q. A caddie casts his shadow on the putting green for the purpose of indicating to the player a line for putting. Is this permissible?

A. Yes, but only if the shadow is removed prior to the stroke.

8-2b/2
Caddie Attending Flagstick Advises Player to Aim at His Foot

Q. A player's ball lies on the putting green and his caddie attends the flagstick for him. The caddie suggests, before the stroke, that the player aim at the caddie's left foot. Is the player in breach of Rule 8-2b?

A. If the caddie had placed his foot in position for the purpose of pointing out the line for putting, the player was in breach of Rule 8-2b as soon as the caddie placed his foot in that position. The breach could not be corrected by the caddie subsequently moving his foot.

If the caddie did not initially place his foot in such a position for the purpose of pointing out the line for putting but subsequently suggested the player aim at his left foot, the player would be in breach of Rule 8-2b if the caddie did not move that foot to another position that does not indicate a line for putting prior to the stroke.

The same answer would apply if a player's partner attends the flagstick for him.

8-2b/3
Caddie Touches Putting Green to Indicate Line of Play Before Player Chips from Off Green

Q. The caddie of a player who is preparing to play a chip shot from off the putting green touches the green with a club to indicate the line of play. What is the ruling?

A. There is no penalty. The prohibition against touching the putting green to indicate the line of play applies only if the player's ball lies on the putting green.

8-2b/4
Whether Team Captain Who Is Authorized to Give Advice May Be Required to Keep Off Putting Greens

Q. In a team competition, the Committee wishes to introduce a condition of competition permitting a Team Captain to give advice to members of his team, including pointing out a line for putting. However, it wishes to stipulate that he must keep off the putting greens. Is such a condition permitted?

A. Yes – see Note to Rule 8.

Related Decisions: See "Team Competition" in the Index.

Other Decisions related to Rule 8-2b: See "Indicating Line for Putting" and "Line of Putt" in the Index.

RULE 9

INFORMATION AS TO STROKES TAKEN

DEFINITIONS

All defined terms are in *italics* and are listed alphabetically in the Definitions section – see pages 6–16.

9-1. GENERAL

The number of *strokes* a player has taken includes any *penalty strokes* incurred.

9-2. MATCH PLAY

a. Information as to Strokes Taken

An *opponent* is entitled to ascertain from the player, during the play of a hole, the number of *strokes* he has taken and, after play of a hole, the number of *strokes* taken on the hole just completed.

b. Wrong Information

A player must not give wrong information to his *opponent*. If a player gives wrong information, he loses the hole.

A player is deemed to have given wrong information if he:

(i)   fails to inform his *opponent* as soon as practicable that he has incurred a penalty, unless (a) he was obviously proceeding under a *Rule* involving a penalty and this was observed by his *opponent*, or (b) he corrects the mistake before his *opponent* makes his next *stroke*; or

(ii) gives incorrect information during play of a hole regarding the number of *strokes* taken and does not correct the mistake before his *opponent* makes his next *stroke*; or

(iii) gives incorrect information regarding the number of *strokes* taken to complete a hole and this affects the *opponent's* understanding of the result of the hole, unless he corrects the mistake before any player makes a *stroke* from the next *teeing ground* or, in the case of the last hole of the match, before all players leave the *putting green*.

A player has given wrong information even if it is due to the failure to include a penalty that he did not know he had incurred. It is the player's responsibility to know the *Rules*.

9-3. STROKE PLAY

A *competitor* who has incurred a penalty should inform his *marker* as soon as practicable.

9/1
Incorrect Information on Rules

A player incurs no penalty for giving incorrect information on the Rules (see Definition of "Rules"); this is not wrong information as that term is used in Rule 9. It is up to each player to know the Rules (Rule 6-1). However, if it is established that a player has knowingly given incorrect information on the Rules, the Committee would be justified in imposing a penalty of disqualification under Rule 33-7.

INFORMATION AS TO STROKES TAKEN IN MATCH PLAY

9-2/1
Meaning of "As Soon as Practicable" in Rule 9-2

Rule 9-2b(i) requires a player who has incurred a penalty to inform his opponent "as soon as practicable." This phrase is purposely broad so as to allow for consideration of the circumstances in each situation, especially the proximity of the player to his opponent. Thus, informing the opponent "as soon as practicable" of a penalty incurred does not, in all circumstances mean that the player must do so before the opponent plays his next stroke.

9-2/2
Incorrect Information Given by Caddie or Partner

Q. If incorrect information as to the number of strokes a player has taken is given to an opponent, not by the player himself, but by the player's partner or caddie, is the player liable to a penalty under Rule 9-2?

A. Yes, provided the error is not corrected before the opponent makes his next stroke.

9-2/3
Wrong Information on Strokes Taken Given Voluntarily

Q. In a match between A and B, A voluntarily told B during play of a hole that he had played three strokes, whereas in fact he had played four strokes. A did not correct the error before B played his next stroke. Was A subject to penalty under Rule 9-2?

A. Yes. When a player gives incorrect information, it is irrelevant whether the error is contained in a response to a question from the player's opponent or in a voluntary statement by the player. Such an error must be corrected before the opponent's next stroke is made.

9-2/3.5
Player Refuses to Tell Opponent How Many Strokes He Has Taken

Q. In a match, B asks A how many strokes he (A) has taken during play of a hole or on a hole just completed. A refuses to give B the information requested. What is the ruling?

A. A incurs the general penalty of loss of hole (Rule 2-6) for failing to act in accordance with the requirements of Rule 9-2a. The penalty applies to the hole being played or, if the hole has been completed, the penalty applies to the last hole played.

9-2/4
Withholding Information on Strokes Taken Until Opponent's Turn to Play

Q. In a match between A and B, A asks B during play of a hole how many strokes he (B) has taken. B, whose turn it is to play, withholds the information until he has played his next stroke. Is B subject to penalty under Rule 9-2?

A. No, provided B gave the information before A played his next stroke.

9-2/5
Incorrect Information Causes Opponent to Lift His Ball-Marker

Q. Rule 9-2 provides that, if during play of a hole a player gives incorrect information to the opponent and does not correct the error before the opponent makes his next stroke, the player loses the hole. During play of a hole, a player gives incorrect information to his opponent and the incorrect information results in the opponent lifting the coin marking the position of his ball. Is the lifting of the coin by the opponent the equivalent of the opponent making his next stroke?

A. Yes; the player loses the hole.

Related Decisions:
- 2-4/3 Player Lifts Ball in Mistaken Belief That Next Stroke Conceded.
- 2-4/3.5 Stroke Conceded by Caddie.
- 20-1/8 Ball-Marker Lifted by Player Who Mistakenly Believes He Has Won Hole.

9-2/6
Player Reporting Wrong Score Causes Opponent with Chance for Half to Pick Up Ball

Q. In match play, A holed out and stated to B, his opponent, that he had scored a 4. B, having played four strokes, picked up assuming he had lost the hole. A then realized that he had scored a 5. He immediately told B.

What is the ruling?

A. A gave wrong information as to the number of strokes taken and, under the principle of Rule 9-2, A would normally lose the hole. However, since A had holed out for no worse than a half, the hole was halved – see Rule 2-2.

Related Decisions:
- 2-5/3 Player Lifts Ball Before Holing Out; Opponent Then Picks Up His Ball Claiming Player Loses Hole.
- 30/5 In Four-Ball Match Player with Putt for Half Picks Up in Error at Suggestion of Opponent Based on Misunderstanding.
- 30-3f/3 Player's Ball Resting Against Flagstick Lifted Before Being Holed; Others in Match Pick Up Mistakenly Believing Player Won Hole.

9-2/7
Incorrect Information Given by Player Corrected Before Opponent Makes Next Stroke But After Opponent Has Conceded Player's Putt

Q. In a match, A's ball was a few inches from the hole. B asked A, "How many will that be in the hole?" A answered "6," whereupon B, lying 5, conceded A's next stroke. Before B putted, A informs B that he (A) had actually scored 5. What is the ruling?

A. A loses the hole under Rule 9-2 for giving wrong information.

The principle of Rule 9-2 applies if, after receiving incorrect information, a player picks up his ball, concedes his opponent's next stroke or takes some similar action before the mistake is corrected.

In this case, the answer does not turn on how close A's ball was to the hole or on the fact that B could not have done any better.

9-2/8
Player Wins Hole with Wrong Ball; Error Discovered at Next Hole; Opponent Claims Previous Hole

Q. In a match, A holed out in 3 at the 5th hole. His opponent, B, holed out in 4. After driving from the next tee, it was discovered that A had played a wrong ball at the 5th hole. B claimed the 5th hole. What is the ruling?

A. Since A failed to inform B as soon as practicable that he had incurred a penalty for playing a wrong ball, he is deemed to have given wrong information even though he was not aware he had incurred a penalty (Rule 9-2). Thus, B's belated claim was valid (Rule 2-5) and the Committee should have ruled that B won the 5th hole.

Related Decisions:
- 2-5/4 Player Wins Hole with Own Ball After Playing Wrong Ball; Opponent Lodges Belated Claim.
- 30-3c/2 Player Wins Hole with Wrong Ball and Partner Picks Up; Error Discovered at Next Hole.

- 30-3c/3 Players on Opposite Sides Exchange Balls During Play of Hole and Their Partners Pick Up; Error Discovered at Next Hole.
- 30-3c/4 Player Plays Partner's Ball; Error Discovered After Opponents Have Played Next Strokes.

9-2/9
Player Reports Wrong Score for Hole; Error Discovered Several Holes Later

Q. In match play, after completion of a hole, A inadvertently reports to B, his opponent, that he scored a 5, whereas in fact he scored a 6. This results in the hole being halved or won by A. A realizes his mistake several holes later. What is the ruling?

A. In either case, A loses the hole and the state of the match must be adjusted accordingly (Rule 9-2).

9-2/10
Player Omits Penalty Stroke When Advising Opponent as to Score for Hole; Error Discovered After Match Conceded by Opponent

Q. In a match, A and B were all square after 18 holes and were playing the 19th hole. A incurred a penalty stroke but was unaware of that fact. A holed out and told B that he had scored a 6. B played his sixth shot, missed the hole and conceded the match to A.

When returning to the clubhouse, A learned that he had incurred a penalty stroke and that his score had been 7, not 6. B claimed the match on the ground that A gave wrong information. What is the ruling?

A. B's claim was valid since the result had not been announced – see Rule 2-5. A lost the hole for giving wrong information, even though he may not have been aware that he had incurred a penalty (Rule 9-2).

Related Decisions: See "Claims and Disputes: late claim" in the Index.

9-2/11
Opponent's Misreading of Number on Player's Ball Results in Agreement That Player Lost Hole

Q. In a match, A and B are playing the same brand of ball (Brand X). The identification number on A's ball is "3" and A's name is imprinted on his ball. The identification number on B's ball is "5."

On completion of the 2nd hole, which A won, B picks up both balls and says, "Both 5's – which is yours?" A states that he was playing a "3" and therefore he must have played a wrong ball. A and B agree that A lost the hole for playing a wrong ball.

B wins the match and then discovers he has in his possession a Brand X ball with the identification number "3" and A's name imprinted on it. A and B conclude that B misread the number at the 2nd hole. Did B give A wrong information?

A. No. Wrong information as the term is used in Rule 9 refers to the number of strokes taken.

The agreement of A and B that A lost the 2nd hole must stand and the match must stand as played. It would have been advisable for A to inspect the two balls at the 2nd hole.

Related Decisions:
- 1-1/4 Player Discovers Own Ball Is in Hole After Playing Wrong Ball.
- 2-4/10 Player Concedes Hole After Which Opponent Plays Wrong Ball.
- 2-4/11 Player with Lost Ball Concedes Hole; Ball Then Found in Hole.
- 2-5/5 Invalid Claim Not Disputed.

9-2/12
Conscious Failure to Correct Opponent's Misunderstanding of State of Match; What Constitutes Wrong Information

Q. In a match, B is 1 up on A playing the 14th hole. A and B take 6's at the 14th hole, but B, assuming A scored a 5, says: "We are now all square." A says nothing although he knows that both have scored a 6 and he is still 1 down.

At the end of the 17th hole, B, believing he is 2 down, concedes the match, although in fact he is only 1 down. Is A subject to penalty under Rule 9-2 for giving wrong information?

A. No. Rule 9-2 deals with giving wrong information as to the number of strokes taken at a hole and would include acquiescence by the player (whether oral or tacit) in a misstatement by his opponent of the number of strokes taken by the player. Wrong information does not include acquiescence by the player in a misstatement by his opponent of the result of a hole or the state of the match.

However, A's conscious failure to correct B's misunderstanding of the state of the match is so contrary to the spirit of the game that the Committee should disqualify A under Rule 33-7 and reinstate B.

Related Decision:
- 2-5/9 Player Agreeing with Opponent That Hole Was Halved Later Realizes He Has Won Hole; Player Then Makes Claim.

9-2/13
Player Who Told Opponent He Would Proceed Under Water Hazard Rule Changes Mind After Opponent Plays

Q. In a match, B hit his tee shot short of a water hazard and A hits his into the hazard. Before B played his second shot he asked A what he was going to do. A said he was going to drop out and take a one-stroke penalty. B then played his second shot, after which A changed his mind and played his ball out of the hazard. Did A give wrong information, contrary to Rule 9-2?

A. No. A could have refused to answer B's question or replied that he would await B's play before deciding his own tactics. The fact that A did tell B what he planned to do does not preclude A from changing his mind.

Related Decisions:

- 3-3/7.5 Competitor Announces Intention to Play Two Balls; Plays Original Ball Before Dropping Second Ball; Elects Not to Play Second Ball.
- 18-2a/12.5 Player Entitled to Relief Without Penalty from Condition Lifts Ball; Chooses Not to Take Relief and Wishes to Proceed Under the Unplayable Ball Rule.
- 18-2a/27.5 Player Who States He Will Proceed Under Unplayable Ball Rule Subsequently Assesses Possibility of Playing Ball as It Lies.
- 28/13 After Deeming Ball Unplayable and Lifting It, Player Discovers Ball Was in Ground Under Repair.

9-2/14
Incorrect Information Causes Opponent Mistakenly to Think He Has Putt for Half; Opponent Holes Putt and Then Error Discovered

Q. In a match between A and B, A's ball was a few inches from the hole. B conceded A's next stroke and then asked, "How many strokes did you take?" A answered, "6." B, lying 5, then holed a putt for a 6 and assumed that he had halved the hole. At that point, A told B that he (A) had actually scored 5. The Committee ruled that A won the hole. Was this correct?

A. Yes. The hole was over when A's putt was conceded and he had won the hole with a 5. Since A corrected the error before either player played from the next tee, no penalty was incurred – see Rule 9-2.

9-2/15
Wrong Information After Play of Hole; When Penalty Applicable

Q. Decision 9-2/14 implies that, if A had not corrected the error before playing from the next tee, he would have lost the hole under Rule 9-2. However, it would seem that A would not incur a penalty because he won the hole, and therefore the incorrect information did not affect the result of the hole. Which answer is correct?

A. There is a penalty for giving incorrect information after play of a hole that is not corrected before play from the next teeing ground unless the incorrect information does not affect the opponent's understanding of the result of the hole just completed. Incorrect information would not affect the opponent's understanding of the result of the hole in the following circumstances: A and B are playing a match. After play of a hole, A states that he scored 5 and B states that he (B) scored 7. After teeing off at the next hole, A states that he was incorrect in saying that he scored 5 and that, in fact, he scored 6.

In Decision 9-2/14, the incorrect information caused B to believe that the hole in question had been halved, when in fact B lost the hole. Accordingly, if A had not corrected the error before playing from the next tee, under Rule 9-2 the hole would have been awarded to B.

9-2/16
Ascertaining Whereabouts of Opponent's Ball Before Playing

Q. In a match, B's tee shot may be lost, out of bounds or in a water hazard. In view of the wording in Rule 9-2a, under which an opponent is entitled to ascertain from the player the number of strokes he has taken, may A go forward to determine the status of B's ball before he (A) plays from the tee?

A. No. A would be in breach of Rule 6-7 (Undue Delay) if he did so. A player may make such a determination only if it can be done without unduly delaying play.

Related Decision:
• 8-1/5 Seeking Information on Whereabouts of Another Player's Ball.

Other Decisions related to Rule 9-2: See "Claims and Disputes," "Information as to Strokes Taken" and "Wrong Information" in the Index.

INFORMATION AS TO STROKES TAKEN IN STROKE PLAY

9-3/1
Competitor in Hole-by-Hole Play-Off Gives Wrong Information

Q. In a stroke-play hole-by-hole play-off, B has completed the hole in 5 strokes. Having no other readily available means for determining B's score at that point, A, who has a putt for a 5, inquires as to the number of strokes B has taken for the hole. B wrongly states that he (B) has holed out in 4 strokes. A picks up his ball without marking its position based on his understanding that B had won the play-off. B then corrects his error. What is the ruling?

A. If B intentionally misled A, B is disqualified under Rule 33-7.

If B simply made a mistake, B incurs no penalty. Rule 9 imposes no penalty for giving wrong information as to the number of strokes in stroke play. In these exceptional circumstances, A incurs no penalty for lifting his ball at rest without marking it. In a stroke-play hole-by-hole play-off, it is not necessary for A to complete the hole if B is the winner (see Decision 33-6/3), and since A had no other readily available means for determining B's score at that point, it was reasonable for A to rely on B's answer. Accordingly, by providing the incorrect information that induced A to lift his ball, B (not A) should be deemed to have caused the movement of A's ball. Therefore, in these limited circumstances, Rule 18-4 applies, i.e., neither player incurs a penalty and A must replace his ball – see Decision 18-1/8 and Decision 18-2a/21. This answer only applies in a stroke-play hole-by-hole play-off. In all other cases during a stroke-play competition, A would be obliged in all events to complete play of the hole and it would therefore not be reasonable for A to lift his ball without marking it. (Revised)

Other Decisions related to Rule 9-3: See "Wrong Information" in the Index.

RULE 10

ORDER OF PLAY

DEFINITIONS
All defined terms are in *italics* and are listed alphabetically in the Definitions section – see pages 6–16.

10-1. MATCH PLAY
a. When Starting Play of Hole
The *side* that has the *honor* at the first *teeing ground* is determined by the order of the draw. In the absence of a draw, the *honor* should be decided by lot.

The *side* that wins a hole takes the *honor* at the next *teeing ground*. If a hole has been halved, the *side* that had the *honor* at the previous *teeing ground* retains it.

b. During Play of Hole
After both players have started play of the hole, the ball farther from the *hole* is played first. If the balls are equidistant from the *hole* or their positions relative to the *hole* are not determinable, the ball to be played first should be decided by lot.

Exception: Rule 30-3b (*best-ball* and *four-ball* match play).

Note: When it becomes known that the original ball is not to be played as it lies and the player is required to play a ball as nearly as possible at the spot from which the original ball was last played (see Rule 20-5), the order of play is determined by the spot from which the previous *stroke* was made. When a ball may be played from a spot other than where the previous *stroke* was made, the order of play is determined by the position where the original ball came to rest.

c. Playing Out of Turn
If a player plays when his *opponent* should have played, there is no penalty, but the *opponent* may immediately require the player to cancel the *stroke* so made and, in correct order, play a ball as nearly as possible at the spot from which the original ball was last played (see Rule 20-5).

10-2. STROKE PLAY
a. When Starting Play of Hole
The *competitor* who has the *honor* at the first *teeing ground* is determined by the order of the draw. In the absence of a draw, the *honor* should be decided by lot.

The *competitor* with the lowest score at a hole takes the *honor* at the next *teeing ground*. The *competitor* with the second lowest score plays next and so on. If two or more *competitors* have the same score at a hole, they play from the next *teeing ground* in the same order as at the previous *teeing ground*.

Exception: Rule 32-1 (handicap bogey, par and Stableford competitions).

b. During Play of Hole

After the *competitors* have started play of the hole, the ball farthest from the *hole* is played first. If two or more balls are equidistant from the *hole* or their positions relative to the *hole* are not determinable, the ball to be played first should be decided by lot.

Exceptions: Rules 22 (ball assisting or interfering with play) and 31-4 (*four-ball* stroke play).

Note: When it becomes known that the original ball is not to be played as it lies and the *competitor* is required to play a ball as nearly as possible at the spot from which the original ball was last played (see Rule 20-5), the order of play is determined by the spot from which the previous *stroke* was made. When a ball may be played from a spot other than where the previous *stroke* was made, the order of play is determined by the position where the original ball came to rest.

c. Playing Out of Turn

If a *competitor* plays out of turn, there is no penalty and the ball is played as it lies. If, however, the *Committee* determines that *competitors* have agreed to play out of turn to give one of them an advantage, they are disqualified.

(Making stroke while another ball in motion after stroke from putting green – see Rule 16-1f)
(Incorrect order of play in foursome stroke play – see Rule 29-3)

10-3. PROVISIONAL BALL OR ANOTHER BALL FROM TEEING GROUND

If a player plays a *provisional ball* or another ball from the *teeing ground*, he must do so after his *opponent* or *fellow-competitor* has made his first *stroke*. If more than one player elects to play a *provisional ball* or is required to play another ball from the *teeing ground*, the original order of play must be retained. If a player plays a *provisional ball* or another ball out of turn, Rule 10-1c or 10-2c applies.

ORDER OF PLAY: GENERAL

10/1
Order of Play When Two Balls Lie in Ground Under Repair and Both Players Take Relief

Q. A and B hit their balls into ground under repair. The balls are approximately 18 inches apart. A's ball is farther from the hole. Both players decide to take relief. Is the order of play for the next shot determined by the relative positions of the balls before relief is taken, or after?

A. The order of play is determined by the relative positions of the balls before relief is taken. A should play before B – see Note to Rules 10-1b and 10-2b.

10/2
Order of Play When Two Balls Lie in Lateral Water Hazard and Both Players Take Relief

Q. A and B hit their balls into a lateral water hazard. The balls are approximately 18 inches apart. A's ball is farther from the hole but B's ball last crossed the hazard margin farther from the hole than A's ball. Both players decide to take relief from the hazard. What is the proper procedure?

A. Since A's ball lies farther from the hole, under the Note to Rule 10-1b or 10-2b, A should play before B.

10/3
Order of Play When Two Balls Are Lost in Lateral Water Hazard

Q. A and B hit their balls into the same general area of a lateral water hazard. Both balls are lost in the hazard and therefore it is not known which ball is farther from the hole. However, B's ball last crossed the hazard margin farther from the hole than A's ball. What is the proper procedure?

A. The ball to be played first should be decided by lot, just as would be the case if the balls were equidistant from the hole – see Rules 10-1b and 10-2b.

10/4
Order of Play for Provisional Ball Other Than from Teeing Ground

Q. In a match between A and B, A hits his approach shot towards an area of trees. As the ball might be lost outside a water hazard, he announces to B that he intends to play a provisional ball. What is the order of play for A's provisional ball?

A. Except when playing a provisional ball from the teeing ground (Rule 10-3), the order of play for a provisional ball is for the player playing the provisional ball to do so immediately. Therefore, A would play his provisional ball before B's next stroke.

If A allows B to play before he (A) states his intention to play a provisional ball, A has abandoned his right to recall B's stroke under Rule 10-1c, but he may still play the provisional ball.

Related Decision:
• 10-3/1 Provisional Balls Played Out of Turn from Teeing Ground.

HONOR IN MATCH PLAY

10-1a/1
Determination of Honor in Handicap Match

Q. A and B are playing a match on a handicap basis. B has the honor at the 1st hole.

Both players score 5's at the 1st hole but A receives a handicap stroke and therefore has a net 4. Does A take the honor at the 2nd hole?

A. Yes. See Rules 2-1 and 10-1a.

10-1a/2
Determination of Honor at Hole Following Claim

Q. A dispute arises in a match between A and B, and A lodges a claim. A and B agree to continue the match and get a ruling later. If the claim could have an effect on determining who has the honor at the next hole, how is the honor decided?

A. In equity (Rule 1-4), the honor is decided by lot.

10-1a/3
Players Agree Not to Tee Off in Prescribed Order to Save Time

Q. In match play, A wins the 4th hole. On his way to the 5th tee, he returns to retrieve a club left at the 4th green and suggests that his opponent B play first to save time, which B does. In view of Rule 10-1a, have the players agreed to waive the Rules in breach of Rule 1-3?

A. No. When starting play of a hole, a player who has the honor may invite his opponent to play first to save time, but if the opponent does so, the player has waived his right under Rule 10-1c to recall the stroke played out of turn. The opponent is under no obligation to accept the offer to tee off first. (Revised – Formerly 1-3/1)

Related Decision:
• 10-2c/2 Competitors in Stroke Play Agree to Play Out of Turn But Not for Purpose of Giving One of Them an Advantage.

Other Decisions related to Rule 10-1a:
• 11-4a/1 Player With Honor Plays from Outside Teeing Ground; Order of Play if Opponent Requires Player to Cancel Stroke.
• 30/3 Determination of Honor in Four-Ball Match in Which Points Awarded for Both Better-Ball and Aggregate Scores.

ORDER OF PLAY IN MATCH PLAY

10-1b/1
Procedure for Referee in Determining Ball Farther from Hole

Q. In a match, A's ball is on one side of the fairway and B's ball is on the other side. Both balls are about 100 yards from the hole. A plays and B questions whether A played out of turn. Is the referee obliged to pace off the distances to the hole to resolve the question?

A. No. In view of the distances involved, the referee would be justified in resolving the question by eye. If he could not do so, he would be justified in deciding by lot which player should have played first. If it was decided by lot that B should have played first, B would have the option of recalling A's stroke under Rule 10-1c.

Other Decisions related to Rule 10-1b:
- 30/4 Player Who Walks Off Green Under Mistaken Impression Partner Halved Hole Returns and Putts for Half.
- 30-3b/2 Waiving Turn to Putt in Four-Ball Match.

PLAYING OUT OF TURN IN MATCH PLAY

10-1c/1
Request for Player to Replay Stroke Withdrawn After Opponent Plays

Q. In a match between A and B, A played his tee shot out of turn. B requested A to abandon the ball and play in the correct order. However, after B played, he told A not to bother playing another ball. What is the ruling?

A. A was not obliged to comply with B's instruction to continue with the original ball. B incurred no penalty for giving the instruction.

Whether A continued with his original ball or played another ball in correct order as was his right, the result of the hole should stand as played.

10-1c/2
Player Requested to Lift Ball Due to Interference Plays Out of Turn Instead

Q. In match play, A's ball is on B's line of putt. B requests A to lift his ball under Rule 22-2. Instead of complying with the request, A putts out of turn. Does A lose the hole for a breach of Rule 22-2 or does Rule 10-1c apply, in which case there would be no penalty but B would have the right to require A to replay the stroke in correct order?

A. Rule 10-1c governs.

Other Decisions related to Rule 10-1c: See "Order of Play" and "Playing Out of Turn" in the Index.

HONOR IN STROKE PLAY

10-2a/1
Determination of Honor in Handicap Stroke Play

Q. In a stroke-play competition on a handicap basis, the handicap is deducted at the end of the round and not at individual holes. In such a competition, how is the honor determined?

A. According to gross scores.

ORDER OF PLAY IN STROKE PLAY

10-2b/1
Competitor Objects to Fellow-Competitor Putting Out of Turn

Q. In stroke play, A's ball is 40 feet from the hole and B's is 30 feet away. A putts and his ball comes to rest four feet from the hole. A prepares to hole out before B putts. B objects and claims that under the Rules (Rule 10-2b) he is entitled to putt before A.

Although putting out of turn in stroke play is generally condoned, should the Committee allow A to putt out of turn in these circumstances?

A. If A had lifted his ball when the objection was lodged, the Committee should rule that A is not entitled to putt out of turn, in view of Rule 10-2b.

If A had not lifted his ball at the time the objection was lodged, the answer depends on whether B would require A to lift his ball under Rule 22 (Ball Assisting or Interfering with Play) before he (B) putts. If so, the Committee should rule that A is entitled to play out of turn, provided he does so without first lifting his ball, i.e., Rule 22-2 permits a competitor in stroke play who is required to lift his ball because of interference to "play first rather than lift."

If B would not require A to lift his ball before he (B) putts, the Committee should rule that A is not entitled to putt out of turn.

Although condoning putting out of turn in stroke play may be questionable in view of the explicit language of Rule 10-2b, there is no penalty for doing so (Rule 10-2c), it is not in conflict with the intent of Rule 10-2b, and it may tend to speed play. Accordingly, it is considered that the practice should not be discouraged.

Other Decisions related to Rule 10-2b:
- 31-4/1 Player Waives Turn to Play; Circumstances Under Which He May Complete Hole.
- 31-4/2 Extent to Which Side May Play in Order It Considers Best.

PLAYING OUT OF TURN IN STROKE PLAY

10-2c/1
Ball Played Out of Turn from Tee Abandoned and Another Ball Played in Proper Order

Q. In stroke play, a competitor played out of turn from the teeing ground and, although he should have continued play with the ball played out of turn without penalty, he abandoned the ball and played another ball in proper order. What is the ruling?

A. When the competitor played another ball from the tee, the original ball was lost and the other ball was in play under penalty of stroke and distance – see Rule 27-1.

Related Decisions:
- 18-2a/1 Player Who Misses Tee Shot Tees Ball Lower Before Making Next Stroke.
- 18-2a/2 Ball Falling Off Tee When Stroke Just Touches It Is Picked Up and Re-Teed.
- 18-2a/11 Tee Shot Wrongly Thought to Be Out of Bounds Lifted; Competitor Plays Another Ball from Tee.
- 27-2b/10 Provisional Ball Lifted Subsequently Becomes Ball in Play; Competitor Then Plays from Wrong Place.
- 29-1/9 Both Player and Partner Drive at Same Tee in Foursome Play.

10-2c/2
Competitors in Stroke Play Agree to Play Out of Turn But Not for Purpose of Giving One of Them an Advantage

Q. In stroke play, A and B agree to play out of turn at the 10th hole to save time. There is no penalty under Rule 10-2c because they did not do so in order to give one of them an advantage. However, are they liable to disqualification under Rule 1-3 for agreeing to exclude the operation of Rule 10-2a or 10-2b as the case may be?

A. No. Rule 10-2c specifically governs and permits the procedure in stroke play. Accordingly, Rule 1-3 does not apply. As to match play, see Decision 10-1a/3. (Revised)

Other Decisions related to Rule 10-2c: See "Order of Play" and "Playing Out of Turn" in the Index.

PROVISIONAL BALL AND SECOND BALL

10-3/1
Provisional Balls Played Out of Turn from Teeing Ground

Q. In match play, A has the honor and plays from the teeing ground, followed by his opponent, B. B, believing that his original ball may be out of bounds, plays a provisional ball while A stands by silently.
  After B has played his provisional ball, A decides that, as his ball may be out of bounds or lost outside a water hazard, he will also play a provisional ball.
  In view of the provisions in Rule 10-3, may A require B to cancel and replay his provisional ball?

A. No. When B played his provisional ball, he did not know that A would do so as well. A may play a provisional ball under these circumstances; however, he abandoned his right to recall B's stroke when he allowed B to play his provisional ball first.

Related Decisions:
- 10/4 Order of Play for Provisional Ball Other Than from Teeing Ground.
- 11-4a/1 Player With Honor Plays from Outside Teeing Ground; Order of Play if Opponent Requires Player to Cancel Stroke.

RULE 11

TEEING GROUND

DEFINITIONS
All defined terms are in *italics* and are listed alphabetically in the Definitions section – see pages 6–16.

11-1. TEEING
When a player is putting a ball into play from the *teeing ground*, it must be played from within the *teeing ground* and from the surface of the ground or from a conforming tee (see Appendix IV) in or on the surface of the ground.

For the purposes of this Rule, the surface of the ground includes an irregularity of surface (whether or not created by the player) and sand or other natural substance (whether or not placed by the player).

If a player makes a *stroke* at a ball on a non-conforming tee, or at a ball teed in a manner not permitted by this Rule, he is disqualified.

A player may stand outside the *teeing ground* to play a ball within it.

11-2. TEE-MARKERS
Before a player makes his first *stroke* with any ball on the *teeing ground* of the hole being played, the tee-markers are deemed to be fixed. In these circumstances, if the player moves or allows to be moved a tee-marker for the purpose of avoiding interference with his *stance*, the area of his intended swing or his *line of play*, he incurs the penalty for a breach of Rule 13-2.

11-3. BALL FALLING OFF TEE
If a ball, when not *in play*, falls off a tee or is knocked off a tee by the player in *addressing* it, it may be re-teed, without penalty. However, if a *stroke* is made at the ball in these circumstances, whether the ball is moving or not, the *stroke* counts, but there is no penalty.

11-4. PLAYING FROM OUTSIDE TEEING GROUND
a. Match Play
If a player, when starting a hole, plays a ball from outside the *teeing ground*, there is no penalty, but the *opponent* may immediately require the player to cancel the *stroke* and play a ball from within the *teeing ground*.

b. Stroke Play
If a *competitor*, when starting a hole, plays a ball from outside the *teeing ground*, he incurs a penalty of two strokes and must then play a ball from within the *teeing ground*.

If the *competitor* makes a *stroke* from the next *teeing ground* without first correcting his mistake or, in the case of the last hole of the round, leaves the *putting green* without first declaring his intention to correct his mistake, he is disqualified.

The *stroke* from outside the *teeing ground* and any subsequent *strokes* by the *competitor* on the hole prior to his correction of the mistake do not count in his score.

11-5. PLAYING FROM WRONG TEEING GROUND

The provisions of Rule 11-4 apply.

TEEING GROUND AND TEEING

Decisions related to Rule 11-1: See "Teeing Ground and Tee-Markers" in the Index.

TEE-MARKERS

11-2/1
Status of Tee-Markers After First Stroke

Q. Under Rule 11-2, tee-markers are deemed to be fixed when playing the first stroke with any ball from the teeing ground. Are tee-markers obstructions thereafter?

A. Yes.

11-2/2
Tee-Marker Moved by Player

Rule 11-2 states that before a player plays his first stroke with any ball from the teeing ground, the tee-markers are deemed to be fixed. Thereafter, Decision 11-2/1 clarifies that they are obstructions and if movable, may be moved (see Definition of "Obstruction").

In view of the fact that tee-markers are initially fixed, and when moved can have a significant effect on the competition, the following are examples of the appropriate ruling in various circumstances. In all cases a moved tee-marker should be replaced. In some cases, the replacement of the tee-marker may affect the penalty to the player.

(a) A player moves a tee-marker before playing his first stroke with any ball from the teeing ground because the tee-marker interferes with the lie of the ball, his stance or his area of intended swing – loss of hole in match play or two strokes in stroke play for breach of Rule 13-2.

(b) A player moves a tee-marker before or after playing a stroke from the teeing ground because, in his view, the tee-markers are too close together, too far back, aimed in the wrong direction, or some similar reason – disqualification under Rule 33-7, unless the tee-marker is replaced before the player or any other player plays from the teeing ground, in which case the penalty is modified to loss of hole in match play or two strokes in stroke play.

(c) A player moves a tee-marker before or after playing a stroke from the teeing ground as a result of falling over the marker – no penalty and the tee-marker should be replaced.

(d) A player moves a tee-marker before or after playing a stroke from the teeing ground as a result of intentionally kicking it or striking it with a club – no penalty and the tee-marker should be replaced.

(e) A player lifts a tee-marker before or after playing a stroke from the teeing ground for no apparent reason and without authority under the Rules – no penalty and the tee-marker should be replaced.

Other Decisions related to Rule 11-2: See "Teeing Ground and Tee-Markers" in the Index.

BALL FALLING OFF TEE

11-3/1
Stroke Misses Ball; Ball Then Accidentally Knocked Off Tee

Q. A player teed his ball within the teeing ground. He made a stroke at the ball but missed it. He addressed the ball again and accidentally knocked it off the tee. What is the ruling?

A. When the player made a stroke at the ball, it was in play and Rule 11-3 no longer applied. When the ball in play moved after it was addressed, the player incurred a penalty stroke and was obliged to replace the ball (Rule 18-2b).

Related Decision:
• 18-2a/2 Ball Falling Off Tee When Stroke Just Touches It Is Picked Up and Re-Teed.

11-3/2 (Reserved)

11-3/3
Original Ball Out of Bounds; Ball Played Under Stroke-and-Distance Procedure Falls Off Tee at Address

Q. A player played his original ball out of bounds from the teeing ground. Under Rule 27-1, he teed up another ball. When addressing the ball, he touched it and it fell off the tee. What is the ruling?

A. There is no penalty, because a teed ball is not in play until a stroke has been made at it (see Definition of "Ball in Play"). The ball may be re-teed (Rule 11-3).

Related Decision:
• 18-2a/19 Ball Moved Accidentally by Practice Swing Prior to Tee Shot.

PLAYING FROM OUTSIDE TEEING GROUND IN MATCH PLAY

11-4a/1
Player with Honor Plays from Outside Teeing Ground; Order of Play If Opponent Requires Player to Cancel Stroke

Q. In match play, the player with the honor plays from outside the teeing ground. His opponent immediately requires the player to cancel his stroke in accordance with Rule 11-4a Does the player retain the honor?

A. Yes. The player's next stroke from the tee is not considered a second ball as the term is used in Rule 10-3.

Other Decisions related to Rule 11-4a:
• 11-5/3 Ball Played Out of Bounds from Wrong Teeing Ground Not Recalled.
• 29-1/1 Ball Played from Outside Teeing Ground in Foursome Match.

PLAYING FROM OUTSIDE TEEING GROUND IN STROKE PLAY

11-4b/1 (Reserved)

11-4b/2
Competitors Estimate Area of Teeing Ground When One Tee-Marker Missing

Q. In stroke play, competitors in a group, finding one tee-marker missing from a teeing ground, determine for themselves the area of the teeing ground based on the position of the remaining tee-marker and the shape of the tee. What is the ruling?

A. The correct procedure is to discontinue play until the Committee resolves the problem.

However, if the Committee is satisfied that the competitors did not gain an advantage by playing from the place they judged to be the teeing ground, it would be appropriate for the Committee, in equity (Rule 1-4), to accept their scores, without penalty. Otherwise, they incur the penalty prescribed in Rule 11-4b.

11-4b/3
Competitors Determine Spot from Which to Play from Tee When Both Tee-Markers Are Missing

Q. In stroke play, the competitors in a group, finding no tee-markers on a particular hole, determine for themselves the spot from which to begin play on the hole, and tee off. What is the ruling?

A. It would be appropriate for the Committee to accept without penalty the scores of the competitors in question if there was evidence as to where the tee-markers were intended to be and the competitors determined the teeing ground from such evidence and played from within such teeing ground. Sufficient evidence might include spots of paint established to show where the tee-markers were to be installed or, if the tee-markers were removed during a round, depressions or other marks on the ground indicating where the tee-markers had been located.

In the absence of such evidence, the competitors should be disqualified under Rule 11-4b unless, before playing from the next tee, they discontinue play, get the Committee to establish tee-markers and replay the hole from within the established teeing ground. Any competitor so replaying would incur a penalty of two strokes (Rule 11-4b).

11-4b/4 (Reserved)

11-4b/5 (Reserved)

11-4b/6
Ball Played from Outside Teeing Ground Goes Out of Bounds

Q. In stroke play, A played from outside the teeing ground and his ball came to rest out of bounds. He played another ball from within the teeing ground. Is he penalized stroke and distance under Rule 27-1, as well as two strokes under Rule 11-4b?

A. No. A is penalized only two strokes under Rule 11-4b. The ball played from outside the teeing ground was not in play. Therefore, the fact that it came to rest out of bounds was irrelevant and the stroke itself did not count.

Other Decisions related to Rule 11-4b:
- 11-5/4 Ball Played from Wrong Teeing Ground in Stroke Play; Error Corrected.
- 29-1/2 Competitor Plays from Outside Teeing Ground in Foursome Stroke Play; Partner Replays Stroke.
- 34-3/4 Dispute as to Whether Competitor Played from Outside Teeing Ground.

PLAYING FROM WRONG TEEING GROUND

11-5/1
Explanation of "Next Teeing Ground" When Competitors Have Played from Wrong Teeing Ground

Q. In stroke play, two competitors, having completed the 11th hole, played from the 15th tee, completed the hole and played from the 16th tee. Before playing their second shots they realized their mistake, returned to the 12th tee and completed the round. On reporting the incident the competitors were each penalized two strokes, as the Committee interpreted the "next teeing ground" referred to in Rule 11-4b to be that of the 12th hole. Was this correct?

A. No. When the competitors played from the 16th tee, they had played from the "next teeing ground" and could not correct their error. Therefore, they should have been disqualified.

11-5/2
Use of Wrong Teeing Ground Attributable to Committee Failure to Indicate Hole Numbers on Teeing Grounds

Q. In a stroke-play competition, the Committee failed to place a sign at each teeing ground indicating the hole number. As a result, a group which had just finished the 4th hole played from the teeing ground of the 12th hole, rather than the 5th hole. Should the members of the group be penalized under Rule 11-4b in the circumstances?

A. Yes.

The Committee was remiss in not placing a sign at each teeing ground. However, each player is responsible for knowing the stipulated round, this being one of the conditions of the competition.

11-5/3
Ball Played Out of Bounds from Wrong Teeing Ground Not Recalled

Q. A played B in a match. A drove out of bounds from the wrong teeing ground. B did not recall the stroke. What is the ruling?

A. As A played from the wrong teeing ground and B did not require him to cancel the stroke and play a ball from within the correct teeing ground, A's ball has been put into play (see Definition of "Ball in Play").

Therefore, under Rule 27-1 A must drop a ball, under penalty of one stroke, as nearly as possible at the spot from which the original ball was played, i.e., on the wrong teeing ground. He could not tee the ball because the original ball was not played from the teeing ground of the hole being played (Rule 20-5).

11-5/4
Ball Played from Wrong Teeing Ground in Stroke Play: Error Corrected

Q. In stroke play, after finishing the 10th hole, A and B played from the teeing ground of the 15th hole instead of the 11th hole. They realized their error before completing the 15th hole, returned to the 11th tee and completed the round. What is the ruling?

A. A and B each incurred a penalty of two strokes under Rule 11-4b. They were correct in discontinuing play at the 15th hole and returning to the 11th hole. Strokes played at the 15th hole, when it was played out of order, did not count.

Related Decisions:
- 11-4b/6 Ball Played from Outside Teeing Ground Goes Out of Bounds.
- 29-1/2 Competitor Plays from Outside Teeing Ground in Foursome Stroke Play; Partner Replays Stroke.

11-5/5
Ball Played from Teeing Ground of Hole to Be Played Later in Round Lifted; Ball Replaced at Spot from Which Lifted and Played Out When That Hole Subsequently Reached

Q. In stroke play, after playing the 8th hole, A, by mistake, played from the teeing ground of the 18th hole, instead of the 9th hole. A marked the position of the ball, lifted it and played from the teeing ground of the 9th hole. He added a two-stroke penalty to his score for the 9th hole under Rule 11-4b for playing from the wrong teeing ground, i.e., playing from the 18th tee. A played the holes from the 10th to the 17th. He then replaced his ball at the spot on the 18th hole from which he had lifted it, played out the hole and returned his score card. Did A proceed correctly?

A. No. A should have disregarded the original stroke played from the 18th tee and replayed from that tee after completion of the 17th hole. In failing to do so, A did not play the stipulated round – see Definition of "Stipulated Round" – and thus did not have an acceptable score.

Related Decision:
- 1-1/1 Two Balls in Play Simultaneously at Different Holes.

RULE 12

SEARCHING FOR AND IDENTIFYING BALL

DEFINITIONS

All defined terms are in *italics* and are listed alphabetically in the Definitions section – see pages 6–16.

12-1. SEEING BALL; SEARCHING FOR BALL

A player is not necessarily entitled to see his ball when making a *stroke*.

In searching for his ball anywhere on the *course*, the player may touch or bend long grass, rushes, bushes, whins, heather or the like, but only to the extent necessary to find or identify the ball, provided that this does not improve the lie of the ball, the area of his intended *stance* or swing or his *line of play*; if the ball is *moved*, Rule 18-2a applies except as provided in clauses a - d of this Rule.

In addition to the methods of searching for and identifying a ball that are otherwise permitted by the *Rules*, the player may also search for and identify a ball under Rule 12-1 as follows:

a. Searching for or Identifying Ball Covered by Sand

If the player's ball lying anywhere on the *course* is believed to be covered by sand, to the extent that he cannot find or identify it, he may, without penalty, touch or move the sand in order to find or identify the ball. If the ball is found, and identified as his, the player must re-create the lie as nearly as possible by replacing the sand. If the ball is *moved* during the touching or moving of sand while searching for or identifying the ball, there is no penalty; the ball must be replaced and the lie re-created.

In re-creating a lie under this Rule, the player is permitted to leave a small part of the ball visible.

b. Searching for or Identifying Ball Covered by Loose Impediments in Hazard

In a *hazard*, if the player's ball is believed to be covered by *loose impediments* to the extent that he cannot find or identify it, he may, without penalty, touch or move *loose impediments* in order to find or identify the ball. If the ball is found or identified as his, the player must replace the *loose impediments*. If the ball is *moved* during the touching or moving of *loose impediments* while searching for or identifying the ball, Rule 18-2a applies; if the ball is *moved* during the replacement of the *loose impediments*, there is no penalty and the ball must be replaced.

If the ball was entirely covered by *loose impediments*, the player must re-cover the ball but is permitted to leave a small part of the ball visible.

c. Searching for Ball in Water in Water Hazard

If a ball is believed to be lying in water in a *water hazard*, the player may, without penalty, probe for it with a club or otherwise. If the ball in water is accidentally *moved* while probing, there is no penalty; the ball must be replaced, unless the player elects to proceed under Rule 26-1. If the *moved* ball was not lying in water or the ball was accidentally *moved* by the player other than while probing, Rule 18-2a applies.

d. Searching for Ball Within Obstruction or Abnormal Ground Condition

If a ball lying in or on an *obstruction* or in an *abnormal ground condition* is accidentally *moved* during search, there is no penalty; the ball must be replaced unless the player elects to proceed under Rule 24-1b, 24-2b or 25-1b as applicable. If the player replaces the ball, he may still proceed under one of those Rules, if applicable.

PENALTY FOR BREACH OF RULE 12-1:
Match Play – Loss of Hole; Stroke Play – Two Strokes.

(Improving lie, area of intended stance or swing, or line of play – see Rule 13-2)

RULE 12-2 LIFTING BALL FOR IDENTIFICATION
The responsibility for playing the proper ball rests with the player. Each player should put an identification mark on his ball.

If a player believes that a ball at rest might be his, but he cannot identify it, the player may lift the ball for identification, without penalty. The right to lift a ball for identification is in addition to the actions permitted under Rule 12-1.

Before lifting the ball, the player must announce his intention to his *opponent* in match play or his *marker* or a *fellow-competitor* in stroke play and mark the position of the ball. He may then lift the ball and identify it, provided that he gives his *opponent*, *marker* or *fellow-competitor* an opportunity to observe the lifting and replacement. The ball must not be cleaned beyond the extent necessary for identification when lifted under Rule 12-2.

If the ball is the player's ball and he fails to comply with all or any part of this procedure, or he lifts his ball in order to identify it without having good reason to do so, he incurs a penalty of one stroke. If the lifted ball is the player's ball, he must replace it. If he fails to do so, he incurs the general penalty for a breach of Rule 12-2, but there is no additional penalty under this Rule.

Note: If the original lie of a ball to be replaced has been altered, see Rule 20-3b.

*PENALTY FOR BREACH OF RULE 12-2:
Match Play – Loss of hole; Stroke Play – Two strokes.

*If a player incurs the general penalty for a breach of Rule 12-2, there is no additional penalty under this Rule.

12-1/1 (Reserved)

12-1/2 (Reserved)

12-1/3
Top of Ball in Hazard Covered by Leaves But Part of Ball Visible from Another Angle

Q. The top of the player's ball in a hazard is covered by leaves so that it is not visible when he takes his stance However, a portion of the ball is visible from another angle. Is it permissible for the player to remove enough leaves to see the ball once he has taken his stance?

A. No. In these circumstances, a player is entitled to remove loose impediments covering a ball in a hazard only if the ball is not visible from any angle. (Revised)

12-1/4
Player Touches Ground in Hazard When Searching for Ball Believed to Be Covered by Loose Impediments in Hazard

Q. A player's ball is believed to be in a bunker covered by leaves. The player probes for the ball with a club which touches the ground in the bunker. What is the ruling?

A. There is no penalty. Rule 12-1 specifically authorizes touching ground in the hazard while probing. Such permission overrides any prohibitions in Rule 13-4.

12-1/5
Player Kicks Ball While Probing for It in Water in Water Hazard

Q. A player is probing for his ball in the water in a water hazard and accidentally kicks the ball which is in fact lying in long grass on the bank within the hazard. What is the ruling?

A. As the moved ball was not lying in water in a water hazard, the player incurs a penalty stroke under Rule 18-2a for moving his ball in play (see Rule 12-1c). The player may replace the ball and play it or, under an additional penalty of one stroke, proceed under Rule 26-1. If the player proceeds under Rule 26-1, he is not required to replace the ball. (Revised)

Related Decision:
• 20-1/13 Ball Accidentally Kicked by Player Asked to Lift It Due to Interference.

Other Decisions related to Rule 12-1: See "Searching for and Identifying Ball" in the Index.

IDENTIFYING BALL

12-2/1
Identifying Ball by Brand, Model and Number Only

Q. In the area in which his ball presumably came to rest, a player finds a ball of the same brand, model and identification number as the ball he is playing. The player assumes it is his ball, even though it does not carry an identification mark as suggested in Rule 12-2, and plays it. Should the player be considered to have played a wrong ball?

A. No, unless (1) there is clear evidence that, because of the ball's condition, it is not the player's ball or (2) subsequently it is established that another ball of the same brand, model and identification number was lying in the area at the time the player played and either ball, from a condition standpoint, could be the player's ball.

Related Decisions:
• 27/10 Player Unable to Distinguish His Ball from Another Ball.
• 27/11 Provisional Ball Not Distinguishable from Original Ball.
• 27/12 Identification of Ball Through Testimony of Spectator.
• 27/13 Refusal to Identify Ball.

12-2/2
Touching and Rotating Half-Buried Ball in Rough for Identification Purposes

Q. A ball is half buried in the rough. Having announced his intention in advance to his opponent, marker or fellow-competitor, the player, for the purpose of identifying the ball, touches the ball and rotates it. By so doing he identifies the ball as his ball. Is there a penalty?

A. Yes, for touching the ball other than as provided for in the Rules (Rule 18-2a). Under Rules 12-2 and 20-1, a ball may be lifted (or touched and rotated) for identification purposes after its position has been marked. If the player had marked the position of the ball before rotating it, there would have been no penalty, assuming the rotating did not result in the ball being cleaned beyond the extent necessary to identify it.

Related Decisions:
• 18-2a/33 Rotating Ball on Putting Green Without Marking Position.
• 20-3a/2 Using Line on Ball for Alignment.

Other Decisions related to Rule 12-2: See "Searching for and Identifying Ball" in the Index.

RULE 13

BALL PLAYED AS IT LIES

DEFINITIONS
All defined terms are in *italics* and are listed alphabetically in the Definitions section – see pages 6–16.

13-1. GENERAL
The ball must be played as it lies, except as otherwise provided in the *Rules*. (Ball at rest moved – see Rule 18)

13-2. IMPROVING LIE, AREA OF INTENDED STANCE OR SWING, OR LINE OF PLAY
A player must not improve or allow to be improved:
* the position or lie of his ball,
* the area of his intended *stance* or swing,
* his *line of play* or a reasonable extension of that line beyond the *hole*, or
* the area in which he is to drop or place a ball,
by any of the following actions:
* pressing a club on the ground,
* moving, bending or breaking anything growing or fixed (including immovable *obstructions* and objects defining *out of bounds*),
* creating or eliminating irregularities of surface,
* removing or pressing down sand, loose soil, replaced divots or other cut turf placed in position, or
* removing dew, frost or water.
However, the player incurs no penalty if the action occurs:
* in grounding the club lightly when *addressing the ball*,
* in fairly taking his *stance*,
* in making a *stroke* or the backward movement of his club for a *stroke* and the *stroke* is made,
* in creating or eliminating irregularities of surface within the *teeing ground* or in removing dew, frost or water from the *teeing ground*, or
* on the *putting green* in removing sand and loose soil or in repairing damage (Rule 16-1).
Exception: Ball in *hazard* – see Rule 13-4.

13-3. BUILDING STANCE
A player is entitled to place his feet firmly in taking his *stance*, but he must not build a *stance*.

13-4. BALL IN HAZARD; PROHIBITED ACTIONS
Except as provided in the *Rules*, before making a *stroke* at a ball that is in a *hazard* (whether a *bunker* or a *water hazard*) or that, having been lifted from a *hazard*, may be dropped or placed in the *hazard*, the player must not:

a. Test the condition of the *hazard* or any similar *hazard*;

b. Touch the ground in the *hazard* or water in the *water hazard* with his hand or a club; or

c. Touch or move a *loose impediment* lying in or touching the *hazard*.

Exceptions:

1. Provided nothing is done that constitutes testing the condition of the *hazard* or improves the lie of the ball, there is no penalty if the player (a) touches the ground or *loose impediments* in any *hazard* or water in a *water hazard* as a result of or to prevent falling, in removing an *obstruction*, in measuring or in marking the position of, retrieving, lifting, placing or replacing a ball under any *Rule* or (b) places his clubs in a *hazard*.

2. At any time, the player may smooth sand or soil in a *hazard* provided this is for the sole purpose of caring for the *course* and nothing is done to breach Rule 13-2 with respect to his next *stroke*. If a ball played from a *hazard* is outside the *hazard* after the *stroke*, the player may smooth sand or soil in the *hazard* without restriction.

3. If the player makes a *stroke* from a *hazard* and the ball comes to rest in another *hazard*, Rule 13-4a does not apply to any subsequent actions taken in the *hazard* from which the *stroke* was made.

Note: At any time, including at *address* or in the backward movement for the *stroke*, the player may touch, with a club or otherwise, any *obstruction*, any construction declared by the *Committee* to be an integral part of the *course* or any grass, bush, tree or other growing thing.

PENALTY FOR BREACH OF RULE:

Match play – Loss of hole; Stroke play – Two strokes.

(Searching for ball – see Rule 12-1)
(Relief for ball in water hazard – see Rule 26)

DEFINITION OF "BUNKER": GENERAL

13/1
Sand Spilling Over Margin of Bunker

Q. If sand spills over the margin of a bunker, is the sand part of the bunker?

A. No.

13/2
Status of Tree in Bunker

Q. Is a tree in a bunker part of the bunker?

A. No. Grass-covered ground within a bunker is not part of the bunker. The same principle applies to a tree. The margin of a bunker does not extend upwards.

13/3
Ball on Edge of Bunker Overhanging Sand

Q. Is a ball in a bunker if it lies on the edge of the bunker overhanging, but not touching, the sand?

A. No. The margin of a bunker, unlike that of a water hazard, does not extend vertically upwards.

13/4
Ball Completely Embedded in Lip of Bunker

Q. A player's ball is completely embedded in the vertical lip of a bunker. The lip is not grass-covered, so it is part of the bunker. Is the ball considered to be lying through the green? If so, the player would be entitled to drop the ball behind the bunker if he deems it unplayable.

A. No. An embedded ball is considered to be lying in the part of the course where it entered the ground.

Related Decisions:
- 16/2 Ball Embedded in Side of Hole; All of Ball Below Lip of Hole.
- 16/3 Ball Embedded in Side of Hole; All of Ball Not Below Lip of Hole.
- 25-2/5 Ball Embedded in Grass Bank or Face of Bunker.
- 33-8/39 Local Rule for Bunker Faces Consisting of Stacked Turf.
- 33-8/39.5 Local Rule Deeming Partially Grass-Covered Wall of Bunker to Be Part of Bunker.

13/5
Ball Lying on Obstruction in Bunker

Q. If a ball is lying on either a movable or an immovable obstruction in a bunker, is the ball considered to be in the bunker?

A. Yes. Although the margin of a bunker does not extend upwards, a ball lying on an obstruction in a bunker is in the bunker.

BALL PLAYED AS IT LIES: GENERAL

Decisions related to Rule 13-1:
- 18-2a/8.5 Ball Played from Ground Under Repair Abandoned and Relief Taken Under Ground Under Repair Rule.
- 20-7c/4 Competitor's Ball Played by Fellow-Competitor; Competitor Substitutes Another Ball at Wrong Place, Plays It and Then Abandons It and Plays Out Original Ball From Right Place.

13-2/0.5
Meaning of "Improve" in Rule 13-2

Q. Rule 13-2 prohibits a player from improving certain areas. What does "improve" mean?

A. In the context of Rule 13-2, "improve" means to change for the better so that the player gains a potential advantage with respect to the position or lie of his ball, the area of his intended stance or swing, his line of play or a reasonable extension of that line beyond the hole, or the area in which he is to drop or place a ball. Therefore, merely changing an area protected by Rule 13-2 will not be a breach of Rule 13-2 unless it creates such a potential advantage for the player in his play.

Examples of changes that are unlikely to create such a potential advantage are if a player:

- repairs a small pitch-mark on his line of play five yards in front of his ball prior to making a 150-yard approach shot from through the green;
- accidentally knocks down several leaves from a tree in his area of intended swing with a practice swing, but there are still so many leaves or branches remaining that the area of intended swing has not been materially affected; or
- whose ball lies in thick rough 180 yards from the green, walks forward and pulls strands of grass on his line of play and tosses them in the air to determine the direction of the wind.

Examples of changes that are likely to create such a potential advantage are if a player:

- repairs a pitch-mark through the green five yards in front of his ball and on his line of play prior to making a stroke from off the putting green that might be affected by the pitch-mark (e.g., a putt or a low-running shot);
- accidentally knocks down a single leaf from a tree in his area of intended swing with a practice swing, but, as this was one of very few leaves that might either interfere with his swing or fall and thereby distract him, the area of intended swing has been materially affected; or
- pulls strands of grass from rough a few inches behind his ball to test the wind, but thereby reduces a potential distraction for the player, or resistance to his club, in the area of his intended swing.

The determination as to whether a player has gained a potential advantage from his actions is made by reference to the situation immediately prior to his stroke. If there is a reasonable possibility that the player's action has created a potential advantage, the player is in breach of Rule 13-2. (New)

13-2/1
Explanation of "Fairly Taking His Stance"

Q. Rule 13-2 states that a player must not improve the position or lie of his ball, the area of his intended stance or swing or his line of play or a reasonable extension of that line beyond the hole by moving, bending or breaking anything growing or fixed (including immovable obstructions and objects defining out of bounds). An exception permits a player to do so in "fairly taking his stance." What is the significance of "fairly"?

A. Without "fairly," the exception would permit improvement of position or lie, area of intended stance or swing or line of play by anything that could be said to be taking a stance. The use of "fairly" is intended to limit the player to what is reasonably necessary to take a stance for the selected stroke without unduly improving the position of the ball, his lie, area of intended stance or swing or line of play. Thus, in taking his stance for the selected stroke, the player should select the least intrusive course of action which results in the minimum improvement in the position or lie of the ball, area of intended stance or swing or line of play. The player is not entitled to a normal stance or swing. He must accommodate the situation in which the ball is found and take a stance as normal as the circumstances permit. What is fair must be determined in the light of all the circumstances.

Examples of actions which do constitute fairly taking a stance are:
- backing into a branch or young sapling if that is the only way to take a stance for the selected stroke, even if this causes the branch to move out of the way or the sapling to bend or break.
- bending a branch of a tree with the hands in order to get under the tree to play a ball.

Examples of actions which do not constitute fairly taking a stance are:
- deliberately moving, bending or breaking branches with the hands, a leg or the body to get them out of the way of the backswing or stroke.
- standing on a branch to prevent it interfering with the backswing or stroke.
- hooking one branch on another or braiding two weeds for the same purpose.
- bending with a hand a branch obscuring the ball after the stance has been taken.
- bending an interfering branch with the hands, a leg or the body in taking a stance when the stance could have been taken without bending the branch.

13-2/1.1
Player Attempts to Take Stance Fairly But Improves Line of Play by Moving Interfering Growing Object

Q. A player's ball lies under the branch of a tree. In attempting to take his stance fairly, the player improves his line of play by moving the branch with his body. Before playing, he realizes he could have taken his stance without moving the branch. He abandons his stance and the branch returns to its original position or is returned to its original position by the player. The player then approaches the ball from a different direction, takes his stance without disturbing the branch and makes his stroke. What is the ruling?

A. There is no penalty. When fairly taking his stance the player is required to take his stance in the least intrusive manner that results in the minimum improvement in the position or lie of the ball, area of intended stance or swing or line of play. However, as the branch moved as a result of the player's attempt to take his stance fairly and was returned to its original position before the stroke was made, there is no penalty. Any doubt as to whether the branch returned to its original position should be resolved against the player.

The same principle would apply to fixed artificial objects (e.g., a boundary stake) if the position or lie of the ball, area of intended stance or swing or line of play is improved as a result of the player's attempt to take his stance fairly but the object is returned to its original position before the player makes a stroke.

Related Decisions:
- 13-2/17 Removal of Boundary Stake Interfering with Swing.
- 13-2/25 Player Removes Boundary Post on Line of Play But Replaces It Before Playing.

13-2/1.5
Player Allowed to Play in Any Direction in "Fairly Taking His Stance"

Q. Decision 13-2/1 clarifies what is meant by a player "fairly taking his stance" and states that a player is not entitled to a normal stance or swing and he must accommodate the situation in which the ball is found. Does the requirement to fairly take a stance restrict the player in the stroke or direction of play he adopts?

A. No. It is a matter for the player to decide on the stroke and direction of play he wishes to adopt and he is entitled to fairly take his stance for that stroke and direction of play.

13-2/1.7
Player Having Fairly Taken Stance Changes Direction of Play

Q. A player's ball lies under a tree. The player fairly takes his stance by backing into the branches of the tree. He then decides to adopt a different direction of play and fairly takes his stance for a second time by backing into the branches of the tree from a different angle. Is this permissible?

A. Yes. A player may change his intended direction of play and re-take his stance with respect to the new stroke. However, if the taking of the original stance improved the position or lie of his ball, the area of his new stance or swing or line of play for the new stroke beyond what occurred in fairly taking the stance for the second time, he is in breach of Rule 13-2.

Related Decisions:
- 13-2/14 Breaking Branch Interfering with Backswing on Teeing Ground.
- 13-2/24 Area of Originally Intended Swing Improved by Breaking Branch; Area of Swing Finally Used Not Affected by Branch.

13-2/2
Player Who Misses Tee Shot Presses Down Irregularities Before Next Stroke

Q. In playing a tee shot A misses the ball. Before playing his next stroke, A presses down turf behind the ball. Is this permissible, since the ball is in play?

A. Yes. Rule 13-2 permits eliminating irregularities of surface on the teeing ground, whether or not the ball is in play.

13-2/3
Breaking Off Grass Behind Ball on Teeing Ground

Q. Under Rule 13-2, it is permissible to eliminate irregularities of surface on the teeing ground. Is it also permissible to break off or pull out grass growing behind a ball on the teeing ground?

A. Yes.

13-2/4
Greenkeeping Staff Member Rakes Bunker When Player's Ball Lies Therein

Q. If a member of the greenkeeping staff rakes a bunker when the player's ball lies therein and the raking improves the lie of the ball or the line of play, is the player penalized under Rule 13-2?

A. If the staff member raked the bunker on the instructions, or with the sanction, of the player, the player would incur a penalty. Otherwise, there would be no penalty.

Related Decisions:
- 13-2/15.5 Position of Ball Worsened When Obstruction Removed; Player Replaces Obstruction.
- 20-1/15.5 Lie Altered by Act of Marking Position of Ball.
- 23-1/10 Removal of Loose Impediments Affecting Player's Play.

13-2/4.5
Divots Replaced in Area in Which Ball Is to Be Dropped

Q. A player makes a stroke. He replaces his divot and other divots nearby. He then discovers that his ball is lost or out of bounds. The player must now drop a ball as nearly as possible at the spot from which his previous stroke was made – Rule 27-1. In these circumstances, is the player in breach of Rule 13-2, which prohibits improving the area in which a ball is to be dropped by eliminating irregularities of surface by replacing a divot?

A. No. When the player replaced the divots, he was unaware that he would be required to drop a ball in the area. Therefore, in equity (Rule 1-4), he is not penalized.

However, if the player wished to play a provisional ball because he thought his original ball might be lost outside a water hazard or out of bounds, he would be prohibited from replacing his or other divots in the area where he would be dropping the provisional ball.

13-2/5
Replacing or Removing Undetached Divot

Q. A player's ball comes to rest in front of a divot which is folded over but not completely detached. The divot interferes with his backswing. May the player replace or remove the divot before playing?

A. No. A divot which is not completely detached is not a loose impediment. It is something fixed and therefore its removal or replacement would be a breach of Rule 13-2 as the lie and area of intended swing would be improved.

13-2/6
Replacing Divot in Divot Hole on Line of Play

Q. A player's ball comes to rest close to the putting green and he wishes to use his putter for his next stroke. However, there is a divot hole just in front of his ball on his line of play. May the player replace the divot before playing his next stroke?

A. No. Rule 13-2 prohibits a player from improving his line of play by eliminating an irregularity of surface.

13-2/7
When Divot Replaced

Q. Under Rule 13-2 a player may not remove or press down a replaced divot. When is a divot considered replaced?

A. When substantially all of it, with the roots downwards, lies in a divot hole. The hole need not be the one from which the divot was extracted.

13-2/8
Player's Lie or Line of Play Affected by Pitch-Mark Made by Partner's, Opponent's or Fellow-Competitor's Ball

Q. A player's lie or line of play through the green is affected by a pitch-mark made by his partner's, his opponent's or a fellow-competitor's ball. Is the player entitled to relief?

A. If the pitch-mark was there before the player's ball came to rest, he is not entitled to relief without penalty.

If the pitch-mark was created after the player's ball came to rest, in equity (Rule 1-4), he may repair the pitch-mark. A player is entitled to the lie which his stroke gave him.

13-2/8.5
Player's Lie Affected by Sand from Partner's, Opponent's or Fellow-Competitor's Stroke from Bunker

Q. A's ball is on the apron between the green and a bunker. A's partner, opponent or fellow-competitor (B) plays from the bunker and deposits sand on and around A's ball. Is A entitled to any relief?

A. Yes. A is entitled to the lie and line of play he had when his ball came to rest. Accordingly, in equity (Rule 1-4), he is entitled to remove the sand deposited by B's stroke and lift his ball and clean it, without penalty.

13-2/8.7
Player's Area of Intended Stance Affected by Another Player's Stroke

Q. The balls of A and B lie near each other through the green. A plays and in doing so affects B's area of intended stance (e.g., by creating a divot hole). What is the ruling?

A. B may play the ball as it lies. In addition, if the original area of intended stance could be easily restored, in equity (Rule 1-4), the area of intended stance may be restored as nearly as possible, without penalty.

If the original area of intended stance could not be easily restored, in equity (Rule 1-4), the player may place his ball, without penalty, on the nearest spot within one club-length of the original lie that provides the most similar lie and area of intended stance to the original lie and area of intended stance. This spot must not be nearer the hole and must not be in a hazard.

Decisions related to 13-2/8 through 13-2/8.7: See "Equity: player entitled to lie, line of play and stance when ball comes to rest after stroke" in the Index.

13-2/9
Lie Through the Green Improved When Sand Behind Ball Removed by Backswing

Q. A player's ball lies in a sandy area through the green and there is a mound of sand a few inches behind his ball. The player makes his stroke and in the process he removes the mound of sand with the clubhead on his backswing, improving his lie. Is the player subject to penalty?

A. No, provided that he did not ground his club other than lightly and that he took a normal backswing.

Related Decisions:
- 13-2/12 Player Presses Down Sand Behind Ball in Grounding Club.
- 13-4/31 Touching Sand in Bunker During Backswing.

13-2/10
Pitch-Mark in Dropping Area Repaired Before Ball Dropped

Q. Through the green, a player's ball was embedded in its own pitch-mark in a closely mown area. He lifted the ball under Rule 25-2 but, before dropping it, repaired the pitch-mark. Is such repair permissible?

A. No. The player was in breach of Rule 13-2 when he improved the area in which his ball was to be dropped by eliminating an irregularity of surface.

Related Decisions:
- 13-2/8 Player's Lie or Line of Play Affected by Pitch-Mark Made by Partner's, Opponent's or Fellow-Competitor's Ball.
- 13-2/21 Area of Intended Swing Improved by Repairing Pitch-Mark Made by Ball on Previous Stroke.

13-2/11
Removing Sand or Loose Soil from Dropping Area

Q. Through the green, may a player remove or brush away sand or loose soil from the area in which he is preparing to drop a ball?

A. No. Rule 13-2 prohibits improving the area in which a ball is to be dropped by removing sand or loose soil. Sand and loose soil are loose impediments only on the putting green.

13-2/12
Player Presses Down Sand Behind Ball in Grounding Club

Q. In addressing his ball through the green, a player grounded his club on sand behind the ball and in so doing pressed down the sand, thereby improving the lie of the ball. What is the ruling?

A. Except in a hazard, Rule 13-2 permits a player to ground his club lightly behind the ball. If the club was grounded only lightly, there is no breach of Rule 13-2 or any other Rule. However, if the club was pressed on the ground, the player was in breach of Rule 13-2.

Related Decisions:
- 13-2/9 Lie Through the Green Improved When Sand Behind Ball Removed by Backswing.
- 13-4/31 Touching Sand in Bunker During Backswing.

13-2/13
Bending Grass in Removal of Loose Impediments

Q. A player whose ball was in long grass rolled a stone away from the ball, pressing down some of the long grass in the process. Was he in breach of Rule 13-2?

A. Yes, if the pressing down of the grass improved the position or lie of his ball, the area of his intended swing or his line of play.

Related Decisions:
- 13-2/26 Natural Object Interfering with Swing Moved to Determine Whether It Is Loose.
- 23-1/4 Breaking Off Part of Large Loose Impediment.

13-2/14
Breaking Branch Interfering with Backswing on Teeing Ground

Q. On the teeing ground, a player broke off a branch of a tree which was interfering with his swing. The player maintained that such action was not a breach of Rule 13-2 because his ball was not yet in play. Was the player correct?

A. No. The player was in breach of Rule 13-2 for improving the area of his intended swing. Although Rule 13-2 allows a player to eliminate irregularities of surface on the teeing ground, it does not allow him to break a branch interfering with his swing. The penalty would apply even if the player, before playing his next stroke, re-teed elsewhere on the teeing ground – see Decision 13-2/24.

Related Decision:
- 13-2/1.7 Player Having Fairly Taken Stance Changes Direction of Play.

13-2/14.5
Branch Broken on Backswing and Swing Discontinued

Q. A player's ball lies under a tree. The player fairly takes his stance and starts his backswing with the intention of making a stroke. Near the top of his backswing his club strikes a branch and breaks it. At that point he discontinues his swing. The breaking of the branch has resulted in an improvement to the area of the player's intended swing.

Rule 13-2 states in part: "... a player must not improve ... the area of his intended stance or swing ... except ... in making a stroke or the backward movement of his club for a stroke." Is the player exempt from penalty under this exception?

A. No, because the swing was discontinued, the backward movement of the club was not in fact the backward movement for a stroke. (Revised)

13-2/15
Area of Intended Swing Improved by Removing Immovable Obstruction

Q. A player's swing is interfered with by an immovable obstruction. The player and his caddie, with great effort, remove the obstruction. Is the player subject to penalty?

A. Yes, for a breach of Rule 13-2. An immovable obstruction is something fixed. Rule 13-2 prohibits a player from improving the area of his intended swing by moving anything fixed.

13-2/15.5
Position of Ball Worsened When Obstruction Removed; Player Replaces Obstruction

Q. A player's ball comes to rest near a tree. A branch of the tree is being held back by a rope installed for gallery control. The player removes the rope (movable obstruction). This releases the branch and worsens the position of the ball. The player then re-installs the rope which results in the branch being held back as before. Was the player in breach of Rule 13-2 when he re-installed the rope?

A. Yes.

If an outside agency had removed the rope without the player's authority or sanction, the player would be entitled to re-install the rope without penalty.

Related Decisions: See "Equity: player entitled to lie, line of play and stance when ball comes to rest after stroke" in the Index.

13-2/16
Stake Supporting Tree Broken in Attempt to Remove It

Q. A stake supporting a young tree interferes with a player's stroke. He tries to remove it, but it cannot readily be removed and it breaks. As a result of the stake being broken, it no longer interferes with the player's stroke. What is the ruling?

A. The player was in breach of Rule 13-2 for breaking the stake. As the stake was not readily removable, it was an immovable obstruction and relief could have been taken, without penalty, under Rule 24-2b. (Revised)

13-2/17
Removal of Boundary Stake Interfering with Swing

Q. A player removes a stake defining out of bounds which interferes with his swing. Is this permissible?

A. No. Objects defining out of bounds are fixed. Improving the position of a ball by moving anything fixed is a breach of Rule 13-2.

Related Decisions:
- 13-2/1.1 Player Attempts to Take Stance Fairly But Improves Line of Play by Moving Interfering Growing Object.
- 13-2/25 Player Removes Boundary Post on Line of Play But Replaces It Before Playing.

13-2/18
Improving Position of Ball by Bending Boundary Fence

Q. Part of a boundary fence is bowed towards the course so that it is inside the out of bounds line formed by the fence posts. A player's ball comes to rest against this part of the fence. Decision 24/4 states that the player is not entitled to drop the ball away from the fence under Rule 24-2b. May the player push back the bowed section of the fence to obtain a measure of relief?

A. No. Such action would be a breach of Rule 13-2, which prohibits improving the position or lie of his ball or the area of his intended stance or swing by moving or bending anything fixed (including objects defining out of bounds).

Related Decision:
- 27/18 Gate in Boundary Fence.

13-2/19
Improving Area of Intended Swing by Moving Growing or Fixed Object Situated Out of Bounds

Q. A young tree or a fixed artificial object situated out of bounds interferes with a player's swing. May the player move, bend or break the tree or fixed artificial object without penalty?

A. No. Such action would be a breach of Rule 13-2.

13-2/20
Part of Fence Off Course Leans Across Boundary and Interferes with Swing

Q. Part of a fence which is beyond white stakes defining out of bounds, and therefore not a boundary fence, leans onto the course and interferes with a player's swing. May the player push the fence back into an upright position or treat it as an obstruction?

A. Rule 13-2 prohibits improving the position of the ball by moving anything fixed, even if such thing is off the course. Therefore, the player may not push the fence back. However, that part of the fence leaning onto the course is an immovable obstruction and the player is entitled to relief under Rule 24-2b.

Decision related to 13-2/19 and 13-2/20:
- 24-2b/21 Interference by Immovable Artificial Object Situated Out of Bounds.

13-2/21
Area of Intended Swing Improved by Repairing Pitch-Mark Made by Ball on Previous Stroke

Q. A pitch-mark made by the ball as a result of the previous stroke interferes with a player's backswing. Before playing his next stroke, the player steps on the pitch-mark, improving the area of his intended swing. Is this permissible?

A. No. The player was in breach of Rule 13-2 which prohibits improving the area of the intended swing by eliminating irregularities of surface.

Related Decisions:
• 13-2/8 Player's Lie or Line of Play Affected by Pitch-Mark Made by Partner's, Opponent's or Fellow-Competitor's Ball.
• 13-2/10 Pitch-Mark in Dropping Area Repaired Before Ball Dropped.

13-2/22 (Reserved)

13-2/23
Shaking Water from Tree Branch Interfering with Backswing

Q. After heavy rain, a player plays a stroke that comes to rest under a tree. A branch of the tree interferes with the player's backswing. Before playing his next stroke, the player shakes the water off this branch in order to eliminate the possibility of dislodged water distracting him. Is this a breach of Rule 13-2?

A. Yes. In moving the branch, the player removed water which could have caused a distraction and thereby improved the area of his intended swing in breach of Rule 13-2.

13-2/24
Area of Originally Intended Swing Improved by Breaking Branch; Area of Swing Finally Used Not Affected by Branch

Q. A player, intending to play in a certain direction, took a practice backswing for a stroke in that direction and broke a branch impeding his backswing. The player then decided to play in a different direction. The area of his intended swing for a stroke in this new direction was not improved by the breaking of the branch. In such circumstances, would the player incur a penalty under Rule 13-2?

A. Yes. The player was in breach of Rule 13-2 as soon as he improved the area of the originally intended swing. The penalty is not avoided if he subsequently plays in another direction, even if the breaking of the branch had no effect on the area of the swing for a stroke in the new direction.

Related Decisions:
• 13-2/1.7 Player Having Fairly Taken Stance Changes Direction of Play.
• 13-2/14 Breaking Branch Interfering with Backswing on Teeing Ground.

13-2/25
Player Removes Boundary Post on Line of Play But Replaces It Before Playing

Q. A player removes a post defining out of bounds on his line of play. He realizes he has made a mistake and replaces it before playing his next stroke. What is the ruling?

A. The player was in breach of Rule 13-2 the moment he moved the post and there was nothing he could do to avoid the penalty. The replacement of the post before the next stroke was irrelevant.

Related Decisions:
- 13-2/1.1 Player Attempts to Take Stance Fairly But Improves Line of Play by Moving Interfering Growing Object.
- 13-2/17 Removal of Boundary Stake Interfering with Swing.

13-2/26
Natural Object Interfering with Swing Moved to Determine Whether It Is Loose

Q. A player cannot determine whether a long blade of grass, a twig, a tumbleweed or some similar natural object interfering with his swing through the green is loose or is attached. The player moves the object to the extent necessary to make a determination and discovers that the object is attached. What is the ruling?

A. A player is entitled to move a natural object for the specific purpose of determining whether the object is loose, provided that if the object is found not to be loose, (1) it has not become detached and (2) it is returned to its original position before the next stroke if failure to do so would result in a breach of Rule 13-2.

Except as otherwise permitted in Rule 13-2 (e.g., in fairly taking the stance), if a player moves a natural object other than to determine whether it is loose and it is found to be attached, the player cannot avoid a breach of Rule 13-2 by returning the object to its original position.

Related Decisions:
- 13-2/13 Bending Grass in Removal of Loose Impediments.
- 16-1a/11 Raised Tuft of Grass on Line of Putt Brushed to Determine Whether It Is Loose.
- 23-1/4 Breaking Off Part of Large Loose Impediment.

13-2/27
Probing Near Ball for Tree Roots

Q. A player's ball comes to rest through the green in such a position that he believes tree roots or rocks may be just below the surface of the ground. May he, without penalty, probe the area around his ball with a tee or the like to see if his club would strike a root or a rock in the course of making a stroke?

A. Yes, provided the lie of the ball, area of intended stance or swing or the line of play is not improved (Rule 13-2) and the ball is not moved (Rule 18-2). The same principle would apply if the player wishes to probe to determine the presence of an immovable obstruction.

13-2/28
Smoothing Irregularities in Bunker Situated Between Ball and Hole

Q. There is a bunker between A's ball and the hole. Before playing, A smoothes footprints and other irregularities in the bunker on his line of play. Was A in breach of Rule 13-2?

A. Yes, such action would improve the line of play, contrary to Rule 13-2.

Related Decision:
• 13-4/37.5 Player Smoothes Irregularities in Bunker After Playing Out Backwards; Smoothed Area on Line of Play.

13-2/29
Worsening and Then Restoring Line of Play

Q. There is a bunker between a player's ball and the hole. The player walks through the bunker, for example, to remove a rake on his line of play or determine the distance to the hole. On his way back to the ball, he smoothes the footprints he made, restoring his line of play to its original condition. Is such smoothing permissible?

A. No. Although Exception 2 to Rule 13-4 permits the player to smooth sand or soil in a hazard at any time for the sole purpose of caring for the course, he may not do so if it would breach Rule 13-2 with respect to his next stroke.

If a player worsens the lie of his ball, the area of his intended stance or swing, his line of play or a reasonable extension of that line beyond the hole, or the area in which he is to drop or place a ball, he is not entitled to restore that area to its original condition. If he does so, he is in breach of Rule 13-2 and incurs a penalty of loss of hole in match play or two strokes in stroke play (but see Decision 13-2/29.3). (Revised)

Related Decisions:
• 13-4/10 Referee Enters a Bunker; Whether Player May Smooth Footprints.
• 13-4/11 Smoothing Footprints Made in Search for Ball in Bunker Before Playing Stroke from Bunker.

13-2/29.3
Creating Footprints in Bunker on Line of Play When Required to Enter Bunker to Retrieve Ball

Q. With reference to Decision 13-2/29, would a player be prohibited from smoothing footprints if he had been required to enter the bunker to retrieve a ball (e.g., a ball that had rolled into the bunker after having been dropped)?

A. No. In such circumstances, the player is entitled to restore the bunker to the condition it was in before he entered it.

13-2/29.5
Extension of Line of Play Affected When Opponent or Fellow-Competitor Creates Footprints in Bunker

Q. A's ball lies behind the green. The ball of his opponent or fellow-competitor (B) lies in a bunker in front of the green, which is on an extension of A's line of play.

It is A's turn to play but before he does so, B walks into the bunker to assess his next stroke, thereby creating footprints. A believes that his ball might come to rest in the bunker. Is A entitled to have the bunker restored to the condition which existed when A's ball came to rest?

A. Yes. In equity (Rule 1-4) A may have the bunker restored to its former condition because the footprints were created by B after A's ball came to rest. The bunker may be restored by anyone.

Decisions related to 13-2/29.3 and 13-2/29.5: See "Equity: player entitled to lie, line of play and stance when ball comes to rest after stroke" in the Index.

13-2/30
Testing Condition of Bunker Before Deciding Whether to Play Through It

Q. A player's ball lies behind a bunker. May he test the condition of the bunker to determine whether it is feasible to putt through it?

A. The Rules do not prohibit a player from testing the condition of a hazard except when his ball lies in or touches the hazard – see Rule 13-4. However, if such testing improved the line of play, the player would be in breach of Rule 13-2.

13-2/31
Ball Outside Bunker; Stone in Bunker on Line of Play Pressed Down or Removed

Q. A player's ball is lying behind a bunker and he decides to putt through the bunker. There is a small stone (loose impediment) in the bunker on his line of play. May he push the stone down into the sand or remove it?

A. Sand may not be pressed down if the act would improve the line of play (Rule 13-2). However, Rule 23-1 permits the removal of a loose impediment in a hazard when the ball is not lying in the hazard.

13-2/32
Improving Line of Play by Removing Stone from Wall

Q. A stone wall on the course is on A's line of play. A removes a stone from the top of the wall. Is this permissible?

A. No. The wall as a whole does not meet the definition of a movable obstruction and the individual stones are intended not to be moved. Therefore, the wall is an immovable obstruction and all parts of the wall are deemed to be fixed. In removing part of an immovable obstruction, A was in breach of Rule 13-2. The same ruling would apply if the wall had been declared an integral part of the course. (Revised)

Related Decisions:
• 24-2b/14 Window of Clubhouse Opened and Ball Played Through Window.
• 24-2b/15 Opening Barn Doors to Play Shot Through Barn.
• 24-2b/15.3 Status of Movable Part of Drainage Hose.
• 24-2b/15.5 Door of Building In Open or Closed Position.

13-2/33
Outside Agency Removes Immovable Obstruction on Player's Line of Play

Q. A stake supporting a young tree has been deemed an immovable obstruction by the Committee. A player's ball comes to rest in such a position that the stake intervenes on his line of play but does not interfere with his swing or stance. At that point, an outside agency removes the stake. What is the ruling?

A. If the player allowed the outside agency to remove the stake, the player loses the hole in match play or incurs a penalty of two strokes in stroke play for a breach of Rule 13-2.

If the player did not know the stake had been removed, or if he knew it but was not in a position to prevent it, there is no penalty and the player may replace the stake but he is not required to do so.

Related Decisions:
• 23-1/10 Removal of Loose Impediments Affecting Player's Play.
• 33-7/7 Competitor Seeks Help from Fellow-Competitor to Avoid Penalty.

13-2/34
Mopping Up Casual Water on Line of Play

Q. A pool of casual water was on the putting green between the player's ball, which was lying short of the green, and the hole. The player's caddie mopped up the water. Was this permissible?

A. No. When the player's caddie improved the line of play by removing the water, the player was in breach of Rule 13-2 and incurred a penalty of loss of hole in match play or two strokes in stroke play.

Related Decision:
• 16-1a/1 Brushing Aside or Mopping Up Casual Water on Line of Putt.

13-2/35
Removal of Dew or Frost

Except on the teeing ground, the removal of dew or frost from the area immediately behind or to the side of a player's ball, or from a player's line of play is a breach of Rule 13-2 if such removal creates a potential advantage (see Decision 13-2/0.5).

Additionally, the removal of dew or frost from the player's line of putt is not permitted. Such action is a breach of Rule 16-1a, unless it occurs incidentally to some other action permitted under the Rules, such as in removing loose impediments, repairing ball marks on the putting green or addressing the ball. (Revised)

Related Decision:
• 16-1a/3 Removing Dew or Frost from Line of Putt.

13-2/36
Competitor Sanctions Repair of Spike Damage on His Line of Putt by Fellow-Competitor

Q. If a fellow-competitor purposely improves the competitor's line of putt by repairing spike damage, the fellow-competitor is penalized under Rule 1-2. If the fellow-competitor's action is sanctioned, tacitly or otherwise, by the competitor, is the competitor also subject to penalty?

A. Yes, under Rule 13-2, for allowing his line of play to be improved.

Related Decisions:
• 16-1a/16 Spike Mark on Line of Putt Repaired During Repair of Ball Mark.
• 16-1c/4 Repair of Spike Mark Damage Around Hole.

13-2/37
Status of Moss or Creepers in Tree

Q. May moss, or a creeper, in a tree be removed if its removal would improve the line of play?

A. No. Trees are the natural habitat of some mosses and creepers. Accordingly, such plants growing in a tree may not be moved – see Rule 13-2.

Moss or a creeper which has fallen to the ground, and is not growing there, is a loose impediment and may be removed, without penalty – see Rule 23-1.

Other Decisions related to Rule 13-2: See "Improving Area of Intended Stance or Swing, Position or Lie of Ball, or Line of Play or Putt" in the Index

BUILDING STANCE

13-3/1
Standing on Mat on Teeing Ground

Q. Is it permissible for a player to carry a mat and stand on it when playing from the teeing ground?

A. No. The player would be building a stance in breach of Rule 13-3.

13-3/2
Making Stroke While Kneeling on Towel

Q. A player's ball was under a tree in such a position that he found it expedient to make his next stroke while on his knees. Because the ground was wet, the player placed a towel on the ground at the spot where his knees would be situated so that the knees of his trousers would not get wet. He then knelt on the towel and made the stroke. Was the player subject to penalty under Rule 13-3 for building a stance?

A. Yes. The same answer would apply if he had wrapped the towel around his knees and knelt on it to make the stroke.

It would have been permissible for the player to have put on waterproof trousers.

Related Decision:
• 1-2/10 Player Wraps Towel Around Self or Places Towel on Cactus Before Taking Stance.

13-3/3
Knocking Down Side of Bunker to Get Level Stance

Q. A player knocks down the side of a bunker with his foot in an effort to get his feet on the same level. Is this permissible?

A. No. Such action constitutes building a stance in breach of Rule 13-3.

13-3/4 (Reserved)

13-3/5
Player Builds Stance But Corrects Error Before Playing Stroke

Q. A player's ball is lodged in the branch of a tree just beyond his reach with a club. The player positions his motorized golf cart under the tree, stands on the cart and prepares to make a stroke at his ball. At that point, the player is advised that he is building a stance, contrary to Rule 13-3. If the player removes the cart and does not play a stroke while standing on it, does he nevertheless incur a penalty for a breach of Rule 13-3?

A. No. If a player builds a stance through use of an object such as a golf cart, stone or brick, he incurs no penalty if he removes the object before playing his next stroke.

However, if a player builds a stance through alteration of the ground on which he is taking his stance, it is impossible for him to restore the ground to its original state. Accordingly, a player who builds a stance in such a manner incurs the penalty prescribed in Rule 13-3, whether or not he attempts to restore the ground to its original state before playing his next stroke.

BALL IN HAZARD

13-4/0.5
Meaning of "Test the Condition of the Hazard" in Rule 13-4a

Q. What is meant by "test the condition of the hazard" in Rule 13-4a?

A. The term covers all actions by which the player could gain more information about the hazard than could be gained from taking his stance for the stroke to be made, bearing in mind that a certain amount of digging in with the feet in the sand or soil is permitted when taking the stance for a stroke.

Examples of actions that would not constitute testing the condition of the hazard include the following:
- digging in with the feet for a stance, including for a practice swing, anywhere in the hazard or in a similar hazard;
- placing an object, such as clubs or a rake, in the hazard;
- leaning on an object (other than a club) such as a rake while it is touching the ground in the hazard or water in a water hazard;
- touching the hazard with an object (other than a club) such as a towel (touching with a club would be a breach of Rule 13-4b); or
- marking the position of the ball with a tee or otherwise when proceeding under a Rule.

Examples of actions that would constitute testing the condition of the hazard in breach of Rule 13-4a include the following:
- digging in with the feet in excess of what would be done for a stance for a stroke or a practice swing;
- filling in footprints from a previous stance (e.g., when changing stance to make a different type of stroke);
- intentionally sticking an object, such as a rake, into sand or soil in the hazard or water in a water hazard (but see Rule 12-1);
- smoothing a bunker with a rake, a club or otherwise (but see Exception 2 to Rule 13-4);
- kicking the ground in the hazard or water in a water hazard; or
- touching the sand with a club when making a practice swing in the hazard or in a similar hazard (but see Exception 3 to Rule 13-4).

13-4/1
Touching Sand in Bunker When Ball Lies Outside Bunker

Q. A ball lies just outside a bunker. The player takes his stance in the bunker. May the player ground his club on the sand in the bunker or touch the sand during his backswing?

A. Yes. Since the ball was not in or touching the bunker, Rule 13-4 does not apply. However, the player may ground his club only lightly – see Rule 13-2.

Related Decision:
• 13-4/29 Grounding Club Outside Water Hazard When Playing Stroke at Ball in Hazard.

13-4/2
Leaning on Club in Hazard While Waiting to Play

Q. A, whose ball lies in a hazard, casually leans on his club in the hazard while waiting for B to play. What is the ruling?

A. A was in breach of Rule 13-4b for touching the ground in the hazard with his club before making a stroke. The Exceptions to Rule 13-4 do not apply.

13-4/3
Touching Ground in Hazard with Several Practice Swings

Q. In stroke play, a competitor in ignorance of the Rules took several practice swings in a hazard, touching the ground each time. What is the penalty?

A. Two strokes for a breach of Rule 13-4.

Related Decisions:
• 1-4/13 Player Advised of Breach of Rule (making practice swing and touching ground in hazard); Player Breaches Same Rule Prior to Stroke.
• 13-4/28 Grounding Club, Moving Loose Impediments and Improving Area of Intended Swing in Hazard.

Other Decisions related to whether multiple penalties apply: See "Multiple Penalty Situations" in the Index.

13-4/3.5
Player Uses Cane or Club to Enter or Leave Hazard When Ball Lies in Hazard

Q. A player, to prevent falling, uses a cane or club to enter or leave a hazard when his ball lies in the hazard. Is the player in breach of Rule 13-4?

A. No, provided nothing is done which constitutes testing the condition of the hazard or improves the lie of the ball – see Exception 1 to Rule 13-4.

13-4/4
Touching Grass with Club During Practice Swing in Hazard

Q. A player takes a practice swing in a water hazard without grounding his club, but his club touches some long grass. Is there a penalty?

A. No – see Note to Rule 13-4. However, the player must ensure that his actions do not breach Rule 13-2 or constitute testing the condition of the hazard.

Related Decisions:
• 13-4/8 When Club Touches Ground in Grass in Water Hazard.
• 18-2b/5 Ball Moves When Club Rested on Grass Immediately Behind Ball.

13-4/5
Touching Mound Made by Burrowing Animal with Backswing in Bunker

Q. A player's ball and a mound made by a burrowing animal are in a bunker. The mound interferes with the player's backswing, but the player elects not to take relief under Rule 25-1b(ii). During his backswing, the player's club touches the mound. Is the player in breach of Rule 13-4?

A. Yes. Rule 13-4 prohibits touching the ground in a hazard with a club before making a stroke, which is the forward movement of the club. In a hazard, a mound made by a burrowing animal is ground in the hazard.

Related Decision:
• 25-1b/18 Crawfish Mound Interferes with Stance or Swing.

13-4/6
Touching Solidly Embedded Stone in Hazard with Club During Backswing

Q. A player's ball lies in a hazard. In making his backswing for the stroke, the player's club touches a solidly embedded stone in the hazard. Is the stone considered "ground in the hazard"?

A. Yes.

Related Decision:
• 13-4/13 Accidentally Moving Loose Impediment in Hazard.

13-4/7
Touching Casual Water in Bunker with Club

Q. A player's ball lies in casual water in a bunker. The player elects to play his ball as it lies and touches the casual water with his club prior to making the stroke. The player's club does not touch the sand in the bunker except in making the stroke. What is the ruling?

A. The player incurs no penalty as he did not touch the ground in the bunker with his club prior to making his stroke – see Rule 13-4b. (Revised)

13-4/8
When Club Touches Ground in Grass in Water Hazard

Q. If a player's ball lies in a water hazard, when is his club in tall grass considered to be touching the ground in the water hazard, in breach of Rule 13-4b?

A. When the grass is compressed to the point where it will support the weight of the club (i.e., when the club is grounded).

Related Decisions:
• 13-4/4 Touching Grass with Club During Practice Swing in Hazard.
• 18-2b/5 Ball Moves When Club Rested on Grass Immediately Behind Ball.

13-4/9
Player Creates and Smoothes Footprints in Bunker Prior to Making Stroke

Q. A player's ball lies in a bunker and a rake has been left in another part of the bunker. Prior to making his stroke in the bunker, the player retrieves the rake. Having lifted the rake, the player smoothes the footprints that he has just created, and some others in the process. What is the ruling?

A. There is no penalty provided the smoothing was done for the sole purpose of caring for the course and nothing was done to breach Rule 13-2 in relation to the player's next stroke (see Exception 2 to Rule 13-4).

If, however, a player is regularly creating and smoothing footprints close to his ball prior to making strokes from bunkers, it would be appropriate to question the player about the purpose of the smoothing. In such circumstances, the smoothing might be for the purpose of gaining knowledge of the condition of the bunker rather than being for the sole purpose of caring for the course. If so, the player would be in breach of Rule 13-4a for testing the condition of the hazard. (New)

13-4/9.5
Loose Impediment in Bunker Moved When Player Smoothes Sand in Bunker for Sole Purpose of Caring for Course

Q. A player's ball lies in a bunker. The player picks up a rake that is lying ten yards behind his ball and, solely for the purpose of caring for the course, smoothes his footprints as he walks towards his ball. While raking his footprints, he also moves a loose impediment in the bunker. Is the player in breach of Rule 13-4c?

A. When a player's ball lies in a bunker, Exception 2 to Rule 13-4 allows a player to smooth sand in the bunker for the sole purpose of caring for the course provided nothing is done to breach Rule 13-2 with respect to his next stroke. Therefore, there is no breach of Rule 13-4c provided that (a) the movement of the loose impediment is incidental to the act permitted by the Rules (i.e., the raking of the footprints), and (b) the lie of the ball, area of intended stance or swing or line of play is not improved by moving the loose impediment. The player is not required to replace the loose impediment so moved. (New)

13-4/10
Referee Enters Bunker; Whether Player May Smooth Footprints

Q. A player whose ball lies in a bunker asks for a ruling from a referee, who enters the bunker to make the ruling. After the ruling, may the footprints of the referee be smoothed?

A. Yes. Exception 2 to Rule 13-4 allows the player to smooth the bunker provided it is for the sole purpose of caring for the course and nothing is done to breach Rule 13-2 with respect to his next stroke. However, even if the area disturbed by the referee is an area covered by Rule 13-2 with respect to his next stroke, in equity (Rule 1-4), the player would be entitled to restore this area of the bunker to its original condition by raking or other means. The bunker may be restored by anyone. (Revised)

13-4/11
Smoothing Footprints Made in Search for Ball in Bunker Before Playing Stroke from Bunker

Q. A player searches for his ball in a bunker and in the process makes numerous footprints. He subsequently finds his ball in the bunker. Before playing his stroke, may the player or his caddie smooth the footprints?

A. Exception 2 to Rule 13-4 would allow the player to smooth the footprints provided it is done for the sole purpose of caring for the course and nothing is done to improve any area covered by Rule 13-2 with respect to his next stroke. Therefore, any footprints made that have worsened any area covered by Rule 13-2 with respect to his next stroke must not be smoothed. (Revised)

Decision related to 13-4/10 and 13-4/11:
• 13-2/29 Worsening and Then Restoring Line of Play.

13-4/12
Ball Touched Accidentally with Club in Hazard But Not Moved

Q. A player, in preparing to make a stroke at his ball that was lying in a bunker or was partially submerged in water in a water hazard, accidentally touches the ball with his club, but without moving it. Does this constitute touching the ground in a hazard or water in a water hazard in breach of Rule 13-4?

A. No. (Revised)

13-4/13
Accidentally Moving Loose Impediment in Hazard

Q. A player accidentally moves a loose impediment in a hazard. Does the player incur a penalty?

A. No, provided the loose impediment was not moved in making the backswing and the lie of the ball or area of the intended stance or swing was not improved.

Related Decision:
• 13-4/6 Touching Solidly Embedded Stone in Hazard with Club During Backswing.

13-4/13.5
Player Moves Loose Impediments When Approaching Ball in Hazard

Q. A player's ball lies in a bunker that is covered with many loose twigs and leaves. In approaching the ball and taking his stance, the player touches and moves loose impediments with his feet. Does he incur a penalty?

A. There is no penalty provided the lie of the ball or area of intended stance or swing is not improved.

13-4/14
Player Accidentally Kicks Pine Cone into Bunker and Picks It Up

Q. A player's ball went into a bunker. The player accidentally kicked a pine cone, and it rolled into the bunker. He picked up the pine cone which was not interfering with his stance or the area of his intended swing. Did he incur a penalty?

A. Yes. A pine cone is a loose impediment – see Definition of "Loose Impediments" – and may not be removed when both the impediment and the ball lie in a hazard (Rule 13-4c). By removing the pine cone from the bunker, the player incurred a penalty of loss of hole in match play or two strokes in stroke play for a breach of Rule 13-4c.

13-4/15
Ball in Hazard Moves When Loose Impediment Removed

Q. In stroke play, a competitor's ball is in a hazard. He removes a loose impediment in the hazard that causes his ball to move. What is the ruling?

A. As a single act resulted in two Rules being breached (Rule 13-4 and Rule 18-2a), in equity (Rule 1-4), a single penalty is applied. Therefore, the competitor incurs a two stroke penalty under Rule 13-4 and the ball must be replaced (Rule 18-2a). If the ball is not replaced before the competitor makes his next stroke, the failure to replace the ball is considered a separate act and he incurs an additional penalty of two strokes under Rule 18-2a.

Other Decisions related to whether multiple penalties apply: See "Multiple Penalty Situations" in the Index.

13-4/16
Removal of Loose Impediment in Water Hazard Covering Wrong Ball

Q. A player plays his ball into a water hazard. He finds a ball in the hazard and, in order to identify the ball, removes a loose impediment partially covering it. He discovers that the ball is not his ball. He searches for his ball but does not find it. He proceeds under Rule 26-1. Is the player subject to penalty under Rule 13-4 for removing the loose impediment?

A. No. Rule 12-1b permits the player to touch or remove loose impediments in a hazard in order to find or identify his ball that is believed to be covered by loose impediments.(Revised)

Related Decisions:
- 13-4/35.7 Player Deems Ball Unplayable in Bunker, Lifts Ball and Then Removes Loose Impediment from Bunker.
- 23-1/7 Loose Impediment Affecting Lie Moved When Ball Lifted.
- 23-1/8 Loose Impediments Affecting Lie Removed While Ball Lifted.

13-4/16.5
Flying Insect in Water Hazard

Q. A player's ball is in a water hazard. The player is being distracted by an insect (a loose impediment) flying in the hazard. May the player swat away the insect?

A. Although the margin of a water hazard extends vertically upwards such that the insect is in the hazard, the Rules do not contemplate such a case. Thus, in equity (Rule 1-4), the player may swat away the insect whether it be flying or on the player.

Related Decisions:
- 23-1/5 Removal of Insect on Ball.
- 23-1/5.5 Status of Insect on Ball in Bunker.
- 23-1/12 After Ball Addressed on Putting Green Ball Moved in Removal of Loose Impediment.

13-4/17
Loose Impediment Removed from Water Hazard; Player Then Decides Not to Play from Hazard

Q. A player whose ball was in a water hazard removed a loose impediment from the hazard. He then decided not to play from the hazard. He proceeded under Rule 26-1. Was the player absolved from the penalty incurred under Rule 13-4 for removing the loose impediment in view of the fact that he subsequently invoked Rule 26-1 and did not play his ball from the hazard?

A. No.

Related Decisions:
- 30-3f/1 Player Lifts Loose Impediment in Bunker When His Ball and Partner's Ball in Bunker.
- 31-8/1 Competitor Lifts Loose Impediment in Bunker When His Ball and Partner's Ball Are in Bunker.

13-4/18
Partner's, Opponent's or Fellow-Competitor's Divot Comes to Rest Near Player's Ball in Bunker

Q. A player's partner, opponent or fellow-competitor plays a stroke from near a bunker and the divot comes to rest near the player's ball lying in the bunker. May the divot be removed?

A. A player is entitled to the lie which his stroke gave him. Accordingly, in equity (Rule 1-4), the divot may be removed without penalty.

The same would apply if the player's ball was lying in a water hazard.

13-4/18.5
Pine Cone Falls from Tree and Comes to Rest Behind Ball Lying in Bunker

Q. A pine cone falls from a tree and comes to rest behind a ball which is lying in a bunker. Under the principle in Decision 13-4/18, may the player remove the pine cone without penalty?

A. No. The principle in Decision 13-4/18 is applied only in cases in which the lie of a ball has been altered as a result of an act by another player or caddie, or by a spectator or other animate outside agency. In this case, the lie was altered through natural causes.

13-4/19
Condition of Bunker Altered by First Player to Play from It

Q. The balls of A and B lie in the same bunker, with B's ball farther from the hole. B plays and his ball comes to rest nearer the hole than A's ball. Is A entitled to have the bunker restored to its original condition?

A. Yes. In addition to Exception 2 to Rule 13-4, which allows the player to smooth sand or soil in a hazard at any time for the sole purpose of caring for the course, A would be entitled, in equity (Rule 1-4), to restore the bunker to its original condition by raking or other means, even if this involves an area covered by Rule 13-2 with respect to his next stroke. The bunker may be restored by anyone. (Revised)

Decisions related to 13-4/18 through 13-4/19: See "Equity: player entitled to lie, line of play and stance when ball comes to rest after stroke" in the Index.

13-4/20 (Reserved)

13-4/21
Rake Thrown into Bunker Before Stroke

Q. A player's ball lies in a bunker. He casually throws a rake into the bunker for use after his stroke. The rake does not move his ball or improve the lie of the ball. Does the player incur a penalty?

A. No. Placing a rake in a bunker is permissible. In this case, throwing the rake into the bunker was the equivalent of placing it.

If the rake had moved the ball, the player would incur a penalty of one stroke for causing his ball to move; and the ball would have to be replaced – Rule 18-2a.

13-4/22 (Reserved)

13-4/23 (Reserved)

13-4/24
Stance in Bunker Taken Without Club

Q. A player whose ball was in a bunker entered it without a club, dug in with his feet and simulated a stroke. He then left the bunker, got a club, dug in again with his feet at the same place and made a stroke.

The Committee asked the player why he had gone through this exercise. He replied that he had wanted to get the "feel" of the shot he was about to make and that the purpose of the simulated stroke was to determine which club to use and what kind of stroke to make. He stated that he was not testing the condition of the hazard or building a stance when he dug his feet in for the simulated stroke.

How should the Committee have ruled?

A. The Committee should have ruled that no penalty was incurred.

Rule 13-3 states: "A player is entitled to place his feet firmly in taking his stance."

The Definition of "Stance" states: "Taking the 'stance' consists in a player placing his feet in position for and preparatory to making a stroke."

On the first occasion, the player was "placing his feet in position for and preparatory to making a stroke," even though he had no club in his hands.

Related Decision:
• 13-4/0.5 Meaning of 'Test the Condition of the Hazard' in Rule 13-4a.

13-4/25 (Reserved)

13-4/26
Taking Stance in Bunker and Then Changing Clubs

Q. A player takes his stance in a bunker and firmly places his feet in the sand. He then leaves his position to change clubs and thereafter takes his stance a second time. Is the player considered to have tested the condition of the hazard, contrary to Rule 13-4?

A. No. Rule 13-3 allows a player to place his feet firmly in taking his stance in a bunker or elsewhere. There is nothing in the Rules to prohibit changing clubs or taking a stance twice in a bunker.

13-4/27 (Reserved)

13-4/28
Grounding Club, Moving Loose Impediments and Improving Area of Intended Swing in Hazard

Q. In stroke play, a competitor's ball is in a hazard. He takes a practice swing and in so doing moves loose impediments and touches the ground in the hazard. He also bends a shrub with his hand, improving the area of his intended swing. What is the penalty?

A. As a single act (i.e., the practice swing) resulted in two Rules being breached (Rule 13-4b and Rule 13-4c), in equity (Rule 1-4), a single penalty of two strokes is applied. However, the competitor also incurs a penalty of two strokes for improving the area of his intended swing by bending a shrub (Rule 13-2).

The practice swing and the bending of the shrub are different acts that resulted in the breach of two Rules and both penalties are applied giving a total penalty of four strokes.

Other Decisions related to whether multiple penalties apply: See "Multiple Penalty Situations" in the Index.

13-4/29
Grounding Club Outside Water Hazard When Playing Stroke at Ball in Hazard

Q. A player's ball touches a line defining the margin of a water hazard. So the ball is in the hazard. In addressing the ball for his next stroke, may the player's club be grounded outside the hazard?

A. Yes.

Related Decision:
• 13-4/1 Touching Sand in Bunker When Ball Lies Outside Bunker.

13-4/30
Grounding Club on Bridge in Water Hazard

Q. A player's ball lies on a bridge over a water hazard within the margins of the hazard when extended upwards. May the player ground his club?

A. Yes. A bridge is an obstruction. In a hazard, the club may touch an obstruction at address or in the backward movement for the stroke – see Note under Rule 13-4. Touching the bridge prior to address is also permissible, since an obstruction in a water hazard is not "ground in the hazard."

This applies even if the bridge has been declared an integral part of the course.

13-4/31
Touching Sand in Bunker During Backswing

Q. A player playing a shot in a bunker accidentally touched the sand when making his backswing. What is the ruling?

A. The player was in breach of Rule 13-4b when he touched the ground in the bunker with his club before making the stroke – see Definition of "Stroke."

Related Decisions:
- 13-2/9 Lie Through the Green Improved When Sand Behind Ball Removed by Backswing.
- 13-2/12 Player Presses Down Sand Behind Ball in Grounding Club.

13-4/32 (Reserved)

13-4/33
Bunker Covered by Leaves; Player Touches Leaves During Backswing

Q. A player hits a ball into a bunker which is covered by leaves (loose impediments). The player removes as many leaves as will enable him to see a part of the ball in accordance with Rule 12-1. If the player then touches some of the leaves on his backswing, is he in breach of the Rules?

A. Yes. If the player touches leaves on his backswing, he is in breach of Rule 13-4c which prohibits a player from touching a loose impediment in a hazard before making a stroke in the hazard. A stroke does not begin until after the completion of the player's backswing – see Definition of "Stroke."

If fallen leaves in bunkers seasonally create an abnormal problem, the Committee may make a Local Rule declaring accumulations of leaves in bunkers to be ground under repair. Rule 25-1b(ii) would then apply.

13-4/34
Touching Bare Earth Wall of Bunker on Backswing

Q. In playing from a bunker, a player touches a bare earth wall of the bunker with his club on his backswing. What is the ruling?

A. The player touched the ground in the hazard in breach of Rule 13-4b. The Note to Rule 13-4 permits a player's club to touch an obstruction (such as an artificial wall) on his backswing. However, an earth wall of a bunker is not an artificial wall.

13-4/35
Hitting Sand in Bunker with Club After Failing to Extricate Ball

Q. A made a stroke in a bunker and failed to get the ball out. He then swung his club into the sand, but his action did not affect his new lie in the bunker. However, since A had to make another stroke in the bunker, was he in breach of Rule 13-4?

A. Yes. None of the Exceptions under Rule 13-4 apply to A's action.

Related Decisions:
- 29/5 Hitting Sand in Bunker with Club After Failing to Extricate Ball; Foursome Match.
- 30-3f/2 Hitting Sand in Bunker with Club After Failing to Extricate Ball; Partner's Ball in Same Bunker.

13-4/35.5
Ball Played from Bunker onto Grass Bank; Player Hits Sand with Club; Ball Then Rolls Back into Bunker

Q. A player plays from a bunker and the ball lands on the grass bank of the bunker. Before the ball comes to rest, the player swings his club into the sand, after which the ball rolls back into the bunker.

Rule 13-4b prohibits touching the ground in a hazard with a club when the ball lies in the hazard. Does the player incur a penalty under this Rule even though the ball was outside the bunker when the club was swung into the sand?

A. No. However, if the club was still touching the sand when the ball rolled back into the bunker, a breach of Rule 13-4 occurred, and any doubt on this point should be resolved against the player.

13-4/35.7
Player Deems Ball Unplayable in Bunker, Lifts Ball and Then Removes Loose Impediment from Bunker

Q. A player's tee shot comes to rest in a bunker. He lifts his ball from the bunker after deeming it unplayable. Before selecting an option under Rule 28, he removes a loose impediment from the bunker. Since this action took place while his ball was lifted, i.e., it was not lying in the hazard, was the player in breach of Rule 13-4?

A. Yes. The prohibitions of Rule 13-4 apply when a ball is in a hazard or when a ball, having been lifted from a hazard, may be dropped or placed in the hazard. Under the unplayable ball Rule, two of the player's options require him to drop a ball in the bunker. The player would incur the penalty even if he subsequently elected to put a ball into play outside the bunker under Rule 28a. However, the player would not incur the penalty if, before removing the loose impediment, he had indicated that he would put a ball into play outside the bunker under Rule 28a and subsequently did so.

Related Decisions:
- 1-4/5 Removal of Obstruction in Hazard Would Move Loose Impediment.
- 13-4/16 Removal of Loose Impediment in Water Hazard Covering Wrong Ball.
- 23-1/7 Loose Impediment Affecting Lie Moved When Ball Lifted.
- 23-1/8 Loose Impediments Affecting Lie Removed While Ball Lifted.

13-4/35.8
Player Deems Ball Unplayable in Bunker, Announces His Intention to Proceed Under Rule 28a Outside Bunker and Then Rakes Bunker on New Line of Play

Q. A player's tee shot comes to rest in a bunker in front of the putting green. He lifts the ball after deeming it unplayable and announces his intention to proceed under Rule 28a. Before walking back to play from the teeing ground again, the player smoothes his footprints in the bunker, which are on his line of play from the teeing ground. He then plays from the teeing ground. What is the ruling?

A. In equity (Rule 1-4), and by analogy to Exception 2 to Rule 13-4, once a player has indicated he will proceed under a Rule that requires him to make his next stroke from outside the hazard, he may smooth sand or soil in the hazard without restriction.

The fact that the smoothing improved the player's line of play for his next stroke from the teeing ground is irrelevant as the right to smooth in these circumstances overrides any conflicting provisions in Rule 13-2.

However, if the player changed his mind and proceeded under Rule 28b or c, he would be in breach of Rule 13-4 if the smoothing of the bunker was not done for the sole purpose of caring for the course or resulted in any area covered by Rule 13-2 with respect to the next stroke being improved. (Revised)

13-4/36
Smoothing Irregularities in Bunker After Stroke But Before Ball Extricated

Q. A makes a stroke in a bunker but fails to extricate his ball from the bunker. He smoothes irregularities in the area where the stroke was made. The smoothing does not breach Rule 13-2 with respect to his next stroke. However, his opponent, B claims that the smoothing assisted A in his subsequent play of the hole because it constituted testing the consistency of the sand. Is B right?

A. No. In such circumstances Exception 2 to Rule 13-4 permits smoothing, provided nothing is done to breach Rule 13-2 with respect to the player's next stroke.

13-4/37
Ball Played from Bunker Is Out of Bounds or Lost; Player Tests Condition of Bunker or Smoothes Footprints Before Dropping Another Ball in Bunker

Q. A player plays from a bunker and his ball comes to rest out of bounds or is lost. He smoothes his footprints in the bunker at the place where he must drop a ball under Rule 27-1 or, before dropping a ball under Rule 27-1, he takes a few practice swings touching the sand in the bunker. Is the player in breach of Rule 13-4?

A. No. The prohibitions in Rule 13-4 apply only when the player's ball is in the hazard or when it has been lifted from a hazard and may be dropped or placed in the hazard. In this case, the player's ball has been played from the hazard rather than lifted.

Furthermore, Exception 2 under Rule 13-4 allows a player, after playing his ball out of a hazard, to smooth sand or soil in the hazard without restriction. This right overrides any conflicting provisions in other Rules, including Rule 13-2.

13-4/37.5
Player Smoothes Irregularities in Bunker After Playing Out Backwards; Smoothed Area on Line of Play

Q. A player plays out of a bunker backwards and smoothes his footprints. He then discovers that the smoothed area of the bunker is on his line of play. Is he in breach of Rule 13-2?

A. No. Exception 2 to Rule 13-4 allows a player, after playing his ball out of a hazard, to smooth sand in the hazard without restriction. This right overrides any conflicting provisions in other Rules, including Rule 13-2.

Related Decisions:
• 13-2/28 Smoothing Irregularities in Bunker Situated Between Ball and Hole.

- 13-2/29 Worsening and Then Restoring Line of Play (creating and then smoothing footprints in bunker on line of play).
- 13-2/29.3 Creating Footprints in Bunker on Line of Play When Required to Enter Bunker to Retrieve Ball.
- 13-4/10 Referee Enters Bunker; Whether Player May Smooth Footprints.

13-4/38
Sand Smoothed After Ball Played Out of Bunker; Ball Later Returns to Smoothed Area

Q. After playing his ball out of a greenside bunker, the player smoothes his footprints. He then discovers that his ball is in another bunker on the other side of the green. He plays out of the second bunker and the ball comes to rest in the smoothed area of the first bunker. What is the ruling?

A. No penalty was incurred. The player did not smooth his footprints in the first bunker while his ball still lay in that bunker – see Exception 2 to Rule 13-4.

If, however, the player failed to extricate his ball from the first bunker with his first stroke and had smoothed his footprints while his ball still lay in that bunker, he would have incurred a penalty if the act of smoothing his footprints had caused a breach of Rule 13-2 with respect to his next stroke.

13-4/39
Player Smoothes Irregularities in Bunker After Playing Out of Turn in Match Play; Opponent Then Recalls Stroke

Q. In a match between A and B, A's ball lay in a bunker near the green and B's ball was on the green. B's ball was farther from the hole but A played first. B recalled the stroke under Rule 10-1c. In the meantime A had raked his footprints. Did A incur a penalty?

A. If A's ball was outside the bunker when he raked his footprints, A incurred no penalty as he was permitted to rake the bunker without restriction – Exception 2 to Rule 13-4.

If A's ball still lay in the bunker then he would, ordinarily, be in breach of Rule 13-4 if his smoothing of the sand improved an area covered by Rule 13-2 with respect to his next stroke (see Exception 2 to Rule 13-4). However, when A raked the bunker, he was unaware that his stroke would be recalled; therefore, in equity (Rule 1-4), A incurs no penalty.

13-4/40
Player Cleans Clubhead in Water Hazard When Ball Lies in Hazard

Q. A player plays a stroke from within a water hazard but does not extricate the ball from the hazard. The player sees the ball land in deep water and it is clearly unreasonable for him to play a stroke at the ball from its new position. Before leaving the hazard, the player cleans mud off his clubhead by rinsing it in the water. Is the player in breach of Rule 13-4?

A. No, provided that there is no doubt or it is reasonable to assume from the player's actions or statements that he will play his next stroke from outside the hazard.

Other Decisions related to Rule 13-4: See "Bunker" and "Water Hazards" in the Index.

RULE 14

STRIKING THE BALL

DEFINITIONS

All defined terms are in *italics* and are listed alphabetically in the Definitions section – see pages 6–16.

14-1. BALL TO BE FAIRLY STRUCK AT

The ball must be fairly struck at with the head of the club and must not be pushed, scraped or spooned.

14-2. ASSISTANCE

a. Physical Assistance and Protection from Elements

A player must not make a *stroke* while accepting physical assistance or protection from the elements.

b. Positioning of Caddie or Partner Behind Ball

A player must not make a *stroke* with his *caddie*, his *partner* or his *partner's caddie* positioned on or close to an extension of the *line of play* or *line of putt* behind the ball.

Exception: There is no penalty if the player's *caddie*, his *partner* or his *partner's caddie* is inadvertently located on or close to an extension of the *line of play* or *line of putt* behind the ball.

PENALTY FOR BREACH OF RULE 14-1 or 14-2:

<u>Match play</u> – Loss of hole; <u>Stroke play</u> – Two strokes.

14-3. ARTIFICIAL DEVICES, UNUSUAL EQUIPMENT AND UNUSUAL USE OF EQUIPMENT

The USGA reserves the right, at any time, to change the *Rules* relating to artificial devices, unusual *equipment* and the unusual use of *equipment*, and to make or change the interpretations relating to these *Rules*.

A player in doubt as to whether use of an item would constitute a breach of Rule 14-3 should consult the USGA.

A manufacturer should submit to the USGA a sample of an item to be manufactured for a ruling as to whether its use during a *stipulated round* would cause a player to be in breach of Rule 14-3. The sample becomes the property of the USGA for reference purposes. If a manufacturer fails to submit a sample or, having submitted a sample, fails to await a ruling before manufacturing and/or marketing the item, the manufacturer assumes the risk of a ruling that use of the item would be contrary to the *Rules*.

Except as provided in the *Rules*, during a *stipulated round* the player must not use any artificial device or unusual *equipment* (see Appendix IV for detailed specifications and interpretations), or use any *equipment* in an unusual manner:

a. That might assist him in making a *stroke* or in his play; or

b. For the purpose of gauging or measuring distance or conditions that might affect his play; or

c. That might assist him in gripping the club, except that:

   (i) gloves may be worn provided that they are plain gloves;

   (ii) resin, powder and drying or moisturizing agents may be used; and

   (iii) a towel or handkerchief may be wrapped around the grip.

Exceptions:

1. A player is not in breach of this Rule if (a) the *equipment* or device is designed for or has the effect of alleviating a medical condition, (b) the player has a legitimate medical reason to use the *equipment* or device, and (c) the *Committee* is satisfied that its use does not give the player any undue advantage over other players.

2. A player is not in breach of this Rule if he uses *equipment* in a traditionally accepted manner.

PENALTY FOR BREACH OF RULE 14-3:
Disqualification.

Note: The *Committee* may make a Local Rule allowing players to use devices that measure or gauge distance only.

14-4. STRIKING THE BALL MORE THAN ONCE

If a player's club strikes the ball more than once in the course of a *stroke*, the player must count the *stroke* and add a *penalty stroke*, making two *strokes* in all.

14-5. PLAYING MOVING BALL

A player must not make a *stroke* at his ball while it is moving.

Exceptions:

• Ball falling off *tee* – Rule 11-3

• Striking the ball more than once – Rule 14-4

• Ball moving in water – Rule 14-6

When the ball begins to *move* only after the player has begun the *stroke* or the backward movement of his club for the *stroke*, he incurs no penalty under this Rule for playing a moving ball, but he is not exempt from any penalty under the following Rules:

• Ball at rest *moved* by player – Rule 18-2a

• Ball at rest moving after *address* – Rule 18-2b

(Ball purposely deflected or stopped by player, partner or caddie – see Rule 1-2)

14-6. BALL MOVING IN WATER

When a ball is moving in water in a *water hazard*, the player may, without penalty, make a *stroke*, but he must not delay making his *stroke* in order to allow the wind or current to improve the position of the ball. A ball moving in water in a *water hazard* may be lifted if the player elects to invoke Rule 26.

PENALTY FOR BREACH OF RULE 14-5 or 14-6:
<u>Match play</u> – Loss of hole; <u>Stroke play</u> – Two strokes.

14/1
Club Stopped on Downswing by Agency Other Than Player

Q. If a player starts his downswing and his clubhead is deflected or stopped by an agency other than himself, e.g., the branch of a tree, is he deemed to have made a stroke?

A. Yes.

14/1.5
Intent to Strike Ball Ceases During Downswing; Club Not Stopped But Path of Clubhead Altered to Avoid Striking Ball

Q. A player begins his downswing with the intention of striking the ball but decides during the downswing not to strike the ball. The player is unable to stop the club before it reaches the ball, but he is able to swing intentionally over the top of the ball. Is the player deemed to have made a stroke?

A. No. The player is considered to have checked his downswing voluntarily by altering the path of his downswing and missing the ball even though the swing carried the clubhead beyond the ball.

   If the player had not successfully checked his downswing (i.e., he had struck the ball), he is considered to have made a stroke.

   Any doubt regarding the player's intent must be resolved against the player.

14/2
Club Breaks During Backswing; Swing Completed

Q. The head of a player's club separated from the shaft during his backswing. The player completed the swing but missed the ball. Is the player deemed to have made a stroke?

A. No. A stroke is "the forward movement of the club …" A shaft by itself is not a club – see Rule 4-1a.

14/3
Clubhead Separates from Shaft on Downswing

Q. A player starts his downswing and the clubhead separates from the shaft. The player continues his swing but no contact is made with the ball. Did the player make a stroke?

A. Yes.

14/4
Club Breaks During Downswing; Swing Stopped Short of Ball; Clubhead Falls and Moves Ball

Q. The shaft of a player's club broke during his downswing. The player stopped his swing short of the ball, but the clubhead fell and moved the ball. What is the ruling?

A. The player did not make a stroke – see Definition of "Stroke."

If the ball was not in play, i.e., the incident involved a tee shot, no penalty was incurred, and a ball must be played from the teeing ground.

If the ball was in play, the player would incur a one-stroke penalty under Rule 18-2a or -2b and the ball must be replaced.

14/5
Club Breaks During Downswing; Swing Completed But Misses Ball; Clubhead Falls and Moves Ball

Q. The shaft of a player's club broke during his downswing. The player continued his swing and missed the ball. However, the clubhead fell and moved the ball. What is the ruling?

A. The stroke counts but the player incurs no penalty. The ball must be played as it lies.

14/6 (Reserved)

14/7
Striking at Tree Branch to Move Ball Lodged Higher in Branch

Q. A player's ball is lodged in a tree branch beyond the reach of a club. The player swings at a lower part of the branch with a club for the purpose of dislodging the ball, and the ball falls to the ground. Has the player made a stroke?

A. No, because the player did not strike at the ball – see Definition of "Stroke." The player incurred a one-stroke penalty under Rule 18-2a (Ball at Rest Moved by Player) and must replace the ball.

Since the spot where the ball lay is unreachable and the ball therefore cannot be replaced, the player must proceed under the unplayable ball Rule, incurring an additional penalty stroke – see Decisions 18-1/9 and 18-2a/29.

Other Decisions related to Striking the Ball: See "Stroke" in the Index.

14-1/1
Playing Stroke with Back of Clubhead

Q. May a player play a left-handed stroke with the back of the head of a right-handed club?

A. Yes. A player may play a stroke with any part of the clubhead, provided the ball is fairly struck at (Rule 14-1) and the club conforms with Rule 4-1.

14-1/2
Striking Ball with Billiard-Type Motion

Q. A player holed a short putt by squatting behind the ball (but not on an extension of the line of putt behind the ball) and striking the ball with the bottom of the clubhead, using a motion similar to that used in playing a shot in billiards or shuffleboard. Was the player in breach of Rule 14-1?

A. Yes. Such a manner of moving the ball constitutes a push in golf.

14-1/3
Putting with Wrong End of Putter

Q. A player misses a short putt and hastily holes the ball with the wrong (handle) end of his putter. What is the ruling?

A. The player incurs a penalty of loss of hole in match play or two strokes in stroke play for a breach of Rule 14-1, which requires that the ball be struck at with the head of the club. In stroke play, the stroke with the wrong end of the putter counts, and, since the ball was holed, the player had completed play of the hole.

14-1/4
Striking Ball with Half an Inch Backswing

Q. A player's ball lies close to an out of bounds fence, but there is room behind the ball to insert an iron club or a putter and leave a space of half an inch between the ball and the face of the club. If the player plays a stroke with such a limited backswing, is he in breach of Rule 14-1?

A. It is possible to strike a ball fairly with a half inch backswing. However, in most such cases the player would be pushing the ball, contrary to Rule 14-1. In the absence of strong evidence to the contrary, it should be ruled that the player has pushed the ball.

In order to strike the ball fairly, it must be swung at with the clubhead. If the ball is moved by any other method, it has been pushed, scraped or spooned.

If a ball is fairly struck at, there is only momentary contact between the clubhead and the ball or whatever intervenes between the clubhead and the ball.

14-1/5
Moving Ball Lying Against Fence by Striking Other Side of Fence

Q. A player's ball lies against a board at the base of an out of bounds fence. He swings a club from the out of bounds side of the fence against the board, i.e., swings at the ball with the board intervening between the club and the ball. The stroke moves the board which causes the ball to move away from the fence. Is such a stroke permissible?

A. Yes. The player fairly struck at the ball even though other material intervened between the club and the ball. The Definition of "Out of Bounds" allows a player to "stand out of bounds to play a ball lying within bounds."

14-1/6
Player Holds Club with Left Hand and Moves Ball by Striking Shaft with Other Hand

Q. A player addresses his ball lying in high grass on a steep bank. His ball does not move, but the player believes it will move if he takes a backswing. Accordingly, the player holds the club with his left hand and strikes the shaft of the club with his right hand, thereby moving the ball. Is this permissible?

A. No. The player pushed the ball, contrary to Rule 14-1.

14-1/7
Using More Than One Club to Make Stroke

Q. A player, whose ball was lodged in a bush, swung at the ball with three clubs to minimize the chance of missing it. Is this permissible?

A. No. Rule 14-1 requires that the ball be struck at with the "head of the club"; the word "club" is in the singular. The player was in breach of this Rule when he swung at the ball with three clubs.

Other Decisions related to Rule 14-1: See "Stroke" in the Index.

ASSISTANCE IN MAKING STROKE

14-2/0.5
Meaning of "Elements"

Q. What are considered "elements" under Rule 14-2a?

A. Elements include sunlight, rain, wind, snow and other weather conditions.

14-2/1
Player Aligns Partner's Club Before Stroke

Q. A player aligns his partner's putter and then moves away before his partner plays. Is this permissible?

A. Yes. Rule 14-2 (Assistance) does not apply prior to making a stroke.

14-2/2
Player Holds Umbrella Over Own Head When Playing Stroke

Q. A player playing in the rain holds an umbrella over his head with one hand while holing a very short putt, gripping the putter with the other hand. Is this permissible?

A. Yes. Rule 14-2a prohibits a player, while making a stroke, from accepting protection from the elements from someone other than himself. However, it does not prohibit him from protecting himself. (Revised)

14-2/2.5
Player Positions Bag for Purpose of Providing Shade for Ball

Q. A player positions his golf bag near the teeing ground for the purpose of blocking the sunlight from the position where he tees his ball. He then makes a stroke. Is he in breach of Rule 14-2?

A. Yes. As the player was not in contact with the golf bag, he accepted protection from the elements in breach of Rule 14-2a. This answer differs from that in Decision 14-2/2 as, in that case, the player was in contact with the umbrella.

While a player may not place an object or position a person for the purpose of blocking the sunlight from his ball, he may ask a person (e.g., a spectator) who is already in position not to move, so that a shadow remains over the ball, or to move, so that his shadow is not over the ball. (Revised)

14-2/3
Caddie Shields Player from Sun During Stroke

Q. May a player's caddie purposely stand between the player and the setting sun so that the sun's glare is not in the player's face while he is playing a stroke?

A. No. Such procedure is a breach of Rule 14-2a.(Revised)

Decision related to 14-2/2.5 and 14-2/3:
• 4-1/5 Material Applied to Clubhead to Reduce Glare or For Protection.

Other Decisions related to Rule 14-2: See "Assistance and Protection, Acceptance of" in the Index.

14-3/0.5
Local Rule Permitting Use of Distance-Measuring Device

Q. May a Committee, by Local Rule, permit the use of distance-measuring devices?

A. Yes. A Committee may establish a Local Rule allowing players to use devices that measure or gauge distance only (see the Note to Rule 14-3). However, the use of a distance-measuring device that is designed to gauge or measure other conditions that might affect a player's play (e.g., gradient, wind speed, temperature, etc) is not permitted regardless of whether such an additional function is used.

   In the absence of such a Local Rule, the use of a distance-measuring device would be contrary to Rule 14-3.

14-3/0.7
Player Obtains Distance Information Measured with Electronic Device

Q. During a stipulated round, a player himself uses an electronic measuring device to obtain distance information. The Committee has not adopted a Local Rule allowing players to use devices to measure or gauge distance (see Note to Rule 14-3). What is the ruling?

A. The player is disqualified. The prohibition in Rule 14-3 against using an electronic device to obtain distance information extends to the player or a member of his side using such a device to obtain distance information. This prohibition in Rule 14-3 would also extend to a player who asks an outside agency to use an artificial device to obtain such distance information for him. However, the player would not be disqualified merely because a spectator or other outside agency provided such information to him without being requested to do so. Similarly, a player is not prohibited from obtaining distance information from scoreboards or from a referee (e.g., when using an artificial device to determine the order of play). (New)

Decisions related to 14-3/0.5 and 14-3/0.7:
• 8-1/2 Exchanging Distance Information.
• 17/3.5 Reflector on Flagstick.

14-3/1
Distance Meter Attached to Golf Cart

Q. May a player attach a meter to his golf cart for the purpose of measuring the distances of shots?

A. No. Such a meter is an artificial device and its use for the purpose of measuring distance is a breach of Rule 14-3. However, see also the Note to Rule 14-3.

14-3/2
Pencil or Score Card Used to Assist in Gauging Distance

Q. It is possible to gauge distance to a putting green by holding a score card or pencil at arm's length and comparing it with the height of the flagstick. Is such a practice permissible?

A. Yes. Provided the score card or pencil has not been specially marked, its use in this manner is traditionally accepted and Exception 2 to Rule 14-3 applies.

Use of anything specially marked to gauge distance is a breach of Rule 14-3. However, see also the Note to Rule 14-3.

14-3/3
Eyeglasses and Binoculars

Standard eyeglasses and binoculars that have no range-finder attachments are not artificial devices within the meaning of the term in Rule 14-3. However, see also the Note to Rule 14-3.

14-3/4
Use of Compass During Round

Q. A player uses a compass during a round to assist him in determining wind direction or the direction of the grain in the greens or for some other similar reason. Is the player in breach of Rule 14-3?

A. Yes. A compass is considered to be an artificial device and must not be used for these purposes.

14-3/5
Booklet Providing Distances Between Various Points

Q. A booklet contains illustrations of the holes on a course, including isolated trees, bunkers, etc. Superimposed on each illustration is a yardage scale in increments of ten yards. Thus, a player using such a booklet can estimate how far his ball lies from a putting green or a tee. Is use of such a booklet during a round contrary to Rule 14-3?

A. No. Although such a booklet is an artificial device, its use has been traditionally accepted and Exception 2 to Rule 14-3 applies.

14-3/5.5
Electronic Device Providing Distances Between Various Points

Q. With regard to Decision 14-3/5, may a player use an electronic device containing the same information?

A. Yes. Exception 2 to Rule 14-3 applies, but the player must not use a device with a measuring or distance calculating function. However, see also the Note to Rule 14-3.

14-3/6
Holding Ball in Hand Against Grip When Putting

Q. A player putts with a golf ball held in his left hand against the grip. He claims the pressure transmitted to the grip through the ball assists him in putting. Is such use of a ball permissible?

A. No. The player is using equipment in an unusual manner to assist him in making a stroke and is in breach of Rule 14-3.

14-3/6.5
Holding Ball in Hand Against Grip for Practice Swings or Practice Strokes

Q. Decision 14-3/6 clarifies that a player may not make a stroke while holding a golf ball in his hand against the grip to assist him. May the player make a practice swing or practice stroke (when permitted by Rule 7-2) while holding a golf ball in the same manner?

A. Yes. The prohibition in Rule 14-3 against using equipment in an unusual manner applies to strokes that count in the player's score and not to practice swings or practice strokes.

14-3/7
Player with Injured Right Wrist Inserts Left Thumb Under Elastic Bandage on Right Wrist and Hand

Q. A player, who wore an elastic bandage around his right wrist and hand because of an injury, inserted his left thumb under the bandage where it crosses his right palm, and played a number of strokes with his left thumb so located. Is this permissible?

A. No. Although a player may wear an elastic bandage for medical purposes in accordance with Exception 1 to Rule 14-3, there is no need for him to insert his thumb under the bandage. Therefore, such an action would constitute use of equipment in an unusual manner in breach of Rule 14-3.

14-3/8
Adhesive Tape

Q. May a player wear adhesive tape on his hands or apply such tape to a golf glove?

A. The use of adhesive tape, or similar coverings of the hand, for any medical reasons, e.g., to reduce blisters or to eliminate the possibility of skin splits between the fingers, is not contrary to the Rules. However, the application of tape to the hand or the construction of a similar covering must not be excessive (i.e., must not otherwise assist the player in gripping and its thickness must be comparable to that of a standard golf glove). Also, applying tape to a golf glove to prevent the glove from slipping or to reduce wear is not a breach of Rule 14-3.

However, if the tape is used solely to aid the player in gripping the club (e.g., it is used to bind two fingers together), the player is in breach of Rule 14-3 as such use of tape is the use of equipment in an unusual manner.

14-3/9
Player Putts with One Hand and Steadies Himself with Club Held in Other Hand

Q. A player, while putting with one hand, uses another club to lean on and steady himself. Is the use of the club in this manner considered to be use of equipment in an unusual manner, contrary to Rule 14-3?

A. Yes.

Related Decision:
• 17-1/5 Holding Flagstick With One Hand and Putting with Other Hand.

14-3/10
Use of Training or Swing Aid During Round

Q. During a round, may a player make a stroke or a practice swing using a club with a weighted headcover or "doughnut" on it, or use any other device designed as a training or swing aid?

A. No. The player would be using an artificial device to assist him in his play in breach of Rule 14-3, but see also Decision 4-4a/7 for use of a weighted training club.

14-3/10.3
Use of Rod During Round for Alignment or as Swing Aid

Q. During a stipulated round, a player uses a rod to check his alignment or his swing plane. What is the ruling?

A. The player is disqualified under Rule 14-3 as the rod is unusual equipment and such use, during the stipulated round, is not permitted.

Carrying the rod is not, of itself, a breach of a Rule.

Related Decision:
•8-2a/1 Club Placed on Ground to Align Feet.

14-3/10.5
Use of Stretching Devises

Q. Rule 14-3a prohibits a player, during a stipulated round, from using any artificial device or unusual equipment, or using any equipment in an unusual manner, that "might assist him in making a stroke or in his play." Would the use of a stretching device during a stipulated round be a breach of Rule 14-3?

A. During a stipulated round, it is permissible to use a device designed for stretching unless the device is designed specifically to be used in a golf swing and is used during a golf swing (see Decision 14-3/10). For example, the following stretching devices may be used:

- Items designed specifically for golf but not used in a golf swing (e.g., a bar to place across the shoulders);
- Items designed for general stretching (e.g., rubber tubing); and
- Items not originally designed for stretching (e.g., a section of pipe).

14-3/11
Plumb-Line

Q. Is a plumb-line, i.e., a weight suspended on a string, an artificial device within the meaning of the term in Rule 14-3?

A. Yes. If a player uses such a device to assist him in his play, he is in breach of Rule 14-3.

14-3/12
Club Used as Plumb-Line

Q. May a player use his putter as a plumb-line to assist him in determining the slope on a putting green?

A. Yes. Use of a club in this manner is traditionally accepted and Exception 2 to Rule 14-3 applies.

14-3/12.5
Bottled Drink Used as a Level

Q. A player places a bottled drink on the putting green in order to gauge the slope of the green. Is the player in breach of Rule 14-3?

A. Yes. The player is using equipment in an unusual manner to assist him in his play contrary to Rule 14-3. However, if the placing of the bottle on the putting green was not for the purpose of gauging the slope, the player would not be in breach of Rule 14-3.

14-3/13
Hand Warmer

Q. A player uses a device to warm his hands during a round. Is the player in breach of Rule 14-3?

A. No. Although a hand warmer is an artificial device, its use to warm the hands is traditionally accepted, and Exception 2 to Rule 14-3 applies.

14-3/13.5
Golf Ball Artificially Warmed

Q. Is the use of a golf ball that was purposely warmed during a stipulated round with a golf ball warmer, hand warmer or any such device a breach of Rule 14-3?

A. Yes. Use of a ball that has been purposely warmed during a stipulated round with an artificial device constitutes a breach of Rule 14-3. However, it would not be a breach of Rule 14-3 to use a ball that was artificially warmed prior to the stipulated round.

14-3/14
Electronic Instrument Used to Find Ball

Q. A radio-frequency identification chip has been embedded in a golf ball. When used with a special radio receiver, a player may find such a ball readily because the receiver emits a signal that grows louder as the person holding the receiver moves closer to the ball. Is the use of such a ball and receiver permissible?

A. No. Use of such a ball in conjunction with the receiver is a breach of Rule 14-3.

However, use of such a ball without the receiver is permissible, provided the ball conforms to the Rules, the embedded chip has no capability other than identifying the ball and its use is in accordance with any conditions of competition that may have been adopted (e.g., the List of Conforming Golf Balls Condition). (Revised)

14-3/15
Artificial Limbs

An artificial leg or arm is an artificial device within the meaning of the term in Rule 14-3. However, as such a device is used to alleviate a medical condition and the player has a legitimate medical reason to use the device, Exception 1 to Rule 14-3 applies, even if an artificial leg has been modified to aid a player in playing the game or an artificial arm has a fitting specially designed for gripping a golf club. However, the Committee must be satisfied that an artificial limb so modified does not give the player any undue advantage over other players. If the Committee is not satisfied of this, Exception 1 to Rule 14-3 does not apply and use of the device would constitute a breach of Rule 14-3.

Clubs used by a player with an artificial arm must conform with Rule 4-1 except that an attachment may be fitted to the grip or shaft to assist the player to hold the club. However, if the Committee believes that the use of a club modified in this way would give the player an undue advantage over other players, it should deem the attachment an artificial device contrary to Rule 14-3.

Players in doubt about the use of a device should raise the matter as soon as possible with the Committee.

14-3/15.5
Use of Swing Aid for Medical Reasons

While Exception 1 to Rule 14-3 authorizes a Committee to allow the use of a device for medical reasons, a Committee should not normally allow the use of a device originally designed as a swing aid, as such a device is likely to give a player an undue advantage over other players.

14-3/16
Use of Electronic Devices

As provided in the Etiquette Section, players should ensure that any electronic device taken onto the course does not distract other players.

The use of an electronic device such as a mobile phone, hand-held computer, calculator, television or radio is not of itself a breach of Rule 14-3. For example, the following uses of an electronic device during a stipulated round are not a breach of the Rules:
- Using the device for matters unrelated to golf (e.g., to call home);
- Using the device to access information on advice-related matters that was produced prior to the start of the player's round (e.g., an electronic yardage book, swing tips);
- Using the device to access (but not interpret or process) playing information from previous rounds (e.g., driving distances, individual club yardages, etc); or
- Using the device to obtain information related to the competition being played (e.g., the leader board or projected "cut").

However, examples of uses of an electronic device during a stipulated round that are a breach of Rule 14-3, for which the penalty is disqualification, include:
- Using the device (e.g., a television or radio) to watch or listen to a broadcast of the competition being played;
- Using the device to ask for or give advice in breach of Rule 8-1 (e.g., calling a swing coach);
- Using the device to access information on advice-related matters that was not produced prior to the start of his round (e.g., analysis of strokes made during that round); or
- Using the device to interpret or process any playing information obtained from current or previous rounds (e.g., driving distances, individual club yardages, etc) or to asssist in calculating the effective distance between two points (i.e., distance after considering gradient, wind speed and/or direction, temperature or other environmental factors).

14-3/17
Player Listens to Music or Broadcast During Round

Q. A player uses a device to listen to music, a radio broadcast or any other type of broadcast during a stipulated round. What is the ruling?

A. Under Rule 14-3a, a player may not use any artificial device or unusual equipment that "might assist him in making a stroke or in his play." Listening to music or a broadcast while making a stroke or for a prolonged period might assist the player in his play, for example, by eliminating distractions or promoting a good tempo. Therefore, the use of an artificial device to listen to music or a broadcast, whether or not through headphones, while making a stroke or for a prolonged period of time during a stipulated round is a breach of Rule 14-3. However, it would not be a breach of Rule 14-3 for a player to listen to a device briefly, for example, to obtain the results of another sporting event or traffic information, while walking between the putting green of one hole and the teeing ground of the next hole.

A Committee will have to consider all available facts and circumstances in determining whether a player using an artificial device to listen to music or a broadcast has done so for a prolonged period such that the action might have assisted the player in his play.

There is no restriction on listening to music or other broadcasts while practicing (whether on the practice ground or on the golf course, and whether by oneself or while playing with others), although club rules and disciplinary codes could apply in such circumstances. (New)

Other Decisions related to Rule 14-3: See "Artificial Devices, Unusual Equipment and Unusual Use of Equipment" in the Index.

STRIKING BALL MORE THAN ONCE

14-4/1
Ball Falls on Club Face After Stroke and Sticks to Mud Thereon

Q. A player, making a stroke at his ball on the bank of a bunker, hit the ball straight up. The ball came down and adhered to mud on the face of the club. Was the player in breach of Rule 14-4?

A. No. However, the player stopped his ball and was in breach of Rule 19-2.

In match play and stroke play, the player incurs a penalty of one stroke and must drop the ball as near as possible to the spot where the ball adhered to the club (Rule 19-2).

But see Decision 1-4/2.

14-4/2
Ball Strikes Pipeline and on Rebound Is Deflected by Face of Club

Q. A player's ball strikes a pipeline and on the rebound hits the face of his club. Is the player considered to have struck the ball more than once in breach of Rule 14-4?

A. No. The player did not strike the ball more than once. He struck it once and it rebounded and hit the face of his club. Rule 19-2 applies.

14-4/3
Player Hits Behind Ball and Then Strikes Moving Ball

Q. In playing a chip shot, a player's club strikes the ground several inches behind the ball and does not come into contact with the ball. However, the ground is struck with enough force to cause the ball to move. The player's club continues and strikes the ball while it is moving. What is the ruling?

A. The player must count his stroke and add a penalty stroke under Rule 14-4.

Even though the club itself did not initially strike the ball, the ball was put into motion due to the stroke; therefore, Rule 14-4 applies.

Other Decisions related to Rule 14-4: See "Ball in Motion Struck by Club" in the Index.

PLAYING MOVING BALL

14-5/1
Ball Moving During Backswing Struck While Still Moving

Q. A player's ball starts moving during his backswing and he strikes the ball while it is still moving. What is the ruling?

A. There is no penalty under Rule 14-5 because the ball began to move after the player had begun his backswing. However, if the player had caused the ball to move or addressed it, he incurred a penalty stroke – Rule 18-2a or b.

14-5/2
Making Stroke at Oscillating Ball

Q. A player's ball lies on the putting green. The ball is oscillating because of the wind. May the player make a stroke at the ball while it oscillates?

A. Yes. As an oscillating ball is not moving as defined by the Rules of Golf, there is no penalty for making a stroke at an oscillating ball. The player must continue play without undue delay. (New)

Related Decisions:
• 1-2/9 Player Presses Ball into Surface of Putting Green
• 18/2 Ball Oscillates During Address

Other Decisions related to Rule 14-5: See "Ball in Motion Struck by Club" in the Index.

14-6/1
Ball Moves in Water in Water Hazard After Stance Taken

Q. A ball was at rest in shallow, rapidly-running water in a water hazard. After the player had carefully entered the water, walked to the ball and taken his stance, the ball moved, presumably due to the current. What is the ruling?

A. When a ball is in water in a water hazard and it is not clear whether the player's actions caused the ball to move, he should be given the benefit of the doubt and no penalty should be applied. However, if the player's actions clearly caused the ball to move, he would be subject to a penalty stroke under Rule 18-2a and required to replace the ball. For example, if a player jumped into the water close to the ball and in so doing created a splash that moved the ball, he would be subject to penalty under Rule 18-2a. (Revised)

Related Decisions:
• 18/10 Ball Falls into Bunker When Person Walks Nearby.
• 18-2a/30 Ball Moves After Player Takes Several Practice Swings Near Ball and Touches Grass Behind Ball.
• 18-2a/30.5 Ball Moves After Removal of Loose Impediment Near Ball.
• 18-2b/3 Ball Moves After Player Has Taken Stance in Bunker.
• 18-2b/4 Ball Moves After Player Grounds Club Short Distance Behind Ball But Before Grounding Club Immediately Behind Ball.

RULE 15

SUBSTITUTED BALL; WRONG BALL

DEFINITIONS
All defined terms are in *italics* and are listed alphabetically in the Definitions section – see pages 6–16.

15-1. GENERAL
A player must hole out with the ball played from the *teeing ground*, unless the ball is *lost* or *out of bounds* or the player *substitutes* another ball, whether or not substitution is permitted (see Rule 15-2). If a player plays a *wrong ball*, see Rule 15-3.

15-2. SUBSTITUTED BALL
A player may *substitute* a ball when proceeding under a *Rule* that permits the player to play, drop or place another ball in completing the play of a hole. The *substituted ball* becomes the *ball in play*.

If a player *substitutes* a ball when not permitted to do so under the *Rules*, that *substituted ball* is not a *wrong ball*; it becomes the *ball in play*. If the mistake is not corrected as provided in Rule 20-6 and the player makes a *stroke* at a wrongly *substituted ball*, he loses the hole in match play or incurs a penalty of two strokes in stroke play under the applicable *Rule* and, in stroke play, must play out the hole with the *substituted ball*.

Exception: If a player incurs a penalty for making a *stroke* from a wrong place, there is no additional penalty for substituting a ball when not permitted.

(Playing from wrong place – see Rule 20-7)

15-3. WRONG BALL
a. Match Play
If a player makes a *stroke* at a *wrong ball*, he loses the hole.

If the *wrong ball* belongs to another player, its owner must place a ball on the spot from which the *wrong ball* was first played.

If the player and *opponent* exchange balls during the play of a hole, the first to make a *stroke* at a *wrong ball* loses the hole; when this cannot be determined, the hole must be played out with the balls exchanged.

Exception: There is no penalty if a player makes a *stroke* at a *wrong ball* that is moving in water in a *water hazard*. Any *strokes* made at a *wrong ball* moving in water in a *water hazard* do not count in the player's score. The player must correct his mistake by playing the correct ball or by proceeding under the *Rules*.

(Placing and Replacing – see Rule 20-3)

b. Stroke Play
If a *competitor* makes a *stroke* or *strokes* at a *wrong ball*, he incurs a penalty of two strokes.

The *competitor* must correct his mistake by playing the correct ball or by proceeding under the *Rules*. If he fails to correct his mistake before making a *stroke* on the next *teeing ground* or, in the case of the last hole of the round, fails to declare his intention to correct his mistake before leaving the *putting green*, he is disqualified.

Strokes made by a *competitor* with a *wrong ball* do not count in his score. If the *wrong ball* belongs to another *competitor*, its owner must place a ball on the spot from which the *wrong ball* was first played.

Exception: There is no penalty if a *competitor* makes a *stroke* at a *wrong ball* that is moving in water in a *water hazard*. Any *strokes* made at a *wrong ball* moving in water in a *water hazard* do not count in the *competitor's* score.

(Placing and Replacing – see Rule 20-3)

PLAYING A WRONG BALL: GENERAL

15/1
Stroke Misses Wrong Ball

Q. A player swings at and misses a wrong ball. What is the ruling?

A. Since the player made a stroke with a wrong ball, he lost the hole in match play (Rule 15-3a) or incurred a two-stroke penalty in stroke play (Rule 15-3b).

15/2
Player's Stroke at Own Ball Dislodges Concealed Ball

Q. A player plays a stroke with his own ball in the rough and also hits an old abandoned ball which was hidden beneath his ball. Since he struck the hidden ball, did he play a wrong ball?

A. No. The player played a stroke with his own ball, not with the hidden ball. Since he did not play a stroke with the hidden ball, Rule 15-3 is not applicable. The player must play his ball as it lies.

Related Decision:
• 7-2/7 Practice Swing Dislodges Concealed Ball.

15/3
Player Plays Stroke at Part of Abandoned Ball Which Had Broken into Pieces

Q. A ball had broken into pieces and had been abandoned. Part of it was lying in heavy grass. A player mistook the part for his ball in play and played a stroke with it. The player asserts that part of a ball is not a ball and, therefore, that he has not played a wrong ball. Is the player correct?

A. No. Since the player made a stroke with a wrong ball, he lost the hole in match play (Rule 15-3a) or incurred a two-stroke penalty in stroke play (Rule 15-3b).

15/4
Player Lifts Ball, Sets It Aside and Plays It from Where Set Aside

Q. A player marks the position of his ball on the putting green, lifts the ball and sets it aside. By mistake, he putts the ball from the spot at which he set it aside. What is the ruling?

A. When a ball is lifted under Rule 20-1, it is out of play – see Definition of "Ball in Play." When the player played a stroke with his ball while it was out of play, he played a wrong ball (Rule 15-3).

In match play, the player lost the hole (Rule 15-3a).

In stroke play, he incurred a penalty of two strokes and was required to correct the error before playing from the next tee; otherwise, he would be disqualified (Rule 15-3b).

Related Decisions:
- 15-3b/3 Fellow-Competitor Lifts Competitor's Ball and Sets It Aside; Competitor Plays Ball from Where Set Aside.
- 20-4/2 Ball Lifted by Player from Putting Green and Placed by Caddie Behind Ball-Marker.

15/5
Original Ball Found and Played After Another Ball Put into Play

Q. A player unable to find his ball after a brief search drops another ball (Ball B) under Rule 27-1 and plays it. His original ball is then found within five minutes after search for it began. The player lifted Ball B and continued to play with the original ball. Was this correct?

A. No. When the player put the substituted ball into play at the spot of the previous stroke with the intent to play a ball under Rule 27-1, he proceeded under an applicable Rule. Therefore, Rule 20-6 does not apply, and he must continue with the substituted ball (see Decision 27-1/2). The original ball was lost when Ball B was dropped under Rule 27-1 (see Definition of "Lost Ball").

When the player lifted Ball B, he incurred a penalty of one stroke under Rule 18-2a. When he made a stroke with the original ball after it was out of play, he played a wrong ball (see Definitions of "Ball in Play" and "Wrong Ball") and incurred a penalty of loss of hole in match play or an additional penalty of two strokes in stroke play (Rule 15-3). In stroke play, the player would be disqualified if, before playing from the next teeing ground, he did not correct his error (Rule 15-3b).

Related Decisions:
- 27/8 Ball Found After Search Exceeding Five Minutes Is Then Played.
- 27-1/2.3 Original Ball Found Within Five-Minute Search Period After Another Ball Dropped (at spot from which original last played); Original Ball Played.

• 27-2b/5 Original Ball Played After Provisional Ball Played from Point Nearer Hole Than Original Ball Is Likely to Be.

15/6
Stroke Played with Ball Lying Out of Bounds

Q. A player plays a stroke at his ball which is lying out of bounds. What is the ruling?

A. A ball lying out of bounds is no longer in play and thus is a wrong ball – see Definitions of "Ball in Play" and "Wrong Ball." Accordingly, in match play, the player loses the hole. In stroke play, he incurs a two-stroke penalty and must proceed under Rule 27-1, incurring the additional one-stroke penalty prescribed in that Rule.

Related Decision:
• 33-8/43 Stroke Played from Environmentally-Sensitive Area.

15/6.5
Ball Changed During Play of Hole to Aid Identification

Q. A and B realized after playing their tee shots on a par-5 hole that they were playing balls with identical markings. Based on the location of both tee shots, A knew which ball was his. To avoid subsequent confusion, A lifted his ball before playing his second shot, substituted a ball with different markings and played out the hole. Is this permissible?

A. No. A was not entitled to substitute a ball.

In match play, A loses the hole – Rule 15-2.

In stroke play, A incurs the general penalty of two strokes under Rule 18 for incorrectly substituting a ball, but there is no additional penalty for lifting the ball without authority (see Rule 15-2 and the penalty statement under Rule 18).

Other Decisions related to whether multiple penalties apply: See "Multiple Penalty Situations" in the Index.

15/7
Wrong Ball Played in Belief It Is Provisional or Second Ball

Q. A player, thinking his original ball may be lost or out of bounds, plays a provisional ball under Rule 27-2a. Before reaching the place where his original ball is likely to be, he plays a wrong ball, believing it is his provisional ball. He then finds his original ball in bounds and, correctly, abandons the provisional ball. Does the player incur a penalty under Rule 15-3 for playing a wrong ball, even though that wrong ball was played in mistake for a provisional ball which never became the ball in play?

A. Yes. Although a penalty incurred in play of a provisional ball is normally canceled if the provisional ball has to be abandoned under Rule 27-2c (e.g., a one-stroke penalty under Rule 18-2b if the provisional ball moves after being addressed), this does not apply when the penalty is for playing a wrong ball.

The same ruling would apply if a competitor played a wrong ball in the belief that it was a second ball played under Rule 3-3 (Doubt as to Procedure in Stroke Play) or Rule 20-7c (Serious Breach of Playing from a Wrong Place in Stroke Play). However, in similar circumstances, there would have been no penalty under Rule 15-3b if the competitor had first holed out with his ball in play and then played a stroke with a wrong ball when proceeding under Rule 3-3 or 20-7c.

Related Decision:

• 20-7c/5 Competitor Plays Second Ball Under Rule 20-7c; Clarification of "Penalty Strokes Incurred Solely by Playing the Ball Ruled Not to Count."

15/8
Ball Played Under Rule for Ball Lost in Ground Under Repair After Another Ball Played Under Stroke-and-Distance Procedure

Q. A player's ball was lost in ground under repair. He played another ball under Rule 27-1. The player then realized that Rule 25-1c provides for relief without penalty for a ball in ground under repair that cannot be found. He decided to proceed under that Rule, lifted the ball played under Rule 27-1, dropped another ball in accordance with Rule 25-1c and played out the hole. What is the ruling?

A. The ball played under Rule 27-1 was the player's ball in play and he should have continued with that ball. The player, having put another ball into play under Rule 27-1, was no longer entitled to proceed under Rule 25-1c. Therefore, when he lifted his ball in play, dropped another ball elsewhere under Rule 25-1c and played it, he was in breach of Rule 18 (for lifting his ball in play and failing to replace it) and Rule 15-2 (for wrongly substituting a ball).

In match play, he loses the hole – Rule 15-2 or Rule 18.

In stroke play, in addition to the stroke-and-distance penalty incurred when he proceeded under Rule 27-1, the player incurs the general penalty of two strokes under Rule 18 for lifting his ball in play and failing to replace it, but there is no additional penalty for incorrectly substituting a ball (see Rule 15-2 and the penalty statement under Rule 18).

Related Decisions:

• 18-2a/8.5 Ball Played from Ground Under Repair Abandoned and Relief Taken Under Ground Under Repair Rule.
• 20-7c/4 Competitor's Ball Played by Fellow-Competitor; Competitor Substitutes Another Ball at Wrong Place, Plays It and Then Abandons It and Plays Out Original Ball From Right Place.
• 25-1c/2 Ball Dropped and Played Under Ground Under Repair Rule in Absence of Knowledge or Virtual Certainty That Original Ball in Ground Under Repair.

15/9
Ball Thrown into Bounds by Outside Agency and Played; Caddie Aware of Action of Outside Agency

Q. A's ball was found lying in bounds and A played a shot towards the green. Then a man appeared and said that A's ball had come to rest out of bounds in his garden. He said he had thrown it onto the course and had told A's caddie what he had done. The caddie had not reported this to A. What is the ruling?

A. Under Rule 6-1, A is responsible for his caddie's failure to tell him what the man had said.

A's ball was no longer the ball in play when it came to rest out of bounds. Therefore, it was a wrong ball – see Definitions of "Ball in Play" and "Wrong Ball." When A made a stroke with the wrong ball, he incurred the penalty prescribed in Rule 15-3 and, in stroke play, was obliged to proceed under Rule 27-1.

15/10
Ball Thrown into Bounds by Outside Agency and Played; Neither Player Nor His Caddie Aware of Action of Outside Agency

Q. Decision 15/9 states that, if an outside agency throws a player's ball back onto the course from out of bounds and advises the player's caddie to this effect, the player is penalized for playing a wrong ball if he plays the ball from its position in bounds. What would be the ruling if neither the player nor his caddie knew the player's ball had been thrown back onto the course?

A. In match play, in equity (Rule 1-4), there would be no penalty for playing a wrong ball (Rule 15-3). If the player learns of the actions of the outside agency after playing the wrong ball, but before the opponent makes another stroke or takes some action (e.g., picks up or concedes the player's next stroke) that the opponent might not have taken if the wrong ball had not been played, then the player must correct his mistake and proceed correctly. If the player learns of the mistake later than this, he must proceed with the wrong ball without penalty and the score with the wrong ball must count.

In stroke play, in equity (Rule 1-4), there would be no penalty for playing a wrong ball (Rule 15-3). If the player discovers before playing from the next teeing ground that the original ball was out of bounds, he must go back and proceed under Rule 27-1. If the discovery is not made until later than this, the score with the wrong ball stands.

Related Decisions:
• 18-1/3 Player Unaware Ball Moved by Outside Agency Does Not Replace Ball.
• 18-5/3 Competitor and Fellow-Competitor Unaware Ball Moved by Fellow-Competitor's Ball Until After Completion of Hole.

15/11
Wrong Ball Hit Out of Bounds; Another Ball Played Under Rule 27-1; Original Ball Then Found Nearby

Q. A player plays what he believes to be his ball and hits it out of bounds. He plays another ball under Rule 27-1 and then discovers that the ball he hit out of bounds was a wrong ball and that his original ball is lying in bounds. What is the ruling?

A. In match play, the player loses the hole for playing a wrong ball (Rule 15-3a).

In stroke play, the ball the player hit out of bounds was a wrong ball, and the ball played under Rule 27-1 was a continuation of the play of that wrong ball. The player incurred a penalty of two strokes under Rule 15-3b and he was obliged to hole out with his original ball.

Related Decisions:
- 15-3b/2 Play of Two Different Wrong Balls Between Strokes with Ball in Play.
- 26/6 Ball Assumed to Be in Water Hazard Found Outside Hazard After Another Ball Played Under Stroke-and-Distance Procedure.

15/12
Stray Ball Found Out of Bounds Played Under Stroke-and-Distance Procedure; Original Ball Then Found in Bounds

Q. A player finds a ball out of bounds, thinks it is his original ball, plays it at the spot from which the original ball was played and then finds his original ball in bounds. What is the ruling?

A. The original ball is lost and the ball found out of bounds is in play under penalty of stroke and distance. See Rule 27-1a.

15/13
Stray Ball Dropped Under Unplayable Ball Rule But Not Played

Q. A player finds a ball he believes is his original ball, deems it unplayable and drops it under Rule 28b or c. He then discovers that the ball is not his but is, in fact, a stray ball. What is the ruling?

A. When the player dropped the stray ball, it became a substituted ball. However, the player was not entitled to proceed under Rule 28b or c without finding the original ball. Since a stroke has not been made with the substituted ball, the player is entitled to correct his error under Rule 20-6 by abandoning the substituted ball and resuming search for the original ball. If the player's ball is lost, the player must proceed under Rule 27-1.

15/14
Ball in Bunker Deemed Unplayable, Dropped in Bunker and Played; Ball Then Discovered to Be Stray Ball

Q. A player, believing that a ball lying very badly in a bunker is his ball, deems it unplayable, drops it in the bunker and plays it out. He then discovers that the ball he has played is not his original ball. Has he played a wrong ball?

A. No. The procedures in Rules 28b and 28c may not be applied except with reference to the position of the player's ball in play, and this must first be found and identified (see Decision 28/1). Before proceeding under option b or c of Rule 28, the player should ensure he is doing so with reference to his ball in play. The player was permitted to identify the ball following the procedure in Rule 12-2 or, having lifted it under Rule 28, could have inspected the ball to verify that it was his ball in play. In this case, the ball dropped and played by the player was not his original ball; it was a substituted ball. Since the location of the original ball was not known at the time the substituted ball was dropped, he was required to proceed under Rule 27-1. As the substituted ball was not dropped at the spot required by Rule 27-1, he played from a wrong place (see Decision 28/15).

In match play, he incurred a penalty of loss of hole (Rule 20-7b).

In stroke play, he incurred a penalty of one stroke under Rule 27-1 and an additional penalty of two strokes under Rule 20-7c for playing from a wrong place. If the breach was a serious one, he is subject to disqualification unless he corrected his error as provided in Rule 20-7c.

Decisions related to 15/13 and 15/14:
• 20-7c/3 Ball Believed to Be Lost in Bunker; Competitor Drops Another Ball in Bunker and Plays It; Original Ball Then Found Outside Bunker.
• 28/14 Stray Ball Deemed Unplayable Played Under Stroke-and-Distance Procedure; Original Ball Then Found.

Other Decisions related to Rule 15: See "Substituted Ball" and "Wrong Ball" in the Index.

CHANGING OR EXCHANGING BALLS

15-1/1
Balls Inadvertently Exchanged by Players Between Holes

Q. After completion of a hole, the balls of A and B were inadvertently exchanged and A played B's ball from the next teeing ground. Did A play a wrong ball?

A. No. A ball played from the teeing ground into the hole is not a wrong ball, even if it does not belong to the player – see Definitions of "Ball in Play" and "Wrong Ball."

15-1/2
Balls Inadvertently Exchanged by Competitors at Unknown Place

Q. In stroke play, it was discovered after play of a hole that A had holed out with B's ball and vice versa. Both A and B were certain that they had holed out at this hole with the balls they played from the teeing ground. Thus, it was concluded that they had exchanged balls during play of a previous hole or between two holes. What is the ruling?

A. If it cannot be established that the balls were exchanged during play of a hole, A and B should be given the benefit of the doubt and it should be assumed that the balls were inadvertently exchanged between play of two holes, in which case no penalty would be imposed.

15-1/2.5
Balls Inadvertently Exchanged by Players After One Ball Struck and Moved the Other; One Player Substitutes Balls

Q. A plays to the putting green, and his ball strikes and moves the ball of his opponent or fellow-competitor, B, which was lying on the green. Both balls come to rest on the green. B, acting under Rules 18-5 and 20-3c, lifts A's ball by mistake and places it as near as possible to where his (B's) ball lay before it was moved. B holes out with A's ball. Without having lifted B's ball, A then, by mistake, holes out with B's ball. What is the ruling?

A. A has played a wrong ball, whereas B has substituted another ball when not so permitted.

In match play, B incurred a penalty stroke for lifting A's ball without authority (Rule 18-3b) and was required to inform A of that penalty stroke (Rule 9-2b). However, B lost the hole when he played A's ball (Rules 15-2 and 18-5). A's subsequent play of a wrong ball is irrelevant.

In stroke play, B incurs a penalty of two strokes (Rules 15-2 and 18-5). A incurs a penalty of two strokes, must retrieve his ball from B, replace it on the spot from which B had lifted it and hole out with it before playing from the next teeing ground; otherwise A is disqualified (Rule 15-3b).

15-1/3
Hole at Which Wrong Ball Played Unknown

Q. A player discovers after the 6th hole that he is not playing the ball with which he started the round. He does not know when he first played the different ball. What is the ruling in:
  (a) stroke play?
  (b) match play when:
    (i) he has won every hole?
    (ii) he has lost every hole?
    (iii) he has won 4 holes, lost 1 hole and halved 1 hole?
    (iv) he has lost 4 holes, won 1 hole and halved 1 hole?

A. The Committee must determine whether the different ball is a wrong ball or not and give the player the benefit of any doubt – see Decision 15-1/2. Thus, if the different ball might have been put into play under a Rule or if the player might have put the different ball into play at the start of a hole, the Committee should rule in favor of the player and the player incurs no penalty in either match play or stroke play.

If, however, the conclusion is that a wrong ball has been played:

(a) in stroke play, the player is disqualified, unless the conclusion is that the wrong ball was played at the 6th hole and the player rectifies his mistake as prescribed in Rule 15-3b.

(b) in match play, the Committee must determine on a balance of probabilities the hole at which the wrong ball was played and the player loses the hole, the state of the match being adjusted accordingly, if necessary. If it is impossible to determine the hole at which the wrong ball was played, in equity (Rule 1-4):

    (i) the player loses one of the holes which he had won and becomes 4 up instead of 6 up.

    (ii) the player remains 6 down.

    (iii) the player becomes one hole worse off, i.e., he becomes 2 up instead of 3 up.

    (iv) as in (iii), i.e., he becomes 4 down instead of 3 down.

15-1/4
Players Inadvertently Exchange Balls Recovered from Water Hazard

Q. A and B played into a water hazard at approximately the same spot. One caddie was authorized to retrieve both balls and he handed A's ball to B and B's ball to A. Each player dropped the ball handed to him behind the hazard under Rule 26-1b and played to the green. On reaching the green, they discovered the exchange of balls. Should they be penalized under Rule 15-2?

A. No. Rule 26-1b authorizes the player to drop "a ball." Accordingly, the substitution of another ball is permissible.

Other Decisions related to Rule 15-1: See "Exchanging Balls" in the Index.

SUBSTITUTED BALL

15-2/1
Player Substitutes Another Ball on Putting Green Because Original Ball Thrown to Caddie for Cleaning Came to Rest in Lake

Q. A player, whose ball was on the putting green, marked the ball's position, lifted it and threw it to his caddie for cleaning. The caddie failed to catch the ball and it went into a lake and could not be retrieved. The player holed out with another ball. Should he be penalized under Rule 15-2?

A. Yes. Rule 16-1b, under which the ball was lifted, does not permit substitution of another ball. Accordingly, the player incurred a penalty of loss of hole in match play or two strokes in stroke play.

Related Decisions:
- 5-3/3.5 Player Lifts Ball on Putting Green, Throws Ball into Lake and Then Announces That Ball Is Unfit for Play.
- 18-2a/13.5 Ball Lifted and Thrown into Pond in Anger.

15-2/2
Player Mistakenly Substitutes Another Ball on Putting Green; Error Discovered Before Stroke Played

Q. A player marks the position of his ball on the putting green and lifts the ball. By mistake he places another ball on the spot from which his original ball was lifted. He discovers his error before playing his next stroke, places his original ball on the spot from which it was lifted and holes out with it. What is the ruling?

A. There is no penalty. The player corrected the error and did not make a stroke with the other ball. Therefore, a penalty under Rule 15-2 was not applicable. Further, the other ball effectively marked the position of his original ball. So a penalty under Rule 20-1 was not applicable.

Related Decisions:
- 20-1/5 Competitor's Ball Lifted Without Authority by Fellow-Competitor's Caddie Who Subsequently Substitutes Another Ball Which Competitor Plays.
- 20-6/3 Ball Mistakenly Substituted When Dropped; Correction of Error.

15-2/3
Competitor Mistakenly Substitutes Another Ball on Putting Green; Error Discovered After Stroke Played from Next Teeing Ground

Q. A competitor in stroke play lifted his ball on the putting green and by mistake replaced it with another ball. He holed out and drove off the next tee. What is the ruling?

A. The competitor incurs a penalty of two strokes (Rule 15-2).

15-2/4
Competitor Who Lifts His Ball and Fellow-Competitor's Ball Inadvertently Exchanges Balls When Replacing Them

Q. In stroke play, A's ball and B's ball are in the same area on the putting green. A marks the position of, and lifts, both balls with B's consent. When A replaces them, they are inadvertently exchanged and A putts out, from the right place, with B's ball and vice versa. What is the ruling?

A. Each player is penalized two strokes under Rule 15-2.

As B authorized A to lift and replace his ball, B cannot be exempted from penalty (Rules 20-1 and 20-3a).

Other Decisions related to Rule 15-2: See "Substituted Ball" in the Index.

WRONG BALL: MATCH PLAY

Decisions related to Rule 15-3a: See "Wrong Ball: match play" in the Index.

WRONG BALL: STROKE PLAY

15-3b/1
Competitor Plays Wrong Ball and Loses It; Wrong Ball May Have Been Fellow-Competitor's Ball

Q. In stroke play, A and B drive into the same area in the rough. B finds a ball and hits it into the middle of a deep water hazard. A finds a ball that turns out to be B's ball. No other ball is found in the area, so presumably B played A's ball. B incurs a penalty of two strokes under Rule 15-3b and must play his own ball. What is the proper procedure for A?

A. As it was virtually certain that B played A's ball, A must place another ball at the spot from which B played the wrong ball, without penalty – Rule 15-3b.

Related Decision:
• 27/6 Player Unable to Find His Ball Because Another Player Played It.

15-3b/2
Play of Two Different Wrong Balls Between Strokes with Ball in Play

Q. In stroke play, a competitor plays a wrong ball to a putting green. He discovers his error and returns to the spot from which the wrong ball was played. He finds another ball and plays it to the green. He then discovers that he has played another wrong ball. Is the penalty two strokes or four strokes?

A. Four strokes. The competitor's discovery that he had played a wrong ball is an intervening event that breaks the relationship between the two strokes. The subsequent playing of another wrong ball is therefore an unrelated act. Accordingly, the player is separately penalized for play of each wrong ball, under Principle 6 of Decision 1-4/12 and Decision 1-4/13. (Revised)

Related Decisions:
• 15/11 Wrong Ball Hit Out of Bounds; Another Ball Played Under Rule 27-1; Original Ball Then Found Nearby.
• 26/6 Ball Assumed to Be in Water Hazard Found Outside Hazard After Another Ball Played Under Stroke-and-Distance Procedure.

Other Decisions related to whether multiple penalties apply: See "Multiple Penalty Situations" in the Index.

15-3b/3
Fellow-Competitor Lifts Competitor's Ball and Sets It Aside; Competitor Plays Ball from Where Set Aside

Q. In stroke play, B marked the position of A's ball on the putting green, lifted it and placed it nearby on the green. A failed to replace the ball. He putted it from where it lay and holed out. The error was then discovered. What is the ruling?

A. When a ball is lifted, it is out of play – see Definition of "Ball in Play." When A played a stroke with his ball which was out of play, he played a wrong ball.

If A knew that B had lifted his ball, he incurred a penalty of two strokes under Rule 15-3b and was required to replace his ball on the correct spot and play out the hole.

If A did not know that B had lifted his ball, A could not be penalized for playing a wrong ball. If he became aware of the mistake before playing from the next tee, he was required to replace his ball on the correct spot, without penalty, and complete the hole. If he learned of the mistake after playing from the next tee, the score with the wrong ball would stand and there would be no penalty.

Related Decisions:
• 15/4 Player Lifts Ball, Sets It Aside and Plays It from Where Set Aside.
• 20-4/2 Ball Lifted by Player from Putting Green and Placed by Caddie Behind Ball-Marker.

Other Decisions related to Rule 15-3: See "Wrong Ball" in the Index.

THE PUTTING GREEN

DEFINITIONS
All defined terms are in *italics* and are listed alphabetically in the Definitions section – see pages 6–16.

16-1. GENERAL
a. Touching Line of Putt
The *line of putt* must not be touched except:
(i)   the player may remove *loose impediments*, provided he does not press anything down;
(ii) the player may place the club in front of the ball when *addressing* it, provided he does not press anything down;
(iii) in measuring – Rule 18-6;
(iv) in lifting or replacing the ball – Rule 16-1b;
(v)   in pressing down a ball-marker;
(vi) in repairing old *hole* plugs or ball marks on the *putting green* – Rule 16-1c; and
(vii) in removing movable *obstructions* – Rule 24-1.

(Indicating line for putting on putting green – see Rule 8-2b)

b. Lifting and Cleaning Ball
A ball on the *putting green* may be lifted and, if desired, cleaned. The position of the ball must be marked before it is lifted and the ball must be replaced (see Rule 20-1). When another ball is in motion, a ball that might influence the movement of the ball in motion must not be lifted.

c. Repair of Hole Plugs, Ball Marks and Other Damage
The player may repair an old *hole* plug or damage to the *putting green* caused by the impact of a ball, whether or not the player's ball lies on the *putting green*. If a ball or ball-marker is accidentally *moved* in the process of the repair, the ball or ball-marker must be replaced. There is no penalty, provided the movement of the ball or ball-marker is directly attributable to the specific act of repairing an old *hole* plug or damage to the *putting green* caused by the impact of a ball. Otherwise, Rule 18 applies.

   Any other damage to the *putting green* must not be repaired if it might assist the player in his subsequent play of the hole.

d. Testing Surface
During the *stipulated round*, a player must not test the surface of any *putting green* by rolling a ball or roughening or scraping the surface.
Exception: Between the play of two holes, a player may test the surface of any practice *putting green* and the *putting green* of the hole last played, unless the *Committee* has prohibited such action (see Note 2 to Rule 7-2).

e. Standing Astride or on Line of Putt

The player must not make a *stroke* on the *putting green* from a *stance* astride, or with either foot touching, the *line of putt* or an extension of that line behind the ball.

Exception: There is no penalty if the *stance* is inadvertently taken on or astride the *line of putt* (or an extension of that line behind the ball) or is taken to avoid standing on another player's *line of putt* or prospective *line of putt*.

f. Making Stroke While Another Ball in Motion

The player must not make a *stroke* while another ball is in motion after a *stroke* from the *putting green*, except that if a player does so, there is no penalty if it was his turn to play.

(Lifting ball assisting or interfering with play while another ball in motion – see Rule 22)

PENALTY FOR BREACH OF RULE 16-1:

<u>Match play</u> – Loss of hole; <u>Stroke play</u> – Two strokes.

(Position of caddie or partner – see Rule 14-2)
(Wrong putting green – see Rule 25-3)

16-2. BALL OVERHANGING HOLE

When any part of the ball overhangs the lip of the *hole*, the player is allowed enough time to reach the *hole* without unreasonable delay and an additional ten seconds to determine whether the ball is at rest. If by then the ball has not fallen into the *hole*, it is deemed to be at rest. If the ball subsequently falls into the *hole*, the player is deemed to have *holed* out with his last *stroke*, and must add a *penalty stroke* to his score for the hole; otherwise, there is no penalty under this Rule.

(Undue delay – see Rule 6-7)

THE PUTTING GREEN: GENERAL

16/1
Mud on Ball Touches Putting Green But Ball Itself Does Not Touch Green

Q. A player's ball lies off the putting green, overhanging but not touching the green. A clump of mud adhering to the ball touches the green. Is the ball considered to be on the green?

A. No. However, if a ball lies on the green but does not actually touch the green because it is perched on mud, the ball is considered to be on the green.

16/2
Ball Embedded in Side of Hole; All of Ball Below Lip of Hole

Q. A player's ball embeds in the side of a hole. All of the ball is below the level of the lip of the hole. What is the ruling?

A. The ball should be considered holed even though all of the ball is not within the circumference of the hole as required by the Definition of "Holed."

16/3
Ball Embedded in Side of Hole; All of Ball Not Below Lip of Hole

Q. A player's ball embeds in the side of a hole. Part of the ball is above the level of the lip of the hole. What is the ruling?

A. The ball is not holed – see Definition of "Holed." The player may play the ball as it lies or lift the ball under Rule 16-1b, repair the damage under Rule 16-1c and place the ball on the lip of the hole.

Decisions related to 16/2 and 16/3:
• 13/4 Ball Completely Embedded in Lip of Bunker.
• 25-2/5 Ball Embedded in Grass Bank or Face of Bunker.
• 33-8/39 Local Rule for Bunker Faces Consisting of Stacked Turf.
• 33-8/39.5 Local Rule Deeming Partially Grass-Covered Wall of Bunker to Be Part of Bunker.

16/4
Hole-Liner Not Sunk Deep Enough

Q. Players discover that a hole-liner is not sunk at least one inch below the putting green surface as prescribed in the Definition of "Hole." What should they do?

A. The players should call the matter to the attention of a member of the Committee if one is present. If feasible, the member of the Committee should attempt to have the fault corrected.

However, the players must not discontinue play in the meantime, because correction might not be possible and, if possible, might take considerable time. (Revised)

16/5
Ball Strikes Edge of Hole-Liner and Bounces Out of Hole

Q. A player's ball struck the rim of a hole-liner, which had not been sunk deep enough, and bounced out of the hole. Should the ball be considered holed in such circumstances?

A. No. Under the Definition of "Holed," the ball must be at rest within the circumference of the hole.

16/5.5
Player Holes Short Putt and Allegedly Removes Ball from Hole Before It Is at Rest

Q. A player strikes a short putt into the hole and removes the ball from the hole. His opponent or a fellow-competitor claims he heard the ball bouncing in the bottom of the hole-liner at the time the player was removing the ball from the hole, and therefore the ball cannot be considered holed in view of the Definition of "Holed" which states: "A ball is holed when it is at rest within the circumference of the hole … ." What is the ruling?

A. The ball is holed. The words "at rest" are in the Definition of "Holed" to make it clear that if a ball falls below the lip and thereafter bounces out, it is not holed.

Related Decision:
• 1-2/5 Player Putts with One Hand and Catches Ball in Hole with Other Hand.

16/6 (Reserved)

16/7
Two Holes on Each Green of Nine-Hole Course

Q. 1. Is it permissible for a Committee to make two holes on each green of a nine-hole course, one (A) for use in play of the first nine holes and the other (B) for use in play of the second nine?

2. If so, what is the status of hole B on each green when hole A is in use, and vice versa?

A. 1. Yes.

2. The hole not in use on each green is a hole made by a greenkeeper – see Definition of "Ground Under Repair" – and Rule 25-1 is applicable.

Related Decision:
• 16-1c/3 Old Hole Plug Sunk or Raised on Line of Putt.

Other Decisions related to "The Putting Green: General": See "Ball Lifted," "Ball Placed or Replaced" and "Putting Green" in the Index.

TOUCHING LINE OF PUTT

16-1a/1
Brushing Aside or Mopping Up Casual Water on Line of Putt

Q. May a player whose ball lies on the putting green brush aside casual water on his line of putt, or mop it up with a towel?

A. No. Such action would be a breach of Rule 16-1a (Touching Line of Putt).

Related Decision:
• 13-2/34 Mopping Up Casual Water on Line of Play.

16-1a/2 (Reserved)

16-1a/3
Removing Dew or Frost from Line of Putt

Q. May a player brush dew or frost from his line of putt?

A. No. Rule 16-1a prohibits touching the line of putt except in removal of loose impediments, repair of ball marks, etc. Dew or frost are not loose impediments – see Definition of "Loose Impediments." Accordingly, such action would be a breach of Rule 16-1a.

Related Decision:
• 13-2/35 Removal of Dew or Frost.

16-1a/4
Removing Casual Water from Hole

Q. A player, whose ball lies on the putting green, removes casual water from the hole without touching the inside of the hole. Is this permissible?

A. As the player has not touched the line of putt, he is not in breach of Rule 16-1a. However, the player is in breach of Rule 13-2 which prohibits improving the line of play by removing water. The player incurs a penalty of loss of hole in match play or two strokes in stroke play.

Related Decisions:
• 16-1d/4 Testing for Wetness of Surface of Putting Green Behind Ball.
• 33/1 Removal of Casual Water or Loose Impediments on Putting Green by Committee.

16-1a/5
Touching Inside of Hole

Q. Prior to putting, a player touched the inside of the hole. Should he be considered to have touched his line of putt in breach of Rule 16-1a?

A. Yes, unless the hole was materially damaged and the player was entitled to repair it – see Decision 16-1a/6. The line of putt includes the hole except in the unusual case when a player makes a stroke from the putting green away from the hole.

16-1a/6
Damaged Hole; Procedure for Player

Q. Prior to putting, a player discovers that the hole has been damaged. What is the proper procedure?

A. If the damage is not clearly identifiable as a ball mark, then:

(a) If the damage is such that the proper dimensions of the hole have not been changed materially, the player should continue play without repairing the hole. If he touches the hole in such circumstances, a breach of Rule 16-1a occurs.

(b) If the proper dimensions of the hole have been changed materially, the player should request the Committee to have the hole repaired. If a member of the Committee is not readily available, the player may repair the damage, without penalty.

If a player repairs a materially damaged hole when a member of the Committee is readily available, he incurs a penalty for a breach of Rule 16-1a. (Revised)

Decisions related to 16-1a/5 and 16-1a/6:
• 1-2/3.5 Player Repairs Hole After Holing Out But Before Opponent, Fellow-Competitor or Partner Holes Out.
• 33-2b/1.5 Committee Wishes to Move Hole During Stroke-Play Round Due to Severity of Location.
• 33-2b/2 Relocating Hole After Ball Already Positioned Nearby on Putting Green.

16-1a/7
Player Repairs Depression on Line of Putt Created When Partially Embedded Acorn Removed

Q. A player removed with his hand an embedded acorn on his line of putt. The acorn was not solidly embedded, so it was a loose impediment. The player then repaired the depression in which the acorn lay. Was the repair of the depression a breach of Rule 16-1a?

A. Yes.

Related Decision:
• 23/9 Embedded Acorn.

16-1a/8
Loose Impediments Removed from Line of Putt with Cap or Towel

Q. A player touches his line of putt in brushing aside loose impediments with his cap or with a towel. Is this permissible?

A. Yes, provided he did not press anything down.

16-1a/9
Brushing Loose Impediments Off Line of Putt with Palm of Hand

Q. A player, with about one dozen strokes with the whole palm of his hand, attempted to remove small leaves, which are difficult to remove by any method, from his line of putt. Is this permissible?

A. Yes, provided the player did not press anything down (Rule 16-1a(i)) and, if the surface were roughened, he did not do so with the intention of testing the surface of the putting green (Rule 16-1d). Given the nature of his acts, any doubt as to whether he pressed anything down should be resolved against the player.

Related Decision:
• 16-1d/6 Caddie Roughens Surface of Putting Green But Player Does Not Benefit.

16-1a/10
Loose Impediments Brushed Along Line of Putt Rather Than to Side

Q. In removing loose impediments from his line of putt by brushing with a putter, a player brushed along the line for about one foot before brushing the impediments to the side. Did the player infringe Rule 16-1?

A. Under Rule 16-1a, a player is allowed to brush aside loose impediments on his line of putt. The casual movement of the putter along the line of putt would not be a breach of the Rules unless in the process the player did something to the putting green that improved his line of putt, (e.g., pressed down a raised tuft of grass), in which case he would be in breach of Rule 13-2. (Revised)

16-1a/11
Raised Tuft of Grass on Line of Putt Brushed to Determine Whether It Is Loose

Q. A player cannot determine whether a raised tuft of grass on his line of putt is loose or is attached to its roots. The player brushes the raised tuft lightly with his hand to make a determination and discovers that the tuft is attached. What is the ruling?

A. A player is entitled to touch and move a natural object on his line of putt for the specific purpose of determining whether the object is loose, provided that if the object is found not to be loose, (1) it has not become detached and (2) it is returned to its original position before the next stroke if failure to do so would result in a breach of Rule 13-2. The touching of the line of putt in these circumstances is not a breach of Rule 16-1a.

Except as otherwise permitted in the Rules (e.g., in repairing a ball mark), if a player touches or moves a natural object on his line of putt other than to determine whether it is loose and it is found to be attached, the player cannot avoid a breach of Rule 16-1a by returning the object to its original position.

Related Decision:
• 13-2/26 Natural Object Interfering with Swing Moved to Determine Whether It Is Loose.

16-1a/12
Player Walks on Line of Putt

Q. A player walked on his line of putt. Did he incur a penalty for a breach of Rule 16-1a?

A. Yes, if he did so intentionally. No, if he did so accidentally and the act did not improve the line.

16-1a/13
Line of Putt Damaged Accidentally by Opponent, Fellow-Competitor or Their Caddies

Q. An opponent, fellow-competitor or one of their caddies accidentally steps on and damages the player's line of putt. What is the ruling?

A. There is no penalty. Rule 1-2 is not applicable as the physical conditions were not altered with the intent of affecting the playing of the hole.

In equity (Rule 1-4), the player may have the line of putt restored to its original condition. The player is entitled to the lie and line of putt he had when his ball came to rest. The line of putt may be restored by anyone.

If it is not possible to restore the line of putt, the player would be justified in requesting the Committee to grant relief. If the damage is severe enough, the Committee may declare the area to be ground under repair, in which case the competitor may take relief under Rule 25-1b(iii). (Revised)

Related Decisions: See "Equity: player entitled to lie, line of play and stance when ball comes to rest after stroke" in the Index.

16-1a/14 (Reserved)

16-1a/15
Mushroom Growing on Line of Putt

Q. A mushroom is growing on a player's line of putt. Is the player entitled to relief?

A. The player would be justified in discontinuing play and requesting the Committee to remove the mushroom. The Committee should comply.

If such an abnormal condition is a recurring problem on a course, the Committee should make a Local Rule to the effect that mushrooms on the putting green are to be treated as ground under repair.

Related Decision:
16-1c/3 Old Hole Plug Sunk or Raised on Line of Putt.

16-1a/16
Spike Mark on Line of Putt Repaired During Repair of Ball Mark

Q. A player stepped on a ball mark in the act of repairing it and incidentally pressed down a spike mark on his line of putt. Did the player incur a penalty under Rule 16-1a?

A. Yes, unless the spike mark was so close to the ball mark that it was impractical to repair the ball mark without affecting the spike mark.

Related Decisions:
• 13-2/36 Competitor Sanctions Repair of Spike Damage on His Line of Putt by Fellow-Competitor.
• 16-1c/4 Repair of Spike Mark Damage Around Hole.

16-1a/16.5
Spike Mark on Line of Putt Pressed Down When Player Repairs Old Hole Plug

Q. An old hole plug is raised on the player's line of putt. The player steps on the hole plug to make it level with the surface of the putting green. In so doing he presses down a spike mark within the hole plug. Was the player in breach of Rule 16-1a when he pressed down the spike mark?

A. No. Rule 16-1a permits touching the line of putt "in repairing old hole plugs."

If the spike mark had been near but not within the old hole plug, the ruling would be different. In these circumstances, the player would have been able to step on the hole plug without affecting the spike mark.

16-1a/17
Ball Lifted on Putting Green Placed Ahead of Ball-Marker and Then Moved Back to Original Position

Q. When replacing his ball on the putting green, a player has a habit of placing the ball ahead of his ball-marker and then rolling or sliding the ball to its original position. Is such a procedure permissible?

A. Such a procedure is not recommended but is not a breach of Rule 16-1a, which permits touching the line of putt in lifting (or replacing) the ball. However, if in the process the player does something to the putting green that improves his line of putt (e.g., presses down a raised tuft of grass), he is in breach of Rule 13-2. (Revised)

Related Decisions:
• 16-1d/3 Player Returns Ball to Spot from Which It Was Lifted by Rolling It with Putter.
• 20-1/19 Placing Object Marking Position of Ball Other Than Behind Ball.

Other Decisions related to Rule 16-1a: See "Line of Putt" and "Putting Green: line of putt" in the Index.

LIFTING BALL ON PUTTING GREEN

16-1b/1
Ball on Putting Green Lifted Because Player Feared Ball Might Move

Q. A player lifted his ball on the putting green under Rule 16-1b, cleaned it and replaced it. As the player approached the ball to make his next stroke, he feared the ball might move. So he lifted the ball again, replaced it and played. What is the ruling?

A. There is no penalty, provided the player marked the position of his ball both times. Rule 16-1b permits the lifting of a ball on the putting green in these circumstances. (Revised)

16-1b/2
Ball Lifted from Putting Green; Ball Replaced While Another Ball in Motion But Then Lifted Because Moving Ball Might Strike It

Q. A's ball comes to rest on the putting green 20 feet from the hole. He marks the position of and lifts his ball so that B, whose ball is also on the putting green, but farther from the hole, can play first. While B's ball is in motion, A replaces his ball. He then realizes that B's ball might strike his ball. A re-marks the position of and lifts his ball to ensure the balls will not collide. What is the ruling?

A. There is no penalty. The replacing and subsequent lifting of A's ball is considered to be an extension of his initial authority to lift the ball under Rule 16-1b, and accordingly the prohibition in that Rule against lifting a ball while another ball is in motion does not apply. Rule 22 does not apply in this case because the ball was initially lifted under Rule 16-1b. (Revised)

16-1b/3
Ball Lifted from Putting Green; Ball Replaced While Another Ball in Motion Subsequently Deflects Ball

Q. A's ball comes to rest on the putting green 20 feet from the hole. He marks the position of and lifts his ball so that B, whose ball is also on the putting green, but farther from the hole, can play first. While B's ball is in motion, A replaces his ball. B's ball strikes A's ball. What is the ruling?

A. If A's action was unintentional (i.e., not for the purpose of deflecting B's ball), Rule 19-5a applies. There is no penalty to either player since A had lifted his ball and it was not lying on the putting green immediately prior to B's stroke. A must replace his ball, and B must play his ball as it lies.

If A's action was for the purpose of deflecting B's ball, A is in breach of Rule 1-2 (Exerting Influence on Movement of Ball or Altering Physical Conditions). The penalty is loss of hole in match play or two strokes in stroke play, unless the Committee decides to impose a penalty of disqualification – see the penalty statement under Rule 1-2. In stroke play, B must replay his stroke, without penalty – see Note under Rule 19-1. Rule 16-1b does not apply as this Rule deals with the lifting of a ball on a putting green, but not its placement. (Revised)

16-1b/4
Ball Lifted from Putting Green by Opponent or Fellow-Competitor While Player's Ball in Motion

Q. A's ball is on the putting green 20 yards from the hole. The ball of B, his opponent or fellow-competitor, is also on the putting green five yards to the right of the hole. A putts and, while the ball is in motion and still 15 yards from the hole, B marks and lifts his ball in order to clean it prior to making his stroke. A played a poor putt and his ball came to rest a yard short of B's ball-marker. What is the ruling?

A. Under Rule 16-1b, B is penalized if lifting his ball might have influenced the movement of A's ball. The determination as to whether there is a reasonable possibility that B's ball might have influenced the movement of A's ball is made by reference to the situation at the time B lifted his ball.

In this case, as B's ball was lying some distance from A's intended line of putt and A's ball had only traveled a short distance at the time that B lifted his ball, it was reasonable for B to assume that the lifting of his ball would not influence the movement of A's ball, despite the fact that A's ball came to rest quite close to the spot from which B's ball was lifted.

When assessing the possibility that A's ball might have collided with B's ball and thus that, by lifting his ball, B might have influenced the movement of A's ball, the following are among the factors that should be taken into account:
- the distance of B's ball from A's line of putt
- the line on which A's ball was moving, and
- the contours of the putting green.

Any doubt as to whether there is a reasonable possibility that the lifting of the ball might have influenced the movement of the ball in motion is resolved against the player who lifted his ball. (New)

Decisions related to 16-1b/3 and 16-1b/4:
- 1-2/0.5 Serious Breach of Rule 1-2.
- 1-2/1 Line of Putt Altered Purposely by Opponent or Fellow-Competitor by Stepping on It.
- 17-3/2 Opponent or Fellow-Competitor Attending Flagstick for Player Fails to Remove It; Player's Ball Strikes Flagstick.
- 19-1/5 Ball Deliberately Deflected or Stopped on Putting Green by Fellow-Competitor.

Other Decisions related to Rule 16-1b: See "Ball Lifted: putting green" in the Index.

REPAIR OF HOLE PLUGS AND BALL MARKS ON PUTTING GREEN

16-1c/1
Repair of Ball Mark a Second Time

Q. A ball mark has been repaired by a player. The ball mark is on the line of putt of a following player. May the following player further repair the ball mark?

A. Yes, provided it is still clearly identifiable as a ball mark.

16-1c/1.5
Ball Mark Partially on and Partially Off Putting Green Is on Line of Play

Q. If a player's ball lies just off the putting green and there is a ball mark on his line of play, he is entitled to repair the ball mark if it is on the green (Rule 16-1c), but not if it is off the green (Rule 13-2). What is the ruling if a ball mark on the line of play is partially on and partially off the green?

A. Since it is impracticable to allow the repair of only that part of the ball mark which is on the putting green, the player may repair the entire ball mark.

16-1c/2
Ball Mark in Position to Assist Opponent

Q. A and B are playing a match. At a par-3 hole, both are on the green with their tee shots. A's ball comes to rest four feet from the hole. B's ball is fifteen feet from the hole. Upon reaching the green, A prepares to repair his ball mark. B tells A not to do so until he (B) has putted because A's ball mark is so situated that B's ball might be deflected into the hole by it. A objects, stating that he wishes to repair his ball mark immediately. May A do so?

A. No. If A were to repair the ball mark, he would lose the hole under Rule 1-2. A has no right to repair a ball mark affecting B's play if B requests A not to repair it, unless the ball mark also physically affects A's play and it is A's turn to play.

16-1c/3
Old Hole Plug Sunk or Raised on Line of Putt

Q. A player's ball lies on the green. An old hole plug is sunk or raised on the player's line of putt. What relief is available to the player?

A. The player may attempt to raise or lower the plug to make it level with the surface of the putting green – Rule 16-1c. If this is impossible, he may discontinue play and request the Committee to raise or lower the plug. If the Committee cannot level the plug without unduly delaying play, the

Committee should declare the plug to be ground under repair, in which case the player would be entitled to relief under Rule 25-1b(iii).

Related Decisions:
- 16/7 Two Holes on Each Green of Nine-Hole Course.
- 16-1a/15 Mushroom Growing on Line of Putt.
- 25/17 Sunken Hole Plug.
- 25/18 Hole of Removed Stake Defining Water Hazard.
- 33-8/30 Local Rule Permitting the Repair of Turf Plugs on the Putting Green That Are Not 4¼ Inches in Diameter.

16-1c/4
Repair of Spike Mark Damage Around Hole

Q. A player's ball lies on or near the putting green. Before playing his next stroke, he taps down spike marks in the vicinity of the hole. Is this permissible?

A. No. Such action would be a breach of Rule 16-1c since repair of spike marks in the vicinity of the hole might assist the player in his subsequent play of the hole.

Related Decisions:
- 13-2/36 Competitor Sanctions Repair of Spike Damage on His Line of Putt by Fellow-Competitor.
- 16-1a/16 Spike Mark on Line of Putt Repaired During Repair of Ball Mark.

TESTING SURFACE OF PUTTING GREEN

16-1d/1
Player Concedes Opponent's Next Stroke and Rolls or Knocks Ball to Opponent

Q. A player concedes his opponent's next stroke and either picks up the opponent's ball and rolls it to the opponent or knocks it back to him with a club. The player did so only for the purpose of returning the opponent's ball to him, not to test the surface of the putting green. Was the player in breach of Rule 16-1d (Testing Surface)?

A. No. Such casual action is not a breach of Rule 16-1d.

16-1d/2
Player Concedes Opponent's Next Stroke and Knocks His Ball Away Along Own Line of Putt

Q. A player concedes his opponent's next stroke and knocks his ball away on the same line on which he (the player) must subsequently putt. Is this a breach of Rule 16-1d?

A. It is a question of fact whether or not the player's action was for the purpose of testing the surface of the putting green. The manner and apparent purpose of the action would be the determining factors in each individual case.

16-1d/3
Player Returns Ball to Spot from Which It Was Lifted by Rolling It with Putter

Q. A player marks the position of his ball on the putting green, lifts the ball and sets it aside. When it is his turn to putt, he rolls the ball with his putter back to the spot from which it was lifted. Was the player in breach of Rule 16-1d (Testing Surface)?

A. No, provided the action of rolling the ball was not for the purpose of testing the surface of the green. This method of replacing a ball is not recommended, but it is not a breach of the Rules.

Decision related to 16-1d/1 through 16-1d/3:
• 16-1a/17 Ball Lifted on Putting Green Placed Ahead of Ball-Marker and Then Moved Back to Original Position.

16-1d/4
Testing for Wetness of Surface of Putting Green Behind Ball

Q. A player placed the palm of his hand on the putting green behind his ball to determine if the green was wet. He did not roughen or scrape the surface. Was the player in breach of Rule 16-1d (Testing Surface)?

A. No. Rule 16-1d only prohibits rolling a ball or roughening or scraping the putting surface for testing purposes. Since the line of putt was not touched, Rule 16-1a also was not infringed.

Related Decisions:
• 16-1a/4 Removing Casual Water from Hole.
• 33/1 Removal of Casual Water or Loose Impediments on Putting Green by Committee.

16-1d/5
Rubbing Ball on Putting Green for Cleaning Purposes

Q. May a player clean his ball by rubbing it on the putting green?

A. Yes, provided the act is not for the purpose of testing the surface of the putting green. It is recommended that a ball be cleaned in other ways to eliminate any question as to the player's intentions.

16-1d/6
Caddie Roughens Surface of Putting Green But Player Does Not Benefit

Q. A player's caddie tests the surface of the putting green by roughening the grass. The player tells him immediately that he is not allowed to do that under the Rules. The player receives no information from the caddie about the condition of the green. Is the player penalized under Rule 16-1d?

A. Yes. The reference to the player in Rule 16-1d includes his caddie. Thus, the Rule prohibits the caddie, as well as the player, from testing the surface of the putting green. Under Rule 6-1, the player incurs the applicable penalty for a breach of a Rule by his caddie.

Related Decisions:
- 8-1/17 Request for Advice Made in Error to Opponent's Caddie Withdrawn Before Advice Given.
- 16-1a/9 Brushing Loose Impediments Off Line of Putt with Palm of Hand.

STANDING ASTRIDE OR ON LINE OF PUTT

16-1e/1
Meaning of "Line of Putt" in Context of "Standing Astride or on Line of Putt"

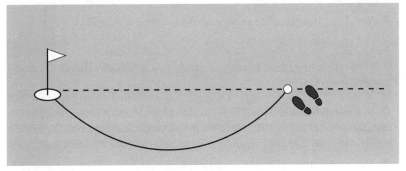

Q. With reference to the above illustration, the broken line is a direct line from the ball to the hole and the solid line is the line on which the player intends his ball to travel. Which line is the "line of putt" for purposes of application of Rule 16-1e (Standing Astride or on Line of Putt)? If the broken line is the "line of putt," the player will be in breach of Rule 16-1e. If the solid line is the "line of putt," he will not be in breach of the Rule.

A. The solid line is the "line of putt."

BALL OVERHANGING HOLE

16-2/0.5
Ball Overhanging Hole Is Lifted, Cleaned and Replaced; Ball Then Falls into Hole

Q. After an approach shot, a player's ball is overhanging the hole. The player walks up to the hole without unreasonable delay and notices that there is mud on the ball. The player marks the position of the ball and lifts it. He then cleans the ball and replaces it. The ball remains on the lip of the hole for about five seconds and then, as the player is preparing to tap it into the hole, the ball falls into the hole. What is the ruling?

A. Under Rule 16-2, if a ball falls into the hole after it is deemed to be at rest, the player is deemed to have holed out with his last stroke and he shall add a penalty stroke to his score for the hole. In this case, when the player marked the position of the ball it must have been at rest. The ball must be considered to have been at rest when it was replaced; otherwise, it would have to be replaced again (Rule 20-3d).

Accordingly, the player is deemed to have holed out with his last stroke and must add a penalty stroke to his score for the hole.

16-2/1
Ball Overhanging Hole Falls into Hole After Player Waits 40 Seconds

Q. A player's ball overhangs the edge of the hole. The player walks up to the hole. He then waits about 40 seconds, after which the ball falls into the hole. Is the player subject to penalty?

A. Yes. The player incurs a penalty of one stroke (Rule 16-2).

16-2/2
Ball Overhanging Hole Knocked Away by Opponent Before Player Determines Status

Q. In a match between A and B, A putts and his ball apparently comes to rest, but is overhanging the hole. Within five seconds, B concedes A's next stroke and knocks his ball away. Was B entitled to knock A's ball away?

A. No. Under Rule 16-2, A is allowed a reasonable time to reach the hole and an additional ten seconds to determine whether his ball is at rest. Since B infringed A's rights, in equity (Rule 1-4), B lost the hole, assuming that A's putt was not for a half, in which case Rule 2-2 (Halved Hole) would apply.

Related Decisions:
• 1-2/4 Player Jumps Close to Hole to Cause Ball to Drop; Ball Moves.
• 2-4/2 Ball Falls into Hole After Concession of Next Stroke.
• 18-2b/10 Ball Falls into Hole After Being Addressed.

16-2/3 (Reserved)

16-2/4
Ball Overhanging Lip of Hole Moves When Flagstick Removed

Q. After a stroke from just off the putting green, a player's ball comes to rest overhanging the lip of the hole but not resting against the unattended flagstick. The player reaches the hole without unreasonable delay and removes the flagstick. The ball either rolls away from the hole or falls into the hole. What is the ruling?

A. It is a question of fact whether the player's actions caused the ball to move and any doubt should be resolved against the player.

The flagstick is a movable obstruction. If the movement of the ball was directly attributable to the removal of the flagstick, the ball must be replaced on the lip of the hole without penalty (Rule 24-1a). If the player caused the ball to move but the movement of the ball was not directly attributable to the removal of the flagstick, the ball must be replaced on the lip of the hole, and the player incurs a penalty stroke under Rule 18-2a.

If the player's actions did not cause the ball to move and the ball fell into the hole, the provisions of Rule 16-2 apply, whether the removal of the flagstick occurs before or after the lapse of time contemplated by Rule 16-2.

If the player's actions did not cause the ball to move and the ball moved to another position, the player must play the ball from that new position.

If an opponent or fellow-competitor were to remove the flagstick without the player's authority, before the ball is deemed to be at rest under Rule 16-2 and as a result of this action causes the ball to move, the opponent or fellow-competitor has infringed the player's rights as, under Rule 16-2, the player is allowed a reasonable time to reach the hole and an additional ten seconds to determine whether his ball is at rest. In equity (Rule 1-4), the opponent or fellow-competitor incurs the loss-of-hole penalty in match play or a two-stroke penalty in stroke play. The player incurs no penalty and, in stroke play, must place the ball on the lip of the hole.

If an opponent or fellow-competitor were to remove the flagstick without the player's authority, before the ball is deemed to be at rest under Rule 16-2, and this does not cause the ball to move, and the ball falls into the hole, the provisions of Rule 16-2 apply.

Related Decisions:
- 2-4/8 Player Concedes Opponent's Next Stroke and Plays Before Opponent Has Opportunity to Lift Ball.
- 3-4/1 Competitor Not Given Opportunity to Lift Ball Assisting Fellow-Competitor.
- 17-4/2 Ball Resting Against Flagstick; Putt Conceded and Ball Removed Before Player Can Remove Flagstick.
- 22/6 Competitor Requests That Ball in Position to Assist Him Not Be Lifted.
- 30-3f/11 Request to Lift Ball That Might Assist Partner Not Honored.

16-2/5
Ball Overhanging Lip of Hole Moves and Strikes Flagstick During Removal of Flagstick

Q. After a stroke from off the putting green, a player's ball overhangs the lip of the hole. While the player is removing the flagstick, the ball falls into the hole, striking the flagstick. The player's actions did not cause the ball to move. What is the ruling?

A. In equity (Rule 1-4), there is no penalty under Rule 17. If the ball came to rest within the circumference of the hole with all of it below the level of the lip of the hole, the ball is holed. If, after striking the flagstick, the ball is deflected out of the hole, the ball must be placed on the lip of the hole without penalty.

The answer with regard to Rule 17 is not affected by how much time elapses before the ball falls into the hole after the player reaches the hole.

There would be a penalty stroke under Rule 16-2 if the ball falls into the hole after it is deemed to be at rest under that Rule.

If, prior to the lapse of the period specified by Rule 16-2, an opponent or fellow-competitor were removing the flagstick without the player's authority and the ball fell into the hole and struck the flagstick before coming to rest outside the hole, the opponent or fellow-competitor would, in equity (Rule 1-4), incur the loss-of-hole penalty in match play or a two-stroke penalty in stroke play as he would be considered to have infringed the player's rights under Rule 16-2. In such a case in stroke play, the player would be required to replace the ball on the lip of the hole.

RULE 17

THE FLAGSTICK

DEFINITIONS

All defined terms are in *italics* and are listed alphabetically in the Definitions section – see pages 6–16.

17-1. FLAGSTICK ATTENDED, REMOVED OR HELD UP

Before making a *stroke* from anywhere on the *course*, the player may have the *flagstick* attended, removed or held up to indicate the position of the *hole*.

If the *flagstick* is not attended, removed or held up before the player makes a *stroke*, it must not be attended, removed or held up during the *stroke* or while the player's ball is in motion if doing so might influence the movement of the ball.

Note 1: If the *flagstick* is in the *hole* and anyone stands near it while a *stroke* is being made, he is deemed to be attending the *flagstick*.

Note 2: If, prior to the *stroke*, the *flagstick* is attended, removed or held up by anyone with the player's knowledge and he makes no objection, the player is deemed to have authorized it.

Note 3: If anyone attends or holds up the *flagstick* while a *stroke* is being made, he is deemed to be attending the *flagstick* until the ball comes to rest.

(Moving attended, removed or held-up flagstick while ball in motion – see Rule 24-1)

17-2. UNAUTHORIZED ATTENDANCE

If an *opponent* or his *caddie* in match play or a *fellow-competitor* or his *caddie* in stroke play, without the player's authority or prior knowledge, attends, removes or holds up the *flagstick* during the *stroke* or while the ball is in motion, and the act might influence the movement of the ball, the *opponent* or *fellow-competitor* incurs the applicable penalty.

*PENALTY FOR BREACH OF RULE 17-1 or 17-2:

<u>Match play</u> – Loss of hole; <u>Stroke play</u> – Two strokes.

*In stroke play, if a breach of Rule 17-2 occurs and the *competitor's* ball subsequently strikes the *flagstick*, the person attending or holding it or anything carried by him, the *competitor* incurs no penalty. The ball is played as it lies, except that if the *stroke* was made on the *putting green,* the *stroke* is canceled and the ball must be replaced and replayed.

17-3. BALL STRIKING FLAGSTICK OR ATTENDANT

The player's ball must not strike:

a. The *flagstick* when it is attended, removed or held up;

b. The person attending or holding up the *flagstick* or anything carried by him; or

c. The *flagstick* in the *hole*, unattended, when the *stroke* has been made on the *putting green*.

Exception: When the *flagstick* is attended, removed or held up without the player's authority – see Rule 17-2.

PENALTY FOR BREACH OF RULE 17-3:
Match play – Loss of hole; Stroke play – Two strokes and the ball must be played as it lies.

17-4. BALL RESTING AGAINST FLAGSTICK

When a player's ball rests against the *flagstick* in the *hole* and the ball is not *holed*, the player or another person authorized by him may move or remove the *flagstick*, and if the ball falls into the *hole*, the player is deemed to have *holed* out with his last *stroke*; otherwise, the ball, if *moved*, must be placed on the lip of the *hole*, without penalty.

THE FLAGSTICK: GENERAL

17/1
Attachment to Flagstick to Indicate Position of Hole on Green

Q. A thin disc or sleeve is attached to the flagstick to indicate the distance of the hole from the front of the green. If the disc is placed near the bottom of the flagstick it means that the hole is at the front of the green; if it is placed near the top of the flagstick it means that the hole is at the back of the green. Is this permitted?

A. Yes, provided the attachment is circular in cross-section.

17/2
Different Colored Flags Used to Indicate Position of Hole on Green

Q. May a Committee use flagsticks with flags of two different colors, one color being used when the hole is at the front of the green and the other when the hole is at the back?

A. Yes.

17/3
Flagstick Tapered or of Varying Diameters

Q. May a flagstick be tapered or have a slender metal ferrule at the base?

A. Yes. The Definition does not prohibit sections of varying diameters. The Definition requires that the flagstick be circular in cross-section. This is to prohibit non-circular features in the lower part of the flagstick.

17/3.5
Reflector on Flagstick

Q. To aid in the use of distance measuring devices, a course has reflectors on its flagsticks. However, the reflectors are not circular in cross-section. Is the use of such reflectors permissible?

A. Yes. The use of small non-circular reflectors is an exception to the requirement in the Definition of "Flagstick" that a flagstick and any attachment to it must be circular in cross-section.

Related Decisions:
• 8-1/2 Exchanging Distance Information.
• 14-3/0.5 Local Rule Permitting Use of Distance-Measuring Device.
• 14-3/0.7 Player Obtains Distance Information Measured with Electronic Device.

17/4
Adjustment of Flagstick; Player's Rights

Q. A player playing from off the putting green and wishing to leave the flagstick in the hole may find that the flagstick is leaning towards his ball (a disadvantage) or away from his ball (an advantage). What are the player's rights in such a situation?

A. The flagstick may be left as it is or centered in the hole, as contemplated by the Definition of "Flagstick."

The flagstick may not be intentionally adjusted to a more favorable position than centered. To do so would infringe Rule 1-2 (Exerting Influence on Movement of Ball or Altering Physical Conditions).

An opponent or fellow-competitor who centers the flagstick incurs no penalty, but the player may have it restored to its original position. (Revised)

17/5 (Reserved)

17/6
Ball Lodged in Flag Attached to Flagstick

Q. A player's ball lodges in the flag attached to a flagstick. What is the procedure?

A. A flagstick is a movable obstruction and Rule 24-1 applies. However, in taking relief the player may not place the ball in the hole. Therefore, in equity (Rule 1-4), the player must place the ball on the lip of the hole when taking relief.

17/7
Hole-Liner Pulled Out by Flagstick Attendant and Ball Falls into Unlined Hole

Q. A flagstick attendant removes the flagstick and, in the process, pulls out the hole-liner. The player's ball rolls into the unlined hole. What is the ruling?

A. The player incurs no penalty and the ball is holed. A hole need not contain a lining – see Definition of "Hole."

17/8
Ball Strikes Hole-Liner Pulled Out with Flagstick

Q. A player played a stroke from the putting green. The ball struck the hole-liner, which had stuck to the bottom of the flagstick and had come out of the hole when the person attending the flagstick removed the flagstick. Is there any penalty?

A. No. A hole-liner is an outside agency. Accordingly, if the hole-liner was moving when the ball struck it, the stroke is canceled and the ball must be replaced – Rule 19-1b. If the hole-liner was not moving, the ball must be played as it lies – Rule 19-1. In case of doubt, the ball must be played as it lies.

17/9
Attendant Removes Flagstick Whereupon Knob Falls from Top of Flagstick and Deflects Ball

Q. After a player putts, the flagstick attendant removes the flagstick and a knob attached to the top of the flagstick falls off. The knob strikes the player's moving ball and deflects it. What is the ruling?

A. Once detached the knob was no longer a part of the flagstick. It was an outside agency. Therefore, the stroke is canceled and the ball must be replaced – Rule 19-1b.

Other Decisions related to Rule 17: See "Flagstick" in the Index.

FLAGSTICK ATTENDED, REMOVED OR HELD UP

17-1/1
Meaning of "Stands Near the Hole"

Q. Note 1 to Rule 17-1 states that, if anyone "stands near the hole," he is deemed to be attending the flagstick. Is such a person considered to be standing "near the hole" if he is close enough to touch the flagstick?

A. Yes.

17-1/2
Opponent or Fellow-Competitor Declines to Attend Flagstick

Q. Does a player have any redress if he requests his opponent or a fellow-competitor to attend the flagstick for him and the opponent or fellow-competitor declines?

A. No.

17-1/3
Flagstick Attended by Referee, Observer or Marker at Player's Request

Q. A player requests a referee, observer or marker to attend the flagstick and the referee, observer or marker does so. Is the player subject to penalty?

A. A referee or observer should not attend the flagstick – see Definitions of "Referee" and "Observer." However, a player incurs no penalty if he makes such a request and the referee or observer complies.

A marker may attend the flagstick even if he is not a fellow-competitor.

17-1/4
Flagstick Attendant Stands Behind Hole

Q. May a person attending the flagstick stand directly behind the hole, instead of to the side of it?

A. Yes. A flagstick attendant might have to stand behind the hole to avoid standing on the line of putt of another player.

17-1/4.5
Flagstick Attendant Removes Flagstick and Holds It Upright Behind Hole; End of Flagstick Touches Green

Q. A player preparing to putt asks his caddie to attend the flagstick. The caddie removes the flagstick from the hole and holds it upright two or three inches directly behind the hole, with the end of the flagstick touching the putting green. He attends the flagstick in this manner to eliminate the risk of the flagstick sticking in the hole. Is such a procedure a breach of the Rules?

A. No, but such a practice is not recommended because of the possibility of damage to the putting green.

17-1/5
Holding Flagstick with One Hand and Putting with Other Hand

Q. A player holds the flagstick with one hand and holes a short putt, gripping the putter with his other hand. Is this permissible?

A. Yes, provided the flagstick has been removed from the hole and the ball therefore does not strike it. If the ball were to strike the flagstick, a breach of Rule 17-3a would occur.

Related Decision:
• 14-3/9 Player Putts with One Hand and Steadies Himself with Club Held in Other Hand.

17-1/6 (Reserved)

17-1/7
Removed Flagstick Placed on Ground Subsequently Lifted

Q. A, the opponent or fellow-competitor of B, removes the flagstick from the hole and places it on the ground. B putts and A, who is standing within reach of the removed flagstick, realizes that B's ball might strike the removed flagstick, so he picks the flagstick up. What is the ruling?

A. There is no penalty – see Rule 24-1.

UNAUTHORIZED ATTENDANCE

17-2/1
Opponent or Fellow-Competitor Attends Flagstick Without Authority But Ceases Attendance on Instruction of Player

Q. While a player is preparing to play from near the putting green, his opponent or fellow-competitor attends the flagstick without the player's authority or prior knowledge. The player makes the stroke, looks up and sees the flagstick being attended. While the ball is in motion, the player tells the opponent or fellow-competitor to leave the flagstick in the hole and step away, which he does. What is the ruling?

A. Since the unauthorized attendance might have influenced the movement of the ball, the opponent or fellow-competitor was in breach of Rule 17-2. The opponent or fellow-competitor does not avoid the penalty under Rule 17-2 by ceasing his attendance of the flagstick.

In match play, the opponent loses the hole (Rule 17-2).

In stroke play, the fellow-competitor is penalized two strokes and the ball is played as it lies. If the player's ball strikes the flagstick, the player incurs no penalty (Rule 17-2).

17-2/2
Flagstick Attended by Opponent or Fellow-Competitor Without Authority While Player's Ball in Motion

Q. A player plays from just off the putting green with the flagstick in the hole. While the ball is in motion and still 20 yards from the hole, an opponent or fellow-competitor, without the authority of the player, removes the flagstick as he mistakenly believes that the player will be penalized if his ball strikes the flagstick in the hole. The ball comes to rest five yards short of the hole. What is the ruling?

A. Under Rule 17-2, the opponent or fellow-competitor is penalized if the removal of the flagstick might have influenced the movement of the ball. The determination as to whether there is a reasonable possibility that the removal of the flagstick might have influenced the movement of the ball is made by reference to the situation at the time the flagstick was removed.

In this case, since the flagstick was removed before it was possible to know what the result of the stroke might be, and since the intention of the player making the stroke was to get the ball as close to the hole as possible, at the moment the flagstick was removed it was reasonably possible that its removal might have influenced the movement of the ball. Therefore, the opponent loses the hole in match play or the fellow-competitor incurs a penalty of two strokes in stroke play for a breach of Rule 17-2.

If a flagstick is removed, attended, or held up without authority by an opponent or fellow-competitor while a ball is in motion, but at the time of the action it is not reasonably possible that the ball will reach the hole or, having gone past the hole, will return to the hole (e.g., as a result of the slope of the putting green, wind, etc.), there is no breach of Rule 17-2. (Revised)

BALL STRIKING FLAGSTICK OR ATTENDANT

17-3/1
Holing Out Without Ball Touching Flagstick

Q. A player plays a stroke from the putting green without having the flagstick attended. The ball stops momentarily on the lip of the hole and then falls into the hole. The player claims that the ball fell into the hole without striking the flagstick and therefore he incurs no penalty under Rule 17-3. Is the claim valid?

A. No. A ball is not holed until it is at rest in the hole – see Definition of "Holed." If the flagstick is in the hole, it is impossible for a ball to come to rest in the hole without striking the flagstick.

17-3/2
Opponent or Fellow-Competitor Attending Flagstick for Player Fails to Remove It; Player's Ball Strikes Flagstick

Q. A's ball lies on the putting green. A requests B, his opponent or fellow-competitor, to attend the flagstick, and B complies. A putts and B fails to remove the flagstick. A's ball strikes the flagstick. What is the ruling?

A. If B failed to remove the flagstick for the purpose of causing A to incur a penalty, B is disqualified, in both match play and stroke play, under Rule 33-7 for taking an action contrary to the spirit of the game. In stroke play, in equity (Rule 1-4), A must replay the stroke without penalty.

If B's failure to remove the flagstick was with the intent to influence the movement of A's ball (e.g., for the purpose of preventing A's ball from going beyond the flagstick), B is in breach of Rule 1-2, and loses the hole in match play or incurs a two-stroke penalty in stroke play, whether the ball strikes the flagstick or not. In stroke play, if the ball struck the flagstick and as a result A suffered significant advantage or disadvantage, then the Committee could consider B to have committed a serious breach of Rule 1-2, the penalty for which is disqualification. Whether or not B has committed a serious breach of Rule 1-2, in stroke play, if A's ball struck the flagstick, in equity (Rule 1-4), A must replay the stroke without penalty – see Note 2 to Rule 1-2.

If B's failure to remove the flagstick was not deliberate (e.g., the flagstick stuck in the hole-liner or B was distracted and did not see A putt), since B was acting on A's behalf, A incurs a penalty of loss of hole in match play or two strokes in stroke play under Rule 17-3. A must play the ball as it lies. B incurs no penalty. (Revised)

Related Decisions:
- 1-2/0.5 Serious Breach of Rule 1-2.
- 1-2/1 Line of Putt Altered Purposely by Opponent or Fellow-Competitor by Stepping on It.
- 16-1b/3 Ball Lifted from Putting Green; Ball Replaced While Another Ball in Motion Subsequently Deflects Ball.
- 16-1b/4 Ball Lifted from Putting Green by Opponent or Fellow-Competitor While Player's Ball in Motion.
- 19-1/5 Ball Deliberately Deflected or Stopped on Putting Green by Fellow-Competitor.

17-3/3
Ball Strikes Flagstick Lying on Ground

Q. Generally, the player's ball must not strike the flagstick when removed from the hole (Rule 17-3). What is the ruling in the following situations:

    (a) A player putts too strongly and his ball strikes the flagstick which has been removed by someone in his match or group and placed on the ground behind the hole.

    (b) A player plays his second shot to the green and the ball strikes the flagstick, which had been blown down by the wind and was lying on the ground.

    (c) A player, not believing he can reach the green which is occupied by the preceding match or group, plays his second shot at a par-5 hole and the ball rolls onto the green and strikes the flagstick which has been removed from the hole and placed on the ground by someone in the preceding match or group.

A. (a) The player incurs a penalty of loss of hole in match play or two strokes in stroke play under Rule 17-3a.

    (b)&(c) No penalty is incurred. Rule 17-3a is not applicable in either case. It applies only when the flagstick has been removed with the player's authority or prior knowledge by someone in the player's match or group.

17-3/4
Flagstick Attended by Partner Without Express Authority of Player; Ball Strikes Flagstick or Partner

Q. In four-ball play, A is preparing to play from off the putting green. B, A's partner, attends the flagstick without A's knowledge or express authority. A plays and his ball strikes B or the flagstick. What is the ruling?

A. If the flagstick is attended by the player's caddie, his partner or his partner's caddie, i.e., by a member of the player's side, it is deemed to be attended with the player's knowledge and authority.

Accordingly, in match play A is disqualified from the hole (Rule 17-3b), but B incurs no penalty (Rule 30-3f).

In stroke play, A incurs a penalty of two strokes and must play the ball as it lies (Rule 17-3b), but B incurs no penalty (Rule 31-8).

17-3/5
Flag Struck by Ball When Flagstick Attended

Q. While the flagstick was being attended, a player's ball struck the flag attached to the flagstick. Did the player incur a penalty under Rule 17-3a?

A. Yes. The flag is part of the flagstick.

17-3/6
Marking Position of Hole with Club

Q. The flagstick has been removed. A wants the position of the hole marked but he does not want to waste time retrieving the flagstick. So A asks B to place the grip end of his putter in the hole. Is this permissible?

A. Yes, but a putter used to mark the position of the hole must be treated as a flagstick for the purposes of applying the Rules.

BALL RESTING AGAINST FLAGSTICK

17-4/1
Ball Resting Against Flagstick Lifted Before Being Holed

Q. A player's ball is resting against the flagstick, but it is not holed because all of it is not below the level of the lip of the hole. However, the player, believing the ball is holed, picks it up. What is the ruling?

A. The player incurs a penalty stroke under Rule 20-1 for lifting his ball without marking its position. The player must replace the ball against the flagstick and may then apply Rule 17-4.

Related Decision:
• 30-3f/3 Player's Ball Resting Against Flagstick Lifted Before Being Holed; Others in Match Pick Up Mistakenly Believing Player Won Hole.

17-4/2
Ball Resting Against Flagstick; Putt Conceded and Ball Removed Before Player Can Remove Flagstick

Q. In a match, A plays a stroke from off the green and his ball comes to rest against the flagstick. B, A's opponent, concedes A's next stroke and removes A's ball. Despite B's concession, is A entitled to have the ball replaced to enable him to exercise his rights under Rule 17-4?

A. Yes. When A's ball was resting against the flagstick, Rule 17-4 applied and A was entitled to have the flagstick moved or removed to see whether the ball would fall into the hole. B had no right to remove the ball and concede the next stroke until A had had an opportunity to proceed under Rule 17-4. By removing A's ball, B was in breach of Rule 18-3b and incurred a penalty stroke; A should then have replaced his ball against the flagstick and applied Rule 17-4.

17-4/3
Ball Resting Against Flagstick Moves Away from Hole When Flagstick Removed by Opponent or Fellow-Competitor

Q. A player's ball is resting against the flagstick. Without the player's authority, his opponent or a fellow-competitor removes the flagstick and the ball moves away from the hole. What is the ruling?

A. In match play, the opponent incurs a penalty stroke and the ball must be replaced against the flagstick (Rule 18-3b).

In stroke play, the ball must be replaced against the flagstick without penalty to anyone (Rule 18-4).

In either form of play, the player may then move or remove the flagstick as prescribed in Rule 17-4.

17-4/4
Ball Resting Against Flagstick Moves Away from Hole When Flagstick Removed by Player; Ball Not Placed on Lip of Hole

Q. A player's ball is resting against the flagstick. The player removes the flagstick and the ball moves away from the hole. The player plays the ball from its new position, holing the putt. What is the ruling?

A. The player was required to place the ball on the lip of the hole (Rule 17-4). In match play, the player loses the hole – Rules 17-4 and 2-6.

In stroke play, the player incurs a penalty of two strokes and the ball is holed – Rules 17-4 and 3-5.

Other Decisions related to Rule 17-4:
- 16-2/4 Ball Overhanging Lip of Hole Moves When Flagstick Removed
- 16-2/5 Ball Overhanging Lip of Hole Moves and Strikes Flagstick During Removal of Flagstick

BALL AT REST MOVED

DEFINITIONS
All defined terms are in *italics* and are listed alphabetically in the Definitions section – see pages 6–16.

18-1. BY OUTSIDE AGENCY
If a ball at rest is *moved* by an *outside agency*, there is no penalty and the ball must be replaced.

Note: It is a question of fact whether a ball has been *moved* by an *outside agency*. In order to apply this Rule, it must be known or virtually certain that an *outside agency* has *moved* the ball. In the absence of such knowledge or certainty, the player must play the ball as it lies or, if the ball is not found, proceed under Rule 27-1.

(Player's ball at rest moved by another ball – see Rule 18-5)

18-2. BY PLAYER, PARTNER, CADDIE OR EQUIPMENT
a. General
Except as permitted by the *Rules*, when a player's ball is *in play*, if
(i) the player, his *partner* or either of their *caddies*:
- lifts or *moves* the ball,
- touches it purposely (except with a club in the act of *addressing* the ball), or
- causes the ball to *move*, or

(ii) the *equipment* of the player or his *partner* causes the ball to *move*, the player incurs a penalty of one stroke.

If the ball is *moved*, it must be replaced, unless the movement of the ball occurs after the player has begun the *stroke* or the backward movement of the club for the *stroke* and the *stroke* is made.

Under the *Rules* there is no penalty if a player accidentally causes his ball to *move* in the following circumstances:
- In searching for a ball covered by sand, in the replacement of *loose impediments* moved in a *hazard* while finding or identifying a ball, in probing for a ball lying in water in a *water hazard* or in searching for a ball in an *obstruction* or an *abnormal ground condition* – Rule 12-1
- In repairing a *hole* plug or ball mark – Rule 16-1c
- In measuring – Rule 18-6
- In lifting a ball under a *Rule* – Rule 20-1
- In placing or replacing a ball under a *Rule* – Rule 20-3a
- In removing a *loose impediment* on the *putting green* – Rule 23-1
- In removing movable *obstructions* – Rule 24-1

b. Ball Moving After Address

If a player's *ball in play moves* after he has *addressed* it (other than as a result of a *stroke*), the player is deemed to have *moved* the ball and incurs a penalty of one stroke.

The ball must be replaced, unless the movement of the ball occurs after the player has begun the *stroke* or the backward movement of the club for the *stroke* and the *stroke* is made.

Exception: If it is known or virtually certain that the player did not cause his ball to *move*, Rule 18-2b does not apply.

18-3. BY OPPONENT, CADDIE OR EQUIPMENT IN MATCH PLAY

a. During Search

If, during search for a player's ball, an *opponent*, his *caddie* or his *equipment* moves the ball, touches it or causes it to *move*, there is no penalty. If the ball is *moved*, it must be replaced.

b. Other Than During Search

If, other than during search for a player's ball, an *opponent*, his *caddie* or his *equipment moves* the ball, touches it purposely or causes it to *move*, except as otherwise provided in the *Rules*, the *opponent* incurs a penalty of one stroke. If the ball is *moved*, it must be replaced.

(Playing a wrong ball – see Rule 15-3)
(Ball moved in measuring – see Rule 18-6)

18-4. BY FELLOW-COMPETITOR, CADDIE OR EQUIPMENT IN STROKE PLAY

If a *fellow-competitor*, his *caddie* or his *equipment* moves the player's ball, touches it or causes it to *move*, there is no penalty. If the ball is *moved*, it must be replaced.

(Playing a wrong ball – see Rule 15-3)

18-5. BY ANOTHER BALL

If a *ball in play* and at rest is *moved* by another ball in motion after a *stroke*, the *moved* ball must be replaced.

18-6. BALL MOVED IN MEASURING

If a ball or ball-marker is *moved* in measuring while proceeding under or in determining the application of a *Rule*, the ball or ball-marker must be replaced. There is no penalty, provided the movement of the ball or ball-marker is directly attributable to the specific act of measuring. Otherwise, the provisions of Rule 18-2a, 18-3b or 18-4 apply.

*PENALTY FOR BREACH OF RULE:

<u>Match play</u> – Loss of hole; <u>Stroke play</u> – Two strokes.

*If a player who is required to replace a ball fails to do so, or if he makes a *stroke* at a *ball substituted* under Rule 18 when such *substitution* is not permitted, he incurs the general penalty for breach of Rule 18, but there is no additional penalty under this Rule.

Note 1: If a ball to be replaced under this Rule is not immediately recoverable, another ball may be *substituted*.

Note 2: If the original lie of a ball to be placed or replaced has been altered, see Rule 20-3b.

Note 3: If it is impossible to determine the spot on which a ball is to be placed or replaced, see Rule 20-3c.

BALL AT REST MOVED: GENERAL

18/1
Ball Moves Vertically Downwards

Q. A ball lying in long grass slips vertically downwards. Or a ball is accidentally stepped on and pressed down, say a quarter of an inch, in the grass or into the ground. In each case, has the ball moved?

A. Yes, unless the ball returns to its original position. The direction of movement is immaterial.

Related Decision:
• 20-3d/3 Ball in Rough Moves Downward When Addressed; Ball Will Not Remain at Rest When Replaced.

18/2
Ball Oscillates During Address

Q. In addressing the ball, a player accidentally causes the ball to oscillate, but it returns to its original position. Has the ball "moved"?

A. No.

Related Decisions:
• 1-2/9 Player Presses Ball into Surface of Putting Green.
• 14-5/2 Making Stroke at Oscillating Ball.

18/3
Ball in Fork of Tree Moves in Relation to Ground But Not in Relation to Fork

Q. A ball rests in the fork of a branch of a tree. The player climbs the tree to play his next stroke. The branch bends under his weight. Although the ball has moved relative to the ground, it has not moved relative to the fork. Is the ball deemed to have moved?

A. The ball is deemed not to have moved since it did not move in relation to the fork of the tree in which it was lodged.

18/4 (Reserved)

18/5 (Reserved)

18/6 (Reserved)

18/7
Explanation of "Any Ball He Has Played"

Q. The Definition of "Equipment" excludes "any ball he (the player) has played at the hole being played." What does this mean?

A. The phrase means any ball the player has played at the hole being played except during any period when it has been lifted and has not been put back into play. Accordingly, the ball in play, a provisional ball, a second ball played under Rule 3-3 or Rule 20-7c and a ball being used for practice are not equipment.

18/7.5
Player's Ball Moved by Ball Accidentally Dropped by Opponent or Fellow-Competitor

Q. A lifts his ball on the putting green. He then accidentally drops the ball and it strikes and moves B's ball, which is in play and at rest. What is the ruling?

A. A ball that has been lifted and not put back into play is equipment – see Note 1 under the Definition of "Equipment."

In match play, A incurs a penalty stroke and B must replace his ball – Rule 18-3b.

In stroke play, there is no penalty and B must replace his ball – Rule 18-4.

18/8
Ball Moved by Golf Cart Shared by Two Players

Under the Definition of "Equipment," equipment includes a golf cart, whether or not motorized. If two or more players share a golf cart, the cart and everything in it are deemed to be the equipment of one of the players sharing the cart. If the cart is being moved by one of the players (or the partner of one of the players) sharing it, the cart and everything in it are deemed to be that player's equipment. Otherwise, the cart and everything in it are deemed to be the equipment of the player sharing the cart whose ball (or whose partner's ball) is involved.

Thus, for example, in a singles match, if A and B are sharing a cart and the cart moves A's ball which was at rest, A would be penalized one stroke if he was driving or pulling the cart (Rule 18-2a). B would be penalized one stroke if he was driving or pulling the cart (Rule 18-3b), unless the incident occurred during search (Rule 18-3a).

Related Decision:
• 19/1 Ball Deflected or Stopped by Golf Cart Shared by Two Players.

18/9 (Reserved)

18/10
Ball Falls into Bunker When Person Walks Nearby

Q. A ball at rest on the edge of a bunker falls into the bunker when X (a spectator, the player, an opponent or a fellow competitor) walks nearby. Should the ball be replaced in accordance with Rules 18-1 or 18-4 or must the ball be played as it lies in the bunker?

A. The answer depends on whether X in any way caused the ball to move. If it is determined that X did not in any way cause the ball to move, there is no penalty and the ball must be played as it lies.

If it is determined that X caused the ball to move, it must be replaced. If X is the player, the player incurs a penalty stroke under Rule 18-2a; if X is an opponent, the opponent incurs a penalty stroke under Rule 18-3b. In all other cases, there is no penalty.

Whether X caused the ball to move is a question of fact to be determined in the light of all the circumstances. Relevant circumstances might include the distance between X and the ball and the nature of the ground. In the absence of evidence that X caused the ball to move, it should be concluded that the ball's movement was a coincidence.

Related Decisions:
• 14-6/1 Ball Moves in Water in Water Hazard After Stance Taken.
• 18-2a/30 Ball Moves After Player Takes Several Practice Swings Near Ball and Touches Grass Behind Ball.
• 18-2a/30.5 Ball Moves After Removal of Loose Impediment Near Ball.
• 18-2b/3 Ball Moves After Player Has Taken Stance in Bunker.
• 18-2b/4 Ball Moves After Player Grounds Club Short Distance Behind Ball But Before Grounding Club Immediately Behind Ball.

18/11
Meaning of "Immediately Recoverable"

Q. With reference to Note 1 under Rule 18, when is a ball to be replaced deemed not to be "immediately recoverable"?

A. When it cannot be retrieved within a few seconds.

BALL AT REST MOVED BY OUTSIDE AGENCY

18-1/1 (Reserved)

18-1/2
Status of Air When Artificially Propelled

Q. What is the status of air from a blower operated by an outside agency or from a fan?

A. Although the Definition of "Outside Agency" states that wind is not an outside agency, in this case the artificially-propelled air is considered to be an outside agency.

If such artificially-propelled air moves a ball at rest, Rule 18-1 applies.

18-1/3
Player Unaware Ball Moved by Outside Agency Does Not Replace Ball

Q. In stroke play, a player's ball was moved by an outside agency. Neither the player nor his caddie was aware that his ball had been moved, so the player played the ball without replacing it. He then learned that his ball had been moved. What is the ruling?

A. As it was not known or virtually certain that the ball had been moved by an outside agency when the player played the ball, he proceeded properly and incurred no penalty – see the Note to Rule 18-1.

Related Decisions:
• 15/10 Ball Thrown into Bounds by Outside Agency and Played; Neither Player Nor His Caddie Aware of Action of Outside Agency.
• 18-5/3 Competitor and Fellow-Competitor Unaware Ball Moved by Fellow-Competitor's Ball Until After Completion of Hole.

18-1/4
Spectator Says Ball Was Moved by Outside Agency But Player Not Sure

Q. A spectator tells a player that his ball has been moved by an outside agency. Neither the player nor his caddie was aware the ball had been moved. Is the player obliged to take the spectator's word and replace the ball on the spot from which the spectator said it was moved?

A. No. In stroke play, if it is impractical to get a decision from the Committee, the player should, under Rule 3-3, hole out both with the original ball and a second ball played from the spot from which the original ball is alleged to have been moved, and request the Committee to decide the matter at the end of the round. In reaching a decision the Committee should interrogate the spectator, if possible.

In match play, if there is no referee or representative of the Committee available within a reasonable time, the player and his opponent should, if possible, agree on the place from which the player should play his next stroke. If agreement cannot be reached, the player must proceed as he thinks best, and if the opponent does not agree with the action taken, he should lodge a claim under Rule 2-5 so that the Committee may make a decision under Rule 34-3.

18-1/5
Ball Stolen by Outside Agency from Unknown Spot

Q. At a par-3 hole, part of the green and the adjoining area cannot be seen from the tee. In this unseen area are a bunker, fairway and a dry water hazard.

A player plays towards this obscured area and cannot tell where the ball comes to rest. When the players are near the green, they see a boy running away with a ball in his hand. The boy throws the ball back and the player identifies it as his ball.

The player is unable to determine from where to play his next stroke under Rule 18-1. He does not know whether the ball was on the green, on the fairway or in one of the hazards.

How should he proceed?

A. As it was impossible to know where the ball should have been replaced under Rule 18-1, the player should, in equity (Rule 1-4), drop the ball in an area which was neither the most, nor the least, favorable of the various areas where it was equally possible that the ball originally lay.

18-1/6
Ball at Rest Moved by Blowing Tumbleweed

Q. A tumbleweed blowing across the course strikes a ball at rest and knocks it into the hole. What is the procedure?

A. In the circumstances, a tumbleweed is an outside agency. Rule 18-1 applies and the ball must be replaced without penalty.

Related Decision:
• 18-2a/17 Towel Dropped by Player Is Blown onto and Moves Ball.

18-1/7
Ball in Plastic Bag Moves When Bag Blown to New Position by Wind

Q. A player's ball comes to rest in a plastic bag that is lying on the ground. Before the player can invoke Rule 24-1b, a gust of wind blows the bag and the ball to a new position. In proceeding under Rule 24-1b, should the player drop the ball directly under the place where it originally lay in the bag or where it now lies in the bag?

A. Wind is not an outside agency. However, if an object being moved by the wind moves a ball, the object is an outside agency in the circumstances – see Decision 18-1/6.

In this case, the bag, not the wind, caused the ball to move. Accordingly, under Rules 18-1 and 24-1b, the player must drop the ball directly under the place where it originally lay in the bag.

18-1/8
Ball Moved by Stone Dislodged by Partner's or Opponent's Stroke

Q. In match play, a player made a stroke and dislodged an embedded stone. The stone struck his partner's or an opponent's ball which was lying about four yards ahead and moved it. What is the ruling?

A. The player is not deemed to have caused the other ball to move.

In playing his ball as it lies, the player could not, through reasonable care, have avoided dislodging the stone through his stroke. Moreover, in these circumstances it was not reasonable to expect the player to ask the partner or opponent to lift his ball under Rule 22-2 because the player could not have reasonably foreseen that his stroke would dislodge the stone ultimately leading to the movement of the opponent's ball.

Accordingly, the player's actions are deemed not to have caused the movement of the other ball, and Rules 18-2a(i) and 18-3b do not apply. The stone is deemed to have caused the movement of the other ball and, as the stone is an outside agency, Rule 18-1 applies. The player incurs no penalty, and the partner or opponent must replace his ball.

Related Decisions:
- 18-2a/20.5 Player's Practice Swing Moves Loose Impediment Which Moves Ball.
- 18-2a/21 Ball Moved Accidentally by Player in Playing Wrong Ball.
- 18-3b/1 Ball Moved Accidentally by Opponent in Playing His Own Ball.
- 18-3b/2 Opponent's Stroke Disturbs Bushes Causing Player's Ball to Move.
- 19-2/9 Divot Taken After Stroke Strikes Ball in Motion.

18-1/9
Ball Lodged in Tree Knocked Down by Outside Agency

Q. A player's ball is lodged in a tree about eight feet off the ground. A spectator knocks the ball down from the tree. In complying with Rule 18-1, it is impossible to replace the ball in the prescribed manner in the tree because the spot where it lay in the tree is unknown or unreachable. What is the ruling?

A. Rules 20-3c and 20-3d cover cases in which the spot where a ball is to be placed or replaced is not determinable or a ball fails to come to rest on the spot on which it is placed. However, these Rules do not contemplate a case such as this one. Thus, in equity (Rule 1-4), if the position of the ball in the tree was such that the player could have made a stroke at it, the ball must be placed in the tree as near as possible to the spot from which it was moved, without penalty. Otherwise, the player must proceed under the unplayable ball Rule.

Related Decisions:
- 14/7 Striking at Tree Branch to Move Ball Lodged Higher in Branch.
- 18-2a/29 Ball Dislodged from Tree; Replacement of Ball Not Possible.

18-1/10
Ball at Rest Kicked Away from Hole by Spectator Attending Flagstick

Q. In stroke play, a competitor asked a spectator to attend the flagstick. The competitor putted and his ball stopped one inch short of the hole. The spectator then kicked the ball away. What is the ruling?

A. There was no infringement of Rule 17-3b because the competitor's ball had come to rest short of the hole. The spectator was not the competitor's caddie and so he was an outside agency. Under Rule 18-1 the competitor was required to replace his ball and hole out without penalty.

18-1/11 (Reserved)

18-1/12
Ball Replaced and at Rest Is Thereafter Moved by Wind

Q. A player replaces his ball on the putting green and the ball is at rest. Before the player addresses the ball, a sudden gust of wind blows the ball farther from the hole. The player plays the ball from its new position. Is that correct?

A. Yes. Wind is not an outside agency – see Definition of "Outside Agency." Accordingly, Rule 18-1 does not apply.

Related Decisions:
• 18-2a/7 Ball Moved by Wind Replaced.
• 20-2c/3.5 Dropped Ball Comes to Rest and Then Rolls Out of Bounds.
• 20-3d/1 Placed Ball Rolls into Hole.
• 20-4/1 Ball Replaced on Putting Green But Ball-Marker Not Removed; Ball Then Moves.

BALL AT REST MOVED BY PLAYER, PARTNER, CADDIE OR EQUIPMENT

18-2a/1
Player Who Misses Tee Shot Tees Ball Lower Before Making Next Stroke

Q. A player playing from the teeing ground misses the ball completely. He pushes his tee further into the ground and plays. What is the ruling?

A. When the player made a stroke, the ball was in play (see Definition of "Ball in Play"). By pushing the tee further into the ground, he moved the ball and incurred a penalty of one stroke under Rule 18-2a and was required to replace it. However, when the player made a stroke at the ball without replacing it, he played under penalty of stroke and distance (see Rule 27-1a). This procedure overrides Rule 18-2a and, therefore, the penalty under Rule 18-2a does not apply.

18-2a/2
Ball Falling Off Tee When Stroke Just Touches It Is Picked Up and Re-Teed

Q. A player making his first stroke on a hole just touched the ball and it fell off the tee. He picked up the ball, re-teed it and played out the hole. What is the ruling?

A. When the player made a stroke, the ball was in play (see Definition of "Ball in Play"). When he lifted the ball, he incurred a penalty of one stroke under Rule 18-2a and was required to replace it. However, when the player made a stroke at the re-teed ball, he played a ball under penalty of stroke and distance (see Rule 27-1a). This procedure overrides Rule 18-2a and, therefore, the penalty under Rule 18-2a does not apply.

Decisions related to 18-2a/1 and 18-2a/2:
• 10-2c/1 Ball Played Out of Turn from Tee Abandoned and Another Ball Played in Proper Order.
• 18-2a/11 Tee Shot Wrongly Thought to Be Out of Bounds Lifted; Competitor Plays Another Ball from Tee.
• 27-2b/10 Provisional Ball Lifted Subsequently Becomes Ball in Play; Competitor Then Plays from Wrong Place.
• 29-1/9 Both Player and Partner Drive at Same Tee in Foursome Play.

18-2a/3
Ball Lifted and Dropped Away from Boundary Stake Under Obstruction Rule

Q. A player's swing is interfered with by a stake defining out of bounds. The player mistakenly considers the stake an obstruction and he lifts his ball and drops it in the manner prescribed in Rule 24-2b. What is the ruling?

A. The player incurs a penalty of one stroke under Rule 18-2a and he must replace his ball before playing his next stroke. Otherwise, he loses the hole in match play or he incurs a total penalty of two strokes in stroke play – see penalty statement under Rule 18.

Related Decision:
• 34-3/6 Player Proceeds Under an Inapplicable Rule; Committee's Decision.

18-2a/4
Ball Lifted and Dropped Away from Movable Obstruction

Q. A player's ball comes to rest against a movable obstruction. The player lifts the ball and drops it away from the obstruction instead of removing the obstruction as provided in Rule 24-1. What is the ruling?

A. The player incurs a penalty of one stroke under Rule 18-2a and he must replace his ball before playing his next stroke. Otherwise, he loses the hole in match play or he incurs a total penalty of two strokes in stroke play – see penalty statement under Rule 18.

18-2a/5 (Reserved)

18-2a/6 (Reserved)

18-2a/7
Ball Moved by Wind Replaced

Q. In stroke play, a competitor's ball was moved by wind. Since wind is not an outside agency (see Definition of "Outside Agency"), he should have played it from where it came to rest, but he replaced it. What is the ruling?

A. The competitor incurred one penalty stroke under Rule 18-2a, and, before playing his next stroke, he should have replaced the ball on the spot where it came to rest after being moved by the wind. If he did not do so, he incurred a total penalty of two strokes – see penalty statement under Rule 18.

Related Decisions:
• 18-1/12 Ball Replaced and at Rest Is Thereafter Moved by Wind.
• 20-2c/3.5 Dropped Ball Comes to Rest and Then Rolls Out of Bounds.
• 20-3d/1 Placed Ball Rolls into Hole.
• 20-4/1 Ball Replaced on Putting Green But Ball-Marker Not Removed; Ball Then Moves.

18-2a/8
Ball Played from Ground Under Repair Picked Up and Relief Taken Under Ground Under Repair Rule

Q. A player, unaware that his ball was in ground under repair, played the ball as it lay. The player then learned that his ball had been in ground under repair, picked up the ball played from the ground under repair, dropped it in accordance with Rule 25-1b and played out the hole. What is the ruling?

A. When the player played from the ground under repair, which is permissible, relief under Rule 25-1b was no longer available and the ball was in play where it lay.

When the player picked up his ball in play, he incurred a penalty stroke – Rule 18-2a. Since he did not replace the ball, he incurred a penalty of loss of hole in match play or a total penalty of two strokes in stroke play – see penalty statement under Rule 18.

18-2a/8.5
Ball Played from Ground Under Repair Abandoned and Relief Taken Under Ground Under Repair Rule

Q. In Decision 18-2a/8, the player picked up the ball played from ground under repair and played it from another spot. What would be the ruling if the player abandoned the original ball by dropping and playing another ball under ground under repair procedures?

A. After the player played from ground under repair, which is permissible, relief under Rule 25-1b was no longer available, and the player was required to play his ball as it lay (Rule 13-1). When he dropped the other ball, he was substituting a ball and that ball became the ball in play (Rule 20-4).

If the location of the original ball was known at the time the substituted ball was dropped, the substitution was not permitted. When he did not correct his error as provided in Rule 20-6 and made a stroke at the wrongly substituted ball, he was in breach of Rule 15-2 as well as Rule 20-7 for playing from a wrong place and the applicable Rule is Rule 13-1. In match play, he incurred a penalty of loss of hole (Rule 15-2 or 20-7b). In stroke play, he incurred a penalty of two strokes for playing from a wrong place (Rule 20-7c). There is no additional penalty for incorrectly substituting a ball (see Exception to Rule 15-2).

If the location of the original ball was not known at the time the substituted ball was dropped, he was required to proceed under Rule 27-1, in which case the substitution was permitted. Since the substituted ball was not dropped at the spot required by Rule 27-1, he played from a wrong place. In match play, he incurred a penalty of loss of hole (Rule 20-7b). In stroke play, he incurred a penalty of one stroke under Rule 27-1 and an additional penalty of two strokes under Rule 20-7c for playing from a wrong place. If the breach was a serious one, he is subject to disqualification unless he corrected his error as provided in Rule 20-7c.

Related Decisions:
- 15/8 Ball Played Under Rule for Ball Lost in Ground Under Repair After Another Ball Played Under Stroke-and-Distance Procedure.
- 20-7c/4 Competitor's Ball Played by Fellow-Competitor; Competitor Substitutes Another Ball at Wrong Place, Plays It and Then Abandons It and Plays Out Original Ball From Right Place.
- 25-1c/2 Ball Dropped and Played Under Ground Under Repair Rule in Absence of Knowledge or Virtual Certainty That Original Ball in Ground Under Repair.

18-2a/9
Ball Lifted Without Authority Dropped Instead of Being Replaced

Q. A player lifted his ball without being entitled to under the Rules and incurred a penalty stroke under Rule 18-2a. He then learned of his error, dropped the ball at the spot from which it was lifted instead of replacing it as required by Rule 18-2a, and played it. What is the ruling?

A. The player failed to replace his ball as required by Rule 18-2a, and therefore incurred a penalty of loss of hole in match play or a total of two strokes in stroke play – see penalty statement under Rule 18. (Revised)

Related Decisions:
- 18-2a/21.5 Ball Moved Accidentally; Spot Where Ball Originally Lay Not Determinable; Player Places Ball Instead of Dropping It.
- 20-2c/2 Ball Dropped Third Time When Placement Required After Second Drop.
- 20-6/1 Ball Placed When Required to Be Dropped or Dropped When Required to Be Placed; Correction of Error.

18-2a/10
Dropped Ball Lifted and Re-Dropped When It Should Have Been Played as It Lay; Ball Then Lifted Again and Placed

Q. In stroke play, a competitor whose ball was in a lateral water hazard elected to take relief under Rule 26-1c(i). When a ball was dropped, it rolled towards the hole but came to rest not more than two club-lengths from where it first struck the ground and not nearer the hole than the point where the original ball last crossed the margin of the water hazard.

Incorrectly believing that Rule 20-2c applied, the competitor lifted the ball and re-dropped it, whereupon the ball rolled towards the hole as before. The competitor again lifted the ball, placed it where it first struck the ground when re-dropped and played his next stroke. Is the competitor penalized two strokes or four strokes?

A. Two strokes. The ball when first dropped was in play – see Rule 20-4. The competitor was in breach of Rule 18-2a when he lifted it. Because the competitor failed to replace his ball at the spot at which it came to rest when first dropped, he incurred a total penalty of two strokes – see penalty statement under Rule 18.

Other Decisions related to whether multiple penalties apply: See "Multiple Penalty Situations" in the Index.

18-2a/11
Tee Shot Wrongly Thought to Be Out of Bounds Lifted; Competitor Plays Another Ball from Tee

Q. In stroke play, a competitor hits his tee shot into a practice area. Thinking that the ball is out of bounds, he lifts it and plays another ball from the tee. He then discovers that the practice area is not out of bounds. What is the ruling?

A. When the player lifted his ball in play, he incurred a penalty of one stroke under Rule 18-2a and was required to replace it. However, when the player made a stroke from where the previous stroke was made (Rule 20-5), he played a ball under penalty of stroke and distance (see Rule 27-1a). This procedure overrides Rule 18-2a and, therefore, the penalty under Rule 18-2a does not apply.

Related Decisions:
• 10-2c/1 Ball Played Out of Turn from Tee Abandoned and Another Ball Played in Proper Order.
• 18-2a/1 Player Who Misses Tee Shot Tees Ball Lower Before Making Next Stroke.
• 18-2a/2 Ball Falling Off Tee When Stroke Just Touches It Is Picked Up and Re-Teed.
• 27-2b/10 Provisional Ball Lifted Subsequently Becomes Ball in Play; Competitor Then Plays from Wrong Place (by returning to the teeing ground and playing it).
• 29-1/9 Both Player and Partner Drive at Same Tee in Foursome Play.

18-2a/12
Player Entitled to Relief from Condition Lifts Ball; Player Then Replaces Ball and Plays It from Original Position

Q. A player elects to take relief from an immovable obstruction or abnormal ground condition and lifts his ball. He then realizes that the only area in which he may drop under the Rules is such that his ball, when dropped, will almost certainly be unplayable. He replaces his ball and plays it from its original position. What is the ruling?

A. The player was entitled to lift the ball to take relief under Rule 24 or 25. However, by subsequently deciding not to take relief, his right to lift the ball was negated and he incurred a penalty stroke under Rule 18-2a for having lifted his ball in play.

Related Decisions:
• 20-6/5 Player Drops Ball Under Rules and Then Wishes to Replace Ball in Original Position.
• 20-7/2 Ball Deemed Unplayable in Water Hazard Is Dropped in Hazard and Played.
• 25-1b/26 Player Unaware Ball in Water Hazard Takes Relief from Interference by Burrowing Animal Hole.
• 27/17 Competitor Plays Out of Turn Other Than From Teeing Ground and Puts Another Ball into Play at Spot of Previous Stroke.

18-2a/12.5
Player Entitled to Relief Without Penalty from Condition Lifts Ball; Chooses Not to Take Relief and Wishes to Proceed Under the Unplayable Ball Rule

Q. A player elects to take relief from an immovable obstruction or abnormal ground condition and lifts his ball. He then realizes that the only area in which he may drop under the Rules is such that his ball, when dropped, will almost certainly be unplayable. May the player deem the ball unplayable and proceed under Rule 28?

A. Yes. The player has the following options:

1. replace the ball in its original position under penalty of one stroke (Rule 18-2a) and then proceed under Rule 28, incurring an additional penalty of one stroke; or
2. proceed directly under Rule 28b or c, without replacing the ball and using the spot where the ball originally lay as the reference point for the relief procedure, incurring a penalty stroke under Rule 28 and an additional penalty stroke under Rule 18-2a; or
3. drop the ball in accordance with Rule 24 or 25 and then, using its new position as a reference point, proceed under Rule 28 incurring a penalty of one stroke; or
4. proceed directly under Rule 28a, without dropping the ball in accordance with Rule 24 or 25, incurring a penalty of one stroke under Rule 28 and no penalty under Rule 18-2a, as he does not need to establish a new reference point before proceeding under Rule 28a.

Related Decisions:
• 3-3/7.5 Competitor Announces Intention to Play Two Balls; Plays Original Ball Before Dropping Second Ball; Elects Not to Play Second Ball.
• 9-2/13 Player Who Told Opponent He Would Proceed Under Water Hazard Rule Changes Mind After Opponent Plays.
• 18-2a/27.5 Player Who States He Will Proceed Under Unplayable Ball Rule Subsequently Assesses Possibility of Playing Ball as It Lies.
• 28/13 After Deeming Ball Unplayable and Lifting It, Player Discovers Ball Was in Ground Under Repair.

18-2a/13
Ball Lifted Without Authority and Cleaned

Q. A player's ball comes to rest on the apron of a green. Mistakenly believing that the ball is on the green, the player marks, lifts and cleans it. The player incurs a penalty stroke under Rule 18-2a for lifting the ball without authority under the Rules. Does the player incur an additional penalty stroke under Rule 21 for cleaning the ball?

A. No. Rule 21 states that a ball may be cleaned when lifted except when it has been lifted in accordance with Rule 5-3, 12-2 or 22.

Related Decision:
• 34-3/3.5 Player Lifts Ball Without Authority Due to Misunderstanding Referee's Instructions.

18-2a/13.5
Ball Lifted and Thrown into Pond in Anger

Q. A player played a poor shot and his ball came to rest through the green near a lake. In anger, the player lifted his ball and threw it into the lake from where it could not be retrieved. The player placed another ball on the spot from which the original ball was lifted and holed out. What is the ruling?

A. Although Note 1 to Rule 18 states "If a ball to be replaced under this

Rule is not immediately recoverable, another ball may be substituted," as the player's ball became irrecoverable only due to the player's subsequent actions after his breach of Rule 18-2a, the Note is not applicable.

The player lost the hole in match play – Rule 15-2.

In stroke play, the player incurred the general penalty of two strokes under Rule 18 for incorrectly substituting a ball, but there is no additional penalty for lifting the ball without authority (see Rule 15-2 and the penalty statement under Rule 18).

Related Decisions:
• 5-3/3.5 Player Lifts Ball on Putting Green, Throws Ball into Lake and Then Announces That Ball Is Unfit for Play.
• 15-2/1 Player Substitutes Another Ball on Putting Green Because Original Ball Thrown to Caddie for Cleaning Came to Rest in Lake.

18-2a/14
Caddie on Own Initiative Lifts Ball for Identification

Q. During search for A's ball, A's caddie found a ball and lifted it for identification without the authority of A and without A's announcing in advance his intention to do so. The ball was identified as A's. What is the ruling?

A. Since the ball was lifted other than in accordance with the Rules, Rule 18-2a applies and A incurs a penalty of one stroke. Rule 18-2a overrides Rule 12-2 in the circumstances. Accordingly, an additional penalty of one stroke under Rule 12-2 for failing to announce the intention to lift the ball for identification purposes is not applicable.

18-2a/15
Caddie on Own Initiative Lifts Ball Considering It Unplayable

Q. A player's caddie, considering the player's ball to be in an unplayable lie, lifted the ball before the player had an opportunity to inspect the lie. What is the ruling?

A. A player's caddie may not deem the player's ball to be unplayable (Rule 28). Therefore, the player incurred a penalty of one stroke under Rule 18-2a when the caddie lifted the ball. The player may replace the ball and play it or invoke the unplayable ball Rule (Rule 28). If the player invokes Rule 28, he may choose to estimate the original location of the ball rather than replace it, but in either case, by invoking Rule 28, the player incurs an additional penalty of one stroke under that Rule.

Decisions related to 18-2a/14 and 18-2a/15:
• 2-4/3.5 Stroke Conceded by Caddie.
• 26-1/9 Caddie Lifts Ball in Water Hazard Without Player's Authority.
• 34-3/3.5 Player Lifts Ball Without Authority Due to Misunderstanding Referee's Instructions.

18-2a/16
Competitor's Ball Picked Up by Fellow-Competitor at Competitor's Request

Q. A competitor, mistakenly thinking his ball in play in the rough was a wrong ball, asked his fellow-competitor to pick up the ball. The fellow-competitor did so and then the error was discovered. Is the competitor subject to penalty under Rule 18-2a or exempt from penalty by virtue of Rule 18-4?

A. Because the lifting of the ball by the fellow-competitor was at the request of the competitor, it would not be correct to exonerate the competitor under Rule 18-4.

The competitor incurred a one-stroke penalty under Rule 18-2a and he was required to replace his ball.

18-2a/17
Towel Dropped by Player Is Blown onto and Moves Ball

Q. A player dropped a towel on the ground. The wind blew the towel onto the player's ball and moved it. What is the ruling?

A. As the player's equipment caused the ball to move, the player incurred a penalty stroke and must replace the ball – Rule 18-2a.

Related Decision:
• 18-1/6 Ball at Rest Moved by Blowing Tumbleweed.

18-2a/18
Opponent's Ball Knocked Away by Player After Concession Moves Player's Ball

Q. In singles match play, A concedes B's next stroke and knocks B's ball away. B's ball in motion moves A's ball. What is the ruling?

A. As A caused his own ball to move, he incurred a penalty of one stroke under Rule 18-2a, and he must replace his ball.

18-2a/19
Ball Moved Accidentally by Practice Swing Prior to Tee Shot

Q. Before playing from the teeing ground, a player took a practice swing, in the course of which he accidentally struck and moved the teed ball with his club. Did the player play a stroke or incur a penalty?

A. The player did not make a stroke – see Definition of "Stroke." Since the ball was not in play – see Definition of "Ball in Play" – he incurred no penalty under Rule 18-2a. The player must put a ball into play from the teeing ground.

18-2a/20
Ball in Play Moved Accidentally by Practice Swing

Q. A player makes a practice swing and accidentally moves his ball in play with his club. Has he made a stroke?

A. No. He had no intention of moving the ball – see Definition of "Stroke." However, he incurs a penalty stroke under Rule 18-2a for moving his ball in play, and the ball must be replaced.

Decisions related to 18-2a/19 and 18-2a/20:
• 7-2/7 Practice Swing Dislodges Concealed Ball.
• 11-3/3 Original Ball Out of Bounds; Ball Played Under Stroke-and-Distance Procedure Falls Off Tee at Address.
• 15/2 Player's Stroke at Own Ball Dislodges Concealed Ball.

18-2a/20.5
Player's Practice Swing Moves Loose Impediment Which Moves Ball

Q. In making a practice swing near his ball, a player moves a loose impediment (e.g., a stone), which causes his ball in play to move. What is the ruling?

A. The player is deemed to have caused his ball in play to move in breach of Rule 18-2a; he incurs a one-stroke penalty and must replace the ball.

This ruling differs from that in Decision 18-1/8 both because it is reasonably foreseeable that a practice swing will move loose impediments that may in turn cause a ball in play to move, and because a player can, through reasonable care, avoid taking practice swings that might produce such a result.

18-2a/21
Ball Moved Accidentally by Player in Playing Wrong Ball

Q. In stroke play, in a bunker, A plays a wrong ball. In so doing, he accidentally moves a nearby ball, which was not visible before he played and which is, in fact, his ball. What is the ruling?

A. Player A incurs a two-stroke penalty for playing a wrong ball – Rule 15-3b.

As the nearby ball was not visible before A played, it was not reasonably foreseeable that the ball could be moved by the stroke at the wrong ball; therefore, A is not penalized for moving his ball. A must replace his ball in play, and if necessary, the lie must be re-created. If the ball is not replaced correctly before A makes his next stroke, the failure to replace the ball is considered a separate act and he incurs a total penalty of four strokes (Rules 15-3b and 18-2a).

Decisions related to 18-2a/20.5 and 18-2a/21:
- 18-1/8 Ball Moved by Stone Dislodged by Partner's or Opponent's Stroke.
- 18-3b/1 Ball Moved Accidentally by Opponent in Playing His Own Ball.
- 18-3b/2 Opponent's Stroke Disturbs Bushes Causing Player's Ball to Move.
- 19-2/9 Divot Taken After Stroke Strikes Ball in Motion.
- 30-3f/9 Player's Ball Moved by Partner in Playing His Own Ball.

18-2a/21.3
Ball Moved Accidentally and Original Lie Altered; Player Places Ball in Wrong Place and Plays

Q. A player accidentally steps on his ball in the rough and pushes it into the ground, incurring a penalty stroke under Rule 18-2a. The original lie of the ball was known and, instead of placing the ball in the nearest most similar lie within one club-length of the original lie as required by Rule 20-3b, the player places the ball almost two club-lengths away from the original lie and makes his next stroke.

In match play, it is clear that the player incurs the general penalty for a breach of Rule 18 or 20-3b, and loses the hole.

In stroke play, does the player incur an additional penalty of two strokes for a breach of Rule 20-3b or a total penalty of two strokes under Rule 18?

A. In stroke play, the player incurs a total penalty of two strokes under Rule 18.

Rule 18 requires replacement of a ball moved accidentally. If some other Rule – in this case Rule 20-3b – requires a moved ball to be placed somewhere else, the player is considered to be in breach of Rule 18 if he places the ball other than as prescribed by the other Rule.

18-2a/21.5
Ball Moved Accidentally; Spot Where Ball Originally Lay Not Determinable; Player Places Ball Instead of Dropping It

Q. A player accidentally moves his ball in the rough, incurring a penalty stroke under Rule 18-2a. The spot where the ball originally lay is not determinable. Instead of dropping the ball as near as possible to the spot where it originally lay as required by Rule 20-3c, the player places the ball as near as possible to that spot and plays his next stroke.

In match play, it is clear that the player incurs the general penalty for a breach of Rule 18 or 20-3c and loses the hole.

In stroke play, does the player incur an additional penalty of two strokes for a breach of Rule 20-3c or a total penalty of two strokes under Rule 18?

A. In stroke play, the player incurs a total penalty of two strokes under Rule 18 – see Decision 18-2a/21.3.

Related Decisions:
- 18-2a/9 Ball Lifted Without Authority Dropped Instead of Being Replaced.
- 20-2c/2 Ball Dropped Third Time When Placement Required After Second Drop.

• 20-6/1 Ball Placed When Required to Be Dropped or Dropped When Required to Be Placed; Correction of Error.

18-2a/22
Ball Moved Accidentally by Backward Movement of Club After Stroke Misses; Ball Comes to Rest Out of Bounds

Q. A player misses a shot completely and, in swinging his club back, he accidentally knocks his ball backwards. Was the backward swing a stroke? If the ball comes to rest out of bounds, how does the player proceed?

A. The backward swing was not a stroke. A stroke is the forward movement of the club made with the intention of striking at, and moving, the ball – see Definition of "Stroke."

In addition to counting the missed stroke, the player incurs a penalty stroke for moving his ball with the backward swing (Rule 18-2a), and the ball must be replaced. The fact that the ball lay out of bounds is irrelevant.

18-2a/23
Ball Knocked from Lip of Hole in Disgust

Q. In stroke play, a competitor's ball stops on the lip of the hole. In disgust the competitor knocks his ball off the green with the back of his putter. What is the ruling?

A. The competitor must replace the ball under penalty of one stroke (Rule 18-2a). The competitor is not considered to have made a stroke.

Related Decision:
• 1-2/4 Player Jumps Close to Hole to Cause Ball to Fall into Hole.

18-2a/24 (Reserved)

18-2a/25
Ball Moved Accidentally by Player During Suspension of Play

Q. During a suspension of play, a player elects to leave his ball in position on the course. Prior to the resumption of play, the player accidentally causes his ball to move (e.g., he drops his club on the ball). What is the ruling?

A. Although play was suspended when the player accidentally moved his ball, the ball was in play (see Definition of "Ball in Play"). Therefore, the player incurred a penalty of one stroke under Rule 18-2a and the ball must be replaced.

Related Decision:
• 6-8d/4 Ball Visible from Tee Disappears While Play Suspended.

18-2a/26
Ball Dislodged from Tree When Player Climbs Tree to Play Stroke

Q. As a player is climbing a tree to play a ball lodged in the tree, the ball falls to the ground. Does the player incur a penalty?

A. Yes, one stroke under Rule 18-2a, and the ball must be replaced.

18-2a/27
Ball Dislodged from Tree; Circumstances in Which Player Not Penalized

Q. A player whose ball is lodged high in a tree wishes to dislodge it by shaking the tree or throwing a club so that he can identify it and proceed under the unplayable ball Rule. Is this permissible?

A. Yes. The player should state his intention before taking such action to avoid any question being raised as to whether a penalty would be incurred under Rule 18-2a.

18-2a/27.5
Player Who States He Will Proceed Under Unplayable Ball Rule Subsequently Assesses Possibility of Playing Ball as It Lies

Q. A player's ball is in a bad lie and in such a position that he considers that he may move the ball in breach of Rule 18-2a when he gets close to it. As provided in Decision 18-2a/27, the player may protect himself against penalty by stating that he will proceed under Rule 28. The player makes such an announcement, but, upon reaching the area where his ball lies and finding that the ball did not move, takes a club and begins to assess the possibility of playing the ball as it lies. What would be the ruling if the player then accidentally caused the ball to move?

A. Despite the fact that the player has stated that he intends to proceed under Rule 28, if it becomes clear from the player's actions that he is considering playing the ball as it lies, the Committee should rule that the player's intention to deem the ball unplayable has ceased and, therefore, the player would incur a penalty stroke under Rule 18-2a if he thereafter caused his ball to move.

Related Decisions:
• 3-3/7.5 Competitor Announces Intention to Play Two Balls; Plays Original Ball Before Dropping Second Ball; Elects Not to Play Second Ball.
• 9-2/13 Player Who Told Opponent He Would Proceed Under Water Hazard Rule Changes Mind After Opponent Plays.
• 18-2a/12.5 Player Entitled to Relief Without Penalty from Condition Lifts Ball; Chooses Not to Take Relief and Wishes to Proceed Under the Unplayable Ball Rule.
• 28/13 After Deeming Ball Unplayable and Lifting It, Player Discovers Ball Was in Ground Under Repair.

18-2a/28
Ball Dislodged from Tree; Circumstances in Which Player Penalized

Q. A player could not find his ball. Believing the ball might be lodged in a tree, he shook the tree and his ball fell to the ground. He played the ball from where it came to rest. What is the ruling?

A. The player incurred one penalty stroke under Rule 18-2a for moving his ball. He should have replaced the ball. Since he did not do so, in match play he lost the hole and in stroke play he incurred a total penalty of two strokes – see penalty statement under Rule 18.

18-2a/29
Ball Dislodged from Tree; Replacement of Ball Not Possible

Q. A player, believing his ball is lodged in a tree, shakes the tree in order to dislodge it. His ball falls to the ground. According to Decision 18-2a/28, the player incurs a penalty of one stroke under Rule 18-2a and must replace his ball. Suppose, however, that the player cannot replace his ball either:

    (1) because the spot where it lay in the tree is not determinable, or
    (2) because the ball fails to remain on the correct spot when replaced, or
    (3) because the player cannot reach the spot where the ball lay.

How should the player proceed in each of these three circumstances?

A. Rules 20-3c and 20-3d would normally cover circumstances (1) and (2), but these Rules do not contemplate a situation such as the one described. Accordingly, in equity (Rule 1-4), in the first two circumstances the ball must be placed in the tree as near as possible to the spot from which it was moved, and in the third circumstance the player must proceed under the unplayable ball Rule, incurring an additional penalty stroke.

Related Decisions:
• 14/7 Striking at Tree Branch to Move Ball Lodged Higher in Branch.
• 18-1/9 Ball Lodged in Tree Knocked Down by Outside Agency.

18-2a/30
Ball Moves After Player Takes Several Practice Swings Near Ball and Touches Grass Behind Ball

Q. A player took several practice swings about one foot from his ball which was lying in light rough, and his club came in contact with the ground. He then took his stance, touched grass behind the ball with the clubhead but did not ground the club. At that point the ball moved.

The player claimed that no penalty was incurred because he had not addressed the ball. However, the Committee judged that the practice swings and the touching of the grass behind the ball caused the ball to move, and therefore the player incurred a penalty stroke under Rule 18-2a. Was the Committee correct?

A. It is a question of fact whether the player caused his ball to move and thus incurred a penalty under Rule 18-2a. Because of the practice swings and touching of the grass, the weight of evidence is against the player and therefore the Committee's decision was correct.

18-2a/30.5
Ball Moves After Removal of Loose Impediment Near Ball

Q. Through the green, a player's ball moves after the player removed a loose impediment near, but not touching, the ball. What is the ruling?

A. It is a question of fact whether the player caused his ball to move and thus incurred a penalty under Rule 18-2a. The Committee should evaluate all the evidence and make a decision based on the weight of that evidence. The Committee should consider a number of factors, including the proximity of the loose impediment to the ball, the force and means with which the loose impediment was removed, the presence of a strong wind and the delay, if any, between the removal of the loose impediment and the movement of the ball. Any doubt as to whether the player caused the ball to move should be resolved against the player.

Decisions related to 18-2a/30 and 18-2a/30.5:
• 14-6/1 Ball Moves in Water in Water Hazard After Stance Taken.
• 18/10 Ball Falls into Bunker When Person Walks Nearby.
• 18-2b/3 Ball Moves After Player Has Taken Stance in Bunker.
• 18-2b/4 Ball Moves After Player Grounds Club Short Distance Behind Ball But Before Grounding Club Immediately Behind Ball.

18-2a/31
Ball Touched Accidentally in Removing Loose Impediments

Q. In removing loose impediments from the vicinity of his ball lying through the green, the player accidentally touches the ball with his hand but does not move it. Is there any penalty?

A. No. Under Rule 18-2a there is only a penalty if the player, his partner or either of their caddies purposely touches the player's ball; it may be touched accidentally provided it does not move.

18-2a/32
Ball Touched with Fir Cone or Stick to Prevent Movement When Loose Impediments Removed

Q. A player placed a fir cone or stick against his ball to prevent the ball from moving when he moved some loose impediments. Is this permissible?

A. No. The player purposely touched his ball in play, contrary to Rule 18-2a, and incurred a penalty of one stroke.

Decisions related to 18-2a/31 and 18-2a/32:
• 23-1/11 Ball Moved Accidently by Foot During Removal of Loose Impediment on Putting Green.
• 24-1/4 Holding Ball in Place While Removing Obstruction.

18-2a/33
Rotating Ball on Putting Green Without Marking Position

Q. A player rotates his ball on the putting green to line up the trademark with the hole. He did not lift the ball, mark its position or change its position. Is there a penalty?

A. Yes, one stroke for touching the ball other than as provided for in the Rules (Rule 18-2a). Under Rules 16-1b and 20-1, a ball on the putting green may be lifted (or touched and rotated) after its position has been marked. If the player had marked the position of the ball before rotating it, there would have been no penalty.

Related Decisions:
• 12-2/2 Touching and Rotating Half-Buried Ball in Rough for Identification Purposes.
• 20-3a/2 Using Line on Ball for Alignment.

BALL MOVING AFTER ADDRESS

18-2b/1
Ball Moves After Stance Taken But Before Address

Q. Outside a hazard, the player took his stance but did not ground his club. The ball moved. What is the ruling?

A. As the player had not addressed the ball, he did not incur a penalty under Rule 18-2b (see Definition of "Addressing the Ball").

If, however, the player caused the ball to move, he was subject to penalty and the ball should have been replaced (Rule 18-2a).

18-2b/2
Ball Addressed in Hazard

Q. Can a player address his ball in a hazard?

A. As the definition of addressing the ball states that "the player has addressed the ball when he has grounded the club immediately in front of or immediately behind the ball, whether or not he has taken his stance," generally the player cannot address his ball in a hazard without incurring the general penalty under Rule 13-4. (New)

18-2b/3
Ball Moves After Player Has Taken Stance in Bunker

Q. In a bunker, a player's ball moved after he had taken his stance. What is the ruling?

A. If the player's approach to the ball or the act of taking his stance caused the ball to move, the player incurred a penalty stroke under Rule 18-2a and the ball must be replaced. Otherwise, he incurs no penalty. (Revised)

18-2b/4
Ball Moves After Player Grounds Club Short Distance Behind Ball But Before Grounding Club Immediately Behind Ball

Q. A player's routine prior to making a stroke is as follows: he first grounds the club a short distance behind, but not immediately behind the ball. Then, he places the clubhead immediately behind the ball and makes the stroke.

If the ball moves after he grounds the club a short distance behind, but before he grounds it immediately behind, the ball, does he incur a penalty stroke under Rule 18-2b (Ball Moving After Address)?

A. No. A player has not addressed the ball until he has placed the clubhead immediately in front of or behind the ball – see Definition of "Addressing the Ball."

However, it is a question of fact to be resolved by reference to all available evidence whether the player in fact caused the ball at rest to move. If the player did so, he incurs a one stroke penalty under Rule 18-2a and must replace his ball. Otherwise, the ball must be played from its new location without penalty unless another Rule applies. (Revised)

18-2b/5
Ball Moves When Club Rested on Grass Immediately Behind Ball

Q. A player's ball is at rest. He rests his club on the grass immediately behind the ball and the ball moves. What is the ruling?

A. If the grass had been compressed to the point where it would support the weight of the club, the club is considered grounded. Therefore, the player has addressed the ball and Rule 18-2b applies. The player incurs a one-stroke penalty and must replace his ball unless it is known or virtually certain that some other agency (e.g., a dog or wind) caused the ball to move.

If the grass had not been compressed to the point where it would support the weight of the club, the player has not grounded his club and, therefore, has not addressed his ball. The player incurs no penalty under Rule 18-2b, but he is subject to penalty under Rule 18-2a if the player's actions caused the ball to move. (New)

Decisions related to 18-2b/3 and 18-2b/4:
- 14-6/1 Ball Moves in Water in Water Hazard After Stance Taken.
- 18/10 Ball Falls into Bunker When Person Walks Nearby.

- 18-2a/30 Ball Moves After Player Takes Several Practice Swings Near Ball and Touches Grass Behind Ball.
- 18-2a/30.5 Ball Moves After Removal of Loose Impediment Near Ball.

18-2b/5.5
Placing Clubhead on Ground in Front of Ball When Addressing

Q. A player places his clubhead on the ground immediately in front of the ball without pressing anything down. Before the player grounds the club behind the ball, the ball moves. Has the player "addressed the ball" so that he is subject to penalty under Rule 18-2b?

A. Yes. (Revised)

18-2b/5.7
When Player Who Putts "Side-Saddle" Has Addressed Ball

Q. A player who putts "side-saddle" usually stands directly behind the ball, places the clubhead on the ground immediately behind the ball and aligns the clubhead. The player then moves to the side so as not to infringe Rule 16-1e and makes his stroke. When is the player deemed to have addressed the ball?

A. The player has addressed the ball when he has placed the clubhead on the ground immediately behind the ball regardless of the location of his feet. (Revised)

18-2b/6 (Reserved)

18-2b/7
Ball Moves After Player Addresses It and Then Steps Away

Q. A player addresses his ball. Realizing that the ball is precariously balanced and may move, he steps away from the ball and starts again. This time he does not address the ball, but before he strikes the ball, it moves. What is the ruling?

A. The player incurs a penalty stroke under Rule 18-2b and the ball must be replaced, unless it is known or virtually certain that something else (e.g., wind) caused the ball to move. (Revised)

18-2b/8
Player Addresses Ball, Steps Away, Lifts Ball and Replaces It; Ball Then Moves

Q. On the putting green, a player addressed the ball. He stepped away from the ball, marked its position and lifted it. He then replaced the ball and, before he addressed it, the ball moved. Since the ball was lifted and out of play after it was addressed, was the player subject to penalty under Rule 18-2b when it moved after it was put back into play?

A. No. The ball must be played as it lies. Once the ball has been lifted the presumption inherent in the Rule that the act of addressing the ball caused the ball to move is no longer valid.

Related Decisions:
- 18-2b/11 Ball Moved By Another Agency After Address.
- 20-2a/4 Ball Dropped in Improper Manner Moves When Addressed; Player Then Lifts Ball and Drops It in Proper Manner.
- 23-1/12 After Ball Addressed on Putting Green Ball Moved in Removal of Loose Impediment.

18-2b/9
Ball Moves After Address and Comes to Rest Out of Bounds; Player Plays Ball

Q. A player's ball in play is lying on a slope. When he addresses the ball, it moves and comes to rest out of bounds. He then plays the ball from out of bounds. What is the ruling?

A. When the player's ball in play moved after he had addressed it, he was required to replace the ball, with a penalty stroke, under Rule 18-2b. However, by making a stroke at the ball lying out of bounds, the player has played a wrong ball (Decision 15/6).

In match play, the player loses the hole (Rule 15-3a).

In stroke play, the player incurs a penalty of two strokes under Rule 15-3b and must correct the error. He must place a ball on the spot where the original ball lay before it moved after address, incurring an additional penalty of one stroke as prescribed by Rule 18-2b, for a total penalty of three strokes. If he does not correct the error, he is disqualified.

18-2b/10
Ball Falls into Hole After Being Addressed

Q. A player's ball overhangs the lip of the hole. He addresses the ball and it falls into the hole. What is the ruling?

A. The ball is not holed. The player incurs a penalty stroke and the ball must be replaced. Although Rule 16-2 applies when a player's ball overhangs the lip of the hole, Rule 18-2b, which specifically applies when a player's ball moves after he has addressed it, overrides Rule 16-2 in this case.

If the player does not replace the ball and hole out, in stroke play he is disqualified under Rule 3-2.

Related Decisions:
- 1-2/4 Player Jumps Close to Hole to Cause Ball to Drop; Ball Moves.
- 2-4/2 Ball Falls into Hole After Concession of Next Stroke.
- 16-2/2 Ball Overhanging Hole Knocked Away by Opponent Before Player Determines Status.

18-2b/11
Ball Moved by Another Agency After Address

Q. After a player has addressed his ball in play, some other agency (e.g., a ball played by another player) moves the player's ball. Is the player subject to penalty under Rule 18-2b?

A. No. As it is known or virtually certain that the player did not cause the ball to move, Rule 18-2b does not apply – see Exception under Rule 18-2b. In such a case where an agency directly causes a ball to move, the Rule applicable to that agency (e.g., Rule 18-1, 18-2a, 18-3, 18-4 or 18-5) applies.

The same principle applies if it is known or virtually certain that a ball in play has been moved by wind, water or some other element after the player has addressed it; there is no penalty and the ball must be played from its new location. Gravity is not in itself an element that should be considered when applying the Exception to Rule 18-2b; therefore, unless it is known or virtually certain that some agency other than gravity (e.g., outside agency or wind) caused the ball to move after address, the player is subject to a one stroke penalty under Rule 18-2b and must replace the ball. (Revised)

Related Decisions:
- 18-2b/8 Player Addresses Ball, Steps Away, Lifts Ball and Replaces It; Ball Then Moves.
- 20-2a/4 Ball Dropped in Improper Manner Moves When Addressed; Player Then Lifts Ball and Drops It in Proper Manner.
- 23-1/12 After Ball Addressed on Putting Green Ball Moved in Removal of Loose Impediment.

18-2b/12
Ball Moves After Address and Is Stopped by Player's Club

Q. After a player addresses his ball, the ball moves backward. Before the player can remove his club, the ball is stopped by the clubhead. What is the ruling?

A. The player incurs a penalty stroke under Rule 18-2b and the ball must be replaced. A further penalty under Rule 19-2 (Ball in Motion Deflected or Stopped by Player) does not apply in these circumstances, as the act of his clubhead stopping the ball was related to the initial act of his ball moving after address – see Principle 4 of Decision 1-4/12.

If it is known or virtually certain that the player did not cause the ball to move, Rule 18-2b does not apply (see Exception to Rule 18-2b). In such circumstances, the player would incur a one-stroke penalty under Rule 19-2 for accidentally deflecting or stopping his ball in motion with his equipment, and must play the ball as it lies. (Revised)

Related Decisions:
- 19-2/1 Ball Stopped by Player's Foot Moves When Foot Removed.
- 19-2/1.5 Ball Moves Prior to Address and Is Accidentally Stopped by Player's Club; Player Removes Club and Ball Rolls Away.

Other Decisions related to Rule 18-2b: See "Addressing the Ball: ball moves after being addressed" and "Ball At Rest Moved: after address" in the Index.

BALL MOVED BY OPPONENT OTHER THAN DURING SEARCH

18-3b/1
Ball Moved Accidentally by Opponent in Playing His Own Ball

Q. In singles match play, A's ball is lying close to B's. It is B's turn to play. Although B has the right under Rule 22-2 to require A to mark the position of and lift his ball, he fails to do so. In making a stroke at his ball, B causes A's ball to move. What is the procedure?

A. B incurs a one-stroke penalty under Rule 18-3b for having caused A's ball in play to move. A must replace his ball; if A's lie has been altered, Rule 20-3b applies.

This ruling differs from that in Decision 18-1/8, because it was reasonably foreseeable that B's stroke could cause A's ball to move, and because B could, through the exercise of reasonable care, have avoided causing A's ball to move by having A's ball lifted prior to his stroke.

Related Decisions:
- 18-2a/21 Ball Moved Accidentally by Player in Playing Wrong Ball.
- 30-3f/9 Player's Ball Moved by Partner in Playing His Own Ball.

18-3b/2
Opponent's Stroke Disturbs Bushes Causing Player's Ball to Move

Q. In playing a stroke, an opponent disturbed some bushes, causing the player's ball to move. What is the ruling?

A. The answer depends on whether it was reasonably foreseeable that the stroke would cause the player's ball to move.

If it was reasonably foreseeable, the opponent incurs a penalty stroke (Rule 18-3b) as the opponent, through exercising reasonable care by having the player's ball lifted under Rule 22-2, could have avoided causing the player's ball to move. If it was not reasonably foreseeable, then the opponent incurs no penalty. In either case, the player must replace the ball.

Related Decisions:
- 18-1/8 Ball Moved by Stone Dislodged by Partner's or Opponent's Stroke.
- 18-2a/20.5 Player's Practice Swing Moves Loose Impediment Which Moves Ball.
- 19-2/9 Divot Taken After Stroke Strikes Ball in Motion.

18-3b/3
Ball Accidentally Stepped on and Moved by Opponent's Caddie

Q. The opponent's caddie accidentally stepped on the player's ball and moved it. What is the ruling?

A. The opponent incurs a one-stroke penalty (Rule 18-3b) unless the caddie was searching for the ball, in which case there would be no penalty (Rule 18-3a).

18-3b/4
Opponent's Caddie Lifts Player's Ball After Player Claims Another Ball

Q. In a match, the player finds a ball and claims it as his. The opponent's caddie then finds another ball and lifts it. It is subsequently discovered that the ball the opponent's caddie lifted was the player's ball. Should the opponent incur a penalty under Rule 18-3b?

A. No. Rule 18-3b does not contemplate an opponent or his caddie moving a player's ball in such circumstances. In equity (Rule 1-4), the ball must be replaced without penalty to anyone.

18-3b/5
Opponent's Caddie Lifts Player's Ball Which May or May Not Have Been Out of Bounds

Q. An opponent's caddie lifted the player's ball and informed the player that the ball was out of bounds. The player claimed that his ball might have been in bounds. What is the ruling?

A. If the Committee establishes that the ball was in bounds, the opponent incurs a penalty stroke under Rule 18-3b and the player must replace his ball.

If the ball was out of bounds, the opponent incurs no penalty.

If the position of the ball cannot be established, the benefit of the doubt should be given to the player.

Other Decisions related to Rule 18-3: See "Ball At Rest Moved: by opponent" in the Index.

BALL MOVED BY FELLOW-COMPETITOR

18-4/1 (Reserved)

18-4/2
Competitor's Ball Knocked Out of Bunker by Fellow-Competitor's Stroke at Own Ball

Q. In stroke play, B, in playing a stroke at his ball in a bunker, accidentally hits A's ball that was also in the bunker. Both balls come to rest outside the bunker. A plays his ball from the spot to which it has been moved by B's stroke. What is the ruling?

A. A was required to replace his ball in the bunker (Rule 18-4). A's breach of Rule 18-4 was a serious one and he should have been disqualified under Rule 20-7c unless the serious breach was rectified as prescribed in that Rule. B incurred no penalty (Rule 18-4).

Related Decision:
• 28/10 Ball Dropped Outside Bunker Under Option Requiring Drop in Bunker.

18-4/3
Fellow-Competitor Lifts Competitor's Ball Conceding Next Stroke in Stroke-Play Play-Off

Q. In a stroke-play play-off, B picks up A's ball, conceding A a 4. B then holed a putt for a 3 to win the play-off. Is B subject to penalty for conceding a putt in stroke play?

A. B incurs no penalty (Rule 18-4). If B had not holed in 3 to win the play-off, A would have been obliged to replace his ball and hole out (Rule 18-4).

Other Decisions related to Rule 18-4: See "Ball At Rest Moved: by fellow-competitor" in the Index.

BALL MOVED BY ANOTHER BALL

18-5/1 (Reserved)

18-5/2
Original Ball Struck by Provisional Ball

Q. A player's provisional ball played from the tee strikes and moves his original ball. What is the ruling?

A. There is no penalty. The original ball must be replaced (Rule 18-5).

Related Decisions:
• 3-3/7 Original Ball Strikes Second Ball or Vice Versa.
• 19-5/5 Provisional Ball Struck by Original Ball.

18-5/3
Competitor and Fellow-Competitor Unaware Ball Moved by Fellow-Competitor's Ball Until After Completion of Hole

Q. In stroke play, A then B play their second strokes to the green but, due to the contours of the green, they cannot see where their balls come to rest. Both competitors complete the hole from about 12 feet with two putts each. On their way to the next tee, it was established that A's ball had come to rest about one foot from the hole, but that B's ball in motion had struck A's ball and moved it. What is the ruling?

A. B proceeded correctly by playing his ball as it lay – Rule 19-5a.

As it was not known or virtually certain that A's ball had been moved by B's ball when A made his next stroke, he proceeded properly and incurred no penalty – see the Note to Rule 18-1.

Related Decisions:

- 15/10 Ball Thrown into Bounds by Outside Agency and Played; Neither Player Nor His Caddie Aware of Action of Outside Agency.
- 18-1/3 Player Unaware Ball Moved by Outside Agency Does Not Replace Ball.
- 19-2/6 Ball Deflected or Stopped by Player's Golf Cart Being Pulled by Opponent or Fellow-Competitor.

Other Decisions related to Rule 18-5: See "Ball At Rest Moved: by another ball" in the Index.

BALL MOVED IN MEASURING

18-6/1
Ball Moved in Measuring to Determine If Re-Drop Required

Q. A player drops his ball in accordance with the Rules. The ball rolls and the player is uncertain whether it has come to rest more than two club-lengths from where it first struck a part of the course. The player measures to determine whether he must re-drop under Rule 20-2c(vi) and in doing so accidentally causes the ball to move. What is the ruling if (a) the ball had rolled more than two club-lengths or (b) the ball had not rolled more than two club-lengths?

A. The player incurs no penalty for causing his ball to move in either case (see Rule 18-6). If the ball had rolled more than two club-lengths, it must be re-dropped. If the ball had not rolled more than two club-lengths, it must be replaced.

18-6/2
Ball Moved by Flagstick When Measuring

Q. In measuring with the flagstick to determine the order of play, the player accidentally moves his ball in play with the flagstick. What is the ruling?

A. The answer depends on whether the movement of the ball was directly attributable to the specific act of measuring – see Rule 18-6.

If the player was holding or touching the flagstick in the act of measuring when it touched and moved the ball, the movement of the ball was directly attributable to the specific act of measuring. There is no penalty and the ball must be replaced.

If the movement of the ball was not directly attributable to the specific act of measuring (e.g., the player dropped the flagstick on the ball), the player incurs a penalty stroke under Rule 18-2a and the ball must be replaced.

RULE 19

BALL IN MOTION DEFLECTED OR STOPPED

DEFINITIONS

All defined terms are in *italics* and are listed alphabetically in the Definitions section – see pages 6–16.

19-1. BY OUTSIDE AGENCY

If a player's ball in motion is accidentally deflected or stopped by any *outside agency*, it is a *rub of the green*, there is no penalty and the ball must be played as it lies, except:

a. If a player's ball in motion after a *stroke* other than on the *putting green* comes to rest in or on any moving or animate *outside agency*, the ball must *through the green* or in a *hazard* be dropped, or on the *putting green* be placed, as near as possible to the spot directly under the place where the ball came to rest in or on the *outside agency*, but not nearer the *hole*, and

b. If a player's ball in motion after a *stroke* on the *putting green* is deflected or stopped by, or comes to rest in or on, any moving or animate *outside agency*, except a worm, insect or the like, the *stroke* is canceled. The ball must be replaced and replayed.

If the ball is not immediately recoverable, another ball may be *substituted*.

Exception: Ball striking person attending or holding up *flagstick* or anything carried by him – see Rule 17-3b.

Note: If a player's ball in motion has been deliberately deflected or stopped by an *outside agency*:

(a) after a *stroke* from anywhere other than on the *putting green*, the spot where the ball would have come to rest must be estimated. If that spot is:
  (i) *through the green* or in a *hazard*, the ball must be dropped as near as possible to that spot;
  (ii) *out of bounds*, the player must proceed under Rule 27-1; or
  (iii) on the *putting green*, the ball must be placed on that spot.

(b) after a *stroke* on the *putting green*, the *stroke* is canceled. The ball must be replaced and replayed.

If the *outside agency* is a *fellow-competitor* or his *caddie*, Rule 1-2 applies to the *fellow-competitor*.

(Player's ball deflected or stopped by another ball – see Rule 19-5)

19-2. BY PLAYER, PARTNER, CADDIE OR EQUIPMENT

If a player's ball is accidentally deflected or stopped by himself, his *partner* or either of their *caddies* or *equipment*, the player incurs a penalty of one stroke. The ball must be played as it lies, except when it comes to rest in or on the player's, his *partner's* or either of their *caddies'* clothes or *equipment*, in which case the ball must *through the green* or in a *hazard* be dropped, or on the *putting green* be placed, as near as possible to the spot directly under the place where the ball came to rest in or on the article, but not nearer the *hole*.

Exceptions:

1. Ball striking person attending or holding up *flagstick* or anything carried by him – see Rule 17-3b.

2. Dropped ball – see Rule 20-2a.

(Ball purposely deflected or stopped by player, partner or caddie – see Rule 1-2)

19-3. BY OPPONENT, CADDIE OR EQUIPMENT IN MATCH PLAY

If a player's ball is accidentally deflected or stopped by an *opponent*, his *caddie* or his *equipment*, there is no penalty. The player may, before another *stroke* is made by either *side*, cancel the *stroke* and play a ball, without penalty, as nearly as possible at the spot from which the original ball was last played (Rule 20-5) or he may play the ball as it lies. However, if the player elects not to cancel the *stroke* and the ball has come to rest in or on the *opponent's* or his *caddie's* clothes or *equipment*, the ball must *through the green* or in a *hazard* be dropped, or on the *putting green* be placed, as near as possible to the spot directly under the place where the ball came to rest in or on the article, but not nearer the hole.

Exception: Ball striking person attending or holding up *flagstick* or anything carried by him – see Rule 17-3b.

(Ball purposely deflected or stopped by opponent or caddie – see Rule 1-2)

19-4. BY FELLOW-COMPETITOR, CADDIE OR EQUIPMENT IN STROKE PLAY

See Rule 19-1 regarding ball deflected by *outside agency*.

Exception: Ball striking person attending or holding up *flagstick* or anything carried by him – see Rule 17-3b.

19-5. BY ANOTHER BALL

a. At Rest

If a player's ball in motion after a *stroke* is deflected or stopped by a *ball in play* and at rest, the player must play his ball as it lies. In match play, there is no penalty. In stroke play, there is no penalty, unless both balls lay on the *putting green* prior to the *stroke*, in which case the player incurs a penalty of two strokes.

b. In Motion

If a player's ball in motion after a *stroke* other than on the *putting green* is deflected or stopped by another ball in motion after a *stroke*, the player must play his ball as it lies, without penalty.

If a player's ball in motion after a *stroke* on the *putting green* is deflected or stopped by another ball in motion after a *stroke*, the player's *stroke* is canceled. The ball must be replaced and replayed, without penalty.

Note: Nothing in this Rule overrides the provisions of Rule 10-1 (Order of Play in Match Play) or Rule 16-1f (Making Stroke While Another Ball in Motion).

PENALTY FOR BREACH OF RULE:
Match play – Loss of hole; Stroke play – Two strokes.

BALL IN MOTION DEFLECTED OR STOPPED: GENERAL

19/1
Ball Deflected or Stopped by Golf Cart Shared by Two Players

Under the Definition of "Equipment," equipment includes a golf cart, whether or not motorized. If two or more players share a golf cart, the cart and everything in it are deemed to be the equipment of one of the players sharing the cart. If the cart is being moved by one of the players (or the partner of one of the players) sharing it, the cart and everything in it are deemed to be that player's equipment. Otherwise, the cart and everything in it are deemed to be the equipment of the player sharing the cart whose ball (or whose partner's ball) is involved.

Thus, for example, in a singles match, if A and B are sharing a cart and A's ball in motion is deflected or stopped by the cart, A incurs a penalty of one stroke (Rule 19-2) unless the cart is being driven or pulled by B when the incident occurs. If B is driving or pulling the cart, there is no penalty, and A would have the option of playing his ball as it lies or replaying the stroke (Rule 19-3).

Related Decision:
• 18/8 Ball Moved by Golf Cart Shared by Two Players.

19/2
Status of Person in Shared Golf Cart

Q. In Note 2 of the Definition of "Equipment" does the phrase "and everything in it" include any person in the cart?

A. Yes.

Related Decisions:
• 6-4/2.5 Status of Individual Who Transports Player's Clubs on Motorized Golf Cart or Trolley.
• 33-1/9.5 Breach of Transportation Condition by Caddie.
• 33-8/4 Local Rule for Events in Which Motorized Golf Carts Permitted.

BALL DEFLECTED OR STOPPED BY OUTSIDE AGENCY

19-1/1
Ball Deflected by Direction Post

Q. A ball is deflected by a direction post. What is the ruling?

A. It is a rub of the green and the ball must be played as it lies, without penalty.

19-1/2
Player's Ball Deflected by Stroke of Player in Another Group

Q. A hit his ball over onto another fairway where, before it came to rest, it was struck by X in the course of striking his own ball. X's ball went 20 yards. A's ball could not be found. What is the ruling?

A. Each player was an outside agency in relation to the other.

Under Rule 19-1, A would have been obliged to play his ball as it lay, without penalty, if it had been found. Since it was not found, A must proceed under Rule 27-1.

X must play his ball as it lies, without penalty.

19-1/3
Ball Played from Putting Green Deflected by Moving Outside Agency; Stroke Not Replayed

Q. In stroke play, a competitor putts and his ball is deflected by a moving outside agency other than a worm, insect or the like. The competitor did not replay the stroke as required by Rule 19-1b, holed out and then played from the next tee. What is the ruling?

A. The stroke that was deflected by the outside agency does not count in the competitor's score. When the competitor failed to replay the stroke he played from a wrong place. If the breach was a serious one, he is disqualified – Rule 20-7c. Otherwise, the score with the original ball counts and he incurs a penalty of two strokes for breach of Rule 19.

19-1/4 (Reserved)

19-1/4.1
Ball Deliberately Deflected or Stopped Through the Green by Spectator

Q. A player overshoots a green. A spectator (X) who is standing behind the green deliberately deflects or stops the ball. According to the Note to Rule 19-1, the spot where the ball would have come to rest must be estimated. How does the player estimate the spot in such circumstances?

A. In a case where the ball might have come to rest where X was situated if he had not deliberately deflected or stopped it, the spot where X was situated should be the estimated spot for the purposes of dropping the ball in accordance with the Note. For example, if another spectator (Y) had been behind X, the ball might have struck Y if X had avoided it, and come to rest where X was situated.

If there is no question that the ball would have come to rest somewhere else if X had not deflected or stopped it, a judgment must be made as to where the ball would have come to rest, and the player should be given the benefit of any doubt. For example, if no person or object had been behind X and without any doubt the ball would have come to rest either in a lateral water hazard behind the green or in the rough just short of the hazard, the estimated spot for dropping the ball should be in the rough just short of the hazard. (Revised)

19-1/5
Ball Deliberately Deflected or Stopped on Putting Green by Fellow-Competitor

Q. At the last hole of a stroke-play event, A's ball lies on the putting green. A has a putt to beat B by one stroke. A putts and B, seeing that A's ball might go into the hole, deliberately deflects it. What is the ruling?

A. A must replay his stroke, without penalty – see Note under Rule 19-1. As B's act of deliberately deflecting his fellow-competitor's ball placed A at a significant disadvantage, B should be considered to have committed a serious breach of Rule 1-2 (Exerting Influence on Movement of Ball or Altering Physical Conditions) and should be disqualified. (Revised)

Related Decisions:
• 1-2/0.5 Serious Breach of Rule 1-2.
• 1-2/1 Line of Putt Altered Purposely by Opponent or Fellow-Competitor by Stepping on It.
• 16-1b/3 Ball Lifted from Putting Green; Ball Replaced While Another Ball in Motion Subsequently Deflects Ball.
• 16-1b/4 Ball Lifted from Putting Green by Opponent or Fellow-Competitor While Player's Ball in Motion.
• 17-3/2 Opponent or Fellow-Competitor Attending Flagstick for Player Fails to Remove It; Player's Ball Strikes Flagstick.

19-1/6
Ball Picked Up or Deflected by Dog on Putting Green After Stroke from Off Green

Q. A ball played from off the green was about a foot from the hole and still in motion when it was moved by a dog to a spot about ten feet from the hole. The ball was either deflected by the dog or the dog picked it up, ran with it and dropped it. What is the ruling?

A. If the ball was deflected, it would be played as it lay, without penalty, from the spot to which it was moved by the dog (Rule 19-1).

If the dog picked up the ball, the player should have placed the ball, without penalty, as near as possible to the spot where the original ball was when the dog picked it up (Rule 19-1a).

19-1/7
Ball Picked Up or Deflected by Dog on Putting Green After Stroke on Green

Q. A player plays a stroke on the putting green and, while the ball is still in motion, it is picked up and carried away, or is deflected, by a dog. What is the ruling?

A. In either case, the stroke is canceled and the ball must be replaced (Rule 19-1b).

Other Decisions related to Rule 19-1: See "Ball Deflected or Stopped: by outside agency" in the Index.

BALL DEFLECTED OR STOPPED BY PLAYER, PARTNER, CADDIE OR EQUIPMENT

19-2/1
Ball Stopped by Player's Foot Moves When Foot Removed

Q. A player making a stroke on the bank of a bunker hits the ball to the top of the bank. The ball then rolls down the bank and is accidentally stopped by the player's foot. The player removes his foot and the ball rolls into the footprint. What is the ruling?

A. The player incurs a penalty of one stroke (Rule 19-2) and must replace the ball on the spot at which it came to rest against his foot. A further penalty under Rule 18-2a (Ball at Rest Moved by Player) does not apply in these circumstances provided the player replaces the ball, as related acts have resulted in two Rules being breached – see principle 4 in Decision 1-4/12. If the ball is not replaced before the player makes his next stroke, the failure to replace the ball is considered an unrelated act – see principle 5 in Decision 1-4/12 – and he loses the hole in match play or incurs an additional penalty of two strokes in stroke play under Rule 18-2a, for a total penalty of three strokes. (Revised)

19-2/1.5
Ball Moves Prior to Address and Is Accidentally Stopped by Player's Club; Player Removes Club and Ball Moves Away

Q. A player's ball lies on a steep slope through the green. The player takes his stance but, fearing the ball might move, does not ground his club and so has not addressed the ball. The ball rolls backwards and is stopped accidentally by the player's club. The player then removes his club and the ball rolls farther down the slope. Is the player subject to the penalty of one stroke under Rule 19-2?

A. Yes, and the ball must be replaced on the spot at which it was stopped. A further penalty under Rule 18-2a (Ball at Rest Moved by Player) does not apply in the circumstances provided the player replaces the ball, as related acts have resulted in two Rules being breached – see principle 4 in Decision 1-4/12. If the ball is not replaced before the player makes his next stroke, the failure to replace the ball is considered an unrelated act (see principle 5 in Decision 1-4/12) and he loses the hole in match play or incurs an additional penalty of two strokes in stroke play under Rule 18-2a, for a total penalty of three strokes. (Revised)

Decision related to 19-2/1 and 19-2/1.5:
• 18-2b/12 Ball Moves After Address and Is Stopped by Player's Club.

19-2/2
Player's Ball Strikes Own Caddie and Comes to Rest Out of Bounds

Q. A player's ball accidentally strikes his caddie, who is standing in bounds, and the ball comes to rest out of bounds. What is the ruling?

A. The player incurs a penalty of one stroke (Rule 19-2) and, since the ball lies out of bounds, he must proceed under Rule 27-1, incurring another penalty stroke.

19-2/3
Player's Ball Strikes Own Caddie Standing Out of Bounds and Comes to Rest on Course

Q. A player's ball accidentally strikes his caddie standing out of bounds and comes to rest in bounds. What is the ruling?

A. The player incurs a penalty of one stroke and, since the ball came to rest in bounds, it is in play – Rule 19-2.

19-2/4
Player's Ball Strikes Own Caddie Standing Out of Bounds and Comes to Rest Out of Bounds

Q. A player's ball accidentally strikes his caddie standing out of bounds and comes to rest out of bounds. What is the ruling?

A. The player incurs a penalty of one stroke (Rule 19-2) and, since the ball lies out of bounds, he must proceed under Rule 27-1, incurring another penalty stroke.

19-2/5
Ball Deflected or Stopped by Clubs Belonging to Different Side But Carried in Same Bag

Q. A had his bag of clubs on a golf cart. B had only a few clubs, which A carried for him in his bag. B played a stroke that was deflected by the clubs. What is the ruling?

A. Under the principle in the Definition of "Equipment," the clubs are deemed B's equipment.

B incurred a penalty of one stroke and must play his ball as it lies – Rule 19-2.

19-2/6
Ball Deflected or Stopped by Player's Golf Cart Being Pulled by Opponent or Fellow-Competitor

Q. A player's ball strikes his own golf cart while it is being pulled by an opponent or a fellow-competitor. What is the ruling?

A. Since the player is not sharing the cart with any other player, it remains his equipment even when it is being pulled by an opponent or a fellow-competitor (see Note 2 to the Definition of "Equipment").

If the player was aware that his cart was being pulled by an opponent or a fellow-competitor, he incurs a penalty of one stroke and must play the ball as it lies – Rule 19-2. But if he was not aware, in equity (Rule 1-4), no penalty is incurred, and the ball must be played as it lies.

Related Decisions:
- 15/10 Ball Thrown into Bounds by Outside Agency and Played; Neither Player Nor His Caddie Aware of Action of Outside Agency.
- 18-1/3 Player Unaware Ball Moved by Outside Agency Does Not Replace Ball.
- 18-5/3 Competitor and Fellow-Competitor Unaware Ball Moved by Fellow-Competitor's Ball Until After Completion of Hole.

19-2/7
Ball Strikes Player's Golf Bag and Then His Caddie

Q. A player's ball strikes his golf bag lying on the ground and then bounces off it and hits his caddie. Is the penalty one stroke or two strokes?

A. One stroke – Rule 19-2.

19-2/8
Player's Ball Strikes Opponent's or Fellow-Competitor's Bag Left Ahead By Shared Caddie

Q. A and B are either opponents in match play or fellow-competitors in stroke play and they are sharing a caddie. They are on the teeing ground and the caddie is positioned where their tee shots would be expected to come to rest. A's tee shot comes to rest well short of the caddie and B's tee shot comes to rest near the caddie. Without specific directions from either A or B, the caddie leaves B's bag near B's ball and returns with A's bag to A's ball. A's next stroke strikes B's bag. What is the ruling?

A. The Definition of "Caddie" states in part: "When one caddie is employed by more than one player, he is always deemed to be the caddie of the player sharing the caddie whose ball (or whose partner's ball) is involved, and equipment carried by him is deemed to be that player's equipment, except when the caddie acts upon specific directions of another player..." As no specific directions were given to the caddie by B, B's bag is deemed to be A's equipment in this case. It is irrelevant that the caddie was not carrying B's bag at the time A's ball struck it.

A incurs a penalty of one stroke and must play his ball as it lies unless the ball has come to rest in or on B's bag – Rule 19-2.

Related Decision:
• 6-4/1 Meaning of "Specific Directions" in Definition of "Caddie."

19-2/9
Divot Taken After Stroke Strikes Ball in Motion

Q. A player has a short pitch shot to the green. He makes a stroke and, while the ball is still in motion, he makes a subsequent swing and takes a divot out of the ground with his club. The divot deflects or stops the moving ball. What is the ruling?

A. The player is deemed to have accidentally deflected or stopped his ball in motion. He incurs a penalty of one stroke and must play the ball as it lies (Rule 19-2).

Related Decisions:
• 18-1/8 Ball Moved by Stone Dislodged by Partner's or Opponent's Stroke.
• 18-2a/20.5 Player's Practice Swing Moves Loose Impediment Which Moves Ball.
• 18-3b/2 Opponent's Stroke Disturbs Bushes Causing Player's Ball to Move.

19-2/10
Ball Stopped or Deflected by Rake Held by Player's Caddie

Q. A player's ball lies in a bunker. He plays, and his ball is accidentally stopped or deflected by a rake that is being held by his caddie. What is the ruling?

A. When a ball is accidentally deflected or stopped by a rake held by or in contact with a player's caddie, the caddie has accidentally deflected or stopped the player's ball in motion in breach of Rule 19-2. The player is responsible for this breach of the Rules by his caddie (see Rule 6-1). The player incurs a penalty of one stroke and must play the ball as it lies. (Revised)

Other Decisions related to Rule 19-2: See "Ball Deflected or Stopped: by equipment of player or partner," "Ball Deflected or Stopped: by player or partner," and "Ball Deflected or Stopped: by player's own caddie" in the Index.

BALL DEFLECTED OR STOPPED BY OPPONENT ACCIDENTALLY

19-3/1
Ball Accidentally Strikes Opponent Standing Out of Bounds and Comes to Rest Out of Bounds

Q. In match play, a player's ball accidentally strikes his opponent, who is standing out of bounds. The ball comes to rest out of bounds. What is the ruling?

A. There is no penalty and the player is entitled to replay the stroke (Rule 19-3).

19-3/2
Dropped Ball Accidentally Deflected by Opponent or His Caddie

Q. In match play, a player drops his ball under a Rule and the ball is accidentally deflected by the opponent or his caddie. What is the ruling?

A. The ball must be re-dropped without penalty (Rule 20-2a).

19-3/3
Player's Ball Strikes Opponent's or Fellow-Competitor's Trolley Then Own Trolley

Q. A player's ball strikes his opponent's or fellow-competitor's trolley and then strikes his own trolley. What is the ruling?

A. In match play, because the ball first struck his opponent's equipment the player may replay the stroke, without penalty, regardless of what happens thereafter to the ball (Rule 19-3). The player may also play the ball as it lies, but would do so under penalty of one stroke because, after striking his opponent's equipment, his ball struck his own equipment (Rule 19-2).

In stroke play, although the ball first struck a fellow-competitor's equipment, the competitor incurs a penalty of one stroke and must play the ball as it lies (Rules 19-4, 19-1 and 19-2).

Other Decisions related to Rule 19-3: See "Ball Deflected or Stopped: by opponent, caddie or equipment in match play" in the Index.

BALL DEFLECTED OR STOPPED BY FELLOW-COMPETITOR

For Decisions related to Rule 19-4: See "Ball Deflected or Stopped: by outside agency" in the Index.

BALL DEFLECTED OR STOPPED BY ANOTHER BALL

19-5/1
Player Lifts His Ball on Putting Green and Sets It Aside; Opponent's or Fellow-Competitor's Ball Played from Green Subsequently Strikes Player's Ball

Q. B lifts his ball on the putting green and sets it aside elsewhere on the green. A then putts and his ball is deflected or stopped by B's ball. What is the ruling?

A. Since A's ball was deflected by B's equipment (see Note 1 under Definition of "Equipment"), Rules 19-3 and 19-4 apply.

In match play, A incurs no penalty and has the option of playing his ball as it lies or canceling and replaying the stroke – Rule 19-3.

In stroke play, A incurs no penalty and must play his ball as it lies – Rules 19-4 and 19-1.

In either form of play, B must replace his ball on the spot from which it was lifted – Rule 20-3a.

Rule 19-5a does not apply because B's ball was not in play.

19-5/1.5
Ball Lifted and Replaced; Ball Then Rolls and Strikes Ball on Putting Green

Q. In stroke play, after a stroke from the putting green, a competitor marks the position of and lifts his ball from the putting green. After he replaces the ball at rest, and before he addresses it, the ball rolls and strikes his fellow-competitor's ball, which was lying on the putting green. Is the player in breach of Rule 19-5a?

A. No. The competitor incurs no penalty and must play the ball from its new position. After the competitor had lifted and replaced his ball, any subsequent movement is not considered to be "after a stroke" for the purposes of Rule 19-5a.

19-5/1.7
Ball Dropped on Putting Green by Opponent or Fellow-Competitor Falls on Player's Moving Ball

Q. A makes a stroke on the putting green. B, A's opponent or a fellow-competitor, accidentally drops his ball, which he had lifted, and it falls on A's ball, which is still in motion. What is the ruling?

A. In match play, since A's ball was deflected by B's equipment (see Note I under Definition of "Equipment"), Rule 19-3 applies. A has the option of playing his ball as it lies or canceling and replaying the stroke. Neither A nor B incurs a penalty.

In stroke play, A's ball was deflected by a moving outside agency. Therefore, A must cancel and replay his stroke, without penalty, under Rule 19-1b. B incurs no penalty.

In either form of play, B must replace his ball on the spot from which it was lifted – Rule 20-3a.

Rule 19-5b does not apply because B's ball was not in motion after a stroke.

19-5/2
Competitor's Ball Played from Putting Green Strikes Ball on Green Belonging to Competitor Playing in Another Group

Q. In stroke play, C and D are playing together. A and B are playing immediately behind C and D. C's ball lies on the putting green and, since D is searching for his ball, C and D invite A and B to play through. Subsequently, A putts and his ball strikes C's ball. What is the ruling?

A. A incurs a penalty of two strokes and must play his ball as it lies (Rule 19-5). C must replace his ball without penalty (Rule 18-5).

19-5/3 (Reserved)

19-5/4
Competitor's Ball Played from Putting Green Touches But Does Not Move Ball of Fellow-Competitor Lying on Green

Q. In stroke play, A putts and his ball comes to rest touching B's ball. B's ball did not move nor did B's ball prevent A's from rolling any farther. What is the ruling?

A. Since A's ball was not deflected or stopped by B's ball, A incurs no penalty under Rule 19-5 or any other Rule. However, if there is any doubt as to whether B's ball moved or prevented A's ball from rolling any farther, it should be resolved against A.

19-5/5
Provisional Ball Struck by Original Ball

Q. A player's original ball strikes and moves his provisional ball. What is the ruling?

A. Rule 19-5 does not apply because the provisional ball was not in play. Rule 19-2 does not apply because the provisional ball is not the equipment of the player – see Decision 18/7. In equity (Rule 1-4) and by analogy to Rule

19-5a, the player shall play the ball as it lies and no penalty is incurred except that, in stroke play, if both balls lay on the putting green prior to the stroke, the player incurs a penalty of two strokes.

Related Decisions:
• 3-3/7 Original Ball Strikes Second Ball or Vice Versa.
• 18-5/2 Original Ball Struck by Provisional Ball.

Other Decisions related to Rule 19-5: See "Ball Deflected or Stopped: by ball at rest" in the Index.

RULE 20

LIFTING, DROPPING AND PLACING; PLAYING FROM WRONG PLACE

DEFINITIONS

All defined terms are in *italics* and are listed alphabetically in the Definitions section – see pages 6–16.

20-1. LIFTING AND MARKING

A ball to be lifted under the *Rules* may be lifted by the player, his *partner* or another person authorized by the player. In any such case, the player is responsible for any breach of the *Rules*.

The position of the ball must be marked before it is lifted under a *Rule* that requires it to be replaced. If it is not marked, the player incurs a penalty of one stroke and the ball must be replaced. If it is not replaced, the player incurs the general penalty for breach of this Rule but there is no additional penalty under Rule 20-1.

If a ball or ball-marker is accidentally *moved* in the process of lifting the ball under a *Rule* or marking its position, the ball or ball-marker must be replaced. There is no penalty, provided the movement of the ball or ball-marker is directly attributable to the specific act of marking the position of or lifting the ball. Otherwise, the player incurs a penalty of one stroke under this Rule or Rule 18-2a.

Exception: If a player incurs a penalty for failing to act in accordance with Rule 5-3 or 12-2, there is no additional penalty under Rule 20-1.

Note: The position of a ball to be lifted should be marked by placing a ball-marker, a small coin or other similar object immediately behind the ball. If the ball-marker interferes with the play, *stance* or *stroke* of another player, it should be placed one or more clubhead-lengths to one side.

20-2. DROPPING AND RE-DROPPING
a. By Whom and How

A ball to be dropped under the *Rules* must be dropped by the player himself. He must stand erect, hold the ball at shoulder height and arm's length and drop it. If a ball is dropped by any other person or in any other manner and the error is not corrected as provided in Rule 20-6, the player incurs a penalty of one stroke.

If the ball, when dropped, touches any person or the *equipment* of any player before or after it strikes a part of the *course* and before it comes to rest, the ball must be re-dropped, without penalty. There is no limit to the number of times a ball must be re-dropped in these circumstances.

(Taking action to influence position or movement of ball – see Rule 1-2)

b. Where to Drop

When a ball is to be dropped as near as possible to a specific spot, it must be dropped not nearer the *hole* than the specific spot which, if it is not precisely known to the player, must be estimated.

A ball when dropped must first strike a part of the *course* where the applicable *Rule* requires it to be dropped. If it is not so dropped, Rules 20-6 and 20-7 apply.

c. When to Re-Drop

A dropped ball must be re-dropped, without penalty, if it:

(i) rolls into and comes to rest in a *hazard;*

(ii) rolls out of and comes to rest outside a *hazard*;

(iii) rolls onto and comes to rest on a *putting green*;

(iv) rolls and comes to rest *out of bounds*;

(v) rolls to and comes to rest in a position where there is interference by the condition from which relief was taken under Rule 24-2b (immovable obstruction), Rule 25-1 (abnormal ground conditions), Rule 25-3 (wrong putting green) or a Local Rule (Rule 33-8a), or rolls back into the pitch-mark from which it was lifted under Rule 25-2 (embedded ball);

(vi) rolls and comes to rest more than two club-lengths from where it first struck a part of the *course*; or

(vii) rolls and comes to rest nearer the *hole* than:

    (a) its original position or estimated position (see Rule 20-2b) unless otherwise permitted by the *Rules*; or

    (b) the *nearest point of relief* or maximum available relief (Rule 24-2, 25-1 or 25-3); or

    (c) the point where the original ball last crossed the margin of the *water hazard* or *lateral water hazard* (Rule 26-1).

If the ball when re-dropped rolls into any position listed above, it must be placed as near as possible to the spot where it first struck a part of the *course* when re-dropped.

Note 1: If a ball when dropped or re-dropped comes to rest and subsequently *moves*, the ball must be played as it lies, unless the provisions of any other *Rule* apply.

Note 2: If a ball to be re-dropped or placed under this Rule is not immediately recoverable, another ball may be *substituted*.

(Use of dropping zone – see Appendix 1; Part B; Section 8)

20-3. PLACING AND REPLACING
a. By Whom and Where

A ball to be placed under the *Rules* must be placed by the player or his *partner*.

A ball to be replaced under the *Rules* must be replaced by any one of the following: (i) the person who lifted or *moved* the ball, (ii) the player, or (iii) the player's *partner*. The ball must be placed on the spot from which it was lifted or *moved*. If the ball is placed or replaced by any other person and the error is not corrected as provided in Rule 20-6, the player incurs a penalty of one stroke. In any such case, the player is responsible for any other breach of the *Rules* that occurs as a result of the placing or replacing of the ball.

If a ball or ball-marker is accidentally *moved* in the process of placing or replacing the ball, the ball or ball-marker must be replaced. There is no penalty, provided the movement of the ball or ball-marker is directly attributable to the specific act of placing or replacing the ball or removing the ball-marker. Otherwise, the player incurs a penalty of one stroke under Rule 18-2a or 20-1.

If a ball to be replaced is placed other than on the spot from which it was lifted or *moved* and the error is not corrected as provided in Rule 20-6, the player incurs the general penalty, loss of hole in match play or two strokes in stroke play, for a breach of the applicable *Rule*.

b. Lie of Ball to be Placed or Replaced Altered

If the original lie of a ball to be placed or replaced has been altered:

(i) except in a *hazard*, the ball must be placed in the nearest lie most similar to the original lie that is not more than one club-length from the original lie, not nearer the *hole* and not in a *hazard*;

(ii) in a *water hazard*, the ball must be placed in accordance with Clause (i) above, except that the ball must be placed in the *water hazard*;

(iii) in a *bunker*, the original lie must be re-created as nearly as possible and the ball must be placed in that lie.

Note: If the original lie of a ball to be placed or replaced has been altered and it is impossible to determine the spot where the ball is to be placed or replaced, Rule 20-3b applies if the original lie is known, and Rule 20-3c applies if the original lie is not known.

Exception: If the player is searching for or identifying a ball covered by sand – see Rule 12-1a.

c. Spot Not Determinable

If it is impossible to determine the spot where the ball is to be placed or replaced:

(i) *through the green,* the ball must be dropped as near as possible to the place where it lay but not in a *hazard* or on a *putting green*;

(ii) in a *hazard*, the ball must be dropped in the *hazard* as near as possible to the place where it lay;

(iii) on the *putting green*, the ball must be placed as near as possible to the place where it lay but not in a *hazard*.

Exception: When resuming play (Rule 6-8d), if the spot where the ball is to be placed is impossible to determine, it must be estimated and the ball placed on the estimated spot.

d. Ball Fails to Come to Rest on Spot

If a ball when placed fails to come to rest on the spot on which it was placed, there is no penalty and the ball must be replaced. If it still fails to come to rest on that spot:

(i) except in a *hazard*, it must be placed at the nearest spot where it can be placed at rest that is not nearer the *hole* and not in a *hazard*;

(ii) in a *hazard*, it must be placed in the *hazard* at the nearest spot where it can be placed at rest that is not nearer the *hole*.

If a ball when placed comes to rest on the spot on which it is placed, and it subsequently *moves*, there is no penalty and the ball must be played as it lies, unless the provisions of any other *Rule* apply.

*PENALTY FOR BREACH OF RULE 20-1, 20-2 or 20-3:

<u>Match play</u> – Loss of hole; <u>Stroke play</u> – Two strokes.

*If a player makes a *stroke* at a ball *substituted* under one of these Rules when such *substitution* is not permitted, he incurs the general penalty for breach of that Rule, but there is no additional penalty under that Rule. If a player drops a ball in an improper manner and plays from a wrong place or if the ball has been put into play by a person not permitted by the *Rules* and then played from a wrong place, see Note 3 to Rule 20-7c.

20-4. WHEN BALL DROPPED OR PLACED IS IN PLAY

If the player's *ball in play* has been lifted, it is again in play when dropped or placed.

A *substituted ball* becomes the *ball in play* when it has been dropped or placed.

(Ball incorrectly substituted – see Rule 15-2)
(Lifting ball incorrectly substituted, dropped or placed – see Rule 20-6)

20-5. MAKING NEXT STROKE FROM WHERE PREVIOUS STROKE MADE

When a player elects or is required to make his next *stroke* from where a previous *stroke* was made, he must proceed as follows:

(a) <u>On the Teeing Ground</u>: The ball to be played must be played from within the *teeing ground*. It may be played from anywhere within the *teeing ground* and may be teed.

(b) <u>Through the Green</u>: The ball to be played must be dropped and when dropped must first strike a part of the *course through the green*.

(c) <u>In a Hazard</u>: The ball to be played must be dropped and when dropped must first strike a part of the *course* in the *hazard*.

(d) <u>On the Putting Green</u>: The ball to be played must be placed on the *putting green*.

PENALTY FOR BREACH OF RULE 20-5:

<u>Match play</u> – Loss of hole; <u>Stroke play</u> – Two strokes.

20-6. LIFTING BALL INCORRECTLY SUBSTITUTED, DROPPED OR PLACED

A ball incorrectly *substituted*, dropped or placed in a wrong place or otherwise not in accordance with the *Rules* but not played may be lifted, without penalty, and the player must then proceed correctly.

313

20-7. PLAYING FROM WRONG PLACE
a. General

A player has played from a wrong place if he makes a *stroke* at his *ball in play*:

(i) on a part of the *course* where the *Rules* do not permit a *stroke* to be made or a ball to be dropped or placed; or

(ii) when the *Rules* require a dropped ball to be re-dropped or a *moved* ball to be replaced.

Note: For a ball played from outside the *teeing ground* or from a wrong *teeing ground* – see Rule 11-4.

b. Match Play

If a player makes a *stroke* from a wrong place, he loses the hole.

c. Stroke Play

If a *competitor* makes a *stroke* from a wrong place, he incurs a penalty of two strokes under the applicable *Rule*. He must play out the hole with the ball played from the wrong place, without correcting his error, provided he has not committed a serious breach (see Note 1).

If a *competitor* becomes aware that he has played from a wrong place and believes that he may have committed a serious breach, he must, before making a *stroke* on the next *teeing ground*, play out the hole with a second ball played in accordance with the *Rules*. If the hole being played is the last hole of the round, he must declare, before leaving the *putting green*, that he will play out the hole with a second ball played in accordance with the *Rules*.

If the *competitor* has played a second ball, he must report the facts to the *Committee* before returning his score card; if he fails to do so, he is disqualified. The *Committee* must determine whether the *competitor* has committed a serious breach of the applicable *Rule*. If he has, the score with the second ball counts and the competitor must add two penalty strokes to his score with that ball. If the *competitor* has committed a serious breach and has failed to correct it as outlined above, he is disqualified.

Note 1: A *competitor* is deemed to have committed a serious breach of the applicable *Rule* if the *Committee* considers he has gained a significant advantage as a result of playing from a wrong place.

Note 2: If a *competitor* plays a second ball under Rule 20-7c and it is ruled not to count, *strokes* made with that ball and *penalty strokes* incurred solely by playing that ball are disregarded. If the second ball is ruled to count, the *stroke* made from the wrong place and any *strokes* subsequently taken with the original ball including *penalty strokes* incurred solely by playing that ball are disregarded.

Note 3: If a player incurs a penalty for making a *stroke* from a wrong place, there is no additional penalty for:

(a) *substituting* a ball when not permitted;

(b) dropping a ball when the *Rules* require it to be placed, or placing a ball when the *Rules* require it to be dropped;

(c) dropping a ball in an improper manner; or

(d) a ball being put into play by a person not permitted to do so under the *Rules*.

20-1
Club to Be Used in Measuring

Q. A player, taking relief under a Rule, uses his driver to measure the one club-length or two club-lengths prescribed in the relevant Rule. He drops a ball correctly and the ball rolls less than two driver-lengths, but more than two putter-lengths, from where the ball first struck a part of the course when dropped.

Under Rule 20-2c, a dropped ball must be re-dropped if it rolls more than two club-lengths. If the ball comes to rest in a poor lie, may the player opt to use his putter to measure the distance his ball has rolled, in which case he would re-drop under Rule 20-2c and escape the poor lie?

A. No. The player must continue to use the club he originally used for measuring for all measuring in a given situation.

20/2
Borrowing Club for Measuring Purposes

The Rules require that a ball to be dropped must be dropped by the player himself. For the purpose of measuring, the player who is required to drop a ball may use any club he has selected for the round (Rule 4-4). He may also borrow a club for measuring from anyone, including his partner. If he borrows a club and drops a ball and plays it, he incurs no penalty provided that the same outcome could have been achieved with one of the player's own clubs selected for the round. If he could not have achieved the same outcome by measuring with one of his own clubs, he incurs the penalty under the applicable Rule for playing from a wrong place (see Rule 20-7).

Decisions related to 20/1 and 20/2:
• 20-2b/2 Measuring Club-Lengths.
• 25-1b/15 Measuring Across Ground Under Repair in Obtaining Relief.

LIFTING AND MARKING BALL

20-1/0.5
Whether Player Himself Must Lift Ball

Q. Rule 20-1 states: "A ball to be lifted under the Rules may be lifted by the player, his partner or another person authorized by the player." On the other hand, other Rules, e.g., Rules 24-2b(i) and 25-1b(i), state that the player shall lift the ball. Does Rule 20-1 override other Rules which imply that the player himself must lift the ball?

A. Yes.

Related Decision:
• 20-3a/0.5 Whether Player Himself Must Place or Replace Ball.

20-1/0.7
Lifting Ball to Determine Application of Rule

Q. May a player lift his ball to determine whether he is entitled to relief under a Rule (e.g., to determine whether his ball is in a hole made by a burrowing animal or is embedded)?

A. In equity (Rule 1-4), if a player has reason to believe he is entitled to relief from a condition, the player may lift his ball, without penalty, provided he announces his intention in advance to his opponent in match play or his marker or fellow-competitor in stroke play, marks the position of the ball before lifting it, does not clean the ball and gives his opponent or fellow-competitor an opportunity to observe the lifting.

If the ball lies in a position that entitles the player to relief, he may take relief under the applicable Rule. If the player is entitled to relief and fails to comply with this procedure, there is no penalty provided he takes relief under the applicable Rule (see Decision 18-2a/12).

If the ball does not lie in a position from which the player is entitled to relief, or if the player is entitled to relief but decides not to take it, the ball must be replaced, and the opponent, marker or fellow-competitor must be given the opportunity to observe the replacement. If a player who is required to replace the ball fails to do so before making a stroke, he incurs a penalty of loss of hole in match play or two strokes in stroke play under Rule 20-3a, but there is no additional penalty for failure to comply with the procedure for lifting or under Rule 20-1 or 21.

If the player lifts a ball without having reason to believe that it lies in a position from which he is entitled to relief without penalty or if the ball does not lie in a position which entitles the player to relief and the player fails to comply with this procedure, he incurs a penalty of one stroke but there is no additional penalty under Rule 20-1 or 21.

Related Decision:
• 5-3/7 Ball Thought to Be Unfit for Play; Committee Involvement.

20-1/1
Ball Lifted from Putting Green in Mistaken Belief It Is Wrong Ball

Q. A player, mistakenly believing the ball he has played onto a putting green is a wrong ball, picks the ball up without marking its position. He then discovers that the ball is his ball in play. What is the ruling?

A. The player incurs a penalty stroke and he must replace his ball (Rule 20-1).

20-1/2
Player's Ball Lifted by Opponent Without Authority

Q. In a match between A and B, B without A's authority, marked the position of, and lifted, A's ball on the putting green. Is B subject to penalty?

A. Yes. Under Rule 20-1, a player's ball may be lifted by his opponent only with the authority of the player. Since B was not entitled to lift A's ball, B incurred a penalty stroke (Rule 18-3b).

20-1/3
Ball Marked and Lifted by Opponent Without Player's Authority; Player Lifts Ball-Marker, Claims Hole and Opponent Disputes Claim

Q. In a match, B marks the position of A's ball and lifts it without A's authority. B holes out. A picks up the ball-marker with which B had marked the position of his (A's) ball and claims the hole. B disputes the claim. What is the ruling?

A. B incurs a penalty stroke (Rule 18-3b) for lifting A's ball without authority. A incurs a penalty stroke for lifting the ball-marker (Rule 20-1). A must replace his ball and hole out; otherwise, A loses the hole.

20-1/4
Competitor's Ball Lifted Without Authority by Fellow-Competitor

Q. In stroke play, a fellow-competitor lifts a competitor's ball on the putting green without the authority of the competitor. Such action is contrary to Rule 20-1. What is the ruling?

A. There is no penalty and the ball must be replaced (Rule 18-4).

Decision related to 20-1/2, 20-1/3 and 20-1/4:
• 30-3f/10 Player's Ball Lifted Without Authority by Opponent in Four-Ball Match.

20-1/5
Competitor's Ball Lifted Without Authority by Fellow-Competitor's Caddie Who Subsequently Substitutes Another Ball Which Competitor Plays

Q. A competitor's ball lying on the putting green is lifted by a fellow-competitor's caddie without the authority of the competitor. Subsequently, the fellow-competitor's caddie by mistake substitutes another ball and the competitor plays it. The error is then discovered. What is the ruling?

A. When a competitor authorises another person to lift his ball, the competitor is responsible for any breach of the Rules (Rule 20-1). The converse is generally true, i.e., the competitor is not responsible for a breach of a Rule caused by the unauthorized lifting of his ball. Thus, in this case, the competitor should not be penalized under Rule 15-2. The competitor should hole out with the substituted ball, without penalty.

Related Decisions:
- 15-2/2 Player Mistakenly Substitutes Another Ball on Putting Green; Error Discovered Before Stroke Played.
- 20-6/3 Ball Mistakenly Substituted When Dropped; Correction of Error.

20-1/5.5
Ball-Marker Moved Accidentally by Player

Q. A player marked the position of his ball on the putting green and lifted the ball. When it was the player's turn to play, he could not find his ball-marker. Subsequently, he found the ball-marker stuck to the sole of his shoe. He concluded that he had accidentally stepped on it while assisting his partner in lining up a putt. What is the ruling?

A. The player incurs a penalty stroke under Rule 20-1 which requires that the position of a ball be marked before it is lifted, and contemplates that the ball-marker will remain in position until the ball is replaced. The player must place the ball as near as possible to its original position but not nearer the hole – Rule 20-3c.

Under the last paragraph of Rule 20-1, a player is exempt from penalty if his ball-marker is accidentally moved in the process of lifting the ball or marking its position. In this case the ball-marker was not moved during such process.

20-1/6
Ball-Marker Moved Accidentally by Player in Process of Marking Position of Ball

Q. A player marked the position of his ball with a coin, lifted the ball and pressed down the coin with the sole of his putter. He walked to the edge of the green and then noticed that the coin had stuck to the sole of the putter. What is the ruling?

A. In this case, the movement of the ball-marker was directly attributable to the specific act of marking the position of the ball.

Accordingly, no penalty is incurred and the ball or the ball-marker must be replaced. If the spot where the ball or the ball-marker lay is not known, it must be placed as near as possible to where it lay but not nearer the hole (Rule 20-3c).

20-1/6.5
Ball-Marker Pressed Down by Opponent

Q. In a match, the player's ball-marker on the putting green is pressed down by the opponent. Is the opponent in breach of the Rules?

A. No. Rule 18-3b does not apply to ball-markers. However, if the ball-marker were moved such that it no longer accurately marked the position of the ball, in equity (Rule 1-4), the opponent would incur a penalty of one stroke. If the opponent pressed down the ball-marker with the authority of the player and that act caused it to move, there would be no penalty to either player (see Decision 20-1/6).

20-1/7
Ball-Marker Moved by Opponent's Caddie Accidentally

Q. A player's caddie accidentally kicked his opponent's ball-marker closer to the hole. What is the ruling?

A. In equity (Rule 1-4), the ball-marker should have been replaced as near as possible to the spot where it lay and the player should incur a penalty of one stroke.

Related Decisions:
• 2-4/5 Whether Lifting Opponent's Ball-Marker Is Concession of Next Stroke.
• 30/5 In Four-Ball Match Player with Putt for Half Picks Up in Error at Suggestion of Opponent Based on Misunderstanding.

20-1/8
Ball-Marker Lifted by Player Who Mistakenly Believes He Has Won Hole

Q. A player, mistakenly believing he has won a hole, picks up his ball-marker. What is the ruling?

A. The player incurs a one-stroke penalty (Rule 20-1) and must replace his ball.

Related Decision:
• 2-4/3 Player Lifts Ball in Mistaken Belief That Next Stroke Conceded.
• 2-4/3.5 Stroke Conceded by Caddie.
• 9-2/5 Incorrect Information Causes Opponent to Lift His Ball-Marker.

20-1/9
Ball-Marker Lifted by Outside Agency

Q. A marked the position of his ball on the putting green while a following match or group was playing through. After the following match or group had played through, A could not find his ball-marker. It apparently had been lifted by one of the players playing through. What is the ruling?

A. Under Rule 20-3c, A must place his ball as near as possible to where it lay on the green.

20-1/10 (Reserved)

20-1/10.5
Ball-Marker Moved by Wind or Casual Water During Stipulated Round

Q. During a stipulated round, a player marked the position of and lifted his ball under a Rule. Prior to the player replacing his ball, wind or casual water moved his ball-marker. What is the procedure?

A. The ball or ball-marker must be replaced without penalty. If a ball has been lifted under a Rule which requires it to be replaced, it must be placed on the spot from which it was lifted (Rule 20-3a).

20-1/11
Ball-Marker in Position to Assist Another Player

Q. A player marks the position of his ball on the putting green and the ball-marker is so located that it might be of assistance to the opponent or a fellow-competitor in lining up his putt. Accordingly, the player prepares to move his ball-marker one or two clubhead-lengths to the side, but the opponent or fellow-competitor says he wants the ball-marker left where it is. What is the ruling?

A. The player is entitled to move his ball-marker to the side. The opponent or fellow-competitor may not insist on its being left where it is in view of the purposes of Rules 8-2b and 22-1.

Related Decision:
• 22/6 Competitor Requests That Ball in Position to Assist Him Not Be Lifted.

20-1/12
Ball-Marker Moved Accidentally by Player After Having Moved Loose Impediments

Q. A player marked the position of his ball on the putting green with a coin and lifted the ball. He then placed his finger on the coin, while he brushed aside some loose impediments so that he did not move the coin. On lifting his finger the coin initially stuck to his finger before falling to the ground and coming to rest in a different position. What is the ruling?

A. The act of placing the finger on the coin is considered to be an extension of the marking process (see Decision 20-1/6). Therefore, as the movement of the coin was directly attributable to the specific act of marking the position of the ball, the player incurs no penalty and the ball or ball-marker must be replaced (Rule 20-1).

20-1/13
Ball Accidentally Kicked by Player Asked to Lift It Due to Interference

Q. A requests B to lift his (B's) ball because it interferes with A's play. As B is walking up to his ball to lift it, he accidentally kicks it. What is the ruling?

A. B incurs a penalty stroke under Rule 18-2a because the movement of the ball was not directly attributable to the specific act of marking the position of or lifting the ball. B must replace his ball.

Related Decision:
• 12-1/5 Player Kicks Ball While Probing for It in Water in Water Hazard.

20-1/14
Ball Moved by Putter Dropped by Player Approaching Ball to Lift It

Q. A player, approaching his ball on the putting green to lift it, dropped his putter on his ball and moved it. Is it correct that there is no penalty in view of Rule 20-1 under which a player incurs no penalty if he accidentally moves his ball in the process of lifting it?

A. No. The player incurred a penalty stroke under Rule 18-2a because the movement of the ball was not directly attributable to the specific act of marking the position of or lifting the ball.

20-1/15
Meaning of "Directly Attributable" in Rules 20-1 and 20-3a

Q. What is meant by the phrase "directly attributable to the specific act" in Rules 20-1 and 20-3a?

A. In Rule 20-1 the phrase means the specific act of placing a ball-marker behind the ball, placing a club to the side of the ball, or lifting the ball such that the player's hand, the placement of the ball-marker or the club, or the lifting of the ball causes the ball or the ball-marker to move.

In Rule 20-3a the phrase means the specific act of placing or replacing a ball in front of a ball-marker, placing a club to the side of a ball-marker or lifting the ball-marker such that the player's hand, the placement of the ball or club, or the lifting of the ball-marker causes the ball or the ball-marker to move.

Under either Rule, any accidental movement of the ball or the ball-marker which occurs before or after this specific act, such as dropping the ball or ball-marker, regardless of the height from which it was dropped, is not considered to be "directly attributable" and would result in the player incurring a penalty stroke.

20-1/15.5
Lie Altered By Act of Marking Position of Ball

Q. A player marks the position of his ball, and as a result of the act of marking, there is a change in the lie of the ball. Is the player required to restore the lie he had before marking the position of the ball?

A. No. The act of placing a marker may result in some change in the lie of the ball, for example, from grass being depressed by the weight of the marker, or grains of sand being moved in the placement or removal of a marker. Such occurrences may improve or worsen the lie of the ball, and the player must accept the result.

If the player attempted to restore the lie under these circumstances, or if the lie was improved from actions which exceeded what was necessary to the process of marking, he would be subject to penalty under Rule 13-2.

Related Decisions:
- 13-2/15 Area of Intended Swing Improved by Removing Immovable Obstruction.
- 13-2/15.5 Position of Ball Worsened When Obstruction Removed; Player Replaces Obstruction.

20-1/16
Method Used to Mark Position of Ball

Q. The Note to Rule 20-1 provides that "the position of a ball to be lifted should be marked by placing a ball-marker, a small coin or other similar object immediately behind the ball." Is a player penalized if he uses an object that is not similar to a ball-marker or small coin to mark the position of his ball?

A. No. The provision in the Note to Rule 20-1 is a recommendation of best practice, but there is no penalty for failing to act in accordance with the Note.

Examples of methods of marking the position of a ball that are not recommended, but are permissible, are as follows:
- placing the toe of a club at the side of, or behind, the ball;
- using a tee;
- using a loose impediment;
- scratching a line, provided the putting green is not tested (Rule 16-1d) and a line for putting is not indicated (Rule 8-2b). As this practice may cause damage to the putting green, it is discouraged.

However, under Rule 20-1 it is necessary to physically mark the position of the ball. Reference to an existing mark on the ground does not constitute marking the position of a ball. For example, it is not permissible to mark the position with reference to a blemish on the putting green.

When moving a ball or ball-marker to the side to prevent it from interfering with another player's stance or stroke, the player may measure from the side of the ball or ball-marker. In order to accurately replace the ball on the spot from which it was lifted, the steps used to move the ball or ball-marker to the side should be reversed.

20-1/17
Tee Marking Position of Player's Ball Deflects Opponent's Ball

Q. In a match, B used a wooden tee to mark the position of his ball. A's ball was deflected by the tee. What is the ruling?

A. The tee was not B's equipment – see Definition of "Equipment." There is no penalty. A must play his ball as it lies.

A should have requested B to move the tee one or more clubhead-lengths to the side or to mark the position of his ball with a ball-marker, a small coin or other similar object – see Note under Rule 20-1.

20-1/18 (Reserved)

20-1/19
Placing Object Marking Position of Ball Other Than Behind Ball

Q. When marking the position of a ball, must the ball-marker be placed behind the ball, or may it also be placed to the side of or in front of the ball?

A. There is no restriction. However, if a player positions his ball-marker in front of the ball on the putting green and in the process does something to the green that improves the line of putt (e.g., presses down a raised tuft of grass), he is in breach of Rule 13-2.

Placing a ball-marker in front of the ball is not recommended but it is not a breach of Rule 16-1a because this Rule permits touching the line of putt in lifting a ball, and marking the position of the ball is part of the lifting process. (Revised)

20-1/20
Player Places Ball-Marker Approximately Two Inches Behind Ball

Q. A player consistently places his ball-marker approximately two inches behind the ball on the green. He says that he does so to ensure that he does not accidentally move the ball. Does such a procedure comply with the Rules?

A. No. A player who places a ball-marker two inches behind his ball cannot be considered to have marked the position of the ball with sufficient accuracy. Accordingly, each time he does so, the player incurs a penalty of one stroke, as provided in Rule 20-1, and must place the ball as near as possible to the spot from which it was lifted (Rule 20-3c).

The player's action was unnecessary because Rule 20-1 states that no penalty is incurred if a ball is accidentally moved in the process of marking or lifting it under a Rule.

Decision related to 20-1/19 and 20-1/20:

• 16-1a/17 Ball Lifted on Putting Green Placed Ahead of Ball-Marker and Then Moved Back to Original Position.

20-1/21 (Reserved)

20-1/22
Knocking Ball Aside After Marking Position Instead of Lifting

Q. A player, whose ball is on the putting green, marks the position of his ball and knocks the ball aside with his putter instead of lifting it. What is the ruling?

A. Knocking the ball aside was the equivalent of lifting it under Rule 20-1. There would be no penalty unless the act was for the purpose of testing the putting surface (Rule 16-1d) or playing a practice stroke (Rule 7-2).

Other Decisions related to Rule 20-1: See "Ball Lifted" and "Marking Position of Ball" in the Index.

DROPPING AND RE-DROPPING BALL: BY WHOM AND HOW

20-2a/1
Penalty When Ball Dropped in Other Than Prescribed Manner

Q. If a ball is dropped in a manner other than that prescribed in Rule 20-2a and the error is not corrected, it is stated in that Rule that the penalty is one stroke. However, the general penalty for a breach of Rule 20-2 is loss of hole in match play or two strokes in stroke play. Which penalty applies?

A. The one-stroke penalty specifically prescribed in Rule 20-2a applies.

20-2a/2
Spinning Ball When Dropping

Q. A player puts spin on a ball purposely when dropping it. What is the ruling?

A. The player incurs a penalty of one stroke under Rule 20-2a for dropping the ball in an improper manner, unless he corrects his mistake as permitted by Rule 20-6.

20-2a/3
Ball Dropped in Improper Manner and in Wrong Place

Q. A player obtaining relief from ground under repair dropped a ball in a manner not conforming with Rule 20-2a and in a wrong place. What is the ruling?

A. If the player corrected the errors before making his next stroke, there was no penalty – Rule 20-6.

If the player failed to correct the errors before making his next stroke:

(a) In match play, he lost the hole for playing from a wrong place – Rule 20-7b.

(b) In stroke play, he incurred a penalty of two strokes. Although the player breached both Rule 20-2a for dropping in an improper manner and Rule 25-1b by taking relief in the wrong place and then making a stroke from that wrong place, the player incurs only the two stroke penalty for playing from a wrong place (see Note 3 under Rule 20-7c). (Revised)

20-2a/4
Ball Dropped in Improper Manner Moves When Addressed; Player Then Lifts Ball and Drops It in Proper Manner

Q. A player drops his ball other than in the manner prescribed in Rule 20-2a. He addresses the ball and the ball moves. He then is advised that he dropped his ball improperly. So, as permitted by Rule 20-6, he lifts the ball, drops it properly and plays. According to Rule 20-6, the player incurs no penalty for the improper drop. Does he incur a penalty stroke under Rule 18-2b because the ball moved after it was addressed, even though the ball was subsequently lifted and re-dropped?

A. Yes. The ball was in play when it was first dropped, even though it was dropped in an improper manner (Rule 20-4). When it moved after being addressed, the penalty prescribed in Rule 18-2b was applicable.

Related Decision:
• 29/4 Dropping Ball in Foursome Competition.

20-2a/5
Caddie Holds Back Tree Branch to Prevent Branch from Deflecting Dropped Ball

Q. May a player have his caddie hold back a tree branch that is waist high and situated at the spot at which the player wishes to drop his ball under a Rule?

If the branch is not held back, the dropped ball might lodge in the branch or, in any case, the branch will be likely to deflect the dropped ball.

A. No. Such an act would be a breach of Rule 13-2, which prohibits a player from improving the area in which he is to drop or place a ball by, among other things, moving or bending anything that is growing or fixed. The branch is part of the course in the area in which the player is to drop, and the player must accept that his ball may first strike the branch when proceeding under a Rule that requires the player to drop (see Decision 20-2c/1.3). The player would be in breach of Rule 13-2 at the moment that his caddie moves the branch. The penalty is not avoided if the branch is released prior to the player dropping the ball; the fact that the branch may return to its original location is irrelevant. (Revised)

Related Decisions:
- 20-2b/1 Dropped Ball Never Strikes Ground.
- 20-2c/1.3 Dropped Ball Strikes Tree Branch Then Ground: Whether Re-Drop Required.

20-2a/6
Ball Dropped Under One Option of Unplayable Ball Rule Strikes Player; Player Wishes to Change Relief Option

Q. A player deems his ball unplayable and elects to proceed under Rule 28c, by dropping a ball within two club-lengths of the spot where it lay. The dropped ball strikes the player's foot, so he is required by Rule 20-2a to re-drop. May the player change his relief option and, for example, proceed under Rule 28b?

A. No. A player may not change his relief option when re-dropping a ball under Rule 20-2a.

Other Decisions related to whether a player may change a selected relief option after taking further action: See "Ball Dropped or Re-Dropped: changing relief option" in the Index.

20-2a/7
Whether Glove Used as Indicating Mark Is Equipment

Q. A player entitled to drop a ball marks with his glove the spot on which the ball is to be dropped or the outer limit of the area within which the ball is to be dropped. The dropped ball then strikes the glove.

If the glove is a "small object," it is not equipment of the player, and the ball would not be re-dropped. Otherwise, the glove is equipment and the ball must be re-dropped under Rule 20-2a.

What is the status of the glove?

A. A glove is not a "small object" within the meaning of that term in the Definition of "Equipment." Therefore, it is equipment and the ball must be re-dropped.

20-2a/8
Player Drops Ball to Determine Where Original Ball May Roll if Dropped

Q. A player's ball lies on an artificially-surfaced path. The player determines his nearest point of relief and measures the one club-length in which the ball may be dropped under Rule 24-2b. As the player is concerned that the ball, when dropped, may roll into an unplayable lie, he takes a ball from his bag and drops it in the area to test where his original ball may roll to if he elects to take relief from the path. He did not intend to put the second ball into play. What is the ruling?

A. As the player had no intention of putting the dropped ball into play, that ball did not become the ball in play, and his original ball on the path remained the ball in play. However, it is contrary to the purpose and spirit of the Rules for a player to test what may happen when he drops his ball. Therefore, in equity (Rule 1-4), the player incurs a penalty of loss of hole in match play or two strokes in stroke play. In stroke play, the player may play the original ball as it lies on the path or take relief under Rule 24-2.

Other Decisions related to Rule 20-2a: See "Ball Dropped or Re-Dropped: by whom and how to drop" in the Index.

WHERE TO DROP

20-2b/1
Dropped Ball Never Strikes Ground

Q. A player drops a ball where the applicable Rule requires. It lodges in a bush without striking the ground. What is the ruling?

A. The ball is in play. It struck a part of the course where required by the applicable Rule and did not roll into a position requiring it to be re-dropped under Rule 20-2c.

Related Decisions:
• 20-2a/5 Caddie Holds Back Tree Branch to Prevent Branch from Deflecting Dropped Ball.
• 20-2c/1.3 Dropped Ball Strikes Tree Branch Then Ground; Whether Re-Drop Required.

20-2b/2
Measuring Club-Lengths

In measuring a distance of one club-length or two club-lengths when proceeding under a Rule, a player is entitled to measure directly across a ditch or through a fence, a tree or a constructed wall. However, a player may not measure through a natural undulation of the ground. (Revised)

Related Decision:
• 20/1 Club to Be Used in Measuring.
• 20/2 Borrowing Club for Measuring Purposes.
• 25-1b/15 Measuring Across Ground Under Repair in Obtaining Relief.

WHEN TO RE-DROP

20-2c/0.5
Ball Dropped from Ground Under Repair Area Rolls to Position Where Area Interferes with Stance; Whether Re-Drop Required

Q. A player's ball lies in ground under repair through the green. The player elects to take relief and drops the ball in accordance with Rule 25-1b(i). The ball remains outside the ground under repair area but it rolls to a position where the player would have to stand in the area to play his stroke. Must the player re-drop the ball?

A. Yes. The ball has rolled and come to rest "in a position where there is interference by the condition from which relief was taken" – see Rule 20-2c(v). The same applies if a player is taking relief from an immovable obstruction.

Related Decision:
• 3-3/12 Competitor Drops One Ball in Accordance with Two Different Rules Instead of Playing Second Ball; Dropped Ball Rolls Back into the Condition from Which Relief Taken.

20-2c/0.7
Ball Dropped from Immovable Obstruction Rolls Nearer Obstruction than Nearest Point of Relief; Whether Re-Drop Required If Player Changes Clubs and Obstruction No Longer Interferes

Q. A player's ball lies behind a tree and he would play a low shot with a 4-iron, under the tree's branches, except that a protective fence interferes with the area of his intended swing. He determines the nearest point of relief using his 4-iron and measures a one club-length area within which to drop the ball. After he drops the ball in accordance with the Rules, the ball rolls and comes to rest nearer the fence than the nearest point of relief. Therefore, there is still interference by the fence for the intended stroke with the 4-iron. However, the ball is now in a position where it would be reasonable for the player to play his next shot over the tree with a pitching-wedge, and the fence would not interfere with this stroke. May the player play the dropped ball or must it be re-dropped?

A. The ball must be re-dropped because it came to rest at a point where the player still had interference from the fence for a stroke with the club used to determine the nearest point of relief – see Rule 20-2c(v).

20-2c/0.8
Player Takes Relief from an Area of Ground Under Repair; Whether Re-Drop Required if Condition Interferes for Stroke with Club Not Used to Determine "Nearest Point of Relief"

Q. A player finds his ball in heavy rough approximately 230 yards from the green. He selects a wedge to play his next shot and finds that his stance touches a line defining an area of ground under repair. He determines the nearest point of relief and drops the ball within one club-length of this point. The ball rolls into a good lie from where he believes he can play a 3-wood for his next stroke. If the player used a wedge for his next stroke he would not have interference from the ground under repair, but adopting a normal stance with the 3-wood, he again touches the ground under repair with his foot. Must the player re-drop his ball under Rule 20-2c?

A. No. The player proceeded in accordance with Rule 25-1b by determining his nearest point of relief using the club with which he expected to play his next stroke and he would only be required to re-drop the ball under Rule 20-2c if interference still existed for a stroke with this club – see analogous Decision 20-2c/0.7.

As it was expedient for the player to play his next stroke with another club, which resulted in interference from the condition, he would have the option of playing the ball as it lies or proceeding again under Rule 25-1b.

Decision related to 20-2c/0.7 and 20-2c/0.8:
• 24-2b/4 Club Used to Determine Nearest Point of Relief Not Used for Next Stroke.

20-2c/1
Dropped Ball Rolling Out of Prescribed Dropping Area

Q. A player taking relief under the Rules sometimes appears to obtain more relief than he is entitled to because the relevant Rule allows him some latitude within which to drop and the dropped ball then rolls some distance from the place where it was dropped. When a Rule prescribes an area within which a ball must be dropped, e.g., within one or two club-lengths of a particular point, should it be re-dropped if it rolls outside the area so prescribed?

A. No, not necessarily. Provided the ball has been correctly dropped (Rule 20-2a) and does not roll into any of the positions listed in Rule 20-2c, it is in play and must not be re-dropped. In particular, under Rule 20-2c(vi), the ball may roll up to two club-lengths from the point where it first struck a part of the course when dropped, and this may result in its coming to rest an appreciable distance farther from the condition from which relief is being taken. For example:

   (a) a ball dropped within two club-lengths of the margin of a lateral water hazard may come to rest almost four club-lengths from the hazard margin without the player being required to re-drop it under Rule 20-2c; and

   (b) a ball dropped away from an immovable obstruction within one club-length of the nearest point of relief may come to rest almost three club-lengths from the nearest point of relief without the player being required to re-drop it under Rule 20-2c.

20-2c/1.3
Dropped Ball Strikes Tree Branch Then Ground; Whether Re-Drop Required

Q. A player drops a ball within the area prescribed by the applicable Rule. It bounces off a tree branch and as a result strikes the ground outside that area. What is the ruling?

A. The ball struck a part of the course (the branch) where the applicable Rule requires (Rule 20-2b). Therefore, provided it does not roll into any of the positions listed in Rule 20-2c, it is in play and must not be re-dropped. In measuring the two club-lengths to determine if a re-drop is required under Rule 20-2c(vi), the point on the ground immediately below the spot where the ball first struck a part of the course (the branch) shall be used for measuring purposes.

Related Decisions:
- 20-2a/5 Caddie Holds Back Tree Branch to Prevent Branch from Deflecting Dropped Ball.
- 20-2b/1 Dropped Ball Never Strikes Ground.

20-2c/1.5
Ball Rolls Towards Hole When Dropped at Spot from Which Previous Stroke Played

Q. A player is required or elects to play his next stroke at the spot from which his previous stroke was played. He is able to identify that specific spot by reference to the divot hole which his previous stroke made. He drops a ball immediately behind that divot hole. The ball rolls nearer the hole than the spot from which the previous stroke was played, but not more than two club-lengths from where it first struck the ground. What is the ruling?

A. Rule 20-2c(vii)(a) requires a ball to be re-dropped if it rolls and comes to rest nearer the hole than "its original position or estimated position … unless otherwise permitted by the Rules." The original position is the spot from which the previous stroke was played. Since the dropped ball rolled nearer the hole than that spot, it must be re-dropped.

However, in many such cases the player cannot determine exactly the spot from which his previous stroke was played. In those cases, the player has satisfied the requirements of the Rule if he uses his best endeavours to estimate the spot. The estimated spot is treated as the specific spot (see Rule 20-2b) and the ball must be re-dropped if it rolls nearer the hole than the estimated spot.

The same principle applies if the spot where a ball is to be placed is not determinable and the player is required, under Rule 20-3c, to drop the ball as near as possible to the spot where it lay.

20-2c/1.7
Whether Re-Drop Required if Ball Dropped Under Rule 24-2b Rolls Nearer Hole Than Nearest Point of Relief but Not Nearer Than Where it Originally Lay

Q. A player's ball comes to rest on a cart path such that his nearest point of relief is behind the obstruction. He properly determines this point and lifts and drops the ball in accordance with Rule 24-2b. The ball rolls and comes to rest nearer the hole than the nearest point of relief, but not nearer the hole than where it lay originally on the path. Must the ball be re-dropped?

A. Yes – see Rule 20-2c(vii)(b).

20-2c/2
Ball Dropped Third Time When Placement Required After Second Drop

Q. A player dropped his ball twice under a Rule and each time the ball rolled nearer the hole. He then dropped the ball a third time instead of placing it as required by Rule 20-2c. What is the ruling?

A. Before making a stroke, the player may lift the ball and place it as prescribed in Rule 20-2c, without penalty (Rule 20-6). If he fails to do so and plays the ball, the player has played from a wrong place and has dropped the ball when it should have been placed. The player incurs a penalty of loss of hole in match play or two strokes in stroke play for playing from the wrong place (Rule 20-2c and Rule 20-7), but there is no additional penalty in stroke play for dropping the ball when Rule 20-2c required it to be placed (see Note 3 to Rule 20-7c). (Revised)

Related Decisions:
- 18-2a/9 Ball Lifted Without Authority Dropped Instead of Being Replaced.
- 18-2a/21.5 Ball Moved Accidentally; Spot Where Ball Originally Lay Not Determinable; Player Places Ball Instead of Dropping It.
- 20-6/1 Ball Placed When Required to Be Dropped or Dropped When Required to Be Placed; Correction of Error.

20-2c/3
Placing Ball Instead of Dropping When Obvious Dropped Ball Will Roll into Hazard, Etc.

Q. A player is required to drop a ball. However, it is obvious that the ball when dropped will roll into a hazard, more than two club-lengths, etc., in which case it must be re-dropped and then placed under Rule 20-2c. In such a case, is it permissible to waive the dropping requirement and allow the player initially to place the ball?

A. No. Dropping and then re-dropping are necessary to resolve any doubt as to whether the ball will roll into a hazard, etc., and to establish the spot at which the ball must be placed, if necessary.

20-2c/3.5
Dropped Ball Comes to Rest and Then Rolls Out of Bounds

Q. A player's ball comes to rest against a boundary stake. He deems the ball unplayable and drops it within two club-lengths of where the ball originally lay, as prescribed by Rule 28c. After the ball has been at rest, it rolls and comes to rest out of bounds. What is the ruling?

A. If a dropped ball comes to rest, but subsequently moves, the ball must be played as it lies (see Note 1 to Rule 20-2). In this case the ball is out of bounds and the player must proceed under Rule 27-1. Since the ball was at rest before moving, Rule 20-2c is not applicable.

Related Decisions:
- 18-1/12 Ball Replaced and at Rest Is Thereafter Moved by Wind.
- 20-3d/1 Placed Ball Rolls into Hole.
- 20-4/1 Ball Replaced on Putting Green But Ball-Marker Not Removed; Ball Then Moves.

20-2c/4
Caddie Stops Dropped Ball Before It Comes to Rest; When Penalty Incurred

Q. A player's caddie deliberately stops a ball dropped by the player. What is the ruling?

A. There is no penalty if the caddie stops the ball after it has rolled to a position from which the player would be required to re-drop it under Rule 20-2c, provided it is reasonable to assume that the ball would not return to a position at which Rule 20-2c would be inapplicable.

However, if a player's caddie acts prematurely and stops a dropped ball before it has reached such a position, the player incurs a penalty of loss of hole in match play or two strokes in stroke play under Rule 1-2 (see reference to Rule 1-2 under Rule 20-2a). In stroke play, he must play the ball as it lies where it was stopped. If the ball was lifted at the time it was stopped, the ball must be replaced where it was stopped with no additional penalty. In these circumstances, the acts of stopping the ball and lifting the ball are close to one another in terms of time and there are no intervening acts. Accordingly the two acts are related acts and a single penalty (two strokes under Rule 1-2) is appropriate (see Principle 4 in Decision 1-4/12).

The same ruling would apply if the player's ball was deliberately stopped by the player, his partner, his partner's caddie or someone else authorized by the player (e.g., an opponent or fellow-competitor). (Revised)

Related Decision:
- 1-2/5.5 Player Purposely Stops or Deflects Ball; Where Next Stroke Must Be Played From.

20-2c/5
Changing Relief Option When Re-Dropping Required

Q. A player declares his ball unplayable. Of the three options available under Rule 28, he elects Rule 28c and drops the ball within two club-lengths of the spot where it lay. The ball rolls and comes to rest nearer the hole than its original position, so the player is required by Rule 20-2c to re-drop. May the player now proceed under a different option, e.g., Rule 28b?

A. No. If the player did so, he would be in breach of Rule 20-2c. The same principles would apply when proceeding under Rule 26-1.

Other Decisions related to whether a player may change a selected relief option after taking further action: See "Ball Dropped or Re-Dropped: changing relief option" in the Index.

20-2c/6
Player's Club Strikes Immovable Obstruction During Stroke After Relief Taken

Q. A player correctly determines the nearest point of relief from an artificially-surfaced path (immovable obstruction) and drops the ball within the area prescribed by Rule 24-2b. However, when the player makes the stroke, his club strikes the path. Is he subject to penalty under Rule 20-2c for not re-dropping the ball when there was still interference by the obstruction?

A. Yes. However, there would be no penalty if the reason that the club struck the obstruction was that the limits of the obstruction were not entirely known when relief was taken (e.g., part of the path was covered with turf) or the club traveled a significantly different path than originally intended due to an unexpected occurrence (e.g., because the player's feet slipped or he was stung by a bee).

20-2c/7
Player Takes Relief from Area of Casual Water and Ball Comes to Rest in a Position Where Another Area of Casual Water Interferes; Whether Re-Drop Required

Q. Through the green, there are two areas of casual water which are close together. There is interference from one area and the player elects to take relief. He drops the ball in accordance with Rule 25-1b(i) and it rolls to a position where interference no longer exists from the first area of casual water, but there is interference from the second area. Does Rule 20-2c(v) require the player to re-drop the ball?

A. No, the ball is in play. The player may play the ball as it lies or take relief from the second area in accordance with Rule 25-1b(i).

The same procedure applies to ground under repair or a hole, cast or runway made by a burrowing animal, a reptile or a bird.

Related Decision:
- 1-4/8 Nearest Point of Relief from Cart Path Is in Casual Water; Nearest Point of Relief from Casual Water Is Back on Cart Path.
- 24-2b/9 After Relief from Obstruction Second Obstruction Interferes.

Other Decisions related to Rule 20-2c: See "Ball Dropped or Re-Dropped: whether re-drop required" in the Index.

PLACING AND REPLACING BALL: BY WHOM AND WHERE

20-3a/0.5
Whether Player Himself Must Place or Replace Ball

Q. Rule 20-3a provides that, in some instances, a person other than the player may place or replace the player's ball. On the other hand, other Rules, e.g., Rule 12-2, state that the player must place or replace the ball. Does Rule 20-3a override other Rules that imply that the player himself must place or replace the ball?

A. Yes. (Revised)

Related Decision:
• 20-1/0.5 Whether Player Himself Must Lift Ball.

20-3a/1
Ball Moved in Removing Ball-Marker After Replacing Ball

Q. A player replaces his ball under a Rule and, in the act of removing the object marking its position, accidentally moves the ball. What is the ruling?

A. Removal of the ball-marker is part of the replacement process. Accordingly, under Rule 20-3a, no penalty is incurred, and the ball must be replaced.

Related Decision:
• 20-1/15 Meaning of "Directly Attributable" in Rules 20-1 and 20-3a.

20-3a/2
Using Line on Ball for Alignment

Q. May a player draw a line on his ball and, when replacing his ball, position the ball so that the line or the trademark on the ball is aimed to indicate the line of play?

A. Yes.

Related Decision:
• 18-2a/33 Rotating Ball on Putting Green Without Marking Position.

20-3a/3
Whether Ball Must Be Replaced If Other Rule Applies

Q. If a Rule requires a ball at rest that was moved to be replaced (e.g., Rule 18-2a), must the player replace the ball if he wishes to proceed under another Rule that involves dropping or placing the ball in another place (e.g., Rule 24-2)?

A. No. If a player is proceeding under a Rule that requires him to replace the ball but another Rule applies, he may proceed directly under the other Rule.

The ruling would be the same even if the original spot were not known, in which case the estimated position of the ball would be the reference point for proceeding under the other Rule.

Other Decisions related to Rule 20-3a: See "Ball Placed or Replaced" in the Index.

LIE OF BALL TO BE PLACED OR REPLACED ALTERED

20-3b/1
Lie of Lifted Ball in Bunker Altered by Another Player's Stroke

Q. The balls of A and B are in the same heel mark in a bunker. B's ball is farther from the hole. A lifts his ball under Rule 22-2, and B plays and obliterates the heel mark. What should A do?

A. Under Rule 20-3b, A is required to recreate his original lie as nearly as possible, including the heel mark, and place his ball in that lie.

20-3b/2
Lie in Bunker Changed by Another Player Taking His Stance

Q. In playing from a bunker, B, in taking his stance, pushed up a mound of sand behind A's ball, which had not been lifted. What is the ruling?

A. Since A's ball did not move when B took his stance, Rule 20-3b does not apply. In equity (Rule 1-4), A's original lie may be restored as nearly as possible by removing the mound of sand.

20-3b/3
Lie Changed by Removal of Gallery-Control Stake

Q. A ball comes to rest adjacent to a gallery-control stake. A marshal, without the sanction of the player, removes the stake and in so doing raises the turf in front of the ball without causing the ball to move. Is the player entitled to proceed under Rule 20-3b?

A. No. As the ball has not moved, Rule 20-3b does not apply.

However, as the marshal acted without the sanction of the player, if the original lie could be easily restored, in equity (Rule 1-4), the raised turf may be pressed down so that the original lie is restored as nearly as possible.

If the original lie could not be easily restored, in equity (Rule 1-4), the player may place his ball, without penalty, in the nearest lie most similar to that which it originally occupied, but not more than one club-length from the original lie, not nearer the hole and not in a hazard.

Had the player sanctioned the action of the marshal or had he removed the stake himself, he would have to accept any resultant worsening of the lie.

Decisions related to 20-3b/1 through 20-3b/3: See "Equity: player entitled to lie, line of play and stance when ball comes to rest after stroke" in the Index.

20-3b/4
Lie of Ball Through the Green Altered; Original Lie of Ball Known But Spot Where Ball Lay Not Determinable

Q. In stroke play, B plays A's ball, which was lying through the green, and in the process removes a divot. The original lie of A's ball was known and has been altered. It is impossible to determine the exact spot where A's ball originally lay. Should A proceed under Rule 20-3b or Rule 20-3c?

A. As A knew the original lie of the ball, Rule 20-3b applies (see Note to Rule 20-3b). The spot where the ball lay will need to be estimated, and a ball must be placed in the nearest lie most similar to the original lie that is not more than one club-length from the estimated spot, not nearer the hole and not in a hazard. (Revised)

20-3b/5
Lie of Ball in Rough Altered by Outside Agency; Original Lie of Ball Not Known and Spot Where Ball Lay Not Determinable

Q. An outside agency accidentally steps on A's ball in tall grass through the green and presses the ball into the ground. The original lie of A's ball was not known, but the lie has clearly been altered. It is impossible to determine the spot where A's ball originally lay. Should A proceed under Rule 20-3b or Rule 20-3c?

A. As A did not know the original lie of the ball, Rule 20-3c applies and the player must drop the ball as near as possible to where it lay but not in a hazard and not on a putting green (see Note to Rule 20-3b). (Revised)

20-3b/6
Lie of Ball in Bunker Altered; Original Lie of Ball Known But Spot Where Ball Lay Not Determinable

Q. At B's request, A has marked the position of and lifted his ball in a bunker under Rule 22-2 as it interfered with B's stroke. B makes his stroke and, in the process, accidentally moves A's ball-marker. The original lie of A's ball was known and has been altered. It is impossible to determine the exact spot where A's ball originally lay. Should A proceed under Rule 20-3b or Rule 20-3c?

A. As A knew the original lie of the ball, Rule 20-3b applies (see Note to Rule 20-3b). The original lie of the ball must be recreated as nearly as possible in its original spot (which will need to be estimated), and the ball must be placed in that lie. (Revised)

Related Decisions:
- 6-8d/1 Resuming Play from Where It Was Discontinued; Lie Altered by Natural Causes.
- 6-8d/2 Lie in Bunker Altered Prior to Resumption of Play.

20-3b/7
Whether Original Lie May Be "Nearest Lie Most Similar"

Q. A player finds a ball he believes to be his lying in a water hazard. When he lifts the ball for identification under Rule 12-2, the original lie is altered. When proceeding under Rule 20-3b, if the altered lie is the nearest lie most similar to the original lie within one club-length of the original lie not nearer the hole and inside the water hazard, is the player required to replace the ball in the original lie in its altered condition?

A. Yes. Although in most situations the nearest most similar lie within one club-length will be located elsewhere, there may be circumstances when the nearest lie most similar to the original lie will be the original lie in its altered condition.

20-3b/8
Loose Impediment Affecting Lie of Ball Moved

Q. A's ball lies in a bunker, with a loose impediment immediately behind the ball. The ball of B, his opponent or fellow-competitor, lies near A's ball in the same bunker, but farther from the hole. B asks A to lift his ball under Rule 22-2, which A does. B's stroke moves the loose impediment that was behind A's ball. Is A's lie considered to have been altered as a result of the removal of the loose impediment, in which case Rule 20-3b would apply?

A. No. Although the loose impediment may have affected the lie of A's ball, loose impediments are not part of the lie of the ball as contemplated by Rule 20-3b. Therefore, A is not required to replace the loose impediment before his next stroke. If he did replace the loose impediment, there would be no penalty.

The same answer would apply on any part of the course. (Revised)

Other Decisions related to Rule 20-3b: See "Ball Placed or Replaced: lie of ball to be replaced altered" in the Index.

REPLACING BALL: SPOT NOT DETERMINABLE

Decisions related to Rule 20-3c: See "Ball Placed or Replaced: spot not determinable" in the Index.

20-3d/1
Placed Ball Rolls into Hole

Q. A replaces his ball on the putting green three feet from the hole. As he is about to address the ball, it rolls into the hole. Should the ball be replaced or is A deemed to have holed out with his previous stroke?

A. The answer depends on whether the ball, when replaced, came to rest on the spot on which it was placed before it started rolling. If it did, A is deemed to have holed out with his previous stroke. If not, A is required to replace the ball (Rule 20-3d). However, if the ball had been overhanging the hole when it was lifted, the provisions of Rule 16-2 would override those of Rule 20-3d.

Related Decisions:
- 18-1/12 Ball Replaced and at Rest Is Thereafter Moved by Wind.
- 18-2a/7 Ball Moved by Wind Replaced.
- 20-4/1 Ball Replaced on Putting Green But Ball-Marker Not Removed; Ball Then Moves.

20-3d/2
Ball in Bunker Moves Closer to Hole When Obstruction Removed and Ball Will Not Remain at Rest When Replaced; All Other Parts of Bunker Are Nearer Hole

Q. A ball came to rest against a movable obstruction, a rake, in a bunker. When the rake was moved the ball rolled nearer the hole. According to Rule 24-1, the ball had to be replaced. Due to the slope and the fact that the sand was firm, the ball, when replaced, rolled closer to the hole.

Under Rule 20-3d, if a ball will not come to rest on the spot where it originally lay, it must be placed at the nearest spot not nearer the hole where it can be placed at rest. The spot where the ball originally lay was farther from the hole than any other part of the bunker. Thus, there was nowhere to place the ball at rest in the bunker that was not nearer the hole. What is the proper procedure if:

1. The only way the ball would remain at rest at the spot where it lay would be to press it lightly into the sand?
2. The sand is so hard that it is impossible to replace the ball?

A. There is nothing in the Rules permitting a player to press his ball lightly into the sand or ground to make it remain at rest. Accordingly, in either case, since the player could not place the ball in conformity with the Rules, he should proceed under the stroke-and-distance option of the unplayable ball Rule (Rule 28a) or, in equity (Rule 1-4), drop the ball, under penalty of one stroke, outside the bunker, keeping the point where the ball lay directly between the hole and the spot on which the ball is dropped.

The same principle would apply if a player is proceeding under any Rule and the ball will not come to rest in the bunker at a spot not nearer to the hole than the appropriate reference point.

Related Decisions:
• 1-2/9 Player Presses Ball into Surface of Putting Green.
• Misc./2 Whether Rakes Should Be Placed In or Outside Bunkers.

20-3d/3
Ball in Rough Moves Downward When Addressed; Ball Will Not Remain at Rest When Replaced

Q. A player's ball is sitting up in the rough about three inches above the ground. He addresses the ball. It moves downward about two inches and comes to rest at Point X. The player attempts to replace the ball as required by Rule 18-2b, but the ball falls downward to Point X. Under Rule 20-3d, he again attempts to replace the ball, with the same result. The player must now place the ball at the nearest spot not nearer the hole where it can be placed at rest – Rule 20-3d.

If the nearest spot where the ball will remain at rest is Point X, must the player place the ball there, even though that point is vertically below the original lie?

A. Yes.

Related Decision:
• 18/1 Ball Moves Vertically Downward.

BALL IN PLAY WHEN DROPPED OR PLACED

20-4/1
Ball Replaced on Putting Green But Ball-Marker Not Removed; Ball Then Moves

Q. A player replaces his ball on the putting green but does not remove his ball-marker. Subsequently the wind moves his ball to a new position. What is the ruling?

A. Under Rule 20-4, a ball is in play when it is replaced, whether or not the object used to mark its position has been removed. Consequently the ball must be played from the new position – see Decision 18-1/12.

Related Decisions:
• 18-1/12 Ball Replaced and at Rest Is Thereafter Moved by Wind.
• 18-2a/7 Ball Moved by Wind Replaced.
• 20-2c/3.5 Dropped Ball Comes to Rest and Then Rolls Out of Bounds.
• 20-3d/1 Placed Ball Rolls into Hole.

20-4/2
Ball Lifted from Putting Green and Placed by Caddie Behind Marker

Q. A player marks the position of his ball on the putting green by placing a coin immediately behind the ball. He lifts the ball and gives it to his caddie to have it cleaned. The caddie then places the ball immediately behind the coin, i.e., not in the ball's original position. Is the ball in play when the caddie places the ball?

A. The answer depends on whether the caddie intended to put the ball into play when he placed it.

If the caddie did not place the ball with the intention of putting it into play (e.g., he positioned the ball to serve as a reference point for reading the line of putt from the other side of the hole), the ball was not in play when so placed. The ball is not considered to be in play until it is repositioned with the intention of replacing the ball as required by Rule 16-1b. If the player made a stroke with his ball while it was out of play, he would be playing a wrong ball (Rule 15-3).

If the caddie placed the ball with the intention of putting it into play, the ball is in play. If the player played the ball that was so placed, he would lose the hole in match play and in stroke play would incur a penalty of two strokes for playing from a wrong place (Rules 16-1b and 20-7). In stroke play, there would be no additional penalty for the ball having been replaced by a person not permitted to do so by Rule 20-3a (see Note 3 to Rule 20-7c).

If the caddie had placed the ball on the original spot, the presumption is that he intended to put it into play unless there is strong evidence to the contrary. (Revised)

Related Decisions:
- 15/4 Player Lifts Ball, Sets It Aside and Plays It from Where Set Aside.
- 15-3b/3 Fellow-Competitor Lifts Competitor's Ball and Sets It Aside; Competitor Plays Ball from Where Set Aside.

MAKING NEXT STROKE FROM WHERE PREVIOUS STROKE MADE

20-5/1
Teed Ball Missed Then Hit Out of Bounds

Q. A player plays a stroke from a teeing ground and misses the ball. He plays a second stroke and hits the ball out of bounds. In proceeding under Rule 27-1, may he tee a ball anywhere within the teeing ground or must he drop a ball where the original ball was teed?

A. The player may tee a ball anywhere within the teeing ground.

20-5/2
Player Proceeding Under Rule 20-5 Drops Ball on Different Part of Course

Q. A player whose ball lies in, and close to the edge of, a bunker hits the ball out of bounds. When proceeding under Rule 27-1, the player drops a ball within a few inches of, and not nearer the hole than, the spot where the original ball was last played, but the ball first strikes a part of the course through the green. What is the ruling?

A. Under Rule 20-6 the player must correct his error by dropping a ball so that, when dropped, it first strikes the bunker (Rule 20-5). If he fails to do so and plays the dropped ball, he has played from a wrong place (Rules 20-7 and 27-1).

Other Decisions related to Rule 20-5: See "Stroke and Distance" and "Stroke Canceled or Recalled" in the Index.

LIFTING BALL WRONGLY DROPPED OR PLACED

20-6/1
Ball Placed When Required to Be Dropped or Dropped When Required to Be Placed; Correction of Error

Q. A player placed a ball when he should have dropped it or dropped it when he should have placed it. Before playing a stroke, may the player lift the ball, without penalty, under Rule 20-6 and proceed correctly?

A. Yes. Otherwise the player would lose the hole in match play or incur a penalty of two strokes in stroke play for a breach of the applicable Rule.

Related Decisions:
- 18-2a/9 Ball Lifted Without Authority Dropped Instead of Being Replaced.
- 18-2a/21.5 Ball Moved Accidentally; Spot Where Ball Originally Lay Not Determinable; Player Places Ball Instead of Dropping It.
- 20-2c/2 Ball Dropped Third Time When Placement Required After Second Drop.

20-6/2
Changing Relief Option After Ball Dropped in a Wrong Place

Q. A player deems his ball unplayable and elects to take relief under Rule 28c. He drops the ball in a wrong place and is advised of this fact. He then lifts his ball under Rule 20-6 and states that he wishes to proceed under Rule 28b. Is the player entitled to proceed under Rule 28b?

A. Yes. Decisions 20-2a/6 and 20-2c/5 suggest a different conclusion. However, in those cases Rules 20-2a and 20-2c are invoked and those Rules imply that a ball to be re-dropped must be re-dropped under the option originally invoked.

Other Decisions related to whether a player may change a selected relief option after taking further action: See "Ball Dropped or Re-Dropped: changing relief option" in the Index.

20-6/3
Ball Mistakenly Substituted When Dropped; Correction of Error

Q. A player's ball lies on a paved cart path. In taking relief from the obstruction, he mistakenly drops a ball other than the original ball. He discovers his error before making his next stroke. How should he proceed?

A. The player is not entitled to substitute a ball when proceeding under Rule 24-2b, unless the ball is not immediately recoverable. Under Rule 20-6, the player must correct his error by dropping the original ball in accordance with the Rules. If he fails to do so and plays the substituted ball, he incurs the general penalty for a breach of Rule 24-2b – see Rule 15-2.

Related Decisions:
• 15-2/2 Player Mistakenly Substitutes Another Ball on Putting Green; Error Discovered Before Stroke Played.
• 20-1/5 Competitor's Ball Lifted Without Authority by Fellow-Competitor's Caddie Who Subsequently Substitutes Another Ball Which Competitor Plays.

20-6/4
Substituting Ball When Re-Dropping

Q. In taking relief from a water hazard, a player drops a ball in a wrong place but realizes his error before playing it. When he corrects the error under Rule 20-6, may he drop a different ball than the one originally dropped?

A. Yes. When correcting the error under Rule 20-6, the player is proceeding under the original Rule, in this case Rule 26-1. As the player is proceeding under a Rule that allows substitution (Rule 26-1), he may substitute balls. If he had been proceeding under a Rule that did not allow substitution (e.g., Rule 24-2b), he would have been required to drop the original ball, unless that ball is not immediately recoverable.

A player re-dropping a ball under Rule 20-2c may not substitute balls unless the ball that was originally dropped is not immediately recoverable.

20-6/5
Player Drops Ball Under Rules and Then Wishes to Replace Ball in Original Position

Q. A player's ball lies under a tree. The player deems the ball unplayable and drops a ball three club-lengths from where the ball originally lay. Before playing, he is informed that he dropped the ball in a wrong place. The player lifts the dropped ball under Rule 20-6 and realizes that, if he drops the ball within two club-lengths of the spot where the ball originally lay, it is likely to be unplayable. May the player replace the ball in its original position, incurring a penalty stroke under Rule 18-2a?

A. No. Once the player has put a ball into play under an applicable Rule, he must continue to proceed under that Rule until he has correctly put a ball into play. In this case, the player may change options under Rule 28 when correcting the error of dropping a ball in a wrong place (see Decision 20-6/2), but he may not proceed under another Rule or replace the ball in its original position.

After lifting a ball, a player is entitled to replace it in its original position only if he has not yet put it back into play under an applicable Rule. However, in that case, the player may incur a penalty of one stroke under Rule 18-2a for having lifted his ball without authority (see Decision 18-2a/12).

Related Decisions:
- 20-7/2 Ball Deemed Unplayable in Water Hazard Is Dropped in Hazard and Played.
- 25-1b/26 Player Unaware Ball in Water Hazard Takes Relief from Interference by Burrowing Animal Hole.

Other Decisions related to whether a player may change a selected relief option after taking further action: See "Ball Dropped or Re-Dropped: changing relief option" in the Index.

PLAYING FROM WRONG PLACE: GENERAL

20-7/1
Ball Played from Spot Where Original Ball Deflected Out of Bounds by Maintenance Vehicle

Q. A player's tee shot travels about 175 yards and, while still in motion, is deflected out of bounds by a golf course maintenance vehicle. The player, claiming the vehicle should not have been there, dropped a ball near the spot where the vehicle deflected the original ball, completed play of the hole and stated that he had incurred no penalty. Was the player correct?

A. No. A maintenance vehicle is an outside agency. The original ball would have been played as it lay, without penalty, if it had been in bounds – Rule 19-1. Since the ball was out of bounds, the player was obliged to proceed under Rule 27-1.

The player, in dropping a ball near where the original ball was deflected and playing it, played from a wrong place.

In match play, he incurred a penalty of loss of hole – Rule 20-7b.

In stroke play, he incurred the stroke-and-distance penalty prescribed by Rule 27-1 and an additional penalty of two strokes for a breach of that Rule. Since the breach was a serious one, he was subject to disqualification unless he corrected the error as prescribed in the second paragraph of Rule 20-7c.

20-7/2
Ball Deemed Unplayable in Water Hazard Is Dropped in Hazard and Played

Q. On the 7th hole a player deems his ball unplayable in a water hazard and, thinking that Rule 28b or c is applicable, drops the ball in the water hazard and plays it. What is the ruling?

A. Rule 28 does not apply when the player's ball lies in a water hazard. As Rule 26-1 was the Rule applicable to the player's situation, he is considered to have played from a wrong place under that Rule.

In match play, the player loses the hole (Rule 20-7b).

In stroke play, if a serious breach of the water hazard Rule was not involved, the player, in addition to incurring the penalty stroke provided for in Rule 26-1, incurs a two-stroke penalty for playing from a wrong place and must play out the hole with the ball played from within the water hazard – see first paragraph of Rule 20-7c and Rule 26-1.

In stroke play, if a serious breach of the water hazard Rule was involved, before playing from the next teeing ground, the player must either (1) place a ball on the spot where the original ball originally lay in the water hazard, with a one-stroke penalty under Rule 18-2a, or (2) play a ball in accordance with Rule 26-1; in either case the player would add two penalty strokes to the score with that ball (Rule 20-7c). If the player fails to correct the mistake, he is disqualified – see second and third paragraphs of Rule 20-7c.

Related Decisions:
- 18-2a/12 Player Entitled to Relief from Condition Lifts Ball; Player Then Replaces Ball and Plays It from Original Position.
- 20-6/5 Player Drops Ball Under Rules and Then Wishes to Replace Ball in Original Position.
- 25-1b/26 Player Unaware Ball in Water Hazard Takes Relief from Interference by Burrowing Animal Hole.
- 34-3/6 Player Proceeds Under an Inapplicable Rule; Committee's Decision.

20-7/2.5
Ball Deemed Unplayable in Water Hazard; Another Ball Is Dropped in Hazard But Player Realizes Error Before Playing

Q. A player deems his ball unplayable in a water hazard, does not lift the ball and drops another ball in the water hazard, thinking that Rule 28b or c is applicable. He realizes his error before playing the dropped ball. What is the ruling?

A. When the player dropped a ball under Rule 28, he proceeded under an inapplicable Rule. Under Rule 20-6 he must abandon the dropped ball and, without penalty, play the original ball or, under penalty of one stroke, proceed under the water hazard Rule (Rule 26-1) with respect to the original ball.

20-7/3
Whether Player May Drop Ball into Area from Which Play Prohibited

Q. In proceeding under a Rule, a player wishes to drop a ball on a part of the course from which play is prohibited (e.g., a wrong putting green or an area of ground under repair from which play is prohibited). Is this permissible?

A. Yes. There is nothing in the Rules to prohibit a player from dropping a ball on a part of the course from which play is prohibited. However, the player must then take relief as prescribed by the applicable Rule. He would be penalized if he played the ball from such an area.

Related Decision:
• 25-1b/14.5 Ball Deemed Unplayable Dropped in Ground Under Repair from Which Play Prohibited; Ball Then Dropped Under Ground Under Repair Rule.

PLAYING FROM WRONG PLACE IN STROKE

20-7c/1
Ball Replaced at Wrong Place on Putting Green and Holed

Q. In stroke play, a competitor in replacing his ball on the putting green inadvertently put the ball in a wrong place nearby and holed out. The error was then discovered and the competitor put his ball in the right place and holed out. What is the ruling?

A. The score with the ball played from the wrong place counts and the competitor must add two penalty strokes to that score (Rule 16-1b or 20-3a and 20-7c).

The competitor incurs no penalty for having putted from the right place after holing out from a wrong place.

20-7c/2
Ball Putted from Wrong Place Lifted and Putted from Right Place

Q. In stroke play, A mistakenly replaced his ball in front of B's ball-marker (which was near A's ball-marker) and putted. The ball came to rest about one foot from the hole. The error was then discovered and A lifted his ball without marking its position, placed it in front of his own ball-marker and finished the hole. What is the ruling?

A. When A replaced his ball in front of B's ball-marker and putted, he played from a wrong place and incurred a penalty of two strokes; the ball was in play (Rule 20-7c).

When A then lifted his ball from where it lay about one foot from the hole without marking its position and did not replace it, he incurred the general penalty (two strokes) for a breach of Rule 20-1 – see second paragraph of Rule 20-1.

Thus, A incurred a total penalty of four strokes.

20-7c/3
Ball Believed to Be Lost in Bunker; Competitor Drops Another Ball in Bunker and Plays It; Original Ball Then Found Outside Bunker

Q. In stroke play, A played a long shot to the green and the ball appeared to have come to rest in a bunker beside the green. The ball was not found in the bunker. A dropped a ball in the bunker and played it onto the green. A then discovered his original ball behind the green. What is the ruling?

A. When A dropped another ball in the bunker, it became the ball in play under penalty of stroke and distance and the original ball was lost – see Definition of "Lost Ball."

Since the place where the ball was dropped and played from was well in advance of the spot from which the original ball was last played, A was guilty of a serious breach of the relevant Rule (Rule 27-1) in failing to go back to that spot. He should have been disqualified unless he rectified the breach as prescribed in Rule 20-7c, in which case he would have incurred an additional penalty of two strokes. (Revised)

Related Decisions:
- 15/13 Stray Ball Dropped Under Unplayable Ball Rule But Not Played.
- 15/14 Ball in Bunker Deemed Unplayable, Dropped in Bunker and Played; Ball Then Discovered to Be Stray Ball.
- 28/14 Stray Ball Deemed Unplayable Played Under Stroke-and-Distance Procedure; Original Ball Then Found.
- 28/15 Stray Ball Deemed Unplayable, Dropped Within Two Club-Lengths and Played Before Error Discovered.

20-7c/4
Competitor's Ball Played by Fellow-Competitor; Competitor Substitutes Another Ball at Wrong Place, Plays It and Then Abandons It and Plays Out Original Ball from Right Place

Q. In stroke play, A, B and C hit their tee shots into the same area. After B and C have played their second shots, A discovers that the remaining ball is not his and, although it is clear that either B or C has played his ball, A assumes that his ball has been played by B. The final paragraph of Rule 15-3b requires A to place a ball on the spot from which his ball was played. A places another ball on the spot from which B played his second shot and plays it to the green. There it is discovered that it was C, not B, who wrongly played A's ball and that A has therefore played the substituted ball from a wrong place. A accepts a two-stroke penalty under the applicable Rule (Rules 15-3b and 20-7c), but he then abandons the substituted ball, thinking he must correct his error. A picks up his original ball, goes back to the spot where C played his second shot, plays it from there onto the putting green and takes two putts to hole out. A then drives from the next tee. What is the ruling, and what did A score on the hole?

A. A's procedure was correct up to the point he abandoned the substituted ball. It is a question of fact who actually played A's ball, and this fact was something that A could have determined prior to playing the substituted ball. The substituted ball, albeit played from a wrong place, was now A's ball in play, and his original ball was out of play. As A's breach was not serious, he was not required to correct the error of playing from a wrong place. Instead of abandoning the substituted ball, A should have played out the hole with it (Rule 13-1) in accordance with Rule 20-7c, adding to his score the two-stroke penalty he had correctly accepted under Rule 15-3b.

When A went back and played his original ball from the right place (i.e., from where C had wrongly played it), he was substituting a ball for his ball in play in breach of Rule 15-2 as well as playing from the wrong place. Therefore, he incurred an additional penalty of two strokes (Rules 13-1, 15-2 and 20-7c) for a total of four penalty strokes. A's score for the hole was 9.

Related Decisions:
- 15/8 Ball Played Under Rule for Ball Lost in Ground Under Repair After Another Ball Played Under Stroke-and-Distance Procedure.
- 18-2a/8.5 Ball Played from Ground Under Repair Abandoned and Relief Taken Under Ground Under Repair Rule.
- 25-1c/2 Ball Dropped and Played Under Ground Under Repair Rule in Absence of Knowledge or Virtual Certainty That Original Ball in Ground Under Repair.

20-7c/5
Competitor Plays Second Ball Under Rule 20-7c; Clarification of "Penalty Strokes Incurred Solely by Playing the Ball Ruled Not to Count"

Note 2 under Rule 20-7c permits a player who has played a second ball to disregard penalty strokes incurred solely in playing a ball ruled not to count, such as accidentally causing the ball to move (Rule 18-2a) or proceeding under the water hazard Rule (Rule 26-1). However, a player cannot disregard a breach of the Rules which might apply to either ball, such as a breach of the practice Rule (Rule 7-2), the advice Rule (Rule 8-1) or playing a wrong ball (Rule 15-3).

Related Decisions:
- 15/7 Wrong Ball Played in Belief It Is Provisional or Second Ball.
- 27-2c/4 Original Ball and Provisional Ball Found Out of Bounds.

20-7c/6
Ball in Bunker Played by Another Player; Ball Not Replaced by Player

Q. In stroke play, A's ball in a bunker was played by his fellow-competitor, B. B failed to get the ball out of the bunker and then discovered he had played a wrong ball. A played his ball from the spot to which B had played it and then learned that he should have replaced his ball. What is the ruling?

A. Rule 15-3b required A to replace his ball. A played from a wrong place (Rules 15-3b and 20-7) incurring a penalty of two strokes when he made a stroke with his ball from the spot to which it had been played by B. Provided A's breach was not serious, he must play out the hole with the ball played from the wrong place.

B incurred a two-stroke penalty under Rule 15-3b and must correct his error.

Other Decisions related to Rule 20-7: See "Wrong Place" and "Serious Breach of Rules: playing from wrong place" in the Index.

RULE 21

CLEANING BALL

DEFINITIONS

All defined terms are in *italics* and are listed alphabetically in the Definitions section – see pages 6–16.

A ball on the *putting green* may be cleaned when lifted under Rule 16-1b. Elsewhere, a ball may be cleaned when lifted, except when it has been lifted:

a. To determine if it is unfit for play (Rule 5-3);

b. For identification (Rule 12-2), in which case it may be cleaned only to the extent necessary for identification; or

c. Because it is assisting or interfering with play (Rule 22).

If a player cleans his ball during play of a hole except as provided in this Rule, he incurs a penalty of one stroke and the ball, if lifted, must be replaced.

If a player who is required to replace a ball fails to do so, he incurs the general penalty under the applicable *Rule*, but there is no additional penalty under Rule 21.

Exception: If a player incurs a penalty for failing to act in accordance with Rule 5-3, 12-2 or 22, there is no additional penalty under Rule 21.

CLEANING BALL

21/1
Removing Paint from Ball

Q. Paint has been used to mark lines on the ground for defining ground under repair. A ball lands on such a line and some paint adheres to the ball. May the player remove the paint?

A. No, unless the ball is in a position from which it may be lifted under the Rules and cleaned under Rule 21, in which case the player may attempt to remove the paint. (Revised)

Related Decision:
• 24-2b/20 Interference by Line or Mark on Ground Consisting of Lime or Paint.

21/2
Removing Grass Adhering to Ball

Q. Through the green, is it permissible to remove cut grass adhering to a ball?

A. No. Such action is prohibited by Rule 21. Anything adhering to a ball is not a loose impediment – see Definition of "Loose Impediments."

Related Decision:
• 23-1/5 Removal of Insect on Ball.

21/3
Whether Ball Cleaned Through Act of Caddie Throwing It to Player

Q. A player is asked to lift his ball, which is lying through the green or in a hazard, because the ball interferes with the play of another player. The player authorises the caddie to lift the ball and, having marked its position and lifted the ball, the caddie throws the ball to the player who catches it. Except when the ball lies on the putting green, it is not permissible to clean a ball lifted because of interference. Does the act of throwing and catching the ball constitute cleaning it?

A. Whether the ball is cleaned is a question of fact. The action described could result in a ball being cleaned. Any doubt should be resolved against the player.

21/4
Position of Ball Lifted for Identification Not Marked, Intention to Lift Not Announced and Ball Cleaned Beyond Extent Necessary to Identify It

Q. A player lifted his ball for identification purposes without announcing his intention to his opponent, marker or a fellow-competitor. Thus, he was in breach of Rule 12-2. He also failed to mark the position of the ball before he lifted it in breach of Rule 20-1 and cleaned the ball more than was necessary for it to be identified, a breach of Rule 21. The penalty for breach of each of these Rules is one stroke. Does the player incur a penalty of three strokes?

A. No. The player incurs a penalty of one stroke for failing to act in accordance with Rule 12-2. An additional penalty under Rule 20-1 or Rule 21 is not justified – see Rule 12-2 and Exception under Rule 21.

Other Decisions related to whether multiple penalties apply: See "Multiple Penalty Situations" in the Index.

21/5
Player Lifts Ball Under Rule Not Permitting Cleaning and Rotates It When Replaced

Q. A piece of mud adheres to a player's ball. The player lifts the ball under a Rule which does not permit cleaning. When he replaces the ball, may he place it facing another direction so that the mud would not interfere between the clubface and the ball?

A. Yes, provided the ball is replaced on the spot from which it was lifted. However, if the player rotated the ball in such a way so as to "tee" it on the mud, he would be in breach of Rule 20-3a.

Other Decisions related to Rule 21: See "Cleaning Ball" in the Index.

BALL ASSISTING OR INTERFERING WITH PLAY

DEFINITIONS

All defined terms are in *italics* and are listed alphabetically in the Definitions section – see pages 6–16.

22-1. BALL ASSISTING PLAY

Except when a ball is in motion, if a player considers that a ball might assist any other player, he may:

a. Lift the ball if it is his ball; or

b. Have any other ball lifted.

A ball lifted under this Rule must be replaced (see Rule 20-3). The ball must not be cleaned, unless it lies on the *putting green* (see Rule 21).

In stroke play, a player required to lift his ball may play first rather than lift the ball.

In stroke play, if the *Committee* determines that *competitors* have agreed not to lift a ball that might assist any *competitor*, they are disqualified.

Note: When another ball is in motion, a ball that might influence the movement of the ball in motion must not be lifted.

22-2. BALL INTERFERING WITH PLAY

Except when a ball is in motion, if a player considers that another ball might interfere with his play, he may have it lifted.

A ball lifted under this Rule must be replaced (see Rule 20-3). The ball must not be cleaned, unless it lies on the *putting green* (see Rule 21).

In stroke play, a player required to lift his ball may play first rather than lift the ball.

Note 1: Except on the *putting green*, a player may not lift his ball solely because he considers that it might interfere with the play of another player. If a player lifts his ball without being asked to do so, he incurs a penalty of one stroke for a breach of Rule 18-2a, but there is no additional penalty under Rule 22.

Note 2: When another ball is in motion, a ball that might influence the movement of the ball in motion must not be lifted.

PENALTY FOR BREACH OF RULE:

Match play – Loss of hole; Stroke play – Two strokes.

BALL ASSISTING OR INTERFERING WITH PLAY

22/1
Mental Interference by Another Ball

Q. In order for A to be entitled to have B's ball lifted because of interference, does B's ball have to be on or near A's line of play and thus in a position to interfere physically with A's ball? Or may A also have B's ball lifted if it is off his line of play but catches his eye and thus constitutes mental interference?

A. A player may, under Rule 22-2, have another ball lifted if the ball interferes either physically or mentally with his play.

Related Decision:
• 24-2a/1 Mental Interference by Obstruction.

22/2
Player Claims That Another Ball Lying 30 Yards Away Interferes with His Play

Q. B's ball is three feet from the green on a direct line to the hole with A's ball which is 30 yards from the green. May A require B to lift his ball, on the grounds that the ball interferes with his play?

A. Yes.

22/3
Player Requests Another Player to Lift His Ball in Absence of Reasonable Possibility Ball Might Interfere or Assist

Q. A's ball is on the putting green. B's ball is 100 yards from the green. B requests A to lift his ball under Rule 22-2 as it might interfere with his (B's) play. This happens several times during the round. Is such procedure permissible?

A. Rule 22 is intended to cover situations where there is a reasonable possibility that one ball might assist or interfere with another ball. If the Rule is being abused, as in this case, the Committee would be justified in penalising B for undue delay (Rule 6-7).

22/4 (Reserved)

22/5
Assisting Ball Lifted by Opponent Replaced on Request; Player's Ball Then Strikes Opponent's Ball and Opponent Lodges Claim

Q. In a match between A and B, A's ball is near the hole in a position to serve as a backstop for B's ball. A lifts his ball to clean it. B requests A to replace his ball before he (B) putts. A protests but B insists that, under the Rules, A must replace his ball immediately. A replaces his ball but disputes B's right to require him to do so and claims the hole. B putts and his ball strikes A's ball and stops very close to the hole. A replaces his ball and holes out for a 4. B then holes out for a 4. The match continues and the claim is later referred to the Committee. How should the Committee rule?

A. The hole stands as played. The Rules do not require A to replace his ball, but B was not in breach of the Rules by asking A to replace it – see Rule 22-1.

22/6
Competitor Requests That Ball in Position to Assist Him Not Be Lifted

Q. In stroke play, B's ball lies just off the putting green. A's ball lies near the hole in a position to serve as a backstop for B's ball. B requests A not to lift his ball. Is such a request proper?

A. No. If A and B agree not to lift a ball that might assist B, both players are disqualified under Rule 22-1.

Related Decisions:
- 2-4/8 Player Concedes Opponent's Next Stroke and Plays Before Opponent Has Opportunity to Lift Ball.
- 3-4/1 Competitor Not Given Opportunity to Lift Ball Assisting Fellow-Competitor.
- 20-1/11 Ball-Marker in Position to Assist Another Player (player asks it not be moved).
- 30-3f/11 Request to Lift Ball That Might Assist Partner Not Honored.

22/7
Ball Assisting Fellow-Competitor on Putting Green; Procedure for Referee If Competitor Does Not Lift Ball

Q. In stroke play, a competitor's ball is in a position to assist the play of a fellow-competitor and the competitor is in a position to lift the ball under Rule 22-1 without delaying the fellow-competitor's play. However, the competitor does not take any action to invoke the Rule. Would a referee be justified in intervening and requesting the competitor to invoke the Rule to protect himself and the rest of the field?

A. Yes. If the competitor were to object, there would be strong evidence of an agreement not to lift the ball for the purpose of assisting the fellow-competitor in breach of Rule 22-1. The referee would be justified in so advising the competitors involved and warning that failure to lift the ball would result in disqualification under Rule 22-1. (Revised)

Other Decisions related to Rule 22: See "Ball Assisting or Interfering with Play" in the Index.

RULE 23

LOOSE IMPEDIMENTS

DEFINITIONS
All defined terms are in *italics* and are listed alphabetically in the Definitions section – see pages 6–16.

23-1. RELIEF
Except when both the *loose impediment* and the ball lie in or touch the same *hazard*, any *loose impediment* may be removed without penalty.

If the ball lies anywhere other than on the *putting green* and the removal of a *loose impediment* by the player causes the ball to *move*, Rule 18-2a applies.

On the *putting green*, if the ball or ball-marker is accidentally *moved* in the process of the player removing a *loose impediment*, the ball or ball-marker must be replaced. There is no penalty, provided the movement of the ball or ball-marker is directly attributable to the removal of the *loose impediment*. Otherwise, if the player causes the ball to *move*, he incurs a penalty of one stroke under Rule 18-2a.

When a ball is in motion, a *loose impediment* that might influence the movement of the ball must not be removed.

Note: If the ball lies in a *hazard*, the player must not touch or move any *loose impediment* lying in or touching the same *hazard* – see Rule 13-4c.

PENALTY FOR BREACH OF RULE:
<u>Match play</u> – Loss of hole; <u>Stroke play</u> – Two strokes.

(Searching for ball in hazard – see Rule 12-1)
(Touching line of putt – see Rule 16-1a)

LOOSE IMPEDIMENTS: GENERAL

23/1
When Loose Impediment Transformed into Obstruction

Loose impediments may be transformed into obstructions through processes of construction or manufacturing. For example, a log (loose impediment) that has been split and had legs attached has been changed by construction into a bench (obstruction); or a piece of wood (loose impediment) becomes an obstruction when manufactured into a charcoal briquette.

23/2
Meaning of "Solidly Embedded" in Definition of "Loose Impediments"

Q. The Definition of "Loose Impediments" states that a stone is a loose impediment if it is not "solidly embedded." When is a stone solidly embedded?

A. If a stone is partially embedded and may be picked up with ease, it is a loose impediment. When there is doubt as to whether a stone is solidly embedded or not, it should not be removed.

23/3
Half-Eaten Pear

Q. A half-eaten pear lies directly in front of a ball in a bunker and there is no pear tree in the vicinity of the bunker. In the circumstances, is the pear an obstruction rather than a loose impediment, in which case the player could remove it without penalty?

A. No. A pear is a natural object. When detached from a tree it is a loose impediment. The fact that a pear has been half-eaten and there is no pear tree in the vicinity does not alter the status of the pear.

23/4
Fruit Skins

Q. Is a banana skin or other fruit skin a loose impediment?

A. Yes.

23/5
Ant Hill

Q. Is an ant hill a loose impediment?

A. Yes. A player is entitled to remove an ant hill under Rule 23-1.

Related Decisions:
• 23/11 Loose Soil from Cast of Hole Made by Burrowing Animal.
• 25/23 Molehills.
• 33-8/22 Local Rule Treating Ant Hills as Ground Under Repair.

23/5.5
Status of Insect-Like Creatures

The definition of "Loose Impediments" provides that worms, insects and the like are loose impediments. The term "the like" includes creatures such as spiders. A web made by a spider is considered to be a cast made by an insect and is also a loose impediment, even if attached to another object.

23/6
Dead Land Crab

Q. A ball lodges against a dead land crab in a bunker. May the crab be removed without penalty?

A. No. A dead land crab is a natural object and thus a loose impediment and not an obstruction. Removal of the crab would be a breach of Rule 13-4.

23/6.5
Status of Snake

Q. What is the status of a snake?

A. A live snake is an outside agency. A dead snake is both an outside agency and a loose impediment. It is possible for an item or person to fall under more than one Definition.

23/7
Fallen Tree

Q. Is a fallen tree a loose impediment?

A. If it is still attached to the stump, no; if it is not attached to the stump, yes.

23/8
Worm Partially Underground

Q. Is a worm, when half on top of the surface of the ground and half below, a loose impediment which may be removed? Or is it fixed or solidly embedded and therefore not a loose impediment?

A. A worm which is half underground is not "fixed or growing" or "solidly embedded" within the meaning of those terms in the Definition of "Loose Impediments." Accordingly, such a worm may be removed under Rule 16-1a(i) or Rule 23.

23/9
Embedded Acorn

Q. Is an embedded acorn a loose impediment?

A. Not if the acorn is solidly embedded – see Definition of "Loose Impediments."

Related Decision:
• 16-1a/7 Player Repairs Depression on Line of Putt Created When Partially Embedded Acorn Removed.

23/10
Ball Embedded in Fruit

Q. A ball is embedded in an orange lying under an orange tree. What is the ruling?

A. The player must play the ball as it lies or deem it unplayable. Since the orange was adhering to the ball, it was not a loose impediment.

23/11
Loose Soil from Cast of Hole Made by Burrowing Animal

Q. A player's ball lies through the green in the cast of a hole made by a burrowing animal. In addition to his relief options under Rule 25, may the player remove the loose soil, which forms the cast, from around his ball?

A. No – see Definition of "Loose Impediments."

Related Decisions:
• 23/5 Ant Hill.
• 25/23 Molehills.

23/12
Aeration Plugs

Q. Are plugs of compacted soil produced through aeration of fairways loose impediments?

A. Yes. Loose soil is not a loose impediment. However, such plugs, since they consist of compacted soil, are loose impediments.

Related Decision:
• 25/15 Aeration Holes.

23/13
Clod of Earth

Q. Is a loose clod of earth a loose impediment?

A. Yes. Loose soil is not a loose impediment except on the putting green. However, a clod of earth is not loose soil.

23/14
Loose Impediments Used to Surface Road

Q. A player hits his ball onto a gravel-covered road. Even though he is entitled to relief from this obstruction, he prefers to play the ball from the road. May he remove gravel that might interfere with his stroke?

A. Yes. Gravel is a loose impediment and a player may remove loose impediments under Rule 23-1. This right is not canceled by the fact that, when a road is covered with gravel, it becomes an artificially-surfaced road and thus an immovable obstruction. The same principle applies to roads or paths constructed with stone, crushed shell, wood chips or the like.

Related Decisions:
• 13-2/32 Improving Line of Play by Removing Stone from Wall
• 24/9 Artificially-Surfaced Road or Path.

Other Decisions related to Rule 23: See "Loose Impediments" and "Status of Object" in the Index.

RELIEF FROM LOOSE IMPEDIMENTS

23-1/1
Means by Which Loose Impediments May Be Removed

Q. Worm casts are loose impediments. By what means may such casts be removed?

A. Loose impediments may be removed by any means, except that, in removing loose impediments on the line of putt, the player must not press anything down (Rule 16-1a).

23-1/2
Large Stone Removable Only with Much Effort

Q. A player's ball lies in the rough directly behind a loose stone the size of a watermelon. The stone can be removed only with much effort. Is it a loose impediment which may be removed?

A. Yes. Stones of any size (not solidly embedded) are loose impediments and may be removed, provided removal does not unduly delay play (Rule 6-7).

23-1/3
Assistance in Removing Large Loose Impediment

Q. May spectators, caddies, fellow-competitors, etc. assist a player in removing a large loose impediment?

A. Yes.

23-1/4
Breaking Off Part of Large Loose Impediment

Q. If part of a large branch which has fallen from a tree (and thus is a loose impediment) interferes with a player's swing, may the player break off the interfering part rather than move the whole branch?

A. Yes.

Related Decisions:
• 13-2/13 Bending Grass in Removal of Loose Impediments.

• 13-2/26 Natural Object Interfering with Swing Moved to Determine Whether It Is Loose.

23-1/5
Removal of Insect on Ball

Q. A live insect is stationary or crawling on a player's ball which is lying through the green. May the player remove the insect with his fingers or blow the insect off the ball?

A. Yes, in both cases, under Rule 23-1. A live insect is not considered to be adhering to the ball and therefore is a loose impediment – see Definition of "Loose Impediments."

23-1/5.5
Status of Insect on Ball in Bunker

Q. With regard to Decision 23-1/5, what is the ruling if the ball was in a bunker?

A. The insect is considered to be in the bunker and because it is, by definition, a loose impediment, the player may not touch or physically remove the insect from the ball (Rule 13-4c). However, as the insect is animate and capable of moving on its own, the player may take action, such as waving his hand or a club or towel, to encourage the insect to move. If the insect moves, there is no penalty provided the player has not touched the insect or the ground in the bunker, or moved another loose impediment in the bunker.

Decisions related to 23-1/5 and 23-1/5.5:
• 13-4/16.5 Flying Insect in Water Hazard.
• 23-1/12 After Ball Addressed on Putting Green Ball Moved in Removal of Loose Impediment.

23-1/6
Removal of Loose Impediments from Area in Which Ball to Be Dropped

Q. Through the green, is it permissible for a player to remove loose impediments from the area in which he is preparing to drop his ball?

A. Yes.

23-1/6.5
Removal of Loose Impediments from Spot Where Ball to Be Placed

Q. A player taking relief under a Rule drops his ball and it rolls more than two club-lengths. He re-drops under Rule 20-2c, with the same result. He must now place the ball as near as possible to the spot where it first struck a part of the course when re-dropped – Rule 20-2c. Before he places the ball, may he remove loose impediments on or around the spot on which the ball is to be placed?

A. Yes.

23-1/7
Loose Impediment Affecting Lie Moved When Ball Lifted

Q. A loose impediment affecting a player's lie is moved when the player lifts his ball under a Rule that requires him to replace the ball. In equity (Rule 1-4), should the player be required to replace the loose impediment?

A. Yes. If he fails to do so when his ball lies through the green, in equity (Rule 1-4), the player incurs a penalty of one stroke in both match play and stroke play. If he fails to do so when the ball lies in a hazard and the loose impediment was originally lying in or touching the same hazard, in equity (Rule 1-4), the player loses the hole in match play or incurs a penalty of two strokes in stroke play.

23-1/8
Loose Impediments Affecting Lie Removed While Ball Lifted

Q. A player's ball lies in an area through the green where there are a number of loose impediments, including a tree branch against which the ball has come to rest. It appears likely that the ball will move if the player moves the tree branch. The player wishes to lift the ball under Rule 5-3 (Ball Unfit for Play) or Rule 12-2 (Identifying Ball), or he is requested to lift it under Rule 22 (Ball Assisting or Interfering with Play). He lifts the ball but, before replacing it, he removes the loose impediments in the area, including the tree branch against which the ball was resting. Is this permissible?

A. No. Under Rule 18-2a, through the green a player incurs a penalty if he causes his ball to move as a result of moving a loose impediment. It would circumvent this Rule if, before a ball is replaced, it was permissible to remove loose impediments which affected the player's lie before the ball was lifted. In equity (Rule 1-4), the player should be penalized one stroke.

In such circumstances, if a player wishes to remove loose impediments affecting his lie, he should do so either before lifting the ball or after replacing it. If his ball then moves as a result of moving the loose impediments, the player incurs a penalty stroke under Rule 18-2a and must replace the ball.

Decisions related to 23-1/7 and 23-1/8:
- 1-4/5 Removal of Obstruction in Hazard Would Move Loose Impediment.
- 13-4/16 Removal of Loose Impediment in Water Hazard Covering Wrong Ball.
- 13-4/35.7 Player Deems Ball Unplayable in Bunker, Lifts Ball and Then Removes Loose Impediment from Bunker.

23-1/9
Removal of Loose Impediment Lying Out of Bounds

Q. A loose impediment lying out of bounds interferes with a player's stance. May the player remove the impediment?

A. Yes.

Related Decision:
• 24-1/3 Movable Artificial Object Lying Out of Bounds.

23-1/10
Removal of Loose Impediments Affecting Player's Play

Q. A player with a downhill putt picks up loose impediments between his ball and the hole but leaves some behind the hole. An opponent or fellow-competitor removes loose impediments behind the hole that might have served as a backstop for the player's ball. What is the ruling?

A. In equity (Rule 1-4), the player is entitled, but not required, to replace the loose impediments.

The opponent or fellow-competitor is permitted to remove the loose impediments by Rule 23-1, and accordingly he is not in breach of Rule 1-2 (see Exception 1 to Rule 1-2). However, if the opponent or fellow-competitor has refused to comply with a request from the player not to remove the loose impediments, the opponent loses the hole (see Decision 2/3) or the fellow-competitor is disqualified (Rule 3-4) for intentionally denying the player's right to have the loose impediments left in position.

The same principles apply to the removal of a movable obstruction in similar circumstances. (Revised)

Related Decisions:
• See "Equity: player entitled to lie, line of play and stance when ball comes to rest after stroke" in the Index.

23-1/11
Ball Moved Accidentally by Foot During Removal of Loose Impediment on Putting Green

Q. A player in the process of removing a loose impediment on the putting green accidentally moved his ball with his foot. What is the ruling?

A. The player incurs a penalty stroke under Rule 18-2a, and the ball must be replaced.

Rule 23-1 provides that the player incurs no penalty if, on the putting green, his ball is accidentally moved in the process of removing a loose impediment. However, this Rule applies only where the moving of a ball is directly attributable to removal of a loose impediment. In this case, removal of the loose impediment did not cause the ball to move.

23-1/12
After Ball Addressed on Putting Green Ball Moved in Removal of Loose Impediment

Q. After a player addresses his ball on the putting green, an insect alights on the ball. The player bends over without moving his feet and, in attempting to brush the insect off the ball, moves the ball several inches. Is the player subject to a penalty stroke under Rule 18-2b?

A. No. An insect is a loose impediment – see Definition of "Loose Impediments" and Decision 23-1/5.

Under Rule 23-1, a player incurs no penalty if a ball on the putting green moves while he is in the process of removing a loose impediment. Rule 23-1 overrides Rule 18-2b in this case.

Related Decisions:
- 13-4/16.5 Flying Insect in Water Hazard.
- 20-1/12 Ball-Marker Moved Accidentally By Player After Having Moved Loose Impediments.
- 23-1/5 Removal of Insect on Ball.
- 23-1/5.5 Status of Insect on Ball in Bunker.

RULE 24

OBSTRUCTIONS

DEFINITIONS
All defined terms are in *italics* and are listed alphabetically in the Definitions section – see pages 6–16.

24-1. MOVABLE OBSTRUCTION
A player may take relief, without penalty, from a movable *obstruction* as follows:

a. If the ball does not lie in or on the *obstruction*, the *obstruction* may be removed. If the ball *moves*, it must be replaced, and there is no penalty, provided that the movement of the ball is directly attributable to the removal of the *obstruction*. Otherwise, Rule 18-2a applies.

b. If the ball lies in or on the *obstruction*, the ball may be lifted and the *obstruction* removed. The ball must *through the green* or in a *hazard* be dropped, or on the *putting green* be placed, as near as possible to the spot directly under the place where the ball lay in or on the *obstruction*, but not nearer the *hole*.

The ball may be cleaned when lifted under this Rule.

When a ball is in motion, an *obstruction* that might influence the movement of the ball, other than *equipment* of any player or the *flagstick* when attended, removed or held up, must not be moved.

(Exerting influence on ball – see Rule 1-2)

Note: If a ball to be dropped or placed under this Rule is not immediately recoverable, another ball may be *substituted*.

24-2. IMMOVABLE OBSTRUCTION
a. Interference
Interference by an immovable *obstruction* occurs when a ball lies in or on the *obstruction*, or when the *obstruction* interferes with the player's *stance* or the area of his intended swing. If the player's ball lies on the *putting green*, interference also occurs if an immovable *obstruction* on the *putting green* intervenes on his *line of putt*. Otherwise, intervention on the *line of play* is not, of itself, interference under this Rule.

b. Relief
Except when the ball is in a *water hazard* or a *lateral water hazard*, a player may take relief from interference by an immovable *obstruction* as follows:

(i) <u>Through the Green</u>: If the ball lies *through the green*, the player must lift the ball and drop it, without penalty, within one club-length of and not nearer the *hole* than the *nearest point of relief*. The *nearest point of relief* must not be in a *hazard* or on a *putting green*. When the ball is dropped within one club-length of the *nearest point of relief*, the ball must first strike a part of the *course* at a spot that avoids interference by the immovable *obstruction* and is not in a *hazard* and not on a *putting green*.

(ii) <u>In a Bunker</u>: If the ball is in a *bunker*, the player must lift the ball and drop it either:

   (a) Without penalty, in accordance with Clause (i) above, except that the *nearest point of relief* must be in the *bunker* and the ball must be dropped in the *bunker*; or

   (b) Under penalty of one stroke, outside the *bunker* keeping the point where the ball lay directly between the *hole* and the spot on which the ball is dropped, with no limit to how far behind the *bunker* the ball may be dropped.

(iii) <u>On the Putting Green</u>: If the ball lies on the *putting green*, the player must lift the ball and place it, without penalty, at the *nearest point of relief* that is not in a *hazard*. The *nearest point of relief* may be off the *putting green*.

(iv) <u>On the Teeing Ground</u>: If the ball lies on the *teeing ground*, the player must lift the ball and drop it, without penalty, in accordance with Clause (i) above.

The ball may be cleaned when lifted under this Rule.

(Ball rolling to a position where there is interference by the condition from which relief was taken – see Rule 20-2c(v))

Exception: A player may not take relief under this Rule if (a) interference by anything other than an immovable *obstruction* makes the *stroke* clearly impracticable or (b) interference by an immovable *obstruction* would occur only through use of a clearly unreasonable *stroke* or an unnecessarily abnormal *stance*, swing or direction of play.

Note 1: If a ball is in a *water hazard* (including a *lateral water hazard*), the player may not take relief from interference by an immovable *obstruction*. The player must play the ball as it lies or proceed under Rule 26-1.

Note 2: If a ball to be dropped or placed under this Rule is not immediately recoverable, another ball may be *substituted*.

Note 3: The *Committee* may make a Local Rule stating that the player must determine the *nearest point of relief* without crossing over, through or under the *obstruction*.

24-3. BALL IN OBSTRUCTION NOT FOUND

It is a question of fact whether a ball that has not been found after having been struck toward an *obstruction* is in the *obstruction*. In order to apply this Rule, it must be known or virtually certain that the ball is in the *obstruction*. In the absence of such knowledge or certainty, the player must proceed under Rule 27-1.

a. Ball in Movable Obstruction Not Found

If it is known or virtually certain that a ball that has not been found is in a movable *obstruction*, the player may *substitute* another ball and take relief, without penalty, under this Rule. If he elects to do so, he must remove the *obstruction* and *through the green* or in a *hazard* drop a ball, or on the *putting green* place a ball, as near as possible to the spot directly under the place where the ball last crossed the outermost limits of the movable *obstruction*, but not nearer the hole.

b. Ball in Immovable Obstruction Not Found

If it is known or virtually certain that a ball that has not been found is in an immovable *obstruction*, the player may take relief under this Rule. If he elects to do so, the spot where the ball last crossed the outermost limits of the *obstruction* must be determined and, for the purpose of applying this Rule, the ball is deemed to lie at this spot and the player must proceed as follows:

(i) Through the Green: If the ball last crossed the outermost limits of the immovable *obstruction* at a spot *through the green*, the player may *substitute* another ball, without penalty, and take relief as prescribed in Rule 24-2b(i).

(ii) In a Bunker: If the ball last crossed the outermost limits of the immovable *obstruction* at a spot in a *bunker*, the player may *substitute* another ball, without penalty, and take relief as prescribed in Rule 24-2b(ii).

(iii) In a Water Hazard (including a Lateral Water Hazard): If the ball last crossed the outermost limits of the immovable *obstruction* at a spot in a *water hazard*, the player is not entitled to relief without penalty. The player must proceed under Rule 26-1.

(iv) On the Putting Green: If the ball last crossed the outermost limits of the immovable *obstruction* at a spot on the *putting green*, the player may *substitute* another ball, without penalty, and take relief as prescribed in Rule 24-2b(iii).

PENALTY FOR BREACH OF RULE:

Match play – Loss of hole; Stroke play – Two strokes.

OBSTRUCTIONS: GENERAL

24/1
Stile Attached to Boundary Fence

Q. Is a stile attached to a boundary fence an obstruction?

A. Yes, unless the Committee declares it to be an integral part of the course under Rule 33-2a(iv).

24/2
Angled Supports or Guy Wires Supporting Boundary Fence

Q. Angled supports or guy wires support a boundary fence or a protective net above such a fence. If the angled supports or guy wires extend onto the course, are they obstructions?

A. Any part of such an angled support or guy wire which is in bounds is an obstruction.

24/3
Concrete Bases of Boundary Fence Posts

Q. Posts of a boundary fence have been set in concrete bases 14 inches in diameter. Are the parts of the bases within the boundary of the course obstructions?

A. No. Such a base is part of the fence and thus no part of it is an obstruction – see Definition of "Obstructions." If such bases are at or below ground level, the boundary line is the inside points of the fence posts at ground level. If they are above ground level, the Committee should clarify the location of the boundary line.

24/4
Part of Boundary Fence Within Boundary Line

Q. Part of a boundary fence is bowed towards the course so that it is inside the boundary line formed by the fence posts. A player's ball comes to rest against this part of the fence. Is the player entitled to relief under Rule 24-2b?

A. No. A fence defining out of bounds is not an obstruction even if part of it is inside the boundary line formed by the fence posts – see Definitions of "Obstructions" and "Out of Bounds."

24/5
Boundary Stakes Having No Significance in Play of Hole Being Played

Q. White stakes installed between the 7th and 8th holes define out of bounds during play of the 7th hole, but they have no significance during play of the 8th hole. Are such stakes obstructions during play of the 8th hole?

A. No, the Definition of "Out of Bounds" states that such stakes are not obstructions. However, in this case it is recommended that, by Local Rule, the stakes be deemed immovable obstructions during play of the 8th hole.

Related Decision:
• 33-8/14 Local Rule Deeming Interior Boundary Fence to Be an Obstruction.

Decisions related to 24/1 through 24/5:
• See "Boundary Fence, Line, Wall or Stake; Wall" in the Index.

24/6
Stone Broken Away from Retaining Wall in Water Hazard

Q. A player's ball in a water hazard is in a playable lie but it is directly behind a stone which has broken away from a retaining wall in the hazard. The wall is an immovable obstruction from which the player is not entitled to relief without penalty. Is the stone which has broken away a movable obstruction, in which case the player may remove it before playing a stroke?

A. Yes.

24/7
Stone Serving as Part of Drain in Bunker

Q. A large stone has been placed at the entrance to a drain in a bunker to prevent sand from washing into the drain. What is the status of such a stone?

A. The stone is an immovable obstruction since it serves as part of the drain which is itself an immovable obstruction. The status of such a stone should be clarified by the Committee.

24/8
Parked Car

Q. A player's ball lies under a parked car. What is the procedure?

A. If the car is readily movable, it should be treated as a movable obstruction and moved – see Rule 24-1.

If the car is not readily movable, it should be treated as an immovable obstruction and the player is entitled to relief as provided in Rule 24-2b.

24/9
Artificially-Surfaced Road or Path

Q. An artificially-surfaced road or path is an obstruction. What constitutes artificial surfacing?

A. A road or path to which any foreign material, e.g., concrete, tar, gravel, wood chips, etc. has been applied is artificially surfaced and thus an obstruction.

Related Decision:
• 23/14 Loose Impediments Used to Surface Road.

24/10 (Reserved)

24/11
Wooden Planks

Q. Is wood which has been manufactured into planks an obstruction?

A. Yes.

24/12
Wooden or Earthen Steps

Wooden steps which have been constructed on a steep bank are obstructions – see Decision 23/1.

Steps which have been cut into a steep bank but which have not been covered with any artificial material such as wooden planks are not obstructions.

24/13 (Reserved)

24/14
Turf Raised by Underground Pipe

Q. A water pipe is partly underground and partly above ground. In some areas where the pipe is underground it has raised the turf. Is such turf, which has been raised by an obstruction, considered part of the obstruction?

A. No.

Other Decisions related to Rule 24: See "Obstructions" and "Status of Object" in the Index.

MOVABLE OBSTRUCTIONS

24-1/1 (Reserved)

24-1/2
Abandoned Ball

Q. A player's ball comes to rest against an abandoned ball. What is the procedure?

A. An abandoned ball is a movable obstruction. The player may remove it under Rule 24-1.

Rule 22-2, which deals specifically with one ball interfering with another, does not apply. It applies only if a ball in play interferes with another ball in play.

24-1/3
Movable Artificial Object Lying Out of Bounds

Q. A movable artificial object lying out of bounds interferes with a player's stance. May the player remove it?

A. Yes. Rule 24-1 applies.

Related Decision:
• 23-1/9 Removal of Loose Impediment Lying Out of Bounds.

24-1/4
Holding Ball in Place While Removing Obstruction

Q. During removal of a movable obstruction, may a player hold his ball to prevent it from moving?

A. No. Such procedure would be a breach of Rule 18-2a. There is no penalty if a ball moves during removal of a movable obstruction provided the movement of the ball is directly attributable to the removal of the obstruction.

Related Decisions:
• 18-2a/31 Ball Touched Accidentally in Removing Loose Impediments.
• 18-2a/32 Ball Touched with Fir Cone or Stick to Prevent Movement When Loose Impediments Removed.

24-1/5
Position of Ball Marked Before Obstruction Removed; Ball Moves When Ball-Marker Removed

Q. A player's ball lies against a movable obstruction. Before removing the obstruction, the player marks the position of his ball so that he will be able to replace the ball precisely if the ball moves when the obstruction is removed. The player removes the obstruction and the ball does not move. However, the ball moves when the ball-marker is removed. What is the ruling?

A. The ball-marker is itself a movable obstruction. Accordingly, under Rule 24-1, the player incurs no penalty and he must replace the ball.

Related Decision:
• 20-1/15 Meaning of "Directly Attributable" in Rules 20-1 and 20-3a.

Other Decisions related to Rule 24-1: See "Obstructions" in the Index.

INTERFERENCE BY IMMOVABLE OBSTRUCTIONS

24-2a/1
Mental Interference by Obstruction

Q. A player's ball lies several inches to the side of a sprinkler head. The sprinkler head does not physically interfere with the player's stance or the area of his intended swing. However, the sprinkler head bothers the player mentally. Is the player entitled to relief under Rule 24-2b?

A. No. See Rule 24-2a.

Related Decision:
• 22/1 Mental Interference by Another Ball.

RELIEF FROM IMMOVABLE OBSTRUCTIONS

24-2b/1
Determining "Nearest Point of Relief"

Q. The Note to the Definition of "Nearest Point of Relief" provides that the player should determine this point by using "the club with which he would have made his next stroke if the condition were not there to simulate the address position, direction of play and swing for such stroke." May the player use any club, address position, direction of play or swing in determining the nearest point of relief?

A. No. In determining the nearest point of relief accurately it is recommended that the player use the club, address position, direction of play and swing (right or left-handed) that he would have used had the obstruction or condition not been there. For example, the player has interference from an immovable obstruction and, were it not for the obstruction, he would have used a right-handed stroke with a 4-iron to play the ball from its original position towards the green. To determine the nearest point of relief accurately, he should use a right-handed stroke with a 4-iron and the direction of play should be towards the green. See also Decisions 20-2c/0.7 and 20-2c/0.8.

Related Decisions:
• 24-2b/3.7 Diagram Illustrating Player Unable to Determine Nearest Point of Relief.
• 24-2b/4 Club Used to Determine Nearest Point of Relief Not Used for Next Stroke.
• 25-1b/2 Diagrams Illustrating "Nearest Point of Relief."

24-2b/2
Player Does Not Follow Recommended Procedure in Determining Nearest Point of Relief

Q. A player's ball lies on an artificially-surfaced path, which is an immovable obstruction, through the green. The ball is situated at the left edge of the obstruction and the player is right-handed. The player elects to take relief under Rule 24-2b(i) but does not go through the procedure recommended in the Note to the Definition of "Nearest Point of Relief" for determining the nearest point of relief. Instead, he lifts the ball and drops it within one club-length of the nearest edge of the obstruction, not nearer the hole than the ball's original position, and plays it. What is the ruling?

A. Provided the ball is dropped on a spot that satisfies the requirements of Rule 24-2b(i) and the ball did not roll into a position requiring a re-drop under Rule 20-2c, the player incurs no penalty.

Although there is a recommended procedure for determining the nearest point of relief, the Rules do not require a player to determine this point when proceeding under Rule 24-2, 24-3, 25-1 or 25-3. If a player does not determine a nearest point of relief accurately or identifies an incorrect nearest point of relief, a penalty only arises if, as a result, the player drops his ball at a spot which does not satisfy the requirements of the Rule under which he is proceeding and he then plays the ball (e.g., the spot is more than one-club length from the correct nearest point of relief or the ball is dropped nearer to the hole than the nearest point of relief). In such circumstances, the player would be penalized for playing from a wrong place (Rule 20-7).

24-2b/3
Player Determines Nearest Point of Relief But Physically Unable to Play Intended Stroke

Q. In proceeding under Rule 24-2b(i) or Rule 25-1b(i), the Definition of "Nearest Point of Relief" provides that to determine the nearest point of relief accurately, the player should use the club, address position, direction of play and swing (right or left-handed) that he would have used to make his next stroke had the obstruction or condition not been there. What is the procedure if, having determined the stroke he would have used, he is unable physically to make such a stroke from, what would appear to be, the nearest point of relief because either (a) the direction of play is blocked by a tree, or (b) he is unable to take the backswing for the intended stroke due to a bush?

A. The point identified is the nearest point of relief. The fact that at this point the player cannot make the intended stroke due to something other than the obstruction or condition from which relief is being taken does not alter this result. The player must drop the ball within one club-length of the nearest point of relief, not nearer the hole. Once the ball is in play, the player must then decide what type of stroke he will make. This stroke may be different from the one he would have made from the ball's original position had the obstruction or condition not been there.

24-2b/3.5
Player Unable Physically to Determine Nearest Point of Relief

Q. In proceeding under Rule 24-2b(i) or Rule 25-1b(i), the Definition of "Nearest Point of Relief" provides that to determine the nearest point of relief accurately, the player should use the club, address position, direction of play and swing (right or left-handed) that he would have used from the original position had the obstruction or condition not been there. What is the procedure if a player is unable physically to determine the nearest point of relief because, for example, that point is within the trunk of a tree or a boundary fence prevents the player from adopting the required address position?

A. The nearest point of relief in both cases must be estimated and the player must drop the ball within one club-length of the estimated point, not nearer the hole.

Decision related to 24-2b/3 and 24-2b/3.5:
• 33-8/19 Local Rule Permitting Relief on Specified Side of Paved Path.

24-2b/3.7
Diagram Illustrating Player Unable to Determine Nearest Point of Relief

The diagram illustrates the point raised in Decision 24-2b/3.5 where a player may be unable to determine the nearest point of relief from an immovable obstruction and will need to estimate this point under Rule 24-2b.

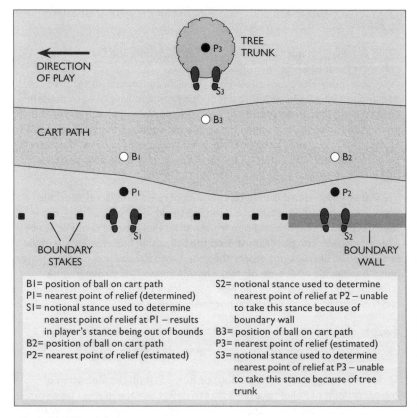

BI= position of ball on cart path
PI= nearest point of relief (determined)
SI= notional stance used to determine nearest point of relief at PI – results in player's stance being out of bounds
B2= position of ball on cart path
P2= nearest point of relief (estimated)

S2= notional stance used to determine nearest point of relief at P2 – unable to take this stance because of boundary wall
B3= position of ball on cart path
P3= nearest point of relief (estimated)
S3= notional stance used to determine nearest point of relief at P3 – unable to take this stance because of tree trunk

Related Decisions:
• 24-2b/1 Determining "Nearest Point of Relief."
• 25-1b/2 Diagrams Illustrating "Nearest Point of Relief."

24-2b/4
Club Used to Determine Nearest Point of Relief Not Used for Next Stroke

Q. The Note to the Definition of "Nearest Point of Relief" states: "In order to determine the nearest point of relief accurately, the player should use the club with which he would have made his next stroke if the condition were not there to simulate the address position, direction of play and swing for such stroke." If the subsequent lie of the ball were such that it was expedient for the player to play his next stroke with some other club, may the player use the other club?

A. Yes.

Related Decisions:
- 20-2c/0.7 Ball Dropped from Immovable Obstruction Rolls Nearer Obstruction Than Nearest Point of Relief; Whether Re-Drop Required If Player Changes Clubs and Obstruction No Longer Interferes.
- 20-2c/0.8 Player Takes Relief from an Area of Ground Under Repair; Whether Re-Drop Required If Condition Interferes for Stroke with Club Not Used to Determine "Nearest Point of Relief."

24-2b/5
Player Who Lifts Ball Under First Option of Rule 24-2b(ii) Then Wishes to Proceed Under Second Option

Q. A player elects to take relief from an immovable obstruction in a bunker. He lifts the ball to take relief without penalty under the first option of clause (ii) but realizes that where he will have to drop the ball will result in a very difficult shot. May he now elect to proceed under the second option of clause (ii) incurring the penalty stroke and drop outside the bunker?

A. Yes. The player lifted the ball to take relief from the immovable obstruction and is entitled to proceed under either of the options under Rule 24-2b(ii), irrespective of the fact that his original intention was to proceed under the first option. However, the player would be precluded from using the second option under Rule 24-2b(ii) if he had put the ball into play under the first option – see Decision 25-1b/9.

Other Decisions related to whether a player may change a selected relief option after taking further action: See "Ball Dropped or Re-Dropped: changing relief option" in the Index.

24-2b/6
Relief from Immovable Obstruction Incidentally Results in Relief from Boundary Fence

Q. A player's ball is in such a position that a boundary fence and an immovable obstruction near the fence both interfere with the area of the player's intended swing. It is reasonable for him to play the stroke despite the interference from the boundary fence. If the player takes relief from the obstruction under Rule 24-2b, he will incidentally get relief from the fence. Is the player entitled to invoke Rule 24-2b in such circumstances?

A. Yes.

24-2b/7
Relief from Obstruction Interfering with Swing Incidentally Gives Relief from Intervention on Line of Play

Q. A player's ball lies behind an immovable obstruction. The obstruction interferes with the player's swing and also intervenes on his line of play. In obtaining relief from interference with his swing, must the player drop the ball in such a position that intervention on the line of play is maintained?

A. No. Since the obstruction interferes with the player's swing, the player is entitled to relief under Rule 24-2b. If, in proceeding under this Rule, the player could drop the ball in a place which would also avoid intervention on his line of play, he is entitled to do so.

24-2b/8
Dropping from Rough to Fairway in Obtaining Relief from Obstruction

Q. A player whose ball lies in the rough close to the fairway is entitled to relief from an immovable obstruction. In obtaining relief under Rule 24-2b(i), may the player drop the ball on the fairway?

A. Yes. There is no distinction in the Rules between fairway and rough; both are covered by the term "through the green."

24-2b/9
After Relief from Obstruction Second Obstruction Interferes

Q. A player obtaining relief from an immovable obstruction drops his ball in such a position that another immovable obstruction interferes with his swing. What is the procedure?

A. The player is entitled to relief from the second obstruction as provided in Rule 24-2b.

Related Decision:
• 20-2c/7 Player Takes Relief from Area of Casual Water and Ball Comes to Rest in a Position Where Another Area of Casual Water Interferes; Whether Re-Drop Required.

24-2b/9.5
After Relief Taken from Obstruction for Stroke Towards Green, Obstruction Interferes with Stance for Necessary Sideways Stroke

Q. With regard to the diagram, Point X is the original position of the ball and Point A is the nearest point of relief from the obstruction (cart path). The player drops his ball within one club-length of Point A (within the shaded area) and it comes to rest on the cart path at Point B. He re-drops as required by Rule 20-2c, again dropping within one club-length of Point A and the ball comes to rest at Point C.

At Point C there is no interference by the cart path for a stroke towards the green. However, the player cannot play towards the green from Point C because of intervention by the tree. His only reasonable stroke is sideways to the fairway, and his stance for such a stroke would be on the cart path. Is the player now required to place the ball as near as possible to the spot where it first struck the ground when re-dropped in accordance with Rule 20-2c?

A. No. The player is not entitled to place the ball because at Point C there is no interference by the cart path for a stroke towards the green, the intended direction of play when relief was taken. However, as a result of the tree, the player has a new situation. He is entitled to take relief under Rule 24-2b(i) for the sideways stroke since this is not an unnecessarily abnormal direction of play – see Exception under Rule 24-2b – and his nearest point of relief would be Point D. After the ball is dropped within one club-length of Point D (within the shaded area) and it comes to rest at Point E, the player may play in any direction he wishes.

Related Decisions:
- 24-2b/17 Obstruction Interferes with Abnormal Stroke; Abnormal Stroke Reasonable in Circumstances.
- 25-1b/22 Cast of Burrowing Animal Interferes with Sideways Stroke; When Relief Granted.

24-2b/10
Obstruction in Ground Under Repair Interferes with Player's Swing

Q. An immovable obstruction situated within an area defined as ground under repair interferes with the area of the player's intended swing. May the player take relief from the obstruction under Rule 24-2b, drop his ball in the ground under repair and then have the option of playing the ball as it lies or proceeding under Rule 25-1b which provides relief from ground under repair?

A. Yes.

Related Decisions:
- 24-2b/19 Stroke at Ball Not Practicable Due to Interference by Immovable Obstruction and Casual Water.
- 25-1b/11 Ball in Casual Water Within Ground Under Repair.
- 25-1b/11.5 Ball in Casual Water Within Ground Under Repair; Whether Player Entitled to Take Relief from Both Conditions in Single Procedure.
- 25-2/4 Ball Embedded in Ground Under Repair in Closely Mown Area.

24-2b/11
Ball Lying on Elevated Part of Immovable Obstruction

Q. A ball comes to rest on the elevated part of an immovable obstruction, such as the walkway of a bridge over a deep hollow. What is the ruling?

A. If the player elects to take relief, vertical distance is disregarded. The nearest point of relief (Point X) is deemed to be at the point on the ground directly beneath where the ball lies on the obstruction, provided the player would not have interference, as defined in Rule 24-2a, at this point. The player may proceed under Rule 24-2b by dropping the ball within one club-length of Point X.

In a situation where there would be interference with some part of the obstruction (e.g., a supporting column) for a ball positioned at Point X, the ball is deemed to lie at Point X. The player may proceed under Rule 24-2b by determining the nearest point of relief for a ball lying at Point X.

The procedure is different where a ball lies underground (e.g., in a tunnel). In such a case, all distance, whether vertical or horizontal, is taken into account when determining the nearest point of relief. In some cases, the nearest point of relief would be near the entrance to the tunnel, and in other cases it would be above the tunnel and would need to be estimated.

Related Decisions:
- 25-1b/23 Ball Enters Burrowing Animal Hole Out of Bounds and Comes to Rest in Bounds.
- 25-1b/24 Ball Enters Burrowing Animal Hole in Bounds and Comes to Rest Out of Bounds.
- 25-1b/25 Ball Enters Burrowing Animal Hole in Bunker and Is Found Underneath Putting Green.

- 25-1b/25.5 Application of Exception to Rule 25-1b When Ball Lies Underground in Burrowing Animal Hole.
- 28/11 Ball Unplayable in Tree and Player Opts to Drop Within Two Club-Lengths.
- 28/12 Ball Unplayable at Base of Cliff and Player Wishes to Drop Within Two Club-Lengths of Point Above Ball.

24-2b/12
Ball in Drainpipe Under Course; Entrance to Drainpipe Is Out of Bounds

Q. A ball enters an underground drainpipe the entrance to which is out of bounds. The ball is found in the drainpipe under an area that is through the green. What is the ruling?

A. Under Rule 24-2b(i), the player is entitled to drop the ball, without penalty, within one club-length of the spot on the ground immediately above its resting place in the drainpipe, but not nearer the hole and not in a hazard or on a putting green. A boundary line extends vertically upwards and downwards – see Definition of "Out of Bounds."

If the player cannot find or identify the ball and it is known or virtually certain that the ball is in the drainpipe within the boundaries of the course, the player may invoke Rule 24-3b. As that part of the drainpipe situated off the course is not an obstruction (see Definition of "Obstruction") the ball "last crossed the outermost limits of the immovable obstruction" where the underground drainpipe coincides with the boundary line. Therefore, as stated above, the player may drop a ball, without penalty, within one club-length of the spot on the ground immediately above where the drainpipe coincides with the boundary line, on a part of the course that is not nearer the hole, not in a hazard or on a putting green.

If it is neither known nor virtually certain that the ball is in the drainpipe, the player must proceed under Rule 27-1.

Related Decision:
- 24-3b/1 Ball Lost in Underground Drainpipe.

24-2b/13 (Reserved)

24-2b/14
Window of Clubhouse Opened and Ball Played Through Window

Q. A competitor hit a ball into a clubhouse which was not out of bounds and had not been declared an integral part of the course.

In order to play it out, he opened a window, claiming that it was a movable (or partially movable) obstruction. Was this permissible?

A. Yes. The clubhouse was an immovable obstruction. However, any part of it designed to be movable, such as a window or door, may be moved to any position if this can be done without undue delay.

The same principle would apply if the clubhouse had been declared an integral part of the course.

24-2b/15
Opening Barn Doors to Play Shot Through Barn

Q. May a player open the doors of a barn to enable him to play a shot through the barn?

A. Yes. A barn is an immovable obstruction, but the doors are movable and may be opened. See also Decision 24-2b/14.

24-2b/15.3
Status of Movable Part of Drainage Hose

Q. In a water hazard, a player's swing is interfered with by a drainage hose. One end of the hose is immovable, i.e., it is anchored in the ground. However, that part of the hose interfering with the player's swing can readily be moved to one side or the other. Is the player entitled to move the hose to one side so that it does not interfere with his swing?

A. Yes, since the part of the hose interfering with the player's swing is designed to be movable.

24-2b/15.5
Door of Building in Open or Closed Position

Q. A player's ball lies through the green and near the open door of a building on the course (immovable obstruction). When open, the door interferes with the player's area of intended swing, but when the door is closed the player does not have interference from the door or building. How may the player proceed?

A. With the door in the open position in which he found it, the player has interference, as defined by Rule 24-2a, from an immovable obstruction; therefore, he is entitled to relief without penalty in accordance with Rule 24-2b. Additionally, as the door is designed to be movable, the player may move the door to any other position to eliminate interference (see Decisions 24-2b/14 and 24-2b/15).

If the player did not have interference from the door, he was not entitled to move the door to another position for the purpose of giving himself interference under Rule 24-2a.

Decision related to 24-2b/14 through 24-2b/15.5:
• 13-2/32 Improving Line of Play by Removing Stone from Wall.

24-2b/16
Obstruction Interferes But Ball Unplayable Due to Some Other Condition

Q. A player's ball lies between two exposed tree roots. The ball is clearly unplayable due to the roots. An immovable obstruction is so located that it would interfere with the player's backswing if the player could play the ball. The player claims he is entitled to relief, without penalty, under Rule 24-2b(i). Is the player correct?

A. No. See Exception under Rule 24-2b. The player must invoke Rule 28.

Related Decision:
• 25-1b/19 Ball Lies on Mound Made by Burrowing Animal; Impracticable to Make Stroke Due to Bush.

24-2b/17
Obstruction Interferes with Abnormal Stroke; Abnormal Stroke Reasonable in Circumstances

Q. A right-handed player's ball is so close to a boundary fence on the left of a hole that the player, in order to play towards the hole, must play left-handed. In making a left-handed stroke, the player's backswing would be interfered with by an immovable obstruction. Is the player entitled to relief from the obstruction?

A. The player is entitled to relief since use of an abnormal (left-handed) stroke is reasonable in the circumstances – see Exception under Rule 24-2b.

The proper procedure is for the player to take relief for a left-handed stroke in accordance with Rule 24-2b(i).

The player may then use a normal right-handed swing for his next stroke. If the obstruction interferes with the swing or stance for the right-handed stroke, the player may take relief for the right-handed stroke in accordance with Rule 24-2b(i). (Revised)

Related Decisions:
• 24-2b/9.5 After Relief Taken from Obstruction for Stroke Towards Green, Obstruction Interferes with Stance for Necessary Sideways Stroke.
• 25-1b/22 Cast of Burrowing Animal Interferes with Sideways Stroke; When Relief Granted.

24-2b/18
Obstruction Interferes with Abnormal Stroke; Abnormal Stroke Not Reasonable in Circumstances

Q. A right-handed player's ball is in a poor lie. A nearby immovable obstruction would not interfere with a normal right-handed swing but it would interfere with a left-handed swing. The player says he wishes to make his next stroke left-handed and, since the obstruction would interfere with such a stroke, he is entitled to proceed under Rule 24-2b. May the player invoke Rule 24-2b?

A. No. If the only reason for the player to use a left-handed stroke is to escape a poor lie, use of an abnormal (left-handed) stroke is clearly unreasonable and the player is not entitled to invoke Rule 24-2b – see Exception under Rule 24-2b. (Revised)

24-2b/19
Stroke at Ball Impracticable Due to Interference by Immovable Obstruction and Casual Water

Q. A player's ball lies against an immovable obstruction in casual water. It is clearly impracticable for him to make a stroke because of interference by either of them. The Exceptions to Rule 24-2b and Rule 25-1b appear to preclude free relief from either because of interference by the other. Is this correct?

A. No. The player may take relief without penalty under either Rule 24-2b or Rule 25-1b. The purpose of the Exception to each of these Rules is to prevent the player from fortuitously obtaining free relief when it is clearly impracticable for him to make a stroke because of interference by something from which free relief is not available. (Revised)

Related Decisions:
- 1-4/8 Nearest Point of Relief from Cart Path Is in Casual Water; Nearest Point of Relief from Casual Water Is Back on Cart Path.
- 24-2b/10 Obstruction in Ground Under Repair Interferes with Player's Swing.
- 25-1b/11.5 Ball in Casual Water Within Ground Under Repair; Whether Player Entitled to Take Relief from Both Conditions in Single Procedure.
- 25-2/4 Ball Embedded in Ground Under Repair in Closely Mown Area.

24-2b/20
Interference by Line or Mark on Ground Consisting of Lime or Paint

Q. A ball comes to rest on a line or other mark on the ground consisting of lime or paint that has been drawn for gallery-control purposes or for providing fixed reference points relating to yardage. Is the player entitled to relief under Rule 24-2b?

A. No. Such lines or marks are not obstructions.

However, the Committee may, by Local Rule, declare such areas to be ground under repair.

Related Decision:
- 21/1 Removing Paint from Ball.

24-2b/21
Interference by Immovable Artificial Object Situated Out of Bounds

Q. An immovable artificial object situated out of bounds interferes with a player's swing. May the player obtain relief as provided in Rule 24-2b?

A. No. Immovable artificial objects off the course are not obstructions (see Definition of "Obstructions"); therefore, the Rules provide no relief without penalty.

Related Decisions:
- 13-2/19 Improving Area of Intended Swing by Moving Growing or Fixed Object Situated Out of Bounds.
- 13-2/20 Part of Fence Off Course Leans Across Boundary and Interferes with Swing.

BALL IN IMMOVABLE OBSTRUCTION NOT

24-3b/1
Ball Lost in Underground Drainpipe

Q. A player's ball goes into an underground drainpipe, but he cannot reach or identify it. What is the ruling?

A. An underground drainpipe or culvert is an obstruction. If it is known or virtually certain that the ball is in the immovable obstruction, the player may invoke Rule 24-3b. Under Rule 24-3b the ball is deemed to lie at the spot where it last crossed the outermost limits of the obstruction.

If the entrance to the underground drainpipe or culvert is in a water hazard, Rule 24-3b(iii) applies and the player is not entitled to relief without penalty and must proceed under Rule 26-1.

If the entrance to the underground drainpipe or culvert is out of bounds and it is neither known nor virtually certain that the ball is within the boundaries of the course, the player must proceed under Rule 27-1 – see Decision 24-2b/12.

Related Decisions:
- 25/10 Ball Lost in Tree in Ground Under Repair.
- 25-1c/1.5 Clarification of Point Where Ball "Last Crossed Outermost Limits" of Abnormal Ground Condition.

Other Decisions related to Rule 24-3: See "Virtually Certain (or Known)" in the Index.

ABNORMAL GROUND CONDITIONS, EMBEDDED BALL AND WRONG PUTTING GREEN

DEFINITIONS

All defined terms are in *italics* and are listed alphabetically in the Definitions section – see pages 6–16.

25-1. ABNORMAL GROUND CONDITIONS

a. Interference

Interference by an *abnormal ground condition* occurs when a ball lies in or touches the condition or when the condition interferes with the player's *stance* or the area of his intended swing. If the player's ball lies on the *putting green*, interference also occurs if an *abnormal ground condition* on the *putting green* intervenes on his *line of putt*. Otherwise, intervention on the *line of play* is not, of itself, interference under this Rule.

Note: The *Committee* may make a Local Rule stating that interference by an *abnormal ground condition* with a player's *stance* is deemed not to be, of itself, interference under this Rule.

b. Relief

Except when the ball is in a *water hazard* or a *lateral water hazard*, a player may take relief from interference by an *abnormal ground condition* as follows:

(i)   Through the Green: If the ball lies *through the green*, the player must lift the ball and drop it, without penalty, within one club-length of and not nearer the *hole* than the *nearest point of relief*. The *nearest point of relief* must not be in a *hazard* or on a *putting green*. When the ball is dropped within one club-length of the *nearest point of relief*, the ball must first strike a part of the *course* at a spot that avoids interference by the condition and is not in a *hazard* and not on a *putting green*.

(ii) In a Bunker: If the ball is in a *bunker*, the player must lift the ball and drop it either:

(a) Without penalty, in accordance with Clause (i) above, except that the *nearest point of relief* must be in the *bunker* and the ball must be dropped in the *bunker* or, if complete relief is impossible, as near as possible to the spot where the ball lay, but not nearer the *hole*, on a part of the *course* in the *bunker* that affords maximum available relief from the condition; or

(b) Under penalty of one stroke, outside the *bunker* keeping the point where the ball lay directly between the *hole* and the spot on which the ball is dropped, with no limit to how far behind the *bunker* the ball may be dropped.

(iii) On the Putting Green: If the ball lies on the *putting green*, the player must lift the ball and place it, without penalty, at the *nearest point of relief* that is not in a *hazard* or, if complete relief is impossible, at the nearest position to where it lay that affords maximum available relief from the condition, but not nearer the *hole* and not in a *hazard*. The *nearest point of relief* or maximum available relief may be off the *putting green*.

(iv) <u>On the Teeing Ground</u>: If the ball lies on the *teeing ground*, the player must lift the ball and drop it, without penalty, in accordance with Clause (i) above.

The ball may be cleaned when lifted under Rule 25-1b.

(Ball rolling to a position where there is interference by the condition from which relief was taken – see Rule 20-2c(v))

Exception: A player may not take relief under this Rule if (a) interference by anything other than an *abnormal ground condition* makes the *stroke* clearly impracticable or (b) interference by an *abnormal ground condition* would occur only through use of a clearly unreasonable *stroke* or an unnecessarily abnormal *stance*, swing or direction of play.

Note 1: If a ball is in a *water hazard* (including a *lateral water hazard*), the player is not entitled to relief, without penalty, from interference by an *abnormal ground condition*. The player must play the ball as it lies (unless prohibited by Local Rule) or proceed under Rule 26-1.

Note 2: If a ball to be dropped or placed under this Rule is not immediately recoverable, another ball may be *substituted*.

c. Ball in Abnormal Ground Condition Not Found

It is a question of fact whether a ball that has not been found after having been struck toward an *abnormal ground condition* is in such a condition. In order to apply this Rule, it must be known or virtually certain that the ball is in the *abnormal ground condition*. In the absence of such knowledge or certainty, the player must proceed under Rule 27-1.

If it is known or virtually certain that a ball that has not been found is in an *abnormal ground condition*, the player may take relief under this Rule. If he elects to do so, the spot where the ball last crossed the outermost limits of the *abnormal ground condition* must be determined and, for the purpose of applying this Rule, the ball is deemed to lie at this spot and the player must proceed as follows:

(i) <u>Through the Green</u>: If the ball last crossed the outermost limits of the *abnormal ground condition* at a spot *through the green*, the player may *substitute* another ball, without penalty, and take relief as prescribed in Rule 25-1b(i).

(ii) <u>In a Bunker</u>: If the ball last crossed the outermost limits of the *abnormal ground condition* at a spot in a *bunker*, the player may *substitute* another ball, without penalty, and take relief as prescribed in Rule 25-1b(ii).

(iii) <u>In a Water Hazard (including a Lateral Water Hazard)</u>: If the ball last crossed the outermost limits of the *abnormal ground condition* at a spot in a *water hazard*, the player is not entitled to relief without penalty. The player must proceed under Rule 26-1.

(iv) <u>On the Putting Green</u>: If the ball last crossed the outermost limits of the *abnormal ground condition* at a spot on the *putting green*, the player may *substitute* another ball, without penalty, and take relief as prescribed in Rule 25-1b(iii).

25-2. EMBEDDED BALL

A ball embedded in its own pitch-mark in the ground in any closely mown area *through the green* may be lifted, cleaned and dropped, without penalty, as near as possible to the spot where it lay but not nearer the *hole*. The ball when dropped must first strike a part of the *course through the green*. "Closely mown area" means any area of the *course*, including paths through the rough, cut to fairway height or less.

25-3. WRONG PUTTING GREEN
a. Interference

Interference by a *wrong putting green* occurs when a ball is on the *wrong putting green*.

Interference to a player's *stance* or the area of his intended swing is not, of itself, interference under this Rule.

b. Relief

If a player's ball lies on a *wrong putting green*, he must not play the ball as it lies. He must take relief, without penalty, as follows:

The player must lift the ball and drop it within one club-length of and not nearer the *hole* than the *nearest point of relief*. The *nearest point of relief* must not be in a *hazard* or on a *putting green*. When dropping the ball within one club-length of the *nearest point of relief*, the ball must first strike a part of the *course* at a spot that avoids interference by the *wrong putting green* and is not in a *hazard* and not on a *putting green*. The ball may be cleaned when lifted under this Rule.

PENALTY FOR BREACH OF RULE:

Match play – Loss of hole; Stroke play – Two strokes.

CASUAL WATER: DEFINITION

25/1
Soft, Mushy Earth

Q. Is soft, mushy earth casual water?

A. No. Soft, mushy earth is not casual water unless water is visible on the surface before or after the player takes his stance – see Definition of "Casual Water."

25/2
Overflow from Water Hazard

Q. If a pond (water hazard) has overflowed, is the overflow casual water?

A. Yes. Any overflow of water from a water hazard which is outside the margin of the hazard is casual water.

Related Decision:
• 1-4/7 Ball Lost In Either Water Hazard or Casual Water Overflowing Hazard.

25/3
Pitch-Mark Filled with Casual Water

Q. A player's ball plugged deeply in short rough. No casual water was visible on the surface, but the pitch-mark in which the ball came to rest was filled with water. Was the player's ball in casual water?

A. Yes.

25/4
Water Visible as Result of Undue Effort with Feet

Q. In a wet area, casual water is not visible before or after the player takes his normal stance. However, by pressing down hard with one foot, the player causes water to appear around the sole of his shoe. Is the player entitled to relief under Rule 25-1b?

A. No. Water visible through undue effort with the feet is not casual water – see Definition of "Casual Water."

25/5
Casual Water on Putting Green Visible When Player Walks Beside Line of Putt But Not Visible Elsewhere

Q. A player's ball lies on a putting green. Casual water is not visible on the green. However, when the player walks beside his line of putt, casual water is visible around the player's feet. Is the player entitled to relief?

A. Not unless there is casual water visible around the player's feet when he takes his stance – see Definition of "Casual Water."

25/6
Status of Saliva

Q. What is the status of saliva?

A. In equity (Rule 1-4), saliva may be treated as either an abnormal ground condition (Rule 25-1) or a loose impediment (Rule 23-1), at the option of the player.

Other Decisions related to Casual Water: See "Casual Water" in the Index.

25/7
Fallen Tree in Process of Being Removed

Q. A greenkeeper is in the process of sawing up a fallen tree and stacking the wood. What is the status of such a tree?

A. The tree in its entirety is ground under repair as it constitutes "material piled for removal" – see Definition of "Ground Under Repair."

25/8
Tree Stump

Q. Do the Rules provide relief without penalty from a tree stump?

A. No, not unless it has been marked as ground under repair or it is in the process of being unearthed or cut up for removal, in which case it is "material piled for removal" and thus automatically ground under repair – see Definition of "Ground Under Repair."

A tree stump which the Committee intends to remove, but which is not in the process of being removed, is not automatically ground under repair.

25/9
Fallen Tree Attached to Stump

Q. A tree has fallen onto a fairway due to a windstorm and is still attached to the stump. Does it constitute ground under repair?

A. No. However, a player could request relief from the Committee and the Committee would be justified in declaring the area covered by the tree to be ground under repair.

25/9.5
Tree Falls onto Fairway During Stipulated Round

Q. A large tree falls onto a fairway during a stipulated round and cannot readily be removed. What should the Committee do?

A. The most appropriate course of action will depend on the circumstances in each case. The Committee has the following options:
  (1) require play to continue, providing no additional relief from the fallen tree;
  (2) suspend play and have the tree removed;
  (3) declare the tree and the area covered by the tree to be ground under repair (Rule 25-1) and may, as an additional option, establish a dropping zone; or
  (4) in equity (Rule 1-4), adopt the relief procedures under the Local Rule for Temporary Obstructions, thus providing intervention relief from the fallen tree.

25/10
Ball Lost in Tree in Ground Under Repair

Q. A ball is lost in a tree rooted in an area marked as ground under repair. Is the player entitled to relief without penalty under Rule 25-1c?

A. As all ground and any grass, bush, tree or other growing thing within ground under repair is considered to be part of the ground under repair (see Definition of "Ground Under Repair"), the ball is lost in ground under repair and the player is entitled to relief under Rule 25-1c.

In this case, the reference point for taking relief is the spot where the ball last crossed the outermost limits of the area of ground under repair.

Related Decision:
• 25-1c/1.5 Clarification of Point Where Ball "Last Crossed Outermost Limits of" Abnormal Ground Condition.

25/10.5
Ball in Tree in Ground Under Repair

Q. A player's ball is found through the green in a tree rooted in an area marked as ground under repair. The spot on the ground directly under where the ball lies is outside the white-lined area defining the ground under repair. Is the player entitled to relief under Rule 25-1b(i)?

A. Yes, because the ball lies in or touches the ground under repair – see Definition of "Ground Under Repair." In this case, the reference point for taking relief is the spot on the ground immediately below the place where the ball lay in the tree.

25/10.7
Status of Roots Outside Ground Under Repair Growing from Tree Inside Ground Under Repair

Q. A player's ball comes to rest against a tree root. The tree is within ground under repair, but the ball is against a part of the root outside the ground under repair. Is the player entitled to relief without penalty under Rule 25-1?

A. No. The margin of ground under repair extends vertically downwards, so part of a growing thing within ground under repair that extends beyond the area at or below ground level is not ground under repair.

Decision related to 25/10.5 and 25/10.7:
• 25-1a/1 Ball Outside Ground Under Repair Area But Tree Within Area Interferes with Swing.

25/10.9
Status of Non-Growing Plants Within Area of Ground Under Repair

Q. A bush, tree or other plant is rooted within an area of ground under repair, but there is a possibility that it may not be growing, e.g., because it is dead or dormant. The Definition of "Ground Under Repair" states in part: "All ground and any grass, bush, tree or other growing thing within the ground under repair is part of the ground under repair." Is the bush, tree or other plant considered ground under repair?

A. Yes. Provided the bush, tree or other plant is rooted within the ground under repair and thus fixed, it is part of the condition. It is often difficult to differentiate between plant life that is alive, dead or dormant.

25/11
Grass Cuttings

Grass cuttings are ground under repair only if they have been piled for removal – see Definition of "Ground Under Repair." If cuttings piled for removal interfere with a player's stance or swing, the player is entitled to relief under Rule 25-1b.

Grass cuttings are loose impediments (see Definition of "Loose Impediments"), whether or not they are piled for removal, and may be removed by the player – Rule 23-1.

25/12
Cracks in Earth

Q. Are cracks in the earth which occur in hot and dry conditions ground under repair? Do the Rules of Golf provide relief?

A. No. However, a player whose ball is in a large crack would be justified in requesting the Committee to declare the crack to be ground under repair, and the Committee would be justified in doing so.

Related Decision:
• 25/16 Rut Made by Tractor.

25/13
Bunker Totally Under Repair

If a bunker is being renovated and the Committee defines the entire bunker as ground under repair, the bunker loses its status as a hazard and is automatically classified as "through the green." Therefore, unless a Committee specifically states otherwise, Rule 25-1b(i) applies, not Rule 25-1b(ii).

Related Decisions:
- 25-1b/8 Player's Options When Bunker Completely Covered by Casual Water.
- 33-8/27 Local Rule Providing Relief Without Penalty from Bunker Filled with Casual Water.

25/14
Explanation of "Hole Made by Greenkeeper" in Definition of "Ground Under Repair"

Q. What constitutes a "hole made by a greenkeeper"?

A. A "hole made by a greenkeeper" is usually ground temporarily dug up in connection with course maintenance, such as a hole made in removing turf or a tree stump, laying pipelines, etc.

25/15
Aeration Holes

Q. Is an aeration hole a hole made by a greenkeeper within the meaning of that term in the Definition of "Ground Under Repair"?

A. No.

Related Decision:
- 23/12 Aeration Plugs.

25/16
Rut Made by Tractor

Q. Is a rut made by a tractor considered a hole made by a greenkeeper and thus ground under repair? If not, should the Committee declare such a rut to be ground under repair?

A. Such a rut is not a hole made by a greenkeeper. The Committee would be justified in declaring a deep rut to be ground under repair, but not a shallow indentation made by greenkeeping equipment.

Related Decision:
- 25/12 Cracks in Earth.

25/17
Sunken Hole Plug

Q. Is an old hole plug which has sunk below the level of the surface of the putting green a hole made by a greenkeeper and therefore ground under repair?

A. No. Rule 16-1c applies.

25/18
Hole of Removed Stake Defining Water Hazard

Q. A stake defining the margin of a water hazard is removed. Is the hole in which the stake was previously located a "hole made by a greenkeeper" and thus ground under repair?

A. Yes. However, such a hole is in a water hazard (see Definition of "Water Hazard") and a player would not be entitled to relief from the hole if his ball was in the water hazard – see first paragraph of Rule 25-1b.

Decisions related to 25/17 and 25/18:
• 16/7 Two Holes on Each Green of Nine-Hole Course.
• 16-1c/3 Old Hole Plug Sunk or Raised on Line of Putt.

Other Decisions related to Ground Under Repair: See "Ground Under Repair" in the Index.

HOLE MADE BY BURROWING ANIMAL, ETC.: DEFINITION

25/19 (Reserved)

25/19.5
Footprint of Burrowing Animal, Reptile or Bird

Q. Is the footprint of a burrowing animal, a reptile or a bird a "hole, cast or runway" within the meaning of these terms in the Definition of "Abnormal Ground Conditions"?

A. No. A footprint is an irregularity of surface from which there is no relief without penalty.

25/20 (Reserved)

25/21 (Reserved)

25/22 (Reserved)

25/23
Molehills

Molehills are casts made by a burrowing animal. Accordingly, a player having interference from a molehill, or the remains of a molehill, is entitled to relief under Rule 25-1b, provided, in the latter instance, the remains are still identifiable as a cast made by a burrowing animal.

Related Decisions:
• 23/5 Ant Hill.

• 23/11 Loose Soil from Cast of Hole Made by Burrowing Animal.

Other Decisions related to Hole Made by Burrowing Animals, etc.: See "Burrowing Animal, Reptile or Bird" in the Index.

ABNORMAL GROUND CONDITIONS: GENERAL

25-1/1
Ball in Casual Water Difficult to Retrieve

Q. It is known or virtually certain that a player's ball came to rest in a large puddle of casual water. A ball is visible in the casual water, but the player cannot retrieve it or identify it as his ball without unreasonable effort. The player abandons the ball and proceeds under Rule 25-1c, which provides relief for a ball lost in casual water. Was the player justified in doing so?

A. Yes. A player is not obliged to use unreasonable effort to retrieve a ball in casual water, for identification purposes.

However, if it would not take unreasonable effort to retrieve a ball in casual water, the player must retrieve it. If it turns out to be the player's ball and he elects to take relief, he must proceed under Rule 25-1b; otherwise, he must proceed under Rule 25-1c.

INTERFERENCE BY ABNORMAL GROUND CONDITIONS

25-1a/1
Ball Outside Ground Under Repair Area But Tree Within Area Interferes with Swing

Q. The margins of ground under repair do not extend vertically upwards. If the ball lies outside ground under repair and a tree rooted within the ground under repair interferes with a player's swing, but there is no interference with his stance, is the player entitled to relief?

A. Yes. The Definition of "Ground Under Repair" states: "All ground and any grass, bush, tree or other growing thing within the ground under repair is part of the ground under repair." Therefore, the player may take relief under Rule 25-1 as the tree within the ground under repair interferes with the area of his intended swing.

Related Decisions:
• 25/10.5 Ball in Tree in Ground Under Repair.
• 25/10.7 Status of Roots Outside Ground Under Repair Growing from Tree Inside Ground Under Repair.

25-1a/2
Casual Water on Putting Green Intervenes Between Ball Off Green and Hole

Q. A player's ball lies just off the putting green and casual water on the green intervenes between the ball and the hole. Is the player entitled to relief?

A. No. In addition, Rule 13-2 prohibits the player from removing casual water from his line of play.

Related Decision:
• 25-1b/10.5 Casual Water on Putting Green; Whether Player Entitled to Relief for Intervention If Ball Is on Green and Nearest Point of Relief Is Off Green.

RELIEF FROM ABNORMAL GROUND CONDITIONS: GENERAL

25-1b/1 (Reserved)

25-1b/2
Diagrams Illustrating Nearest Point of Relief

The diagrams illustrate the term "nearest point of relief" in Rule 25-1b(i) in the case of both a right-handed and left-handed player.

The "nearest point of relief" must be strictly interpreted. A player is not permitted to choose on which side of the ground under repair he will drop the ball, unless there are two equidistant "nearest points of relief." Even if one side of the ground under repair is fairway and the other is bushes, if the "nearest point of relief" is in the bushes then the player, if taking relief, must drop the ball within one club-length of that point, even though he may have to drop the ball in a virtually unplayable lie.

The same procedure applies under Rule 24-2b dealing with immovable obstructions.

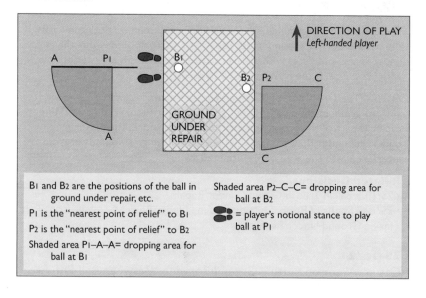

B1 and B2 are the positions of the ball in ground under repair, etc.

P1 is the "nearest point of relief" to B1

P2 is the "nearest point of relief" to B2

Shaded area P1–A–A= dropping area for ball at B1

Shaded area P2–C–C= dropping area for ball at B2

= player's notional stance to play ball at P1

B₁ = position of ball in ground under repair, etc.

P₁ = "nearest point of relief" to B₁

Shaded area P₁–A–A = area within which ball to be dropped, radius of one club-length from P₁, measured with any club

B₂ = position of ball in ground under repair, etc.

= notional stance required to play ball at P₂ with club with which player would expect to play the stroke

P₂ = "nearest point of relief" to B₂

Shaded area P₂–C–C = area within which ball to be dropped, radius of one club-length from P₂, measured with any club

Related Decisions:
• 24-2b/1 Determining "Nearest Point of Relief."
• 24-2b/3.7 Diagram Illustrating Player Unable to Determine Nearest Point of Relief.
• 33-8/19 Local Rule Permitting Relief on Specified Side of Paved Path.

25-1b/3
Improving Line of Play When Taking Relief from Abnormal Ground Condition

Q. In certain circumstances, in complying with Rule 25-1b, it is possible for a player incidentally to improve his line of play, e.g., avoid playing over a bunker or a tree. Is this permissible?

A. Yes. If a player's ball is in one of the conditions covered by Rule 25 and if, in taking relief in accordance with the procedure laid down in Rule 25-1b, his line of play is improved, this is his good fortune.

25-1b/4
Casual Water Covering Teeing Ground

Q. After several groups have played a particular hole, a player arrives at the teeing ground of that hole and the teeing ground has become completely covered with casual water. What is the procedure?

A. Even though the players may remove water from the teeing ground (Rule 13-2), the matter should be brought to the attention of the Committee. Rule 25-1 is not applicable since the player's ball is not in play

– see Definition of "Ball in Play."

In match play, the Committee may relocate the teeing ground.

In stroke play, if the conditions are such that removal of the casual water might be possible, the Committee should suspend play and attempt to remove the casual water. If the removal of the casual water is impossible, the Committee may (I) suspend play until the teeing ground is playable or cancel the round (Rule 33-2d) or (2) relocate the teeing ground if this could be done without giving any competitor an undue advantage or disadvantage.

Related Decisions:
• 33-2b/I Holes Relocated and/or Tee-Markers Moved During Stroke Play Round.
• 33-2d/2 Hole Surrounded by Casual Water.

25-1b/5
Explanation of "Maximum Available Relief" from Casual Water in Bunker

Q. In a bunker completely covered by casual water, is the place providing "maximum available relief" the spot which will provide the most relief for both lie and stance or just lie?

A. The term applies to both lie and stance. The spot providing "maximum available relief" might be such that the ball will be in shallower water than the player's feet after he takes his stance, or vice versa.

25-1b/6
Ball Dropped from Casual Water in Bunker at Point of Maximum Relief Rolls Elsewhere

Q. A player whose ball lies in a bunker completely covered by casual water drops his ball under Rule 25-1b(ii) at a spot where there is $\frac{1}{4}$ inch of casual water. This spot is the nearest spot providing maximum available relief. The ball rolls into a spot where there is about $\frac{1}{2}$ inch of casual water. What is the ruling?

A. In equity (Rule 1-4), and under the principle of Rule 20-2c(v), the player may re-drop and, if the ball so rolls again, place the ball where it first struck a part of the course when re-dropped.

25-1b/7
Ball to Be Dropped in Bunker Dropped Outside Bunker and Rolls into Bunker

Q. A player's ball lies in casual water in a bunker. The player elects to proceed under Rule 25-1b(ii)(a) and determines that the nearest point of relief in the bunker is close to the back of the bunker. The player drops his ball within one club-length of the nearest point of relief on a slope outside the bunker because he fears it will plug in the sand. The ball rolls down the slope and comes to rest in the bunker not nearer the hole than the nearest point of relief. Is the player subject to penalty?

A. Yes, unless he lifts the ball and proceeds correctly, as provided in Rule 20-6. Under Rule 25-1b(ii)(a), the player is required to drop the ball in the bunker. If the player, although proceeding under this Rule, drops the ball outside the bunker and plays it, he is in breach of Rule 25 and the penalty is loss of hole in match play or two strokes in stroke play.

25-1b/8
Player's Options When Bunker Completely Covered by Casual Water

Q. If a player's ball lies in a bunker completely covered by casual water, what are his options?

A. The player may play the ball as it lies or:
  (1) drop the ball in the bunker without penalty at the nearest point, not nearer the hole, where the depth of the casual water is least – Rule 25-1b(ii)(a); or
  (2) drop the ball behind the bunker under penalty of one stroke – Rule 25-1b(ii)(b); or
  (3) deem the ball unplayable and proceed in accordance with Rule 28.

Related Decisions:
• 25/13 Bunker Totally Under Repair.
• 33-8/27 Local Rule Providing Relief Without Penalty from Bunker Filled with Casual Water.

25-1b/9
Player Who Invokes First Option of Rule 25-1b(ii) Then Wishes to Invoke Second Option

Q. A player's ball is in a bunker completely covered by casual water. Under the first option of Rule 25-1b(ii), he drops the ball on ground in the bunker affording maximum available relief. He then decides he would have been better off to invoke the second option and drop behind the bunker. May he invoke the second option?

A. No. Rule 25-1b(ii) permits the player to proceed under one of two options. He is not entitled to invoke one option and then, if he does not like the result, invoke the other. Therefore, as Rule 25-1 no longer applies, the player must play the ball as it lies or proceed under the unplayable ball Rule, incurring the penalty stroke prescribed by that Rule.

Related Decisions:
• 24-2b/5 Player Who Lifts Ball Under First Option of Rule 24-2b(ii) Then Wishes to Proceed Under Second Option.

Other Decisions related to whether a player may change a selected relief option after taking further action: See "Casual Water: changing relief option" in the Index.

25-1b/10
Casual Water on Putting Green; Nearest Point of Relief Is Off Green

Q. A player whose ball is on a putting green is entitled to relief from casual water. However, the nearest position affording complete relief which is not nearer the hole or in a hazard is off the green in the rough. If the player opts to take relief, must he place the ball in the rough?

A. Yes. See Rule 25-1b(iii).

25-1b/10.5
Casual Water on Putting Green; Whether Player Entitled to Relief for Intervention If Ball Is on Green and Nearest Point of Relief Is Off Green

Q. In Diagram X, a player's ball lies at Point 1 in casual water on the putting green. In Diagram Y, a player's ball lies at Point 1 on the putting green with casual water intervening on his line of putt.

Under Rule 25-1b(iii), the player is not entitled to place the ball at Point 4, which is on the green, because Point 4 is farther from Point 1 than either Point 2 or Point 3, both of which are off the green. It would seem that Point 2 may be the correct point because there is no relief if a ball lies off the green and casual water on the green intervenes on the line of play. In taking relief must the player place the ball at Point 2 or Point 3?

A. Since, in both diagrams, the ball lies on the putting green, the player is entitled to relief with respect to the lie of the ball and intervention on his line. Accordingly, in either case the player must place the ball at Point 3, the nearest point which affords complete relief with respect to both situations.

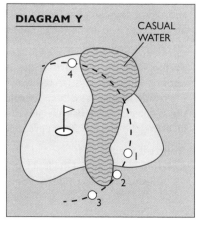

25-1b/11
Ball in Casual Water Within Ground Under Repair

Q. A ball lies in casual water within an area defined as ground under repair. May a player take relief from the casual water under Rule 25-1b, drop the ball in the ground under repair, and then either play the ball as it lies or take relief from the ground under repair under Rule 25-1b?

A. Yes.

25-1b/11.5
Ball in Casual Water Within Ground Under Repair; Whether Player Entitled to Take Relief from Both Conditions in Single Procedure

Q. The diagram shows a player's ball which lies in casual water, at Point X, within an area of ground under repair. May the player, in a single procedure, drop the ball at Point Y, the nearest point of relief from both conditions?

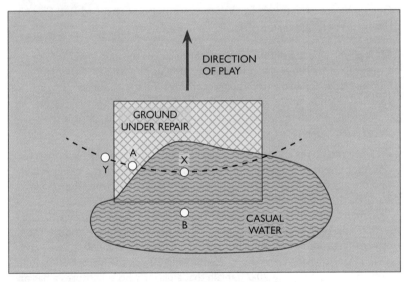

A. No. The player has the option of taking relief from each condition in separate stages but not from both at the same time.

The player may take relief from the casual water at Point A and then may take relief from the ground under repair.

Alternatively, he may take relief from ground under repair at Point B and then may take relief from the casual water.

Decisions related to 25-1b/11 and 25-1b/11.5:
- 1-4/8 Nearest Point of Relief from Cart Path Is in Casual Water; Nearest Point of Relief from Casual Water Is Back on Cart Path.

• 24-2b/10 Obstruction in Ground Under Repair Interferes with Player's Swing.
• 24-2b/19 Stroke at Ball Not Practicable Due to Interference by Immovable Obstruction and Casual Water.

25-1b/12
Casual Water Mistaken for Water Hazard; Original Ball Played Under Water Hazard Rule

Q. A player whose ball is in casual water mistakes the casual water for a water hazard. He retrieves his original ball, drops it 10 yards behind the casual water in accordance with the water hazard Rule and plays it. His error is then discovered. What is the ruling?

A. The player did not follow the procedure prescribed in Rule 25-1b(i) for dropping a ball from casual water; he dropped the ball in a wrong place. In match play, he loses the hole (Rule 20-7b). In stroke play, he incurs a penalty of two strokes (Rules 25-1b(i) and 20-7c).

25-1b/13
Casual Water Mistaken for Water Hazard; Substituted Ball Played Under Water Hazard Rule

Q. A player whose ball is in casual water mistakes the casual water for a water hazard. The player does not retrieve his original ball, although he could have done so without unreasonable effort – see Decision 25-1/1. Rather, he drops another ball ten yards behind the casual water in accordance with the water hazard Rule and plays it. His error is then discovered. What is the ruling?

A. Since the player could retrieve the ball without unreasonable effort, he was not permitted to substitute a ball in taking relief from the casual water. Additionally, as a result of proceeding under the water hazard Rule (Rule 26-1), he dropped the ball in a wrong place.

In match play, the player loses the hole (Rules 15-2, 25-1b(i) and 20-7b).

In stroke play, the player incurs a penalty of two strokes. Although the player substituted a ball when not permitted (Rule 15-2 and Rule 25-1) and played from a wrong place (Rules 25-1b(i) and 20-7c), the Exception to Rule 15-2 and Note 3 to Rule 20-7 explain that a player who substitutes a ball and plays from a wrong place incurs a total penalty of two strokes.

Related Decision:
• 34-3/6 Player Proceeds Under an Inapplicable Rule; Committee's Decision.

25-1b/14 (Reserved)

25-1b/14.5
Ball Deemed Unplayable Dropped in Ground Under Repair from Which Play Prohibited; Ball Then Dropped Under Ground Under Repair Rule

Q. A player deemed his ball unplayable. In proceeding under Rule 28b or 28c, the player dropped his ball in an area of ground under repair from which play was prohibited by Local Rule. He then took the mandatory relief under Rule 25-1b. Is this procedure permitted?

A. Yes.

Related Decision:
• 20-7/3 Whether Player May Drop Ball into Area from Which Play Prohibited.

25-1b/15
Measuring Across Ground Under Repair in Obtaining Relief

Q. A player obtaining relief from a narrow strip of ground under repair through the green determines his nearest point of relief (Point A) which is not in a hazard or on a putting green. Point A is on the right-hand side of the ground under repair. Within one club-length of Point A is a point (Point B) on the left side of the ground under repair which meets the requirements of Rule 25-1b(i). May the player drop his ball at Point B?

A. Yes. There is nothing in Rule 25-1b prohibiting measuring the one club-length across ground under repair in obtaining relief.

Related Decisions:
• 20/1 Club to Be Used in Measuring.
• 20/2 Borrowing Club for Measuring Purposes.
• 20-2b/2 Measuring Club-Lengths.

25-1b/16
Ball Equidistant from Two Points Which Meet Requirements of Ground Under Repair Rule

Q. Through the green, the player's ball lies in ground under repair and he opts for relief under Rule 25-1b(i). There is no single nearest point of relief. Rather, there are two such points equidistant from the spot where the ball lies. May the player drop within one club-length of either point?

A. Yes.

25-1b/17
Pine Needles Piled for Removal Interfere with Line of Play After Ball Dropped Away

Q. A player whose ball lies in pine needles piled for removal drops away under Rule 25-1b. The ball comes to rest in such a position that the pile of pine needles intervenes on his line of play. May the player remove the pine needles from his line of play?

A. Yes. Pine needles piled for removal are loose impediments or ground under repair. Initially, the player was entitled to remove the pine needles under Rule 23-1 (Loose Impediments) or drop away, as he did, under Rule 25-1b.

After the player dropped away a new situation existed and he was no longer entitled to invoke Rule 25-1b. However, he was not prohibited from removing the pine needles under Rule 23-1.

25-1b/18
Crawfish Mound Interferes with Stance or Swing

Q. When a crawfish digs a hole, it creates a sizable mound of mud. If such a mound interferes with a player's stance or swing, does he get relief under Rule 25-1b?

A. Yes, provided the player's ball does not lie in a water hazard – see first paragraph of Rule 25-1b. A crawfish is a burrowing animal.

Related Decision:
• 13-4/5 Touching Mound Made by Burrowing Animal with Backswing in Bunker.

25-1b/19
Ball Lies on Mound Made by Burrowing Animal; Impracticable to Make Stroke Due to Bush

Q. A player's ball lies under a bush and it is clearly impracticable for the player to make a stroke at it. However, the ball lies on a mound made by a burrowing animal. Is the player entitled to relief without penalty under Rule 25-1b?

A. Under the Exception to Rule 25-1b a player may not obtain relief from an abnormal ground condition if it is clearly impracticable for him to make a stroke due to interference by something other than such a condition. Therefore, in the circumstances described, the player is not entitled to relief. (Revised)

Related Decision:
• 24-2b/16 Obstruction Interferes But Ball Unplayable Due to Some Other Condition.

25-1b/20
Stance Interfered with by Burrowing Animal Hole; Impracticable to Make Stroke Because of Other Condition

Q. A player's ball is in an indentation at the base of a tree in such a position that it is clearly impracticable for him to make a stroke. Despite this, the player claims relief without penalty under Rule 25-1 because his stance for a stroke at the ball in the indentation would be on a burrowing animal hole. Is the player entitled to relief without penalty under Rule 25-1b?

A. Under the Exception to Rule 25-1b a player may not obtain relief from an abnormal ground condition if it is clearly impracticable for him to make a stroke due to interference by something other than such a condition. In the circumstances described above, the player's ball is unplayable as it lies in an indentation at the base of a tree. Therefore, the player is not entitled to relief under Rule 25-1 from the burrowing animal hole. (Revised)

25-1b/21
Cast of Burrowing Animal Interferes with Stroke Towards Green; Tree Prevents Such Stroke

Q. A player's ball is immediately behind a tree. A cast behind the ball made by a burrowing animal would interfere with the player's backswing for a stroke towards the green, but not with a sideways stroke, which is the only reasonable stroke. If the player says he intends to play towards the green into the tree, may he take relief without penalty under Rule 25-1b?

A. Under the Exception to Rule 25-1b a player may not obtain relief from an abnormal ground condition if interference from such a condition would only occur through the player using an unnecessarily abnormal direction of play. Therefore, in the circumstances described above, the player is not entitled to relief.

25-1b/22
Cast of Burrowing Animal Interferes with Sideways Stroke; When Relief Granted

Q. A ball is behind a tree so that a sideways stroke is the only reasonable stroke for the player. However, a cast made by a burrowing animal interferes with the backswing for a sideways stroke. Is the player entitled to relief under Rule 25-1b?

A. Yes, and if relief gets the player out from behind the tree, he is entitled to play towards the green.

Related Decisions:
• 24-2b/9.5 After Relief Taken from Obstruction for Stroke Towards Green, Obstruction Interferes with Stance for Necessary Sideways Stroke.
• 24-2b/17 Obstruction Interferes with Abnormal Stroke; Abnormal Stroke Reasonable in Circumstances.

25-1b/23
Ball Enters Burrowing Animal Hole Out of Bounds and Comes to Rest in Bounds

Q. The entrance to a burrowing animal hole is out of bounds, but most of the burrow is in bounds under the course. A ball enters the hole from out of bounds and comes to rest in bounds under ground classified as through the green. What is the procedure?

A. Under Rule 25-1b, the player may drop the ball, without penalty, within one club-length of the point on the ground directly above its position in the burrow. In such cases, vertical distance is disregarded in applying the Rules.

25-1b/24
Ball Enters Burrowing Animal Hole in Bounds and Comes to Rest Out of Bounds

Q. A player's ball entered a rabbit hole, the mouth of which was in bounds but only about a foot from a boundary fence. The rabbit hole sloped steeply down below the fence, so that the ball came to rest beyond the boundary line. What is the ruling?

A. Whether or not a ball is out of bounds depends on where it lies in relation to the boundary of the course and this must be measured vertically upwards or downwards – see Definition of "Out of Bounds."

In the case cited, the ball was lying out of bounds and Rule 27-1 applied. Relief could not be obtained under Rule 25-1, i.e., from a hole made by a burrowing animal.

25-1b/25
Ball Enters Burrowing Animal Hole in Bunker and Is Found Underneath Putting Green

Q. A ball enters a burrowing animal hole in a greenside bunker and is found underneath the putting green. As the ball is not in the bunker or on the putting green, is relief taken in accordance with Rule 25-1b(i), i.e., through the green?

A. Yes. The player would drop the ball without penalty on a part of the course through the green within one club-length of the nearest point to its position in the burrowing animal hole that avoids interference from the condition and is not in a hazard, not on a putting green and not nearer the hole.

Decisions related to 25-1b/23 through 25-1b/25:
• 24-2b/11 Ball Lying on Elevated Part of Immovable Obstruction.
• 28/11 Ball Unplayable in Tree and Player Opts to Drop Within Two Club-Lengths.
• 28/12 Ball Unplayable at Base of Cliff and Player Wishes to Drop Within Two Club-Lengths of Point Above Ball.

25-1b/25.5
Application of Exception to Rule 25-1b When Ball Lies Underground in Burrowing Animal Hole

Q. Through the green, a player's ball comes to rest underground in a hole made by a burrowing animal. A large bush is immediately next to and overhanging the entrance to the hole. Given the Exception to Rule 25-1b, is the player entitled to relief without penalty from the burrowing animal hole?

A. For the purpose of applying the Exception to Rule 25-1b, a ball lying underground in a burrowing animal hole is deemed to lie at the entrance to the hole. If the nature of the area surrounding the entrance to the hole is such that it is clearly impracticable for the player to make a stroke at a ball lying at any part of the entrance to the hole (e.g., because of the overhanging bush), the player is not entitled to relief without penalty under Rule 25-1b. Otherwise, the player is entitled to relief without penalty under Rule 25-1b.

If the ball lies in a hole, but is not underground, it is the position of the ball, rather than the entrance to the hole, which is relevant in determining whether the Exception to Rule 25-1b applies. (Revised)

25-1b/26
Player Unaware Ball in Water Hazard Takes Relief from Interference by Burrowing Animal Hole

Q. A player, unaware that his ball is in a dry water hazard, lifts and drops the ball under Rule 25-1b(i) believing he is entitled to relief from a hole made by a burrowing animal. After dropping the ball in the hazard, he discovers his mistake. What is the ruling?

A. As the player's ball lay in a water hazard, he was not entitled to relief without penalty from a hole made by a burrowing animal – see first paragraph of Rule 25-1b. However, as his ball lay in a water hazard, he is not precluded from taking relief under Rule 26.

As the player had dropped the ball under an inapplicable Rule, he may correct his error under Rule 20-6 by:
1. lifting the ball and replacing it where it originally lay in the water hazard, in which case he incurs a penalty of one stroke under Rule 18-2a – see Decision 18-2a/12; or
2. proceeding under Rule 26-1. He incurs a penalty of one stroke under Rule 26-1, but no additional penalty is incurred.

Related Decisions:
- 20-6/5 Player Drops Ball Under Rules and Then Wishes to Replace Ball in Original Position.
- 20-7/2 Ball Deemed Unplayable in Water Hazard Is Dropped in Hazard and Played.
- 27/17 Competitor Plays Out of Turn Other Than From Teeing Ground and Puts Another Ball into Play at Spot of Previous Stroke.

25-1c/1
Ball Not Found Is in Casual Water or Rough

Q. An area of casual water preceded by high rough is in a hollow not visible from the tee. A ball driven into this area is not found. The ball may be in the casual water or it may be in the high rough. May the player treat the ball as being in the casual water?

A. No. In such circumstances, it is neither known nor virtually certain that the ball is in casual water. The player may not proceed under Rule 25-1c.

25-1c/1.5
Clarification of Point Where Ball "Last Crossed Outermost Limits of" Abnormal Ground Condition

Q. In the diagram, a ball is lost in an area of casual water, having splashed at Point A. Point B represents the point where the ball crossed over the outermost limits of the casual water. For the purposes of proceeding under Rule 25-1c, where is the ball deemed to lie?

A. The ball is deemed to lie at Point B.

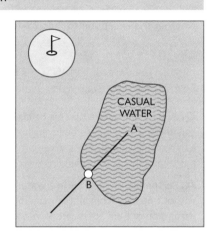

Related Decisions:
- 24-2b/12 Ball in Drainpipe Under Course; Entrance to Drainpipe Is Out of Bounds.
- 24-3b/1 Ball Lost in Underground Drainpipe.
- 25/10 Ball Lost in Tree in Ground Under Repair.

25-1c/2
Ball Dropped and Played Under Ground Under Repair Rule in Absence of Knowledge or Virtual Certainty That Original Ball in Ground Under Repair

Q. A player, after a search of less than one minute, considers that his ball is in ground under repair, although it is neither known nor virtually certain that this is the case. He drops a ball under Rule 25-1c and plays it. His original ball is then found beyond the ground under repair. What is the ruling?

A. When the player dropped and played another ball under Rule 25-1c, it became the ball in play and the original ball was lost.

In the absence of knowledge or virtual certainty that the ball was in ground under repair, the player was not permitted to proceed under Rule 25-1; therefore, he was considered to have put another ball into play under Rule 27-1. In playing the ball dropped under Rule 25-1c, the player played from a wrong place.

In match play, he incurred a penalty of loss of hole (Rule 20-7b).

In stroke play, he incurred the stroke-and-distance penalty prescribed by Rule 27-1 and an additional penalty of two strokes for a breach of that Rule (Rule 20-7c). If the breach was a serious one, he was subject to disqualification unless he corrected the error as provided in Rule 20-7c.

Related Decisions:
- 15/8 Ball Played Under Rule for Ball Lost in Ground Under Repair After Another Ball Played Under Stroke-and-Distance Procedure.
- 18-2a/8.5 Ball Played from Ground Under Repair Abandoned and Relief Taken Under Ground Under Repair Rule.
- 20-7c/4 Competitor's Ball Played by Fellow-Competitor; Competitor Substitutes Another Ball at Wrong Place, Plays It and Then Abandons It and Plays Out Original Ball From Right Place.
- 27-1/2.5 Lost Ball Treated as Moved by Outside Agency in Absence of Knowledge or Virtual Certainty to That Effect.
- 34-3/6 Player Proceeds Under an Inapplicable Rule; Committee's Decision.

25-1c/2.5
Ball Dropped Under Rule 25-1c with Knowledge or Virtual Certainty That Ball Is in Casual Water; Original Ball Then Found

Q. A player's ball is struck towards a large area of casual water. It is known or virtually certain that the player's ball is lost in the casual water and the player drops a ball under Rule 25-1c. Before he plays the dropped ball, his original ball is found within the five-minute search period. What is the ruling?

A. As it was known or virtually certain that the player's ball was in casual water when he put the substituted ball into play, that ball was correctly substituted and he may not play the original ball.

If the original ball was found in the casual water and this discovery affects the reference point for proceeding under Rule 25-1c, resulting in the substituted ball having been dropped in a wrong place, the player must correct the error under Rule 20-6 and drop a ball under Rule 25-1c with respect to the correct reference point. Otherwise, Rule 20-6 does not apply, and the player must continue play with the dropped ball. In either case, the player incurs no penalty.

In the unlikely event that the original ball was found outside the casual water, the player must continue play with the dropped ball without penalty.

The same answer would apply if it is known or virtually certain that the player's ball is in any other abnormal ground condition or an obstruction (Rule 24-3).

Related Decision:
• 26-1/3.5 Ball Dropped Under Water Hazard Rule with Knowledge or Virtual Certainty; Original Ball Then Found.

25-1c/3
Ball Played in Ground Under Repair Area Lost in Same Area

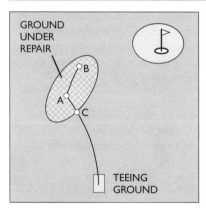

Q. In the diagram, a player's tee shot comes to rest at point A in a large area of ground under repair. He makes a stroke at his ball from within the ground under repair. He advances the ball to point B, which is still in the ground under repair, and the ball never crossed the outermost limits of the ground under repair. The ball cannot be found. What is the ruling?

A. The player may drop a ball outside the ground under repair area, without penalty, as provided in Rule 25-1c and make his third stroke. In this case, the reference point is where the ball last crossed the outermost limits of the ground under repair with the player's tee shot (point C).

Alternatively, the player may, under penalty of one stroke, drop a ball in the ground under repair as near as possible at the spot from which his original ball was last played (point A) under Rule 27-1 and make his fourth stroke. Having dropped a ball under Rule 27-1, if the player then has interference from the ground under repair, he may take relief under Rule 25-1b without further penalty.

Related Decision:
• 27-2c/1.5 Whether Provisional Ball Becomes Ball in Play If Original Ball Lost in Ground Under Repair.

EMBEDDED BALL

25-2/0.5
When Ball Embedded in Ground

For a ball to be considered embedded, it must be in its own pitch-mark with part of the ball below the level of the ground. However, the ball does not necessarily have to touch the soil to be considered embedded, e.g., grass or loose impediments may intervene between the ball and the soil.

25-2/1
Ball Bounces Out of Its Pitch-Mark and Spins Back into It

Q. A player's ball lands in soft ground in a closely mown area through the green, bounces out of its pitch-mark and then spins back into the pitch-mark. Is the player entitled to relief under Rule 25-2?

A. Yes. If a ball spins back into its pitch-mark, it is embedded in the pitch-mark.

25-2/2
Dropped Ball Embeds

Q. A player takes relief under an applicable Rule and drops a ball on a fairway. The ball embeds on impact. Is the player entitled to relief under Rule 25-2?

A. Yes.

25-2/2.5
Dropped Ball Embeds; Procedure If Ball Again Embeds When Re-Dropped

Q. According to Decision 25-2/2, if a ball dropped on a fairway embeds on impact, the player is entitled to relief under Rule 25-2. What is the proper procedure if a ball embeds each time it is dropped?

A. If a ball embeds when dropped and embeds again when re-dropped, the player may, in equity (Rule 1-4), place the ball as near as possible to the spot where it embedded when re-dropped, but not nearer the hole.

If the player drops the ball more than twice, the ball embeds each time and he then becomes aware that he was entitled to place the ball after the second drop, he may place the ball as near as possible to the spot where it embedded on the second drop.

25-2/3
Ball Returns to Pitch-Mark from Prior Stroke

Q. A player's ball embeds in its own pitch-mark in the ground in a closely-mown area through the green. After taking relief under Rule 25-2, the player makes a stroke. The ball climbs a slope but rolls back down it and into the same pitch-mark. Is the player entitled to relief without penalty?

A. No. A player is only entitled to relief under Rule 25-2 when his ball is embedded in a pitch-mark created by the last stroke he made – but see Decision 25-2/2 with regard to a dropped ball that embeds.

25-2/4
Ball Embedded in Ground Under Repair in Closely Mown Area

Q. A player's ball is embedded in ground under repair in a closely mown area through the green. May the player drop the ball within the ground under repair under Rule 25-2 (Embedded Ball) and then elect whether to play the ball as it lies or take relief from the ground under repair under Rule 25-1b?

A. Yes.

Related Decision:
• 25-1b/11.5 Ball in Casual Water Within Ground Under Repair; Whether Player Entitled to Take Relief from Both Conditions in Single Procedure.

25-2/5
Ball Embedded in Grass Bank or Face of Bunker

Q. Are grass banks or faces of bunkers considered to be "closely mown areas" under Rule 25-2 (Embedded Ball) and may relief be taken from them under that Rule?

A. No, not unless they are cut to fairway height or less.

Related Decisions:
• 13/4 Ball Completely Embedded in Lip of Bunker.
• 16/2 Ball Embedded in Side of Hole; All of Ball Below Lip of Hole.
• 16/3 Ball Embedded in Side of Hole; All of Ball Not Below Lip of Hole.
• 33-8/39 Local Rule for Bunker Faces Consisting of Stacked Turf.
• 33-8/39.5 Local Rule Deeming Partially Grass-Covered Wall of Bunker to Be Part of Bunker.

25-2/6
Ball on Steep Bank Driven Straight into Ground

Q. A player's ball lies on a steep bank in the fairway. He plays a stroke and drives the ball straight into the bank, i.e., the ball is never airborne. Is the player entitled to relief without penalty under Rule 25-2?

A. No. Under Rule 25-2, relief is provided if a ball is embedded in its own pitch-mark. The word "pitch-mark" implies that the ball has become airborne.

25-2/7 (Reserved)

25-2/8
Ball Embedded in Teeing Ground

Q. A player's tee shot strikes a tree and returns to the teeing ground, where the ball embeds in the ground. Is the player entitled to relief without penalty?

A. Yes. Although the Rules of Golf do not contemplate such a situation, in equity (Rule 1-4), the player is entitled to relief without penalty and must follow the procedure prescribed in Rule 25-2 for a ball that lies in a closely mown area through the green.

The same principle would apply to other relief situations that do not contemplate relief being required within the teeing ground (e.g., Rule 24-1b).

Other Decisions related to Rule 25-2: See "Embedded Ball" in the Index.

WRONG PUTTING GREEN

25-3/1
Status of Double Green Serving Hole Not Being Played

Q. One half of a U-shaped putting green serves as the 11th green and the other half serves as the 17th green. In play of the 17th hole, if a ball comes to rest on the part of the green serving the 11th hole, does Rule 25-3 (Wrong Putting Green) apply?

A. No, not unless the Committee divides the green by use of stakes or a line and declares one part to be the green of the 11th hole and the other part to be the green of the 17th hole. The Definition of "Putting Green" gives a Committee this right.

Other Decisions related to Rule 25-3: See "Wrong Putting Green" in the Index.

RULE 26

WATER HAZARDS (INCLUDING LATERAL WATER HAZARDS)

DEFINITIONS

All defined terms are in *italics* and are listed alphabetically in the Definitions section – see pages 6–16.

26-1. RELIEF FOR BALL IN WATER HAZARD

It is a question of fact whether a ball that has not been found after having been struck toward a *water hazard* is in the *hazard*. In the absence of knowledge or virtual certainty that a ball struck toward a *water hazard*, but not found, is in the *hazard*, the player must proceed under Rule 27-1.

If a ball is found in a *water hazard* or if it is known or virtually certain that a ball that has not been found is in the *water hazard* (whether the ball lies in water or not), the player may under penalty of one stroke:

a. Proceed under the stroke and distance provision of Rule 27-1 by playing a ball as nearly as possible at the spot from which the original ball was last played (see Rule 20-5); or

b. Drop a ball behind the *water hazard*, keeping the point at which the original ball last crossed the margin of the *water hazard* directly between the *hole* and the spot on which the ball is dropped, with no limit to how far behind the *water hazard* the ball may be dropped; or

c. As additional options available only if the ball last crossed the margin of a *lateral water hazard*, drop a ball outside the *water hazard* within two club-lengths of and not nearer the *hole* than (i) the point where the original ball last crossed the margin of the *water hazard* or (ii) a point on the opposite margin of the *water hazard* equidistant from the *hole*.

When proceeding under this Rule, the player may lift and clean his ball or *substitute* a ball.

(Prohibited actions when ball is in a hazard – see Rule 13-4)
(Ball moving in water in a water hazard – see Rule 14-6)

26-2. BALL PLAYED WITHIN WATER HAZARD
a. Ball Comes to Rest in Same or Another Water Hazard

If a ball played from within a *water hazard* comes to rest in the same or another *water hazard* after the *stroke*, the player may:

(i) proceed under Rule 26-1a. If, after dropping in the *hazard*, the player elects not to play the dropped ball, he may:

    (a) proceed under Rule 26-1b, or if applicable Rule 26-1c, adding the additional penalty of one stroke prescribed by the Rule and using as the reference point the point where the original ball last crossed the margin of this *hazard* before it came to rest in this *hazard*; or

    (b) add an additional penalty of one stroke and play a ball as nearly as possible at the spot from which the last *stroke* from outside a *water hazard* was made (see Rule 20-5); or

(ii) proceed under Rule 26-1b, or if applicable Rule 26-1c; or

(iii) under penalty of one stroke, play a ball as nearly as possible at the spot from which the last *stroke* from outside a *water hazard* was made (see Rule 20-5).

b. Ball Lost or Unplayable Outside Hazard or Out of Bounds

If a ball played from within a *water hazard* is *lost* or deemed unplayable outside the *hazard* or is *out of bounds*, the player may, after taking a penalty of one stroke under Rule 27-1 or 28a:

(i) play a ball as nearly as possible at the spot in the *hazard* from which the original ball was last played (see Rule 20-5); or

(ii) proceed under Rule 26-1b, or if applicable Rule 26-1c, adding the additional penalty of one stroke prescribed by the Rule and using as the reference point the point where the original ball last crossed the margin of the *hazard* before it came to rest in the *hazard*; or

(iii) add an additional penalty of one stroke and play a ball as nearly as possible at the spot from which the last *stroke* from outside a *water hazard* was made (see Rule 20-5).

Note 1: When proceeding under Rule 26-2b, the player is not required to drop a ball under Rule 27-1 or 28a. If he does drop a ball, he is not required to play it. He may alternatively proceed under Rule 26-2b(ii) or (iii).

Note 2: If a ball played from within a *water hazard* is deemed unplayable outside the *hazard*, nothing in Rule 26-2b precludes the player from proceeding under Rule 28b or c.

PENALTY FOR BREACH OF RULE:
Match play – Loss of hole; Stroke play – Two strokes.

WATER HAZARDS: GENERAL

26/1
When Ball Is in Water Hazard

Q. Is a ball in a water hazard when some part of the ball breaks the plane that extends vertically upwards from the margin of the hazard even though the ball does not touch the ground or grass inside the hazard?

A. Yes, since the Definition of "Water Hazard" provides that "the margin of a water hazard extends vertically upwards and downwards."

26/1.5
Status of Ball That Touches Water Hazard and Another Part of the Course

Q. A player's ball touches the line defining the margin of a water hazard but also touches another part of the course (e.g., a bunker or the putting green).

On which part of the course is the player's ball considered to lie?

A. The player's ball is considered to lie in the water hazard.

26/2
Ball Within Natural Margin of Water Hazard But Outside Stakes Defining Margin

Q. Stakes defining the margin of a water hazard were improperly installed. As a result, an area which clearly was part of the water hazard was outside the stakes and, thus, technically was outside the hazard. A player's ball came to rest in water in this area. The player claimed that, in view of the alignment of the stakes, his ball was in casual water through the green. Was the claim valid?

A. No. The Committee erred in not properly defining the margin of the hazard as required by Rule 33-2a, but a player is not entitled to take advantage of such an error. Since it was clear that the place where the player's ball lay was within the natural boundaries of the water hazard, the claim should not be upheld.

Related Decision:
• 33-2a/4 Where to Place Lines or Stakes Defining Margin of Water Hazard.

26/3
Unmarked Water Hazard

Q. An unmarked ditch on the left of a hole is in bounds, but the left-hand margin is out of bounds. Accordingly, it is impossible to drop behind the water hazard under Rule 26-1b. A player's ball comes to rest in the ditch. Is the player restricted to playing the ball as it lies or proceeding under Rule 26-1a?

A. It is the responsibility of the Committee to define accurately the margins of water hazards and lateral water hazards – see Rule 33-2a. However, if the Committee has not done so, the ditch is, by definition, a lateral water hazard and the player should be permitted to proceed under Rule 26-1c(i).

26/3.5
Lateral Water Hazard Defined as Water Hazard

Q. A body of water which is both in front of and to the right of a putting green is so large that it is impossible to drop behind the water hazard as required by Rule 26-1b. May the Committee define the hazard or parts of the hazard as a water hazard even though it meets the Definition of a "Lateral Water Hazard"?

A. Yes – see Note 3 to the Definition of "Lateral Water Hazard." However, this should only be done when a Committee deems it necessary to preserve the integrity of the hole. In such cases the establishment of a dropping zone as an additional option under the water hazard Rule (Rule 26-1) may be justified.

26/4 (Reserved)

26/5 (Reserved)

26/6
Ball Assumed to Be in Water Hazard Found Outside Hazard After Another Ball Played Under Stroke-and-Distance Procedure

Q. A player assumes his original ball to be in a water hazard, despite the absence of knowledge or virtual certainty to that effect. Using the option in Rule 26-1a, he plays another ball at the spot from which the original ball was played. He then finds his original ball outside the hazard. What is the ruling?

A. The original ball is lost and the other ball is in play under penalty of stroke and distance – see Rule 27-1a and the Definition of "Lost Ball." (Revised)

Related Decision:
- 15/11 Wrong Ball Hit Out of Bounds; Another Ball Played Under Rule 27-1; Original Ball Then Found Nearby.

BALL IN WATER HAZARD

26-1/1
Meaning of "Known or Virtually Certain"

When a ball has been struck towards a water hazard and cannot be found, a player may not assume that his ball is in the water hazard simply because there is a possibility that the ball may be in the water hazard. In order to proceed under Rule 26-1, it must be "known or virtually certain" that the ball is in the water hazard. In the absence of "knowledge or virtual certainty" that it lies in a water hazard, a ball that cannot be found must be considered lost somewhere other than in a water hazard and the player must proceed under Rule 27-1.

When a player's ball cannot be found, "knowledge" may be gained that his ball is in a water hazard in a number of ways. The player or his caddie or other members of his match or group may actually observe the ball disappear into the water hazard. Evidence provided by other reliable witnesses may also establish that the ball is in the water hazard. Such evidence could come from a referee, an observer, spectators or other outside agencies. It is important that all readily accessible information be considered because, for example, the mere fact that a ball has splashed in a water hazard would not always provide "knowledge" that the ball is in the water hazard, as there are instances when a ball may skip out of, and come to rest outside, the hazard.

In the absence of "knowledge" that the ball is in the water hazard, Rule 26-1 requires there to be "virtual certainty" that the player's ball is in the water hazard in order to proceed under this Rule. Unlike "knowledge," "virtual certainty" implies some small degree of doubt about the actual location of a ball that has not been found. However, "virtual certainty" also means that, although the ball has not been found, when all readily available information is considered, the conclusion that there is nowhere that the ball could be except in the water hazard would be justified.

In determining whether "virtual certainty" exists, some of the relevant factors in the area of the water hazard to be considered include topography, turf conditions, grass heights, visibility, weather conditions and the proximity of trees, bushes and abnormal ground conditions.

The same principles would apply for a ball that may have been moved by an outside agency (Rule 18-1) or a ball that has not been found and may be in an obstruction (Rule 24-3) or an abnormal ground condition (Rule 25-1c). (Revised)

26-1/1.3
When is it Necessary to Go Forward to Establish "Virtual Certainty"?

Q. Rule 26-1 requires there to be "knowledge or virtual certainty" before proceeding under the provisions of the Rule. In the absence of "knowledge" that a ball is in a water hazard, is it possible to establish the existence of "virtual certainty" without going forward to assess the physical conditions around the water hazard?

A. In the majority of cases, in order for it to be reasonably concluded that the ball does not lie anywhere outside the water hazard, it is necessary to go forward to assess the physical conditions around the hazard. However, there are situations where there will be sufficient evidence that the ball is in the hazard to establish "virtual certainty" without anyone having to go forward to review the physical conditions around the hazard.

In the following examples, the conclusion that it is "virtually certain" that the ball is in the water hazard would be justified without anyone going forward to the water hazard so that the player would be entitled to proceed under the provisions of Rule 26-1.

- It is a clear day, with good visibility. A player's ball is struck towards a water hazard, which has closely mown grass extending right up to its margin. The ball is observed to fall out of sight as it approaches the water hazard but is not seen actually to enter it. From a distance, it can be seen that there is no golf ball lying on the closely mown grass outside the hazard and, from both prior experience and a reasonable evaluation of current course conditions, it is known that the contour of the ground surrounding the hazard causes balls to enter the hazard. In such circumstances, it is reasonable for the conclusion to be reached from a distance that the ball must be in the water hazard.
- It is a clear day, with good visibility. A player's ball is struck towards an island putting green. The margin of the water hazard coincides with the apron of the putting green. Both from prior experience and a reasonable evaluation of current course conditions, it is understood that any ball that comes to rest on the apron or the putting green will be visible from where the stroke was made. In this instance, the

ball is observed to land on the putting green and roll out of sight. It is therefore concluded that the ball has carried over the green and into the water hazard. The player drops a ball in a dropping zone in front of the hazard, which has been provided by the Committee as an additional option to those under Rule 26-1, and plays to the green. When he arrives at the putting green, he discovers his original ball on the back apron of the green lying on a sunken sprinkler head. Nonetheless, in the circumstances, it was reasonable for the conclusion to be reached from where the ball was last played that the ball must be in the water hazard.

In the following example, it cannot be established that there is "virtual certainty" that the ball is in the water hazard without going forward to assess the area surrounding the hazard.

- It is a clear day, with good visibility. A player's ball is struck towards a water hazard, which has closely mown grass extending right up to its margin. The ball is observed travelling in the direction of the water hazard and it is known from prior experience that, with normal turf conditions, the ball would undoubtedly go into the water hazard. However, on this day, the fairways are wet and therefore it is possible that the ball could have embedded in the fairway and thus might not be in the water hazard. (New)

Decision related to 26-1/1 and 26-1/1.3:
- 27-2a/3 Play of Provisional Ball in Absence of Reasonable Possibility Original Ball Is Lost or Out of Bounds.

26-1/1.5
Meaning of "Behind" in Rule 26-1

Q. With regard to the diagram, a player makes a stroke from the tee and his ball comes to rest in the water hazard at Point A, having last crossed the margin of the hazard at Point B. The player wishes to proceed under Rule 26-1b, which requires that the player drop a ball behind the water hazard, keeping the point at which the original ball last crossed the margin of the water hazard directly between the hole and the spot on which the ball is dropped. May the player drop a ball on dotted line Y–Y?

A. Yes. The reference to "behind" in Rule 26-1b means that the ball must be dropped outside the hazard behind the point where the ball last crossed the margin of the water hazard. Therefore, the player may drop a ball on either dotted line X–X or dotted line Y–Y.

26-1/2
Player Proceeding Under Water Hazard Rule Drops Ball in Another Hazard

Q. A player's ball lies in a water hazard. In applying Rule 26-1b, the player drops a ball in a bunker or another water hazard. Is this permissible?

A. Yes.

Related Decision:
• 28/4.5 Ball Deemed Unplayable Through the Green Dropped in Water Hazard; Player Elects Not to Play Ball and Wishes to Proceed Under the Water Hazard Rule.

26-1/3
Ball Played Under Water Hazard Rule; Original Ball Then Found Outside Hazard

Q. A player believed his original ball had come to rest in a water hazard. He searched for about a minute but did not find his ball. He therefore dropped another ball behind the hazard under Rule 26-1 and played it. He then found his original ball outside the hazard within five minutes of having begun to search for it. What is the ruling?

A. When the player dropped and played another ball behind the hazard, it became the ball in play and the original ball was lost.

If it was known or virtually certain that the original ball was in the water hazard, the player was entitled to invoke Rule 26-1. In the absence of knowledge or virtual certainty that the original ball was in the water hazard, the player was required to put another ball into play under Rule 27-1. In playing the ball dropped under Rule 26-1, the player played from a wrong place.

In match play, he incurred a penalty of loss of hole (Rule 20-7b).

In stroke play, he incurred the stroke-and-distance penalty prescribed by Rule 27-1 and an additional penalty of two strokes for a breach of that Rule (Rule 20-7c). If the breach was a serious one, he was subject to disqualification unless he corrected the error as provided in Rule 20-7c.

26-1/3.5
Ball Dropped Under Water Hazard Rule with Knowledge or Virtual Certainty; Original Ball Then Found

Q. A player's ball is struck towards a water hazard. It is known or virtually certain that the player's ball is in the water hazard, and he drops a ball under Rule 26-1b. Before he plays the dropped ball, his original ball is found within the five-minute search period. What is the ruling?

A. As it was known or virtually certain that the ball was in the water hazard when the player put the substituted ball into play, that ball was correctly substituted and he may not play the original ball.

If the original ball was found in the water hazard and this discovery affects the reference point for proceeding under Rule 26-1b, resulting in the substituted ball having been dropped in a wrong place, the player must correct the error under Rule 20-6. The player must proceed in accordance with any of the applicable options under Rule 26-1 with respect to the correct reference point (see Decisions 20-6/2 and 26-1/16). Otherwise, Rule 20-6 does not apply and the player must continue play with the dropped ball. In either case, the player incurs a penalty of one stroke under Rule 26-1.

In the unlikely event that the original ball was found outside the water hazard, the player must continue with the dropped ball under penalty of one stroke (Rule 26-1).

Related Decision:
• 25-1c/2.5 Ball Dropped Under Rule 25-1c with Knowledge or Virtual Certainty That Ball Is In Casual Water; Original Ball Then Found.

26-1/3.7
Ball Dropped Under Water Hazard Rule Without It Being Known or Virtually Certain Ball in Hazard; Original Ball Then Found

Q. A player's ball is struck towards a water hazard and is not found. It is neither known nor virtually certain that the player's ball is in the water hazard, but he drops a ball under Rule 26-1b. Before he plays the dropped ball, his original ball is found within the five-minute search period. What is the ruling?

A. It was neither known nor virtually certain that the player's ball was in the water hazard when he put the substituted ball into play, and, therefore, that ball was incorrectly substituted under an inapplicable Rule.

The player must correct his error under Rule 20-6 by abandoning the substituted ball and continuing play with the original ball. If the original ball was found inside the water hazard, the player may proceed under Rule 26-1.

If the player failed to correct his improper procedure and played the dropped ball, he has proceeded under an inapplicable Rule and incurred a penalty (see Decision 34-3/6). The ruling would be that the player has proceeded under Rule 27-1 (the only Rule that applied to his situation), incurring the one-stroke penalty under that Rule. Additionally, as he played the ball from a wrong place (i.e., a place not permitted by Rule 27-1), he incurred the general penalty, loss of hole in match play or two strokes in stroke play, for a breach of Rule 27-1. In stroke play, the Committee must determine whether the player committed a serious breach when he played from the wrong place (Rule 20-7c).

26-1/4
Ball Played Under Water Hazard Rule Without Knowledge or Virtual Certainty That Original Ball in Hazard; Original Ball Then Found in Hazard

Q. A player's ball carried over a water hazard into some trees. It could not be determined whether the ball bounced back into the hazard or came to rest in the trees. Therefore, it was neither known nor virtually certain that the ball was in the hazard.

The player did not search for his original ball. He assumed that it was in the hazard, dropped a ball behind the hazard at a spot that conformed to Rule 26-1b and played that ball onto the green. As he was walking to the green, he found his original ball in the hazard. What is the ruling?

A. The first paragraph of Rule 26-1 states in part: "In the absence of knowledge or virtual certainty that a ball struck towards a water hazard, but not found, is in the hazard, the player must proceed under Rule 27-1." Therefore, the player was not entitled to assume that his original ball was in the hazard and the fact that it was subsequently found in the hazard is irrelevant. When the player dropped and played another ball behind the hazard, it became the ball in play and the original ball was lost. The player was required to proceed under Rule 27-1. In playing the ball dropped under Rule 26-1b, he played from a wrong place.

In match play, he incurred a penalty of loss of hole (Rule 20-7b).

In stroke play, he incurred the stroke-and-distance penalty prescribed by Rule 27-1 and an additional penalty of two strokes for a breach of that Rule (Rule 20-7c). If the breach was a serious one, he was subject to disqualification unless he corrected the error as provided in Rule 20-7c. (Revised)

26-1/5
Ball Dropped and Played Under Water Hazard Rule; Original Ball Then Found in Hazard and Holed Out as Second Ball

Q. In stroke play, a competitor, unable to find his ball in a water hazard, drops another ball behind the hazard under Rule 26-1 and plays it. He then finds his original ball in the hazard. Not being sure of his rights, he holes out with both balls under Rule 3-3, opting to score with the original ball. What is the ruling?

A. When the competitor dropped and played the ball behind the hazard, that ball became the ball in play (see Definition of "Ball in Play"). The score with that ball was the competitor's score for the hole. The score with the original ball could not count because that ball was no longer the ball in play. However, the competitor incurs no penalty for holing out with the original ball.

Related Decision:
• 3-3/6 Competitor Plays Original Ball After Doubtful Situation Has Arisen and Then Invokes Rule 3-3.

26-1/6
Ball Played Back into Water Hazard from Putting Green Side of Hazard

Q. A player plays his second shot over a water hazard into a bunker behind the green. He skulls his third shot and the ball comes to rest in the water hazard. The ball is not playable. What are the player's options?

A. The player may, under penalty of one stroke:

    (a) drop a ball behind the water hazard, keeping the point at which the original ball last crossed the hazard margin between the hole and the spot on which the ball is dropped – Rule 26-1b. This procedure would probably make it necessary for the player to return to the tee side of the hazard and play over the hazard again; or

    (b) drop a ball in the bunker at the spot where his second shot came to rest – Rule 26-1a.

26-1/7
Ball Moved Out of Bounds by Flow of Water in Water Hazard

Q. The flow of water in a water hazard carries a ball out of bounds. May the player invoke Rule 26-1?

A. No. Since the ball lies out of bounds, the player must proceed under Rule 27-1. Water is not an outside agency – see Definition of "Outside Agency" – and thus the ball would not be replaced under Rule 18-1.

In a situation where it is likely that a ball will be carried out of bounds by the flow of water in a water hazard, it is suggested that a screen be installed to prevent such an occurrence.

26-1/8
Ball Moved into Bounds by Flow of Water in Lateral Water Hazard

Q. With regard to the diagram, a player's ball lands in a river out of bounds at Point A and the flow of the water carries the ball into bounds to Point B. That part of the river which is in bounds is defined as a lateral water hazard. May the player invoke Rule 26-1?

A. Yes. The ball lies on the course in a lateral water hazard and it last crossed the margin of the hazard at Point C. Therefore, in taking relief in accordance with Rule 26-1b or 26-1c, Point C is the reference point. As it is not possible to proceed under Rules 26-1b and 26-1c(i), it is likely that the player will proceed under Rule 26-1c(ii) by dropping a ball within two club-lengths of and not nearer the hole than Point D.

Alternatively, the player may proceed under Rule 26-1a, or play the ball as it lies in the river.

26-1/9
Caddie Lifts Ball in Water Hazard Without Player's Authority

Q. A player's ball lying in a water hazard is lifted by the player's caddie without the player's authority. What is the ruling?

A. There is no penalty under Rule 18-2a if there was no doubt or it was reasonable to assume from the player's actions or statements that he would make his next stroke from outside the water hazard.

In the absence of such circumstances, the player incurred a one-stroke penalty under Rule 18-2a and may either replace the ball as required by Rule 18-2a or proceed under Rule 26-1 and incur an additional one-stroke penalty under that Rule.

In such cases, any doubt should be resolved against the player.

Related Decisions:
- 2-4/3.5 Stroke Conceded by Caddie.
- 18-2a/14 Caddie on Own Initiative Lifts Ball for Identification.
- 18-2a/15 Caddie on Own Initiative Lifts Ball Considering It Unplayable.
- 34-3/3.5 Player Lifts Ball Without Authority Due to Misunderstanding Referee's Instructions.

26-1/10
Placing Ball on Bank of Water Hazard Instead of Dropping to Prevent Ball Rolling into Water

Q. A player's ball lies in a playable position on the bank of a water hazard. The player hits the ball out of bounds. If he proceeds under Rule 27-1 and drops a ball on the bank as nearly as possible at the spot from which the original ball was played, the ball will be likely to roll into deep water. May he place the ball in such circumstances, rather than drop it?

A. No. However, the player is not obliged to drop a ball within the hazard in accordance with Rule 27-1. He may take the penalty stroke provided in Rule 27-1 and then, under an additional penalty of one stroke, put a ball into play outside the hazard in accordance with either Rule 26-2b(ii) or 26-2b(iii).

26-1/11
Water Hazard Treated as Lateral Water Hazard

Q. In stroke play, a competitor played a stroke over a water hazard and the ball spun back into the hazard. The competitor, in error, treated the hazard as a lateral water hazard and dropped the ball under Rule 26-1c(i) within two club-lengths of where it crossed the hazard margin when it spun back into the hazard. He played the ball onto the green and then his procedure was questioned. What is the ruling?

A. The competitor incurred a penalty of one stroke under Rule 26-1. Furthermore, he was guilty of a serious breach of that Rule. He must, under an additional penalty of two strokes, rectify the error as provided in the second paragraph of Rule 20-7c or be disqualified.

26-1/12
Hazard Marked as Water Hazard Where Ball Last Crosses Margin and as Lateral Hazard Where Ball Comes to Rest

Q. A body of water is defined in part as a water hazard and in part as a lateral water hazard. A ball last crosses the hazard margin at a spot where it is marked as a water hazard but it comes to rest in that part of the hazard marked as a lateral water hazard. In addition to playing the ball as it lies, what are the player's options?

A. Since the ball last crossed the margin of the hazard where it is defined as a water hazard, the options in Rule 26-1c are not available. Thus, the player is limited to the options in Rules 26-1a and 26-1b.

26-1/13
Opposite Side of Lateral Water Hazard Defined as Water Hazard

Q. A player hit a ball into a lateral water hazard. The player wanted to drop within two club-lengths of a point on the opposite margin of the hazard equidistant from the hole, as permitted under Rule 26-1c. However, the opposite margin was marked as a water hazard. Was the player entitled to drop a ball within two club-lengths of the point in question on the opposite margin?

A. Yes. In such a case, relief is determined according to the status of the hazard at the point where the ball last crossed the hazard margin.

26-1/14
Clarification of "Opposite Margin" in Rule 26-1c(ii)

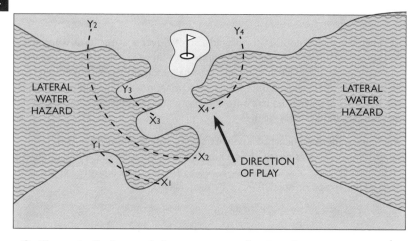

Q. Please clarify the words "opposite margin" in Rule 26-1c. With regard to the diagram, "X1" indicates where a ball in the hazard last crossed the hazard margin. May the player drop a ball within two club-lengths of "Y1"? And, may a player whose ball last crossed the hazard margin at "X2" drop a ball within two club-lengths of "Y2," and so on?

A. With respect to "X1," "Y1" is "a point on the opposite margin of the water hazard equidistant from the hole." Accordingly, the player would be entitled to drop a ball within two club-lengths of "Y1."

The same applies in the cases of "X3"–"Y3" and "X4"–"Y4," but not in the case of "X2"–"Y2." A "point on the opposite margin" is a point across the hazard from "the point where the original ball last crossed the margin of the hazard." "Y2" is not across the hazard from "X2" because an imaginary straight line from "X2" to "Y2" crosses land outside the hazard.

26-1/15
Procedures for Relief from Lateral Water Hazard

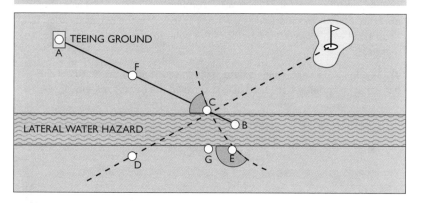

In the diagram, a player has played a ball from the teeing ground (Point A) into the lateral water hazard at Point B. It last crossed the margin of the hazard at Point C. He may play the ball as it lies or, under penalty of one stroke:

(a) play another ball from the teeing ground – Rule 26-1a;

(b) drop a ball anywhere on the far side of the hazard on the dotted line from the hole through Point C, e.g., Point D – Rule 26-1b;

(c) drop a ball in the shaded area on the near side of the hazard which is all ground within two club-lengths of Point C, but not nearer the hole than Point C – Rule 26-1c(i); or

(d) drop a ball in the shaded area on the far side of the hazard which is all ground within two club-lengths of Point E, but not nearer the hole than Point E – Rule 26-1c(ii).

The player may not drop a ball on the so-called "line-of-flight" at Point F or anywhere else on the line the ball followed from A to B, except in the shaded area on the near side. Nor may he drop a ball within two club-lengths of Point G, the point on the far side of the hazard directly opposite Point C.

26-1/16
Point Where Ball Last Crossed Margin of Lateral Water Hazard Determined and Ball Dropped; Point Then Proves to Be Wrong Point

Q. In stroke play, A's ball goes into a lateral water hazard and is not found. A uses his best judgment in determining the point where the ball last crossed the hazard margin. B, A's marker and a fellow-competitor, agrees with that judgment and A drops a ball in accordance with Rule 26-1c, using the agreed point on the margin as the reference point. Before A makes his next stroke, C, another fellow-competitor, says that A's ball last crossed the hazard margin 20 yards beyond the point judged by A to be the point where the ball last crossed. A's ball is then found where C said it would be. What is the ruling?

A. When A dropped the ball under Rule 26-1, it was known or virtually certain that his original ball lay in the lateral water hazard. Therefore, Rule 26-1 was the applicable Rule and the player proceeded correctly in that he was permitted to put a ball into play under that Rule. However, as he dropped his ball in a wrong place, A must correct the error under Rule 20-6. He must proceed in accordance with any of the applicable options under Rule 26-1 with respect to the correct reference point (see Decision 20-6/2). A is precluded from playing the original ball from the hazard.

Other Decisions related to whether a player may change a selected relief option after taking further action: See "Ball Dropped or Re-Dropped: changing relief option" in the Index.

26-1/17
Point Where Ball Last Crossed Margin of Lateral Water Hazard Determined and Ball Dropped and Played; Point Then Proves to Be Wrong Point

Q. In the circumstances described in Decision 26-1/16, what is the ruling if A, having dropped a ball in a wrong place, plays it before his error is discovered?

A. A must continue play with the ball played from a wrong place, without penalty. Applying a penalty under Rule 26-1 for playing from a wrong place (see Rule 20-7) is not appropriate. Otherwise, a competitor would risk incurring a penalty every time he makes an honest judgment as to the point where his ball last crosses a water-hazard margin and that judgment subsequently proves incorrect.

26-1/18
Impossible to Drop Not Nearer Hole Than Point Where Ball Last Crossed Margin of Lateral Water Hazard

Q. When a ball last crosses the margin of a lateral water hazard at the side of a putting green, it is sometimes impossible to drop a ball within two club-lengths of the point where the ball last crossed the hazard margin without dropping nearer the hole than that point. What is the procedure in such a case?

A. It is usually possible to drop a ball on the near side of a lateral water hazard and conform with Rule 26-1c(i) by dropping the ball close to the hazard margin. Where this is impossible, the player must proceed under one of the other options provided in Rule 26-1.

26-1/19
Permissible Dropping Area Under Lateral Water Hazard Rule So Narrow Player Has Difficulty Dropping Within It

When a ball comes to rest in a lateral water hazard and relief is taken under Rule 26-1c(i), the ball must be dropped (1) outside the hazard and (2) not nearer the hole than the point where the ball last crossed the margin of the hazard (Point X). In some circumstances, the permissible dropping area may be very narrow. If the ball, when dropped, first strikes a part of the course in the hazard or nearer the hole than Point X, the drop does not count for the purpose of determining when the ball must be placed under Rule 20-2c. A ball so dropped has been dropped in a wrong place and the player must correct the error under Rule 20-6 by proceeding in accordance with any of his options under Rule 26-1 (see Decision 20-6/2). Only if the ball has been dropped in the permissible dropping area twice and, each time, rolls and comes to rest in a position listed under Rule 20-2c (e.g., into the hazard or nearer the hole than Point X) may it be placed as permitted by Rule 20-2c. If a ball is placed other than as described, and is played, a breach of Rule 26-1c occurs.

Stakes and lines defining the margins of water hazards should be placed along the natural limits of the hazard. However, minor deviation to alleviate such a dropping problem would be appropriate. Alternatively, a dropping zone could be established.

Decisions related to 26-1/18 and 26-1/19:
• 26/2 Ball Within Natural Margin of Water Hazard But Outside Stakes Defining Margin.
• 33-2a/4 Where to Place Lines or Stakes Defining Margin of Water Hazard.
• 33-2a/9 Part of Lateral Water Hazard Where Impossible to Drop Not Nearer Hole.

26-1/20
Allowing Drop Opposite Spot Where Ball Comes to Rest in Lateral Water Hazard

Q. A lateral water hazard is so situated that it is difficult to determine where a ball lying in the hazard last crossed the hazard margin. Would it be permissible to make a Local Rule to the effect that a player whose ball lies in this hazard may drop a ball, under penalty of one stroke, within two club-lengths of the point on the hazard margin opposite where the original ball came to rest in the hazard, instead of within two club-lengths of where the original ball last crossed the hazard margin, i.e., the Local Rule would modify Rule 26-1c.

A. No. Such modification of Rule 26-1c is not authorized. Moreover, the suggested Local Rule would be inoperable if the player's ball was lost in the hazard.

26-1/21
Example of Serious Breach of Lateral Water Hazard Rule

Q. In stroke play, A and B drive into a lateral water hazard. They determine where their original balls last crossed the hazard margin and elect to proceed under Rule 26-1c, taking a penalty of one stroke. A drops a ball slightly closer to the hole than the spot where his ball last crossed the hazard margin; B drops a ball 50 yards closer to the hole. A and B make their next strokes. What is the ruling?

A. A incurs an additional penalty of two strokes for a breach of Rule 26-1c and must play out the hole with the ball dropped in a wrong place and played – see Rule 20-7c.

B is guilty of a serious breach of Rule 26-1c. He incurs an additional penalty of two strokes and, before playing from the next teeing ground, he must drop another ball in accordance with any of his options under Rule 26-1 (see Decision 20-6/2) and play out the hole; otherwise B is disqualified – see Rule 20-7c.

26-2/1
Explanation of Options Under Rules 26-2a and 26-2b

Regarding the diagram, A and B play from the tee. A's ball comes to rest in the water hazard at Point A. B's ball comes to rest at Point B. Both A and B elect to play from the hazard. A fails to get out of the hazard. He plays to Point X, and his ball is not playable. B plays to Point Y, which is out of bounds.

Under penalty of one stroke, A may:

(a) drop a ball at Point A and play again from there, playing 4 (Rule 26-2a(i)); or

(b) drop a ball anywhere on dotted line E–E and play from there, playing 4 (Rule 26-2a(ii)); or

(c) play another ball from the tee, playing 4 (Rule 26-2a(iii)).

If A drops a ball at Point A and the ball comes to rest at a spot from which he judges he cannot play, he may, adding an additional penalty of one stroke, either drop a ball anywhere on the dotted line E–E or play another ball from the tee, playing 5.

B, after taking the penalty stroke prescribed in Rule 27-1, may drop a ball at Point B and play again from there, playing 4 (Rule 26-2b(i)).

Alternatively, B, after taking the penalty stroke prescribed in Rule 27-1, may drop a ball at Point B and elect not to play that ball or elect not to drop a ball at Point B. In either case, he shall then:

(a) under an additional penalty of one stroke, drop a ball anywhere on dotted line F–F and play from there, playing 5 (Rule 26-2b(ii)); or

(b) under an additional penalty of one stroke, play another ball from the tee, playing 5 (Rule 26-2b(iii)).

26-2/2
Ball Played from Within Hazard Comes to Rest in Same Hazard After Exiting Hazard

Q. In the diagram, a player has played a ball from Point A (the teeing ground) into the lateral water hazard at Point B. The ball last crossed the margin of the hazard at Point C.

The player elects to play the ball from the hazard and he succeeds in getting his ball out of the hazard, but it re-enters the hazard at Point E. The ball comes to rest at Point D and it is not playable. What are the player's options?

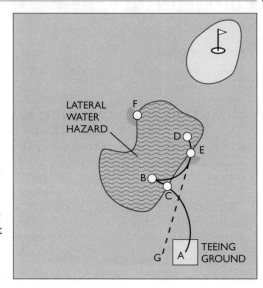

A. The player may under penalty of one stroke:
  (a) drop a ball at Point B and play again from there, playing 4 (Rule 26-2a(i)); or
  (b) drop a ball anywhere on dotted line E–G and play from there, playing 4 (Rule 26-2a(ii)); or
  (c) drop a ball within two club-lengths of and not nearer the hole than Point E, playing 4 (Rule 26-2a(ii)); or
  (d) drop a ball within two club-lengths of and not nearer the hole than Point F, playing 4 (Rule 26-2a(ii)); or
  (e) play another ball from Point A (the teeing ground), playing 4 (Rule 26-2a(iii)).

Point E is the reference point for proceeding under Rule 26-1b or 26-1c as it is the point where the original ball last crossed the margin of the water hazard.

If the player drops a ball at Point B and the ball comes to rest at a spot from which he judges he cannot play, he may, adding an additional penalty of one stroke, either drop a ball anywhere on the dotted line E–G, drop a ball within two club-lengths of and not nearer the hole than Points E or F, or play another ball from Point A (the teeing ground), playing 5.

RULE 27

BALL LOST OR OUT OF BOUNDS; PROVISIONAL BALL

DEFINITIONS
All defined terms are in *italics* and are listed alphabetically in the Definitions section – see pages 6–16.

27-1. STROKE AND DISTANCE; BALL OUT OF BOUNDS; BALL NOT FOUND WITHIN FIVE MINUTES
a. Proceeding Under Stroke and Distance
At any time, a player may, under penalty of one stroke, play a ball as nearly as possible at the spot from which the original ball was last played (see Rule 20-5), i.e., proceed under penalty of stroke and distance.

Except as otherwise provided in the *Rules*, if a player makes a *stroke* at a ball from the spot at which the original ball was last played, he is deemed to have proceeded under penalty of stroke and distance.

b. Ball Out of Bounds
If a ball is *out of bounds,* the player must play a ball, under penalty of one stroke, as nearly as possible at the spot from which the original ball was last played (see Rule 20-5).

c. Ball Not Found Within Five Minutes
If a ball is *lost* as a result of not being found or identified as his by the player within five minutes after the player's *side* or his or their *caddies* have begun to search for it, the player must play a ball, under penalty of one stroke, as nearly as possible at the spot from which the original ball was last played (see Rule 20-5).

Exception: If it is known or virtually certain that the original ball, that has not been found, has been moved by an *outside agency* (Rule 18-1), is in an *obstruction* (Rule 24-3), is in an *abnormal ground condition* (Rule 25-1) or is in a *water hazard* (Rule 26-1), the player may proceed under the applicable *Rule*.

PENALTY FOR BREACH OF RULE 27-1:
<u>Match play</u> – Loss of hole; <u>Stroke play</u> – Two strokes.

27-2. PROVISIONAL BALL
a. Procedure
If a ball may be *lost* outside a *water hazard* or may be *out of bounds,* to save time the player may play another ball provisionally in accordance with Rule 27-1. The player must inform his *opponent* in match play or his *marker* or a *fellow-competitor* in stroke play that he intends to play a *provisional ball,* and he must play it before he or his *partner* goes forward to search for the original ball.

If he fails to do so and plays another ball, that ball is not a *provisional ball* and becomes the *ball in play* under penalty of stroke and distance (Rule 27-1); the original ball is *lost*.

(Order of play from teeing ground – see Rule 10-3)

Note: If a *provisional ball* played under Rule 27-2a might be *lost* outside a *water hazard* or *out of bounds*, the player may play another *provisional ball*. If another *provisional ball* is played, it bears the same relationship to the previous *provisional ball* as the first *provisional ball* bears to the original ball.

b. When Provisional Ball Becomes Ball in Play

The player may play a *provisional ball* until he reaches the place where the original ball is likely to be. If he makes a *stroke* with the *provisional ball* from the place where the original ball is likely to be or from a point nearer the *hole* than that place, the original ball is *lost* and the *provisional ball* becomes the *ball in play* under penalty of stroke and distance (Rule 27-1).

If the original ball is *lost* outside a *water hazard* or is *out of bounds*, the *provisional ball* becomes the *ball in play*, under penalty of stroke and distance (Rule 27-1).

Exception: If it is known or virtually certain that the original ball, that has not been found, has been moved by an *outside agency* (Rule 18-1), or is in an *obstruction* (Rule 24-3) or an *abnormal ground condition* (Rule 25-1c), the player may proceed under the applicable *Rule*.

c. When Provisional Ball to be Abandoned

If the original ball is neither *lost* nor *out of bounds*, the player must abandon the *provisional ball* and continue playing the original ball. If it is known or virtually certain that the original ball is in a *water hazard,* the player may proceed in accordance with Rule 26-1. In either situation, if the player makes any further *strokes* at the *provisional ball,* he is playing a *wrong ball* and the provisions of Rule 15-3 apply.

Note: If a player plays a *provisional ball* under Rule 27-2a, the *strokes* made after this Rule has been invoked with a *provisional ball* subsequently abandoned under Rule 27-2c and penalties incurred solely by playing that ball are disregarded.

BALL LOST OR OUT OF BOUNDS AND PROVISIONAL BALL: GENERAL

27/1
Player Directs Caddie Not to Search for His Ball Until Others Can Assist

Q. A hits a long drive into heavy rough. B hits a short drive into heavy rough. A's caddie starts walking towards the area where A's ball may be to search for A's ball. Everyone else, including A, walks towards the area where B's ball may be to look for B's ball. A directs his caddie also to look for B's ball and delay search for his (A's) ball until everyone else can assist. Is such procedure permitted?

A. Yes.

27/1.5
Time Permitted for Search for Lost Ball if Play Suspended During Search

Q. A player has been searching for his ball for three minutes when play is suspended. How much time is he allowed for further search?

A. The player may continue searching for two more minutes. The suspension of play has no effect on the five-minute search period. Thus, even if the player searches for his ball during the suspension of play, he is still only permitted a total of five minutes to search for his ball.

27/2
Time Permitted for Search for Lost Ball After Wrong Ball Played

Q. In stroke play, a competitor searches for his ball for three minutes, finds a ball, plays it and then discovers he has played a wrong ball. He returns to the area from which the wrong ball was played and resumes search for his ball. How much time is he allowed for further search – two minutes or five minutes?

A. Two minutes – see Definition of "Lost Ball."

27/3
Time Permitted for Search When Lost Ball Found and Then Lost Again

Q. A player finds his ball in high rough after a two-minute search, leaves the area to get a club and, when he returns, is unable to find the ball. Is he allowed three minutes or five minutes to find his ball?

A. Three minutes.

27/4
Time Permitted for Search for Original Ball and Provisional Ball

Q. Is a player allowed five minutes to search for his original ball and five more minutes to search for his provisional ball, or just a total of five minutes?

A. If the two balls are so close together that, in effect, both balls would be searched for simultaneously, a total of five minutes for search is allowed. Otherwise, the player is allowed to search five minutes for each ball.

27/5
Player Searching for Ball Mistakes His Ball for Opponent's

Q. In a match, A begins to search for his ball and after two minutes finds a ball which he believes to be his opponent's ball and resumes his search. The five-minute search period elapses and thereafter it is discovered that the ball which he found and believed to be his opponent's was in fact his ball. What is the ruling?

A. Once a ball has been found a player has an opportunity to identify it as his. In this case, the player had every opportunity to identify the ball as his within the five-minute search period and failed to do so. Therefore, the ball is, by definition, "lost."

27/5.5
Original Ball Found Within Five-Minute Search Period Not Identified Until After Period Has Elapsed

Q. A player plays a second shot, searches for his ball for just over four minutes and then starts to walk back down the fairway to play another ball under Rule 27-1. A ball is then found within the five-minute search period, but as the player is now a considerable distance away, he is unable to identify the ball as his before the search period has elapsed. What is the ruling?

A. As a ball was found within five minutes of beginning search, the player is allowed enough time to reach the area in order to identify it. If the player identifies the ball as his, it is not a "lost ball" even though the identification takes place after the five-minute search period has elapsed.

27/6
Player Unable to Find His Ball Because Another Player Played It

Q. A and B hit their tee shots into the same general area. A found a ball and played it. B went forward to look for his ball and could not find it. After a few minutes, B started back to the tee to put another ball into play. On the way, he found A's ball and knew then that A had played his (B's) ball in error. What is the ruling?

A. In match play, A lost the hole (Rule 15-3a).

In stroke play, A incurred a penalty of two strokes for playing a wrong ball and must then play his own ball (Rule 15-3b). A's ball was not lost even if A and B had been searching for more than five minutes because A had not "begun to search for it (his ball)"; the searching had been for B's ball – see Definition of "Lost Ball."

On the other hand, B began to search for his ball as soon as he went forward to look for it. If less than five minutes had elapsed before B found A's ball, B should have placed a ball on the spot from which A had wrongly played his (B's) ball and continued play, without penalty – see last paragraph of Rule 15-3b. However, if five minutes had expired, B's original ball was lost and he was obliged to put another ball into play under penalty of stroke and distance (Rule 27-1).

Related Decision:
- 15-3b/1 Competitor Plays Wrong Ball and Loses It; Wrong Ball May Have Been Fellow-Competitor's Ball.

27/7
Ball Found in Burrowing Animal Hole After Five-Minute Search

Q. A player's tee shot comes to rest in an area containing heavy rough and a large burrowing animal hole. After a search of five minutes, the players in the group determine that it is neither known nor virtually certain that the ball is in the burrowing animal hole. The player returns to the tee to put another ball into play under Rule 27-1. As the player is returning to the tee, the ball is found in the burrowing animal hole. May the player now proceed under Rule 25-1?

A. No. When five minutes elapsed and it was neither known nor virtually certain that the ball was in the burrowing animal hole, the ball was lost and Rule 27-1 was applicable.

27/8
Ball Found After Search Exceeding Five Minutes Is Then Played

Q. A player searches for his ball for five minutes and does not find it. He continues to search, finds his ball and plays it. What is the ruling?

A. The ball was lost and therefore out of play when the five-minute period allowed for search expired – see Definitions of "Ball in Play" and "Lost Ball." When the player played a stroke with the ball out of play, he played a wrong ball – see Definition of "Wrong Ball" – and incurred a penalty of loss of hole in match play or two strokes in stroke play – Rule 15-3. In stroke play, he was disqualified if he did not correct the error by proceeding under Rule 27-1 before playing from the next tee – Rule 15-3b.

Related Decisions:
- 15/5 Original Ball Found and Played After Another Ball Put into Play.
- 27-1/2.3 Original Ball Found Within Five-Minute Search Period After Another Ball Dropped; Original Ball Played.
- 27-2b/5 Original Ball Played After Provisional Ball Played from Point Nearer Hole Than Original Ball Is Likely to Be.

27/9
Player Searches for Lost Ball After Putting Another Ball into Play

Q. According to Rule 27, if a player hits his tee shot into the woods and tees up and plays another ball without announcing it as a provisional ball, the second ball becomes the ball in play and the original ball is lost. In such a case, is the player precluded from searching for his original ball?

A. No. But the player may not play the ball if he finds it and must not unduly delay play.

27/10
Player Unable to Distinguish His Ball from Another Ball

Q. A and B hit their tee shots into the same area. Both balls were found but, because A and B were playing identical balls and neither had put an identification mark on his ball, they could not determine which ball was A's and which was B's. What is the ruling?

A. Since neither player could identify a ball as his ball, both balls were lost – see Definition of "Lost Ball."

This incident underlines the advisability of the player putting an identification mark on his ball – see Rules 6-5 and 12-2.

27/11
Provisional Ball Not Distinguishable from Original Ball

A player entitled to play a provisional ball from the tee plays it into the same area as his original ball. The balls have identical markings and the player cannot distinguish between them. Following are various situations and the solutions, which are based on equity (Rule 1-4), when the above circumstances exist and one or both of the balls are found within a search of five minutes:

Situation1: One ball is found in a water hazard and the other ball is not found.

Solution 1: The ball that was found must be presumed to be the provisional ball.

Situation 2: Both balls are found in a water hazard.

Solution 2: As the player's original ball is lost in the water hazard due to his inability to identify it (see analogous Decision 27/10), the player must proceed under Rule 26-1 with respect to the original ball (estimating the spot where the ball last crossed the margin of the hazard, if necessary – see Decision 26-1/17); his next stroke would be his third.

Situation 3: One ball is found in bounds and the other ball is lost or is found out of bounds.

Solution 3: The ball in bounds must be presumed to be the provisional ball.

Situation 4: Both balls are found in bounds, whether in a playable or an unplayable lie, and (1) one ball is in a water hazard and the other is not or (2) both balls lie through the green or in a bunker.

Solution 4: One could argue that both balls are lost. However, it would be inequitable to require the player to return to the tee, playing 5, when the player has found both balls but does not know which is the original and which the provisional. Accordingly, the player must select one of the balls, treat it as his provisional ball and abandon the other.

27/12
Identification of Ball Through Testimony of Spectator

Q. A's ball and B's ball came to rest close together. Neither A nor B could identify one of the balls as his ball because they were using balls with identical markings.

A spectator who saw both shots land was able to state which ball belonged to A and which one belonged to B. May his testimony be accepted, or should both balls be deemed lost because they could not be identified by A and B?

A. If the Committee determined that, based on information given by the spectator, A and B were able to identify their balls, the balls should not be deemed lost. Otherwise, they would have to proceed under Rule 27-1.

Decision related to 27/10 through 27/12:
• 12-2/1 Identifying Ball by Brand, Model and Number Only.

27/13
Refusal to Identify Ball

Q. A player purposely refuses to identify a ball as his. What can the opponent or a fellow-competitor do in such a case?

A. An opponent or fellow-competitor has the right to be satisfied about the identification of a player's ball.

If a player has dishonestly not identified his ball, the opponent or fellow-competitor may refer the dispute to the Committee (Rule 34-3). In such a case, the Committee would be justified in imposing a penalty of disqualification under Rule 33-7.

Related Decisions:
• 27-2/2 Member of Committee Finds Player's Original Ball; Player Prefers to Continue with Provisional Ball.
• 27-2b/1 Continuation of Play with Provisional Ball Without Searching for Original Ball.
• 27-2c/2 Ball Believed to Be Original Found; Player Wishes to Ignore It and Continue Play with Provisional Ball.

27/14
Ball in Tree Identified But Not Retrieved

Q. A player's ball is lodged high in a tree. He identifies it with the aid of binoculars but is unable to retrieve it. Is the ball lost, in which case the player must invoke Rule 27-1?

A. No. Since the ball was identified, it was not lost – see Definition of "Lost Ball." The player may invoke the unplayable ball Rule (Rule 28).

27/15
Ball in Tree Visible But Not Identifiable

Q. A player is certain that his ball is lodged high in a tree. He can see a ball in the tree, but he cannot identify it as his ball. Is the player's ball lost, in which case he must proceed under Rule 27-1?

A. Yes.

27/16
Ball Declared Lost Is Found Before Another Ball Put into Play

Q. A player searched for his ball for two minutes, declared it lost and started back to play another ball at the spot from which the original ball was played. Before he put another ball into play, his original ball was found within the five-minute period allowed for search. What is the ruling?

A. A player cannot render a ball lost by a declaration – see Definition of "Lost Ball." The original ball remained in play – see Definition of "Ball in Play."

27/17
Competitor Plays Out of Turn Other Than from Teeing Ground and Puts Another Ball into Play at Spot of Previous Stroke

Q. In stroke play, a competitor whose ball lay through the green played out of turn. He should have continued play with the ball played out of turn without penalty, but he mistakenly believed he needed to cancel and replay the stroke in the correct order. The competitor dropped another ball at the spot from which he made that stroke, but his action was questioned before he played the dropped ball. What is the ruling?

A. As the dropped ball was not dropped with the intention of putting it into play under penalty of stroke and distance, part c of the Definition of "Lost Ball" does not apply and, therefore, the original ball was not lost. As the competitor had put a ball into play under an inapplicable Rule but not played it, Rule 20-6 applies, and the player may correct his error by continuing play with the original ball, without penalty.

Had the competitor played the dropped ball, he would have been considered to have played under penalty of stroke and distance (Rule 27-1a) and the original ball would be lost. (Revised)

Related Decisions:
• 27-1/2 Original Ball Found Within Five-Minute Search Period After Another Ball Dropped.

Other related Decisions – See "Inapplicable Rule or Procedure Used" in the Index.

27/18
Gate in Boundary Fence

Q. A gate in a boundary fence swings onto the course. Sometimes the gate is open and sometimes it is closed. If the gate is open, may a player close it if it interferes with his swing?

A. A gate in a boundary fence, when closed, is part of the boundary fence, is not an obstruction (see Definition of "Obstructions") and may not be moved. A gate in a boundary fence, if open, is not covered by the Rules. In equity (Rule 1-4), a player who finds a gate in a boundary fence open may leave it as he finds it or close it, but he must not move it to any other position.

Related Decisions:
• 13-2/18 Improving Position of Ball by Bending Boundary Fence.
• 24/4 Part of Boundary Fence Within Boundary Line.

27/19
When Ball Inside Boundary Fence Is Out of Bounds

Q. In view of the Definition of "Out of Bounds," is it correct to say that, if the posts of a boundary fence are on the golf course side of the fence, the diameter of the posts is greater than the diameter of a golf ball and the fence is straight, a ball lying against the inside of the fence would be out of bounds?

A. Yes.

Decisions related to 27/18 and 27/19:
• See "Boundary Fence, Line, Wall or Stakes; Wall" in the Index.

27/20
Public Road Defined as Out of Bounds Divides Course; Status of Ball Crossing Road

Q. A public road defined as out of bounds divides a course. A ball crosses the road and comes to rest on the part of the course on the other side of the road. Is the ball out of bounds?

A. No. Since the ball lies on the course, it is in bounds unless a Local Rule provides otherwise. However, because it is unfair that a ball on the road is out of bounds and a ball beyond it is in bounds, it is suggested that the following Local Rule should be adopted:

"A ball which crosses a public road defined as out of bounds and comes to rest beyond that road is out of bounds, even though it may lie on another part of the course."

Related Decisions:
• 33-2a/12 Internal Boundary Between Holes.
• 33-2a/13 Tee Decreed to Be in Bounds for Tee Shot and Out of Bounds Thereafter.

- 33-2a/14 Internal Out of Bounds Applying to Stroke from Teeing Ground Only.
- 33-8/38 Local Rule Deeming Out of Bounds Ball Which Crosses Boundary But Comes to Rest on Course.

STROKE AND DISTANCE; BALL OUT OF BOUNDS; BALL NOT FOUND WITHIN FIVE

27-1/1
Original Ball Found Within Five-Minute Search Period After Another Ball Teed

Q. A player plays from the teeing ground, searches briefly for his ball and then goes back and tees another ball. Before he plays the teed ball, and within the five-minute search period, the original ball is found. May the player abandon the teed ball and play the original ball?

A. Yes. The teed ball was not in play since the player had not yet made a stroke at it – see Definition of "Ball in Play" – and the original ball was not lost – see Definition of "Lost Ball."

27-1/2
Original Ball Found Within Five-Minute Search Period After Another Ball Dropped

Q. A player plays his second shot, searches for his ball briefly and then goes back and drops another ball under Rule 27-1. Before he plays the dropped ball, and within the five-minute search period, the original ball is found. Is the player required to continue with the dropped ball?

A. Yes. When the player put the substituted ball into play at the spot of the previous stroke with the intent to play a ball under penalty of stroke and distance (Rule 27-1), the original ball was lost (see Definition of "Lost Ball"). Therefore, Rule 20-6 does not apply, and he must continue with the substituted ball.

Related Decision:
- 27/17 Competitor Plays Out of Turn Other Than From Teeing Ground and Puts Another Ball into Play at Spot of Previous Stroke.

27-1/2.3
Original Ball Found Within Five-Minute Search Period After Another Ball Dropped; Original Ball Played

Q. In Decision 27-1/2, the player was required to proceed with the dropped ball. What would be the ruling if the player continues play with the original ball?

A. As the original ball is no longer the player's ball in play, it is a wrong ball, and the provisions of Rule 15-3 apply.

- 15/5 Original Ball Found and Played After Another Ball Put into Play.
- 27/8 Ball Found After Search Exceeding Five Minutes Is Then Played.
- 27-2b/5 Original Ball Played After Provisional Ball Played from Point Nearer Hole Than Original Ball Is Likely to Be.

27-1/2.5
Lost Ball Treated as Moved by Outside Agency in Absence of Knowledge or Virtual Certainty to That Effect

Q. A player who is unable to find his ball treats it as moved by an outside agency, rather than lost, in the absence of knowledge or virtual certainty to that effect. Accordingly, he drops a ball where he thinks his original ball came to rest (Rule 18-1) and plays it, rather than taking the stroke-and-distance penalty for a lost ball (Rule 27-1). What is the ruling?

A. In the absence of knowledge or virtual certainty that the ball had been moved by an outside agency, the player was required to put another ball into play under Rule 27-1. In playing the ball dropped under Rule 18-1, the player played from a wrong place.

In match play, he incurred a penalty of loss of hole (Rule 20-7b).

In stroke play, he incurred the stroke-and-distance penalty prescribed by Rule 27-1 and an additional penalty of two strokes for a breach of that Rule (Rule 20-7c). Because the breach was a serious one, he was subject to disqualification unless he corrected the error as provided in the second paragraph of Rule 20-7c.

Related Decision:
- 25-1c/2 Ball Dropped and Played Under Ground Under Repair Rule in Absence of Knowledge or Virtual Certainty That Original Ball in Ground Under Repair.

27-1/3
Ball Dropped in Area Where Original Ball Lost; Ball Then Played

Q. A player, unable to find his ball, drops another ball in the area where his original ball was lost and plays that ball. What is the ruling?

A. In match play, the player loses the hole – Rule 20-7b.

In stroke play, the player incurs the stroke-and-distance penalty prescribed by Rule 27-1 and an additional penalty of two strokes for a breach of that Rule. If the breach was a serious one, he must rectify the error as provided in the second paragraph of Rule 20-7c; otherwise, he is disqualified.

PROVISIONAL BALL: GENERAL

27-2/1
Provisional Ball Serving as Ball in Play If Original Ball Unplayable or in Water Hazard

Q. May a player announce that a second ball he is going to play is both (a) a provisional ball in case the original ball is lost outside a water hazard or out of bounds and (b) the ball in play in case the original ball is unplayable or in a water hazard?

A. No.

27-2/2
Member of Committee Finds Player's Original Ball; Player Prefers to Continue with Provisional Ball

Q. Is a member of a Committee or a forecaddie obliged to inform a player that his original ball has been found, even if it is clear that the player does not plan to search for it because he would prefer to continue play with the provisional ball he has played?

A. Yes.

Related Decisions:
• 27/13 Refusal to Identify Ball.
• 27-2b/1 Continuation of Play with Provisional Ball Without Searching for Original Ball.
• 27-2c/2 Ball Believed to Be Original Found; Player Wishes to Ignore It and Continue Play with Provisional Ball.

PROVISIONAL BALL: PROCEDURE

27-2a/1
Announcement of Provisional Ball

Q. A player hits his ball into an area where it may be lost outside a water hazard or out of bounds. The player then drops another ball and plays it. The player intends the dropped ball to be a provisional ball, but he does not inform his opponent, marker or fellow-competitor that he is "playing a provisional ball." In such a situation, can a player's actions constitute announcement that he is playing a provisional ball?

A. No. Rule 27-2a specifically provides that the player must inform his opponent, marker or a fellow-competitor that he intends to play a provisional ball.

The player's statement must specifically mention the words "provisional ball" or must make it clear that he is proceeding under Rule 27-2a. Therefore, a player who says nothing has put another ball into play.

The following are examples of statements that do not satisfy the

requirement of announcing a provisional ball:
  (a) "That might be lost. I am going to re-load."
  (b) "That might be out of here."
  (c) "I'd better hit another one."
  (d) "I will never find that one. I'll play another."

27-2a/1.3
Player Intends to Play Provisional Ball But No One Present to Hear Announcement

Q. In stroke play, A hits his tee shot into the trees. After a search of five minutes, he does not find his ball and returns to the tee to play a second ball under Rule 27-1c. He hits the second tee shot into the trees as well. He intends to play a provisional ball, but his two fellow-competitors are well down the fairway and unable to hear an announcement from A of his intention. How should he proceed?

A. Rule 27-2a does not contemplate the absence of an opponent, marker or fellow-competitor when the player intends to play a provisional ball. In this case, in the interest of not delaying play A is considered to have fulfilled the announcement requirements of Rule 27-2a if he informs his marker or fellow-competitor as soon as practicable that he has played a provisional ball.

27-2a/1.5
Meaning of "Goes Forward to Search"

Q. With respect to Rule 27-2a, when has a player gone forward to search for the original ball such that a provisional ball cannot be played?

A. The sole purpose of Rule 27-2 is to enable the player to save time. The only way he can effectively do so is to play the provisional ball before going forward for the purpose of searching for the original ball. However, this provision should not be so narrowly interpreted to preclude a player from playing a provisional ball even though he has proceeded from where he last played in the direction of the original ball, e.g., in retrieving a ball or a different club to play the provisional ball. The Committee must consider all of the relevant facts in determining if the player did in fact go forward to search for the original ball.

27-2a/2
Provisional Ball Played Solely in Belief Original Ball Might Be in Water Hazard

Q. A player's tee shot might be in a water hazard, but clearly it is not lost outside a water hazard or out of bounds. The player announces that, since his ball might be in the hazard, he is going to play a provisional ball and he does so. Rule 27-2a seems to prohibit a provisional ball in the circumstances. What is the ruling?

A. The player did not play a provisional ball which, according to the Definition of "Provisional Ball," is a ball played under Rule 27-2 for a ball which may be lost outside a water hazard or may be out of bounds. The second ball from the tee was in play since it was not a provisional ball.

27-2a/2.2
Possibility That Original Ball Is in Water Hazard May Not Preclude Play of Provisional Ball

Q. Is it true that, if a player's original ball may have come to rest in a water hazard, the player is precluded from playing a provisional ball?

A. No. Even though the original ball may be in a water hazard, the player is entitled to play a provisional ball if the original ball might also be lost outside the water hazard or out of bounds. In such a case, if the original ball is found in the water hazard, the provisional ball must be abandoned – Rule 27-2c.

27-2a/2.5
Player Plays Provisional Ball in Belief Original Might Be Lost Outside Water Hazard Then Discovers There Is No Possibility of Its Being Lost Outside Water Hazard

Q. A player's tee shot is struck towards an area of trees, bushes and tall grass. Believing his ball might be lost outside a water hazard, the player announces his intention to play a provisional ball and plays a ball from the tee. When he arrives at the area, he finds that the area in question is wetlands that has been defined as a lateral water hazard and that it is known or virtually certain that his ball is in it. What is the ruling?

A. As the player played the second ball from the tee in the belief that his original ball might be lost outside a water hazard, that ball was a provisional ball. The subsequent discovery that the area in question is in fact a lateral water hazard is irrelevant. Therefore, the player must abandon the provisional ball and proceed under Rule 26-1 – see Rule 27-2c.

27-2a/3
Play of Provisional Ball in Absence of Reasonable Possibility Original Ball Is Lost or Out of Bounds

Q. In the absence of reasonable possibility that a ball is lost outside a water hazard or is out of bounds, may the player play a provisional ball?

A. No. If a player plays a ball under such circumstances, the ball is not a provisional ball but the ball in play – see Decision 27-2a/2.

Related Decisions:
• 26-1/1 Meaning of "Known or Virtually Certain."
• 26-1/1.3 When is it Necessary to Go Forward to Establish "Virtual Certainty"?

27-2a/4
Three Balls Played from Same Spot; Only Second Ball Was Provisional Ball

Q. A player, believing his tee shot might be lost or out of bounds, plays a provisional ball. His provisional ball is struck in the same direction as the original ball and, without any announcement, he plays another ball from the tee. This ball comes to rest on the fairway. What is the ruling?

A. If the original ball is not lost or out of bounds, the player must continue play with that ball without penalty.

If the original ball is lost or out of bounds, the player must continue play with the third ball played from the tee as, when this ball was played without any announcement, it rendered the provisional ball lost, regardless of the provisional ball's location. The player would lie 5 with the third ball played from the tee.

In both situations, the third ball bears a relationship only to the previous ball played, i.e., the provisional ball.

WHEN PROVISIONAL BALL BECOMES BALL IN PLAY

27-2b/1
Continuation of Play with Provisional Ball Without Searching for Original Ball

Q. At a par-3 hole, a player hits his tee shot into dense woods. He then hits a provisional ball which comes to rest near the hole. In view of the position of the provisional ball, the player does not wish to find his original ball. He does not search for it and walks directly towards his provisional ball to continue play with it. His opponent (or fellow-competitor) believes it would be beneficial to him if the original ball were found. May the opponent (or fellow-competitor) search for the player's ball?

A. Yes. In equity (Rule 1-4), he may search for five minutes provided that in the meantime the player does not play a stroke with the provisional ball, it being nearer the hole than the place where the original ball is likely to be. The player is entitled to play such a stroke. If he does, the original ball is then lost under Rule 27-2b and further search for it would serve no purpose. In match play, if the player so proceeds and his provisional ball is closer to the hole than his opponent's ball, his opponent may recall the stroke (Rule 10-1c). However, recalling the stroke would not change the status of the original ball, which was lost when the provisional ball was played out of turn. See also Decision 27-2c/2.

Related Decisions:
- 27/13 Refusal to Identify Ball.
- 27-2/2 Member of Committee Finds Player's Original Ball; Player Prefers to Continue with Provisional Ball.

• 27-2c/2 Ball Believed to Be Original Found; Player Wishes to Ignore It and Continue Play with Provisional Ball.

27-2b/2
When Provisional Ball Holed Becomes Ball in Play

Q. At a short hole, A's tee shot may be out of bounds or lost, so he plays a provisional ball, which he holes. A does not wish to look for his original ball. B, A's opponent or a fellow-competitor, goes to look for the original ball. When does the provisional ball become the ball in play?

A. In equity (Rule 1-4) the provisional ball becomes the ball in play as soon as A picks it out of the hole, provided his original ball has not already been found in bounds within five minutes of B starting to search for it.

27-2b/3
Original Ball Is Beyond Provisional Ball; Player Searches Briefly for Original Ball, Plays Provisional Ball and Then Finds Original Ball

Q. A player's provisional ball comes to rest short of where the original ball is likely to be. After a two-minute search for the original ball, the player goes back, plays a second stroke with the provisional ball and then his original ball is found within the five-minute time limit. What is the ruling?

A. The player must continue play with the original ball. Play of a provisional ball does not render the original ball lost until it has been played from the place where the original ball is likely to be or from a point nearer the hole than that place (Rule 27-2b).

27-2b/4
Provisional Ball Played from Beyond Where Original Ball Likely to Be But Not Beyond Where Original Ball Found

Q. A player, believing his tee shot might be lost or in a road defined as out of bounds, played a provisional ball. He searched for his original ball but did not find it. He went forward and played his provisional ball. Then he went farther forward and found his original ball in bounds. The original ball must have bounced down the road and then come back into bounds, because it was found much farther from the tee than anticipated. Was the original ball still the ball in play?

A. No. The player played a stroke with the provisional ball from a point nearer the hole than the place where the original ball was likely to be. When he did so, the provisional ball became the ball in play and the original ball was lost (Rule 27-2b).

The place where the original ball in fact lay was irrelevant.

27-2b/5
Original Ball Played After Provisional Ball Played from Point Nearer Hole Than Original Ball Is Likely to Be

Q. A player, unable to find his original ball, goes forward and makes a second stroke with his provisional ball from a point nearer the hole than the place where the original ball is likely to be. His original ball is then found and he plays it. What is the ruling?

A. When the player made his second stroke with the provisional ball, the original ball was lost and the provisional ball was in play – Rule 27-2b. In making a stroke with a ball that was no longer in play (the original ball), the player played a wrong ball – see Definition of "Wrong Ball" – and was subject to penalty as prescribed in Rule 15-3.

Related Decisions:
- 15/5 Original Ball Found and Played After Another Ball Put into Play.
- 27/8 Ball Found After Search Exceeding Five Minutes Is Then Played.
- 27-1/2.3 Original Ball Found Within Five-Minute Search Period After Another Ball Dropped; Original Ball Played.

27-2b/6
Player Abandons Original Ball and Walks Forward to Play Provisional Ball; Original Ball Then Found

Q. A player, having searched for a minute for his original ball, abandoned it and walked forward to continue play with his provisional ball. Before he played the provisional ball, some spectators found the original ball before the five-minute search period expired. What is the ruling?

A. The original ball remained the ball in play since it was found within five minutes after search for it had begun and the player had not played a stroke with the provisional ball from the place where the original ball was likely to be or from a point nearer the hole than that place (Rule 27-2b).

27-2b/6.5
Player Deems Provisional Ball Unplayable and Drops Ball; Original Ball Then Found

Q. A player hits his tee shot into heavy rough approximately 150 yards from the teeing ground and, since his ball may be lost outside a water hazard, he plays a provisional ball. After searching briefly for his original ball he goes forward to play his provisional ball which is in a bush approximately 200 yards from the teeing ground. He deems his provisional ball unplayable and drops it within two club-lengths of where it lay under Rule 28c. Before playing the provisional ball, the player's original ball is found by a spectator within five minutes of the player having begun to search for it. What is the ruling?

A. The original ball remained the ball in play since it was found within five minutes after search for it had begun and the player had not played a stroke with the provisional ball (see Rule 27-2b). The fact that the player lifted and dropped the provisional ball under Rule 28c is irrelevant.

27-2b/7
Provisional Ball Played in Erroneous Belief It Is Original Ball

Q. A player, believing his original ball may be out of bounds, plays a provisional ball which comes to rest in the same area. He finds a ball which he believes is his original ball, plays it and then discovers that the ball he played was his provisional ball. What is the ruling?

A. If a player reaches the place where his original ball is likely to be and plays another stroke with a provisional ball, the provisional ball is in play and the original ball is lost (Rule 27-2b).

27-2b/8
Provisional Ball Lifted in Erroneous Belief Original Ball Is in Bounds

Q. A player, believing his original ball might be out of bounds, played a provisional ball which came to rest short of where the original ball came to rest. He walked forward, saw his original ball and, believing the original ball to be in bounds, picked up the provisional ball. He then discovered that the original ball was out of bounds. What is the ruling?

A. Since the original ball was out of bounds, the provisional ball was in play (Rule 27-2b). When the player lifted the ball in play (provisional ball) without authority under the Rules, he incurred a penalty stroke and was required to replace it (Rule 18-2a).

27-2b/9
Provisional Ball Lifted Subsequently Becomes Ball in Play

Q. In stroke play, a competitor, believing his tee shot might be lost, plays a provisional ball. He finds a ball he believes is his original ball, plays a stroke at it, picks up his provisional ball and then discovers that the ball he played was not his original ball, but rather a wrong ball. He resumes search for his original ball but cannot find it. What is the ruling?

A. The competitor lifted a ball which was to become the ball in play, i.e., the provisional ball – see Rule 27-2b. Accordingly, the competitor incurred a stroke-and-distance penalty under Rule 27-1 as a result of losing his original ball, a two-stroke penalty under Rule 15-3b for playing a wrong ball and a one-stroke penalty under Rule 18-2a for picking up his provisional ball. He is required to replace and play out the provisional ball. The competitor would be playing his seventh stroke.

445

27-2b/10
Provisional Ball Lifted Subsequently Becomes Ball in Play; Competitor Then Plays from Wrong Place

Q. With regard to Decision 27-2b/9, what is the ruling if the competitor returns to the tee with the provisional ball and puts it into play again?

A. When the competitor played again from the tee rather than replacing and playing the provisional ball from where it was lifted, he put that ball into play under penalty of stroke-and-distance (see Rule 27-1a). However, the penalty of one stroke for the original lifting of the provisional ball in breach of Rule 18-2a still applies because, at the moment of lifting the provisional ball, the player had no intention of playing it again from the teeing ground. Therefore, the competitor would be playing his eighth stroke from the tee.

Related Decisions:
- 10-2c/1 Ball Played Out of Turn from Tee Abandoned and Another Ball Played in Proper Order.
- 18-2a/1 Player Who Misses Tee Shot Tees Ball Lower Before Making Next Stroke.
- 18-2a/2 Ball Falling Off Tee When Stroke Just Touches It Is Picked Up and Re-Teed.
- 18-2a/11 Tee Shot Wrongly Thought to Be Out of Bounds Lifted; Competitor Plays Another Ball from Tee.
- 29-1/9 Both Player and Partner Drive at Same Tee in Foursome Play.

WHEN PROVISIONAL BALL TO BE ABANDONED

27-2c/1 (Reserved)

27-2c/1.5
Whether Provisional Ball Becomes Ball in Play If Original Ball Lost in Ground Under Repair

Q. A player hits his tee shot into an area of tall rough and, since the ball may be lost, he plays a provisional ball. During search for the original ball, the player discovers that the Committee has marked a large area of the rough as ground under repair. It is established that there is virtual certainty that the original ball is in the ground under repair. Does the provisional ball automatically become the ball in play since the original ball, which has not been found, was outside a water hazard?

A. No. The player may continue play with the provisional ball under Rule 27-2b or he may proceed under Rule 25-1c(i) as it is virtually certain that his ball is in ground under repair – see Exception to Rule 27-2b.

Related Decision:
- 25-1c/3 Ball Played in Ground Under Repair Area Lost in Same Area.

27-2c/2
Ball Believed to Be Original Found; Player Wishes to Ignore It and Continue Play with Provisional Ball

Q. At a par-3 hole, a player plays his tee shot into a heavy thicket. Since his ball may be lost, he hits a provisional ball that comes to rest near the hole. In the circumstances, it is advantageous to the player not to find his original ball. Accordingly, the player does not search for the original ball and walks directly toward his provisional ball. While the player is on his way to his provisional ball, a ball believed to be his original is found. The player is advised that his original ball may have been found. May the player ignore this ball and continue play with the provisional ball?

A. No. The player must inspect the ball that has been found and, if it is the player's original ball, he must continue play with it (or proceed under the unplayable ball Rule). The provisional ball must be abandoned – Rule 27-2c. See also Decision 27-2b/1.

Related Decisions:
• 27/13 Refusal to Identify Ball.
• 27-2/2 Member of Committee Finds Player's Original Ball; Player Prefers to Continue with Provisional Ball.
• 27-2b/1 Continuation of Play with Provisional Ball Without Searching for Original Ball

27-2c/3
Provisional Ball Played from Point Nearer Hole Than Original Ball Because Player Erroneously Thought Original Ball, Which Was Visible, Was Out of Bounds

Q. A player's ball came to rest 20 yards over a green and beyond a white stake which the player's caddie said was a boundary stake. The player played a provisional ball which came to rest short of the green, but closer to the hole than his original ball. The player played the provisional ball onto the green. At that point, he walked behind the green towards his original ball, which had been visible all along, and discovered that the white stake was not a boundary stake and that his original ball was in bounds. What is the ruling?

A. The player should have determined the status of his original ball before playing a second stroke with the provisional ball and, since the original ball was not out of bounds, he should have abandoned the provisional ball. When he failed to do so, the second stroke with the provisional ball was a stroke with a wrong ball – Rule 27-2c.

In match play, the player lost the hole (Rule 15-3a).

In stroke play, he incurred a two-stroke penalty (Rule 15-3b) and was required to hole out with the original ball.

27-2c/4
Original Ball and Provisional Ball Found Out of Bounds

Q. A player finds both his original ball and his provisional ball out of bounds. The balls were played from the tee. When the player returns to the tee and plays another ball, has he taken 3 strokes or 5?

A. The player will have taken 5 strokes when he plays the third ball from the tee. A stroke played with a provisional ball and any penalty related to it are not disregarded unless the provisional ball is abandoned as provided in Rule 27-2c.

Related Decisions:
• 15/7 Wrong Ball Played in Belief It Is Provisional or Second Ball.
• 20-7c/5 Competitor Plays Second Ball Under Rule 20-7c; Clarification of "Penalty Strokes Incurred Solely by Playing the Ball Ruled Not to Count."

RULE 28

BALL UNPLAYABLE

DEFINITIONS

All defined terms are in *italics* and are listed alphabetically in the Definitions section – see pages 6–16.

The player may deem his ball unplayable at any place on the *course*, except when the ball is in a *water hazard*. The player is the sole judge as to whether his ball is unplayable.

If the player deems his ball to be unplayable, he must, under penalty of one stroke:

a. Proceed under the stroke and distance provision of Rule 27-1 by playing a ball as nearly as possible at the spot from which the original ball was last played (see Rule 20-5); or

b. Drop a ball behind the point where the ball lay, keeping that point directly between the *hole* and the spot on which the ball is dropped, with no limit to how far behind that point the ball may be dropped; or

c. Drop a ball within two club-lengths of the spot where the ball lay, but not nearer the *hole*.

If the unplayable ball is in a *bunker*, the player may proceed under Clause a, b or c. If he elects to proceed under Clause b or c, a ball must be dropped in the *bunker*.

When proceeding under this Rule, the player may lift and clean his ball or *substitute* a ball.

PENALTY FOR BREACH OF RULE:

<u>Match play</u> – Loss of hole; <u>Stroke play</u> – Two strokes.

BALL UNPLAYABLE

28/1
When Necessary to Find and Identify Ball Deemed Unplayable

Q. A player hits his tee shot into a deep canyon. The player immediately deems the ball unplayable and plays another ball from the tee under the stroke-and-distance option of Rule 28. May a player deem unplayable a ball which has not been found?

A. Yes. A player may proceed under the stroke-and-distance option (Rule 28a) without finding his ball.

However, since Rules 28b and 28c require reference to where the ball lay, the player must find and identify his ball in order to proceed under either of these options.

28/2
Player Deems First Ball from Tee Unplayable, Abandons Provisional Ball and Claims He Is Lying Three with Third Ball

Q. A player hit his tee shot deep into the woods on the right. The player then hit a provisional ball into the same woods. The player did not search for either ball.

The player deemed his first ball unplayable, said he was abandoning his provisional ball and hit a third ball from the tee. The player maintained that his third ball was in play and that he was lying 3. He based his argument on Rule 28, which states that the player is the sole judge as to whether his ball is unplayable, and on Decision 28/1, which says in effect that a player may proceed under the stroke-and-distance option of the unplayable ball Rule without finding his ball. The Committee ruled that the player's stroke with the third ball was his fifth stroke, but the wording of Decision 28/1 leaves a little doubt. Did the Committee rule correctly?

A. Yes. The player may not deem the first ball from the tee unplayable, disregard the provisional ball and put another ball into play under a stroke-and-distance penalty because, having played the provisional ball, he must find the original ball before he can deem it unplayable. Unless the original ball was found, the provisional ball would automatically become the ball in play.

This case differs from Decision 28/1. No provisional ball was played in that case.

28/3
Ball Dropped Under Unplayable Ball Rule Comes to Rest in Original Position or Another Position at Which Ball Is Unplayable

Q. A player deemed his ball unplayable and, under Rule 28c, dropped his ball within two club-lengths of the spot where it lay. The ball came to rest in the original position or another position at which the ball was unplayable. What is the ruling?

A. The ball was in play when it was dropped – Rule 20-4. Thus, if the ball came to rest in the original position, the player must again invoke the unplayable ball Rule, incurring an additional penalty stroke, unless he decides to play the ball as it lies. The same applies if the ball came to rest in another position at which it was unplayable, assuming that the ball did not roll into a position covered by Rule 20-2c, in which case re-dropping without penalty would be required.

Related Decision:
• 28/6.5 Player Deems Ball Unplayable a Second Time and Wishes to Proceed Under Stroke and Distance After Dropping a Ball Under Other Unplayable Option.

28/4
Ball Deemed Unplayable Through the Green Dropped in Hazard

Q. A player's ball lies through the green. The player deems the ball unplayable. In proceeding under Rule 28b or 28c, the player drops a ball in a hazard. Is this permissible?

A. Yes.

Related Decisions:
- 20-7/3 Whether Player May Drop Ball into Area from Which Play Prohibited.
- 25-1b/14.5 Ball Deemed Unplayable Dropped in Ground Under Repair from Which Play Prohibited; Ball Then Dropped Under Ground Under Repair Rule.

28/4.5
Ball Deemed Unplayable Through the Green Dropped in Water Hazard; Player Elects Not to Play Ball and Wishes to Proceed Under the Water Hazard Rule

Q. With regard to Decision 28/4, if the player drops a ball into a lateral water hazard and the ball rolls into a position where the player is unable to play the ball, how should he proceed?

A. The player's only option is to proceed under Rule 26-1a.

As the player deliberately dropped the ball directly into the water hazard "the point at which the original ball last crossed the margin of the water hazard" cannot be identified. Therefore, in the absence of this reference point, neither Rule 26-1b nor 26-1c can be applied.

Related Decision:
- 26-1/2 Player Proceeding Under Water Hazard Rule Drops Ball in Another Hazard.

28/5
Regression Under Unplayable Ball Rule

Q. A player plays a stroke from Point A to Point B. Point B is in an area from which it is very difficult to extricate the ball. The player considers deeming the ball unplayable but this would result in a stroke-and-distance penalty (Rule 28a). Dropping behind under Rule 28b is impossible due to a boundary fence and dropping within two club-lengths under Rule 28c is not feasible because it would require a considerable number of such drops to escape the area. The player plays from Point B and moves the ball a few feet to Point C, where the ball is clearly unplayable. Under Rule 28a, may the player:

    (a) deem the ball unplayable at Point C and drop a ball under penalty of one stroke at Point B, and then

    (b) deem the ball unplayable at Point B and drop a ball, under an additional penalty of one stroke, at Point A?

A. No. Under Rule 28a, the player would be entitled to drop a ball only at the place from which he played his last stroke (Point B).

In the circumstances, the player's only alternative is to invoke Rule 28c a sufficient number of times (starting at Point C and dropping the ball sideways within two club-lengths each time) to get the ball into a playable position.

28/6
Player Plays Second Shot, Deems Ball Unplayable and Returns to Tee

Q. With regard to Decision 28/5, if Point A is the teeing ground and Point B is the spot from which the second shot was played, what is the penalty if the player, having deemed his ball unplayable at Point C, returns to the tee and plays out the hole from there?

A. The player was entitled to drop and play a ball at Point B under Rule 28a, but not Point A. When he played a ball from Point A, he played from a wrong place.

In match play, the player incurs a penalty of loss of hole for a breach of Rule 28 – see also Rule 20-7b.

In stroke play, a serious breach of Rule 28 is involved. Accordingly, the player is disqualified unless the serious breach is corrected as provided in Rule 20-7c.

Except in the special circumstances covered by Rule 26-2, the Rules do not allow a player to regress beyond the spot from which his last stroke was played, in this case Point B. Such action may constitute a serious breach, as in this case.

28/6.5
Player Deems Ball Unplayable a Second Time and Wishes to Proceed Under Stroke and Distance After Dropping a Ball Under Other Unplayable Option

Q. A player plays a stroke from Point A to Point B. The player deems his ball unplayable and proceeds under either Rule 28b or 28c. After dropping under penalty of one stroke, the ball comes to rest at Point C. The player deems his ball unplayable for a second time and wishes to proceed under Rule 28a, playing from Point A. Is this permissible?

A. Yes. The player may play from Point A because he did not make a stroke at the ball from either Point B or Point C. Point A was the spot from which the original ball was last played. The player would incur a total of two penalty strokes.

Related Decision:
• 28/3 Ball Dropped Under Unplayable Ball Rule Comes to Rest in Original Position or Another Position at Which Ball Is Unplayable.

28/7
Player Misses Ball and Deems It Unplayable

Q. A player's tee shot comes to rest in tree roots. He makes a stroke, fails to move the ball and then deems the ball unplayable. May the player return to the tee, playing 4, under Rule 28a?

A. No. Rule 28a permits the player to play "a ball … at the spot from which the original ball was last played." The original ball was last played from the tree roots, not the tee.

28/8
Ball Deemed Unplayable; Place from Which Previous Stroke Played Is Nearer Hole

Q. A player's ball strikes a rock and bounces farther away from the hole than the spot from which the stroke was played. The player deems the ball unplayable. May the player invoke the stroke-and-distance option of Rule 28 in the circumstances?

A. Yes.

28/9
Ball Lying on Grass-Covered Ground Within Bunker Deemed Unplayable

Q. A player's ball is lying on grass-covered ground within a bunker. The player deems the ball unplayable and elects to drop it under Rule 28b. Must he drop it in the bunker?

A. No. Grass-covered ground within a bunker is not part of the bunker. Accordingly, the player may drop the ball behind the bunker.

28/10
Ball Dropped Outside Bunker Under Option Requiring Drop in Bunker

Q. In stroke play, a competitor deems his ball unplayable in a bunker and, purporting to proceed under Rule 28b or 28c, drops a ball outside the bunker and plays it. What is the ruling?

A. In this case, Rules 28b and 28c require that a ball be dropped in and played from the bunker. Generally, if the ball is played from outside the bunker, the penalty should be disqualification for a serious breach of Rule 28, unless rectified under Rule 20-7c. However, if the position of the ball after it is dropped out of the bunker is not substantially different from what it would have been if the competitor had invoked the stroke-and-distance option under Rule 28a, he incurs the penalty stroke prescribed by Rule 28 and an additional penalty of two strokes for a breach of that Rule, rather than disqualification.

28/11
Ball Unplayable in Tree and Player Opts to Drop Within Two Club-Lengths

Q. A player's ball is eight feet off the ground, lodged in a tree. The player deems the ball unplayable. May the player proceed under option c of Rule 28 which permits him to drop a ball within two club-lengths of where his ball lay unplayable?

A. Yes. The player would be entitled to drop a ball within two club-lengths of the point on the ground immediately below the place where the ball lay in the tree. In some instances this may allow the player to drop a ball on a putting green.

28/12
Ball Unplayable at Base of Cliff and Player Wishes to Drop Within Two Club-Lengths of Point Above Ball

Q. Under Decision 28/11, if a ball in a tree is deemed unplayable, the player may, under Rule 28c, drop a ball within two club-lengths of the spot on the ground directly beneath where the ball lies.

Suppose a player deems unplayable a ball lying at the base of a cliff and wishes to proceed under Rule 28c. May the player drop a ball within two club-lengths of a point directly above where the ball lies in order to get himself onto the top of the cliff?

A. No.

In Decision 28/11, the player was permitted to ignore vertical distance in taking relief under Rule 28c only because his ball was off the ground. In this case, the ball at the base of the cliff is on the ground.

Decisions related to 28/11 and 28/12:
- 24-2b/11 Ball Lying on Elevated Part of Immovable Obstruction.
- 25-1b/23 Ball Enters Burrowing Animal Hole Out of Bounds and Comes to Rest in Bounds.
- 25-1b/24 Ball Enters Burrowing Animal Hole in Bounds and Comes to Rest Out of Bounds.
- 25-1b/25 Ball Enters Burrowing Animal Hole in Bunker and Is Found Underneath Putting Green.
- 25-1b/25.5 Application of Exception to Rule 25-1b When Ball Lies Underground in Burrowing Animal Hole.

28/13
After Deeming Ball Unplayable and Lifting It, Player Discovers Ball Was in Ground Under Repair

Q. A player lifts his ball after deeming it unplayable and then discovers that the ball was lying in ground under repair. Does the deeming and the lifting of the ball commit the player to proceeding under Rule 28?

A. No. Provided the player has not put a ball into play under Rule 28, he is not precluded by that Rule from taking relief, without penalty, under the ground under repair Rule (Rule 25).

Related Decisions:
- 3-3/7.5 Competitor Announces Intention to Play Two Balls; Plays Original Ball Before Dropping Second Ball; Elects Not to Play Second Ball.
- 9-2/13 Player Who Told Opponent He Would Proceed Under Water Hazard Rule Changes Mind After Opponent Plays.
- 18-2a/12.5 Player Entitled to Relief Without Penalty from Condition Lifts Ball; Chooses Not to Take Relief and Wishes to Proceed Under the Unplayable Ball Rule.
- 18-2a/27.5 Player Who States He Will Proceed Under Unplayable Ball Rule Subsequently Assesses Possibility of Playing Ball as It Lies.

28/14
Stray Ball Deemed Unplayable Played Under Stroke-and-Distance Procedure; Original Ball Then Found

Q. A player finds a stray ball, which he mistakenly thinks is his, in a bad lie. He deems it unplayable and decides to adopt the procedure in Rule 28a. After going back, he plays the stray ball under penalty of stroke and distance at the spot from which his original ball was played. He then finds his original ball in a playable position. What is the ruling?

A. The original ball is lost and the stray ball played under penalty of stroke and distance is in play (Definition of "Lost Ball" and Rule 27-1).

The ruling would have been different if the player had decided to proceed under either Rule 28b or 28c – see Decision 28/15.

28/15
Stray Ball Deemed Unplayable, Dropped Within Two Club-Lengths and Played Before Error Discovered

Q. A player finds a stray ball, which he mistakenly thinks is his, in a bad lie. He deems it unplayable and decides to adopt the procedure in Rule 28c. He drops the stray ball within two club-lengths of the spot where it lay and plays it. He then finds his original ball in a playable position. In Decision 28/14 the basic situation is exactly the same, but in that case the player elected to proceed under Rule 28a and it was ruled that the stray ball played under penalty of stroke and distance was in play. What is the ruling in this case?

A. The procedures in Rules 28b and 28c may not be applied except with reference to the position of the player's ball in play, which must first be found and identified (see Decision 28/1). In the present case, the stray ball dropped and played by the player was not his original ball; it was a substituted ball. Since the location of the original ball was not known at the time the substituted ball was dropped, he was required to proceed under Rule 27-1. As the substituted ball was not dropped at the spot required by Rule 27-1, he played from a wrong place (see Decision 15/14).

In match play, he incurred a penalty of loss of hole (Rule 20-7b).

In stroke play, he incurred a penalty of one stroke under Rule 27-1 and an additional penalty of two strokes under Rule 20-7c for playing from a wrong place. If the breach was a serious one, he was subject to disqualification unless he corrected the error as provided in Rule 20-7c.

Decisions related to 28/14 and 28/15:

• 15/13 Stray Ball Dropped Under Unplayable Ball Rule But Not Played.
• 20-7c/3 Ball Believed to Be Lost in Bunker; Competitor Drops Another Ball in Bunker and Plays It; Original Ball Then Found Outside Bunker.

RULE 29

THREESOMES AND FOURSOMES

DEFINITIONS

All defined terms are in *italics* and are listed alphabetically in the Definitions section – see pages 6–16.

29-1. GENERAL

In a *threesome* or a *foursome*, during any *stipulated round* the *partners* must play alternately from the *teeing grounds* and alternately during the play of each hole. *Penalty strokes* do not affect the order of play.

29-2. MATCH PLAY

If a player plays when his *partner* should have played, his *side* loses the hole.

29-3. STROKE PLAY

If the *partners* make a *stroke* or *strokes* in incorrect order, such *stroke* or *strokes* are canceled and the *side* incurs a penalty of two strokes. The *side* must correct the error by playing a ball in correct order as nearly as possible at the spot from which it first played in incorrect order (see Rule 20-5). If the *side* makes a *stroke* on the next *teeing ground* without first correcting the error or, in the case of the last hole of the round, leaves the *putting green* without declaring its intention to correct the error, the *side* is disqualified.

THREESOMES AND FOURSOMES: GENERAL

29/1
Changing Partners After Driving from First Tee

Q. A and B are to play C and D in a foursome match in which the conditions of the competition permit substitutions. D is absent at the time the match is to start. Accordingly, E is substituted for D. C plays the first stroke for Side C–E. At that point, D arrives. May D be reinstated in the match since E has not made a stroke?

A. No. Once any player in a foursome match has played from the first tee, the composition of neither side may be changed.

Related Decision:
• 2/2 Stipulated Round in Match Play.

29/2
Mixed Foursome in Which Different Tees Used by Men and Women; Tee Shot Out of Bounds

Q. In a mixed foursome in which the men play from the back tees and the women play from the forward tees, a man hits a tee shot out of bounds. Does his partner play the next stroke from the back tee or the forward tee?

A. The partner must play from the back tee.

29/3
Player in Foursome Match Practices Putts on Previous Green After Partner Has Driven from Next Tee

Q. A and B are partners in a foursome match. A was practicing putts on the 11th green after B drove off the 12th tee. Was A playing practice strokes during the play of a hole?

A. Yes. A and B lost the 12th hole for a breach of Rule 7-2.

Related Decision:
• 30-3f/12 Player in Four-Ball Practices Putts on Previous Green After Partner Has Driven from Next Tee.

29/4
Dropping Ball in Foursome Competition

Q. Rule 20-2a provides that "the player himself" must drop a ball. Under the Definition of "Partner," it is stated that, in the case of threesomes and foursomes, the term "player" includes his partner where the context so admits. When a side in a foursome is required to drop a ball, may either member of the side drop it?

A. No. In view of the requirement of Rule 20-2a that the player *himself* shall drop the ball, the member of the side whose turn it is to play next must drop the ball.

Related Decision:
• 20-2a/4 Ball Dropped in Improper Manner Moves When Addressed; Player Then Lifts Ball and Drops It in Proper Manner.

29/5
Hitting Sand in Bunker with Club After Failing to Extricate Ball; Foursome Match

Q. In a foursome match, A and B are partners. A plays a bunker shot, fails to get the ball out and takes a swing with his club into the sand. This action does not improve the position of the ball in the bunker. What is the ruling?

A. In a foursome, the word "player" includes his partner, where the context so admits – see Definition of "Partner." In these circumstances, the prohibitions in Rule 13-4 apply to both the player and his partner. Therefore, Side A-B incur a penalty of loss of hole for a breach of Rule 13-4 – see Decision 13-4/35.

Related Decisions:
- 30-3f/2 Hitting Sand in Bunker with Club After Failing to Extricate Ball; Partner's Ball in Same Bunker.
- 30-3f/2.5 Touching Sand with Practice Swing After Partner Has Extricated Ball from Bunker; Four-Ball Match.

29/6
Signing of Score Card in Foursome Stroke Play

Q. Rule 31-3 dealing with scoring in four-ball stroke play states: "Only one of the partners need be responsible for complying with Rule 6-6b." What is the ruling in this regard in foursome stroke play?

A. Although Rule 29 is silent on the matter, in foursome stroke play only one of the partners need comply with Rule 6-6b.

Other Decisions related to Rule 29: See "Foursomes" in the Index.

THREESOMES AND FOURSOMES: ORDER OF PLAY

29-1/1
Ball Played from Outside Teeing Ground in Foursome Match

Q. A and B are playing C and D in a foursome match. A plays from outside the teeing ground and Side A-B is required by C and D to replay the stroke. Should A or B replay it?

A. A must replay the stroke. The original stroke does not count.

29-1/2
Competitor Plays from Outside Teeing Ground in Foursome Stroke Play; Partner Replays Stroke

Q. In foursome stroke play A plays in correct order but from outside the teeing ground. B, his partner, then plays from within the teeing ground, whereas A should have done so. What is the ruling?

A. The side is penalized two strokes for playing from outside the teeing ground (Rule 11-4) and two strokes for playing in incorrect order (Rule 29-3). A must now play another ball from within the teeing ground. Otherwise, the side is disqualified.

Related Decisions:
- 11-4b/6 Ball Played from Outside Teeing Ground Goes Out of Bounds.
- 11-5/4 Ball Played From Wrong Teeing Ground in Stroke Play; Error Corrected.
- 34-3/4 Dispute as to Whether Competitor Played from Outside Teeing Ground.

29-1/3
Who Plays Provisional Ball in Foursome

Q. A and B are partners in a foursome. A drives and there is doubt whether the ball is out of bounds. They decide to play a provisional ball. Who plays it?

A. The provisional ball is played by B.

29-1/4
Provisional Ball Played by Wrong Member of Side in Foursome

Q. A and B were partners in a foursome competition. A drove from the tee and, since the ball might be lost, A-B elected to play a provisional ball. A played the provisional ball, whereas, under Rule 29, B should have played it. What is the ruling?

A. If the original ball was found in bounds and thus the provisional ball did not become the ball in play, there was no penalty.

If the original ball was lost and the provisional ball became the ball in play, A-B lost the hole in match play (Rule 29-2) or incurred a penalty of two strokes in stroke play (Rule 29-3). In stroke play, the provisional ball would have to be abandoned and B would have to play from the tee (Rule 29-3).

29-1/4.5
Play of Provisional Ball in Foursomes When Partner Has Already Gone Ahead

Q. A and B are partners in foursomes play. It is A's turn to play from the teeing ground, and B walks ahead to where he thinks the ball might land. A's tee shot comes to rest in an area where it may not be found. Without searching for the original ball, B immediately returns to the tee with the intention of playing a provisional ball, by which time A has walked forward a considerable distance towards the original ball in the knowledge that it may be lost. Rule 27-2a prohibits the play of a provisional ball after the player or his partner has gone forward to search for the original ball. As a result of A having gone forward to search, is B prohibited from playing a provisional ball under Rule 27-2a?

A. Rule 27-2a does not contemplate such a case and, in view of the fact that the purpose of Rule 27-2 is to enable players to save time and that B's desire and actions to play a provisional ball in such a case are consistent with this purpose, B is permitted to play a provisional ball, provided the original ball has not been found. However, the five-minute period for search for the original ball commences as soon as A has begun to search for it.

29-1/5
Order of Play If Player Accidentally Moves Ball After Address

Q. In a foursome match, a player accidentally moves the ball after addressing it and incurs a penalty of one stroke under Rule 18-2b. Does the player or his partner play the next stroke?

A. The player must play the next stroke. Penalty strokes do not affect the order of play (Rule 29-1).

29-1/6
Player Misses Ball Accidentally When Making Stroke

Q. In a foursome event, A and B are partners. A attempts to strike the ball and misses. Whose turn is it to play?

A. An accidental miss is a stroke – see Definition of "Stroke." It is B's turn to play.

29-1/7
Player Misses Ball Purposely So Partner Would Play Ball Over Water

Q. A and B, partners in a foursome competition, were faced with a difficult shot over a pond. A, a poor player, swung but purposely missed the ball. B, an expert player, then played the ball to the green. Is this permissible?

A. No. Since A had no intention of moving the ball, he did not play a stroke – see Definition of "Stroke" – and it remained his turn to play.

When B played instead of A, A and B incurred a penalty of loss of hole in match play or two strokes in stroke play (Rules 29-2 and 29-3). In stroke play, A must play a ball at the spot from which B played. If A did not do so before the side played from the next teeing ground, A and B were disqualified (Rule 29-3).

29-1/8
Order of Play in Foursome Stroke Play When Wrong Ball Played

Q. In foursome stroke play, A played a wrong ball. Who plays the next shot, A or his partner, B?

A. A must play the next stroke. In a foursome competition, penalty strokes do not affect the order of play – see Rule 29-1. The Side A-B incurs a penalty of two strokes – Rule 15-3b.

29-1/9
Both Player and Partner Drive at Same Tee in Foursome Play

Q. A and B are partners in foursome play. At the 5th hole, forgetting that they were playing a foursome, A and then B drive. What is the ruling:
- (a) if it was A's turn to drive?
- (b) if it was B's turn to drive?

A. (a) If it was A's turn to drive, B's ball would be the side's ball in play and would be lying 3 – see Rule 27-1a.
- (b) If it was B's turn to drive, the side loses the hole in match play or incurs a penalty of two strokes in stroke play (Rules 29-2 and 29-3). In stroke play, the side must continue with B's ball which lies 3.

Related Decisions:
- 10-2c/1 Ball Played Out of Turn from Tee Abandoned and Another Ball Played in Proper Order.
- 18-2a/1 Player Who Misses Tee Shot Tees Ball Lower Before Making Next Stroke.
- 18-2a/2 Ball Falling Off Tee When Stroke Just Touches It Is Picked Up and Re-Teed.
- 18-2a/11 Tee Shot Wrongly Thought to Be Out of Bounds Lifted; Competitor Plays Another Ball from Tee.
- 27-2b/10 Provisional Ball Lifted Subsequently Becomes Ball in Play; Competitor Then Plays from Wrong Place.

Other Decisions related to Rule 29-1: See "Foursomes" in the Index.

THREESOMES AND FOURSOMES: ORDER OF PLAY IN MATCH PLAY

29-2/1
Wrong Partners Drive for Both Sides in Foursome Match

Q. A and B are playing C and D in a foursome match. A and C drive off at a hole at which B and D should have driven. The error is then discovered. What is the ruling?

A. The side which drove first loses the hole under Rule 29-2.

29-2/2
Side Drives for Three Holes in Wrong Order and Then Claim Is Made

Q. In a foursome match, A and B are playing C and D. A drives at the 9th hole and again, in error, at the 10th hole. B drives at the 11th and A drives at the 12th. The error is then discovered. C and D claim the 10th, 11th and 12th holes, and the matter is referred to the Committee. What is the ruling?

A. A and B lose the 12th hole under Rule 29-2.

C and D's claim of the 10th and 11th holes could have been considered only if C and D had been given wrong information by A and B and the claim had been based on facts previously unknown to C and D. A and B are deemed to have given wrong information to C and D – see Rule 9-2b(i). However, C and D must have seen A and B play out of order on all three holes. Therefore, the claim was not based on facts previously unknown to C and D.

Other Decisions related to Rule 29-2: See "Foursomes" in the Index.

RULE 30

THREE-BALL, BEST-BALL AND FOUR-BALL MATCH PLAY

DEFINITIONS

All defined terms are in *italics* and are listed alphabetically in the Definitions section – see pages 6–16.

30-1. GENERAL

The Rules of Golf, so far as they are not at variance with the following specific Rules, apply to *three-ball*, *best-ball* and *four-ball* matches.

30-2. THREE-BALL MATCH PLAY
a. Ball at Rest Moved or Purposely Touched by an Opponent

If an *opponent* incurs a penalty stroke under Rule 18-3b, that penalty is incurred only in the match with the player whose ball was touched or moved. No penalty is incurred in his match with the other player.

b. Ball Deflected or Stopped by an Opponent Accidentally

If a player's ball is accidentally deflected or stopped by an *opponent*, his *caddie* or *equipment*, there is no penalty. In his match with that *opponent* the player may, before another *stroke* is made by either *side*, cancel the *stroke* and play a ball, without penalty, as nearly as possible at the spot from which the original ball was last played (see Rule 20-5) or he may play the ball as it lies. In his match with the other *opponent*, the ball must be played as it lies.
Exception: Ball striking person attending or holding up *flagstick* or anything carried by him – see Rule 17-3b.

(Ball purposely deflected or stopped by opponent – see Rule 1-2)

30-3. BEST-BALL AND FOUR-BALL MATCH PLAY
a. Representation of Side

A *side* may be represented by one *partner* for all or any part of a match; all *partners* need not be present. An absent *partner* may join a match between holes, but not during play of a hole.

b. Order of Play

Balls belonging to the same *side* may be played in the order the *side* considers best.

c. Wrong Ball

If a player incurs the loss of hole penalty under Rule 15-3a for making a *stroke* at a *wrong ball*, he is disqualified for that hole, but his *partner* incurs no penalty even if the *wrong ball* belongs to him. If the *wrong ball* belongs to another player, its owner must place a ball on the spot from which the *wrong ball* was first played.
(Placing and Replacing – see Rule 20-3)

d. Penalty to Side

A *side* is penalized for a breach of any of the following by any *partner*:

- Rule 4 — Clubs
- Rule 6-4 — Caddie
- Any Local Rule or Condition of Competition for which the penalty is an adjustment to the state of the match.

e. Disqualification of Side

(i) A *side* is disqualified if any *partner* incurs a penalty of disqualification under any of the following:

- Rule 1-3 — Agreement to Waive Rules
- Rule 4 — Clubs
- Rule 5-1 or 5-2 — The Ball
- Rule 6-2a — Handicap
- Rule 6-4 — Caddie
- Rule 6-7 — Undue Delay; Slow Play
- Rule 11-1 — Teeing
- Rule 14-3 — Artificial Devices, Unusual Equipment and Unusual Use of Equipment
- Rule 33-7 — Disqualification Penalty Imposed by Committee

(ii) A *side* is disqualified if all *partners* incur a penalty of disqualification under any of the following:

- Rule 6-3 — Time of Starting and Groups
- Rule 6-8 — Discontinuance of Play

(iii) In all other cases where a breach of a *Rule* would result in disqualification, the player is disqualified for that hole only.

f. Effect of Other Penalties

If a player's breach of a *Rule* assists his *partner's* play or adversely affects an *opponent's* play, the *partner* incurs the applicable penalty in addition to any penalty incurred by the player.

In all other cases where a player incurs a penalty for breach of a *Rule*, the penalty does not apply to his *partner*. Where the penalty is stated to be loss of hole, the effect is to disqualify the player for that hole.

THREE-BALL, BEST-BALL AND FOUR-BALL MATCH PLAY: GENERAL

30/1
Caddie Shared by Members of Opposite Sides in Four-Ball Match Moves Ball

Q. A and B were playing C and D in a four-ball match. A caddie shared by A and C moves A's ball. What is the ruling?

A. If the caddie was not acting upon directions of C or D, A is penalized one stroke – see Definition of "Caddie" and Rule 18-2a.

If the caddie was acting upon directions of C or D, C is penalized one stroke under Rule 18-3b.

30/2
Caddie Shared by Opponents' Side in Four-Ball Match Moves Player's Ball

Q. A and B are playing C and D in a four-ball match. A caddie shared by C and D accidentally moves A's ball. Who is penalized?

A. Rule 18-3b provides that, if a player's ball is moved by an opponent's caddie, that opponent incurs a penalty stroke. However, when opponents share a caddie, there is no fair way of assigning the penalty to one member of the side. Accordingly, in equity (Rule 1-4), both C and D incur a penalty stroke.

A must replace his ball – Rule 18-3b.

30/2.5
Player Touches Putting Green in Pointing Out Line for Putting for Partner and Incidentally Touches Own Line of Putt

Q. In a four-ball match, A and B are partners and their balls lie on the putting green. A touches the green in pointing out a line for putting for B. Incidentally, the spot which A touches is on his (A's) line of putt.

B is disqualified for the hole under Rule 8-2b. Is A disqualified for the hole under Rule 16-1a?

A. No.

30/3
Determination of Honor in Four-Ball Match in Which Points Awarded for Both Better-Ball and Aggregate Scores

Q. In a four-ball match, one point is awarded for the better-ball score at each hole and one point is awarded for the aggregate score at each hole. How is the honor determined?

A. The Rules of Golf do not cover such a match – see Definition of "Forms of Match Play." It is recommended that the honor be determined by the better-ball score only.

30/4
Player Who Walks Off Green Under Mistaken Impression Partner Halved Hole Returns and Putts for Half

Q. A and B are playing C and D in a four-ball match. At one hole C and D hole out and their better-ball score is 4. A, who had marked the position of his ball and lifted it, has a putt for a 4 but he mistakenly thinks B has scored a 4. Accordingly, A walks off the green, leaving his ball-marker on the green. B immediately advises A that he (B) scored a 5. So A returns to the green, replaces his ball and holes out for a 4.

C and D claim the hole on the ground that A cannot come back and putt after walking off the green, thinking his partner had halved the hole. Are C and D correct?

A. No. Since A had not waived his turn to putt and there was no undue delay, A was entitled to proceed as he did. If, however, A had not left his ball-marker on the green, and therefore the position of his ball was no longer marked, he would have incurred a penalty stroke under Rule 20-1 and would no longer have had a putt for the half.

Related Decisions:
- 30-3b/2 Waiving Turn to Putt in Four-Ball Match.
- 30-3c/2 Player Wins Hole with Wrong Ball and Partner Picks Up; Error Discovered at Next Hole.

30/5
In Four-Ball Match Player with Putt for Half Picks Up in Error at Suggestion of Opponent Based on Misunderstanding

Q. A and B are playing C and D in a four-ball match. A has holed out in 4, the better ball for his side. When C holes out, A remarks: "Nice 4, C. D, you may pick your ball up." C does not correct A by stating he had a 5 and allows his partner D to pick his ball up although D still has a putt for a half.

Upon leaving the putting green, it occurs to C that he has allowed D to pick up when D had an opportunity to halve the hole. In the circumstances, could A's remark be construed as a concession of D's putt?

A. No. A's suggestion that D might pick up D's ball was based on A's mistaken impression that C had scored a 4 and that therefore D's putt could have no bearing on the result.

C should have corrected A's mistaken impression before D picked up his ball. Since C failed to do so and D did not finish the hole, C's score of 5 for the hole was C-D's better-ball score. Thus, C and D lost the hole.

Related Decisions:
- 2-4/4 Whether Picking Up Opponent's Ball Is Concession of Next Stroke.
- 2-4/5 Whether Lifting Opponent's Ball-Marker Is Concession of Next Stroke.
- 2-4/17 Player in Erroneous Belief Match Is Over Shakes Opponent's Hand and Picks Up Opponent's Ball.

30/6
Player Plays Practice Putt After He and Partner Have Holed Out But Before Opponents Hole Out

Q. In a four-ball match, A plays a practice putt after he and his partner have holed out but before the opponents have holed out. Was A in breach of Rule 7-2?

A. No. Rule 7-2 prohibits practicing during play of a hole. A did not practice during play of the hole because he and his partner had completed it. However, A was guilty of a breach of etiquette.

30-1/1
Side Plays Out of Turn from Tee; Opponents Require One Member of Side to Replay But Not Other

Q. A and B are playing C and D in a four-ball match. At one hole A and B drive out of turn. C and D require that A abandon his ball and replay in correct order and that B continue with his original ball. A and B maintain that if A is required to drive again then B must also do so. What is the ruling?

A. Rule 10-1c states in part: " … the opponent may immediately require the player to cancel the stroke so made …" In this context, "immediately" means before anyone else plays.

Accordingly, if A and B played in that order, C and D could not require A to replay his stroke after B had played, but they could require B to replay.

If A and B played in the order B-A, A could be required to replay, but not B.

Other Decisions related to Rule 30: See "Four-Ball Match Play" and "Three-Ball Match Play" in the Index.

THREE-BALL MATCH PLAY

30-2/1
Player Plays Out of Turn from Tee in Three-Ball Match

The following are the rulings in a three-ball match if A, B and C are scheduled to play in that order from the teeing ground and one of them inadvertently plays out of turn:

(a) If C plays first both A and B may require C to replay the stroke in correct order. If A and B disagree on whether C should be required to replay, C must complete the hole with two balls. He must replay his stroke in his match with the opponent who requires him to replay and continue with his original ball in his match with the other opponent.

(b) If B plays first, A may require him to replay his stroke for their match, but C may not. As B did not play out of turn with respect to C, B must continue play of his original ball in his match with C. If B is required by A to replay his stroke, B must play the hole with a different ball in his match with A.

(c) If C plays after A but before B, only B may require C to replay his stroke for their match. As C did not play out of turn with respect to A, C must continue play of his original ball in his match with A. If C is required by B to replay his stroke, C must play the hole with a different ball in his match with B. (Revised)

Related Decision:
• 2-4/10 Player Concedes Hole After Which Opponent Plays Wrong Ball.

30-3/1
Examples of Rulings in Four-Ball Match with Concurrent Singles Matches

When players are involved in concurrent matches, whenever possible the Rules are applied only to the match affected. When it is not possible to separate the matches, the four-ball match takes precedence.

A and B are playing C and D in a four-ball match. There are also concurrent singles matches between A and C and between B and D. The following are examples of the application of the Rules in such a format:

(1) A concedes the match, a hole, or a stroke to C but stipulates that the concession is solely for their singles match. The concession is not valid in the four-ball match.

(2) A concedes the match, a hole, or a stroke to C and does not specify which match the concession is intended for. The concession applies to both the four-ball and the singles matches.

(3) A concedes the match, a hole, or a stroke to D. The concession applies only to the four-ball match as A has no authority to make a concession in the B-D singles match.

(4) The balls of all four players lie on the putting green and A's ball is the farthest from the hole with B's ball on the same line. Side C-D concedes B's next stroke for the four-ball match only, but B goes ahead and putts before A. In the four-ball match, A is disqualified for the hole (see Decision 2-4/6).

(5) B moves A's ball without authority under the Rules. In the four-ball match, A incurs a penalty stroke (Rule 18-2a) but, in his singles match against C, he incurs no penalty. B incurs no penalty in any match.

(6) Other than during search, A moves D's ball. In the four-ball match, A incurs a penalty stroke (Rule 18-3b) but, in his singles match against C, he incurs no penalty.

(7) On the 3rd hole it is discovered that B started his round with 15 clubs. In the four-ball match, Side A-B has two holes deducted from the state of the match (Rules 4-4a and 30-3d) after the 3rd hole. B has two holes deducted from the state of his singles match against D. A incurs no penalty in his singles match against C.

(8) During the round, B made a stroke with a non-conforming club. In the four-ball match, Side A-B is disqualified (Rules 4-1 and 30-3e). B is disqualified in his singles match against D. A incurs no penalty in his singles match against C.

(9) On the 5th hole, B holes out in 3 to win the hole for Side A-B in the four-ball match. A has a putt left to win or halve the hole in his singles match against C and asks B for advice. There is no penalty to either player. A and B may exchange advice at any time until the four-ball match has been concluded, at which point A and B are no longer partners and become outside agencies with respect to each other.

30-3/2
Effect of State of Match Penalties in Four-Ball Play

Q. In a four-ball match in which A and B are partners, A employs two caddies at the 3rd hole. Before play of the 3rd hole is completed, A discovers and corrects his breach of Rule 6-4. As the penalty for breach of Rule 6-4 requires an adjustment of the state of the match, how should the penalty be applied in four-ball match play?

A. At the conclusion of the 3rd hole, Side A-B must deduct one hole from the state of the match (Rules 6-4 and 30-3d). In four-ball match play, when a player breaches a Rule that requires an adjustment to the state of the match, the side is penalized. If a breach of a Rule that requires an adjustment to the state of the match in match play arises in four-ball stroke play, both partners incur the applicable stroke play penalty.

30-3/3
Application of Rule 2-2 in Four-Ball Match Play

The second paragraph of Rule 2-2 does not apply in four-ball match play.

Related Decision:
• 2-2/1 Player Putting for Half is Given Advice by Opponent.

FOUR-BALL MATCH PLAY: REPRESENTATION OF SIDE

30-3a/1
Absent Partner Joins Match During Play of Hole

Q. Rule 30-3a states in part: "An absent partner may join a match between holes, but not during play of a hole." If A and B are to play C and D in a four-ball match and A is absent when the match begins, what is the ruling if A joins the match during play of a hole?

A. A incurs the general penalty prescribed in Rule 2-6 and thus is disqualified for the hole. If any of A's strokes assisted B's play, B also is disqualified for the hole (Rule 30-3f).

Related Decision:
• 30-3f/8 Player Disqualified for Next Hole Plays That Hole.

30-3a/2
Absent Partner Gives Advice Before Joining Match

Q. A and B are to play C and D in a four-ball match. A is absent when the match begins. A arrives just after B, C and D have teed off at the 3rd hole. According to Decision 30-3a/1, A is prohibited from joining the match until the 4th hole. Is it permissible for A to give B advice during the play of the 3rd hole?

A. Yes.

30-3a/3
Determination of Handicap Allowances in Four-Ball Match If One Player Unable to Compete

Q. In a four-ball handicap match, the player with the lowest handicap is unable to play. Should the absent player be disregarded in determining the handicap allowances?

A. No. Under Rule 30-3a, a side may be represented by one partner for all or any part of the match. In determining handicap allowances, the handicaps of the three players should be reduced by the handicap of the absent player.

If a wrong handicap is declared for the absent player, Rule 6-2a applies.

BEST-BALL AND FOUR-BALL MATCH PLAY: ORDER OF PLAY

30-3b/1
Player Entitled to Putt Stands on Another Player's Line of Putt

Q. A and B are partners in a four-ball match. A's ball is closer to the hole than any other ball and it is B's turn to play. Side A-B decide that A will putt before B – Rule 30-3b. However, in doing so A would be standing on B's line of putt or the line of putt of an opponent. What is the ruling?

A. A would be entitled to putt first even if he would be standing on B's line. Rule 30-3b overrides Rule 16-1a, which prohibits touching the line of putt.

A would also be entitled to putt first if he would be standing on an opponent's line of putt. However, it would be a sporting gesture for Side A-B to relinquish A's right to putt first in these circumstances.

30-3b/2
Waiving Turn to Putt in Four-Ball Match

Q. In a four-ball match, A and B are playing C and D. All four balls are on the green in three strokes. The balls of A and C are about 10 feet from the hole; B's ball is two feet away and D's is three feet away. C picks up his ball. A leaves his ball on the green, but tells B and D to "battle it out." D putts first and holes; B then putts and misses. May A then putt for a half?

A. No. A and B abandoned A's right to complete the hole by allowing D to putt before A and B when it was Side A-B's turn to play. Under Rule 30-3b, Side A-B could have opted for B to putt before A. However, if B had done so and missed, it would then have been A's turn to play.

The answer is different if B's ball is three feet away, D's is two feet away and B putts and misses. In these circumstances, A may putt, provided he does so before D putts.

Related Decisions:
- 30/4 Player Who Walks Off Green Under Mistaken Impression Partner Halved Hole Returns and Putts for Half.
- 30-3c/2 Player Wins Hole with Wrong Ball and Partner Picks Up; Error Discovered at Next Hole.
- 31-4/1 Player Waives Turn to Play; Circumstances Under Which He May Complete Hole.

FOUR-BALL MATCH PLAY: PLAY OF WRONG

30-3c/1
Player Plays Partner's Ball

Q. A and B are partners in a four-ball match. By mistake, A putts B's ball and A is disqualified for the hole under Rule 30-3c for playing a wrong ball. B replaces his ball as required by Rule 30-3c and holes his putt. The opponents then claim that B also is disqualified for the hole under Rule 30-3f because A's act of putting B's ball assisted B in determining how much his putt would break, etc. Is the claim valid?

A. No. Rule 30-3c specifically provides that B incurs no penalty. Rule 30-3f is not applicable.

30-3c/2
Player Wins Hole with Wrong Ball and Partner Picks Up; Error Discovered at Next Hole

Q. In a four-ball match, Side A-B holed out for a 4. C, a member of Side C-D, then holed a putt for a 3 and his partner, D, picked up what he thought was his ball. After playing from the next tee, it was discovered that C had putted out at the previous hole with D's ball. Side A-B claimed the hole. What is the ruling?

A. C gave wrong information to Side A-B when he did not inform Side A-B as soon as practicable that he had incurred a penalty for playing a wrong ball – see Rule 9-2. Accordingly, a belated claim by Side A-B was valid – Rule 2-5.

The Committee should have ruled that C was disqualified for the hole – Rule 9-2 or 30-3c – and, since D did not complete the hole, Side A-B won the hole.

Related Decisions:
- 30/4 Player Who Walks Off Green Under Mistaken Impression Partner Halved Hole Returns and Putts for Half.
- 30-3b/2 Waiving Turn to Putt in Four-Ball Match.

30-3c/3
Players on Opposite Sides Exchange Balls During Play of Hole and Their Partners Pick Up; Error Discovered at Next Hole

Q. A and B were playing C and D in a four-ball match. At the 2nd hole, by mistake A played C's ball and then C played A's. C holed out with A's ball, scoring 5.

A holed out with C's ball, scoring 4. B and D picked up. Thus A and B "won" the hole. The error was discovered during play of the 3rd hole, and Side C-D lodged a claim. What is the ruling?

A. A and C were disqualified for the 2nd hole for playing wrong balls. They should have informed their opponents as soon as practicable, which in this case was as soon as they had the opportunity to discover that they had done so, i.e., when they reached the balls wrongly played to play them again. Because they failed to do so, they gave wrong information (Rule 9-2) and, under Rule 2-5, a belated claim that A (and C as well) was disqualified for the 2nd hole for a breach of Rule 30-3c should be upheld.

It could be argued that B and D's play of the 2nd hole was adversely affected (in that they picked up) and that accordingly Rule 30-3f applies. However, Rule 30-3c specifically provides that the "partner incurs no penalty." This applies even if play of the wrong ball would have assisted the partner – see Decision 30-3c/1 – and by implication it applies in the related case of an adverse effect on an opponent's play.

Furthermore, applying Rule 30-3f for the breaches of Rule 9-2 would not have been proper because those breaches were the direct result of the penalties incurred under Rule 30-3c.

Accordingly, if B picked up before D, Side C-D won the hole. If D picked up before B, Side A-B won the hole. If the order in which B and D picked up was not determinable, the Committee should have ruled that the 2nd hole was halved.

30-3c/4
Player Plays Partner's Ball; Error Discovered After Opponents Have Played Next Strokes

Q. A and B are playing C and D in a four-ball match. At the 2nd hole, after the tee shots A mistakenly plays B's ball. The error is discovered after C and D play their second strokes, and C and D claim the hole. What is the ruling?

A. A is disqualified for the hole because he played a wrong ball (Rule 30-3c). B incurs no penalty for A having played his ball (Decision 30-3c/1) and players B, C and D should continue play of the hole.

Decisions related to 30-3c/2 through 30-3c/4:
• 2-5/4 Player Wins Hole with Own Ball After Playing Wrong Ball; Opponent Lodges Belated Claim.
• 9-2/8 Player Wins Hole with Wrong Ball; Error Discovered at Next Hole; Opponent Claims Previous Hole.

FOUR-BALL MATCH PLAY: DISQUALIFICATION OF SIDE

30-3e/1
Partners Fail to Discontinue Play Immediately Contrary to Condition of Competition

Q. A and B are playing C and D in a four-ball match for which the Committee has adopted the condition of competition, authorized by the Note to Rule 6-8b, requiring players to discontinue play immediately in potentially dangerous situations. The Committee suspends play for a potentially dangerous situation and the players have heard the signal for that suspension. A and B play, and C and D make a claim. What is the ruling?

A. A and B are disqualified.

In four-ball play, when a player is in breach of a condition of competition authorized under a specific Rule, that breach is deemed to come under the appropriate Rule (Rule 6-8 in this case). Both A and B were in breach of the condition of competition and are disqualified – Rule 30-3e(ii).

In four-ball stroke play, Side A-B is disqualified – Rule 31-7b(i).

Related Decisions:
- 6-8b/5 Player Claiming Danger from Lightning Refuses to Resume Play When Resumption Ordered by Committee.
- 6-8b/8 Player Drops Ball After Play Suspended for Dangerous Situation.
- 33-2d/3 Competitor Refuses to Start or Picks Up Because of Weather Conditions; Round Subsequently Canceled.

FOUR-BALL MATCH PLAY: EFFECT OF PENALTY ON PARTNER

30-3f/1
Player Lifts Loose Impediment in Bunker When His Ball and Partner's Ball in Bunker

Q. A and B are partners in a four-ball match. A's ball and B's ball are in the same bunker. A lifts a loose impediment lying in the bunker. A is disqualified for the hole for a breach of Rule 13-4. Does B incur a penalty?

A. If A's infringement assisted B's play, B also is disqualified for the hole (Rule 30-3f). Otherwise, B incurs no penalty.

Related Decisions:
- 13-4/17 Loose Impediment Removed from Water Hazard; Player Then Decides Not to Play from Hazard.
- 31-8/1 Competitor Lifts Loose Impediment in Bunker When His Ball and Partner's Ball Are in Bunker.

30-3f/2
Hitting Sand in Bunker with Club After Failing to Extricate Ball; Partner's Ball in Same Bunker

Q. In a four-ball match, A and B were partners. A played a stroke in a bunker and failed to get the ball out of the bunker. He then swung his club into the sand in the bunker, but this action did not affect his new lie in the bunker:
- (a) What is the ruling if B's ball lay in the same bunker when A swung his club into the sand?
- (b) What is the ruling if B's ball lay elsewhere?

A. In either case, A is disqualified for the hole (Rule 13-4 and Decision 13-4/35). The penalty does not apply to B unless A's action assisted B's play or adversely affected an opponent's play (Rule 30-3f).

30-3f/2.5
Touching Sand with Practice Swing After Partner Has Extricated Ball from Bunker; Four-Ball Match

Q. In a four-ball match, A and B are partners. The balls of A and B lie in the same bunker. A plays a bunker shot and extricates his ball, but it comes to rest in another bunker. Before B makes his stroke in the bunker, B makes a practice swing, touching the sand in the bunker. Is B exempt from penalty by virtue of Exception 3 to Rule 13-4?

A. No. In a four-ball match, the word "player" includes his partner, where the context so admits – see Definition of "Partner." However, in four-ball play, as each partner is playing his own ball, Exception 3 to Rule 13-4 applies only to the player whose ball has been extricated from the bunker. Therefore, while A does not incur any penalty, B is disqualified from the hole (Rules 13-4 and 30-3f).

Decisions related to 30-3f/2 and 30-3f/2.5:
- 13.4/35 Hitting Sand in Bunker with Club After Failing to Extricate Ball.
- 29/5 Hitting Sand in Bunker with Club After Failing to Extricate Ball; Foursome Match.

30-3f/3
Player's Ball Resting Against Flagstick Lifted Before Being Holed; Others in Match Pick Up Mistakenly Believing Player Won Hole

Q. In a four-ball match, A's ball rested against the flagstick but it was not holed in terms of the Definition of "Holed." Instead of proceeding under Rule 17-4, A picked up the ball without marking its position. The other three players, believing that A had won the hole, picked up. Before anyone played from the next tee, a spectator pointed out that A's ball had not been holed. The players immediately asked the Committee for a ruling. What would be the correct ruling?

A. A incurred a penalty stroke under Rule 20-1 when he lifted his ball without marking its position. Since A did not inform the opponents about the penalty before they picked up, A was disqualified for the hole for giving wrong information (Rule 9-2). Since A's infringement adversely affected the opponents, i.e., caused them to pick up, A's partner was also disqualified for the hole (Rule 30-3f). Thus, the opponents won the hole.

Related Decisions:
• 2-5/3 Player Lifts Ball Before Holing Out; Opponent Then Picks Up His Ball Claiming Player Loses Hole.
• 9-2/6 Player Reporting Wrong Score Causes Opponent with Chance for Half to Pick Up Ball.
• 17-4/1 Ball Resting Against Flagstick Lifted Before Being Holed.
• 30/5 In Four-Ball Match Player with Putt for Half Picks Up in Error at Suggestion of Opponent Based on Misunderstanding.

30-3f/4
Wrong Information Given by Player Out of Contention in Four-Ball Match

Q. A and B are playing C and D in a four-ball match, and the situation is as follows:
• A's ball is on the green; he lies 3.
• B's ball is in a bunker; he lies 5 and it is his turn to play.
• C's ball is on the green; he lies 4.
• D has picked up.

B causes his ball in the bunker to move and incurs a penalty stroke under Rule 18-2a. B does not inform anyone that he has incurred a penalty stroke. B then replaces his ball and plays onto the green.

A then holes out for a 5 and C does likewise.

B is disqualified for the hole under Rule 9-2 for failing to inform C or D, before C played his next stroke, that he (B) had incurred a penalty stroke. Is A also disqualified for the hole under Rule 30-3f on the ground that B's failure to inform C or D of his (B's) penalty stroke adversely affected C's play?

A. No. B was clearly out of contention, and the result of the hole was dependent upon A and C alone. Accordingly, B's failure to inform C or D about the penalty could not have adversely affected C's play. (Revised)

30-3f/5
Player Attending Flagstick for Opponent Struck by Ball of Opponent's Partner Who Played Out of Turn

Q. A and B are playing C and D in a four-ball match. It is B's turn to play and C is attending the flagstick at B's request. A, whose ball is in a deep bunker in such position that he cannot see C, plays out of turn and his ball strikes C. What is the ruling?

A. B authorized C to attend the flagstick which is the equivalent of A having authorized attendance of the flagstick. See Definition of "Partner," which provides that in a four-ball match, where the context so admits, the word "player" includes his partner.

Accordingly, A is disqualified for the hole (Rule 17-3b), but the penalty does not apply to B (Rule 30-3f).

30-3f/6
Player Plays Away from Hole to Assist Partner

Q. In a four-ball competition, a player purposely putts away from the hole to a position slightly farther from the hole than the spot where his partner's ball lies and on the same line to the hole as his partner's ball. The player then putts towards the hole, and the roll of his ball is helpful to his partner in determining how much his putt will break, etc. Is such procedure contrary to the Rules?

A. Such procedure is contrary to the spirit of the game. In match play, in equity (Rule 1-4), the player should be disqualified for the hole and, since his action assisted his partner's play, the partner should incur the same penalty (Rule 30-3f).

In stroke play, the player should incur a penalty of two strokes and, under Rule 31-8, the partner should incur the same penalty.

Related Decisions:
• 2-4/6 Putting Out After Concession of Stroke.
• 30-3c/1 Player Plays Partner's Ball.

30-3f/7
Player After Picking Up Drops Ball Where Partner's Ball Lies and Plays Practice Stroke

Q. In four-ball play, A and B are partners. A hits his tee shot out of bounds and decides not to complete play of the hole. B was undecided on club selection for his second shot, so A drops a ball near B's ball and hits a shot towards the green. What penalties were incurred?

A. Since the side, i.e., both A and B, had not completed the play of the hole, A was practicing during play of the hole and thus was in breach of Rule 7-2.

Since it must be assumed that the breach assisted B, he would also be penalized (Rules 30-3f and 31-8).

30-3f/8
Player Disqualified for Next Hole Plays That Hole

Q. In a four-ball match, A practices chip shots to the 18th green between play of the 9th and 10th holes. Thus, A is disqualified for the 10th hole under Rule 7-2. If A plays the 10th hole, is B, A's partner, also subject to disqualification for the 10th hole if A's play of the hole assists B, e.g., with regard to club selection?

A. Since A was disqualified for the 10th hole, the strokes played by him on that hole were practice strokes. Therefore, A was in breach of Rule 7-2 each time he played a stroke on the 10th and, if B was assisted by any such stroke, B incurred the applicable penalty.

Related Decision:
• 30-3a/1 Absent Partner Joins Match During Play of Hole.

30-3f/9
Player's Ball Moved by Partner in Playing His Own Ball

Q. In four-ball match play, A and B are partners. In playing his own ball, B accidentally strikes the nearby ball of A with his club and causes it to move. What is the procedure?

A. The answer depends on whether A's ball was visible before B played.

If A's ball was visible when B made his stroke, it was reasonably foreseeable that B's stroke at his own ball could cause A's ball to move and, through exercising reasonable care by having A's ball lifted under Rule 22-2, B could have avoided causing A's ball to move. In such circumstances, A incurs a one-stroke penalty under Rule 18-2a and must replace his ball. Assuming the infringement did not assist B, B incurs no penalty (Rule 30-3f).

If A's ball was not visible when B made his stroke, it was not reasonably foreseeable that his stroke could cause A's ball to move and A is not penalized provided he replaces his ball.

If A fails to replace his ball before making his next stroke, he is disqualified from the hole for playing from a wrong place (Rules 18 and 20-7).

Related Decisions:
• 18-2a/21 Ball Moved Accidentally by Player in Playing Wrong Ball.
• 18-3b/1 Ball Moved Accidentally by Opponent in Playing His Own Ball.

30-3f/10
Player's Ball Lifted Without Authority by Opponent in a Four-Ball Match

Q. In a four-ball match, an opponent lifted a player's ball on the putting green after marking its position. He did this without the authority of the player. Is the opponent subject to penalty?

A. Yes. Rule 20-1 prohibits such action. Accordingly, the opponent incurs a penalty stroke under Rule 18-3b, but the penalty does not apply to his partner – see Rule 30-3f. The player must replace his ball.

Related Decisions:
• 20-1/2 Player's Ball Lifted by Opponent Without Authority.
• 20-1/3 Ball Marked and Lifted by Opponent Without Player's Authority; Player Lifts Ball-Marker, Claims Hole and Opponent Disputes Claim.

30-3f/11
Request to Lift Ball That Might Assist Partner Not Honored

Q. A and B are playing C and D in a four-ball match. B's ball is near the hole in a position to serve as a backstop for A's ball. C requests B to lift his ball. B does not comply and A putts. What is the ruling?

A. B is disqualified for the hole for failing to comply with Rule 22-1. If A's ball strikes B's ball, A would also be disqualified from the hole since B's infringement assisted A – Rule 30-3f. If the balls do not collide, A is not penalized.

Related Decisions:
• 2/3 Refusal to Comply with Rule in Match Play.
• 2-4/8 Player Concedes Opponent's Next Stroke and Plays Before Opponent Has Opportunity to Lift Ball.
• 16-2/4 Ball Overhanging Lip of Hole Moves When Flagstick Removed.
• 22/6 Competitor Requests That Ball in Position to Assist Him Not Be Lifted.

30-3f/12
Player in Four-Ball Practices Putts on Previous Green After Partner Has Driven from Next Tee

Q. A and B are partners in a four-ball competition. A was practicing putts on the 4th green after B drove from the 5th tee. Was A in breach of Rule 7-2?

A. Yes.

In match play, A is disqualified for the 5th hole. B incurred no penalty since A's breach did not assist him (Rule 30-3f).

In stroke play, A incurred a penalty of two strokes at the 5th hole. B incurred no penalty since A's breach did not assist him (Rule 31-8).

Related Decision:
• 29/3 Player in Foursome Match Practices Putts on Previous Green After Partner Has Driven from Next Tee.

30-3f/13
Partner Stands on Extension of Player's Line of Play Behind Ball

Q. A and B are partners in a four-ball competition. A's ball is on the putting green 30 feet from the hole, and B's ball is 20 feet from the hole on a similar line. To assist him with his own putt, B stands on an extension of the line of putt behind A's ball while A putts. What is the ruling?

A. A was in breach of Rule 14-2b by putting with his partner, B, positioned on or close to an extension of the line of putt behind the ball. As A's breach assisted B, B also incurred the same penalty (Rules 30-3f and 31-8).

In match play, Side A-B loses the hole.

In stroke play, A incurs a penalty of two strokes and B incurs the same penalty. (Revised)

RULE 31

FOUR-BALL STROKE PLAY

DEFINITIONS

All defined terms are in *italics* and are listed alphabetically in the Definitions section – see pages 6–16.

31-1. GENERAL

The Rules of Golf, so far as they are not at variance with the following specific Rules, apply to *four-ball* stroke play.

31-2. REPRESENTATION OF SIDE

A *side* may be represented by either *partner* for all or any part of a *stipulated round*; both *partners* need not be present. An absent *competitor* may join his *partner* between holes, but not during play of a hole.

31-3. SCORING

The *marker* is required to record for each hole only the gross score of whichever *partner's* score is to count. The gross scores to count must be individually identifiable; otherwise, the *side* is disqualified. Only one of the *partners* need be responsible for complying with Rule 6-6b.

(Wrong score – see Rule 31-7a)

31-4. ORDER OF PLAY

Balls belonging to the same *side* may be played in the order the *side* considers best.

31-5. WRONG BALL

If a *competitor* is in breach of Rule 15-3b for making a *stroke* at a *wrong ball*, he incurs a penalty of two strokes and must correct his mistake by playing the correct ball or by proceeding under the *Rules*. His *partner* incurs no penalty, even if the *wrong ball* belongs to him.

If the *wrong ball* belongs to another *competitor*, its owner must place a ball on the spot from which the *wrong ball* was first played.

(Placing and Replacing – see Rule 20-3)

31-6 PENALTY TO SIDE

A *side* is penalized for a breach of any of the following by any *partner*:

- Rule 4   Clubs
- Rule 6-4   Caddie
- Any Local Rule or Condition of Competition for which there is a maximum penalty per round.

31-7. DISQUALIFICATION PENALTIES
a. Breach by One Partner
A *side* is disqualified from the competition if either *partner* incurs a penalty of disqualification under any of the following:

• Rule 1-3	Agreement to Waive Rules
• Rule 3-4	Refusal to Comply with a Rule
• Rule 4	Clubs
• Rule 5-1 or 5-2	The Ball
• Rule 6-2b	Handicap
• Rule 6-4	Caddie
• Rule 6-6b	Signing and Returning Score Card
• Rule 6-6d	Wrong Score for Hole
• Rule 6-7	Undue Delay; Slow Play
• Rule 7-1	Practice Before or Between Rounds
• Rule 10-2c	Sides Agree to Play Out of Turn
• Rule 11-1	Teeing
• Rule 14-3	Artificial Devices, Unusual Equipment and Unusual Use of Equipment
• Rule 22-1	Ball Assisting Play
• Rule 31-3	Gross Scores to Count Not Individually Identifiable
• Rule 33-7	Disqualification Penalty Imposed by Committee

b. Breach by Both Partners
A *side* is disqualified from the competition:
(i) if each *partner* incurs a penalty of disqualification for a breach of Rule 6-3 (Time of Starting and Groups) or Rule 6-8 (Discontinuance of Play), or
(ii) if, at the same hole, each *partner* is in breach of a *Rule* the penalty for which is disqualification from the competition or for a hole.

c. For the Hole Only
In all other cases where a breach of a *Rule* would result in disqualification, the *competitor* is disqualified only for the hole at which the breach occurred.

31-8. EFFECT OF OTHER PENALTIES
If a *competitor's* breach of a *Rule* assists his *partner's* play, the *partner* incurs the applicable penalty in addition to any penalty incurred by the *competitor*.

In all other cases where a *competitor* incurs a penalty for breach of a *Rule*, the penalty does not apply to his *partner*.

FOUR-BALL STROKE PLAY; GENERAL

31/1
Examples of Rulings in Four-Ball Stroke Play with Concurrent Individual Competition

When competitors are involved in concurrent stroke-play competitions, whenever possible the Rules are applied only to the competition affected.

When it is not possible to separate the competitions, the four-ball competition takes precedence. The exception to that is with Rule 8-1 (Advice), as the two partners may not exchange advice if both are playing in the individual competition; if just one of them is playing in the individual competition, they may exchange advice.

A and B are partners in four-ball stroke play, and they are concurrently playing in an individual stroke-play competition. The following are examples of the application of the Rules in such a format:

(1) B moves A's ball without authority under the Rules. In the four-ball competition A incurs a penalty stroke (Rule 18-2a), but he incurs no penalty in the individual competition. B incurs no penalty in either competition.

(2) On the 3rd hole it is discovered that B started his round with 15 clubs. In the four-ball competition Side A-B incurs a total penalty of four strokes (two strokes on each of the first two holes), but A incurs no penalty in the individual competition. B incurs a total penalty of four strokes in the individual competition.

(3) During the round B makes a stroke at a non-conforming ball. In the four-ball competition Side A-B is disqualified (Rules 5-1 and 31-7a), but A incurs no penalty in the individual competition. B is disqualified from the individual competition.

Other Decisions related to Rule 31: See "Four-Ball Stroke Play" in the Index.

FOUR-BALL STROKE PLAY: REPRESENTATION OF SIDE

31-2/1
Absent Player Joins Partner After Fellow-Competitor Plays from Teeing Ground But Before Partner Plays

Q. In four-ball stroke play, A and B are playing with C and D. They have been given a starting time of 9:00 am. D arrives at 9:01 am after A has played but before B and C have played. May D play the first hole?

A. D was late for his starting time and as such, D may play the first hole, adding the penalty of two strokes prescribed by Rule 6-3a to his score for that hole. Rule 31-2 allows an absent player to join his partner before his partner has commenced play of a hole. As C had not yet played from the teeing ground, D may join him.

If D did not arrive until later in the round, he would be able to join his partner between holes without penalty, provided C had not yet played from the next tee, regardless of whether A and/or B had played. (Revised)

31-3/1
Gross Score of Partner with Better Net Score Omitted from Score Card

Q. In four-ball stroke play on a handicap basis, partners A and B both holed out in 4 at the 8th hole; partner A did not receive a handicap stroke at the hole, but partner B did. The marker, who was a fellow-competitor, recorded a gross score of 4 for A, who did not receive a stroke, and no gross score for B. However, the marker also recorded a net 3 in the better-ball column.

On completion of the round, the score card, in all other respects correct, was signed and returned to the Committee. Both the marker and the partners were interviewed, and it was established that in fact both partners had gross scores of 4 at the 8th hole. What is the ruling?

A. Under Rules 6-6b and 31-3, it was the responsibility of one of the partners to check the side's better-ball gross score for each hole before signing the score card.

When checking the score card, the partner concerned should have noticed that there was no gross score recorded for B at the 8th hole and should have corrected this mistake. As he did not do so, A's gross 4 was the side's score for the hole. It is the responsibility of the Committee – and not the competitor – to record the better-ball net score for each hole.

Related Decision:
• 6-6d/1 No Score Entered for One Hole But Total Correct.

31-4/1
Player Waives Turn to Play; Circumstances Under Which He May Complete Hole

Q. A and B are partners in four-ball stroke play. A's tee shot at a par-3 entirely over water comes to rest in the water hazard. As B's tee shot comes to rest on the putting green, A elects not to play a ball under Rule 26-1 and proceeds to the green. B four putts and scores 5 for the hole. May A return to the tee and put another ball into play under Rule 26-1?

A. Yes. However, he may be subject to penalty under Rule 6-7 for unduly delaying play.

Related Decision:
• 30-3b/2 Waiving Turn to Putt in Four-Ball Match.

31-4/2
Extent to Which Side May Play in Order It Considers Best

Rule 31-4, which is an exception to Rule 10-2 (Order of Play), permits a side to play in the order it considers best. Generally, a side will exercise its right under Rule 31-4 for strategic reasons. However, in doing so, the side must not unduly delay play (Rule 6-7).

The following are examples of a side (competitors A and B) playing in an order other than that set forth in Rule 10-2b and whether a penalty under Rule 6-7 would be appropriate:

(a) A's ball is on the putting green five feet from the hole and he plays before B, whose ball is on the putting green 20 feet from the hole – no penalty.

(b) A's ball is in an awkward lie in a hazard 30 yards from the hole and he plays before B, whose ball is in the fairway 50 yards from the hole – no penalty.

(c) A's ball is 220 yards from the hole on a par-5 hole and he plays his second stroke before B, whose ball is 240 yards from the hole, plays – no penalty.

(d) In situation (c) above, A's ball comes to rest 30 yards from the green. The side then elects to have A play his third stroke before B plays his second stroke – B is penalized two strokes for a breach of Rule 6-7.

FOUR-BALL STROKE PLAY: PENALTY TO SIDE

Decisions Related to Rule 31-6:
• 4-4a/10 Breach of 14-Club Rule in Stroke Play Discovered at 8th Hole; Where Penalty Strokes Applied.
• 30-3/2 Effect of State of Match Penalties in Four-Ball Play.

FOUR-BALL STROKE PLAY: DISQUALIFICATION PENALTIES

31-7a/1
Competitor Records Score for Hole Not Completed

Q. A and B are partners in four-ball stroke play. At the 10th hole, A picks up and B holes out in 5 strokes. The marker records a score of 6 for A and a score of 5 for B. The card is returned with these scores recorded. Is any penalty incurred because A-B returned a card containing a score for A at a hole which A did not complete?

A. No. Rule 31-7a provides that disqualification of a side under Rule 6-6d applies only when the recorded score of the partner whose score is to count is lower than actually taken. The score recorded for A was not A-B's lower score for the 10th hole. Accordingly, no penalty is applicable.

Related Decision:
• 32-2a/1 Four-Ball Stableford Competition on Handicap Basis; Side's Scores Transposed at a Hole But Not to Side's Advantage.

31-7a/2
Lower Gross Score Attributed to Wrong Partner

Q. A and B were partners in four-ball stroke play. At the 11th hole, A picked up and B holed out in 4 strokes. The marker inadvertently recorded a score of 4 for A. The card was returned. What is the ruling?

A. It was A's recorded score of 4 which was the side's gross score to count. As this was lower than the score actually taken by A, the side is disqualified under Rule 31-7a.

Related Decision:
• 32-2a/2 Four-Ball Stableford Competition on Handicap Basis; Side's Scores Transposed at a Hole to Side's Advantage.

FOUR-BALL STROKE PLAY: EFFECT OF PENALTY ON PARTNER

31-8/1
Competitor Lifts Loose Impediment in Bunker When His Ball and Partner's Ball Are in Bunker

Q. A and B are partners in a four-ball stroke-play competition. A's ball and B's ball are in the same bunker. A lifts a loose impediment lying in the bunker. A is penalized two strokes for a breach of Rule 13-4. Does B incur a penalty?

A. If A's infringement assisted B's play, B also is penalized two strokes (Rule 31-8). Otherwise, B incurs no penalty.

Related Decisions:
• 13-4/17 Loose Impediment Removed from Water Hazard; Player Then Decides Not to Play from Hazard.
• 30-3f/1 Player Lifts Loose Impediment in Bunker When His Ball and Partner's Ball in Bunker.

RULE 32

BOGEY, PAR AND STABLEFORD COMPETITIONS

DEFINITIONS
All defined terms are in *italics* and are listed alphabetically in the Definitions section – see pages 6–16.

32-1. CONDITIONS
Bogey, par and Stableford competitions are forms of stroke play in which play is against a fixed score at each hole. The *Rules* for stroke play, so far as they are not at variance with the following specific Rules, apply.

In handicap bogey, par and Stableford competitions, the *competitor* with the lowest net score at a hole takes the *honor* at the next *teeing ground*.

a. Bogey and Par Competitions
The scoring for bogey and par competitions is made as in match play.

Any hole for which a *competitor* makes no return is regarded as a loss. The winner is the *competitor* who is most successful in the aggregate of holes.

The *marker* is responsible for marking only the gross number of *strokes* for each hole where the *competitor* makes a net score equal to or less than the fixed score.

Note 1: The *competitor's* score is adjusted by deducting a hole or holes under the applicable *Rule* when a penalty other than disqualification is incurred under any of the following:
- Rule 4   Clubs
- Rule 6-4   Caddie
- Any Local Rule or Condition of Competition for which there is a maximum penalty per round.

The *competitor* is responsible for reporting the facts regarding such a breach to the *Committee* before he returns his score card so that the *Committee* may apply the penalty. If the *competitor* fails to report his breach to the *Committee*, he is disqualified.

Note 2: If the *competitor* is in breach of Rule 6-3a (Time of Starting) but arrives at his starting point, ready to play, within five minutes after his starting time, or is in breach of Rule 6-7 (Undue Delay; Slow Play), the *Committee* will deduct one hole from the aggregate of holes. For a repeated offense under Rule 6-7, see Rule 32-2a.

b. Stableford Competitions
The scoring in Stableford competitions is made by points awarded in relation to a fixed score at each hole as follows:

Hole Played In	Points
More than one over fixed score or no score returned	0
One over fixed score	1
Fixed score	2

One under fixed score	3
Two under fixed score	4
Three under fixed score	5
Four under fixed score	6

The winner is the *competitor* who scores the highest number of points.

The *marker* is responsible for marking only the gross number of *strokes* at each hole where the *competitor's* net score earns one or more points.

Note 1: If a *competitor* is in breach of a *Rule* for which there is a maximum penalty per round, he must report the facts to the *Committee* before returning his score card; if he fails to do so, he is disqualified. The *Committee* will, from the total points scored for the round, deduct two points for each hole at which any breach occurred, with a maximum deduction per round of four points for each *Rule* breached.

Note 2: If the *competitor* is in breach of Rule 6-3a (Time of Starting) but arrives at his starting point, ready to play, within five minutes after his starting time, or is in breach of Rule 6-7 (Undue Delay; Slow Play), the *Committee* will deduct two points from the total points scored for the round. For a repeated offense under Rule 6-7, see Rule 32-2a.

Note 3: For the purpose of preventing slow play, the *Committee* may, in the conditions of a competition (Rule 33-1), establish pace of play guidelines, including maximum periods of time allowed to complete a *stipulated round*, a hole or a *stroke*.

The *Committee* may, in such a condition, modify the penalty for a breach of this Rule as follows:

First offense – Deduction of one point from the total points scored for the round;

Second offense – Deduction of a further two points from the total points scored for the round;

For subsequent offense – Disqualification.

32-2. DISQUALIFICATION PENALTIES
a. From the Competition

A *competitor* is disqualified from the competition if he incurs a penalty of disqualification under any of the following:

• Rule 1-3	Agreement to Waive Rules
• Rule 3-4	Refusal to Comply with a Rule
• Rule 4	Clubs
• Rule 5-1 or 5-2	The Ball
• Rule 6-2b	Handicap
• Rule 6-3	Time of Starting and Groups
• Rule 6-4	Caddie
• Rule 6-6b	Signing and Returning Score Card
• Rule 6-6d	Wrong Score for Hole, i.e., when the recorded score is lower than actually taken, except that no penalty is incurred when a breach of this Rule does not affect the result of the hole

- Rule 6-7   Undue Delay; Slow Play
- Rule 6-8   Discontinuance of Play
- Rule 7-1   Practice Before or Between Rounds
- Rule 11-1   Teeing
- Rule 14-3   Artificial Devices, Unusual Equipment and Unusual Use of Equipment
- Rule 22-1   Ball Assisting Play
- Rule 33-7   Disqualification Penalty Imposed by Committee

b. For a Hole

In all other cases where a breach of a *Rule* would result in disqualification, the *competitor* is disqualified only for the hole at which the breach occurred.

BOGEY, PAR AND STABLEFORD COMPETITIONS: CONDITIONS

32-1/1
Competing Simultaneously in Bogey, Par or Stableford Competition and Stroke-Play Competition

Q. Is it permissible for a player to compete simultaneously in a bogey, par or Stableford competition and a stroke-play competition?

A. Yes, as bogey, par and Stableford competitions are each forms of stroke-play competition.

Related Decision:
- 33-1/6 Players in Match Compete Concurrently in Stroke-Play Competition.

32-1/2
Omitting Holes in Bogey, Par or Stableford Competition

Q. In a bogey, par or Stableford competition, may a player omit, for example, two holes for the round and return a score for 16 holes?

A. Yes. Under Rule 32-1a, any hole for which a competitor makes no return in a bogey or par competition is regarded as a loss. Under Rule 32-1b, if no score is returned on a hole in a Stableford competition, the competitor scores no points for that hole.

32-2a/1
Four-Ball Stableford Competition on Handicap Basis; Side's Scores Transposed at a Hole But Not to Side's Advantage

Q. A and B were partners in a four-ball Stableford competition on a handicap basis. At a hole where A, but not B, received a handicap stroke, A scored a 4 (net 3) and B scored a 5. The marker inadvertently transposed the scores, recording a 5 (net 4) for A and a 4 for B. The card was returned with these scores recorded. What is the ruling?

A. There is no penalty. Although B's recorded score of 4 was lower than the score actually taken by him, since it was not lower than the recorded score of net 4 for A (which was higher than actually taken by A), there was no breach of Rule 31-7a. Nor was there a breach of Rule 32-2a, since the error did not affect the result of the hole.

The same ruling would apply in a four-ball bogey or par competition on a handicap basis.

Related Decision:
• 31-7a/1 Competitor Records Score for Hole Not Completed.

32-2a/2
Four-Ball Stableford Competition on Handicap Basis; Side's Scores Transposed at a Hole to Side's Advantage

Q. A and B were partners in a four-ball Stableford competition on a handicap basis. At a hole, A scored 4 (net 3) and B scored 5 (net 4). The marker inadvertently transposed the scores, recording 5 (net 4) for A and 4 (net 3) for B. The card was returned with these scores recorded. What is the ruling?

A. B's recorded score of 4 (net 3) was the lower recorded score. As this was lower than the score actually taken by B and was also lower than A's recorded score of 5 (net 4), the result of the hole was affected and the side is disqualified under Rule 32-2a for a breach of Rule 31-7a.

The same ruling would apply in a four-ball bogey or par competition on a handicap basis.

Related Decision:
• 31-7a/2 Lower Gross Score Attributed to Wrong Partner.

32-2a/3
Handicap Stableford Competition; Recording of Lower Gross Score Affects Result of Hole

Q. In a handicap Stableford competition against a fixed score of par, a competitor inadvertently returns his score card to the Committee with a score of 6 at the

9th hole when his score for the hole was actually 7. The 9th hole is a par 4 at which the competitor receives a handicap stroke. What is the ruling?

A. As the recording of the lower score affected the result of the hole, i.e., the competitor would be awarded 1 point for the hole when he should have received no points, the competitor is disqualified under Rule 32-2a for a breach of Rule 6-6d.

32-2a/4
Handicap Stableford Competition; Recording of Lower Gross Score Does Not Affect Result of Hole

Q. In a handicap Stableford competition against a fixed score of par, a competitor inadvertently returns his score card to the Committee with a score of 6 at the 11th hole when his score for the hole was actually 7. The 11th hole is a par 4 at which the competitor receives no handicap strokes. What is the ruling?

A. As the recording of the lower score did not affect the result of the hole, i.e., the competitor would be awarded no points for the hole despite recording a 6 instead of a 7, there is no penalty (Rule 32-2a).

32-2a/5
Handicap Bogey or Par Competition; Recording of Lower Gross Score Does Not Affect Result of Hole

Q. In a handicap bogey or par competition, a competitor inadvertently returns his score card to the Committee with a score of 3 at the 10th hole when his score for the hole was actually 4. The 10th hole is a par 4 at which the competitor receives a handicap stroke. What is the ruling?

A. As the recording of the lower score did not affect the result of the hole, i.e., the competitor would be awarded the hole despite recording a 3 instead of a 4, there is no penalty (Rule 32-2a).

BOGEY, PAR AND STABLEFORD COMPETITIONS: DISQUALIFICATION FOR HOLE

32-2b/1
Breach of Rule by Both Partners at Same Hole in Four-Ball Stableford

Q. A and B are partners in a four-ball Stableford competition. During the play of a hole, A and B find they have exchanged balls at the previous hole. What is the ruling?

A. A and B are not disqualified from the competition but only for the hole at which they exchanged balls, for which they score no points.

Other Decisions related to Rule 32: See "Bogey Competition," "Par Competition" and "Stableford Competition" in the Index.

RULE 33

THE COMMITTEE

DEFINITIONS
All defined terms are in *italics* and are listed alphabetically in the Definitions section – see pages 6–16.

33-1. CONDITIONS; WAIVING RULE
The *Committee* must establish the conditions under which a competition is to be played.

The *Committee* has no power to waive a Rule of Golf.

Certain specific *Rules* governing stroke play are so substantially different from those governing match play that combining the two forms of play is not practicable and is not permitted. The result of a match played in these circumstances is null and void and, in the stroke-play competition, the *competitors* are disqualified.

In stroke play, the *Committee* may limit a *referee*'s duties.

33-2. THE COURSE
a. Defining Bounds and Margins
The *Committee* must define accurately:
(i) the *course* and *out of bounds*,
(ii) the margins of *water hazards* and *lateral water hazards*,
(iii) *ground under repair*, and
(iv) *obstructions* and integral parts of the *course*.

b. New Holes
New *holes* should be made on the day on which a stroke-play competition begins and at such other times as the *Committee* considers necessary, provided all *competitors* in a single round play with each *hole* cut in the same position.

Exception: When it is impossible for a damaged *hole* to be repaired so that it conforms with the Definition, the *Committee* may make a new *hole* in a nearby similar position.

Note: Where a single round is to be played on more than one day, the *Committee* may provide, in the conditions of a competition (Rule 33-1), that the *holes* and *teeing grounds* may be differently situated on each day of the competition, provided that, on any one day, all *competitors* play with each *hole* and each *teeing ground* in the same position.

c. Practice Ground
Where there is no practice ground available outside the area of a competition *course*, the *Committee* should establish the area on which players may practice on any day of a competition, if it is practicable to do so. On any day of a stroke-play competition, the *Committee* should not normally permit practice on or to a *putting green* or from a *hazard* of the competition *course*.

d. Course Unplayable

If the *Committee* or its authorized representative considers that for any reason the *course* is not in a playable condition or that there are circumstances that render the proper playing of the game impossible, it may, in match play or stroke play, order a temporary suspension of play or, in stroke play, declare play null and void and cancel all scores for the round in question. When a round is canceled, all penalties incurred in that round are canceled.

(Procedure in discontinuing and resuming play – see Rule 6-8)

33-3. TIMES OF STARTING AND GROUPS

The *Committee* must establish the times of starting and, in stroke play, arrange the groups in which *competitors* must play.

When a match play competition is played over an extended period, the *Committee* establishes the limit of time within which each round must be completed. When players are allowed to arrange the date of their match within these limits, the *Committee* should announce that the match must be played at a stated time on the last day of the period, unless the players agree to a prior date.

33-4. HANDICAP STROKE TABLE

The *Committee* must publish a table indicating the order of holes at which handicap strokes are to be given or received.

33-5. SCORE CARD

In stroke play, the *Committee* must provide each *competitor* with a score card containing the date and the *competitor's* name or, in *foursome* or *four-ball* stroke play, the *competitors'* names.

In stroke play, the *Committee* is responsible for the addition of scores and application of the handicap recorded on the score card.

In *four-ball* stroke play, the *Committee* is responsible for recording the better-ball score for each hole and in the process applying the handicaps recorded on the score card, and adding the better-ball scores.

In bogey, par and Stableford competitions, the *Committee* is responsible for applying the handicap recorded on the score card and determining the result of each hole and the overall result or points total.

Note: The *Committee* may request that each *competitor* records the date and his name on his score card.

33-6. DECISION OF TIES

The *Committee* must announce the manner, day and time for the decision of a halved match or of a tie, whether played on level terms or under handicap.

A halved match must not be decided by stroke play. A tie in stroke play must not be decided by a match.

33-7. DISQUALIFICATION PENALTY; COMMITTEE DISCRETION

A penalty of disqualification may in exceptional individual cases be waived, modified or imposed if the *Committee* considers such action warranted.

Any penalty less than disqualification must not be waived or modified.

If a *Committee* considers that a player is guilty of a serious breach of etiquette, it may impose a penalty of disqualification under this Rule.

33-8. LOCAL RULES
a. Policy

The *Committee* may establish Local Rules for local abnormal conditions if they are consistent with the policy set forth in Appendix I.

b. Waiving or Modifying a Rule

A Rule of Golf must not be waived by a Local Rule. However, if a *Committee* considers that local abnormal conditions interfere with the proper playing of the game to the extent that it is necessary to make a Local Rule that modifies the Rules of Golf, the Local Rule must be authorized by the USGA.

THE COMMITTEE; GENERAL

33/1
Removal of Casual Water or Loose Impediments on Putting Green by Committee

Q. If casual water, leaves, sand or other loose impediments accumulate on a putting green during a round, would it be appropriate for the Committee to remove them?

A. Yes. The Committee may do what is necessary to eliminate the condition, e.g., use a squeegee or brush or blow the surface of the putting green. It is not necessary for the Committee to suspend play to take these actions.

In such cases, the Committee may, when necessary, enlist the help of players to eliminate the condition. However, a player would be in breach of Rule 13-2 if he were to mop up casual water on his line of play or line of putt without the Committee's permission.

Related Decisions:
- 16-1a/4 Removing Casual Water from Hole.
- 16-1d/4 Testing for Wetness of Surface of Putting Green Behind Ball.
- 33-2d/2 Hole Surrounded by Casual Water.

33/2 (Reserved)

33/3
Match-Play Finalists Both Disqualified

If both finalists in a match play competition are disqualified, the Committee may decide to conclude the event without a winner. Alternatively, the Committee could elect to have the defeated semi-finalists play a match to determine the winner of the competition.

33/4 (Reserved)

33/5 (Reserved)

33/6
Map of Putting Green Indicating Hole Position Displayed at Tee

Q. At the teeing ground of each hole, a Committee has displayed a map of the putting green. The position of the hole on the green is indicated on each map. Is this proper?

A. Yes. Displaying such maps is not contrary to the Rules.

33/7
Whether Player Disqualified in Match-Play Event Entitled to Prize Won Prior to Disqualification

Q. If a player in a match play event is disqualified, should he be entitled to any prize he had previously won in the event?

A. Yes.

Related Decision:
• 33-1/13 Competitor Disqualified from Handicap Event Claims Gross Prize.

33/8
Application of Disqualification Penalty in Competition in Which Not All Scores Used to Determine Winner

Q. In a 72-hole stroke-play team competition with each team consisting of three players, a team's score for each round is the aggregate of the two best scores for the round. In the first of four rounds, a player is disqualified under Rule 6-3a. May he play in the subsequent rounds and have his score count?

A. Yes. The disqualification applies only to that round of the competition. This applies to all events in which not all scores are used to determine the winner (e.g., an individual competition in which the player counts his three best scores from four rounds).

However, if the player had been disqualified under Rule 33-7 or for a serious breach of Rule 1-2, it is up to the Committee to determine whether that disqualification should be for the round or the duration of the competition.

Related Decision:
• 6-2b/5 Competition in Which Best Two of Four Scores Used to Determine Winner; Competitor Returns Score Card with Higher Handicap.

Other Decisions related to the Committee: See "Committee" in the Index.

ESTABLISHING CONDITIONS OF COMPETITION

33-1/1
Altering Conditions After Competition Starts

Q. A condition of a stroke-play competition provided that scores must be returned by 7:30 pm. At 5:00 pm, a member of the Committee extended the deadline to accommodate four late-arriving competitors. Is such action proper?

A. No. Once a competition has started, the conditions should be altered only in very exceptional circumstances. In this case, no such circumstances existed.

33-1/2
Number of Holes of Stroke-Play Competition Reduced During the Competition

Q. A 72-hole stroke-play competition is scheduled over four consecutive days. Eighteen holes are to be played each day. On the third day, all competitors finish the first nine holes but a number of competitors are still playing the second nine holes. At that point, the course becomes unplayable due to heavy rain and play is suspended. The rain continues and it is impossible to resume play that day. What are the Committee's options?

A. Under Rules 33-1 and 33-2d, the Committee has the following choices:
   (a) resume play the next day and finish the third round and then play the last 18 holes that day or on a subsequent day,
   (b) cancel the third round, replay it on a subsequent day and then play the last 18 holes that day or on a subsequent day,
   (c) reduce to three the number of rounds of the competition and finish the suspended third round on a subsequent day, or cancel the third round and replay it on a subsequent day, or
   (d) cancel the third and fourth rounds and declare the leader after 36 holes to be the winner.

The third and fourth choices are undesirable. It is preferable not to reduce the number of rounds of a competition when the competition is in progress.

The Committee does not have the authority to reduce the number of holes of a stipulated round once play has commenced on that round.

Related Decision:
• 33-2d/1 Guidelines on Whether to Cancel Round.

33-1/3
Starting Players from 1st and 10th Tees

Q. May the Committee start play in a competition from both the 1st and10th tees?

A. Yes. See Definition of "Stipulated Round," which says that the holes are to be played in correct sequence unless otherwise authorized by the Committee.

33-1/3.5
Restriction on Which Partner in Foursome Competition May Play from 1st Tee

Q. Rule 29-1 states that in a foursome "the partners must play alternately from the teeing grounds and alternately during the play of each hole." However, it is a matter of personal choice which partner drives at the 1st tee.

May a Committee, in the conditions of a foursome competition, stipulate which partner must play from the 1st tee?

A. Yes.

33-1/4
Match Decided by Wrong Form of Play by Agreement of Players

Q. The four participants in a first-round match thought the competition was a foursome competition, whereas it was in fact a four-ball competition. They played the first hole on a foursome basis and then learned of their error. Rather than go back and begin again on a four-ball basis, they agreed (1) to continue playing a foursome and (2) that in the four-ball competition the side losing the foursome match would default to the winning side.

The matter came to the Committee's attention after the side receiving the default reached the semi-finals of the four-ball event. What should the Committee do?

A. The side should be disqualified under Rule 1-3 for agreeing to decide a match other than as prescribed in the conditions, and the Committee should decide how the competition should be concluded.

Related Decisions:
• 2-4/21 Wrong Form of Play Used to Decide Which Side Concedes Match.
• 6-1/1 Wrong Form of Play Used in Match-Play Event.

33-1/5
Competitor in Stroke-Play Event Plays with Two Players Engaged in Match

Q. A competitor in a stroke-play competition had no other competitor with whom to play. So he joined two players engaged in a match and one of those players served as his marker. Is such procedure considered combining stroke play and match play, contrary to Rule 33-1?

A. No. The competitor was playing stroke play only and the other two players were playing match play only. The Committee should retrospectively appoint the player concerned as the competitor's marker – see Definition of "Marker."

Related Decision:
• 6-6a/1 Lone Competitor Appoints Own Marker.

33-1/6
Players in Match Compete Concurrently in Stroke-Play Competition

Q. In ignorance of the Rules, A and B played a match and concurrently competed in a stroke-play competition. What should the Committee do?

A. Under Rule 33-1, the result of the match is null and void, and A and B are disqualified in the stroke-play competition.

If the match was to be played on any day in a prescribed period, A and B must replay the match within the prescribed period. If it was too late for A and B to replay the match within the period, A and B are disqualified from the match-play competition, unless one concedes the match to the other.

Related Decision:
• 32-1/1 Competing Simultaneously in Bogey, Par or Stableford Competition and Stroke-Play Competition.

33-1/7
Making Competitors Responsible for Adding Scores

Q. May the Committee make it a condition of a competition that competitors are responsible for the addition of scores?

A. No. Such a condition would modify Rule 33-5.

Related Decisions:
• 6-6a/6 Requirement That Alteration on Score Card Be Initialled.
• 6-6b/8 Requirement That Score Be Entered into Computer.

33-1/8
Use of Golf Carts in Competition

Q. May a player use a golf cart during a competition?

A. Yes, unless such equipment is prohibited in the conditions of the competition (Rule 33-1).

33-1/9 (Reserved)

33-1/9.5
Breach of Transportation Condition by Caddie

Q. The Committee has adopted the Transportation Condition in Appendix I as a condition of competition. During the stipulated round, a player's caddie accepts a ride on a golf cart without the authority of the Committee. Is the player penalized for the caddie's breach of the condition?

A. Yes. The player is responsible for any breach of a Rule during a stipulated round by his caddie and incurs the applicable penalty (Rule 6-1).

Related Decisions:
- 6-4/2.5 Status of Individual Who Transports Player's Clubs on Motorized Golf Cart or Trolley.
- 33-8/4 Local Rule for Events in Which Motorized Golf Carts Permitted.

33-1/10 (Reserved)

33-1/11 (Reserved)

33-1/11.5
Status of Team Captain or Coach

Q. May a Committee, in the conditions of a team competition, specify that, during the stipulated round, the team captain or coach is part of the match or part of the competitor's side, i.e., he is not an outside agency?

A. Yes. If such a condition is adopted, the player(s) or, in some circumstances, the team would be responsible for any breach of the Rules by the captain or coach.

Related Decisions: See "Team Competition" in the Index.

33-1/12
Wrong Handicap Used Due to Committee Misinformation

Q. The players in a four-ball match were unsure as to the handicaps to which they were entitled under the conditions of the competition. They consulted a member of the Committee who wrongly advised them as to the condition regarding handicaps. This resulted in Player A receiving one less handicap stroke than he was entitled to receive. Player A's side lost the match, 4 and 3. The Committee representative's error was then discovered. What should the Committee do?

A. The Committee should resolve the matter in whatever manner it considers most equitable. The Committee could let the result stand or require a replay of the match.

All players except Player A received the correct number of handicap strokes and Player A received only one less stroke than he should have received. In view of this fact and the rather one-sided result, it is recommended that the fairest solution would be to let the result stand.

Related Decisions:
- 6-2a/5 Wrong Handicap Used in Match by Mistake; Error Discovered After Result Officially Announced.
- 6-2a/6 Wrong Handicap Allowance Used in Match.
- 30-3a/3 Determination of Handicap Allowances in Four-Ball Match If One Player Unable to Compete.

33-1/13
Competitor Disqualified from Handicap Event Claims Gross Prize

Q. In a stroke-play event, a competitor played off a higher handicap than that to which he was entitled. Although the event was primarily a handicap one, there was also a gross prize, and the competitor concerned had the lowest gross score.

The competitor was disqualified from the handicap competition under Rule 6-2b, but he claimed the gross prize. Should he receive the gross prize?

A. Yes.

Related Decision:
- 33/7 Whether Player Disqualified in Match-Play Event Entitled to Prize Won Prior to Disqualification.

33-1/14
Condition Regarding Footwear

Q. May a Committee, in the conditions of a competition, prohibit the use of shoes with metal or traditionally designed spikes?

A. Yes.

Other Decisions related to Rule 33-1: See "Conditions of Competition" in the Index.

DEFINING BOUNDS, MARGINS, GROUND UNDER REPAIR AND OBSTRUCTIONS

33-2a/1
Exposed Water Pipe Adjacent and Parallel to Boundary Fence Causes Problems; Suggested Procedure

Q. An exposed water pipe (obstruction) which is parallel to, and about six inches inside, a boundary fence is causing a problem. If a ball lies near the boundary fence, the prohibition against free relief from the fence is effectively negated because in most cases the player would be entitled to drop away from the fence by taking free relief from the water pipe under Rule 24-2b. Is there a solution to this dilemma?

A. It is suggested that the water pipe be declared an integral part of the course and thus not an obstruction – see Definition of "Obstructions" – in which case the player would have to play the ball as it lies or deem it unplayable.

33-2a/2
Declaring Area as Ground Under Repair During Competition Round

Q. A's ball is in a poor lie in a washed-out area which warrants being marked as ground under repair but is not so marked. He deems the ball unplayable and proceeds under Rule 28, incurring a one-stroke penalty.

Subsequently, in the same competition round, B's ball is in the same area. B requests the Committee to declare the area ground under repair. Would the Committee be justified in declaring the area ground under repair in such circumstances?

A. Yes; this applies in either match or stroke play. However, it is preferable that all areas which warrant marking as ground under repair should be so marked before the start of a competition.

Related Decision:
• 34-2/1 Referee's Authority to Declare Ground Under Repair.

33-2a/3
Extensive Damage Due to Heavy Rain and Traffic

When heavy rains have resulted in many areas of unusual damage to the course (such as deep ruts caused by vehicles or footprints by spectators) and it is not feasible to define them with stakes or lines, a notice to players along the following lines is suggested:

"Ground under repair may include areas of unusual damage, including areas where spectators or other traffic have combined with wet conditions to affect materially the ground surface, but only when so declared by a Committee member."

Without such a notice, Committee members have authority to declare unusual damage to be ground under repair, if so authorized. However, a notice has the advantage of advising all players that relief from unusual damage might be given.

33-2a/4
Where to Place Lines or Stakes Defining Margin of Water Hazard

Lines and stakes defining the margins of a water hazard should be placed as nearly as possible along the natural limits of the hazard, i.e., where the ground breaks down to form the depression containing the water. See also Decision 26-1/19.

Related Decisions:
- 26/2 Ball Within Natural Margin of Water Hazard But Outside Stakes Defining Margin.
- 26-1/18 Impossible to Drop Not Nearer Hole Than Point Where Ball Last Crossed Margin of Lateral Water Hazard.
- 26-1/19 Permissible Dropping Area Under Lateral Water Hazard Rule So Narrow Player Has Difficulty Dropping Within It.
- 33-2a/9 Part of Lateral Water Hazard Where Impossible to Drop Not Nearer Hole.
- 33-8/37.5 Local Rule for Water Hazard with Bunker Adjacent

33-2a/5 (Reserved)

33-2a/6
Pond Is Water Hazard from Back Tee and Lateral Water Hazard from Forward Tee

Q. A pond on a par-3 hole meets the Definition of a lateral water hazard in play from the forward tee but not from the back tee. How should the Committee handle this situation?

A. The pond should be defined as a water hazard with yellow stakes or a yellow line and there should be a Local Rule to the effect that the hazard is a lateral water hazard in play from the forward tee.

33-2a/7
Deeming Body of Water as Both Water Hazard and Lateral Water Hazard

A given part of a body of water must not be defined as both a water hazard and a lateral water hazard in play of a particular hole, except in the circumstances described in Decision 33-2a/6.

A given part of a body of water may be defined as a water hazard in play of one hole and a lateral water hazard in play of another hole.

A given part of a body of water may be defined as a water hazard and another part of the same body of water as a lateral water hazard.

33-2a/8
Treating Ocean and Beach as Through the Green

There is no authority in the Rules for a Committee to treat the ocean and adjoining beach and rocks as through the green.

Such treatment results in a more severe penalty in many instances than is the case if the ocean, beach and rocks are properly defined as a water hazard or lateral water hazard.

33-2a/9
Part of Lateral Water Hazard Where Impossible to Drop Not Nearer Hole

If part of a lateral water hazard at the side of a putting green is so configured that it may be impossible to drop a ball within two club-lengths of the point where the ball last crossed the hazard margin without dropping nearer the hole than that point, the following is suggested:

(1) the part of the hazard where the situation exists should be distinctively marked;

(2) one or more dropping zones should be established; and

(3) a Local Rule should state that, if a ball in the lateral water hazard last crossed the margin of the hazard in the marked area, the player may, under penalty of one stroke, drop a ball in the dropping zone or, if more than one dropping zone has been established, in the nearest dropping zone.

Related Decisions:
- 26/2 Ball Within Natural Margin of Water Hazard But Outside Stakes Defining Margin.
- 26-1/18 Impossible to Drop Not Nearer Hole Than Point Where Ball Last Crossed Margin of Lateral Water Hazard.
- 26-1/19 Permissible Dropping Area Under Lateral Water Hazard Rule So Narrow Player Has Difficulty Dropping Within It.
- 33-2a/4 Where to Place Lines or Stakes Defining Margin of Water Hazard.

33-2a/10
How to Mark Island Green

Q. A putting green is situated on an island in a lake. The water between the tee and the green is defined as a water hazard. The water on each side is marked as a lateral water hazard. How should the water behind the island be marked?

A. The Committee would be justified in marking the water behind the island as a lateral water hazard.

Alternatively, the Committee might consider defining the entire lake as a water hazard, establishing a dropping zone and adopting a Local Rule giving a player whose ball lies in the hazard the option of dropping a ball in the dropping zone, under penalty of one stroke.

33-2a/10.5
Status of Tree Basins

Q. What is the status under the Rules of tree wells or tree basins?

A. There is no relief under the Rules from tree basins which are not made of artificial materials.

If a tree basin has an artificial wall, the wall is an obstruction unless the Committee deems it to be an integral part of the course under Rule 33-2a.

33-2a/11
Defining Body of Water Adjacent to Course

Q. A body of water (e.g., a river, lake or ocean) is adjacent to a hole and is off club property. The Definition of "Water Hazard" refers to a body of water "on the course." How may the Committee define the body of water?

A. The Committee may define the body of water as a water hazard (or lateral water hazard), even though it is off the club's property. The phrase "on the course" in the Definition of "Water Hazard" does not mean on property owned by the club; rather, it refers to any area not defined as out of bounds by the Committee.

When it is possible for a ball to finish on ground on the opposite side of a body of water, but it is impracticable for the Committee to define the opposite margin, the Committee may adopt a Local Rule stating that when marked on just one side, a water hazard is deemed to extend to infinity. Accordingly, all ground and water beyond the defined margin of the hazard is in the hazard.   When it is not possible for a ball to finish on the opposite side of the body of water (e.g., as with a wide river, large lake or ocean), such a Local Rule is not necessary.

In some situations the Committee may decide to define such a body of water as out of bounds for safety reasons (e.g., to prevent players playing from an unstable bank or cliff) or to ensure that a hole plays as designed (e.g., not to give the players the ability to play from the beach).

33-2a/12
Internal Boundary Between Holes

Q. It is proposed to install boundary stakes between two holes as a safety measure. It would prevent players playing a dog-leg hole from driving onto the fairway of another hole in order to cut the "dog-leg." Is it permissible to establish such a boundary?

A. Yes. For the recommended status of such boundary stakes, see Decision 24/5.

33-2a/13
Tee Decreed to Be in Bounds for the Tee Shot and Out of Bounds Thereafter

Q. A Committee has decreed that ground surrounding a certain teeing ground is in bounds for tee shots and out of bounds thereafter. Is this permissible?

A. No. In play of a particular hole, an area cannot be both in bounds and out of bounds.

33-2a/14
Internal Out of Bounds Applying to Stroke from Teeing Ground Only

A Committee may make a Local Rule under Rule 33-2a declaring part of an adjoining hole to be out of bounds when playing a particular hole, but it is not permissible for a Committee to make a Local Rule placing an area of the course out of bounds to a stroke played from the teeing ground only.

Related Decision:
• 33-8/20 Local Rule Providing Relief from Unsurfaced Road for Tee Shot Only.

Decisions related to 33-2a/12 through 33-2a/14:
• 27/20 Public Road Defined as Out of Bounds Divides Course; Status of Ball Crossing Road.
• 33-8/38 Local Rule Deeming Out of Bounds Ball Which Crosses Boundary But Comes to Rest on Course.

33-2a/15
Establishing Boundary Line Inside Fence on Property Line

Q. Along a fence on our property line, i.e., the fence is a boundary fence, there are flower beds. To save time and protect the flowers, it is proposed to move the boundary line inward several feet by establishing white stakes along the inside edge of the flower bed. Is this permitted by the Rules?

A. Yes.

33-2a/16
Deeming Ball in Bounds Until Beyond Boundary Wall

Q. Because a boundary wall is in disrepair and the inside face is irregular, the Committee has declared by Local Rule that a ball is not out of bounds until it is beyond the wall. Is this permissible or must the inside face of the wall serve as the boundary line?

A. Such procedure is permissible. There is nothing in the Rules stating that, in the case of a boundary wall, the inside face of the wall serves as the boundary line.

33-2a/17 (Reserved)

33-2a/18 (Reserved)

33-2a/19
Boundary Altered by Unauthorized Removal of Boundary Stake

In stroke play, a boundary line has been altered through unauthorized removal of a boundary stake and, therefore, there is an area (Area X) which is in bounds if the removed stake is disregarded and out of bounds if the removed stake is replaced.

Q1 A's ball comes to rest in Area X. A is aware that the boundary has been altered. He asks the Committee for a ruling. What is the ruling?

A1 The Committee should replace the removed stake, i.e., restore the original boundary line and require A to proceed under Rule 27-1, unless the Committee knows that one or more preceding competitors had, in ignorance of the fact that a stake has been removed, played from Area X. In that case, the Committee should allow the altered boundary line to stand for the remainder of the competition, and A would play his ball as it lay.

Q2 What would be the ruling if the Committee determined that one or more competitors had, in ignorance of the fact that a stake was missing, played from Area X and one or more other competitors had treated Area X as out of bounds and proceeded under Rule 27-1?

A2 If the inconsistent treatment of Area X could significantly affect the result of the competition, the round should be canceled and replayed. Otherwise, the round should stand.

33-2a/20
Displaced Boundary Stake

Q. A boundary stake has fallen down, or has been removed without authority of the Committee. The stake is lying several feet from the hole in which it had been situated. It is obvious that the stake had been displaced.

A player's ball comes to rest in bounds near the hole in which the boundary stake had been situated. The ball is in such a position that, if the boundary stake were reinstalled, it would interfere with the player's swing.

Is the player required to replace the stake before playing his next stroke?

A. No. If a boundary fence or stake is leaning towards the course and as a result interferes with a player's swing, the player is not allowed to straighten the fence or the stake – see Decision 13-2/18. It follows that, if the boundary fence or stake is leaning away from the course the player is not allowed to straighten it.

A displaced boundary stake is a movable obstruction. Therefore, the player may replace it but he is not required to do so.

Other Decisions related to Rule 33-2a: See "Margins of Areas of the Course" and "Marking or Defining Course" in the Index.

CUTTING OF NEW HOLES

33-2b/1
Holes Relocated and/or Tee-Markers Moved During Stroke-Play Round

Q. During a round in a stroke-play competition, one or more holes were relocated and/or tee-markers moved. What is the proper procedure?

A. If this was authorized by the Committee, the round should be declared null and void. In stroke play, the Committee is prohibited from relocating a hole and from moving tee-markers except as provided in the Exception and Note to Rule 33-2b or in circumstances such as those in Decisions 25-1b/4 or 33-2b/1.5.

If this was done without the authority or sanction of the Committee, generally the round should be declared null and void. However, if the course has not been altered significantly and no competitor has been given an undue advantage or disadvantage, the Committee would be justified in letting the round stand.

33-2b/1.5
Committee Wishes to Move Hole During Stroke-Play Round Due to Severity of Location

Q. During a round in a stroke-play competition, the Committee discovers that one of the holes is positioned such that the ball will not stop near the hole due to the severity of the slope at the hole. As a result, the majority of players who have played the hole have taken an excessive number of putts to hole out. What are the Committee's options in such circumstances?

A. There is no good solution in such a case, and the Committee, taking into account all factors (e.g., how severe the hole location is, how many players have completed play of the hole and where the hole is in the round), should take the course of action that it considers to be the fairest to all the players. In the circumstances described, the following are examples of actions the Committee may take:

(a) Have play continue with the hole location unchanged on the basis that the conditions are the same for all players in the field;

(b) Keep the hole in the same location but take some action, e.g., watering the putting green between groups, to make the hole location less severe;

(c) Declare the round null and void and have all players start the round again.

(d) Suspend play, relocate the hole and have the players who played the hole return at the conclusion of their rounds to replay the hole. The score for the hole for these players is the score achieved when the hole is replayed;

(e) Have all players disregard their score for the hole in question and play another hole (whether on the competition course or elsewhere) for their score for the hole.

Options (d) and (e) should be taken only in extreme circumstances because they alter the stipulated round for some or all players.

33-2b/2
Relocating Hole After Ball Already Positioned Nearby on Putting Green

Q. A's ball comes to rest on the putting green four feet from the hole. B's ball then strikes the hole, severely damaging the hole before coming to rest off the putting green, 30 feet from the hole. The players attempt to repair the damage caused by the impact of the ball as permitted by Rule 16-1c, but they are unable to restore the hole to its proper dimensions and call for a ruling. What should the Committee do?

A. The Committee should attempt to repair the hole so that it conforms with the Definition of "Hole." If this is not possible, the players may complete the hole with the hole in its damaged state. It is not desirable to relocate the hole, as provided in the Exception to Rule 33-2b, before all players in the group have completed play of the hole. However, the Committee may relocate the hole in a nearby similar position if it is necessary to ensure the proper playing of the game.

If it was necessary to relocate the hole before A and B made their next strokes, as A's ball was on the putting green, in equity (Rule 1-4), the Committee should require A to relocate his ball to a position comparable to that which his stroke had given him originally. As B's ball was off the putting green, the Committee should require B to play his ball as it lies. The same principle would apply in match play.

Decisions related to 33-2b/1 through 33-2b/2:
• 16-1a/6 Damaged Hole; Procedure for Player.
• 25-1b/4 Casual Water Covering Teeing Ground.

SUSPENDING PLAY OR CANCELLING SCORES

33-2d/1
Guidelines on Whether to Cancel Round

Q. In stroke play, in what circumstances should a Committee cancel a round?

A. There is no hard-and-fast rule. The proper action depends on the circumstances in each case and must be left to the judgment of the Committee.

Generally, a round should be canceled only in a case where it would be grossly unfair not to cancel it. For example, if some competitors begin a round under extremely adverse weather conditions, conditions subsequently worsen and further play that day is impossible, it would be unfair to the competitors who started not to cancel the round.

Related Decision:
• 33-1/2 Number of Holes of Stroke-Play Competition Reduced During the Competition.

33-2d/2
Hole Surrounded by Casual Water

If all the area around a hole contains casual water, in stroke play the course should be considered unplayable and the Committee should suspend play under Rule 33-2d. In match play, the Committee should relocate the hole.

Related Decisions:
• 16-1a/6 Damaged Hole; Procedure for Player.
• 25-1b/4 Casual Water Covering Teeing Ground.

33-2d/3
Competitor Refuses to Start or Picks Up Because of Weather Conditions; Round Subsequently Canceled

Q. In stroke play, A refuses to start at the time arranged by the Committee because of inclement weather, and B picks up during the round for the same reason. Subsequently, the course becomes unplayable and the Committee cancels the round and reschedules it for the next day. Are A and B entitled to play the next day?

A. Yes. When a round is canceled all penalties incurred in the round are canceled – see Rule 33-2d.

Related Decisions:
• 6-8b/5 Player Claiming Danger from Lightning Refuses to Resume Play When Resumption Ordered by Committee.
• 6-8b/8 Player Drops Ball After Play Suspended for Dangerous Situation.
• 30-3e/1 Partners Fail to Discontinue Play Immediately Contrary to Condition of Competition.

33-2d/4
Match Begun in Ignorance That Course Closed

Q. Two players began a match at 10:00 am. After the players had played two holes, a member of the Committee arrived and advised them that the course had been closed since 9:00 am, but no notice to this effect had been posted at the 1st tee. Should the match be replayed entirely or resumed at the 3rd hole?

A. The match should be replayed entirely. Play on the course while it was closed should be considered null and void.

ESTABLISHING TIMES OF STARTING AND ARRANGING STROKE-PLAY GROUPS

33-3/1
Status of Starting Time Fixed by Players

Q. It was a condition of a match-play competition that each match must be played on the day and at the time published unless the players agreed to a prior date and time. A and B agreed to play their match at a specified time on a prior date. However, B arrived late. Was B subject to disqualification under Rule 6-3a?

A. Yes. The starting time agreed by A and B had the same status as a starting time fixed by the Committee.

33-3/2
Player Not Present at Time of Starting; Course Closed at the Time

Q. A and B were scheduled to play a match at 9.00 am, at which time the course was closed due to weather conditions. A was present at the appointed time. B, assuming the course would be closed, was not present. B arrived at noon, at which time the course was still closed. A claimed the match because B was not present at 9.00 am. Was the claim valid?

A. No. As the course was closed, and it was impossible for A and B to start at the appointed time or within a reasonable time thereafter, a new starting time for the match should be arranged.

Related Decision:
• 6-3a/4 Time of Starting; Player is Late but Group Unable to Play Due to Delay.

33-3/3
Competitors Determining Own Groupings and Starting Times

Q. May a Committee permit competitors in a stroke-play competition to determine their own groupings and starting times?

A. Yes. Rule 33-3 does not prohibit such an arrangement.

33-3/4
Groupings for Stroke-Play Play-Off

Q. Is there any Rule limiting the number of competitors in a group in a stroke-play play-off? For example, if 11 competitors are in a play-off, should they be separated into a group of five and group of six? Or should they be separated into two groups of four and one group of three?

A. There is no Rule. The matter is up to the Committee. However, it is suggested that normally there should be no more than five competitors in any group.

Other Decisions related to Rule 33-3: See "Groups and Grouping" and "Time of Starting" in the Index.

PUBLISHING HANDICAP STROKE TABLE

33-4/1
Alteration of Handicap Stroke Table

Q. As provided in the Definition of a "Stipulated Round," the Committee has authorized certain matches to begin at the 6th hole. The higher-handicapped player in such matches is disadvantaged because, under the Handicap Stroke Table, the first handicap stroke is allocated to the 5th hole and, thus, it is not used if a match is concluded in less than 18 holes. Would it be permissible to alter the Handicap Stroke Table for such matches?

A. Yes.

SCORE CARDS; COMMITTEE RESPONSIBILITIES

33-5/1
Score Cards in Hole-by-Hole Play-Off

Q. Must competitors involved in a hole-by-hole play-off in stroke play complete score cards and return them to the Committee?

A. Yes, but only if the Committee has issued a score card for each competitor in accordance with Rule 33-5. Otherwise, the competitors should not be penalized if they fail to return score cards.

33-5/2
Wrong Handicap Applied by Committee Results in Player Not Receiving Prize

Q. In a stroke-play competition, A returns a card showing the handicap to which he is entitled and the Committee applies the wrong handicap or miscalculates the correct net score. This results in another competitor receiving a prize to which A was entitled. The error is discovered after the competition has closed. What is the ruling?

A. The Committee should correct its error by retrieving the prize and awarding it to A. There is no time limit for correcting such an error. Rule 34-1b is not applicable since it deals with penalties and not with Committee errors.

Related Decisions:
• 6-2b/3 Competitor Wins Competition with Handicap Which Was Incorrect Due to Committee Error; Error Discovered Several Days Later.
• 34-1b/6 Winner's Score Not Posted Due to Committee Error.

33-5/3
Misapplication of Handicap Affects Match-Play Draw

Q. Misapplication of a player's handicap by the Committee on a score card for the qualifying round of a match-play event results in an incorrect draw. The error is discovered during the first round of match play. What should the Committee do?

A. The Committee should deal with the matter in the fairest way possible. The Committee should consider amending the draw and cancelling the matches affected by the amendment if this is practicable.

Other Decisions related to Rule 33-5: See "Scores and Score Cards" in the Index

ANNOUNCING MANNER FOR DECISION OF TIES

33-6/1 (Reserved)

33-6/2 (Reserved)

33-6/3
Determining Winner and Positions in Stroke-Play Play-Off

If there is a stroke-play play-off between two competitors and one of them is disqualified or concedes defeat, it is not necessary for the other to complete the play-off hole or holes to be declared the winner.

If there is a play-off involving more than two competitors and not all of them complete the play-off hole or holes, the order in which the competitors are disqualified or decide to withdraw shall determine their positions in the play-off.

33-6/4
Players Decide Method of Settling Tie When Committee Fails to Do So

Q. A and B, in a club match-play event in which the Committee had not prescribed how a halved match would be decided, finished their stipulated round all square. A suggested that the tie be decided by an 18-hole play-off. B reluctantly agreed. A won the play-off. B protested to the Committee. He argued that the match should have been settled by a hole-by-hole play-off, since that is the customary manner of deciding a tie in club events. What should the Committee do?

A. Since the Committee did not prescribe the method of settling the tie, it was appropriate for the players to determine the method. Since the players agreed to an 18-hole play-off, the match should stand as played.

Other Decisions related to Rule 33-6: See "Play-Off and Ties" in the Index.

WAIVING, MODIFYING OR IMPOSING PENALTY OF DISQUALIFICATION

33-7/1
Authority to Waive or Modify Disqualification Penalty

Only the Committee as a whole has authority to waive or modify a penalty of disqualification under Rule 33-7. A referee or an individual member of the Committee may not take such action.

33-7/2
Modifying Penalty for Not Holing Out in Stroke Play

Q. In stroke play, a competitor missed a short putt at the 16th hole, knocked his ball off the green, picked it up and teed off at the next hole without having holed out at the 16th.

After the competitor returned his score card, a fellow-competitor brought the matter to the attention of the Committee. The competitor admitted the error and expressed the view that his fellow-competitors were unsportsmanlike in not calling the error to his attention when the incident occurred.

In such circumstances, would the Committee be justified in modifying to two strokes the disqualification penalty provided in Rule 3-2?

A. No. Rule 33-7 should never be invoked in the case of disqualification for failing to hole out in stroke play. The competitor in such a case has not played the course.

Failure of the fellow-competitors to advise the competitor of his error is not a good reason for modifying the penalty. It is the responsibility of the competitor to know the Rules.

33-7/3
Competitor's Failure to Countersign Card Blamed on Lack of Time Provided by Committee

Q. In a 36-hole stroke-play competition played in one day over two courses, a competitor returned his first-round score card to the Committee but he failed to countersign it. After the second round the Committee informed him that he was disqualified. The competitor blamed the Committee for the error. He said the Committee, in attempting to get him to leave promptly for the course on which the second round was being played, caused him to return his first-round card hurriedly and that he had been given insufficient time to check and countersign the card. The competitor requested the Committee to waive the penalty under Rule 33-7. Would the Committee be justified in doing so?

A. No. If the competitor did not feel he was given sufficient time to check and sign his first-round card, he should have protested before he returned the card.

Related Decisions:
- 6-6b/3 Competitor Fails to Sign First-Round Card; Error Discovered on Completion of Last Round.
- 34-1b/2 Competitor's Failure to Sign Score Card Discovered After Competition Closed.

33-7/4
Modifying Penalty for Returning Wrong Score

Q. A marker inadvertently recorded a 4 for a competitor on a hole at which the competitor's score was actually 5. The competitor failed to check his score for each hole and therefore did not discover the error. The competitor returned his card to the Committee.

Later, the competitor discovered the error while observing the scoreboard. He immediately reported the error to the Committee. Would it be appropriate in such circumstances to invoke Rule 33-7 and waive or modify the disqualification penalty prescribed in Rule 6-6d?

A. No. A penalty of disqualification may be waived or modified only in exceptional circumstances. Under Rule 6-6d, the competitor is responsible for the correctness of the score recorded for each hole.

33-7/4.5
Competitor Unaware of Penalty Returns Wrong Score; Whether Waiving or Modifying Disqualification Penalty Justified

Q. A competitor returns his score card. It later transpires that the score for one hole is lower than actually taken due to his failure to include a penalty stroke(s) which he did not know he had incurred. The error is discovered before the competition has closed.

Would the Committee be justified, under Rule 33-7, in waiving or modifying the penalty of disqualification prescribed in Rule 6-6d?

A. Generally, the disqualification prescribed by Rule 6-6d must not be waived or modified.

However, if the Committee is satisfied that the competitor could not reasonably have known or discovered the facts resulting in his breach of the Rules, it would be justified under Rule 33-7 in waiving the disqualification penalty prescribed by Rule 6-6d. The penalty stroke(s) associated with the breach would, however, be applied to the hole where the breach occurred.

For example, in the following scenarios, the Committee would be justified in waiving the disqualification penalty:
- A competitor makes a short chip from the greenside rough. At the time, he and his fellow-competitors have no reason to suspect that the competitor has double-hit his ball in breach of Rule 14-4. After the competitor has signed and returned his score card, a close-up, super-

slow-motion video replay reveals that the competitor struck his ball twice during the course of the stroke. In these circumstances, it would be appropriate for the Committee to waive the disqualification penalty and apply the one-stroke penalty under Rule 14-4 to the competitor's score at the hole in question.

- After a competitor has signed and returned his score card, it becomes known, through the use of a high-definition video replay, that the competitor unknowingly touched a few grains of sand with his club at the top of his backswing on a wall of the bunker. The touching of the sand was so light that, at the time, it was reasonable for the competitor to have been unaware that he had breached Rule 13-4. It would be appropriate for the Committee to waive the disqualification penalty and apply the two-stroke penalty to the competitor's score at the hole in question.

- A competitor moves his ball on the putting green with his finger in the act of removing his ball-marker. The competitor sees the ball move slightly forward but is certain that it has returned to the original spot, and he plays the ball as it lies. After the competitor signs and returns his score card, video footage is brought to the attention of the Committee that reveals that the ball did not precisely return to its original spot. When questioned by the Committee, the competitor cites the fact that the position of the logo on the ball appeared to be in exactly the same position as it was when he replaced the ball and this was the reason for him believing that the ball returned to the original spot. As it was reasonable in these circumstances for the competitor to have no doubt that the ball had returned to the original spot, and because the competitor could not himself have reasonably discovered otherwise prior to signing and returning his score card, it would be appropriate for the Committee to waive the disqualification penalty. The two-stroke penalty under Rule 20-3a for playing from a wrong place would, however, be applied to the competitor's score at the hole in question.

A Committee would not be justified under Rule 33-7 in waiving or modifying the disqualification penalty prescribed in Rule 6-6d if the competitor's failure to include the penalty stroke(s) was a result of either ignorance of the Rules or of facts that the competitor could have reasonably discovered prior to signing and returning his score card.

For example, in the following scenarios, the Committee would not be justified in waiving or modifying the disqualification penalty:

- As a competitor's ball is in motion, he moves several loose impediments in the area in which the ball will likely come to rest. Unaware that this action is a breach of Rule 23-1, the competitor fails to include the two-stroke penalty in his score for the hole. As the competitor was aware of the facts that resulted in his breaching the Rules, he should be disqualified under Rule 6-6d for failing to include the two-stroke penalty under Rule 23-1.

- A competitor's ball lies in a water hazard. In making his backswing for the stroke, the competitor is aware that his club touched a branch in the hazard. Not realising at the time that the branch was detached, the competitor did not include the two-stroke penalty for a breach of Rule

13-4 in his score for the hole. As the competitor could have reasonably determined the status of the branch prior to signing and returning his score card, the competitor should be disqualified under Rule 6-6d for failing to include the two-stroke penalty under Rule 13-4. (Revised)

33-7/5
Play of Wrong Ball Not Rectified on Advice of Referee

Q. In stroke play, a competitor plays two strokes on the 14th hole and then plays a wrong ball for what he believed to be his third stroke. He plays a total of four strokes with the wrong ball, holing out with it. He then discovers the error. Before teeing off at the 15th, he asks a referee as to the procedure. The referee told the competitor to proceed and consult the Committee when the round was completed, instead of telling him to rectify the error as prescribed in Rule 15-3b.

Should the competitor be disqualified as prescribed in Rule 15-3b?

A. No. In the circumstances, the competitor should incur a penalty of two strokes for a breach of Rule 15-3b. The disqualification penalty that he also incurred under that Rule should be waived by the Committee under Rule 33-7, since the competitor's failure to correct his mistake was due to the error of the referee.

Generally, strokes played with a wrong ball do not count in the competitor's score. However, in this case such strokes must be counted. Otherwise, the competitor would not have a score for the hole. In equity (Rule 1-4), his score for the hole would be 8: the two strokes he played with his ball, the two penalty strokes for playing a wrong ball and the four strokes he played with the wrong ball. (Revised)

Related Decisions:
- 34-3/3 Player in Match Makes Stroke From Wrong Place Due to Incorrect Ruling; Procedure for Player When Error is Discovered.
- 34-3/3.3 Competitor in Stroke Play Makes Stroke From Wrong Place Due to Incorrect Ruling; Procedure for Competitor When Error is Discovered.

33-7/6
Competitor Repeatedly Replaces Ball Nearer Hole on Green

Q. On completion of a round in stroke play, a competitor's marker reports that the competitor, after lifting his ball on the putting green, repeatedly placed it nearer the hole than the spot from which it was lifted. The Committee, after gathering all available evidence, concludes that the marker's report is correct. What should the Committee do?

A. The competitor should be disqualified under Rule 33-7.

33-7/7
Competitor Seeks Help from Fellow-Competitor to Avoid Penalty

Q. A competitor's ball is lying through the green. He asks a fellow-competitor to remove a loose impediment lying near his ball because he believes that the removal of the loose impediment might cause his ball to move and knows that if the loose impediment is removed by an outside agency, the competitor incurs no penalty. The fellow-competitor removes the loose impediment. What is the ruling?

A. Irrespective of whether the ball moves as a result of removing the loose impediment, the action of the competitor is so contrary to the spirit of the game that the Committee should disqualify him under Rule 33-7.

The fellow-competitor incurs no penalty for removing the loose impediment unless the Committee is satisfied that he was aware of the competitor's intention to circumvent a Rule. In that instance, he should also be disqualified under Rule 33-7.

Related Decisions:
• 13-2/33 Outside Agency Removes Immovable Obstruction on Player's Line of Play.
• 23-1/10 Removal of Loose Impediments Affecting Player's Play.

33-7/8
Meaning of "Serious Breach of Etiquette"

Q. In Rule 33-7, what is meant by a "serious breach of etiquette"?

A. A serious breach of etiquette is behavior by a player that shows a significant disregard for an aspect of the Etiquette Section, such as intentionally distracting another player or intentionally offending someone.

Although a Committee may disqualify a player under Rule 33-7 for a single act that it considers to be a serious breach of etiquette, in most cases it is recommended that such a penalty should be imposed only in the event of a further serious breach.

Ultimately, the application of a penalty for a serious breach of etiquette under Rule 33-7 is at the discretion of the Committee.

33-7/9
Competitor Who Knows Player Has Breached Rules Does Not Inform Player or Committee in Timely Manner

The responsibility for knowing the Rules lies with all players. In stroke play, the player and his marker have an explicit responsibility for the correctness of the player's score card.

There may, however, be exceptional individual cases where, in order to protect the interests of every other player in the competition, it would be reasonable to expect a fellow-competitor or another competitor to bring to light a player's breach of the Rules by notifying the player, his marker or the Committee.

In such exceptional circumstances, it would be appropriate for the Committee to impose a penalty of disqualification under Rule 33-7 on a fellow-competitor or another competitor if it becomes apparent that he has failed to advise the player, his marker or the Committee of a Rules breach with the clear intention of allowing that player to return an incorrect score.

Related Decisions:
- 1-3/6 Marker Attests Wrong Score Knowingly and Competitor Aware Score Wrong.
- 6-6a/5 Marker Attests Wrong Score Knowingly But Competitor Unaware Score Wrong.

Other Decisions related to Rule 33-7: See "Penalties Imposed, Modified or Waived by Committee" in the Index.

COMMITTEE'S AUTHORITY TO MAKE LOCAL RULES

33-8/1
Local Rule for Temporary Putting Green Waives Requirement to Hole Out

Q. A course has been going through a period of renovation necessitating the use of temporary putting greens from time to time.

A Local Rule states that a player whose ball lies on a temporary green may either pick up his ball, counting two putts, or putt out.

Is such a Local Rule authorized?

A. No. Rule 1-1 provides: "The Game of Golf consists in playing a ball with a club from the teeing ground into the hole by a stroke or successive strokes in accordance with the Rules." Any Local Rule under which a player would not be required to play the ball into the hole waives this basic Rule and is not authorized.

33-8/2
Local Rule Allows Drop on Green Side of Water Hazard When Ball Fails to Clear Hazard

Q. The design of a hole is such that a player must hit the ball about 100 yards in order to carry a water hazard. A Local Rule has been adopted to assist players who cannot drive over the hazard by allowing them to drop a ball, under penalty of two strokes, in a dropping zone that is located across the hazard. Is such a Local Rule authorized?

A. No. Such a Local Rule substantially alters Rule 26-1b as it allows the player to drop a ball on a part of the course (i.e., on the green side of the water hazard) that the Rule would not have permitted him to reach. Furthermore, the penalty for taking relief under the water hazard Rule (Rule

26) is one stroke, and may not be increased to two strokes by a Committee through a Local Rule – see Rule 33-8b.

33-8/3
Local Rule Allowing Play of Second Ball in Match Play

Q. May a Committee make a Local Rule allowing play of a second ball in match play when a player is in doubt as to his rights?

A. No. Rule 3-3 specifically restricts the play of a second ball to stroke play.

Related Decision:
• 3-3/9 Second Ball Played in Match Play.

33-8/4
Local Rule for Events in Which Motorized Golf Carts Permitted

Q. A competition involving stroke play qualifying followed by match play is to be held. Motorized golf carts will be permitted. Play will be in couples. There are enough carts available to provide each couple with a cart. No caddies will be available. Should a Local Rule clarifying the status of the carts be made?

A. It is suggested that the following Local Rule be adopted:
"A motorized cart is part of the player's equipment:
(1) When one cart is shared by two players, the cart and everything in it are deemed to be the equipment of the player whose ball is involved except that, when the cart is being moved by one of the players, the cart and everything in it are deemed to be the equipment of that player.
(2) A player or players using a cart may appoint someone to drive the cart, in which case the driver is considered to be the caddie of the player or players.
(3) Use of a cart by anyone other than the player or players using it or the appointed driver is prohibited. Any player allowing unauthorized use of his cart is subject to penalty as follows:
Match play – At the conclusion of the hole at which the breach is discovered, the state of the match shall be adjusted by deducting one hole for each hole at which a breach occurred. Maximum deduction per round: two holes.
Stroke play – Two strokes for each hole at which any breach occurred; maximum penalty per round: four strokes (two strokes at each of the first two holes at which any breach occurred).
Match play or stroke play – If a breach is discovered between the play of two holes, it is deemed to have been discovered during play of the next hole, and the penalty must be applied accordingly.
In either form of play – Use of any unauthorized automotive vehicle must be discontinued immediately upon discovering that a breach has occurred. Otherwise, the player is disqualified."
If some caddies are available, it is suggested that they be assigned in an

equitable way and that the above suggested Local Rule be adopted with item (2) amended to read as follows:

"A player or players using a cart may appoint someone to drive the cart if no caddie is available, in which case the driver is considered to be the caddie of the player or players." (Revised)

Related Decisions:
- 6-4/2.5 Status of Individual Who Transports Player's Clubs on Motorized Golf Cart or Trolley.
- 19/2 Status of Person in Shared Golf Cart.
- 33-1/9.5 Breach of Transportation Condition by Caddie.

33-8/5
Local Rule Permitting Competitors to Discontinue Play by Agreement in Bad Weather

Q. May the Committee for a stroke-play event make a Local Rule permitting competitors to discontinue play by agreement among themselves in bad weather?

A. No. Such a Local Rule would modify Rule 6-8a.

33-8/6
Local Rule for Breach of Sportsmanship Code or Competition Policy

Q. May a Committee make a Local Rule assessing a penalty for breach of a sportsmanship code (e.g., for offensive language) or of a competition policy (e.g., for use of a mobile phone when such use is prohibited)?

A. No. A Local Rule assessing a penalty for a breach of a sportsmanship code or competition policy is not authorized. Penalties for breaches of such items should take a more generalised form, e.g., censure, suspension or revocation of the privilege of playing in events.

However, a Committee may disqualify a player under Rule 33-7 for a serious breach of etiquette – see Decision 33-7/8.

33-8/7
Local Rule Requiring Player to Play Out of Turn on Putting Green

Q. A proposed Local Rule would require that, on the putting green, a player must play continuously until he has holed out. Would such a Local Rule be acceptable?

A. No. Such a Local Rule would modify Rules 10-1b and 10-2b, which require that the ball farther from the hole shall be played first.

33-8/8
Local Rule Providing Relief from Tree Roots

Q. May a Committee make a Local Rule providing relief without penalty if a player's stroke is interfered with by exposed tree roots?

A. No. A Local Rule is authorized only if an abnormal condition exists. The existence of exposed tree roots is not abnormal.

33-8/9
Local Rule Providing Relief from Damage to Bunkers Caused by Children

Q. Some holes are accessible to the general public, and children play in the bunkers leaving footprints, holes and sand castles.

May the Committee make a Local Rule allowing a player, without penalty, either to drop his ball outside a bunker damaged by children or to lift his ball from such damage, smooth out the sand and replace the ball?

A. No. This would be a modification of Rule 13-4.

33-8/10
Local Rule Prohibiting Removal of Flagstick

Q. May a Committee make a Local Rule for winter-time play prohibiting removal of the flagstick? The purpose would be to reduce traffic around the hole in the winter when the putting greens are very soft.

A. No. Such a Local Rule would modify the Rules of Golf.

33-8/11
Local Rule Waiving Penalty for Ball Striking Unattended Flagstick

Q. Is it permissible for a Committee to make a Local Rule for winter play waiving the penalty incurred under Rule 17-3c (Ball Striking Flagstick When Unattended) in order to reduce the damage caused to the area around the hole and to speed up play?

A. No.

33-8/12
Local Rule for Ball Deflected by Sprinkler Head

Q. May a Committee make a Local Rule allowing a player to replay a stroke, without penalty, if his ball has been deflected by a sprinkler head?

A. No. A sprinkler head is an outside agency (see Definition of "Outside Agency"). The deflection of a ball by it is a rub of the green and the ball must be played as it lies – see Rule 19-1.

33-8/13
Local Rule for Ball Deflected by Power Line

Q. An overhead power line is so situated that it interferes with the play of a hole. Would it be appropriate for the Committee to make a Local Rule allowing a player whose ball is deflected by this power line the option to replay the stroke, without penalty, if he wishes?

A. No. However, a Local Rule requiring a player to replay the stroke would be acceptable. The following text is suggested:

"If a ball strikes the power line during play of the _____ hole, the stroke is canceled and the player must play a ball as nearly as possible at the spot from which the original ball was played in accordance with Rule 20-5 (Making Next Stroke from Where Previous Stroke Made)."

In some cases the Committee may wish to include in the Local Rule the towers or poles supporting such lines when the towers or poles are positioned such that they interfere with the play of the hole.

33-8/14
Local Rule Deeming Interior Boundary Fence to Be an Obstruction

Q. There is a practice range in the middle of the course. The range is surrounded by a fence which defines the range as out of bounds. Would a Local Rule be authorized under which this particular boundary fence, since it is within the course, is treated as an obstruction?

A. No, such a Local Rule is not authorized. An interior boundary fence is not an abnormal condition.

Related Decision:
• 24/5 Boundary Stakes Having No Significance in Play of Hole Being Played.

33-8/15
Local Rule Providing Relief from Interference by Immovable Water Hazard Stake for Ball Lying in Water Hazard

Q. If the stakes defining the margins of water hazards are immovable, may the Committee make a Local Rule providing relief without penalty if a player's ball lies in a water hazard and such a stake interferes with his swing or stance?

A. No. Such stakes are immovable obstructions – see Note 1 to Rule 24-2.

33-8/16
Local Rule Deeming All Stakes on Course to Be Immovable Obstructions

Q. It is proposed to adopt a Local Rule providing that all stakes on the course, i.e., stakes defining the margins of water hazards, ground under repair, etc., are deemed to be immovable obstructions. The Local Rule would not, of course, apply to boundary stakes since they are not on the course. Is such a Local Rule permissible?

A. Yes.

33-8/17
Local Rule Providing Line-of-Sight Relief from Irrigation-Control Boxes

Q. Irrigation-control boxes, which are about two feet wide and four feet high, have been installed near a number of fairways. Would it be appropriate for a Committee to adopt a Local Rule under which relief would be provided from such boxes when they intervene on the line of play, i.e., line-of-sight relief?

A. No. Providing line-of-sight relief from permanent immovable obstructions is not authorized, except in very unusual circumstances. It is not unusual for irrigation-control boxes to be located near fairways.

33-8/18
Local Rule Providing Line-of-Sight Relief from Protective Fence Near Line of Play

If a wire fence is erected to protect players on the tee of one hole from errant shots played at another hole, and it is relatively close to the line of play of the other hole, it would be permissible to make a Local Rule allowing a player whose ball is in such a position that the fence intervenes on his line of play to drop the ball, without penalty, not nearer the hole in a specified dropping zone.

33-8/19
Local Rule Permitting Relief on Specified Side of Paved Path

Q. A paved path is parallel to the left side of the 12th hole. If a ball is on the path and the nearest point of relief under Rule 24-2b is on the left side of the path, the player effectively gets no relief as there is a very sharp incline on the left of the path that goes down 30 feet. Would it be appropriate to make a Local Rule giving relief in all cases on the fairway side of this path?

A. No. Rule 33-8 states: "The Committee may establish Local Rules for local abnormal conditions." It is not abnormal for areas adjacent to paved paths to have dense underbrush, trees, sharp slopes, etc., thereby providing no practical relief.

Furthermore, it would not be appropriate to establish dropping zones on the fairway side of the path to alleviate the problem.

33-8/20
Local Rule Providing Relief from Unsurfaced Road for Tee Shot Only

Q. A road which is not artificially surfaced crosses a fairway 225 yards from the tee. May the Committee adopt a Local Rule granting relief of the type afforded by Rule 24-2b(i) or Rule 25-1b(i) for tee shots, but not subsequent shots, coming to rest on the road?

A. No. The Committee has authority to provide relief from interference by the road but does not have authority so to limit its application.

Related Decision:
• 33-2a/14 Internal Out of Bounds Applying to Stroke from Teeing Ground Only.

33-8/21
Local Rule for Damage Made by Insects

Q. Some types of insects, e.g., mole crickets, can create damage on a golf course that results in unreasonable playing conditions. May a Committee make a Local Rule treating this damage as ground under repair?

A. Yes. However, in some instances a Committee would be justified in stating that interference by this condition with a player's stance is deemed not to be, of itself, interference under this Local Rule – see Note under Rule 25-1a.

33-8/22
Local Rule Treating Ant Hills as Ground Under Repair

Q. An ant hill is a loose impediment and may be removed, but there is no other relief without penalty. Some ant hills are conical in shape and hard, and removal is not possible, but relief under Rule 25-1b is not available since an ant is not a burrowing animal. If such ant hills interfere with the proper playing of the game, would a Local Rule providing relief be authorized?

A. Yes. A Local Rule stating that such ant hills are to be treated as ground under repair would be justified.

Such a Local Rule is also justified on courses where fire-ants exist. A fire-ants' mound or hill is removable, but its removal will cause the fire-ants to swarm out of the ground. When this occurs, anyone in the vicinity is in danger of being bitten by the ants, and the bite of a fire-ant can cause serious illness.

If a Local Rule giving relief from fire-ants has not been adopted and a ball is so close to a fire-ants' mound that the player is in danger, the player is, in equity, entitled to relief as prescribed in Decision 1-4/10.

33-8/23
Local Rule Denying Relief from Ground Under Repair During Play of Particular Hole

Q. An area of ground under repair is situated on the fairway of the 2nd hole, which is parallel to the 1st hole. Is it permissible to make a Local Rule prohibiting relief from this ground under repair during the play of the 1st hole?

A. No.

33-8/24
Local Rule Permitting Relief from Edging Grooves Around Putting Green

Q. Edging grooves are cut at the perimeters of the putting greens, or just beyond the fringes of the greens, to prevent creeping grasses (e.g., bermuda-grass) from encroaching. If a ball comes to rest in or on such a groove, it is impossible to play the ball with any degree of accuracy. Would a Local Rule providing relief be authorized?

A. Yes. If an edging groove touches the green, the Committee may make a Local Rule giving relief if a ball lies in or on such a groove or the groove interferes with the area of intended swing, but not solely because the groove might affect the player's stance. The Local Rule should read as follows:

"If a ball lies in or on an edging groove around a putting green, or if the groove interferes with the area of the player's intended swing, the ball may, without penalty, be lifted, cleaned and placed in the nearest position to where it lay that is not nearer the hole and avoids interference by the condition, whether on or off the putting green."

If edging grooves do not touch the green, the Committee may declare them to be ground under repair and provide relief under Rule 25-1 as follows:

"The grooves around the fringes of the putting greens are ground under repair. However, interference by a groove with the player's stance is deemed not to be, of itself, interference under Rule 25-1. If the ball lies in or touches the groove or the groove interferes with the area of intended swing, relief is available under Rule 25-1."

33-8/25
Local Rule for Ground Under Repair Adjacent to Artificially-Surfaced Cart Path

Q. When ground under repair is adjacent to an artificially-surfaced cart path (an obstruction), sometimes a player, after obtaining relief from one condition, is interfered with by the other condition. Thus, another drop under another Rule results. This is cumbersome and could lead to complications. Would it be proper to eliminate the problem by means of a Local Rule under which ground under repair adjacent to an artificially-surfaced cart path would have the same status as the cart path?

A. Yes. If white lines are used to define ground under repair, a Local Rule is suggested as follows:

"White-lined areas tying into artificially-surfaced roads or paths are declared to have the same status as the roads or paths, i.e., they are obstructions, not ground under repair. Relief, without penalty, is provided under Rule 24-2b(i)."

33-8/26
Local Rule Altering Ground Under Repair Relief Procedure

Q. It is planned to define an area containing young trees as ground under repair. Would it be permissible to make a Local Rule requiring that, if a player elects to take relief from this area, he must drop the ball behind the area, keeping the trees between himself and the hole?

A. No. However, if it is not feasible to proceed in conformity with the ground under repair Rule, establishment of dropping zones is authorized. The Local Rule providing such dropping zones may establish them as an additional option under Rule 25-1 or may require their use.

33-8/27
Local Rule Providing Relief Without Penalty from Bunker Filled with Casual Water

Q. May a Committee make a Local Rule allowing a player to drop out of any bunker filled with casual water, without penalty, contrary to Rule 25-1b(ii)?

A. No. The Committee may not make a Local Rule providing generally that flooded bunkers are ground under repair through the green, as such a Local Rule waives a penalty imposed by the Rules of Golf, contrary to Rule 33-8b.

However, in exceptional circumstances, where certain specific bunkers are completely flooded and there is no reasonable likelihood of the bunkers drying up during the round, the Committee may introduce a Local Rule providing relief without penalty from specific bunkers. Prior to introducing such a Local Rule, the Committee must be convinced that such exceptional circumstances exist and that providing relief without penalty from specific bunkers is more appropriate than simply applying Rule 25-1b(ii). If the Committee elects to introduce a Local Rule, the following wording is suggested:

"The flooded bunker on [insert location of bunker; e.g., left of 5th green] is ground under repair. If a player's ball lies in that bunker or if that bunker interferes with the player's stance or the area of his intended swing and the player wishes to take relief, he must take relief outside the bunker, without penalty, in accordance with Rule 25-1b(i). All other bunkers on the course, regardless of whether they contain water, maintain their status as hazards and the Rules apply accordingly."

In a competition played over more than one round, such a Local Rule may be introduced or rescinded between rounds. (Revised)

Related Decisions:
• 25/13 Bunker Totally Under Repair.
• 25-1b/8 Player's Options When Bunker Completely Covered by Casual Water.

33-8/28
Local Rule Permitting Re-Dropping or Placing When Dropped Ball Embeds in Bunker

Q. Our bunkers frequently have casual water in them. The texture of the sand in the bunkers is such that a ball dropped under Rule 25-1b(ii)(a) embeds itself in the wet sand to the depth of the ball or deeper.

Would it be proper to make a Local Rule permitting a ball that embeds in a bunker after being dropped from casual water in the bunker to be re-dropped or placed?

A. No. It is not abnormal for a ball dropped in a bunker to embed itself in the sand.

33-8/29
Local Rule Requiring Player to Take Relief Under Penalty from Tree Nursery or Plantation

Q. May a Committee make a Local Rule requiring that a ball lying in a tree nursery or plantation be dropped outside it under penalty of one stroke?

A. No. If the Committee wishes to prohibit play in such an area, it may declare it to be ground under repair from which relief without penalty is mandatory. However, a Local Rule imposing a penalty of one stroke is not permitted.

33-8/30
Local Rule Permitting the Repair of Turf Plugs On the Putting Green That are Not 4¼ Inches in Diameter

Q. Turf plugs which are not 4¼ inches in diameter or are not circular have been cut on some putting greens to repair damaged areas of turf. May a Committee adopt a Local Rule permitting the repair of these plugs?

A. Yes. If such areas exist it is recommended that a Local Rule permitting the repair of these plugs under Rule 16-1c be adopted. Otherwise, the repair of such turf plugs would be contrary to Rule 16-1c.

33-8/31
Local Rule Providing Relief from Accumulations of Leaves Through the Green

The Committee may make a temporary Local Rule declaring accumulations of leaves through the green at certain holes to be ground under repair (see Definition of "Ground Under Repair") and Rule 25-1 will apply.

The Local Rule should be restricted to the hole(s) at which trouble with leaves occurs and it should be withdrawn as soon as conditions permit. Particular attention is drawn to the opening paragraph of Rule 25-1c; unless it is known or virtually certain that a ball that has not been found is in the leaves, it must be treated as lost elsewhere and Rule 27-1 applies.

For fallen leaves in a bunker – see Decision 13-4/33.

33-8/32 (Reserved)

33-8/32.5
Local Rule Treating Severe Damage by Non-Burrowing Animals as Ground Under Repair

Q. May a Committee make a Local Rule declaring areas severely damaged by non-burrowing animals to be ground under repair without marking them as such?

A. Yes. Furthermore, in some instances a Committee would be justified in specifying that interference with the player's stance is not, of itself, interference from the condition – see the Note under Rule 25-1a.

33-8/33
Local Rule Prohibiting Dropping on Apron When Ball on Wrong Putting Green

Q. Balls from the 13th tee frequently come to rest on the 15th green, and the point of nearest relief under Rule 25-3 is the closely mown apron of the green. Much damage is being caused to this apron. May the Committee make a Local Rule requiring that a ball be dropped not only clear of the putting surface but also clear of the apron of this green?

A. Yes. The following wording for a Local Rule is suggested:
"For the purpose of Rule 25-3, the putting green of the 15th hole includes the apron surrounding the green."

33-8/34
Relief from Divot Holes

Q. May a Committee make a Local Rule providing relief without penalty from divot holes or repaired divot holes (e.g., holes that have been filled with sand and/or seed mix)?

A. No. Such a Local Rule would modify Rule 13-1 and is not authorized.

33-8/35
Local Rule Treating Rough as a Lateral Water Hazard

Q. The areas immediately adjacent to the fairways consist of large embedded boulders, thick desert brush and prickly cactus. A player whose ball comes to rest in such areas has no opportunity to play a stroke. Would it be proper to make a Local Rule under which such areas would be treated as lateral water hazards?

A. No. There are many courses where the areas adjacent to the fairways are of such a nature that a ball therein is almost always lost or unplayable. Thus, such a situation is not abnormal.

33-8/36
Local Rule Giving Free Relief for Ball in Water Hazard

Q. A drainage ditch crosses a hole 190 yards from the tee. The Committee has marked that portion of the ditch within the limits of the fairway and a Local Rule allows a player relief, without penalty, if his tee shot lies in the ditch within the fairway limits.

Is this a proper Local Rule?

A. No. A drainage ditch is a water hazard – see Definition of "Water Hazard." Under Rule 26-1, the penalty for relief from a water hazard is one stroke. Rule 33-8b prohibits waiving this penalty by Local Rule.

33-8/37
Local Rule Allowing Drop in Water Hazard Behind Point Where Ball Lies Unplayable in Hazard

Q. A water hazard varies from 100 yards to 250 yards in width, and there is little or no water in it. In most cases, a ball in the hazard can be played. However, it sometimes happens that a ball fails by a few yards to carry the hazard and ends up unplayable in water.

Under Rule 26-1, the player must either drop behind the hazard or at the spot from which his previous stroke was played. In either case, the relief point is up to 250 yards away. In such circumstances, may the Committee make a Local Rule permitting a player to drop a ball in the hazard under penalty of one stroke, as well as out of the hazard?

A. No.

Related Decisions:
• 26-1/20 Allowing Drop Opposite Spot Where Ball Comes to Rest in Lateral Water Hazard.
• 33-2a/9 Part of Lateral Water Hazard Where Impossible to Drop Not Nearer Hole.

33-8/37.5
Local Rule for Water Hazard with Bunker Adjacent

Q. Due to the proximity of a bunker to the margin of a lateral water hazard, it is likely that a player, when dropping a ball under Rule 26-1c(i), will be required to drop a ball in the bunker.

Would it be permissible to place the line defining the lateral water hazard along the fairway side of the bunker (i.e., making the bunker part of the lateral water hazard), or alternatively, make a Local Rule to the effect that, when obtaining relief under the lateral water hazard Rule, the player may drop a ball to the fairway side of the bunker?

A. In all cases, the hazard should be marked along its natural boundary – see Decision 33-2a/4.

If the Committee does not wish to require a player to drop a ball in the bunker when proceeding under the lateral water hazard Rule, the Committee may establish a dropping zone or series of dropping zones on the fairway side of the bunker and make a Local Rule stating that a player whose ball is in the lateral water hazard (having last crossed the hazard margin between defined points) may drop a ball, under penalty of one stroke, in the nearest dropping zone that is not nearer the hole. (New)

33-8/38
Local Rule Deeming Out of Bounds Ball Which Crosses Boundary But Comes to Rest on Course

Q. Is it permissible to make a Local Rule that a ball is out of bounds if it crosses a boundary, even if it recrosses the boundary and comes to rest on the same part of the course? The purpose of the Local Rule would be to prevent players from cutting across a "dog-leg."

A. No. A ball is out of bounds only when all of it lies out of bounds – see Definition of "Out of Bounds."

The Local Rule suggested in Decision 27/20 deals with a different situation, i.e., one in which a ball crosses an out of bounds area and comes to rest on a different part of the course.

Related Decisions:
• 33-2a/12 Internal Boundary Between Holes.
• 33-2a/13 Tee Decreed to Be in Bounds for Tee Shot and Out of Bounds Thereafter.
• 33-2a/14 Internal Out of Bounds Applying to Stroke from Teeing Ground Only.

33-8/39
Local Rule for Bunker Faces Consisting of Stacked Turf

Q. The face of a bunker that consists of stacked turf may be grass-covered or earthen. May a Committee make a Local Rule deeming that such faces are not "closely mown areas" (Rule 25-2)?

A. Yes.

33-8/39.5
Local Rule Deeming Partially Grass-Covered Wall of Bunker to Be Part of Bunker

Q. The bunkers on a course are designed to have earthen walls (not consisting of stacked turf), which are therefore intended to be part of the bunkers. However, parts of some of the bunker walls have become grass-covered. Under the Definition of "Bunker," such grass-covered areas are through the green. In such a situation, may a Committee make a Local Rule deeming the "mixed" bunker walls to be part of the bunker?

A. Yes. Conversely, if the bunkers had been designed to have grass-covered walls, but some parts had worn bare, the Committee could deem the "mixed" bunker walls to be through the green and not part of the bunker. (New)

Decisions related to 33-8/39 and 33-8/39.5:
• 13/4 Ball Completely Embedded in Lip of Bunker.
• 16/2 Ball Embedded in Side of Hole; All of Ball Below Lip of Hole.
• 25-2/5 Ball Embedded in Grass Bank or Face of Bunker.

33-8/40
Local Rule Clarifying Status of Material Similar to Sand

Q. A course has material other than sand (e.g., finely crushed shell or lava dust) filling its bunkers. May the Committee establish a Local Rule stating that such material is deemed to have the same status as sand or loose soil (i.e., loose impediments on the putting green but not elsewhere)?

A. Yes.

33-8/41
Marking Environmentally-Sensitive Areas

If an appropriate authority prohibits entry into and/or play from an area for environmental reasons, it is the Committee's responsibility to decide whether an environmentally-sensitive area should be defined as ground under repair, a water hazard or out of bounds.

However, the Committee may not define the area as a water hazard or a lateral water hazard unless it is, by Definition, a water hazard. The Committee should attempt to preserve the character of the hole.

As examples:
(a) A small area of rare plants close to a putting green has been declared an environmentally-sensitive area. The Committee may define the area to be ground under repair or out of bounds, but it may not be defined as a water hazard or lateral water hazard. In view of the area's proximity to a putting green, it should not be defined as out of bounds because a stroke-and-distance penalty would be unduly harsh. It would be more appropriate to define the area as ground under repair.

(b) A large area of sand dunes along the side of a hole has been declared an environmentally-sensitive area. In contrast to (a) above, it should not be defined as ground under repair because the absence of a penalty would be unduly generous. It would be more appropriate to define the area as out of bounds.

(c) A large area of wetlands along the side of a hole has been declared an environmentally-sensitive area. As in (b) above, it could be defined as out of bounds, but it would be more appropriate to define it as a lateral water hazard.

An environmentally-sensitive area should be physically protected to deter players from entering the area (e.g., by a fence, warning signs and the like) and it should be marked in accordance with the recommendations in the Rules of Golf (i.e., by yellow, red or white stakes, depending on the status of the area). It is recommended that stakes with green tops be used to designate an environmentally-sensitive area.

33-8/42
Player Enters Environmentally-Sensitive Area to Retrieve Ball

Q. A player wrongfully enters an environmentally-sensitive area to retrieve his ball. What is the ruling?

A. There is no penalty under the Rules of Golf, but the player may have broken the law or be subject to other disciplinary action. A Local Rule which imposes a penalty for entering an environmentally-sensitive area is not authorized.

33-8/43
Stroke Played from Environmentally-Sensitive Area

Q. A player played a stroke at his ball in an environmentally-sensitive area from which play is prohibited or took his stance in such an area in playing a stroke. What is the ruling?

A. The answer depends on how the Committee has defined the environmentally-sensitive area.

Ground Under Repair, Water Hazard or Lateral Water Hazard: If the ball was in the environmentally-sensitive area, or if the player took his stance in the environmentally-sensitive area to play a stroke at his ball which was lying outside the environmentally-sensitive area, he loses the hole in match play or he incurs a penalty of two strokes in stroke play for a breach of the Local Rule. In stroke play, he must play out the hole with that ball unless a serious breach of the Local Rule has occurred – see Decision 33-8/44.

Out of Bounds: If the ball was in the environmentally-sensitive area, the player played a wrong ball – see Decision 15/6. Accordingly, in match play, the player loses the hole. In stroke play, he incurs a two stroke penalty and is required to proceed under Rule 27-1, incurring the additional one stroke penalty prescribed by that Rule.

If the player took his stance in the environmentally-sensitive area to play a ball which was in bounds, the ruling would be the same as that for Ground Under Repair, Water Hazard or Lateral Water Hazard.

In all cases, the player may have broken the law or be subject to other disciplinary action for having entered the environmentally-sensitive area.

33-8/44
Significant Advantage Gained When Player Plays Stroke from Environmentally-Sensitive Area Defined as Water Hazard

Q. A player makes a stroke at his ball which is lying in an environmentally-sensitive area from which play is prohibited and which has been defined as a water hazard.

The point where his ball last crossed the margin of the water hazard is 150 yards behind the place where he made a stroke at his ball. What is the ruling?

A. In match play, the player loses the hole for a breach of the Local Rule.

In stroke play, playing from an environmentally-sensitive area does not, by itself, constitute a serious breach of the Local Rule. However, in this case the player gained a significant advantage by doing so and, consequently, was guilty of a serious breach of the Local Rule. Therefore, the player must correct his error and follow the procedure outlined in Rule 20-7c by playing a ball in accordance with Rule 26-1, incurring the penalty stroke prescribed by that Rule and an additional penalty of two strokes for a breach of the Local Rule; otherwise the player is disqualified. The stroke made with the original ball from within the environmentally-sensitive area and all subsequent strokes, including penalty strokes, with this ball do not count in the player's score.

33-8/44.5
Status of Growing Things Rooted Within Environmentally-Sensitive Area

Q. A player's ball comes to rest through the green but near an environmentally-sensitive area that has been defined as a lateral water hazard. The player's backswing is interfered with by a branch of a tree that is rooted within the environmentally-sensitive area but overhangs ground outside the hazard. With the Local Rule for Environmentally-Sensitive Areas in effect, is the player required to take relief from the branch without penalty?

A. No. The player must play the ball as it lies or deem it unplayable (Rule 28). The part of the tree that extends beyond the margin of the lateral water hazard is not part of the lateral water hazard and therefore not part of the environmentally-sensitive area. Consequently, the Local Rule does not apply to that part of the branch.

The same result would apply if the environmentally-sensitive area had been defined as out of bounds, as the out of bounds line, like that of a lateral water hazard, extends vertically upwards and downwards.

If, however, the environmentally-sensitive area had been defined as ground under repair, the player would be required to take relief, without penalty, from the branch as the entire tree is part of the ground under repair (see Definition of "Ground Under Repair").

To avoid such situations, it is recommended that, where possible, the Committee define the margins of an environmentally-sensitive area so that any overhanging branches are within the area.

33-8/45
Local Rule Treating Temporary Immovable Obstructions as Immovable Obstructions or Temporary Immovable Obstructions

Q. May a Committee make a Local Rule stating that a player may, at his option, treat a temporary immovable obstruction (TIO) either as an immovable obstruction (in which case Rule 24-2 applies) or a TIO (in which case the Local Rule for TIOs applies)?

A. Yes.

Other Decisions related to Rule 33-8: See "Local Rules" in the Index.

RULE 34

DISPUTES AND DECISIONS

DEFINITIONS
All defined terms are in *italics* and are listed alphabetically in the Definitions section – see pages 6–16.

34-1. CLAIMS AND PENALTIES
a. Match Play
If a claim is lodged with the *Committee* under Rule 2-5, a decision should be given as soon as possible so that the state of the match may, if necessary, be adjusted. If a claim is not made in accordance with Rule 2-5, it must not be considered by the *Committee*.

There is no time limit on applying the disqualification penalty for a breach of Rule 1-3.

b. Stroke Play
In stroke play, a penalty must not be rescinded, modified or imposed after the competition has closed. A competition is closed when the result has been officially announced or, in stroke play qualifying followed by match play, when the player has teed off in his first match.

Exceptions: A penalty of disqualification must be imposed after the competition has closed if a *competitor*:

(i) was in breach of Rule 1-3 (Agreement to Waive Rules); or

(ii) returned a score card on which he had recorded a handicap that, before the competition closed, he knew was higher than that to which he was entitled, and this affected the number of strokes received (Rule 6-2b); or

(iii) returned a score for any hole lower than actually taken (Rule 6-6d) for any reason other than failure to include a penalty that, before the competition closed, he did not know he had incurred; or

(iv) knew, before the competition closed, that he had been in breach of any other *Rule* for which the penalty is disqualification.

34-2. REFEREE'S DECISION
If a *referee* has been appointed by the *Committee*, his decision is final.

34-3. COMMITTEE'S DECISION
In the absence of a *referee*, any dispute or doubtful point on the *Rules* must be referred to the *Committee*, whose decision is final.

If the *Committee* cannot come to a decision, it may refer the dispute or doubtful point to the Rules of Golf Committee of the USGA, whose decision is final.

If the dispute or doubtful point has not been referred to the Rules of Golf Committee, the player or players may request that an agreed statement be referred through a duly authorized representative of the *Committee* to the Rules of Golf Committee for an opinion as to the correctness of the decision given. The reply will be sent to this authorized representative.

If play is conducted other than in accordance with the Rules of Golf, the Rules of Golf Committee will not give a decision on any question.

CLAIMS AND PENALTIES IN MATCH PLAY

34-1a/1
Player Who Has Reached Third Round of Match Play Disqualified for Agreeing to Waive Rules in First-Round Match

Q. Rule 34-1a provides that there is no time limit on applying the disqualification penalty under Rule 1-3 for agreeing to waive a Rule. If A, who agreed with his opponent to waive a Rule in a first-round match, has advanced to the third round before the Committee becomes aware of the breach of Rule 1-3, what should the Committee do?

A. As A is disqualified, the Committee must rule in accordance with equity (Rule 1-4). For guidelines, see Decision 34-1b/8.

CLAIMS AND PENALTIES IN STROKE PLAY

34-1b/1
Omission of Penalty Stroke When Score Returned

Q. In stroke play, a competitor returned an incorrect score for a hole due to failure to include a penalty stroke. After the competition closed the error was discovered. Does Rule 34-1b allow imposition of a disqualification penalty for a breach of Rule 6-6d?

A. As stated in Rule 34-1b, the Committee should impose a penalty of disqualification if the competitor knew, before the competition closed, that he had incurred the penalty but intentionally or unintentionally failed to add the penalty to his score, but not if the competitor did not know he had incurred the penalty.

Related Decision:
• 34-3/1 Correction of Incorrect Ruling in Stroke Play.

34-1b/1.5
Competitor Correctly Advised by Fellow-Competitor That He Had Incurred a Penalty Disagrees with Fellow-Competitor and Fails to Include Penalty in His Score; Committee Advised of Incident After Competition Had Closed

Q. In stroke play, A, in ignorance of the Rules and with the concurrence of B, his marker, removed a stone from a water hazard when his ball lay in the hazard. Subsequently, A was advised by C, a fellow-competitor, that he (A) was in breach of Rule 13-4. A disagreed, failed to settle the doubtful point with the Committee at the end of the round and returned his score card without including a two-stroke penalty for a breach of Rule 13-4.

After the competition had closed, C advised the Committee of the incident. Should A be disqualified?

A. Yes. Rule 34-1b says in effect that a competitor shall be disqualified after the competition has closed if he had returned a score, failing to include a penalty which, before the competition closed, he knew he had incurred. As C pointed out to A that he had proceeded incorrectly and A took no action to check whether he had incurred a penalty before returning his card, the Committee should decide that A knew that he had incurred a penalty.

34-1b/2
Competitor's Failure to Sign Score Card Discovered After Competition Closed

Q. Shortly after a stroke-play competition had closed, it was discovered that the score card of the winner had not been signed by him. Should the Committee take any action?

A. The Committee must decide whether the competitor knew, before the competition closed, that he was in breach of the Rules by failing to sign his score card (Rule 6-6b). If he knew, he is disqualified. Otherwise, as provided in Rule 34-1b, no penalty may be imposed and the result of the competition must stand.

Related Decisions:
• 6-6b/3 Competitor Fails to Sign First-Round Card; Error Discovered on Completion of Last Round.
• 33-7/3 Competitor's Failure to Countersign Card Blamed on Lack of Time Provided by Committee.

34-1b/3
Play of Wrong Ball in Stroke Play Not Rectified; Error Discovered After Competition Closed

Q. In stroke play, A played a wrong ball at the 5th hole but he did not realize it until he had holed out at that hole. Before teeing off at the 6th hole, A and B, who was A's marker, concluded that A had incurred a two-stroke penalty. Accordingly, B added two penalty strokes to A's score for the 5th hole and A and B teed off at the 6th hole without A having rectified his mistake as required under Rule 15-3b. A was not aware that he should have rectified the error.

Before returning his card, A advised the Committee of the incident. The Committee confirmed that the penalty was two strokes but did not ask A whether the error had been rectified.

A won the competition. Several days later the runner-up claimed that A should be disqualified under Rule 15-3b. What is the ruling?

A. The competition stands as played, with A the winner. Under Rule 34-1b, a penalty of disqualification may not be imposed after a competition is closed if the competitor did not know he had incurred the penalty.

34-1b/4
Competitor Changes Weight of Club During Round; Breach Discovered After Competition Closed

Q. It was reported a few days after the conclusion of a stroke-play competition that the winner had changed the weight of his putter during a stipulated round. Should he be penalized?

A. The Committee must determine whether the competitor knew, between the time of the breach and the close of competition, that he had incurred a penalty under the Rules for changing the weight of his putter during the stipulated round (Rule 4-2). If he knew he had incurred a penalty under the Rules, he is disqualified. Otherwise, as provided in Rule 34-1b, no penalty may be imposed.

34-1b/5
Disqualification Penalty Wrongly Applied to Winner of Event; Error Discovered After Two Other Competitors Play Off for First Place

Q. In the final round of a stroke-play competition, the Committee disqualified A for recording on his score card a total score which was one stroke less than his actual score. A's hole by hole scores were correct. The Committee was in error. A would have won the event if he had not been disqualified.

As a result of A's disqualification, B and C play off for first place and B wins the play-off. Before the result of the competition is announced, the Committee discovers that A should not have been penalized.

Should the Committee rectify its error?

A. Yes. The penalty applied to A should be rescinded and A should be declared the winner – see Rule 34-1b.

34-1b/6
Winner's Score Not Posted Due to Committee Error

Q. In a stroke-play event, the winner's prize is awarded to B. The next day A advises the Committee that he had returned a lower score than B. A check reveals that A is correct and that, in error, the Committee had failed to post A's score. What should be done?

A. Rule 34-1b does not apply to Committee errors of this kind. The prize should be retrieved from B and given to A, the rightful winner.

Related Decisions:
• 6-2b/3 Competitor Wins Competition with Handicap Which Was Incorrect Due to Committee Error; Error Discovered Several Days Later.

• 33-5/2 Wrong Handicap Applied by Committee Results in Player Not Receiving Prize.

34-1b/7
Wrong Score in Qualifying Round Discovered During Match Play

Q. On completion of the stroke-play qualifying round for a match-play competition, a player unintentionally failed to include in his score for a hole a penalty he knew he had incurred. After the player had advanced in the match-play phase, the error was discovered. What should be done?

A. The player should be disqualified. Under Rule 34-1b, the penalty for a breach of Rule 6-6d was applicable after the qualifying competition was closed.

34-1b/8
Player Who Has Advanced in Match Play Is Disqualified for Wrong Score in Qualifying Round

Q. The Committee discovers that by mistake A, who has advanced to the fourth round of a match-play competition, returned a score lower than actually taken in the qualifying round. A was disqualified. What is the proper procedure with regard to the players beaten by A?

A. The Committee must determine further procedure in equity (Rule 1-4). The choices are:
  (a) cancel the competition;
  (b) consider the disqualification penalty applicable only from the time of its discovery, thus giving A's next opponent a default;
  (c) reinstate the player last eliminated by A; or
  (d) require all players eliminated by A to play off for his position.

34-1b/9
Breach of Anti-Doping Condition Discovered After Competition Closed

Q. In stroke play, a Committee discovers after a competition has closed that a player was in breach of that competition's anti-doping condition, which carries a penalty of disqualification. If the player claims no prior knowledge of the breach, how should Rule 34-1b(iv) be interpreted?

A. Anti-doping conditions adopt a policy whereby a player is held to be responsible for a breach of the condition regardless of how this may have happened. Therefore, from a Rules of Golf perspective, a player who commits a breach of such an anti-doping condition is deemed to have known he was in breach of a Rule, for which the penalty is disqualification. Accordingly, Exception (iv) to Rule 34-1b applies and the player must be disqualified.

34-2/1
Referee's Authority to Declare Ground Under Repair

Q. Does the referee of a match have authority to declare an area ground under repair during the match?

A. Yes.

Related Decision:
• 33-2a/2 Declaring Area as Ground Under Repair During Competition Round.

34-2/2
Referee Authorises Player to Infringe a Rule

Q. In error, a referee authorized a player to infringe a Rule of Golf. Is the player absolved from penalty in such a case?

A. Yes. Under Rule 34-2, a referee's decision is final, whether or not the decision is correct.

34-2/3
Referee Warning Player About to Infringe Rule

Q. If the referee observes a player about to break a Rule, may he warn the player and thus prevent a breach?

A. Yes, but he is under no obligation to do so. If he volunteers information about the Rules, he should do so uniformly to all players.

34-2/4
Disagreement with Referee's Decision

Q. In match play, if a player disagrees with a referee's decision, may the player demand that the matter be considered by the Committee?

A. No. A referee's decision may be referred to the Committee only if the referee consents.

34-2/5
Referee Reverses Ruling Made at Last Hole of Match After Players Leave Putting Green

Q. In a match, A and B are all square playing the last hole. An incident occurs on the putting green and the referee rules incorrectly that A loses the last hole and the match, whereas he should have ruled that B lost the last hole and the match. A and B walk off the putting green without disputing the ruling. Subsequently, but before the result of the match is officially announced, the referee learns of his error, reverses his ruling and decides that B lost the last hole and the match. Did the referee act properly in reversing his ruling?

A. Yes. As the result of the match had not been officially announced and neither player had made any further strokes, the referee was correct in reversing his ruling (see also Decisions 2-5/14, 34-2/6, 34-3/3 and 34-3/3.3).

34-2/6
Referee Reverses Ruling After Player Subsequently Plays a Ball

Q. In a match, an incident occurs on the putting green of the 17th hole and the referee rules incorrectly that A loses the hole. A and B walk off the putting green without disputing the ruling. After the players play from the next tee, the referee learns of his error, reverses the ruling and rules that B lost the 17th hole. Did the referee act properly in reversing the ruling?

A. No. If, after a referee has given a ruling, either player makes a stroke on the hole or, in circumstances where no more strokes are made on the hole, either player makes a stroke from the next teeing ground, the referee may not reverse his ruling. In the case of the last hole of the match, see Decision 34-2/5.

If the referee becomes aware of his error prior to a player making a stroke or, in circumstances where no more strokes are made on the hole, either player making a stroke from the next teeing ground, in equity (Rule 1-4), the referee must correct the error. Although Rule 34-2 states that the referee's decision is final, it is final only in the sense that the player has no right to appeal unless the referee consents.

34-2/7
Correction of Incorrect Ruling by Referee in Match Play

Q. In singles match play, the players obtain a ruling from the referee, and the referee incorrectly advises one of the players that he has incurred a loss of hole penalty. Both players lift their balls and walk to the next tee. The referee then learns of the incorrect ruling. Should the referee correct the error?

A. If neither player has made a stroke from the next teeing ground or, in the case of the last hole of the match, if the result of the match has not been officially announced, in equity (Rule 1-4), the referee must correct the error. The referee must direct the players to replace their balls and complete the hole, with the correct ruling applied. Otherwise, it is too late to correct the error and the loss of hole penalty must stand.

COMMITTEE'S DECISION

34-3/1
Correction of Incorrect Ruling in Stroke Play

Q. During the first round of a 36-hole stroke-play competition, a competitor plays a wrong ball from a bunker at the 6th hole and the ball comes to rest on the green. He then realizes that he has played a wrong ball and corrects his mistake. The competitor reports the facts to the Committee before returning his card and is incorrectly advised that he has incurred no penalty since the wrong ball was played from a hazard.

During the second round the Committee realizes that it made a mistake and retrospectively adds to the competitor's first-round score two penalty strokes at the 6th hole, but does not disqualify the competitor under Rule 6-6d.

The competitor objects on the ground that the Committee reached a decision on the matter the previous day and that, as Rule 34-3 states that the Committee's decision is final, it cannot now impose a penalty.

Was the Committee's procedure correct?

A. Yes. Under Rule 34-3, a Committee's decision is final in that the competitor has no right to appeal. However, Rule 34-3 does not prevent a Committee from correcting an incorrect ruling and imposing or rescinding a penalty provided that no penalty is imposed or rescinded after the competition is closed, except in the circumstances set forth in Rule 34-1b.

Related Decision:
• 34-1b/1 Omission of Penalty Stroke When Score Returned.

34-3/1.3
Competitor Incorrectly Advised to Cancel Stroke

Q. In stroke play, a competitor's second stroke on a hole strikes the equipment of a player in another group. The competitor consults a referee before making his next stroke, and the referee incorrectly advises him that he must cancel and replay the stroke without penalty, which he does. Having replayed the stroke, the competitor then takes two more strokes to hole out. The competitor plays from the next tee and, prior to returning his score card, the referee's error comes to light. What is the ruling?

A. The referee's decision to require the competitor to cancel and replay the stroke stands. In such circumstances, the competitor's score for the hole concerned would be 4. (New)

Related Decisions:
• 33-7/5 Play of Wrong Ball Not Rectified on Advice of Committee Member
• 34-3/3 Player in Match Makes Stroke From Wrong Place Due to Incorrect Ruling; Procedure for Player When Error is Discovered
• 34-3/3.3 Competitor in Stroke Play Makes Stroke From Wrong Place Due to Incorrect Ruling; Procedure for Competitior When Error is Discovered

A player is responsible for knowing the Rules (Rule 6-1), but there may be situations, immediately before and during a stipulated round, when an official representative of the Committee provides the player with incorrect information on the Rules. The player is entitled to act on such information in his subsequent play. Consequently, the Committee may be required to make a judgment as to both the duration of the player's entitlement and his proper score when, as a result of proceeding according to the incorrect information provided by the official, he is liable to a penalty under the Rules.

In these situations, the Committee should resolve the matter in whatever manner it considers most equitable, in light of all the facts and with the objective of ensuring that no player receives an undue advantage or disadvantage. In cases where the incorrect information significantly affects the results of the competition, the Committee may have no option but to cancel the round. The following principles, in equity (Rule 1-4), are applicable:

1. **General Guidance on the Rules**

   When a member of the Committee or a referee provides incorrect information in the nature of general guidance about the Rules, the player should not be exempt from penalty.

2. **Specific Ruling**

   When a referee makes a specific ruling that is contrary to the Rules in a specific situation, the player should be exempt from penalty. The Committee has the authority to extend this exemption for the duration of the round in circumstances where the player proceeds incorrectly on his own in exactly the same manner as advised by a referee earlier in the round. However, that exemption would cease if, in that round, the player becomes aware of the proper procedure or has his actions questioned.

3. **Guidance on Local Rules or Conditions of Competition**

   When a member of the Committee or a referee gives incorrect information on whether a Local Rule or condition of the competition is in effect, the player should be exempt from penalty for acting on that information. This exemption should be for the duration of the round unless corrected earlier, in which case, the exemption should cease at that point.

4. **Equipment Ruling**

   When a member of the Committee or a referee rules that a non-conforming club is conforming, the player should be exempt from penalty for carrying or using the club. This exemption should be for the duration of the competition unless corrected earlier, in which case, the exemption should cease at the completion of the round during which the correction was made. (Revised)

34-3/2
Committee Does Not Penalize Player in Breach of Pace of Play Condition Believing Player Had Already Lost Hole

Q. In a match between A and B, a pace of play condition was in effect. During play of the 10th hole, B was observed by a referee to breach the pace of play condition. The referee did not advise either player of the loss of hole penalty because he mistakenly believed that A had won the hole. During play of the 14th hole, another referee began to monitor the match's pace of play and informed B that he had previously breached the pace of play condition on the 10th hole. The referee also indicated that neither player was advised of the breach and the resulting loss of hole penalty because it was thought that A had already won the hole. The players indicated that A did not win the 10th hole and that the hole was halved. What is the ruling?

A. The result of the 10th hole stands as played. The first referee erred in failing to impose the loss of hole penalty for B's breach of the pace of play condition and it may not be imposed after either player has played from the 11th tee. A was not given wrong information by B and could not therefore make a later claim when the referee's error came to his attention (Rule 2-5). (Revised)

34-3/3
Player in Match Makes Stroke from Wrong Place Due to Incorrect Ruling; Procedure for Player When Error is Discovered

Q. In a match, a player obtains a ruling from a referee and proceeds on the basis of that ruling, which involves dropping a ball and playing from a wrong place. The Committee then learns of the incorrect ruling by the referee. Should the Committee require the player to disregard the stroke or strokes made after the incorrect ruling and proceed correctly?

A. Unless a serious breach is involved or the player has been seriously disadvantaged due to his playing from a wrong place, the ruling may not be reversed or corrected once the player has made the stroke from the wrong place.

If a serious breach is involved or the player has been seriously disadvantaged due to playing from a wrong place, in equity (Rule 1-4), the error must be corrected by the Committee up to the point where an opponent makes his next stroke on the hole concerned. If an opponent does not make a stroke on the hole after the ruling was given, the incorrect ruling may be corrected before either player makes a stroke from the next teeing ground or, in the case of the last hole of the match, before the result of the match is officially announced. Therefore, even if, for example, the player has conceded the opponent's next stroke and the opponent has lifted his ball, the Committee should direct the player to proceed correctly and the opponent to replace his ball, without penalty. If it is too late to correct the error, the strokes made after the incorrect ruling must stand with no penalty. (Revised)

34-3/3.3
Competitor in Stroke Play Makes Stroke from Wrong Place Due to Incorrect Ruling; Procedure for Competitor When Error is Discovered

Q. In stroke play, a competitor obtains a ruling from a referee and proceeds on the basis of that ruling, which involves dropping a ball and playing from a wrong place. The Committee then learns of the incorrect ruling by the referee. Should the Committee require the competitor to disregard the stroke or strokes made after the incorrect ruling and proceed correctly?

A. Unless a serious breach is involved or the competitor has been seriously disadvantaged due to his playing from a wrong place, the strokes made after the incorrect ruling must stand with no penalty.

If a serious breach is involved or the competitor has been seriously disadvantaged due to his playing from a wrong place, and the competitor has not played from the next teeing ground or, in the case of the last hole of the round, has not left the putting green, in equity (Rule 1-4), the Committee must correct the error. The Committee must direct the competitor to cancel the stroke made from the wrong place and any subsequent strokes and proceed correctly. The competitor incurs no penalty for playing from a wrong place. If it is too late to correct the error, the strokes made after the incorrect ruling must stand with no penalty. (Revised)

Decisions related to 34-3/3 and 34-3/3.3:
• 33-7/5 Play of Wrong Ball Not Rectified on Advice of Committee Member.
• 34-3/1.3 Competitor Incorrectly Advised to Cancel Stroke.

34-3/3.5
Player Lifts Ball Without Authority Due to Misunderstanding Referee's Instructions

Q. A player's ball comes to rest against a movable obstruction and he seeks relief. A referee correctly advises him that he may remove the obstruction under Rule 24-1 and that he should mark the position of the ball in case it moves during the removal of the obstruction. The player marks the position of the ball and lifts it before the referee can stop him. The player was under the misapprehension that, having been requested to mark the position of the ball, he was entitled to lift it before the obstruction was removed. Should the player be penalized under Rule 18-2a in these circumstances?

A. No. Provided the referee is satisfied that the player misunderstood the instruction, the ball should be replaced without penalty. (Revised)

Related Decision:
• 18-2a/13 Ball Lifted Without Authority and Cleaned.

34-3/3.7
Player Incorrectly Advised to Continue with Provisional Ball

Q. In stroke play, a competitor's tee shot is struck towards an area of trees, bushes and tall grass. Believing his ball might be lost outside a water hazard, the player announces his intention to play a provisional ball and plays a ball from the tee. When he arrives at the area, he finds that his ball is in a lateral water hazard. A referee incorrectly tells the competitor that a provisional ball is not allowed in such circumstances and, therefore, the second ball has become the ball in play under penalty of stroke and distance. The competitor continues with the second ball, taking three additional strokes to finish the hole, and plays from the next tee. The Committee then learns of this incorrect ruling. What score should it assign to the player for the hole?

A. As the competitor played the second ball from the tee in the belief that his original ball might have been lost outside a water hazard, that ball was a provisional ball, and the competitor should have abandoned it and continued with the original ball (Rule 27-2c).

By directing the competitor to continue with the provisional ball, the referee had the player play a wrong ball. However, the competitor incurs no penalty under Rule 15-3b for playing a wrong ball as he did so at the instruction of a referee.

The Committee should determine that the competitor's score for the hole is 4: his tee shot with the original ball plus the three strokes made with the wrong ball after the incorrect ruling. However, if it would have been clearly unreasonable for the competitor to play the original ball as it lay in the water hazard, he must, in equity (Rule 1-4), add one penalty stroke under Rule 26-1 to his score. (Revised)

34-3/3.9
Committee Makes Incorrect Ruling Under Rule 3-3; Whether Ruling May Be Corrected

Q. In stroke play, a competitor plays two balls (X and Y) under Rule 3-3. When he reports the facts to the Committee before returning his score card, the Committee determines that he must score with Ball Y. Subsequently, the Committee realizes it made an incorrect ruling and that the score with Ball X should have been the competitor's score for the hole. May the Committee correct this mistake?

A. Such a mistake is an incorrect ruling and not an administrative error. Therefore Rule 34 applies and the answer depends on when the Committee learns of its incorrect ruling.

If the Committee learns of the incorrect ruling before the competition closes, it should correct the ruling without penalty to the competitor by changing his score for the hole in question to that with Ball X (Decision 34-3/1).

If the Committee learns of the incorrect ruling after the competition has closed, the score with Ball Y must remain the competitor's score for the hole in question. Under Rule 34-3, such a ruling is final once the competition has closed.

34-3/4
Dispute as to Whether Competitor Played from Outside Teeing Ground

Q. In stroke play, B, A's fellow-competitor and marker, claimed at the completion of the round that A had played from outside the teeing ground at the 15th hole. A stated that he had played from within the teeing ground.

The Committee ruled that the claim was invalid because it was not made at the 15th tee and because A disputed the claim. Was the ruling correct?

A. It is a question of fact whether A played from outside the teeing ground. The matter should be resolved on the basis of the weight of evidence. The timing of a claim is not necessarily a factor.

In this case, it was B's word against A's and the weight of evidence did not favor either competitor. In such a case, the benefit of the doubt should be given to A, the player of the stroke.

Related Decisions:
• 6-6a/4 Marker Refuses to Sign Competitor's Card After Dispute Resolved in Favor of Competitor.
• 6-6d/5 Spectators Allege Competitor's Score Incorrect.

34-3/5
True State of Match Not Determinable

Q. On completion of a match, A claims he is 1 up and B claims the match is all square. The matter is referred to the Committee. The Committee gathers all available evidence and is unable to determine the true state of the match. What should the Committee do?

A. It should resolve the matter in the fairest way. An equitable solution would be to order that the match be replayed.

34-3/6
Player Proceeds Under an Inapplicable Rule; Committee's Decision

When a player proceeds under a Rule that does not apply to his situation and then makes a stroke, the Committee must determine the Rule to apply in order to give a ruling based on the player's actions.

For examples of appropriate Committee decisions in such cases, see Decisions 18-2a/3, 20-7/2, 25-1b/13 and 25-1c/2 and the explanations below:

In Decision 18-2a/3, the player has proceeded under an inapplicable Rule (Rule 24-2). As Rule 28 (Ball Unplayable) requires the player to have the intention to proceed under it before lifting the ball, the Committee may not apply Rule 28 to the player's actions. As there was no Rule that allowed the player to lift his ball in such a situation, the Committee determined that Rule 18-2a must apply.

In Decision 20-7/2, the player deemed his ball unplayable in a water hazard, dropped it according to the procedure of option b or c of Rule 28 and played it from the water hazard. As Rule 26-1 was the only Rule that allowed the player to lift his ball for relief in that situation, the Committee determined that Rule 26 applied and ruled accordingly. As a result, the player was considered to have played from a wrong place (i.e., a place not permitted by Rule 26-1).

In Decision 25-1b/13, the player's ball lay in casual water that he mistook for a water hazard. He dropped and played a ball according to the procedure of option b under Rule 26-1. As Rule 25-1 was the only Rule that allowed the player to lift his ball for relief in that situation, the Committee determined that Rule 25 applied and ruled accordingly. As a result, the player was considered to have played from a wrong place (i.e. a place not permitted by Rule 25-1) and to have wrongly substituted a ball in breach of Rule 25-1 (see Rule 15-2).

In Decision 25-1c/2, the player did not know the location of his original ball but assumed, without knowledge or virtual certainty, that it was in ground under repair. He dropped and played another ball under Rule 25-1c. As the player did not know the location of his original ball, in these circumstances, Rule 27-1 was the only Rule that the player could have proceeded under. Therefore, the Committee determined that Rule 27-1 applied and ruled accordingly. As a result, the player was considered to have put a ball into play under penalty of stroke and distance and to have played from a wrong place (i.e. a place not permitted by Rule 27-1).

34-3/7
Player Proceeds on Basis of Ruling; Subsequent Facts Prove Ruling to Be Incorrect

Q. A player believes his ball in play may have moved after he addressed it and asks for a ruling from a referee. Based on the evidence available at the time, the referee determines that the ball did not move and instructs the player to play the ball as it lies without penalty. After the player plays, the referee becomes aware of evidence that indicates that the ball had in fact moved. What is the ruling?

A. As the ball moved after the player had addressed it, he was required to replace the ball with a penalty stroke under Rule 18-2b. When he failed to do so, he played from a wrong place. As he did so at the instruction of a referee, he does not incur the general penalty under Rule 18 for playing from a wrong place. However, he does incur the penalty stroke under Rule 18-2b as the ball had moved after address before the ruling from the referee. The player must continue with the ball played from the wrong place. (Revised)

34-3/8
Player Proceeds on Basis of Ruling; Player's Version of Facts Subsequently Found to Be Incorrect

Q. A player's ball in play moves, and the player asks for a ruling from a referee. When asked, the player informs the referee that he had not addressed the ball. As the player had done nothing else to cause the ball to move, the referee instructs the player to play the ball from its new location without penalty. After the player plays, the referee becomes aware that the player had in fact addressed the ball. What is the ruling?

A. As the ball moved after the player had addressed it, he was required to replace the ball with a penalty stroke under Rule 18-2b. When he failed to do so, he played from a wrong place and loses the hole in match play or incurs a penalty of two strokes in stroke play under Rule 18.

The player must continue with the ball played from the wrong place except that, in stroke play, if a serious breach is involved and the player has not yet played from the next teeing ground or, in the case of the last hole of the round, before the player leaves the putting green, the referee must require the player to cancel the stroke made with the ball from the wrong place and any subsequent strokes and play from the original location of the ball.

The imposition of the general penalty in this situation is different from the ruling in Decision 34-3/7 in that, in this case, the player provided the incorrect information that led to the incorrect ruling. The player is responsible for providing the correct facts to the referee and is subject to penalty under the applicable Rule if his incorrect version of the facts led to his playing from a wrong place. (Revised)

34-3/9
Resolution of Questions of Fact; Referee and Committee Responsibility

Resolving questions of fact is among the most difficult actions required of a referee, or the Committee as a whole. For example, these situations include a broad array of incidents such as determining whether a player caused a ball to move (Decisions 18/10, 18-2a/30 and 18-2a/30.5), whether a player played from outside the teeing ground (Decision 34-3/4), whether a stroke was made (Decision 14/1.5), the hole at which a wrong ball was played (Decision 15-1/3) and the state of a match (Decision 34-3/5).

In all situations involving questions of fact, resolution of the doubt must be made in light of all the relevant circumstances and evaluation of the weight of the evidence, including the balance of probabilities where applicable (Decision 15-1/3). When the Committee is unable to determine the facts to its satisfaction, it must resolve the matter in the fairest way (Decision 34-3/5).

Testimony of the players involved is important and must be given due consideration. In some situations where the facts are not decisive, the doubt should be resolved in favor of the player (Decisions 15-1/2 and 19-1/4.1); in others, the doubt should be resolved against the player (Decision 13-4/35.5 and 21/3). There is no hard-and-fast rule for evaluating the testimony of the players or for assigning the weight to be given to such testimony and each situation must be treated on its own merits. The proper action depends on the circumstances in each case and must be left to the judgment of the referee, or the Committee as a whole.

Testimony of those who are not a part of the competition, including spectators, must be accepted and evaluated (Decision 27/12). It is also appropriate to use television footage and the like to assist in resolving doubt.

It is important that any questions of fact be resolved in a timely manner such that the competition may proceed in an orderly way. Thus, the referee may be limited to evaluating the evidence available to him in a timely manner. Any such ruling is always subject to further review by the referee, or Committee as a whole as additional evidence becomes available.

If a judgment is made by a referee, the player is entitled to proceed on the basis of that ruling whether it is an interpretation of the Rules of Golf (Decision 34-3/1.5) or a resolution of a question of fact (Decision 34-3/7). In situations arising in both circumstances, if the ruling is found to be incorrect, the Committee may have the authority to make a correction (Decisions 34-3/1 and 34-3/7). However, in all circumstances, including both match play and stroke play, the referee or Committee is limited in its ability to make corrections by the guidance contained in Decisions 34-2/5, 34-2/6, 34-2/7, 34-3/3 and 34-3/3.3. (Revised)

MISCELLANEOUS

Misc./1
Course Record

The term "course record" is not defined in the Rules of Golf. However, it is generally accepted that a record score should be recognized as the official "course record" only if made in an individual stroke-play competition (excluding bogey, par or Stableford competitions) with the holes and tee-markers in their proper medal or championship positions.

It is recommended that a record score should not be recognized as the official "course record" if a Local Rule permitting preferred lies is in operation.

Misc./2
Whether Rakes Should Be Placed in or Outside Bunkers

Q. Should rakes be placed in or outside bunkers?

A. There is not a perfect answer for the position of rakes, but on balance it is felt there is less likelihood of an advantage or disadvantage to the player if rakes are placed outside bunkers.

It may be argued that there is more likelihood of a ball being deflected into or kept out of a bunker if the rake is placed outside the bunker. It could also be argued that if the rake is in the bunker it is most unlikely that the ball will be deflected out of the bunker.

However, in practice, players who leave rakes in bunkers frequently leave them at the side which tends to stop a ball rolling into the flat part of the bunker, resulting in a much more difficult shot than would otherwise have been the case. This is most prevalent at a course where the bunkers are small. When the ball comes to rest on or against a rake in the bunker and the player must proceed under Rule 24-1, it may not be possible to replace the ball on the same spot or find a spot in the bunker which is not nearer the hole – see Decision 20-3d/2.

If rakes are left in the middle of the bunker the only way to position them is to throw them into the bunker and this causes damage to the surface. Also, if a rake is in the middle of a large bunker it is either not used or the player is obliged to rake a large area of the bunker resulting in unnecessary delay.

Therefore, after considering all these aspects, it is recommended that rakes should be left outside bunkers in areas where they are least likely to affect the movement of the ball.

Ultimately, it is a matter for the Committee to decide where it wishes rakes to be placed.

APPENDIX I

LOCAL RULES; CONDITIONS OF THE COMPETITION

PART A

LOCAL RULES

DEFINITIONS

All defined terms are in *italics* and are listed alphabetically in the Definitions section – see pages 6–16.

As provided in Rule 33-8a, the *Committee* may make and publish Local Rules for local abnormal conditions if they are consistent with the policy established in this Appendix. In addition, detailed information regarding acceptable and prohibited Local Rules is provided in "Decisions on the Rules of Golf" under Rule 33-8 and in "How to Conduct a Competition."

If local abnormal conditions interfere with the proper playing of the game and the *Committee* considers it necessary to modify a Rule of Golf, authorization from the USGA must be obtained.

I. DEFINING BOUNDS AND MARGINS

Specifying means used to define *out of bounds, water hazards, lateral water hazards, ground under repair, obstructions* and integral parts of the *course* (Rule 33-2a).

2. WATER HAZARDS
a. Lateral Water Hazards
Clarifying the status of *water hazards* that may be *lateral water hazards* (Rule 26).

b. Ball Played Provisionally Under Rule 26-1
Permitting play of a ball provisionally under Rule 26-1 for a ball that may be in a *water hazard* (including a *lateral water hazard*) of such character that, if the original ball is not found, it is known or virtually certain that it is in the *water hazard* and it would be impracticable to determine whether the ball is in the *hazard* or to do so would unduly delay play.

3. AREAS OF THE COURSE REQUIRING PRESERVATION; ENVIRONMENTALLY-SENSITIVE AREAS
Assisting preservation of the *course* by defining areas, including turf nurseries, young plantations and other parts of the *course* under cultivation, as *ground under repair* from which play is prohibited.

When the *Committee* is required to prohibit play from environmentally-sensitive areas that are on or adjoin the *course*, it should make a Local Rule clarifying the relief procedure.

4. COURSE CONDITIONS – MUD, EXTREME WETNESS, POOR CONDITIONS AND PROTECTION OF COURSE
a. Lifting an Embedded Ball, Cleaning
Temporary conditions that might interfere with proper playing of the game, including mud and extreme wetness, warranting relief for an embedded ball anywhere *through the green* or permitting lifting, cleaning and replacing a ball anywhere *through the green* or on a closely mown area *through the green*.

b. "Preferred Lies" and "Winter Rules"
Adverse conditions, including the poor condition of the *course* or the existence of mud, are sometimes so general, particularly during winter months, that the *Committee* may decide to grant relief by temporary Local Rule either to protect the *course* or to promote fair and pleasant play. The Local Rule should be withdrawn as soon as the conditions warrant.

5. OBSTRUCTIONS
a. General
Clarifying status of objects that may be *obstructions* (Rule 24).

Declaring any construction to be an integral part of the *course* and, accordingly, not an *obstruction*, e.g., built-up sides of *teeing grounds*, *putting greens* and *bunkers* (Rules 24 and 33-2a).

b. Stones in Bunkers
Allowing the removal of stones in *bunkers* by declaring them to be movable *obstructions* (Rule 24-1).

c. Roads and Paths
(i) Declaring artificial surfaces and sides of roads and paths to be integral parts of the *course*, or
(ii) Providing relief of the type afforded under Rule 24-2b from roads and paths not having artificial surfaces and sides if they could unfairly affect play.

d. Immovable Obstructions Close to Putting Green
Providing relief from intervention by immovable *obstructions* on or within two club-lengths of the *putting green* when the ball lies within two club-lengths of the immovable *obstruction*.

e. Protection of Young Trees
Providing relief for the protection of young trees.

f. Temporary Obstructions
Providing relief from interference by temporary obstructions (e.g., grandstands, television cables and equipment, etc).

6. DROPPING ZONES
Establishing special areas on which balls may or must be dropped when it is not feasible or practicable to proceed exactly in conformity with Rule 24-2b or 24-3 (Immovable Obstruction), Rule 25-1b or 25-1c (Abnormal Ground Conditions), Rule 25-3 (Wrong Putting Green), Rule 26-1 (Water Hazards and Lateral Water Hazards) or Rule 28 (Ball Unplayable).

APPENDIX I

LOCAL RULES; CONDITIONS OF THE COMPETITION

PART B

SPECIMEN LOCAL RULES

Within the policy established in Part A of this Appendix, the *Committee* may adopt a Specimen Local Rule by referring, on a score card or notice board, to the examples given below. However, Specimen Local Rules of a temporary nature should not be printed on a score card.

1. WATER HAZARDS; BALL PLAYED PROVISIONALLY UNDER RULE 26-1

If a *water hazard* (including a *lateral water hazard*) is of such size and shape and/or located in such a position that:

(i) it would be impracticable to determine whether the ball is in the *hazard* or to do so would unduly delay play, and

(ii) if the original ball is not found, it is known or virtually certain that it is in the *water hazard*,

the *Committee* may introduce a Local Rule permitting the play of a ball provisionally under Rule 26-1. The ball is played provisionally under any of the applicable options under Rule 26-1 or any applicable Local Rule. In such a case, if a ball is played provisionally and the original ball is in a *water hazard*, the player may play the original ball as it lies or continue with the ball played provisionally, but he may not proceed under Rule 26-1 with regard to the original ball.

In these circumstances, the following Local Rule is recommended:

"If there is doubt whether a ball is in or is lost in the water hazard (specify location), the player may play another ball provisionally under any of the applicable options in Rule 26-1.

If the original ball is found outside the water hazard, the player must continue play with it.

If the original ball is found in the water hazard, the player may either play the original ball as it lies or continue with the ball played provisionally under Rule 26-1.

If the original ball is not found or identified within the five-minute search period, the player must continue with the ball played provisionally.

PENALTY FOR BREACH OF LOCAL RULE:
<u>Match play</u> – Loss of hole; <u>Stroke play</u> – Two strokes."

2. AREAS OF THE COURSE REQUIRING PRESERVATION; ENVIRONMENTALLY- SENSITIVE AREAS

a. Ground Under Repair; Play Prohibited

If the *Committee* wishes to protect any area of the *course*, it should declare it to be *ground under repair* and prohibit play from within that area. The following Local Rule is recommended:

"The _____(defined by _____) is ground under repair from which play is prohibited. If a player's ball lies in the area, or if it interferes with the player's stance or the area of his intended swing, the player must take relief under Rule 25-1.

PENALTY FOR BREACH OF LOCAL RULE:
<u>Match play</u> – Loss of hole; <u>Stroke play</u> – Two strokes."

b. Environmentally-Sensitive Areas

If an appropriate authority (i.e., a Government Agency or the like) prohibits entry into and/or play from an area on or adjoining the *course* for environmental reasons, the *Committee* should make a Local Rule clarifying the relief procedure.

The *Committee* has some discretion in terms of whether the area is defined as *ground under repair*, a *water hazard* or *out of bounds*. However, it may not simply define the area to be a *water hazard* if it does not meet the Definition of a "*Water Hazard*" and it should attempt to preserve the character of the hole.

The following Local Rule is recommended:

"I. Definition

An environmentally-sensitive area (ESA) is an area so declared by an appropriate authority, entry into and/or play from which is prohibited for environmental reasons. These areas may be defined as ground under repair, a water hazard, a lateral water hazard or out of bounds at the discretion of the Committee, provided that in the case of an ESA that has been defined as a water hazard or a lateral water hazard, the area is, by definition, a water hazard.
Note: The Committee may not declare an area to be environmentally-sensitive.

II. Ball in Environmentally-Sensitive Area
a. Ground Under Repair

If a ball is in an ESA defined as ground under repair, a ball must be dropped in accordance with Rule 25-1b.

If it is known or virtually certain that a ball that has not been found is in an ESA defined as ground under repair, the player may take relief, without penalty, as prescribed in Rule 25-1c.

b. Water Hazards and Lateral Water Hazards

If the ball is found in or if it is known or virtually certain that a ball that has not been found is in an ESA defined as a water hazard or lateral water hazard, the player must, under penalty of one stroke, proceed under Rule 26-1.
Note: If a ball, dropped in accordance with Rule 26 rolls into a position where the ESA interferes with the player's stance or the area of his intended swing, the player must take relief as provided in Clause III of this Local Rule.

c. Out of Bounds

If a ball is in an ESA defined as out of bounds, the player must play a ball, under penalty of one stroke, as nearly as possible at the spot from which the original ball was last played (see Rule 20-5).

III. INTERFERENCE WITH STANCE OR AREA OF INTENDED SWING

Interference by an ESA occurs when the ESA interferes with the player's stance or the area of his intended swing. If interference exists, the player must take relief as follows:

(a) <u>Through the Green</u>: If the ball lies through the green, the point on the course nearest to where the ball lies must be determined that (a) is not nearer the hole, (b) avoids interference by the ESA and (c) is not in a hazard or on a putting green. The player must lift the ball and drop it, without penalty, within one club-length of the point so determined on a part of the course that fulfils (a), (b) and (c) above.

(b) <u>In a Hazard</u>: If the ball is in a hazard, the player must lift the ball and drop it either:

   (i) Without penalty, in the hazard, as near as possible to the spot where the ball lay, but not nearer the hole, on a part of the course that provides complete relief from the ESA; or

   (ii) Under penalty of one stroke, outside the hazard, keeping the point where the ball lay directly between the hole and the spot on which the ball is dropped, with no limit to how far behind the hazard the ball may be dropped. Additionally, the player may proceed under Rule 26 or 28 if applicable.

(c) <u>On the Putting Green</u>: If the ball lies on the putting green, the player must lift the ball and place it, without penalty, in the nearest position to where it lay that affords complete relief from the ESA, but not nearer the hole or in a hazard.

   The ball may be cleaned when lifted under Clause III of this Local Rule.

Exception: A player may not take relief under Clause III of this Local Rule if (a) interference by anything other than an ESA makes the stroke clearly impracticable or (b) interference by an ESA would occur only through use of a clearly unreasonable stroke or an unnecessarily abnormal stance, swing or direction of play.

PENALTY FOR BREACH OF LOCAL RULE:
<u>Match play</u> – Loss of hole; <u>Stroke play</u> – Two strokes.

Note: In the case of a serious breach of this Local Rule, the Committee may impose a penalty of disqualification."

3. PROTECTION OF YOUNG TREES

When it is desired to prevent damage to young trees, the following Local Rule is recommended:

"Protection of young trees identified by _____. If such a tree interferes with a player's stance or the area of his intended swing, the ball must be lifted, without penalty, and dropped in accordance with the procedure prescribed in Rule 24-2b (Immovable Obstruction). If the ball lies in a water hazard, the player must lift and drop the ball in accordance with Rule 24-2b(i), except that the nearest point of relief must be in the water hazard and the ball must be dropped in the water hazard or the player may proceed under Rule 26. The ball may be cleaned when lifted under this Local Rule.

Exception: A player may not obtain relief under this Local Rule if (a) interference by anything other than such a tree makes the stroke clearly impracticable or (b) interference by such a tree would occur only through use of a clearly unreasonable stroke or an unnecessarily abnormal stance, swing or direction of play.

PENALTY FOR BREACH OF LOCAL RULE:
Match play – Loss of hole; Stroke play – Two strokes."

4. COURSE CONDITIONS – MUD, EXTREME WETNESS, POOR CONDITIONS AND PROTECTION OF THE COURSE

a. Relief for Embedded Ball

Rule 25-2 provides relief, without penalty, for a ball embedded in its own pitch-mark in any closely mown area *through the green*. On the *putting green*, a ball may be lifted and damage caused by the impact of a ball may be repaired (Rules 16-1b and c). When permission to take relief for an embedded ball anywhere *through the green* would be warranted, the following Local Rule is recommended:

"Through the green, a ball that is embedded in its own pitch-mark in the ground may be lifted, without penalty, cleaned and dropped as near as possible to where it lay but not nearer the hole. The ball when dropped must first strike a part of the course through the green.

Exceptions:
1. A player may not take relief under this Local Rule if the ball is embedded in sand in an area that is not closely mown.
2. A player may not take relief under this Local Rule if interference by anything other than the condition covered by this Local Rule makes the stroke clearly impracticable.

PENALTY FOR BREACH OF LOCAL RULE:
Match play – Loss of hole; Stroke play – Two strokes."

b. Cleaning Ball

Conditions, such as extreme wetness causing significant amounts of mud to adhere to the ball, may be such that permission to lift, clean and replace the ball would be appropriate. In these circumstances, the following Local Rule is recommended:

"(Specify area) a ball may be lifted, cleaned and replaced without penalty.
Note: The position of the ball must be marked before it is lifted under this Local Rule – see Rule 20-1.

PENALTY FOR BREACH OF LOCAL RULE:
Match play – Loss of hole; Stroke play – Two strokes."

c. "Preferred Lies" and "Winter Rules"

Ground under repair is provided for in Rule 25 and occasional local abnormal conditions that might interfere with fair play and are not widespread should be defined as *ground under repair.*

However, adverse conditions, such as heavy snows, spring thaws, prolonged rains or extreme heat can make fairways unsatisfactory and sometimes prevent use of heavy mowing equipment. When such conditions are so general throughout a *course* that the *Committee* believes "preferred lies" or "winter rules" would promote fair play or help protect the *course*, the following Local Rule is recommended:

"A ball lying on a closely mown area through the green (or specify a more restricted area, e.g., at the 6th hole) may be lifted, without penalty, and cleaned. Before lifting the ball, the player must mark its position. Having lifted the ball, he must place it on a spot within (specify area, e.g., six inches, one club-length, etc.) of and not nearer the hole than where it originally lay, that is not in a hazard and not on a putting green.

A player may place his ball only once, and it is in play when it has been placed (Rule 20-4). If the ball fails to come to rest on the spot on which it is placed, Rule 20-3d applies. If the ball when placed comes to rest on the spot on which it is placed and it subsequently moves, there is no penalty and the ball must be played as it lies, unless the provisions of any other Rule apply.

If the player fails to mark the position of the ball before lifting it or moves the ball in any other manner, such as rolling it with a club, he incurs a penalty of one stroke.

Note: "Closely mown area" means any area of the course, including paths through the rough, cut to fairway height or less.

*PENALTY FOR BREACH OF LOCAL RULE:
<u>Match play</u> – Loss of hole; <u>Stroke play</u> – Two strokes.

*If a player incurs the general penalty for a breach of this Local Rule, no additional penalty under the Local Rule is applied."

d. Aeration Holes

When a *course* has been aerated, a Local Rule permitting relief, without penalty, from an aeration hole may be warranted. The following Local Rule is recommended:

"Through the green, a ball that comes to rest in or on an aeration hole may be lifted, without penalty, cleaned and dropped, as near as possible to the spot where it lay but not nearer the hole. The ball when dropped must first strike a part of the course through the green.

On the putting green, a ball that comes to rest in or on an aeration hole may be placed at the nearest spot not nearer the hole that avoids the situation.

PENALTY FOR BREACH OF LOCAL RULE:
<u>Match play</u> – Loss of hole; <u>Stroke play</u> – Two strokes."

e. Seams of Cut Turf

If a *Committee* wishes to allow relief from seams of cut turf, but not from the cut turf itself, the following Local Rule is recommended:

557

"Through the green, seams of cut turf (not the turf itself) are deemed to be ground under repair. However, interference by a seam with the player's stance is deemed not to be, of itself, interference under Rule 25-1. If the ball lies in or touches the seam or the seam interferes with the area of intended swing, relief is available under Rule 25-1. All seams within the cut turf area are considered the same seam.

PENALTY FOR BREACH OF LOCAL RULE:
<u>Match play</u> – Loss of hole; <u>Stroke play</u> – Two strokes."

5. STONES IN BUNKERS

Stones are, by definition, *loose impediments* and, when a player's ball is in a *hazard*, a stone lying in or touching the *hazard* may not be touched or moved (Rule 13-4). However, stones in *bunkers* may represent a danger to players (a player could be injured by a stone struck by the player's club in an attempt to play the ball) and they may interfere with the proper playing of the game.

When permission to lift a stone in a *bunker* is warranted, the following Local Rule is recommended:

"Stones in bunkers are movable obstructions (Rule 24-1 applies)."

6. IMMOVABLE OBSTRUCTIONS CLOSE TO PUTTING GREEN

Rule 24-2 provides relief, without penalty, from interference by an immovable *obstruction*, but it also provides that, except on the *putting green*, intervention on the *line of play* is not, of itself, interference under this Rule.

However, on some courses, the aprons of the *putting greens* are so closely mown that players may wish to putt from just off the green. In such conditions, immovable *obstructions* on the apron may interfere with the proper playing of the game and the introduction of the following Local Rule providing additional relief, without penalty, from intervention by an immovable *obstruction* would be warranted:

"Relief from interference by an immovable obstruction may be taken under Rule 24-2.

In addition, if a ball lies through the green and an immovable obstruction on or within two club-lengths of the putting green and within two club-lengths of the ball intervenes on the line of play between the ball and the hole, the player may take relief as follows:
The ball must be lifted and dropped at the nearest point to where the ball lay that (a) is not nearer the hole, (b) avoids intervention and (c) is not in a hazard or on a putting green.
If the player's ball lies on the putting green and an immovable obstruction within two club-lengths of the putting green intervenes on his line of putt, the player may take relief as follows:
The ball must be lifted and placed at the nearest point to where the ball lay that (a) is not nearer the hole, (b) avoids intervention and (c) is not in a hazard.
The ball may be cleaned when lifted.

Exception: A player may not take relief under this Local Rule if interference by anything other than the immovable obstruction makes the *stroke* clearly impracticable.

PENALTY FOR BREACH OF LOCAL RULE:
Match play – Loss of hole; Stroke play – Two strokes."

Note: The *Committee* may restrict this Local Rule to specific holes, to balls lying only in closely mown areas, to specific *obstructions*, or, in the case of *obstructions* that are not on the *putting green*, to *obstructions* in closely mown areas if so desired. "Closely mown area" means any area of the *course*, including paths through the rough, cut to fairway height or less.

7. TEMPORARY OBSTRUCTIONS

When temporary obstructions are installed on or adjoining the *course*, the *Committee* should define the status of such obstructions as movable, immovable or temporary immovable obstructions.

a. Temporary Immovable Obstructions

If the *Committee* defines such obstructions as temporary immovable obstructions, the following Local Rule is recommended:

"I. Definition

A temporary immovable obstruction (TIO) is a non-permanent artificial object that is often erected in conjunction with a competition and is fixed or not readily movable.

Examples of TIOs include, but are not limited to, tents, scoreboards, grandstands, television towers and lavatories.

Supporting guy wires are part of the TIO, unless the Committee declares that they are to be treated as elevated power lines or cables.

II. Interference

Interference by a TIO occurs when (a) the ball lies in front of and so close to the TIO that the TIO interferes with the player's stance or the area of his intended swing, or (b) the ball lies in, on, under or behind the TIO so that any part of the TIO intervenes directly between the player's ball and the hole and is on his line of play; interference also exists if the ball lies within one club-length of a spot equidistant from the hole where such intervention would exist.

Note: A ball is under a TIO when it is below the outer most edges of the TIO, even if these edges do not extend downwards to the ground.

III. Relief

A player may obtain relief from interference by a TIO, including a TIO that is out of bounds, as follows:

(a) Through the Green: If the ball lies through the green, the point on the course nearest to where the ball lies must be determined that (a) is not nearer the hole, (b) avoids interference as defined in Clause II and (c) is not in a hazard or on a putting green. The player must lift the ball and drop it, without penalty, within one club-length of the point so determined on a part of the course that fulfils (a), (b) and (c) above.

(b) In a Hazard: If the ball is in a hazard, the player must lift and drop the ball either:

(i) Without penalty, in accordance with Clause III(a) above, except that the nearest part of the course affording complete relief must be in the hazard and the ball must be dropped in the hazard or, if complete relief is impossible, on a part of the course within the hazard that affords maximum available relief; or

(ii) Under penalty of one stroke, outside the hazard as follows: the point on the course nearest to where the ball lies must be determined that (a) is not nearer the hole, (b) avoids interference as defined in Clause II and (c) is not in a hazard. The player must drop the ball within one club-length of the point so determined on a part of the course that fulfils (a), (b) and (c) above.

The ball may be cleaned when lifted under Clause III.

Note 1: If the ball lies in a hazard, nothing in this Local Rule precludes the player from proceeding under Rule 26 or Rule 28, if applicable.

Note 2: If a ball to be dropped under this Local Rule is not immediately recoverable, another ball may be substituted.

Note 3: A Committee may make a Local Rule (a) permitting or requiring a player to use a dropping zone when taking relief from a TIO or (b) permitting a player, as an additional relief option, to drop the ball on the opposite side of the TIO from the point established under Clause III, but otherwise in accordance with Clause III.

Exceptions: If a player's ball lies in front of or behind the TIO (not in, on or under the TIO), he may not obtain relief under Clause III if:

1. Interference by anything other than the TIO makes it clearly impracticable for him to make a stroke or, in the case of intervention, to make a stroke such that the ball could finish on a direct line to the hole;

2. Interference by the TIO would occur only through use of a clearly unreasonable stroke or an unnecessarily abnormal stance, swing or direction of play; or

3. In the case of intervention, it would be clearly impracticable to expect the player to be able to strike the ball far enough towards the hole to reach the TIO.

A player who is not entitled to relief due to these exceptions may, if the ball lies through the green or in a bunker, obtain relief as provided in Rule 24-2b, if applicable. If the ball lies in a water hazard, the player may lift and drop the ball in accordance with Rule 24-2b(i), except that the nearest point of relief must be in the water hazard and the ball must be dropped in the water hazard, or the player may proceed under Rule 26-1.

IV. Ball in TIO Not Found

If it is known or virtually certain that a ball that has not been found is in, on or under a TIO, a ball may be dropped under the provisions of Clause III or Clause V, if applicable. For the purpose of applying Clauses III and V, the ball is deemed to lie at the spot where it last crossed the outermost limits of the TIO (Rule 24-3).

V. Dropping Zones

If the player has interference from a TIO, the Committee may permit or require the use of a dropping zone. If the player uses a dropping zone in taking relief, he must drop the ball in the dropping zone nearest to where his ball originally lay or is deemed to lie under Clause IV (even though the nearest dropping zone may be nearer the hole).

Note: A Committee may make a Local Rule prohibiting the use of a dropping zone that is nearer the hole.

PENALTY FOR BREACH OF LOCAL RULE:
Match play – Loss of hole; Stroke play – Two strokes."

b. Temporary Power Lines and Cables

When temporary power lines, cables, or telephone lines are installed on the *course*, the following Local Rule is recommended:

"Temporary power lines, cables, telephone lines and mats covering or stanchions supporting them are obstructions:
1 If they are readily movable, Rule 24-1 applies.
2. If they are fixed or not readily movable, the player may, if the ball lies through the green or in a bunker, obtain relief as provided in Rule 24-2b. If the ball lies in a water hazard, the player may lift and drop the ball in accordance with Rule 24-2b(i), except that the nearest point of relief must be in the water hazard and the ball must be dropped in the water hazard or the player may proceed under Rule 26.
3. If a ball strikes an elevated power line or cable, the stroke is canceled and the player must play a ball as nearly as possible at the spot from which the original ball was played in accordance with Rule 20-5 (Making Next Stroke from Where Previous Stroke Made).

Note: Guy wires supporting a temporary immovable obstruction are part of the temporary immovable obstruction, unless the Committee, by Local Rule, declares that they are to be treated as elevated power lines or cables.

Exception: A stroke that results in a ball striking an elevated junction section of cable rising from the ground must not be replayed.
4. Grass-covered cable trenches are ground under repair, even if not marked, and Rule 25-1b applies.

PENALTY FOR BREACH OF LOCAL RULE:
Match play – Loss of hole; Stroke play – Two strokes."

8. DROPPING ZONES

If the *Committee* considers that it is not feasible or practicable to proceed in accordance with a Rule providing relief, it may establish dropping zones in which balls may or must be dropped when taking relief. Generally, such dropping zones should be provided as an additional relief option to those available under the Rule itself, rather than being mandatory.

Using the example of a dropping zone for a *water hazard*, when such a dropping zone is established, the following Local Rule is recommended:

"If a ball is in or it is known or virtually certain that a ball that has not been found is in the water hazard (specify location), the player may:
(i) proceed under Rule 26; or
(ii) as an additional option, drop a ball, under penalty of one stroke, in the dropping zone.

PENALTY FOR BREACH OF LOCAL RULE:

<u>Match play</u> – Loss of hole; <u>Stroke play</u> – Two strokes."

Note: When using a dropping zone the following provisions apply regarding the dropping and re-dropping of the ball:

(a) The player does not have to stand within the dropping zone when dropping the ball.

(b) The dropped ball must first strike a part of the *course* within the dropping zone.

(c) If the dropping zone is defined by a line, the line is within the dropping zone.

(d) The dropped ball does not have to come to rest within the dropping zone.

(e) The dropped ball must be re-dropped if it rolls and comes to rest in a position covered by Rule 20-2c(i-vi).

(f) The dropped ball may roll nearer the *hole* than the spot where it first struck a part of the *course*, provided it comes to rest within two club-lengths of that spot and not into any of the positions covered by (e).

(g) Subject to the provisions of (e) and (f), the dropped ball may roll and come to rest nearer the *hole* than:

- its original position or estimated position (see Rule 20-2b);
- the *nearest point of relief* or maximum available relief (Rule 24-2, 25-1 or 25-3); or
- the point where the original ball last crossed the margin of the *water hazard* or *lateral water hazard* (Rule 26-1).

9. DISTANCE-MEASURING DEVICES

If the *Committee* wishes to act in accordance with the Note under Rule 14-3, the following wording is recommended:

"(Specify as appropriate, e.g., In this competition, or For all play at this course, etc.), a player may obtain distance information by using a device that measures distance only. If, during a stipulated round, a player uses a distance-measuring device that is designed to gauge or measure other conditions that might affect his play (e.g., gradient, windspeed, temperature, etc.), the player is in breach of Rule 14-3, for which the penalty is disqualification, regardless of whether any such additional function is actually used."

APPENDIX I

LOCAL RULES; CONDITIONS OF THE COMPETITION

PART C

CONDITIONS OF THE COMPETITION

Rule 33-1 provides, "The *Committee* must establish the conditions under which a competition is to be played." The conditions should include many matters such as method of entry, eligibility, number of rounds to be played, etc. which it is not appropriate to deal with in the Rules of Golf or this Appendix. Detailed information regarding these conditions is provided in "Decisions on the Rules of Golf" under Rule 33-1 and in "How to Conduct a Competition."

However, there are a number of matters that might be covered in the Conditions of the Competition to which the *Committee's* attention is specifically drawn. These are:

1. SPECIFICATION OF CLUBS AND THE BALL

The following conditions are recommended only for competitions involving expert players:

a. List of Conforming Driver Heads

On its web site (www.usga.org) the USGA periodically issues a List of Conforming Driver Heads that lists driving clubheads that have been evaluated and found to conform with the Rules of Golf. If the *Committee* wishes to limit players to drivers that have a clubhead, identified by model and loft, that is on the List, the List should be made available and the following condition of competition used:

"Any driver the player carries must have a clubhead, identified by model and loft, that is named on the current List of Conforming Driver Heads issued by the USGA.

Exception: A driver with a clubhead that was manufactured prior to 1999 is exempt from this condition.

*PENALTY FOR CARRYING, BUT NOT MAKING STROKE WITH, CLUB OR CLUBS IN BREACH OF CONDITION:

<u>Match play</u> – At the conclusion of the hole at which the breach is discovered, the state of the match is adjusted by deducting one hole for each hole at which a breach occurred; maximum deduction per round – Two holes.

<u>Stroke play</u> – Two strokes for each hole at which any breach occurred; maximum penalty per round – Four strokes (two strokes at each of the first two holes at which any breach occurred).

<u>Match play or stroke play</u> – If a breach is discovered between the play of two holes, it is deemed to have been discovered during play of the next hole, and the penalty must be applied accordingly.

<u>Bogey and par competitions</u> – See Note 1 to Rule 32-1a.

Stableford competitions – See Note I to Rule 32-1b.

*Any club or clubs carried in breach of this condition must be declared out of play by the player to his opponent in match play or his marker or a fellow-competitor in stroke play immediately upon discovery that a breach has occurred. If the player fails to do so, he is disqualified.

PENALTY FOR MAKING STROKE WITH CLUB IN BREACH OF CONDITION:
Disqualification."

b. List of Conforming Golf Balls

On its website (www.usga.org) the USGA periodically issues a List of Conforming Golf Balls that lists balls that have been tested and found to conform with the Rules of Golf. If the *Committee* wishes to require players to play a model of golf ball on the List, the List should be made available and the following condition of competition used:

"The ball the player plays must be named on the current List of Conforming Golf Balls issued by the USGA.

PENALTY FOR BREACH OF CONDITION:
Disqualification."

c. One Ball Condition

If it is desired to prohibit changing brands and models of golf balls during a *stipulated round*, the following condition is recommended:

"Limitation on Balls Used During Round: (Note to Rule 5-1)
(i) "One Ball" Condition
During a stipulated round, the balls a player plays must be of the same brand and model as detailed by a single entry on the current List of Conforming Golf Balls.
Note: If a ball of a different brand and/or model is dropped or placed it may be lifted, without penalty, and the player must then proceed by dropping or placing a proper ball (Rule 20-6).

PENALTY FOR BREACH OF CONDITION:
Match play – At the conclusion of the hole at which the breach is discovered, the state of the match is adjusted by deducting one hole for each hole at which a breach occurred; maximum deduction per round – Two holes.
Stroke play – Two strokes for each hole at which any breach occurred; maximum penalty per round – Four strokes (two strokes at each of the first two holes at which any breach occurred).
Bogey and Par competitions – See Note I to Rule 32-1a.
Stableford competitions – See Note I to Rule 32-1b.

(ii) Procedure When Breach Discovered
When a player discovers that he has played a ball in breach of this condition, he must abandon that ball before playing from the next teeing ground and complete the round with a proper ball; otherwise, the player is disqualified. If discovery is made during play of a hole and the player elects to substitute a proper ball before completing that hole, the player must place a proper ball on the spot where the ball played in breach of the condition lay."

2. CADDIE (NOTE TO RULE 6-4)

Rule 6-4 permits a player to use a *caddie*, provided he has only one *caddie* at any one time. However, there may be circumstances where a *Committee* may wish to prohibit *caddies* or restrict a player in his choice of *caddie*, e.g., professional golfer, sibling, parent, another player in the competition, etc. In such cases, the following wording is recommended:

Use of Caddie Prohibited
"A player is prohibited from using a caddie during the stipulated round."

Restriction on Who May Serve as Caddie
"A player is prohibited from having _____ serve as his caddie during the stipulated round.

*PENALTY FOR BREACH OF CONDITION:

<u>Match play</u> – At the conclusion of the hole at which the breach is discovered, the state of the match is adjusted by deducting one hole for each hole at which a breach occurred; maximum deduction per round – Two holes.

<u>Stroke play</u> – Two strokes for each hole at which any breach occurred; maximum penalty per round – Four strokes (two strokes at each of the first two holes at which any breach occurred).

<u>Match play or stroke play</u> – If a breach is discovered between the play of two holes, it is deemed to have been discovered during play of the next hole, and the penalty must be applied accordingly.

<u>Bogey and par competitions</u> – See Note 1 to Rule 32-1a.

<u>Stableford competitions</u> – See Note 1 to Rule 32-1b.

*A player having a caddie in breach of this condition must immediately upon discovery that a breach has occurred ensure that he conforms with this condition for the remainder of the stipulated round. Otherwise, the player is disqualified."

3. PACE OF PLAY (NOTE 2 TO RULE 6-7)

The *Committee* may establish pace of play guidelines to help prevent slow play, in accordance with Note 2 to Rule 6-7.

4. SUSPENSION OF PLAY DUE TO A DANGEROUS SITUATION (NOTE TO RULE 6-8b)

As there have been many deaths and injuries from lightning on golf courses, all clubs and sponsors of golf competitions are urged to take precautions for the protection of persons against lightning. Attention is called to Rules 6-8 and 33-2d. If the *Committee* desires to adopt the condition in the Note under Rule 6-8b, the following wording is recommended:

"When play is suspended by the Committee for a dangerous situation, if the players in a match or group are between the play of two holes, they must not resume play until the Committee has ordered a resumption of play. If they are in the process of playing a hole, they must discontinue play immediately and not resume play until the Committee has ordered a resumption of play. If a player fails to discontinue play immediately, he is disqualified, unless circumstances warrant waiving the penalty as provided in Rule 33-7.

The signal for suspending play due to a dangerous situation will be a prolonged note of the siren."

The following signals are generally used and it is recommended that all *Committees* do similarly:

Discontinue Play Immediately: One prolonged note of siren.
Discontinue Play: Three consecutive notes of siren, repeated.
Resume Play: Two short notes of siren, repeated.

5. PRACTICE

a. General

The *Committee* may make regulations governing practice in accordance with the Note to Rule 7-1, Exception (c) to Rule 7-2, Note 2 to Rule 7 and Rule 33-2c.

b. Practice Between Holes (Note 2 to Rule 7)

If the *Committee* wishes to act in accordance with Note 2 to Rule 7-2, the following wording is recommended:

"Between the play of two holes, a player must not make any practice stroke on or near the putting green of the hole last played and must not test the surface of the putting green of the hole last played by rolling a ball.

PENALTY FOR BREACH OF CONDITION:
Match play – Loss of next hole.
Stroke play – Two strokes at the next hole.
Match play or stroke play – In the case of a breach at the last hole of the stipulated round, the player incurs the penalty at that hole."

6. ADVICE IN TEAM COMPETITIONS (NOTE TO RULE 8)

If the *Committee* wishes to act in accordance with the Note under Rule 8, the following wording is recommended:

"In accordance with the Note to Rule 8 of the Rules of Golf, each team may appoint one person (in addition to the persons from whom advice may be asked under that Rule) who may give advice to members of that team. Such person (if it is desired to insert any restriction on who may be nominated insert such restriction here) must be identified to the Committee before giving advice."

7. NEW HOLES (NOTE TO RULE 33-2b)

The *Committee* may provide, in accordance with the Note to Rule 33-2b, that the *holes* and *teeing grounds* for a single round of a competition being held on more than one day may be differently situated on each day.

8. TRANSPORTATION

If it is desired to require players to walk in a competition, the following condition is recommended:

"Players must not ride on any form of transportation during a stipulated round unless authorized by the Committee.

*PENALTY FOR BREACH OF CONDITION:
Match play – At the conclusion of the hole at which the breach is discovered, the state of the match is adjusted by deducting one hole for each hole at

which a breach occurred; maximum deduction per round – Two holes.
Stroke play – Two strokes for each hole at which any breach occurred; maximum penalty per round – Four strokes (two strokes at each of the first two holes at which any breach occurred).
Match play or stroke play – If a breach is discovered between the play of two holes, it is deemed to have been discovered during play of the next hole, and the penalty must be applied accordingly.
Bogey and par competitions – See Note 1 to Rule 32-1a.
Stableford competitions – See Note 1 to Rule 32-1b.

*Use of any unauthorized form of transportation must be discontinued immediately upon discovery that a breach has occurred. Otherwise, the player is disqualified."

9. ANTI-DOPING

The *Committee* may require, in the conditions of competition, that players comply with an anti-doping policy.

10. HOW TO DECIDE TIES

In both match play and stroke play, a tie can be an acceptable result. However, when it is desired to have a sole winner, the *Committee* has the authority, under Rule 33-6, to determine how and when a tie is decided. The decision should be published in advance.

The USGA recommends:

Match Play

A match that ends all square should be played off hole by hole until one side wins a hole. The play-off should start on the hole where the match began. In a handicap match, handicap strokes should be allowed as in the stipulated round.

Stroke Play

(a) In the event of a tie in a scratch stroke-play competition, a play-off is recommended. The play-off may be over 18 holes or a smaller number of holes as specified by the Committee. If that is not feasible or there is still a tie, a hole-by-hole play-off is recommended.

(b) In the event of a tie in a handicap stroke-play competition, a play-off with handicaps is recommended. The play-off may be over 18 holes or a smaller number of holes as specified by the Committee. It is recommended that any such play-off consist of at least three holes.

In competitions where the handicap stroke allocation table is not relevant, if the play-off is less than 18 holes, the percentage of 18 holes played should be applied to the players' handicaps to determine their play-off handicaps. Handicap stroke fractions of one half stroke or more should count as a full stroke and any lesser fraction should be disregarded.

In competitions where the handicap stroke table is relevant, such as four-ball stroke play and bogey, par and Stableford competitions, handicap strokes should be taken as they were assigned for the competition using the players' respective stroke allocation table(s).

(c) If a play-off of any type is not feasible, matching score cards is recommended. The method of matching cards should be announced in advance and should also provide what will happen if this procedure does not produce a winner. An acceptable method of matching cards is to determine the winner on the basis of the best score for the last nine holes. If the tying players have the same score for the last nine, determine the winner on the basis of the last six holes, last three holes and finally the 18th hole. If this method is used in a competition with a multiple tee start, it is recommended that the "last nine holes, last six holes, etc." is considered to be holes 10-18, 13-18, etc.

For competitions where the handicap stroke table is not relevant, such as individual stroke play, if the last nine, last six, last three holes scenario is used, one-half, one-third, one-sixth, etc. of the handicaps should be deducted from the score for those holes. In terms of the use of fractions in such deductions, the Committee should act in accordance with the recommendations of the relevant handicapping authority.

In competitions where the handicap stroke table is relevant, such as four-ball stroke play and bogey, par and Stableford competitions, handicap strokes should be taken as they were assigned for the competition, using the players' respective stroke allocation table(s).

II. DRAW FOR MATCH PLAY

Although the draw for match play may be completely blind or certain players may be distributed through different quarters or eighths, the General Numerical Draw is recommended if matches are determined by a qualifying round.

General Numerical Draw

For purposes of determining places in the draw, ties in qualifying rounds other than those for the last qualifying place are decided by the order in which scores are returned, with the first score to be returned receiving the lowest available number, etc. If it is impossible to determine the order in which scores are returned, ties are determined by a blind draw.

UPPER HALF	LOWER HALF	UPPER HALF	LOWER HALF
64 QUALIFIERS		32 QUALIFIERS	
1 vs 64	2 vs 63	1 vs 32	2 vs 31
32 vs 33	31 vs 34	16 vs 17	15 vs 18
16 vs 49	15 vs 50	8 vs 25	7 vs 26
17 vs 48	18 vs 47	9 vs 24	10 vs 23
8 vs 57	7 vs 58	4 vs 29	3 vs 30
25 vs 40	26 vs 39	13 vs 20	14 vs 19
9 vs 56	10 vs 55	5 vs 28	6 vs 27
24 vs 41	23 vs 42	12 vs 21	11 vs 22
4 vs 61	3 vs 62	16 QUALIFIERS	
29 vs 36	30 vs 35	1 vs 16	2 vs 15
13 vs 52	14 vs 51	8 vs 9	7 vs 10
20 vs 45	19 vs 46	4 vs 13	3 vs 14
5 vs 60	6 vs 59	5 vs 12	6 vs 11
28 vs 37	27 vs 38	8 QUALIFIERS	
12 vs 53	11 vs 54	1 vs 8	2 vs 7
21 vs 44	22 vs 43	4 vs 5	3 vs 6

APPENDICES II, III AND IV

DEFINITIONS

All defined terms are in *italics* and are listed alphabetically in the Definitions section – see pages 6–16.

The USGA reserves the right, at any time, to change the *Rules* relating to clubs, balls, devices and other equipment and make or change the interpretations relating to these *Rules*. For up to date information, please contact the USGA or refer to www.usga.org.

Any design in a club, ball, device or other equipment that is not covered by the *Rules,* which is contrary to the purpose and intent of the *Rules* or that might significantly change the nature of the game, will be ruled on by the USGA.

The dimensions and limits contained in Appendices II, III and IV are given in the units by which conformance is determined. An equivalent imperial/metric conversion is also referenced for information, calculated using a conversion rate of 1 inch = 25.4 mm.

APPENDIX II

DESIGN OF CLUBS

A player in doubt as to the conformity of a club should consult the USGA.

A manufacturer should submit to the USGA a sample of a club to be manufactured for a ruling as to whether the club conforms with the *Rules*. The sample becomes the property of the USGA for reference purposes. If a manufacturer fails to submit a sample or, having submitted a sample, fails to await a ruling before manufacturing and/or marketing the club, the manufacturer assumes the risk of a ruling that the club does not conform with the *Rules*.

The following paragraphs prescribe general regulations for the design of clubs, together with specifications and interpretations. Further information relating to these regulations and their proper interpretation is provided in "A Guide to the Rules on Clubs and Balls."

Where a club, or part of a club, is required to meet a specification within the *Rules*, it must be designed and manufactured with the intention of meeting that specification.

1. CLUBS

a. General

A club is an implement designed to be used for striking the ball and generally comes in three forms: woods, irons and putters distinguished by shape and intended use. A putter is a club with a loft not exceeding ten degrees designed primarily for use on the *putting green*.

The club must not be substantially different from the traditional and customary form and make. The club must be composed of a shaft and a head and it may also have material added to the shaft to enable the player to obtain a firm hold (see 3 below). All parts of the club must be fixed so that the club is one unit, and it must have no external attachments. Exceptions may be made for attachments that do not affect the performance of the club.

b. Adjustability

All clubs may incorporate features for weight adjustment. Other forms of adjustability may also be permitted upon evaluation by the USGA. The following requirements apply to all permissible methods of adjustment:

(i)   the adjustment cannot be readily made;

(ii)   all adjustable parts are firmly fixed and there is no reasonable likelihood of them working loose during a round; and

(iii)   all configurations of adjustment conform with the *Rules*.

During a *stipulated round*, the playing characteristics of a club must not be purposely changed by adjustment or by any other means (see Rule 4-2a).

c. Length

The overall length of the club must be at least 18 inches (0.457 m) and, except for putters, must not exceed 48 inches (1.219 m).

For woods and irons, the measurement of length is taken when the club is lying on a horizontal plane and the sole is set against a 60 degree plane as

Figure I

Figure II

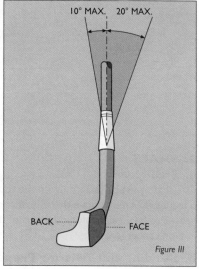

Figure III

shown in Fig. I. The length is defined as the distance from the point of the intersection between the two planes to the top of the grip.

For putters, the measurement of length is taken from the top of the grip along the axis of the shaft or a straight line extension of it to the sole of the club.

d. Alignment

When the club is in its normal address position the shaft must be so aligned that:

(i) the projection of the straight part of the shaft on to the vertical plane through the toe and heel must diverge from the vertical by at least 10 degrees (see Fig. II). If the overall design of the club is such that the player can effectively use the club in a vertical or close-to-vertical position, the shaft may be required to diverge from the vertical in this plane by as much as 25 degrees;

(ii) the projection of the straight part of the shaft on to the vertical plane along the intended *line of play* must not diverge from the vertical by more than 20 degrees forwards or 10 degrees backwards (see Fig. III).

Except for putters, all of the heel portion of the club must lie within 0.625 inches (15.88 mm) of the plane containing the axis of the straight part of the shaft and the intended (horizontal) *line of play* (see Fig. IV).

Figure IV

Figure V

2. SHAFT

a. Straightness

The shaft must be straight from the top of the grip to a point not more than 5 inches (127 mm) above the sole, measured from the point where the shaft ceases to be straight along the axis of the bent part of the shaft and the neck and/or socket (see Fig. V).

b. Bending and Twisting Properties

At any point along its length, the shaft must:

(i)   bend in such a way that the deflection is the same regardless of how the shaft is rotated about its longitudinal axis; and

(ii)   twist the same amount in both directions.

c. Attachment to Clubhead

The shaft must be attached to the clubhead at the heel either directly or through a single plain neck and/or socket. The length from the top of the neck and/or socket to the sole of the club must not exceed 5 inches (127 mm), measured along the axis of, and following any bend in, the neck and/or socket (see Fig. VI).

Exception for Putters: The shaft or neck or socket of a putter may be fixed at any point in the head.

3. GRIP (see Fig. VII)

The grip consists of material added to the shaft to enable the player to obtain a firm hold. The grip must be fixed to the shaft, must be straight and plain in form, must extend to the end of the shaft and must not be molded for any part of the hands. If no material is added, that portion of the shaft designed to be held by the player must be considered the grip.

(i)   For clubs other than putters the grip must be circular in cross-section, except that a continuous, straight, slightly raised rib may be incorporated along the full length of the grip, and a slightly indented spiral is permitted on a wrapped grip or a replica of one.

(ii)   A putter grip may have a non-circular cross-section, provided the cross-section has no concavity, is symmetrical and remains generally similar throughout the length of the grip. (See Clause (v) overleaf).

(iii)   The grip may be tapered but must not have any bulge or waist. Its cross-sectional dimensions measured in any direction must not exceed 1.75 inches (44.45 mm).

(iv)   For clubs other than putters the axis of the grip must coincide with the axis of the shaft.

(v)   A putter may have two grips provided each is circular in cross-section, the axis of each coincides with the axis of the shaft, and they are separated by at least 1.5 inches (38.1 mm).

Figure VI

Figure VII

4. CLUBHEAD
a. Plain in Shape

The clubhead must be generally plain in shape. All parts must be rigid, structural in nature and functional. The clubhead or its parts must not be designed to resemble any other object. It is not practicable to define plain in shape precisely and comprehensively. However, features that are deemed to be in breach of this requirement and are therefore not permitted include, but are not limited to:

(i) All Clubs
* holes through the face;
* holes through the head (some exceptions may be made for putters and cavity back irons);
* facsimiles of golf balls or actual golf balls incorporated into the head;
* features that are for the purpose of meeting dimensional specifications;
* features that extend into or ahead of the face;
* features that extend significantly above the top line of the head;
* furrows in or runners on the head that extend into the face (some exceptions may be made for putters); and

• optical or electronic devices.

(ii) Woods and Irons

• all features listed in (i) above;
• cavities in the outline of the heel and/or the toe of the head that can be viewed from above;
• severe or multiple cavities in the outline of the back of the head that can be viewed from above;
• transparent material added to the head with the intention of rendering conforming a feature that is not otherwise permitted; and
• features that extend beyond the outline of the head when viewed from above.

b. Dimensions, Volume and Moment of Inertia
(i) Woods

When the club is in a 60 degree lie angle, the dimensions of the clubhead must be such that:

• the distance from the heel to the toe of the clubhead is greater than the distance from the face to the back;
• the distance from the heel to the toe of the clubhead is not greater than 5 inches (127 mm); and
• the distance from the sole to the crown of the clubhead, including any permitted features, is not greater than 2.8 inches (71.12 mm).

These dimensions are measured on horizontal lines between vertical projections of the outermost points of:

• the heel and the toe; and
• the face and the back (see Fig. VIII, dimension A);

and on vertical lines between the horizontal projections of the outermost points of the sole and the crown (see Fig. VIII, dimension B). If the outermost point of the heel is not clearly defined, it is deemed to be 0.875 inches (22.23 mm) above the horizontal plane on which the club is lying (see Fig. VIII, dimension C).

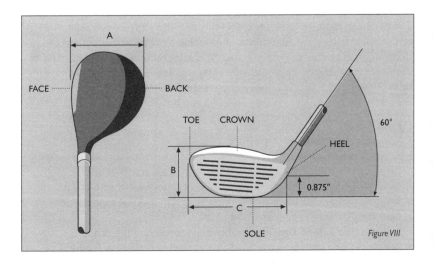

Figure VIII

The volume of the clubhead must not exceed 460 cubic centimeters (28.06 cubic inches), plus a tolerance of 10 cubic centimeters (0.61 cubic inches).

When the club is in a 60 degree lie angle, the moment of inertia component around the vertical axis through the clubhead's center of gravity must not exceed 5900 g cm^2 (32.259 oz in^2), plus a test tolerance of 100 g cm^2 (0.547 oz in^2).

(ii) Irons

When the clubhead is in its normal address position, the dimensions of the head must be such that the distance from the heel to the toe is greater than the distance from the face to the back.

(iii) Putters (see Fig. IX)

When the clubhead is in its normal address position, the dimensions of the head must be such that:

- the distance from the heel to the toe is greater than the distance from the face to the back;
- the distance from the heel to the toe of the head is less than or equal to 7 inches (177.8 mm);

Figure IX

- the distance from the heel to the toe of the face is greater than or equal to two thirds of the distance from the face to the back of the head;
- the distance from the heel to the toe of the face is greater than or equal to half of the distance from the heel to the toe of the head; and
- the distance from the sole to the top of the head, including any permitted features, is less than or equal to 2.5 inches (63.5 mm).

For traditionally shaped heads, these dimensions will be measured on horizontal lines between vertical projections of the outermost points of:
- the heel and the toe of the head;
- the heel and the toe of the face; and
- the face and the back;

and on vertical lines between the horizontal projections of the outermost points of the sole and the top of the head.

For unusually shaped heads, the toe to heel dimension may be made at the face.

c. Spring Effect and Dynamic Properties

The design, material and/or construction of, or any treatment to, the clubhead (which includes the club face) must not:

(i)   have the effect of a spring which exceeds the limit set forth in the Pendulum Test Protocol on file with the USGA; or

(ii) incorporate features or technology including, but not limited to, separate springs or spring features, that have the intent of, or the effect of, unduly influencing the clubhead's spring effect; or

(iii) unduly influence the movement of the ball.

Note: (i) above does not apply to putters.

d. Striking Faces

The clubhead must have only one striking face, except that a putter may have two such faces if their characteristics are the same, and they are opposite each other.

5. CLUB FACE

a. General

The face of the club must be hard and rigid and must not impart significantly more or less spin to the ball than a standard steel face (some exceptions may be made for putters). Except for such markings listed below, the club face must be smooth and must not have any degree of concavity.

b. Impact Area Roughness and Material

Except for markings specified in the following paragraphs, the surface roughness within the area where impact is intended (the "impact area") must not exceed that of decorative sandblasting, or of fine milling (see Fig. X).

Figure X

The whole of the impact area must be of the same material (exceptions may be made for clubheads made of wood).

c. Impact Area Markings

If a club has grooves and/or punch marks in the impact area they must meet the following specifications:

(i) Grooves

- Grooves must be straight and parallel.
- Grooves must have a symmetrical cross-section and have sides which do not converge (see Fig. XI).

Figure XI

- *For clubs that have a loft angle greater than or equal to 25 degrees, grooves must have a plain cross-section.
- The width, spacing and cross-section of the grooves must be consistent throughout the impact area (some exceptions may be made for woods).
- The width (W) of each groove must not exceed 0.035 inches (0.9 mm), using the 30 degree method of measurement on file with the USGA.
- The distance between edges of adjacent grooves (S) must not be less than three times the width of the grooves, and not less than 0.075 inches (1.905 mm).
- The depth of each groove must not exceed 0.020 inches (0.508 mm).
- * For clubs other than driving clubs, the cross-sectional area (A) of a groove divided by the groove pitch (W+S) must not exceed 0.0030 square inches per inch (0.0762 mm²/mm) (see Fig. XII).

$$\frac{A}{W + S} \leq 0.0030\,in^2/in$$

Figure XII

- Grooves must not have sharp edges or raised lips.
- * For clubs that have a loft angle greater than or equal to 25 degrees, groove edges must be substantially in the form of a round having an effective radius which is not less than 0.010 inches (0.254 mm) when measured as shown in Fig. XIII, and not greater than 0.020 inches (0.508 mm). Deviations in effective radius within 0.001 inches (0.0254 mm) are permissible.

CONFORMING

NON-CONFORMING

R=0.010"

0.001"

Figure XIII

(ii) Punch Marks

- The maximum dimension of any punch mark must not exceed 0.075 inches (1.905 mm).

- The distance between adjacent punch marks (or between punch marks and grooves) must not be less than 0.168 inches (4.27 mm), measured from center to center.
- The depth of any punch mark must not exceed 0.040 inches (1.02 mm).
- Punch marks must not have sharp edges or raised lips.
- * For clubs that have a loft angle greater than or equal to 25 degrees, punch mark edges must be substantially in the form of a round having an effective radius which is not less than 0.010 inches (0.254 mm) when measured as shown in Figure XIII, and not greater than 0.020 inches (0.508 mm). Deviations in effective radius within 0.001 inches (0.0254 mm) are permissible.

Note 1: The groove and punch mark specifications above indicated by an asterisk (*) apply only to new models of clubs manufactured on or after January 1, 2010 and any club where the face markings have been purposely altered, for example, by re-grooving. For further information on the status of clubs available before January 1, 2010, please refer to the Informational Club Database at www.usga.org

Note 2: The Committee may require, in the conditions of competition, that the clubs the player carries must conform to the groove and punch mark specifications above indicated by an asterisk (*). This condition is recommended only for competitions involving expert players. For further information, refer to Decision 4-1/1 in "Decisions on the Rules of Golf."

d. Decorative Markings

The center of the impact area may be indicated by a design within the boundary of a square whose sides are 0.375 inches (9.53 mm) in length. Such a design must not unduly influence the movement of the ball. Decorative markings are permitted outside the impact area.

e. Non-Metallic Club Face Markings

The above specifications do not apply to clubheads made of wood on which the impact area of the face is of a material of hardness less than the hardness of metal and whose loft angle is 24 degrees or less, but markings which could unduly influence the movement of the ball are prohibited.

f. Putter Face Markings

Any markings on the face of a putter must not have sharp edges or raised lips. The specifications with regard to roughness, material and markings in the impact area do not apply.

APPENDIX III

THE BALL

I. GENERAL
The ball must not be substantially different from the traditional and customary form and make. The material and construction of the ball must not be contrary to the purpose and intent of the *Rules*.

2. WEIGHT
The weight of the ball must not be greater than 1.620 ounces avoirdupois (45.93 g).

3. SIZE
The diameter of the ball must not be less than 1.680 inches (42.67mm).

4. SPHERICAL SYMMETRY
The ball must not be designed, manufactured or intentionally modified to have properties which differ from those of a spherically symmetrical ball.

5. INITIAL VELOCITY
The initial velocity of the ball must not exceed the limit specified under the conditions set forth in the Initial Velocity Standard for golf balls on file with the *USGA*.

6. OVERALL DISTANCE STANDARD
The combined carry and roll of the ball, when tested on apparatus approved by the USGA, must not exceed the distance specified under the conditions set forth in the Overall Distance Standard for golf balls on file with the USGA.

APPENDIX IV

DEVICES AND OTHER EQUIPMENT

A player in doubt as to whether use of a device or other equipment would constitute a breach of the *Rules* should consult the USGA.

A manufacturer should submit to the USGA a sample of a device or other equipment to be manufactured for a ruling as to whether its use during a *stipulated round* would cause a player to be in breach of Rule 14-3. The sample becomes the property of the USGA for reference purposes. If a manufacturer fails to submit a sample or, having submitted a sample, fails to await a ruling before manufacturing and/or marketing the device or other equipment, the manufacturer assumes the risk of a ruling that use of the device or other equipment would be contrary to the Rules.

The following paragraphs prescribe general regulations for the design of devices and other equipment, together with specifications and interpretations. They should be read in conjunction with Rule 11-1 (Teeing Ground) and Rule 14-3 (Artificial Devices, Unusual Equipment and Unusual Use of Equipment).

1. TEES (Rule 11)
A tee is a device designed to raise the ball off the ground. A tee must not:
- be longer than 4 inches (101.6 mm);
- be designed or manufactured in such a way that it could indicate line of play;
- unduly influence the movement of the ball; or
- otherwise assist the player in making a stroke or in his play.

2. GLOVES (Rule 14-3)
Gloves may be worn to assist the player in gripping the club, provided they are plain.
A "plain" glove must:
- consist of a fitted covering of the hand with a separate sheath or opening for each digit (fingers and thumb); and
- be made of smooth materials on the full palm and gripping surface of the digits;

A "plain" glove must not incorporate:
- material on the gripping surface or inside of the glove, the primary purpose of which is to provide padding or which has the effect of providing padding. Padding is defined as an area of glove material which is more than 0.025 inches (0.635 mm) thicker than the adjacent areas of the glove without the added material;

  Note: Material may be added for wear resistance, moisture absorption or other functional purposes, provided it does not exceed the definition of padding (see above).
- straps to assist in preventing the club from slipping or to attach the hand to the club;
- any means of binding digits together;
- material on the glove that adheres to material on the grip;

- features, other than visual aids, designed to assist the player in placing his hands in a consistent and/or specific position on the grip;
- weight to assist the player in making a stroke;
- any feature that might restrict the movement of a joint; or
- any other feature that might assist the player in making a stroke or in his play.

3. SHOES (Rule 14-3)

Shoes that assist the player in obtaining a firm stance may be worn. Subject to the conditions of competition, features such as spikes on the sole are permitted, but shoes must not incorporate features:

- designed to assist the player in taking his stance and/or building a stance;
- designed to assist the player with his alignment; or
- that might otherwise assist the player in making a stroke or in his play.

4. CLOTHING (Rule 14-3)

Articles of clothing must not incorporate features:

- designed to assist the player with his alignment; or
- that might otherwise assist the player in making a stroke or in his play.

5. DISTANCE-MEASURING DEVICES (Rule 14-3)

During a *stipulated round,* the use of any distance measuring device is not permitted unless the Committee has introduced a Local Rule to that effect (see Note to Rule 14-3 and Appendix I; Part B; Section 9).

Even when the Local Rule is in effect, the device must be limited to measuring distance only. Features that would render use of the device contrary to the Local Rule include, but are not limited to:

- the gauging or measuring of slope;
- the gauging or measuring of other conditions that might affect play (e.g., wind speed or direction, or other climate-based information such as temperature, humidity, etc.);
- recommendations that might assist the player in making a stroke or in his play (e.g., club selection, type of shot to be played, green reading or any other advice related matter); or
- calculating the effective distance between two points based on slope or other conditions affecting shot distance.

Such non-conforming features render use of the device contrary to the Rules, irrespective of whether or not:

- the features can be switched off or disengaged; and
- the features are switched off or disengaged.

A multi-functional device, such as a smartphone or PDA, may be used as a distance measuring device provided it contains a distance measuring application that meets all of the above limitations (i.e., it must measure distance only). In addition, when the distance measuring application is being used, there must be no other features or applications installed on the device that, if used, would be in breach of the Rules, whether or not they are actually used.

INDEX

INTRODUCTION

The Index consists of over 5000 entries, each of which refers to a Decision by number. Decisions relating to a given topic are grouped under a heading, which should be thought of as a keyword. There are over 250 separate headings, of which there are two kinds – those that have entries (Decisions) and those that simply refer to other more appropriate headings. Decisions entered under headings with a larger number of entries are sometimes grouped under subheadings for further efficiency. The Contents section that precedes the actual Index is a listing of all the headings found in the Index. It is the entry point into the Index and a familiarity with these headings will make using the Index easier. Each of the over 1200 Decisions in the book is listed in the Index. Nearly every Decision appears under several separate headings to increase the chances of finding the proper Decision relating to a given situation.

Efficient and timely use of the Decisions book suggests that one should first become skillful in finding in the Index a Decision that most closely relates to the situation at hand. For example, assume a situation in match play where a player lifts his ball without marking its position under a mistaken belief that his next stroke is conceded. Within the Contents, identify the headings (keywords) that might be examined – Ball Lifted, Concession, Marking Position of Ball or Putting Green. The relevant Decision (2–4/3) is found under each of these headings. If the Contents is not consulted first, one might select a keyword that is not listed as a heading, and much effort might be expended without success. For instance, potential keywords such as "ball picked up" or "ball not marked" are not headings in the Index; the proper terms that are found in the Contents are "Ball Lifted" or "Marking Position of Ball." Reference to the Contents will efficiently lead an inquirer to the proper heading and increase the likelihood of finding the appropriate Decision.

INDEX

CONTENTS

ABNORMAL GROUND
CONDITIONS   I-1
See also Burrowing Animal, Reptile or
Bird (and Holes Made by Them); Casual
Water, Embedded Ball; Greenkeeper
and Hole Made by Greenkeeper; Ground
Under Repair; Material Piled for Removal;
Pitch-Mark; Status of Object; Virtually
Certain (or Known)

ABNORMAL STANCE, SWING OR
DIRECTION OF PLAY   I-1

ACCEPTING ASSISTANCE OR
PROTECTION See Assistance or
Protection, Acceptance of

ADDRESSING THE BALL   I-1

ADVICE   I-2

AERATION HOLES AND PLUGS   I-3

AGREEMENT TO WAIVE RULES   I-3

ANIMAL See Ants and Ant Hills; Bees;
Burrowing Animal, Reptile or Bird (and
Holes Made by Them); Dog; Insects;
Snake; Worm

ANTS AND ANT HILLS   I-3
See also Insects; Loose Impediments

AREA OF INTENDED SWING   I-3
See also Improving Area of Intended
Stance or Swing, Position or Lie of Ball,
or Line of Play or Putt

ARTIFICIAL DEVICES, UNUSUAL
EQUIPMENT AND UNUSUAL
USE OF EQUIPMENT   I-4
See also Medical Assistance or Condition;
Status of Object

ARTIFICIAL OBJECTS See Obstructions

ARTIFICIALLY-SURFACED See
Obstructions

ASSISTANCE OR PROTECTION,
ACCEPTANCE OF   I-4
See also Ball Assisting or Interfering with
Play; Exerting Influence on Ball/Altering
Physical Conditions; Four-Ball Match Play;
Four-Ball Stroke Play; Medical Assistance
or Condition

BALL   I-5
See also Addressing the Ball; Ball Assisting
or Interfering with Play; Ball at Rest
Moved; Ball Deflected or Stopped; Ball
Dropped or Re-Dropped; Ball Lifted; Ball

Mark; Ball Overhanging Hole; Ball Placed
or Replaced; Ball Touched; Ball Unfit
for Play; Cleaning Ball; Embedded Ball;
Exchanging Ball; Exerting Influence on
Ball/Altering Physical Conditions; Holed
and Holing Out; Lie of Ball Altered; Lost
Ball; Out of Bounds; Provisional Ball;
Searching for and Identifying Ball; Second
Ball; Status of Object; Stroke; Substituted
Ball; "X-Out" Ball

BALL ASSISTING OR INTERFERING
WITH PLAY   I-6
See also Assistance or Protection,
Acceptance of; Exerting Influence on Ball/
Altering Physical Conditions

BALL AT REST MOVED   I-6
See also Ball Deflected or Stopped; Ball
Touched

BALL DEFLECTED OR STOPPED   I-10
See also Ball at Rest Moved; Ball in Motion
Struck by Club; Exerting Influence on
Ball/Altering Physical Conditions

BALL DROPPED OR RE-DROPPED   I-11
See also Ball Lifted; Ball Placed or
Replaced; Local Rules

BALL IN MOTION STRUCK
BY CLUB   I-14
See also Ball at Rest Moved; Ball Deflected
or Stopped

BALL INTERFERING WITH OR
ASSISTING PLAY See Ball Assisting or
Interfering with Play

BALL LIFTED   I-14

BALL MARK   I-17
See also Ball-Marker; Pitch-Mark

BALL-MARKER   I-17
See also Ball Mark; Marking Position of
Ball; Status of Object

BALL OVERHANGING HOLE   I-17

BALL PLACED OR REPLACED   I-17

BALL TOUCHED   I-19
See also Ball at Rest Moved

BALL UNFIT FOR PLAY   I-19
See also Unplayable Ball

BALL UNPLAYABLE See Unplayable Ball

BANDAGE   I-19

BEACH   I-19

BEES I-19
See also Insects

BIRD See Burrowing Animal, Reptile, or Bird (and Holes Made by Them);

BOGEY COMPETITION I-19
See also Stableford Competition

BOUNDARY FENCE, LINE, WALL OR STAKES I-20
See also Marking or Defining Course; Out of Bounds; Status of Object

BRIDGE I-20

BUNKER I-20
See also Sand

BURROWING ANIMAL, REPTILE OR BIRD (AND HOLES MADE BY THEM) I-23
See also Abnormal Ground Conditions; Casual Water; Ground Under Repair; Reptile; Status of Object; Virtually Certain (or Known);

CADDIE I-24

CANCELING SCORES See Course Unplayable or Closed; Discontinuance and Resumption of Play

CAR See Status of Object

CART See Golf Cart; Trolley

CART PATH See Roads and Paths

CASUAL WATER I-25
See also Abnormal Ground Conditions; Virtually Certain (or Known)

CHIPPER See Clubs, Status of Object

CLAIMS AND DISPUTES I-27
See also Committee; Penalty Imposed, Modified or Waived by Committee; Referee

CLEANING BALL I-29

CLOSE OF COMPETITION I-30
See also Committee; Conditions of Competition; Handicap Competition and Handicap Strokes; Penalties Imposed, Modified or Waived by Committee; Scores and Score Cards

CLUBHOUSE OR HALF-WAY HOUSE I-30

CLUB(S) I-30
See also Grip and Gripping; Grounding Club; Status of Object; Stroke

COMMITTEE I-32
See also Claims and Disputes; Close of Competition; Conditions of Competition; Course Unplayable or

Closed; Discontinuance and Resumption of Play; Doubt Regarding Facts; Local Rules; Marking or Defining Course; Observer; Penalties Imposed, Modified or Waived by Committee; Referee

CONCESSION I-36
See also Default; Four-Ball Match Play; Foursomes; Singles Match; Wrong Information

CONDITIONS OF COMPETITION I-37
See also Committee; Local Rules

CONCURRENT FOUR-BALL AND SINGLES MATCHES See Singles Match

CONCURRENT MATCH AND STROKE PLAY See Singles Match

COURSE See Course Unplayable or Closed; Marking or Defining Course; Out of Bounds

COURSE UNPLAYABLE OR CLOSED I-38
See also Discontinuance and Resumption of Play

COURSE MARKING See Marking or Defining Course

COURSE RECORD I-39

CRAB See Status of Object

CRAWFISH See Burrowing Animal, Reptile or Bird (and Holes Made by Them); Status of Object

DAMAGE I-39
See also Ball Unfit for Play; Club(s); Ground Under Repair; Repair

DANGEROUS SITUATIONS I-39

DEFAULT I-40
See also Concession; Halved Hole

DEFINING COURSE See Marking or Defining Course

DEFLECTED BALL See Ball Deflected or Stopped

DELAY, UNDUE See Undue Delay

DEW I-40

DIRECTLY ATTRIBUTABLE I-40

DIRECTION POST I-40
See also Status of Object

DISCONTINUANCE AND RESUMPTION OF PLAY I-40

DISPUTES See Claims and Disputes

DISTANCE, DISTANCE INFORMATION AND DISTANCE MARKERS   I-41
See also Measuring

DIVOT AND DIVOT HOLE   I-41

DOG   I-42

DOOR See Gate, Door or Window

DOUBT AS TO PROCEDURE   I-42
See also Doubt Regarding Facts; Provisional Ball; Second Ball; Serious Breach of Rules

DOUBT REGARDING FACTS   I-42
See also Committee; Doubt as to Procedure

DRAINPIPE   I-44

DROPPING ZONE   I-44

ELEVATED POWER LINE See Power Line

EMBEDDED BALL   I-44
See also Pitch-Mark

ENVIRONMENTALLY-SENSITIVE AREA   I-45

EQUIPMENT   I-45
See also Artificial Devices and Unusual Equipment; Club(s); Golf Cart; Status of Object; Trolley

EQUITY   I-45

ETIQUETTE   I-48

EXCHANGING BALLS   I-48
See also Substituted Ball

EXCLUDING OPERATION OF RULE See Agreement to Waive Rules

EXERTING INFLUENCE ON BALL/ALTERING PHYSICAL CONDITIONS   I-48
See also Serious Breach of Rules

FAILURE TO HOLE OUT   I-49
See also Holed or Holing Out

FAIRWAY AND CLOSELY MOWN AREAS   I-50
See also Embedded Ball; Through the Green

FENCE   I-50
See also Boundary Fence, Line, Wall or Stake; Wall

FLAGSTICK   I-51
See also Putting Green

FLOWERS   I-52

FOOT, FEET AND FOOTWEAR   I-52

FOOTPRINT(S)   I-52

See also Abnormal Ground Conditions; Bunker; Damage; Ground Under Repair; Spike Mark(s)

FOUR-BALL MATCH PLAY   I-53
See also Default; Four-Ball Stableford Competition; Four-Ball Stroke Play; Wrong Information

FOUR-BALL STABLEFORD COMPETITION   I-54
See also Four-Ball Match Play; Four-Ball Stroke Play

FOUR-BALL STROKE PLAY   I-54
See also Four-Ball Match Play; Four-Ball Stableford Competition

FOURSOMES   I-55

FROST   I-56

FRUIT See Status of Object

GALLERY See Spectator

GALLERY-CONTROL STAKE, ROPE OR LINE   I-56
See also Obstructions; Status of Object

GATE, DOOR OR WINDOW   I-56

GLOVE   I-56
See also Equipment; Tape

GOLF CART   I-56
See also Equipment; Status of Object; Trolley

GRASS OR TURF   I-56
See also Fairway and Closely Mown Areas; Spike Mark(s); Test or Testing

GRAVEL See Stone(s), Rock(s)

GREENKEEPER AND HOLE MADE BY GREENKEEPER   I-57

GRIP AND GRIPPING   I-57
See also Club(s)

GROUND UNDER REPAIR   I-58
See also Abnormal Ground Conditions; Burrowing Animal, Reptile or Bird (and Holes Made by Them); Casual Water; Marking or Defining Course; Tree or Bush; Virtually Certain (or Known)

GROUNDING CLUB   I-60
See also Addressing the Ball

GROUPS AND GROUPING   I-60
See also Time of Starting

GUIDELINES   I-61

HALF-WAY HOUSE See Clubhouse or Half-Way House

HALVED HOLE   I-61
See also Concession; Default

HANDICAP COMPETITION AND
HANDICAP STROKES   I-61
See also Claims and Disputes; Close of
Competition; Scores and Score Cards

HAZARD See Bunker; Water Hazards

HOLE   I-62
See also Ball Overhanging Hole; Claims
and Disputes; Concession; Flagstick;
Holed and Holing Out; Putting Green

HOLE-BY-HOLE PLAY-OFF See Play-off
and Ties

HOLE-LINER See Hole

HOLE MADE BY GREENKEEPER See
Greenkeeper and Hole Made by
Greenkeeper

HOLE PLUG   I-63

HOLED AND HOLING OUT   I-63
See also Failure to Hole Out; Stroke

HONOR   I-64
See also Order of Play; Playing Out of
Turn

ICE See Casual Water; Loose
Impediments; Obstructions

IDENTIFYING BALL See Lost Ball;
Searching for and Identifying Ball

IMPOSED PENALTY See Penalties
Imposed, Modified or Waived by
Committee

IMPROVING AREA OF INTENDED
STANCE OR SWING, POSITION
OR LIE OF BALL, OR LINE OF
PLAY OR PUTT   I-64
See also Area of Intended Swing; Lie of Ball
Altered; Line of Play; Line of Putt; Stance

IMPROVING AREA OF INTENDED
SWING See Area of Intended Swing;
Improving Area of Intended Stance or
Swing, Position or Lie of Ball, or Line of
Play or Putt

IMPROVING LIE OF BALL See Improving
Area of Intended Stance or Swing,
Position or Lie of Ball, or Line of Play or
Putt

IMPROVING LINE OF PLAY See Improving
Area of Intended Stance or Swing,
Position or Lie of Ball, or Line of Play or
Putt; Line of Play

IMPROVING LINE OF PUTT See
Improving Area of Intended Stance or
Swing, Position or Lie of Ball, or Line
of Play or Putt; Line of Putt

IMPROVING POSITION OF BALL See
Improving Area of Intended Stance or
Swing, Position or Lie of Ball, or Line of
Play or Putt

IMPROVING STANCE See Improving Area
of Intended Stance or Swing, Position or
Lie of Ball, or Line of Play or Putt; Stance

INAPPLICABLE RULE OR
PROCEDURE USED   I-65

INCORRECT INFORMATION See
Incorrect Information on Rules; Wrong
Information

INCORRECT INFORMATION
ON RULES   I-66
See also Information as to Strokes Taken;
Wrong Information

INDICATING LINE FOR PUTTING   I-66
See also Improving Area of Intended
Stance or Swing, Position or Lie of Ball, or
Line of Play or Putt; Indicating Line of Play;
Line of Play; Line of Putt; Putting Green

INDICATING LINE OF PLAY   I-66
See also Indicating Line for Putting; Line of
Play; Line of Putt

INFORMATION AS TO STROKES
TAKEN   I-66
See also Wrong Information

INJURY See Physical Problem

INSECTS   I-66
See also Burrowing Animal, Reptile or
Bird (and Holes Made by Them); Loose
Impediments; Status of Object

INSTRUCTION See Advice

INTEGRAL PART OF COURSE   I-67
See also Fence; Gate, Door or Window;
Marking or Defining Course;
Obstructions; Wall

INTERFERENCE See Ball Assisting or
Interfering with Play; Exerting Influence
on Ball/Altering Physical Conditions

KNOWN OR VIRTUALLY CERTAIN See
Virtually Certain (or Known)

LATERAL WATER HAZARDS See Water
Hazards

LEAVES   I-67
See also Pine Needles; Status of
Object; Tree or Bush

LIE OF BALL ALTERED   I-68
See also Improving Area of Intended
Stance or Swing, Position or Lie of Ball,
or Line of Play or Putt

LIGHTNING I-68
See also Dangerous Situations; Discontinuance and Resumption of Play; Rain; Weather Conditions

LINE OF PLAY I-68
See also Improving Area of Intended Stance or Swing, Position or Lie of Ball, or Line of Play or Putt; Indicating Line of Play

LINE OF PUTT I-69
See also Hole; Improving Area of Intended Stance or Swing, Position or Lie of Ball, or Line of Play or Putt; Indicating Line for Putting; Putting Green

LOCAL RULES I-70
See also Conditions of Competition

LOOSE IMPEDIMENTS I-73
See also Status of Object

LOST BALL I-74
See also Provisional Ball; Searching for and Identifying Ball; Virtually Certain (or Known)

MARGINS OF AREAS OF THE COURSE I-76

MARKER I-76
See also Ball-Marker; Scores and Score Cards

MARKING OR DEFINING COURSE I-77
See also Abnormal Ground Conditions; Boundary Fence, Line, Wall or Stakes; Committee; Fence; Ground Under Repair; Local Rules; Obstructions; Out of Bounds; Teeing Ground and Tee-Markers; Water Hazards

MARKING POSITION OF BALL I-78
See also Ball-Marker

MATCH PLAY See Claims and Disputes; Concession; Halved Hole; Information as to Strokes Taken; Wrong Information

MATERIAL PILED FOR REMOVAL I-79
See also Greenkeeper and Hole Made by Greenkeeper; Ground Under Repair; Status of Object

MAXIMUM AVAILABLE RELIEF I-79
See also Nearest Point of Relief

MEASURING I-79
See also Distance, Distance Information and Distance Markers

MEDICAL ASSISTANCE OR CONDITION I-80
See also Artificial Devices, Unusual Equipment or Unusual Use of Equipment; Physical Problem

METHOD OF MAKING STROKE See Stroke

MODIFIED PENALTY See Penalties Imposed, Modified or Waived by Committee

MOLEHILL See Status of Object

MOSS See Status of Object

MOVED AND MOVING BALL See Ball at Rest Moved; Ball Deflected or Stopped; Striking Ball in Motion

MULTIPLE PENALTY SITUATIONS I-80

MUSHROOM See Status of Object

NATURAL OBJECTS See Loose Impediments

NEAREST LIE MOST SIMILAR I-80
See also Lie of Ball Altered

NEAREST POINT OF RELIEF I-81
See also Maximum Available Relief

OBSERVER I-81
See also Committee; Referee

OBSTRUCTIONS I-81
See also Integral Part of Course; Loose Impediments; Status of Object; Virtually Certain (or Known); Wood and Wood Chips

OCEAN I-84

OFFICIAL See Committee; Referee

ORDER OF PLAY I-84
See also Order of Play in Foursomes and Threesomes; Playing Out of Turn; Stroke Canceled or Recalled

ORDER OF PLAY IN FOURSOMES AND THREESOMES I-85

OUT OF BOUNDS I-85
See also Boundary Fence, Line, Wall or Stakes; Marking or Defining Course; Provisional Ball

OUT OF TURN See Order of Play; Playing Out of Turn

OUTSIDE AGENCY I-87
See also Ball Deflected or Stopped; Loose Impediments; Status of Object

PACE OF PLAY I-88
See also Undue Delay

PAR COMPETITION I-88
See also Bogey Competition; Stableford Competition

PATH See Roads and Paths

PENALTIES IMPOSED, MODIFIED OR WAIVED BY COMMITTEE I-88
See also Close of Competition; Committee; Multiple Penalty Situations

PHYSICAL PROBLEM   I-89
See also Artificial Devices, Unusual Equipment and Unusual Use of Equipment; Medical Assistance or condition

PINE NEEDLES See Leaves; Tree or Bush

PITCH-MARK   I-89
See also Ball Mark; Embedded Ball

PLANTS See Flowers; Heather; Status of Object; Tree or Bush; Tumbleweed

PLAYER REPONSIBILITIES   I-90

PLAYING FROM WRONG PLACE See Wrong Place

PLAYING OUT OF TURN   I-90
See also Honor; Order of Play; Order of Play in Foursomes and Threesomes

PLAY-OFF AND TIES   I-91

PLUMB-LINE See Status of Object

POWER LINE   I-91

PRACTICE   I-91

PRACTICE SWING   I-92
See also Practice

PRIZE   I-92

PROTECTION See Assistance or Protection, Acceptance of

PROVISIONAL BALL   I-93
See also Lost Ball; Out of Bounds; Second Ball

PUTTING GREEN   I-94
See also Ball Overhanging Hole; Flagstick; Hole; Hole Plug; Improving Area of Intended Stance or Swing, Position or Lie of Ball, or Line of Play or Putt; Indicating Line for Putting; Line of Putt; Wrong Putting Green

RAIN See Discontinuance and Resumption of Play; Weather Conditions

RAKE   I-96
See also Bunker; Improving Area of Intended Stance or Swing, Position or Lie of Ball, or Line of Play or Putt; Line of Play; Obstructions; Status of Object

RECORDING SCORES See Marker; Scores and Score Cards

RE-DROPPING BALL See Ball Dropped or Re-Dropped

REFEREE   I-97
See also Committee; Observer

REFUSAL TO COMPLY WITH RULE I-97

REPAIR   I-97
See also Damage; Ground Under Repair

REPLACING BALL See Ball Placed or Replaced

REPTILE See Burrowing Animal, Reptile or Bird (and Holes Made by Them);

RESUMPTION OF PLAY See Discontinuance and Resumption of Play

ROADS AND PATHS   I-98
Status of Object

ROCK See Stone(s), Rock(s) or Gravel

ROOTS   I-98
See also Tree or Bush

ROUGH   I-98
See also Through the Green

RULES See Incorrect Information on Rules

SALIVA   I-99
See also Casual Water; Loose Impediments

SAND   I-99
See also Bunker

SCORES AND SCORE CARDS   I-99
See also Information as to Strokes Taken; Marker

SEARCHING FOR AND IDENTIFYING BALL   I-101
See also Lost Ball

SECOND BALL   I-102
See also Doubt as to Procedure; Provisional Ball; Serious Breach of Rules

SERIOUS BREACH OF RULES   I-103
See also Agreement to Waive Rules; Etiquette

SHOES See Foot, Feet and Footwear

SHRUBS See Leaves; Status of Object; Tree or Bush

SINGLES MATCH   I-103

SLOW PLAY See Undue Delay

SNAKE   I-104
See also Burrowing Animal, Reptile or Bird (and Holes Made by Them); Status of Object

SPECTATOR   I-104
See also Outside Agency

SPIKE MARK(S)   I-105

See also Damage; Improving Area of Intended Stance or Swing, Position or Lie of Ball, or Line of Play or Putt; Line of Putt; Putting Green

SPORTSMANSHIP CODE AND/OR COMPETITION POLICY
See Etiquette

STABLEFORD COMPETITION I-105
See also Bogey Competition; Four-Ball Stableford Competition

STAKES I-105
See also Boundary Fence, Line, Wall or Stakes; Status of Object

STANCE I-105
See also Addressing the Ball; Improving Area of Intended Stance or Swing, Position or Lie of Ball, or Line of Play or Putt

STARTING, STARTING TIME *See* Groups and Grouping; Time of Starting

STATUS OF OBJECT I-107

STEPS *See* Obstructions; Status of Object

STIPULATED ROUND I-108
See also Artificial Devices and Unusual Equipment and Unusual Use of Equipment

STONE(S), ROCK(S) OR GRAVEL I-109
See also Loose Impediments; Status of Object; Wall

STOPPED BALL *See* Ball Deflected or Stopped

STRIKING THE BALL *See* Stroke

STRIKING BALL IN MOTION *See* Ball in Motion Struck by Club

STROKE I-109
See also Artificial Devices, Unusual Equipment and Unusual Use of Equipment; Ball in Motion Struck by Club; Concession; Handicap Competition and Handicap Strokes; Practice; Practice Swing; Stroke and Distance; Stroke Canceled or Recalled; Wrong Ball

STROKE AND DISTANCE I-110

STROKE CANCELED OR RECALLED I-112
See also Ball Deflected or Stopped; Order of Play; Order of Play in Foursomes and Threesomes; Stroke and Distance; Teeing Ground and Tee Markers

STROKE PLAY *See* Doubt as to Procedure; Failure to Hole Out; Scores and Score Cards; Second Ball

SUBSTITUTED BALL I-113
See also Exchanging Balls

SUDDEN-DEATH PLAY-OFF *See* Play-Off and Ties

SUSPENSION OF PLAY *See* Discontinuance and Resumption of Play

TAPE I-114

TEAM COMPETITION I-114

TEE I-114
See also Status of Object; Teeing Ground and Tee-Markers

TEEING GROUND AND TEE-MARKERS I-114
See also Marking or Defining Course; Status of Object; Stroke and Distance; Tee

TEMPORARY OBSTRUCTIONS *See* Local Rules

TERMINOLOGY I-115

TEST OR TESTING I-116

THREE-BALL MATCH PLAY I-117

THROUGH THE GREEN I-117
See also Fairway and Closely Mown Areas; Rough

TIES *See* Play-Off and Ties

TIME OF STARTING I-118
See also Course Unplayable or Closed; Groups and Grouping

TOUCHING BALL *See* Ball Touched

TOWEL I-118

TRADEMARK I-118

TREE OR BUSH I-118
See also Leaves; Pine Needles; Status of Object

TROLLEY I-119
See also Equipment; Golf Cart

TUMBLEWEED I-119

TURF *See* Grass and Turf

UMBRELLA I-120

UNDUE DELAY I-120
See also Pace of Play

UNPLAYABLE BALL I-120
See also Ball Unfit for Play

UNUSUAL USE OF EQUIPMENT *See* Artificial Devices, Unusual Equipment and Unusual Use of Equipment

VIRTUALLY CERTAIN (OR KNOWN) I-121

See also Abnormal Ground Conditions; Burrowing Animal, Reptile or Bird (and Holes Made by Them); Casual Water; Ground Under Repair; Lost Ball; Obstructions; Outside Agency; Provisional Ball; Water Hazards

WAIVED PENALTY See Penalties Imposed, Modified or Waived by Committee

WALL   I-122
See also Boundary Fence, Line, Wall or Stakes; Fence; Integral Part of Course; Obstructions; Status of Object

WATER HAZARDS   I-122
See also Marking or Defining Course; Provisional Ball; Virtually Certain (or Known)

WEATHER CONDITIONS   I-125
See also Course Unplayable or Closed; Discontinuance and Resumption of Play

WIND See Weather Conditions

WOOD AND WOOD CHIPS   I-126
See also Loose Impediments; Obstructions

WORM   I-126

WRONG BALL   I-126

WRONG INFORMATION   I-128
See also Claims and Disputes; Incorrect Information on the Rules; Information as to the Strokes Taken

WRONG PLACE   I-129
See also Serious Breach of Rules

WRONG PUTTING GREEN   I-130

WRONG TEEING GROUND   I-130
See also Teeing Ground and Tee-Markers

"X-OUT" BALL   I-131

INDEX

INDEX TO DECISIONS

ABNORMAL GROUND CONDITIONS

See also BURROWING ANIMAL, REPTILE
OR BIRD (AND HOLES MADE BY THEM);
CASUAL WATER, EMBEDDED BALL;
GROUND UNDER REPAIR; MATERIAL PILED
FOR REMOVAL; PITCH-MARK; STATUS OF
OBJECT; VIRTUALLY CERTAIN (OR KNOWN)

aeration holes 25/15

application of exception to Rule
25–1b when ball lies underground
in hole made by burrowing animal,
reptile or bird. 25–1b/25.5

clarification of point where ball
"last entered" abnormal ground
condition when ball in condition
but not found 25–1c/1.5

cracks in earth. 25/12

crawfish mound. 25–1b/18

dropping zone; specimen Local
Rule for establishing as additional
option under Rules 25–1b, 25–1c
and 25–3 . . . . .App I-B-8

edging grooves around putting
green; Local Rule allowing relief 33-8/24

improving line of play when taking
relief from abnormal ground
conditions. 25–1b/3

molehills 25/23

nearest point of relief
– determining club, address
  position, direction of play and
  swing used to identify nearest
  point of relief 24-2b/1
– diagrams illustrating nearest
  point of relief 25–1b/2
– diagram illustrating player
  unable to determine nearest
  point of relief 24-2b/3.7
– player determines nearest point
  of relief but physically unable to
  play intended stroke 24-2b/3
– player does not follow
  recommended procedure in
  determining nearest point of relief .24-2b/2

rut made by tractor 25/16

sod seams; specimen Local Rule
allowing relief from seams of cut
turf . . . . .App I-B-4e

soft, mushy earth 25/1

sunken hole plug 25/17

virtually certain (or known)
– meaning of "known or virtually
  certain" in Rule 25–1c 26-1/1
– missing ball in abnormal ground
  condition; drop made under
  Rule 25–1c; original ball then
  found within five minutes 25–1c/2.5
– unfound ball either in abnormal
  ground condition or high rough;

whether player may treat ball as
in abnormal ground condition 25-1c/1

ABNORMAL STANCE, SWING OR DIRECTION OF PLAY

after relief taken from obstruction
for stroke toward green,
obstruction interferes with stance
for necessary sideways stroke 24-2b/9.5

burrowing animal
– application of exception to Rule
  25–1b when ball lies underground 25.1b/25.5
– cast interferes with stroke
  toward green; tree prevents
  such stroke 25–1b/21
– hole interferes with stance;
  impracticable to make stroke
  because of other condition 25–1b/20
– mound interferes with lie of ball;
  impracticable to make stroke
  due to bush 25–1b/19

obstruction interferes with
abnormal stroke
– abnormal stroke not reasonable
  in circumstances. 24-2b/18
– abnormal stroke reasonable in
  circumstances. 24-2b/17

stroke at ball not practicable due
to interference by immovable
obstruction and casual water. 24-2b/19

ADDRESSING THE BALL

ball dropped in improper manner
moves when addressed; player
then lifts ball and drops it in
proper manner. 20-2a/4

ball moves after being addressed
– and comes to rest out of
  bounds; player plays ball 18-2b/9
– and falls into hole 18-2b/10
– and then stopped by player's club. .18-2b/12
– ball moves downward in rough;
  will not remain at rest when
  replaced. 20-3d/3
– clubhead grounded immediately
  in front of ball 18-2b/5.5
– competitor invokes Rule 3–3;
  second ball played first from
  spot where original ball lay 3-3/14
– on putting green when player
  attempts to brush insect from it . . .23-1/12
– player steps away from ball after
  addressing it; ball then moves. 18-2b/7
– player steps away from ball
  after addressing it, lifts ball and
  replaces it; ball then moves. 18-2b/8
– provisional ball moves after
  being addressed; whether
  penalty canceled if provisional
  ball never becomes ball in play 15/7

– when club rested on grass
immediately behind ball 18-2b/5
– when some other agency strikes it 18-2b/11

ball moves before being addressed
– after club grounded short
distance behind ball but not
immediately behind ball 18-2b/4
– after stance taken but before
club grounded 18-2b/1
– ball replaced at rest; thereafter
ball moved by wind before being
addressed 18-1/12

ball in bunker moves after stance
taken 18-2b/3

ball oscillates during address 18/2

casual water in bunker touched
with club; whether club grounded . . 13-4/7

grounding club
– immediately behind ball, club
rested on grass; whether ball
addressed 18-2b/5
– immediately in front of ball
then ball moves; whether ball
addressed 18-2b/5.5
– in grass in water hazard; when
club considered grounded 13-4/8
– outside water hazard prior to
stroke at ball in hazard 13-4/29
– presses down sand behind ball
through the green 13-2/12

order of play in foursome play if
player accidentally moves ball
after address 29-1/5

original ball out of bounds; ball
re-teed under stroke and distance
touched at address and falls off tee . . 11-3/3

stance in bunker taken
– then player smoothes footprints
after deciding to play different
type of stroke 13-4/0.5
– without club; player tested
condition of hazard or built a
stance 13-4/24

stroke misses ball; ball then
accidentally knocked off tee 11-3/1

when ball addressed
– by player who putts "side-saddle" . 18-2b/5.7
– in hazard 18-2b/2

ADVICE

absent partner gives advice before
joining match 30-3a/2

asking
– accuracy of distance marker 8-1/3
– advice between rounds in
36-hole match 8-1/19
– advice when play suspended 8-1/20
– distance between objects 8-1/2
– whereabouts of another player's
ball 8-1/5

caddies briefly changed by player in
order to receive advice from new
caddie 8-1/26

club selection
– after playing to green, player
asks what club opponent or
fellow-competitor used for
similar stroke 8-1/7
– comment about club selection
made after stroke 8-1/8
– double caddie informs one
employer about club used by
other 8-1/12
– looking into another player's bag
to determine club used 8-1/10
– misleading statement about club
selection purposely made 8-1/9
– player asks opponent or fellow-
competitor about club used at
previous hole 8-1/6
– towel removed covering
another player's clubs to
determine club used 8-1/11

concurrent
– four-ball and individual stroke
play; whether partners may
exchange advice 31/1
– four-ball and single matches;
whether partners may exchange
advice on single match after
result of hole or match in four-
ball decided 30-3/1

electronic device used to seek or
give advice during stipulated round . . 14-3/16

given on request; penalties in
various forms of play 8-1/25

instruction
– caddie swings club to show
player how to play shot 8-1/15
– competitor, after finishing
hole, demonstrates to fellow-
competitor how to play shot 8-1/14
– player gives opponent or fellow-
competitor instruction during
round 8-1/13

play of wrong ball not rectified on
advice of referee 33-7/5

player putting for half given advice
by opponent 2-2/1

player who has not yet played
seeks advice from player who has
finished round 8-1/18

request for advice made in error
to opponent's caddie; withdrawn
before advice given 8-1/17

Rules; whether advice 9/1

suggesting fellow-competitor deem
ball unplayable 8-1/16

team competition
– advice given by team captain or
by team coach not authorized
to give advice 8-1/24
– advice given by team captain
while playing 8/2
– advice given by team mate in
another group in stroke play 8-1/21
– condition of team competition
requires person appointed
to give advice must be team
captain or amateur 8/1

– specimen condition permitting
appointment of one person who
may give advice . . . . App I-C-7
– team mate in gallery hits ball to
green to show player whether
green will hold 8-1/23
– team mates playing as fellow-
competitors exchange advice. . . . 8-1/22
– whether team captain
authorized to give advice may
be required to keep off putting
greens 8-2b/4

AERATION HOLES AND PLUGS
holes 25/15
plugs 23/12
specimen Local Rule allowing relief
from aeration holes. . . . . App I-B-4d

AGREEMENT TO WAIVE RULES
agreement
– not to tee off in prescribed
order in match play to save time . . 10-1a/3
– that side losing after 18 holes of
36-hole match will concede
match 1-3/7
– to concede one or more holes 2-4/22
– to concede short putts 1-3/2
– to consider hole halved during
play of hole 2-1/1.5
– to consider hole halved made
when players not able to resolve
rules problem 2-1/1
– to play out of turn made
between competitors but not
for purpose of giving one of
them an advantage 10-2c/2
– to repair spike marks on one
another's line of putt made by
player and opponent or fellow-
competitor 1-3/3
breach of Rule by opponent
– discussed between player and
opponent; penalty not applied 1-3/4
– neither player nor opponent
aware; penalty not applied 1-3/5
– procedure for valid claim. 2-5/2
handicap stroke given at wrong hole
in error 6-2a/2
incorrect procedure agreed to in
error by player and opponent;
whether valid claim can be made
after procedure followed 2-5/8.5
marker attests wrong score
– knowingly 1-3/6
– knowingly; competitor unaware
score wrong 6-6a/5
player reaching third round of
match play disqualified for
agreeing to waive Rules in first-
round match. 34-1a/1
players unaware penalty incurred. 1-3/5
replaying match when play
discontinued instead of resuming
from where play stopped 2-1/6
two holes purposely omitted in
match 2-1/4

when agreement made between
players becomes breach of Rule
1-3 . . . . 1-3/0.5
wrong form of play used
– in match discovered after play of
9th hole 6-1/1
– in match; players agree losing
side will default to winners 33-1/4
– to decide which side will
concede match 2-4/21

ANTS AND ANT HILLS
See also INSECTS; LOOSE IMPEDIMENTS
danger from fire ants 33-8/22
dangerous situation
– meaning of "dangerous situation" .1-4/11
– relief procedure 1-4/10
Local Rule deeming hard conical ant
hills as ground under repair 33-8/22
status of ant hill 23/5

AREA OF INTENDED SWING
See also IMPROVING AREA OF INTENDED
STANCE OR SWING, POSITION OR LIE OF
BALL, OR LINE OF PLAY OR PUTT
breaking branch
– interfering with backswing on
teeing ground 13-2/14
– on backswing and swing
discontinued 13-2/14.5
– with practice swing; area of
intended swing finally used not
affected by branch 13-2/24
diagram illustrating player unable to
determine nearest point of relief . . 24-2b/3.7
"fairly taking his stance"
– explanation of "fairly taking his
stance". 13-2/1
– player allowed to play in any
direction in "fairly taking his
stance". 13-2/1.5
– player attempts to take stance
fairly but improves line of play
by moving interfering growing
object. 13-2/1.1
– player under tree changes
intended direction of play and
fairly takes stance second time. . . . 13-2/1.7
improved by
– bending boundary fence 13-2/18
– bending branch with hand;
also club grounded and loose
impediments moved in hazard;
whether multiple penalties apply . . 13-4/28
– bending grass in removal of
loose impediments. 13-2/13
– moving growing or fixed object
situated out of bounds. 13-2/19
– pushing off-course fence leaning
across boundary to upright
position 13-2/20
– removing boundary stake
interfering with swing 13-2/17
– removing immovable obstructions 13-2/15
– repairing pitch-mark made by
ball on previous stroke 13-2/21

– replacing or removing
undetached divot 13-2/5
– shaking water from tree branch
interfering with backswing 13-2/23
– taking stance fairly then
changing direction of play 13-2/1.7

movable part of immovable obstruction
– door of building interferes with
player's swing; relief options
available 24-2b/15.5
– drainage hose interferes with
player's swing; relief options
available 24-2b/15.3

natural object interfering with
swing moved to determine if
loose; whether breach of Rule 13–2 .13-2/26

obstruction
– in ground under repair
interferes with player's swing 24-2b/10
– struck by player's swing after
relief taken under Rule 24–2;
whether player subject to penalty .20-2c/6

player breaches two Rules with
different penalties; more severe
penalty applied 1-4/15

player determines nearest point
of relief but physically unable to
make intended stroke 24-2b/3

position of ball worsened when
obstruction removed; player
replaces obstruction; whether
area of intended swing improved . . .13-2/15.5

probing near ball for tree roots or
rocks; whether permitted 13-2/27

removing dew or frost; whether
permitted 13-2/35

stake supporting tree broken in
attempt to remove it. 13-2/16

tree in area of ground under repair
interferes with swing at ball
outside area 25-1a/1

ARTIFICIAL DEVICES, UNUSUAL EQUIPMENT AND UNUSUAL USE OF EQUIPMENT

See also MEDICAL ASSISTANCE OR CONDITION; STATUS OF OBJECT

adhesive tape applied to hand or glove 14-3/8

artificial limbs 14-3/15

binoculars 14-3/3

booklet providing distances
between various points 14-3/5

bottled drink used as level. 14-3/12.5

broadcast listened to during
stipulated round 14-3/17

compass used during round. 14-3/4

distance-measuring device 14-3/0.5

distance meter attached to golf cart .14-3/1

elastic bandage worn 14-3/7

electronic device or instrument
– containing distances between
various points 14-3/5.5
– radio transmitting
chipcontained contained in ball . . .14-3/14
– use of electronic devices 14-3/16

– used to find ball. 14-3/14

eyeglasses. 14-3/3

field glasses 14-3/3

golf ball warmer or hand warmer
used to warm ball 14-3/13

gradient-measuring device. 14-3/0.5

hand warmer 14-3/13.5

headphones used to listen to
broadcast or music during
stipulated round 14-3/17

holding ball in hand against grip
– when putting .14-3/6
– when making practice swing or
practice stroke 14-3/6.5

Local Rule
– permitting use of distance
measuring device 14-3/0.5
– specimen Local Rule permitting
use of devices that measure
distance only . . . . .App I-B-9

music listened to during stipulated
round. 14-3/17

pencil used to gauge distance 14-3/2

player uses distance-measuring
device or obtains distance
information from outside agency
using a device; such devices not
permitted in competition 14-3/0.7

player putts with one hand and
steadies himself with club in other
hand. 14-3/9

player with injured right wrist
inserts left thumb under elastic
bandage on right wrist and hand 14-3/7

plumb-line
– club used as 14-3/12
– used during round 14-3/11

reflectors (non-circular) on
flagsticks aid in use of distance-
measuring devices; whether
permitted 17/3.5

rod used to check alignment or
swing plane. 14-3/10.3

score card used to gauge distance 14-3/2

spectacles. 14-3/3

stretching device. 14-3/10.5

swing aid; whether Committee may
authorise for medical reasons
during stipulated round 14-3/15.5

training or swing aid, such
as weighted head cover or
"doughnut" on club, used to make
stroke or practice swing. 14-3/10

weighted training club 4-4a/7

wind gauge 14-3/0.5

ASSISTANCE OR PROTECTION, ACCEPTANCE OF

See also BALL ASSISTING OR INTERFERING WITH PLAY; EXERTING INFLUENCE ON BALL; FOUR-BALL MATCH PLAY; FOUR-BALL STROKE PLAY; MEDICAL ASSISTANCE OR CONDITION

ball mark in position to assist player;
whether player may prevent
repair by opponent 16-1c/2

ball-marker of player in position
to assist opponent or fellow-
competitor; whether player may
move it if opponent or fellow-
competitor objects 20-1/11

caddie
 – hires boy to carry most of
  player's clubs but does not
  assist player in any other way;
  whether player has two caddies. . .6-4/4
 – shields player from sun during
  stroke. 14-2/3
 – takes player's glove to him at tee
  while another caddie or friend
  assists him by carrying player's
  clubs forward; whether player
  has two caddies 6-4/4.5

golf bag positioned for purpose of
blocking sunlight on ball 14-2/2.5

meaning of "elements" in Rule 14–2a .14-2/0.5

player
 – aligns partner's club before stroke.14-2/1
 – directs caddie not to search for
  ball until others can assist 27/1
 – holds ball in hand against grip to
  assist in putting. 14-3/6
 – holds umbrella over own head
  during stroke 14-2/2
 – late for starting time provided
  medical assistance at
  scene of accident; whether
  circumstances warrant waiving
  penalty of disqualification under
  Rule 6–3a. 6-3a/1.5
 – places club on ground to assist
  in aligning feet for stroke. 8-2a/1
 – places towel on cactus and leans
  against it during stroke 1-2/10
 – repairs spike marks in vicinity
  of hole that might assist him in
  subsequent play of hole. 16-1c/4
 – seeks assistance of others in
  removing large loose impediment .23-1/3
 – smoothes irregularities in
  bunker after playing out of turn
  in match; opponent recalls
  stroke; whether player in
  breach of Rule 13–4. . . . . .13-4/39
 – smoothes irregularities in
  bunker after stroke but before
  ball extricated; opponent
  or fellow-competitor claims
  smoothing assisted player in
  subsequent play of hole. 13-4/36
 – with artificial arm uses club with
  attachment to grip or shaft to
  assist him to hold club; whether
  permitted 14-3/15
 – wraps towel around self and
  leans against cactus during stroke .1-2/10

player's breach of Rule assists partner
 – absent player joins match during
  play of hole; stroke played by
  him assists partner. 30-3a/1
 – loose impediment in bunker
  lifted when player's and

partner's balls lie in bunker;
infringement assists partner's
play (match play). 30-3f/1
 – loose impediment in bunker
  lifted when player's and
  partner's balls lie in bunker;
  infringement assists partner's
  play (stroke play) 31-8/1
 – player allows partner to stand
  on extension of line of play or
  putt behind ball; assists partner
  with similar shot. 30-3f/13
 – player putts partner's ball by
  mistake; opponents claim
  partner also disqualified for hole
  because action assisted him 30-3c/1
 – playing away from hole to assist
  partner 30-3f/6
 – practice stroke made from near
  partner's ball after player picks up.30-3f/7
 – putting out after concession of
  stroke; act assists partner. 2-4/6
 – stroke made by player
  disqualified for hole assists
  partner 30-3f/8

shadow of spectator blocks sunlight
from ball when player makes stroke 14-2/2.5

umbrella
 – carrier (in addition to caddie)
  hired to protect player from sun
  or rain 6-4/5
 – held by player over head with
  one hand while holing short
  putt with other. 14-2/2

BALL

See also ADDRESSING THE BALL; BALL
ASSISTING OR INTERFERING WITH PLAY;
BALL AT REST MOVED; BALL DEFLECTED OR
STOPPED; BALL DROPPED OR RE-DROPPED;
BALL LIFTED; BALL MARK; BALL
OVERHANGING HOLE; BALL PLACED OR
REPLACED; BALL TOUCHED; BALL UNFIT
FOR PLAY; CLEANING BALL; EMBEDDED
BALL; EXCHANGING BALL; EXERTING
INFLUENCE ON BALL; HOLE MADE BY
GREENKEEPER; HOLED AND HOLING OUT;
LIE OF BALL ALTERED; LOST BALL; OUT OF
BOUNDS; PROVISIONAL BALL; SEARCHING
FOR AND IDENTIFYING BALL; SECOND
BALL; STATUS OF OBJECT; STROKE;
SUBSTITUTED BALL; "X-OUT" BALL

artificially warmed 14-3/13.5

borrowing balls from another
player; whether permitted. 5-1/5

effect of state of match penalty for
breach of "One Ball" condition in
four-ball play. .30-3/2

explanation of "any ball he has played" 18/7

holding ball in hand against grip
 – when putting. 14-3/6
 – when making practice swing or
  practice stroke 14-3/6.5

line drawn or on ball aimed to
indicate line of play when ball
replaced 20-3a/2

List of Conforming Golf Balls
  – ball to be removed from List used .5-1/1.7
  – condition in effect; ball not on
    list played as provisional ball 5-1/3
  – penalty for breach of condition
    requiring use of ball on List of
    Conforming Golf Balls changed
    by Committee. 5-1/2
  – status of ball not on List. 5-1/1.5
non-conforming ball
  – concurrent individual and four-
    ball stroke play; application of
    penalties when one player uses
    non-conforming ball. 31/1
  – one stroke made with non-
    conforming ball; whether
    Committee may waive
    disqualification penalty 5-1/1
  – used for stroke with provisional
    ball that never becomes ball in
    play. 5-1/3
optional conditions of competition
  – "One Ball" condition;
    prohibiting changing brands
    or types of golf balls during
    stipulated round . . . . .App I-C-1c
  – requiring use of ball named on
    current List of Conforming Golf
    Balls . . . . .App I-C-1b
status of
  – abandoned ball 24-1/2
  – ball not on List of Conforming
    Golf Balls. .5-1/1.5
  – ball stamped "practice" 5-1/4
  – ball stamped with logo. 5-1/4
  – ball to be removed from List of
    Conforming Golf Balls. 5-1/1.7
  – broken piece of ball swung at
    and struck by player mistaking it
    for his ball lying in heavy grass 15/3
  – "refurbished" ball 5-1/4
  – "X-out" ball. 5-1/4
use of ball containing radio
  transmitting chip 14-3/14

BALL ASSISTING OR INTERFERING WITH PLAY

See also ASSISTANCE OR PROTECTION, ACCEPTANCE OF; EXERTING INFLUENCE ON BALL

ball assisting play
  – competitor not given
    opportunity to lift ball assisting
    fellow-competitor 3-4/1
  – competitor requests ball in
    position to assist him not be
    lifted; whether request proper . . .22/6
  – lifted by opponent then
    replaced at player's request;
    player's putt strikes opponent's
    ball; opponent lodges claim. 22/5
  – on putting green in position
    to assist fellow-competitor;
    procedure for referee if
    competitor does not lift ball. 22/7
  – player requests ball of another
    player be lifted in absence of
    reasonable possibility it might
    assist play. .22/3

  – request to lift ball that might
    assist partner not honored. 30-3f/11
ball interfering with play
  – abandoned ball lies against
    player's ball; procedure for player .24-1/2
  – ball replaced on putting green
    while another ball in motion
    after stroke; player re-lifts ball
    in belief moving ball might strike it.16-1b/2
  – kicked accidentally by player
    asked to lift it due to interference .20-1/13
  – lie of ball lifted from bunker
    altered by another player's stroke .20-3b/1
  – mental interference by another
    ball; whether player may have
    ball lifted under Rule 22–2 . . . . . .22/1
  – mud adheres to ball when lifted
    under Rule not permitting
    cleaning; whether ball may
    be replaced with mud facing
    different direction 21/5
  – player claims ball lying 30 yards
    away interferes with his play;
    whether request reasonable 22/2
  – player plays out of turn instead
    of complying with opponent's
    request to lift ball due to
    interference 10-1c/2
  – player requests ball of another
    player be lifted in absence of
    reasonable possibility it might
    interfere with play 22/3
ball on putting green that might
  influence movement of another
  ball in motion lifted 16-1b/4

BALL AT REST MOVED

See also BALL DEFLECTED OR STOPPED; BALL TOUCHED

after address
  – and comes to rest out of
    bounds; player plays ball 18-2b/9
  – and then stopped by player's club. .18-2b/12
  – ball dropped in improper
    manner moves when addressed;
    player then lifts ball and drops it
    in proper manner 20-2a/4
  – ball falls into hole 18-2b/10
  – ball in rough moves downward
    when addressed; ball will not
    remain at rest when replaced. 20-3d/3
  – ball moves in water hazard after
    stance taken; presumably due to
    current or cause unclear. 14-6/1
  – ball oscillates during address. 18/2
  – by ball played from elsewhere. 18-2b/11
  – competitor invokes Rule 3–3;
    second ball played first from
    spot where original ball lay 3-3/14
  – foursome partner accidentally
    moves ball after address; effect
    on order of play 29-1/5
  – on putting green when player
    removes loose impediment 23-1/12
  – player addresses ball, steps
    away; ball then moves 18-2b/7
  – player addresses ball, steps
    away, lifts ball and replaces it;
    ball then moves. 18-2b/8

– provisional or second ball moves after address; whether penalty canceled if it never becomes ball in play..........................15/7

after club grounded short distance behind ball but not immediately behind ball.......................18-2b/4

after club rested on grass immediately behind ball..........18-2b/5

after loose impediment touched or moved
– ball in hazard moves when loose impediment in hazard removed...13-4/15
– ball through the green moves after removal of nearby loose impediment....................18-2a/30.5
– ball touched with fir cone or stick to prevent movement when loose impediments removed....................18-2a/32

after stance taken but before address .18-2b/1

ball deemed unplayable
– high in tree, player shakes tree to dislodge it; whether player exempt from penalty under Rule 18–2a....................18-2a/27
– may move when neared; player subsequently considers playing ball; ruling if ball thereafter moves.18-2a/27.5

ball falls into bunker when person walks nearby 18/10

ball in tall grass stepped on; original lie altered and spot where ball originally lay not determinable; procedure for player..............20-3b/5

ball in tree moved
– circumstances in which player not penalized...................18-2a/27
– circumstances in which player penalized.....................18-2a/28
– ball in fork of tree moves in relation to ground.............18/3
– knocked down by outside agency..18-1/9
– replacement of ball not possible...18-2a/29
– player climbs tree to make stroke; ball falls to ground........18-2a/26
– striking at tree branch to move ball lodged beyond reach in branch.14/7

ball lifted without authority by player dropped instead of replaced..18-2a/9

ball moved
– after stance taken in bunker......18-2b/3
– by air propelled from fan or blower........................18-1/2
– by backward movement of club after stroke misses; ball comes to rest out of bounds.............18-2a/22
– by fellow-competitor; competitor's ball thought to be wrong ball picked up at competitor's request............18-2a/16
– by foot during removal of loose impediment on putting green.....23-1/11
– by golf cart shared by two players .18/8
– by loose impediment dislodged by partner's or opponent's stroke.18-1/8
– by loose impediment dislodged by practice swing 18-2a/20.5

– by opponent in playing his own ball...........................18-3b/1
– by player accidentally during suspension of play 18-2a/25
– by player in kicking ball accidentally when asked to lift it due to interference 20-1/13
– by player in playing wrong ball in bunker......................18-2a/21
– by player, original lie altered; player places ball in wrong place and plays 18-2a/21.3
– by practice swing prior to tee shot 18-2a/19
– by practice swing when ball in play...........................18-2a/20
– by putter dropped by player approaching ball to lift it 20-1/14
– by removal of player's foot after ball stopped by same foot........19-2/1
– by towel of player dropped on ground and blown onto ball 18-2a/17
– in measuring to determine if re-drop required 18-6/1
– in removing ball-marker after replacing ball..................20-3a/1
– prior to address then accidentally stopped by player's club; player removes club and ball rolls away 19-2/1.5
– vertically downward 18/1

ball played from within ground under repair retrieved by player and relief taken under ground under repair Rule.................18-2a/8

branch of bush or tree broken by player fearing ball may roll nearby after drop 1-2/3

by another ball
– accidentally dropped by opponent or fellow-competitor...18/7.5
– after player addresses ball........18-2b/11
– balls inadvertently exchanged by players after one ball strikes and moves other 15-1/2.5
– competitor and fellow-competitor unaware ball moved by fellow-competitor's ball until after completion of hole 18-5/3
– competitor's ball played from putting green strikes ball on green belonging to competitor playing in another group 19-5/2
– opponent's ball knocked away by player after concession moves player's ball 18-2a/18
– original ball strikes and moves provisional ball 19-5/5
– original ball strikes second ball or vice versa 3-3/7
– provisional ball strikes original ball 18-5/2

by another player making stroke
– competitor's ball knocked out of bunker by fellow-competitor's stroke at own ball...............18-4/2
– opponent's stroke disturbs bushes causing player's ball to move 18-3b/2

B

B

– player plays own ball and
accidentally moves partner's ball
with club during stroke 30-3f/9

by caddie

– ball accidentally stepped on by
opponent's caddie 18-3b/3
– shared by members of opposite
sides in four-ball match 30/1
– shared by opponent's side in
four-ball match 30/2

by fellow-competitor

– ball accidentally dropped by
fellow-competitor moves
competitor's ball 18/7.5
– ball addressed by competitor
subsequently moved by fellow-
competitor prior to stroke 18-2b/11
– ball of competitor in bunker
played by fellow-competitor;
ball not replaced by competitor . 20-7c/6
– ball of competitor knocked from
lip of hole by fellow-competitor
not replaced 3-2/1
– ball of competitor knocked
out of bunker by fellow-
competitor's stroke at own ball . . 18-4/2
– ball of competitor lifted without
authority by fellow-competitor . . 20-1/4
– ball of competitor picked
up by fellow-competitor at
competitor's request............18-2a/16
– ball of competitor resting
against flagstick moves away
from hole when flagstick
removed by fellow-competitor . . 17-4/3
– next stroke of competitor in
stroke-play play-off conceded
by fellow-competitor who lifts
competitor's ball 18-4/3

by opponent

– ball addressed by player
subsequently moved by
opponent prior to stroke 18-2b/11
– ball of player falls into bunker
when opponent walks nearby.....18/10
– ball of player lifted by opponent
without player's authority 20-1/2
– ball of player lifted by opponent
without player's authority in
four-ball match.................30-3f/10
– ball of player marked and
lifted by opponent without
player's authority; player lifts
ball-marker, claims hole and
opponent disputes claim 20-1/3
– ball of player moved accidentally
by opponent in playing his own
ball 18-3b/1
– ball of player moved by ball
dropped accidentally by opponent 18/7.5
– ball of player picked up by
opponent under erroneous
belief match is over 2-4/17
– ball of player picked up by
opponent; whether act is
concession of next stroke........2-4/4
– ball resting against flagstick but
not holed moves away from
hole when flagstick removed by
opponent 17-4/3

– ball resting against flagstick but
not holed; opponent concedes
putt and removes ball before
player can remove flagstick 17-4/2
– balls inadvertently exchanged
by players after one struck and
moved the other; opponent
mistakenly lifts player's ball and
places it on spot from which his
ball was moved 15-1/2.5
– caddie of opponent accidentally
steps on and moves player's ball . .18-3b/3
– caddie of opponent lifts player's
ball after player claims another
ball 18-3b/4
– caddie of opponent lifts player's
ball which may or may not have
been out of bounds 18-3b/5
– caddie shared by members of
opposite sides in four-ball match
moves ball 30/1
– caddie shared by opponents'
side in four-ball match moves
player's ball 30/2
– four-ball opponent moves
player's ball; explanation
of penalties when four-ball
and single matches played
concurrently 30-3/1
– golf cart shared by members of
opposite sides moves ball 18/8
– loose impediment dislodged
by opponent's practice swing
moves player's ball 18-2a/20.5
– loose impediment dislodged
by opponent's stroke moves
player's ball 18-1/8
– stroke made by opponent
disturbs bushes causing player's
ball to move....................18-3b/2

by outside agency

– ball at rest kicked away from
hole by spectator attending
flagstick 18-1/10
– ball in bad lie moved during
suspension of play; player fails to
estimate position sufficiently in
replacing ball...................6-8d/5
– ball in tree knocked down by
outside agency 18-1/9
– ball not found treated as moved
by outside agency in absence of
knowledge or virtual certainty
to that effect...................27-1/2.5
– ball stolen by outside agency
from unknown spot.............18-1/5
– ball visible from tee disappears
or moved by outside agency
while play suspended...........6-8d/4
– meaning of "known or virtually
certain" in Rule 18–1...........26-1/1
– player unaware ball moved by
outside agency does not replace
ball 18-1/3
– spectator says ball moved by
outside agency but player not
sure; procedure for player
if Committee decision not
possible in reasonable time.......18-1/4

by water
- ball moved into bounds by flow
  of water in water hazard 26-1/8
- ball moved out of bounds by
  flow of water in water hazard. 26-1/7
- ball moves in water in water
  hazard after stance taken 14-6/1

by wind
- after being replaced at rest on
  putting green and before being
  addressed 18-1/12
- ball in plastic bag moves when
  bag blown to new position by
  wind 18-1/7
- ball moved by tumbleweed
  blown by wind. 18-1/6
- ball replaced instead of played
  from new location 18-2a/7

club breaks during downswing
- swing completed but misses ball;
  clubhead falls and moves ball 14/5
- swing stopped short of ball;
  clubhead falls and moves ball 14/4

concurrent four-ball and individual
stroke play; application of penalty
when four-ball partner causes
player's ball to move 31/1

concurrent four-ball and single
matches
- application of penalty when
  four-ball partner causes player's
  ball to move. .30-3/1
- player causes opponent's ball to
  move; whether penalty stroke
  applies to player's single match
  with other opponent 30-3/1

dropped ball comes to rest and then
rolls out of bounds 20-2c/3.5

during backswing ball moves; ball
struck while still in motion 14-5/1

flagstick
- ball overhanging hole rolls away
  or falls in hole when flagstick
  removed 16-2/4
- ball overhanging hole moves and
  strikes flagstick being removed . . .16-2/5
- ball resting against flagstick
  moves away from hole when
  flagstick removed by opponent
  or fellow-competitor. 17-4/3
- ball resting against flagstick
  moves away from hole when
  flagstick removed by player; ball
  not placed on lip of hole 17-4/4
- when used for measuring or
  when accidentally dropped on ball 18-6/2

grass behind ball touched by player
then ball moves 18-2a/30

meaning of
- "directly attributable" in Rules
  20-1 and 20-3a 20-1/15
- "known or virtually certain" in
  Rule 24-3 . . . . .26-1/1
- "not immediately recoverable"
  when moved ball to be replaced . .18/11

position of ball marked before
obstruction removed; ball moves
when ball-marker removed 24-1/5

practice swings taken near ball by
player then ball moves 18-2a/30

putting green
- after ball addressed on putting
  green ball moved in removal of
  loose impediment. 23-1/12
- ball blown into hole by
  competitor not replaced and
  holed out. 3-2/2
- ball falls into hole after being
  addressed 18-2b/10
- ball knocked from lip of hole in
  disgust 18-2a/23
- ball oscillating in wind pressed
  into surface of putting green. 1-2/9
- ball replaced at rest thereafter
  moved by wind 18-1/12
- ball replaced on putting green
  but ball-marker not removed;
  ball then moves. 20-4/1
- ball replaced at rest on putting
  green; rolls and strikes another
  ball on green 19-5/1.5
- competitor's ball played from
  putting green strikes ball on
  green belonging to competitor
  playing in another group 19-5/2
- fellow-competitor marks and
  lifts player's ball without
  authority 20-1/4
- fellow-competitor's ball
  knocked from lip of hole by
  competitor not replaced. 3-2/1
- opponent's ball knocked away
  by player after concession
  moves player's ball 18-2a/18
- opponent marks and lifts
  player's ball without authority 20-1/2
- player addresses ball, steps
  away, lifts ball and replaces it;
  ball then moves. 18-2b/8
- player jumps close to hole to
  cause ball to drop; ball falls into
  hole 1-2/4

searching for ball, player
accidentally kicks it lying in grass
while probing for it in water in
water hazard .12-1/5

spot where moved ball originally lay
not determinable; player places
ball instead of dropping it 18-2a/21.5

teeing ground
- ball swung at within teeing
  ground falls off tee when stroke
  just touches it; player lifts,
  re-tees and plays ball 18-2a/2
- player misses tee shot; tees ball
  lower before playing next stroke. .18-2a/1
- stroke misses ball; then
  accidentally knocked off tee 11-3/1

two Rules with different penalties
breached; more severe penalty
applied. 1-4/15

whether act causing movement of
ball reasonably foreseeable
- ball moved accidentally by
  opponent in playing his own ball. .18-3b/1
- ball moved accidentally by player
  in playing wrong ball. 18-2a/21

– opponent's stroke disturbs
bushes causing player's ball to
move 18-3b/2
– practice swing moves loose
impediment which moves ball 18-2a/20.5
– stone dislodged by stroke
moves another player's ball. 18-1/8

whether ball must be replaced after
being moved if player wishes to
proceed under another Rule 20-3a/3

wind causes ball to oscillate,
whether ball considered moving 14-5/2

BALL DEFLECTED OR STOPPED
See also BALL AT REST MOVED; BALL IN
MOTION STRUCK BY CLUB; EXERTING
INFLUENCE ON BALL

by ball at rest
– ball replaced at rest on putting
green; rolls and strikes another
ball on green 19-5/1.5
– ball replaced on putting green
while another ball in motion;
replaced ball subsequently
deflects moving ball 16-1b/3
– competitor not given
opportunity to lift his ball that
assists fellow-competitor 3-4/1
– competitor's ball played from
putting green strikes ball on
green belonging to competitor
playing in another group 19-5/2
– competitor's ball played from
putting green touches but
does not move ball of fellow-
competitor lying on green. 19-5/4
– opponent's or fellow-
competitor's ball played from
putting green strikes player's
ball that was lifted and set aside
on green 19-5/1
– original ball strikes provisional
ball 19-5/5
– original ball strikes second ball
or vice versa 3-3/7
– provisional ball strikes original
ball 18-5/2

by divot taken by player subsequent
to making original stroke 19-2/9

by equipment of player or partner
– club when ball moves after
address 18-2b/12
– club when ball moves prior to
address; player removes club
and ball rolls away 19-2/1.5
– clubs belonging to different side
but carried in same bag 19-2/5
– competitor's golf bag and then
his caddie. 19-2/7
– face of club after striking pipeline. .14-4/2
– face of club after stroke when
ball falls and sticks to mud
thereon 14-4/1
– golf cart being pulled by
opponent or fellow-competitor. . .19-2/6
– opponent's or fellow-
competitor's bag left ahead by
shared caddie 19-2/8

– trolley after first being deflected
by trolley of opponent or
fellow-competitor 19-3/3

by flagstick, flag or hole-liner
– flag when flagstick attended 17-3/5
– flagstick attended by opponent
or fellow-competitor not
removed from hole 17-3/2
– flagstick attended by partner
without authority of player 17-3/4
– flagstick being removed when
ball moves while overhanging
hole 16-2/5
– flagstick lying on ground 17-3/3
– hole-liner and thereafter
bounces out of hole 16/5
– hole-liner pulled out with
flagstick 17/8

by golf cart shared by two players 19/1

by opponent, caddie or equipment
in
match play
– opponent or caddie deflects ball
dropped under Rule by player 19-3/2
– opponent standing out of
bounds and ball comes to rest
out of bounds 19-3/1
– opponent's trolley then strikes
player's trolley 19-3/3
– player attending flagstick for
opponent. 30-3f/5
– tee marking position of ball. 20-1/17

by outside agency
– ball dropped on moving ball by
opponent or fellow-competitor. . .19-5/1.7
– direction post 19-1/1
– dog on putting green when
stroke made from off putting
green 19-1/6
– dog on putting green when
stroke made from on putting
green 19-1/7
– fellow-competitor, deliberately . . .19-1/5
– fellow-competitor's or
opponent's trolley then strikes
player's trolley 19-3/3
– knob falls from top of flagstick
as attendant removes flagstick
and deflects ball 17/9
– other than worm or insect (or
the like) and stroke from putting
green not replayed 19-1/3
– maintenance vehicle deflects
ball out of bounds; substituted
ball played from spot where
original ball deflected. 20-7/1
– pipeline then deflected by face
of club 14-4/2
– stroke of player in another group .19-1/2
– tree branch before striking
ground when dropped. 20-2c/1.3

by player or partner
– ball stopped by player's foot; ball
moves when foot removed 19-2/1
– player catches ball in hole with
one hand after putting with
other hand. .1-2/5

– player knocks partner's putted ball back to him while still in motion after having passed hole...1-2/7
– when flagstick attended by partner without authority of player......................17-3/4
– where next stroke must be played from when ball purposely stopped or deflected by player or partner.....................1-2/5.5

by player's own caddie
– dropped ball rolls toward or into position where re-drop would be required; caddie stops ball before it comes to rest.......20-2c/4
– standing in bounds; ball comes to rest out of bounds...........19-2/2
– standing out of bounds; ball comes to rest on course.........19-2/3
– standing out of bounds; ball comes to rest out of bounds......19-2/4

by rake held by caddie of side (or partner)........................19-2/10

Local Rule for ball deflected by
– power line, tower or pole requiring cancellation and replay of stroke without penalty........33-8/13
– sprinkler head; allowing replay of stroke without penalty; whether authorized.............33-8/12
– temporary power lines, cables, telephone lines and guy wires; specimen Local Rule............App I-B-7b
– unattended flagstick; waiving penalty for ball striking unattended flagstick; whether authorized....................33-8/11

BALL DROPPED OR RE-DROPPED
See also BALL LIFTED; BALL PLACED OR REPLACED; LOCAL RULES

ball accidentally dropped by opponent or fellow-competitor on player's ball
– at rest......................18/7.5
– in motion after stroke from putting green..................19-5/1.7

ball deemed unplayable
– and dropped when deemed unplayable second time; player wishes to proceed under stroke and distance..................28/6.5
– at base of cliff and player wishes to drop within two club-lengths of point above ball.............28/12
– dropped in ground under repair from which play prohibited; ball then dropped under ground under repair Rule...............25-1b/14.5
– dropped outside bunker under option requiring drop in bunker...28/10
– in tree and player opts to drop within two club-lengths.........28/11
– in water hazard; dropped in hazard and played.............20-7/2
– in water hazard; substituted ball dropped in hazard without lifting original; error discovered before stroke made.............20-7/2.5

– player deems provisional ball unplayable and drops ball; original ball then found.........27-2b/6.5
– player who deems ball unplayable under Rule 28a must drop only at place from which last stroke made...............28/5
– through the green dropped in hazard.....................28/4
– through the green dropped in water hazard; player elects not to play ball and wishes to proceed under water hazard Rule..........................28/4.5

ball embeds when dropped
– in fairway......................25-2/2
– procedure if ball again embeds when re-dropped...............25-2/2.5

ball lifted without authority
– and dropped away from boundary stake under obstruction Rule...............18-2a/3
– and dropped away from movable obstruction...................18-2a/4
– ball played from ground under repair abandoned and relief taken under ground under repair Rule.....................18-2a/8.5

ball not found
– ball believed lost in bunker; competitor drops and plays substituted ball in bunker; then original ball found outside bunker.20-7c/3
– explanation of how to determine "estimated spot" for dropping when specific spot cannot be determined precisely..20-2c/1.5
– original ball found within five-minute search period after substituted ball dropped at spot of previous stroke under stroke and distance...................27-1/2
– original ball found within five-minute search period after substituted ball dropped at spot of previous stroke; original ball played....................27-1/2.3
– substituted ball dropped and played under Rule 25-1c in absence of knowledge or virtual certainty original ball lost in ground under repair............25-1c/2
– substituted ball dropped in area where original ball missing then played.....................27-1/3
– substituted ball dropped under water hazard Rule without knowledge or virtual certainty ball in hazard; before substituted ball played original ball found within five minutes.....26-1/3.7

bunker
– ball believed lost in bunker; competitor drops and plays substituted ball in bunker; then original ball found outside bunker.20-7c/3
– ball deemed unplayable through the green dropped in hazard.....28/4

B

– ball dropped outside bunker under option requiring drop in bunker..........................28/10
– ball to be dropped in bunker, dropped outside bunker so it will roll into bunker to avoid ball embedding in bunker............25-1b/7
– smoothing footprints created in bunker on line of play when required to enter bunker to retrieve ball....................13-2/29.3

by whom and how to drop
– ball dropped in improper manner and in wrong place.......20-2a/3
– ball dropped in other than prescribed manner moves after address and before re-drop......20-2a/4
– ball spun by player when dropping.20-2a/2
– ball substituted mistakenly when dropped.........................20-6/3
– caddie holds back tree branch to prevent branch from deflecting dropped ball 20-2a/5
– penalty when ball dropped in other than prescribed manner....20-2a/1
– who drops ball in foursome play...29/4

changing relief option
– dropped ball first strikes course outside where applicable Rule requires; whether player may change relief option when re-dropping....................20-6/2
– dropped ball first strikes course outside where applicable Rule requires; whether player may replace ball in original location....20-6/5
– dropped ball rolls to position requiring re-drop; whether player may change relief option when re-dropping 20-2c/5
– dropped ball strikes player; whether player may change relief option when re-dropping ...20-2a/6
– player drops ball in bunker under first option of Rule 25–1b(ii); player then wishes to proceed under second option to drop outside bunker..........25-1b/9
– player lifts ball from bunker intending to drop under first option of Rule 24–2b(ii); player then wishes to proceed under second option to drop outside bunker.........................24-2b/5
– point where ball last crossed margin of lateral water hazard determined and ball dropped; point then proves to be wrong point; whether player may change relief option when re-dropping...................26-1/16

dropped ball rolls toward or into position where re-drop would be required; caddie stops ball before it comes to rest 20-2c/4

dropping instead of placing or placing instead of dropping

– ball dropped instead of being replaced after being lifted without authority...............18-2a/9
– ball dropped third time when placement required after second drop 20-2c/2
– ball moved accidentally; spot where ball originally lay not determinable; player places ball instead of dropping it............18-2a/21.5
– ball placed instead of dropped on bank of water hazard to prevent ball rolling into water 26-1/10
– ball placed instead of dropped when obvious dropped ball will roll into position where re-drop will be required................20-2c/3
– ball placed when required to be dropped or dropped when required to be placed...........20-6/1

dropping zone; dropping and re-dropping procedures when established by Local Rule ....App I-B-8

improving area in which ball to be dropped
– ball played from bunker either out of bounds or lost; player smoothes footprints or tests condition of bunker before dropping another ball in bunker...13-4/37
– divots replaced in area in which ball to be dropped 13-2/4.5
– loose impediments removed from area in which ball to be dropped.......................23-1/6
– pitch-mark in dropping area repaired before ball dropped 13-2/10
– player smoothes irregularities in bunker after playing out of turn in match play; opponent then recalls stroke and player must drop ball in smoothed area.......13-4/39
– sand or loose soil removed from dropping area 13-2/11

interference from original condition occurs during stroke made after ball dropped for relief; whether penalty incurred 20-2c/6

Local Rule
– allowing drop opposite to spot where ball comes to rest in lateral water hazard; whether authorized....................26-1/20
– permitting re-dropping or placing when dropped ball embeds in bunker; whether authorized....................33-8/28
– wrong putting green; deemed to include apron to prohibit dropping on and play from 33-8/33

measuring for dropping and re-dropping
– ball moved in measuring to determine if re-drop required 18-6/1
– borrowed club used for measuring 20/2
– club to be used in measuring......20/1
– directly through fence, tree or wall or across ditch 20-2b/2

– player must continue measuring with club originally used for subsequent measuring 20/1

player drops ball after play suspended for dangerous situation . .6-8b/8

player invokes Rule 3–3 (doubt as to procedure)
– ball dropped in wrong place and played; second ball dropped in right place; both balls played out . .3-3/3
– ball dropped in wrong place but not played; second ball dropped in right place; both balls played out3-3/4
– competitor announces intention to play two balls; plays original ball before dropping second ball then elects not to play second ball.3-3/7.5
– competitor drops one ball in accordance with two different Rules instead of playing second ball 3-3/11
– competitor drops one ball in accordance with two different Rules instead of playing second ball; dropped ball rolls back into condition from which relief taken .3-3/12
– competitor lifts and drops original ball then places second ball where original ball lay and plays it 3-3/13
– substituted ball dropped under water hazard Rule without knowledge or virtual certainty ball in hazard; before substituted ball played original ball found within five minutes. 26-1/3.7
– whether score with second ball counts if dropped in wrong place and played 3-3/5

player mis-hits ball when distracted by accidentally dropped ball. 1-4/1

player picks up without completing hole; drops ball where partner's ball lies and plays practice stroke . . .30-3f/7

stray ball
– dropped and played under stroke-and-distance procedure; original ball then found 28/14
– dropped under unplayable ball Rule but not played 15/13
– dropped under unplayable ball Rule within two club-lengths and played before error discovered. .28/15
– in bunker deemed unplayable, dropped in bunker and played; ball then discovered to be wrong ball 15/14

test drop made by player to determine where ball will roll if relief taken under a Rule 20-2a/8

virtually certain or known
– missing original ball in abnormal ground condition or obstruction; substituted ball dropped under Rule 25–1c; whether re-drop required if finding original demonstrates drop made in wrong place. 25-1c/2.5
– missing original ball in water hazard; substituted ball dropped under water hazard Rule; whether re-drop required if finding original demonstrates drop made in wrong place. 26-1/3.5

water hazard
– ball deemed unplayable in water hazard, dropped in hazard and played. 20-7/2
– ball deemed unplayable through the green dropped in hazard 28/4
– ball deemed unplayable through the green dropped in water hazard; player elects not to play ball and wishes to proceed under water hazard Rule. 28/4.5
– ball dropped and played under water hazard Rule; original ball found outside hazard. 26-1/3
– ball dropped twice then placed where second drop struck course and played; first drop should have been played as it lay . .18-2a/10
– ball placed instead of dropped on bank of water hazard to prevent ball from rolling into water 26-1/10
– impossible to drop not nearer hole than point where ball last crossed margin of lateral water hazard 26-1/18
– Local Rule allowing drop opposite to spot where ball comes to rest in lateral water hazard; whether authorized 26-1/20
– meaning of "behind" in Rule 26–1 .26-1/1.5
– part of lateral water hazard where impossible to drop not nearer hole 33-2a/9
– permissible dropping area under lateral water hazard Rule so narrow player has difficulty dropping within it. 26-1/19
– player proceeding under water hazard Rule drops ball in another hazard. 26-1/2
– point where ball last crossed margin of lateral water hazard determined; ball dropped but not played; point then proves to be wrong point. 26-1/16
– point where ball last crossed margin of lateral water hazard determined; ball dropped and played; point then proves to be wrong point. 26-1/17

whether ball that has been moved must be replaced before relief taken under another applicable Rule 20-3a/3

whether glove used to mark dropping area is equipment 20-2a/7

whether player may drop ball into area from which play prohibited 20-7/3

whether player may substitute ball
when re-dropping under Rule
allowing substitution 20-6/4

whether re-drop required
 – after relief from obstruction
   taken for stroke toward green,
   same obstruction interferes
   with stance for necessary
   sideways stroke 24-2b/9.5
 – ball accidentally deflected by
   opponent or his caddie when
   dropped. 19-3/2
 – ball dropped from casual water
   in bunker at point of maximum
   relief rolls elsewhere 25-1b/6
 – ball dropped from ground under
   repair area rolls to position
   where area interferes with
   stance. 20-2c/0.5
 – ball dropped under Rule 20–5
   strikes course through the
   green within inches of and not
   nearer hole than spot in bunker
   where previous stroke made 20-5/2
 – ball dropped under Rule 24–2b
   rolls nearer hole than nearest
   point of relief but not nearer
   than where it originally lay 20-2c/1.7
 – ball dropped under unplayable
   ball Rule comes to rest in
   original position or another
   unplayable position 28/3
 – ball never strikes ground when
   dropped. 20-2b/1
 – ball rolls towards hole when
   dropped at spot from which
   previous stroke made 20-2c/1.5
 – ball strikes tree branch then
   ground when dropped. 20-2c/1.3
 – dropped ball comes to rest and
   then rolls out of bounds 20-2c/3.5
 – dropped ball rolls out of
   prescribed dropping area 20-2c/1
 – pine needles piled for removal
   interfere with lie; after drop
   taken pine needles interfere
   with line of play. 25-1b/17
 – player takes relief from area of
   casual water; ball comes to rest
   in position where another area
   of casual water interferes 20-2c/7
 – player takes relief from area
   of ground under repair and
   condition interferes for stroke
   with club not used to determine
   nearest point of relief 20-2c/0.8
 – player takes relief from
   immovable obstruction;
   dropped ball rolls nearer
   obstruction than nearest point
   of relief; player changes clubs
   and obstruction no longer
   interferes. 20-2c/0.7

wrong ball
 – in bunker deemed unplayable,
   dropped in bunker and played;
   ball then discovered to be
   wrong ball 15/14
 – original ball found within five-
   minute search period after

substituted ball dropped;
original ball played 27-1/2.3

BALL IN MOTION STRUCK BY CLUB
See also BALL AT REST MOVED; BALL
DEFLECTED OR STOPPED

ball falls on club face after stroke
and sticks to mud thereon 14-4/1
ball moving during backswing struck
while still moving 14-5/1
ball strikes pipeline; on rebound
deflects off club face 14-4/2
club hits behind ball then strikes ball
while moving 14-4/3

BALL LIFTED

assisting or interfering with play
 – assisting ball lifted by opponent
   replaced on request; player's
   ball then strikes opponent's ball
   and opponent lodges claim 22/5
 – ball assisting fellow-competitor
   on putting green; procedure for
   referee if competitor does not
   lift ball 22/7
 – competitor not given
   opportunity to lift ball assisting
   fellow-competitor 3-4/1
 – competitor requests ball in
   position to assist him not be
   lifted; whether request proper . . .22/6
 – mental interference by another
   ball 22/1
 – player requested to lift ball due
   to interference plays out of turn
   instead 10-1c/2
 – player claims that another ball
   lying 30 yards away interferes
   with his play. 22/2
 – player requests another player
   to lift his ball in absence of
   reasonable possibility ball might
   interfere or assist. 22/3
 – request to lift ball that might
   assist partner not honored. 30-3f/11

ball at rest moved
 – accidentally kicked by player
   asked to lift it due to interference .20-1/13
 – ball dropped in improper
   manner moves when addressed;
   player then lifts ball and drops it
   in proper manner 20-2a/4
 – ball moved by putter dropped by
   player approaching ball to lift it . .20-1/14
 – player addresses ball, steps
   away, lifts ball and replaces it;
   ball then moves. 18-2b/8

ball with mud adhering lifted under
Rule not permitting cleaning,
rotated when replaced 21/5

ball-marker moved accidentally by
player who marked position of
ball and lifted it. 20-1/6

by caddie without authority
 – competitor's ball lifted
   without authority by fellow-
   competitor's caddie who
   subsequently substitutes

another ball which competitor
plays 20-1/5
– considering it unplayable 18-2a/15
– for identification 18-2a/14
– in water hazard 26-1/9
– opponent's caddie lifts player's
ball after player claims another
ball 18-3b/4
– opponent's caddie lifts player's
ball which may or may not have
been out of bounds 18-3b/5

by opponent or fellow-competitor
without authority
– balls inadvertently exchanged by
players after one ball strikes and
moves other 15-1/2.5
– by fellow-competitor 20-1/4
– by opponent 20-1/2
– by opponent after marking it;
player lifts ball-marker and
claims hole; opponent disputes
claim 20-1/3
– by opponent because player
reported wrong score in match
play 9-2/6
– by opponent in four-ball match . . .30-3f/10
– competitor's ball thought to be
wrong ball picked up by fellow-
competitor at competitor's
request 18-2a/16
– fellow-competitor lifts
competitor's ball and sets it
aside; competitor plays ball
from where set aside 15-3b/3

by player (or partner) without
authority
– and cleaned 18-2a/13
– and dropped away from
boundary stake under
obstruction Rule 18-2a/3
– and dropped away from movable
obstruction .18-2a/4
– and re-dropped when it should
have been played as it lay; ball
then lifted again and placed 18-2a/10
– and thrown into pond in anger 18-2a/13.5
– ball in play under stroke-and-
distance procedure lifted when
original ball found and played 15/5
– ball played from teeing ground
of hole to be played later in
round lifted; ball replaced at
spot from which lifted and
played out when that hole
subsequently reached 11-5/5
– ball played from teeing ground
wrongly thought out of bounds
lifted; competitor plays another
ball from tee 18-2a/11
– ball played from within ground
under repair retrieved by player
and relief taken under ground
under repair Rule 18-2a/8
– ball swung at within teeing
ground falls off tee when stroke
just touches it; player lifts,
re-tees and plays ball 18-2a/2
– before being holed out;
opponent then picks up his ball
claiming player loses hole 2-5/3

– competitor picks up second ball,
completes hole with original ball
and plays from next tee 3-3/8
– dropped instead of being replaced.18-2a/9
– due to misunderstanding
referee's instructions. 34-3/3.5
– provisional ball lifted in
erroneous belief original ball in
bounds 27-2b/8
– provisional ball lifted
subsequently becomes ball in play .27-2b/9
– provisional ball lifted;
subsequently becomes ball
in play; ball not replaced but
played from wrong place 27-2b/10

changing relief option
– dropped ball first strikes course
outside where applicable Rule
requires; whether player may
change relief option when
re-dropping. 20-6/2
– dropped ball first strikes course
outside where applicable Rule
requires; whether player may
replace ball in original location . . .20-6/5
– dropped ball rolls to position
requiring re-drop; whether
player may change relief option
when re-dropping 20-2c/5
– dropped ball strikes player;
whether player may change
relief option when re-dropping . . .20-2a/6
– player drops ball in bunker
under first option of Rule
25–1b(ii); player then wishes to
proceed under second option
to drop outside bunker 25-1b/9
– player lifts ball from bunker
intending to drop under first
option of Rule 24–2b(ii); player
then wishes to proceed under
second option to drop outside
bunker 24-2b/5
– point where ball last crossed
margin of lateral water hazard
determined and ball dropped;
point then proves to be wrong
point; whether player may
change relief option when
re-dropping. 26-1/16

competitor invokes Rule 3–3; lifts
and drops original ball 3-3/13

competitor who lifts his and fellow-
competitor's balls inadvertently
exchanges them when replaced. 15-2/4

concessions
– caddie concedes opponent's
next stroke; ball then lifted 2-4/3.5
– fellow-competitor lifts
competitor's ball conceding
next stroke in stroke play 18-4/3
– player concedes match due to
misconception as to opponent's
score at last hole and lifts
opponent's ball 2-4/14
– player concedes opponent's
next stroke and plays before
opponent has opportunity to lift
ball 2-4/8

– player lifts ball in mistaken belief
that next stroke conceded 2-4/3
– whether lifting opponent's ball-
marker considered concession
of next stroke 2-4/5
– whether picking up opponent's
ball considered concession of
next stroke 2-4/4
– player shakes opponent's hand
and picks up opponent's ball in
erroneous belief match over 2-4/17

dropped ball stopped and lifted by
caddie before it rolls into position
where re-drop required 20-2c/4

lie of lifted ball in bunker altered by
another player's stroke 20-3b/1

loose impediments
– affecting lie moved when ball
lifted through the green 23-1/7
– affecting lie removed while ball
lifted through the green 23-1/8
– removed after player lifts ball
deemed unplayable in bunker 13-4/35.7

meaning of
– "directly attributable" in Rules
20–1 and 20–3a 20-1/15
– "good reason to lift" when play
suspended .6-8c/1

player entitled to free relief lifts ball
then chooses not to take relief
– replaces ball and plays it from
original position 18-2a/12
– wishes to proceed under
unplayable ball Rule 18-2a/12.5

position of ball not marked when
lifted for identification, intention
to lift not announced and ball
cleaned beyond extent necessary
to identify it 21/4

provisional ball lifted
– in erroneous belief original ball
in bounds 27-2b/8
– subsequently becomes ball in play .27-2b/9
– subsequently becomes ball in
play; provisional ball not replaced
but played from wrong place 27-2b/10

putting green
– ball knocked aside after marking
position instead of lifted 20-1/22
– ball lifted and thrown into lake;
player then announces ball was
unfit for play 5-3/3.5
– ball lifted because player feared
ball might move. 16-1b/1
– ball lifted by fellow-competitor
who sets it aside; competitor
plays ball from where set aside 15-3b/3
– ball lifted by player while
another ball in motion after
stroke from putting green. 16-1b/4
– ball lifted by player who sets
it aside; opponent's or fellow-
competitor's ball subsequently
strikes player's ball 19-5/1
– ball lifted by player who sets it
aside; played from where set aside .15/4

– ball lifted without its position
being marked in mistaken belief
it is wrong ball. 20-1/1
– ball moved by putter dropped by
player approaching ball to lift it . . .20-1/14
– ball overhanging hole lifted,
cleaned and replaced; ball then
falls into hole. 16-2/0.5
– ball placed ahead of ball-marker
and then rolled or slid back to
original position 16-1a/17
– ball putted from wrong place
lifted and putted from right place. .20-7c/2
– ball replaced while another ball
in motion; player re-lifts ball
thinking moving ball might strike it 16-1b/2
– ball replaced while another ball
in motion; replaced ball deflects
moving ball 16-1b/3
– ball resting against flagstick
lifted before being holed 17-4/1
– ball resting against flagstick
lifted before being holed; others
in match pick up mistakenly
believing player won hole 30-3f/3
– ball returned to spot from
which it was lifted by rolling it
with putter 16-1d/3

referee incorrectly advises player of
loss of hole penalty; both sides lift
their balls; then referee discovers
error 34-2/7

teeing ground
– ball played from teeing ground
of hole to be played later in
round lifted; ball replaced at
spot from which lifted and
played out when that hole
subsequently reached 11-5/5
– ball played within teeing ground
barely moved by first stroke;
player lifts and re-tees ball 18-2a/2

to determine whether embedded in
own pitch-mark or in hole made
by reptile, bird or burrowing animal .20-1/0.7

unfit for play
– ball lifted and thrown into lake;
player then announces ball was
unfit for play 5-3/3.5
– Committee involvement when
opponent, marker or fellow-
competitor not readily available. . .5-3/7
– lifted under another Rule and
cleaned; ball then determined
unfit for play 5-3/6

unplayable ball
– after declaring ball unplayable
and lifting it, player discovers
ball was in ground under repair . . .28/13
– caddie lifts ball considering it
unplayable .18-2a/15
– player deems ball unplayable
in bunker; lifts ball and then
removes loose impediment
from bunker 13-4/35.7
– player entitled to relief without
penalty lifts ball then decides
not to take relief and wishes to

proceed under unplayable ball
Rule 18-2a/12.5

when player entitled to replace
lifted ball in original position 20-6/5

whether player himself must lift ball. . .20-1/0.5

BALL MARK
See also BALL-MARKER; PITCH-MARK

ball embedded in side of hole
– all of ball below lip of hole 16/2
– all of ball not below lip of hole 16/3

removal of dew or frost from line of putt
– incidental to repair of ball marks
on putting green 13-2/35
– other than incidental to repair
of ball marks 16-1a/3

repair of ball mark
– in position to assist opponent. 16-1c/2
– on putting green by caddie
without player's authority;
whether permitted 6-4/10
– partially on and partially off
putting green. 16-1c/1.5
– second time. 16-1c/1
– spike mark on line of putt
repaired during repair of ball mark 16-1a/16
– that damaged hole 16-1a/6

BALL-MARKER
See also BALL MARK; MARKING POSITION
OF BALL; STATUS OF OBJECT

ball lifted from putting green by
player; caddie places ball behind
ball-marker; whether ball in play 20-4/2

ball lifted on putting green placed
ahead of ball-marker and then
rolled or slid back to original
position. 16-1a/17

ball moved in removing ball-marker
after replacing ball 20-3a/1

ball replaced on putting green but
ball-marker not removed; ball
then moves. 20-4/1

ball-marker moved by wind or
casual water during stipulated
round. 20-1/10.5

in position to assist another player. . . .20-1/11

incorrect information causes
opponent to lift ball-marker;
whether lifting of marker
equivalent of next stroke 9-2/5

lie altered by act of marking position
of ball. 20-1/15.5

lifted
– ball marked and lifted by
opponent without player's
authority; player lifts ball-
marker and claims hole;
opponent disputes claim 20-1/3
– by outside agency 20-1/9
– by player mistakenly believing he
won hole 20-1/8

meaning of "directly attributable" in
Rules 20–1 and 20–3a. 20-1/15

method used to
– mark position of ball 20-1/16

– move ball-marker to side. 20-1/16

moved accidentally
– by player after having moved
loose impediments. 20-1/12
– by opponent's caddie 20-1/7
– by player. .20-1/5.5
– by player after having moved
loose impediments. 20-1/12
– by player in process of marking
position of ball 20-1/6

placing object marking position of
ball other than behind ball 20-1/19

player measures clubhead-length to
side of ball and places ball-marker. . .20-1/16

player places ball-marker
approximately two inches behind
ball 20-1/20

position of ball
– marked before obstruction
removed; ball moves when ball-
marker removed 24-1/5
– marked with tee 20-1/17

pressed down by opponent;
whether opponent subject to
penalty 20-1/6.5

tee marking position of player's ball
deflects opponent's ball 20-1/17

whether lifting opponent's ball-
marker considered concession of
next stroke. 2-4/5

BALL OVERHANGING HOLE

falls into hole after
– addressed by player 18-2b/10
– concession of next stroke 2-4/2
– player waits 40 seconds. 16-2/1

fellow-competitor's ball knocked
from lip of hole by competitor not
replaced 3-2/1

flagstick
– ball overhanging hole rolls away
or falls in hole when flagstick
removed 16-2/4
– ball overhanging hole moves and
strikes flagstick being removed . . .16-2/5

knocked away by opponent before
player determines status 16-2/2

lifted cleaned and replaced; ball
then falls into hole 16-2/0.5

player jumps close to hole to cause
overhanging ball to fall in hole 1-2/4

BALL PLACED OR REPLACED

after relief taken from obstruction
for stroke towards green,
obstruction interferes with
stance for necessary sideways
stroke; whether ball should be
re-dropped or placed where it
first struck course 24-2b/9.5

ball dropped instead of placed or
replaced
– ball dropped third time when
placement required after
second drop 20-2c/2

B

– ball dropped when required to
be placed; correction of error 20-6/1
– ball lifted without authority
dropped instead of replaced 18-2a/9

ball placed instead of dropped or
re-dropped
– ball moved accidentally; spot
where ball originally lay not
determinable; player places ball
instead of dropping it 18-2a/21.5
– ball placed on bank of water
hazard instead of dropped to
prevent ball rolling into water 26-1/10
– ball placed when required to be
dropped; correction of error 20-6/1
– when obvious dropped ball will
roll into position where re-drop
will be required 20-2c/3

ball with mud adhering lifted under
Rule not permitting cleaning
rotated when replaced 21/5

ball-marker
– ball moved in removing ball-
marker after replacing ball 20-3a/1
– ball replaced on putting green
but ball-marker not removed;
ball then moves 20-4/1
– lifted by outside agency 20-1/9
– lifted by player mistakenly
believing he won hole 20-1/8
– moved accidentally by player 20-1/5.5
– moved accidentally by player in
process of marking position of ball 20-1/6

competitor invokes Rule 3-3;
second ball played first from spot
where original ball lay 3-3/14

competitor lifts and drops original
ball then places second ball where
original ball lay and plays it 3-3/13

in wrong place
– ball resting against flagstick
moves away from hole when
flagstick removed by player; ball
not placed on lip of hole 17-4/4
– competitor repeatedly replaces
ball nearer hole on green 33-7/6
– on putting green and holed 20-7c/1

lie of ball to be replaced altered
– by act of marking position of ball . 20-1/15.5
– in bunker by another player's
stroke 20-3b/1
– in hazard; lifted to determine
whether unfit for play 5-3/5
– original lie known but spot
where ball originally lay through
the green not determinable 20-3b/4
– original lie known but spot
where ball originally lay in
bunker not determinable 20-3b/6
– original lie not known and spot
where ball originally lay not
determinable; procedure for
player 20-3b/5
– when stepped on accidentally
by player; ball placed in wrong
place and played 18-2a/21.3
– whether original lie may be
"nearest lie most similar" 20-3b/7

Local Rule permitting re-dropping
or placing when dropped ball
embeds in bunker; whether
authorized 33-8/28

meaning of
– "directly attributable" in Rules
20-1 and 20-3a 20-1/15
– "estimated spot" for placing
when specific spot cannot be
determined precisely 20-2c/1.5

method used to
– mark position of ball 20-1/16
– move ball or ball-marker to side . . 20-1/16

moved by wind after being replaced . . 18-1/12

player addresses ball, steps away,
lifts ball and replaces it; ball then
moves 18-2b/8

putting green
– ball lifted by player from putting
green and placed by caddie
behind ball-marker 20-4/2
– ball mistakenly substituted;
error discovered before stroke
made 15-2/2
– ball mistakenly substituted;
error discovered after stroke
made 15-2/3
– ball oscillating in wind pressed
into surface of putting green 1-2/9
– ball overhanging hole lifted,
cleaned and replaced; ball then
falls into hole 16-2/0.5
– ball replaced at rest on putting
green; rolls and strikes another
ball on green 19-5/1.5
– ball replaced at wrong place on
putting green and holed 20-7c/1
– ball replaced on putting green
but ball-marker not removed;
ball then moves 20-4/1
– ball replaced on putting green
while another ball in motion;
player re-lifts ball thinking
moving ball might strike it 16-1b/2
– ball replaced on putting green
while another ball in motion;
replaced ball deflects moving ball . . 16-1b/3
– ball resting against flagstick
moves away from hole when
flagstick removed by player; ball
not placed on lip of hole 17-4/4
– competitor who lifts his and
fellow-competitor's balls
inadvertently exchanges them
when replaced 15-2/4
– competitor repeatedly replaces
ball nearer hole on green 33-7/6
– line drawn or on ball aimed to
indicate line of play when ball
replaced 20-3a/2
– player addresses ball, steps
away, lifts ball and replaces it;
ball then moves 18-2b/8
– player returns ball to spot from
which it was lifted by rolling it
with putter 16-1d/3
– replaced ball rolls into hole 20-3d/1

removal of loose impediments from
spot on which ball to be placed 23-1/6.5

replacement of ball not possible
  – ball dislodged from tree by
    outside agency 18-1/9
  – ball dislodged from tree by player .18-2a/29
  – ball in bunker moves when
    obstruction removed; whether
    player may press ball into sand
    or take relief outside bunker if
    not possible to replace or place
    in bunker not nearer hole 20-3d/2
  – ball in rough moves downward
    when addressed; ball will not
    remain at rest when replaced 20-3d/3
ball on putting green pressed into
  surface to prevent it from moving .1-2/9
spot not determinable
  – ball dislodged from tree;
    replacement not possible 18-2a/29
  – ball lodged in tree knocked
    down by outside agency 18-1/9
  – ball moved accidentally; spot
    where ball originally lay not
    determinable; player places ball
    instead of dropping it 18-2a/21.5
  – ball visible from tee disappears
    while play suspended 6-8d/4
  – ball-marker lifted by outside
    agency 20-1/9
  – ball-marker moved accidentally
    by player 20-1/5.5
  – ball-marker moved accidentally
    by player in process of marking
    position of ball 20-1/6
  – lie of ball through the green
    altered; original lie known
    but spot where ball lay not
    determinable 20-3b/4
  – lie of ball through the green
    (in rough) altered by outside
    agency; original lie not known
    and spot where ball lay not
    determinable 20-3b/5
  – lie of ball in bunker altered;
    original lie known but spot
    where ball lay not determinable . .20-3b/6
  – lie in bunker altered prior to
    resumption of play 6-8d/2
  – spot where ball to be placed not
    exactly determinable 20-2c/1.5
whether
  – ball must be replaced after
    being moved if player wishes to
    proceed under another Rule 20-3a/3
  – player entitled to replace ball in
    original position after dropping
    under Rule .20-6/5
  – player himself must place or
    replace ball 20-3a/0.5

BALL TOUCHED
See also BALL AT REST MOVED
accidentally
  – in removing loose impediments . . .18-2a/31
  – original ball out of bounds;
    ball re-teed under stroke and
    distance touched at address and
    falls off tee .11-3/3
  – with club in bunker or water
    hazard; ball does not move 13-4/12

purposely
  – ball on putting green rotated
    without marking position 18-2a/33
  – half-buried ball rotated for
    identification purposes through
    the green 12-2/2
  – holding ball in place while
    removing obstruction 24-1/4
  – stick or fir cone placed against
    ball to prevent movement when
    loose impediments removed 18-2a/32

BALL UNFIT FOR PLAY
See also UNPLAYABLE BALL
ball breaks into pieces as result of
  striking paved cart path 5-3/4
ball deemed unfit during hole earlier
  in round put back into play later in
  round 5-3/2
ball fit for play deemed unfit during
  play of hole; player substitutes and
  plays another ball 5-3/3
ball thought unfit for play
  – Committee involvement when
    opponent, marker or fellow-
    competitor not readily available. . .5-3/7
  – in bunker or water hazard lifted
    to determine if unfit 5-3/5
  – lifted under another Rule and
    cleaned; ball then determined
    unfit for play 5-3/6
claim that player's ball unfit for play
  disputed by opponent or fellow-
  competitor 5-3/8
loose impediment affecting lie
  – moves when ball lifted to
    determine if unfit 23-1/7
  – removed while ball lifted to
    determine if unfit for play 23-1/8
player claims ball with no visible
  external damage unfit because of
  internal damage 5-3/1
player lifts ball from putting green
  and throws it into lake; announces
  ball was unfit for play 5-3/3.5

BANDAGE
player with injured wrist wears
  elastic bandage 14-3/7
used as aid in gripping 14-3/7

BEACH
treating ocean and beach as through
  the green 33-2a/8

BEES
See also INSECTS
discontinuing play due to bee sting 6-8a/3
interfering with play 1-4/10
meaning of dangerous situation 1-4/11

BOGEY COMPETITION
See also STABLEFORD COMPETITION
competing simultaneously in bogey
  and stroke-play competitions 32-1/1

omitting holes in bogey competition . .32-1/2

recording of lower gross score does
  not affect result of hole. 32-2a/5

when practice between holes
  permitted 7-2/1

BOUNDARY FENCE, LINE, WALL OR STAKES

See also MARKING OR DEFINING COURSE;
OUT OF BOUNDS; STATUS OF OBJECT

ball enters burrowing animal hole
  – in bounds and comes to rest out
    of bounds. 25-1b/24
  – out of bounds and comes to rest
    in bounds. .25-1b/23

ball in underground drainpipe
  – not reachable or identifiable;
    entrance to drainpipe out of
    bounds. 24-3b/1
  – under course; entrance to
    drainpipe out of bounds 24-2b/12

ball in unmarked ditch in bounds;
  opposite margin out of bounds;
  relief options for player 26/3

ball lifted and dropped away from
  boundary stake under obstruction
  Rule. 18-2a/3

boundary altered by unauthorized
  removal of boundary stake. 33-2a/19

dropped ball comes to rest and then
  rolls out of bounds 20-2c/3.5

establishing boundary line inside
  fence on property line 33-2a/15

exposed water pipe adjacent and
  parallel to boundary fence causes
  problems; suggested procedure 33-2a/1

flow of water moves ball
  – into bounds in lateral water
    hazard 26-1/8
  – out of bounds in water hazard 26-1/7

improving position of ball by
  bending boundary fence 13-2/18

internal boundary between holes;
  whether permitted 33-2a/12

Local Rule
  – deeming ball in bounds until
    beyond boundary wall 33-2a/16
  – deeming interior boundary
    fence immovable obstruction;
    whether authorized. 33-8/14
  – to prevent cutting across "dog-
    leg;" deeming ball out of bounds
    that crosses boundary and comes
    to rest on same part of course;
    whether authorized. 33-8/38

marking environmentally-sensitive
  areas; recommendations for
  Committee. 33-8/41

moving ball lying against fence by
  striking other side of fence. 14-1/5

obstruction interferes with
  abnormal stroke; because of
  proximity to boundary fence
  abnormal stroke reasonable in
  circumstances 24-2b/17

part of boundary fence within
  boundary line. 24/4

part of fence off course leans across
  boundary and interferes with swing .13-2/20

provisional ball played from point
  nearer hole than visible original
  ball; player erroneously thought
  original ball out of bounds 27-2c/3

public road defined as out of bounds
  divides course; status of ball
  crossing road 27/20

regression under unplayable ball
  Rule; ball near boundary fence. 28/5

relief from immovable obstruction
  incidentally results in relief from
  boundary fence 24-2b/6

relief from immovable obstruction
  parallel to boundary fence in most
  cases would result in relief from
  boundary fence; recommendation
  for Committee. 33-2a/1

removal of boundary post or stake
  – interfering with swing 13-2/17
  – on line of play; replaced before
    playing 13-2/25

river or other body of water
  adjacent to hole but off club
  property. 33-2a/11

status of
  – angled supports or guy wires
    supporting boundary fence. 24/2
  – boundary stakes having no
    significance in play of hole being
    played. 24/5
  – concrete bases of boundary
    fence posts 24/3
  – displaced boundary stake 33-2a/20
  – gate in boundary fence. 27/18
  – stile attached to boundary fence . .24/1

striking ball interfered with by
  boundary fence with half-inch
  backswing. 14-1/4

when ball inside boundary fence
  considered out of bounds. 27/19

BRIDGE

ball lying on elevated bridge over
  deep hollow; how nearest point of
  relief determined. 24-2b/11

grounding club on bridge in water
  hazard; whether permitted 13-4/30

BUNKER

See also SAND

ball at rest moved
  – accidentally by player in playing
    wrong ball in bunker 18-2a/21
  – after stance taken in bunker 18-2b/3
  – ball falls into bunker when
    person walks nearby 18/10
  – competitor's ball knocked out of
    bunker by fellow-competitor's
    stroke at own ball. 18-4/2
  – competitor's ball played by
    fellow-competitor in bunker not
    replaced. 20-7c/6

– when loose impediment removed .13-4/15

ball believed lost in bunker;
  competitor drops and plays
  substituted ball in bunker; then
  original ball found outside bunker. . .20-7c/3

ball deemed unplayable
  – ball lying on grass-covered
    ground within bunker deemed
    unplayable 28/9
  – dropped in bunker and played;
    ball then discovered to be
    wrong ball 15/14
  – dropped outside bunker under
    option of unplayable ball Rule
    requiring drop in bunker. 28/10
  – in bunker; player lifts ball and
    then removes loose impediment
    from bunker 13-4/35.7
  – through the green dropped in
    hazard 28/4

ball enters burrowing animal hole
  in bunker and comes to rest
  underneath putting green. 25-1b/25

ball hit out of bounds from bunker;
  player's drop under Rule 20–5
  strikes course through the green
  within inches of and not nearer
  hole than spot in bunker where
  previous stroke made 20-5/2

ball overhangs edge of bunker;
  whether considered in bunker 13/3

ball played back into water hazard
  from putting green side of hazard . .26-1/6

bunker totally under repair;
  Committee options. 25/13

casual water
  – ball dropped from casual water
    in bunker at point of maximum
    relief rolls elsewhere 25-1b/6
  – ball dropped in bunker under
    first option of Rule 25–1b(ii);
    player then wishes to proceed
    under second option to drop
    outside bunker 25-1b/9
  – ball lifted from bunker by player
    intending to drop under first
    option of Rule 25–1b(ii); player
    then wishes to proceed under
    second option to drop outside
    bunker 24-2b/5
  – ball required to be dropped in
    bunker, dropped outside bunker
    so it will roll into bunker to
    avoid embedding in bunker 25-1b/7
  – explanation of "maximum
    available relief" from casual
    water in bunker 25-1b/5
  – Local Rule providing relief from
    flooded bunker without penalty
    outside bunker 33-8/27
  – player's options when bunker
    completely covered by casual
    water 25-1b/8
  – touching casual water in bunker
    with club 13-4/7

club accidentally touches ball in
  bunker; ball does not move 13-4/12

embedded ball
  – in bunker lifted to determine
    whether unfit for play 5-3/5
  – in grass bank or face of bunker 25-2/5
  – in lip of bunker 13/4
  – Local Rule permitting
    re-dropping or placing when
    dropped ball embeds in bunker;
    whether authorized. 33-8/28

footprints
  – created retrieving rake
    smoothed by player prior to
    making stroke. 13-4/9
  – made in bunker by referee
    making ruling; whether
    smoothing permitted before
    player plays 13-4/10

grounding club
  – bare earth wall of bunker
    touched on backswing. 13-4/34
  – cane or club used to enter or
    leave bunker when ball lies in
    bunker. 13-4/3.5
  – ground in bunker or water
    hazard touched with club
    while probing for ball believed
    covered by loose impediments. . . .12-1/4
  – leaning on club in bunker while
    waiting to play. 13-4/2
  – loose impediments moved
    and area of intended swing
    improved in hazard; whether
    multiple penalties apply 13-4/28
  – mound made by burrowing
    animal touched with backswing
    in bunker 13-4/5
  – sand in bunker touched during
    backswing .13-4/31
  – sand in bunker touched when
    ball lies outside bunker 13-4/1
  – several practice swings touch
    ground in bunker 13-4/3
  – several practice swings touch
    ground in bunker; player advised
    of breach then makes several
    more practice swings. 1-4/13
  – several practice swings touch
    ground in bunker then player
    makes stroke and ball remains
    in bunker; player makes several
    similar practice swings before
    next stroke .1-4/14
  – solidly embedded stone in
    hazard touched with club during
    backswing .13-4/6

hitting sand in bunker after failing to
  extricate ball
  – in foursome match 29/5
  – in four-ball match; partner's ball
    also in same bunker 30-3f/2
  – in individual play 13-4/35
  – player hits ball from bunker
    into grass bank then hits sand in
    bunker with club; thereafter ball
    rolls back into bunker 13-4/35.5

lie in bunker altered
  – by another player taking stance . . .20-3b/2
  – by another player's stroke. 20-3b/1

  – by another player's stroke;
original lie known but spot
where ball originally lay in
bunker not known 20-3b/6

  – greenkeeper rakes bunker
when player's ball lies therein
improving lie of ball or line of play .13-2/4

  – prior to resumption of play. 6-8d/2

Local Rule
  – allowing free drop outside
bunker or smoothing of sand
in bunker damaged by play of
children; whether authorized. 33-8/9

  – deeming material similar to sand
to have same status as sand 33-8/40

  – deeming partially grass-covered
walls of bunkers to be part of
bunker 33-8/39.5

  – deeming stacked turf bunker
faces (whether grass covered or
earthen) as not closely mown 33-8/39

  – permitting re-dropping or
placing when dropped ball
embeds in bunker; whether
authorized. .33-8/28

  – providing relief without penalty
from flooded bunker 33-8/27

loose impediment
  – accidentally moved in bunker 13-4/13

  – affecting lie of player's ball
moved by another player making
nearby stroke while ball lifted;
whether lie considered altered . . .20-3b/8

  – ball outside bunker; stone in
bunker on line of play pressed
down or removed 13-2/31

  – bunker covered by leaves; player
touches leaves during backswing. .13-4/33

  – competitor lifts loose
impediment in bunker when his
ball and partner's ball in bunker . . .31-8/1

  – ground in bunker or water
hazard touched with club
while probing for ball believed
covered by loose impediments. . . .12-1/4

  – moved as player smoothes sand
for the sole purpose of caring
for the course. 13-4/9.5

  – partner's, opponent's or fellow-
competitor's divot comes to
rest near player's ball in bunker . . .13-4/18

  – pine cone falls from tree and
comes to rest behind ball lying
in bunker 13-4/18.5

  – player accidentally kicks pine
cone into bunker and picks it up . .13-4/14

  – player lifts loose impediment
in bunker when his ball and
partner's ball in bunker 30-3f/1

  – player moves loose impediments
when approaching ball in hazard . .13-4/13.5

  – removal of obstruction in
bunker would move loose
impediment. 1-4/5

  – top of ball in bunker covered
by leaves but part of ball visible
from another angle. 12-1/3

obstruction
  – ball dropped in bunker under
first option of Rule 24–2b(ii);

player then wishes to proceed
under second option to drop
outside bunker 25-1b/9

  – ball lifted from bunker by player
intending to drop under first
option of Rule 24–2b(ii); player
then wishes to proceed under
second option to drop outside
bunker 24-2b/5

  – ball lying on obstruction in bunker.13/5

  – loose impediment in bunker will
move when obstruction lying
against ball removed 1-4/5

  – rake removal causes ball in
bunker to move; whether player
may press ball into sand or take
relief outside bunker if not
possible to replace or place in
bunker not nearer hole 20-3d/2

placing ball instead of dropping
when obvious dropped ball will
roll into bunker requiring re-drop . .20-2c/3

player proceeding under water
hazard Rule drops ball in bunker
or another water hazard 26-1/2

player's lie through the green
affected by sand from partner's,
opponent's, or fellow-
competitor's stroke from bunker . . .13-2/8.5

rake
  – ball in bunker moves when rake
removed; whether player may
press ball into sand or take relief
outside bunker if not possible to
replace or place in bunker not
nearer hole 20-3d/2

  – placed in bunker before stroke
or handle stuck in bunker
before stroke 13-4/0.5

  – thrown into bunker before
stroke. 13-4/21

  – whether rakes should be placed
in or outside bunkers Misc./2

smoothing footprints and/or other
surface irregularities in bunker
  – after ball played from bunker
out of bounds and before ball
dropped in bunker under stroke
and distance 13-4/37

  – after ball played out of bunker;
ball returns to smoothed area
on subsequent stroke 13-4/38

  – after failing to extricate ball
from bunker 13-4/36

  – after lifting ball from bunker
and announcing intention to
proceed under Rule 28a outside
bunker; whether permitted 13-4/35.8

  – after player required to enter
bunker to retrieve ball 13-2/29.3

  – after ball played out of bunker
backwards; smoothed area on
player's new line of play 13-4/37.5

  – after playing out of turn in
match play; opponent recalls
stroke and player must drop ball
in smoothed area 13-4/39

  – created by referee who entered
bunker to give ruling 13-4/10

– created during search for ball in
bunker and ball found in bunker;
whether permitted 13-4/11
– on line of play before stroke
made from outside bunker 13-2/28
– on line of play before stroke
made from outside bunker;
whether multiple penalties apply .1-4/12
– on way back to ball after bunker
walked through to determine
distance to hole or to remove
rake on line of play 13-2/29
– raking by member of
greenkeeping staff improves
players lie or line of play 13-2/4
– whether considered testing
condition of hazard 13-4/0.5

stance
– ball moves after player takes
stance in bunker................18-2b/3
– knocking down side of bunker
to level stance...................13-3/3
– lie in bunker altered by another
player taking stance.............20-3b/2
– taken in bunker then player
changes clubs and takes second
stance.........................13-4/26
– taken in bunker without club 13-4/24

status of
– ball on edge of bunker
overhanging sand 13/3
– ball touching both water hazard
and bunker.....................26/1.5
– dead land crab in bunker 23/6
– half-eaten pear in bunker 23/3
– insect on ball in bunker 23-1/5.5
– sand spilling over margin of bunker 13/1
– stone serving as part of drain in
bunker.........................24/7
– tree in bunker..................13/2

testing condition of bunker
– ball outside bunker; stone in
bunker on line of play pressed
down or removed 13-2/31
– ball played from bunker either
lost or out of bounds; player
tests condition of bunker or
smoothes footprints before
dropping another ball in bunker...13-4/37
– before deciding whether to
make stroke from outside
bunker through it...............13-2/30
– four-ball match play partners
balls lie in same bunker; after one
plays from bunker other makes
practice swing touching sand.....30-3f/2.5
– meaning of "test the condition
of the hazard" in Rule 13-4a....13-4/0.5
– player in bunker takes firm
stance and then smoothes
footprints after deciding to play
different type of shot...........13-4/0.5
– player uses cane or club to enter
or leave bunker when ball lies
therein........................13-4/3.5
– rake placed in bunker or handle
stuck in bunker before stroke 13-4/0.5
– rake thrown into bunker before
stroke.........................13-4/21

– smoothing sand in bunker after
stroke but before ball extricated..13-4/36
– stance in bunker taken without
club............................13-4/24
– taking firm stance in bunker
some distance from ball in
bunker to simulate next stroke ...13-4/0.5
– taking stance in bunker and then
changing clubs...................13-4/26
when ball addressed in hazard 18-2b/2
whether player in match play may
play next stroke from bunker
after result of hole decided 7-2/1.5
wrong ball
– ball deemed unplayable in bunker
dropped in bunker and played; ball
then discovered to be wrong ball ...15/14
– in playing wrong ball in bunker
player accidentally moves own ball 18-2a/21

BURROWING ANIMAL, REPTILE OR BIRD (AND HOLES MADE BY THEM)

See also ABNORMAL GROUND
CONDITIONS; CASUAL WATER; GROUND
UNDER REPAIR; STATUS OF OBJECT;
VIRTUALLY CERTAIN (OR KNOWN)

after five-minute search, ball found
in hole made by burrowing animal,
reptile or bird...................27/7
application of exception to Rule
25–1b when ball lies underground
in hole made by burrowing animal,
reptile or bird...................25-1b/25.5
ball enters burrowing animal, reptile
or bird hole
– in bounds and comes to rest out
of bounds......................25-1b/24
– in bunker and comes to rest
underneath putting green........25-1b/25
– out of bounds and comes to rest
in bounds......................25-1b/23
ball interfered with by hole next to
tree or bush made by burrowing
animal, reptile or bird
– for reasonable sideways stroke ...25-1b/22
– impracticable to make stroke
because of bush 25-b/19
– impracticable to make stroke
because of tree................25-1b/20
– stroke toward green not
reasonable because of position
of tree 25-1b/21
bird nest interferes with stroke 1-4/9
bunker or water hazard
– ball enters burrowing animal,
reptile or bird hole in bunker;
comes to rest underneath
putting green...................25-1b/25
– relief taken from hole made by
burrowing animal, reptile or
bird by player unaware ball in
water hazard; error discovered
before ball played...............25-1b/26
– touching mound made by
burrowing animal, reptile or
bird with backswing............13-4/5

crawfish mound interferes with
stance or swing 25-1b/18

diagram illustrating player unable to
determine nearest point of relief . . .24-2b/3.7

footprint of burrowing animal,
reptile or bird; whether relief
available. 25/19.5

lifting ball
– to determine whether it lies in
hole made by burrowing animal,
reptile or bird; Committee
involvement when opponent,
marker or fellow-competitor
not readily available 5-3/7
– to determine whether it lies in
hole made by reptile, bird or
burrowing animal 20-1/0.7
– with mud adhering to it to
determine whether in hole
made by burrowing animal,
reptile or bird; ball rotated
when replaced 21/5

line of play improved when relief
taken from burrowing animal,
reptile or bird hole 25-1b/3

Local Rule
– declaring severe damage by non-
burrowing animals as ground
under repair 33-8/32.5
– deeming hard conical ant hills as
ground under repair. 33-8/22

nearest point of relief
– determining club, address
position, direction of play and
swing used to identify nearest
point of relief 24-2b/1
– diagrams illustrating nearest
point of relief 25-1b/2
– from cart path in burrowing
animal hole; nearest point of
relief from burrowing animal
hole back on cart path. 1-4/8
– from cart path in burrowing
animal hole; nearest point of
relief from burrowing animal
hole back on cart path; drop
into burrowing animal hole
impracticable 1-4/8.5
– player determines nearest point
of relief but physically unable to
play intended stroke 24-2b/3
– player does not follow
recommended procedure in
determining nearest point of relief 24-2b/2
– player entitled to relief without
penalty from burrowing animal
hole lifts ball; chooses not
to take relief and wishes to
proceed under unplayable ball
Rule 18-2a/12.5

relief taken from hole made by
burrowing animal, reptile or bird
– ball comes to rest in position
where another such hole
interferes. .20-2c/7
– line of play improved 25-1b/3
– player unaware ball in water
hazard; error discovered before
ball played .25-1b/26

snake
– dangerous snake interferes with
play. 1-4/10
– when outside agency; when
loose impediment. 23/6.5

status of
– molehills. .25/23
– footprint of burrowing animal,
reptile or bird 25/19.5
– snake 23/6.5

touching mound made by burrowing
animal, reptile or bird with back
swing in bunker 13-4/5

virtually certain (or known)
unfound ball is in burrowing
animal, reptile or bird hole; drop
made under Rule 25–1c; original
ball then found within five minutes . 25-1c/2.5

CADDIE

acts which caddie may perform 6-4/10

advice
– caddie swings club to show
player how to play shot 8-1/15
– request for advice made in error
to opponent's caddie withdrawn
before advice given. 8-1/17

application of penalty when player
has multiple caddies 6-4/5.5

ball deflected or stopped by caddie
– ball strikes opponent's or
fellow-competitor's bag left
ahead by shared caddie 19-2/8
– ball strikes player's caddie and
comes to rest out of bounds. 19-2/2
– ball strikes player's caddie
standing out of bounds and
comes to rest on course 19-2/3
– ball strikes player's caddie
standing out of bounds and
comes to rest out of bounds. 19-2/4
– competitor's ball strikes golf bag
and then his caddie. 19-2/7
– dropped ball accidentally
deflected by opponent's caddie . . .19-3/2
– dropped ball rolls toward or
into position where re-drop
would be required; caddie stops
ball before it comes to rest. 20-2c/4

ball lifted by caddie
– considering it unplayable
without authority of player. 18-2a/15
– fellow-competitor's caddie
lifts competitor's ball without
authority; caddie subsequently
substitutes another ball when
replaced which competitor plays . .20-1/5
– for identification without
authority of player 18-2a/14
– in water hazard without player's
authority 26-1/9
– opponent's caddie lifts player's
ball after player claims another
ball 18-3b/4
– opponent's caddie lifts player's
ball which may or may not have
been out of bounds 18-3b/5

ball moved by caddie
- of opponent when accidentally
  stepped on .18-3b/3
- shared by members of opposite
  sides in four-ball match 30/1
- shared by opponent's side in
  four-ball match moves player's ball30/2

ball thrown into bounds by outside
agency and played
- caddie aware of action of
  outside agency 15/9
- neither player nor his caddie
  aware of action of outside agency .15/10

casual water mopped up on line of
play by caddie 13-2/34

changed briefly by player in order to
receive advice from new caddie 8-1/26

competitor withdraws during round
and carries fellow-competitor's
clubs for remainder of round 6-4/9

concedes opponent's next stroke;
ball then lifted 2-4/3.5

conditions and restrictions
- acts which caddie may perform . . .6-4/10
- prohibiting use of caddies;
  restricting who may caddie . . . . .App I-C-3

during round caddie gets putter
from clubhouse and gives it to
player; whether player may tell
caddie to take it back and get
different club 4-4a/1

effect of state of match penalty
when one partner has more than
one caddie in four-ball play 30-3/2

incorrect information given by
caddie 9-2/2

meaning of "specific directions" in
definition of caddie 6-4/1

player directs caddie not to search
for ball until others can assist 27/1

player in competition caddies for
another player in same event 6-4/8

putting green
- ball thrown to caddie for
  cleaning comes to rest in lake 15-2/1
- ball-marker moved by
  opponent's caddie accidentally 20-1/7
- caddie practices on or tests
  putting green surfaces of course
  before stroke-play round 7-1b/5
- line of putt damaged accidentally
  by caddie of opponent or
  fellow-competitor 16-1a/13
- shadow cast on putting green by
  caddie to indicate line of putt 8-2b/1
- surface roughened by caddie but
  player does not benefit 16-1d/6
- touched by caddie or partner
  to indicate line of play before
  player chips from off green 8-2b/3
- while attending flagstick caddie
  suggests player aim at foot;
  whether breach of any Rule 8-2b/2

rake held by player's caddie
accidentally stops or deflects
player's ball 19-2/10

shared or double caddie
- ball moved by caddie shared by
  members of opposite sides in
  four-ball match 30/1
- ball moved by caddie shared by
  opponent's side in four-ball
  match 30/2
- ball strikes opponent's or
  fellow-competitor's bag left
  ahead by shared caddie 19-2/8
- ball strikes opponent's or
  fellow-competitor's cart being
  pulled by double caddie 6-4/6
- double caddie informs one
  employer about club used by other. 8-1/12

shields player from sun during stroke .14-2/3

smoothing footprints made in search
for ball in bunker before stroke 13-4/11

status of
- additional clubs carried for
  player during round and
  whether person carrying such
  clubs considered caddie 4-4a/16
- ball placed behind ball-marker
  on putting green by caddie so
  player can assess line of putt 20-4/2
- carts pulled by double caddie 6-4/6
- individual who transports
  player's clubs on motorized golf
  cart or trolley 6-4/2.5

transportation condition breached
by caddie 33-1/9.5

tree branch held back by caddie to
prevent branch from deflecting
dropped ball .20-2a/5

whether ball cleaned by act of
caddie throwing it to player 21/3

whether player has more than one
caddie
- additional person(s) carry items,
  other than clubs, for player 6-4/5.3
- another caddie or friend carries
  clubs while player's caddie
  returns to tee with player's glove. 6-4/4.5
- changing caddies during round 6-4/7
- competitor withdraws
  during round and carries
  fellow-competitor's clubs for
  remainder of round 6-4/9
- player hires boy to carry all of
  player's clubs except putter 6-4/4
- player with clubs transported
  on motorized golf cart hires
  individual to perform all other
  functions of caddie 6-4/3
- umbrella carrier employed in
  addition to caddie 6-4/5

CASUAL WATER
See also ABNORMAL GROUND
CONDITIONS; VIRTUALLY CERTAIN (OR
KNOWN)

ball in casual water
- difficult to retrieve 25-1/1
- within ground under repair 25-1b/11

– within ground under repair; whether player entitled to take relief from both conditions in single procedure................25-1b/11.5

ball not found either in water hazard or casual water overflowing hazard 1-4/7

ball-marker moved by wind or casual water during stipulated round........................20-1/10.5

ball played from area of casual water, lost in same area 25-1c/3

brushing aside or mopping up casual water on line of putt 16-1a/1

bunker completely covered by casual water
– Local Rule providing relief from flooded bunker without penalty outside bunker 33-8/27
– player's options................25-1b/8

changing relief option
– dropped ball first strikes course outside where applicable Rule requires; whether player may change relief option when re-dropping....................20-6/2
– dropped ball first strikes course outside where applicable Rule requires; whether player may replace ball in original location....20-6/5
– dropped ball rolls to position requiring re-drop; whether player may change relief option when re-dropping 20-2c/5
– dropped ball strikes player; whether player may change relief option when re-dropping ...20-2a/6
– player drops ball in bunker under first option of Rule 25–1b(ii); player then wishes to proceed under second option to drop outside bunker 25-1b/9
– player lifts ball from bunker intending to drop under first option of Rule 25–1b(ii); player then wishes to proceed under second option to drop outside bunker 24-2b/5

clarification of point where ball "last entered" casual water when ball lost in condition.................25-1c/1.5

covering teeing ground.............25-1b/4

diagram illustrating player unable to determine nearest point of relief ...24-2b/3.7

explanation of "maximum available relief" from casual water in bunker..25-1b/5

hole surrounded by casual water 33-2d/2

improving line of play when taking relief from casual water 25-1b/3

Local Rule
– permitting re-dropping or placing when dropped ball embeds in bunker; whether authorized.....................33-8/28
– providing relief from flooded bunker without penalty outside bunker 33-8/27

mistaken for water hazard
– original ball played under water hazard Rule 25-1b/12
– substituted ball played under water hazard Rule 25-1b/13

mopping up casual water on line of play 13-2/34

nearest point of relief
– determining club, address position, direction of play and swing used to identify nearest point of relief 24-2b/1
– diagrams illustrating nearest point of relief 25-1b/2
– from cart path in casual water; nearest point of relief from casual water back on cart path....1-4/8
– from cart path in casual water; nearest point of relief from casual water back on cart path; drop into casual water impracticable 1-4/8.5
– player determines nearest point of relief but physically unable to play intended stroke 24-2b/3
– player does not follow recommended procedure in determining nearest point of relief 24-2b/2

on putting green casual water
– intervenes between ball off green and hole 25-1a/2
– nearest point of relief off green ...25-1b/10
– visible when player walks beside line of putt but not visible elsewhere 25/5
– whether player entitled to relief for intervention; ball on green, nearest point of relief off green ..25-1b/10.5

overflow from water hazard 25/2

pitch-mark filled with casual water ...25/3

player entitled to relief without penalty from casual water lifts ball; chooses not to take relief and wishes to proceed under unplayable ball Rule...............18-2a/12.5

player takes relief from area of casual water and ball comes to rest in position where another area of casual water interferes; whether re-drop required 20-2c/7

player unable physically to determine nearest point of relief ...24-2b/3.5

removal of casual water or loose impediments on putting green by Committee......................33/1

removing casual water from hole 16-1a/4

soft, mushy earth 25/1

stroke at ball not practicable due to interference by immovable obstruction and casual water.......24-2b/19

touching casual water in bunker with club.......................13-4/7

virtually certain (or known)
– missing ball either in casual water or high rough; whether player may treat ball as in casual water 25-1c/1

– missing ball is in casual water;
   drop made under Rule 25–1c;
   original ball then found within
   five minutes .25–1c/2.5

water visible as result of undue
   effort with feet. 25/4

CLAIMS AND DISPUTES

See also COMMITTEE; PENALTIES IMPOSED,
MODIFIED OR WAIVED BY COMMITTEE;
REFEREE

after competition closed in stroke play
   – change to weight of club during
      round discovered after close of
      competition 34–1b/4
   – competitor correctly advised
      he incurred penalty by fellow-
      competitor; competitor
      disagrees and fails to include
      penalty in returned score card;
      Committee advised of incident
      after close of competition. 34–1b/1.5
   – failure to sign score card
      discovered. 34–1b/2
   – omission of penalty stroke in
      competitor's score discovered. . . .34–1b/1
   – play of wrong ball not rectified
      in stroke play discovered. 34–1b/3
   – wrong score in qualifying round
      discovered during match play 34–1b/7

after match played to conclusion
   – breach of 14-club Rule
      discovered after match
      concluded but before result
      officially announced 2–5/5.5
   – hole inadvertently omitted in
      match; error discovered after
      match concluded 2–1/3
   – incorrect information on
      penalty applicable to player
      given by opponent; error
      discovered after match result
      announced; player then makes
      claim. 2–5/10
   – player concedes match after
      winning it when opponent
      lodges invalid claim regarding
      strokes taken 2–4/15
   – player omits penalty stroke
      when advising opponent as to
      score for hole; error discovered
      after match conceded by
      opponent. 9–2/10
   – valid timely claim made after
      concession of match 2–4/16
   – wrong handicap used in match
      by mistake; error discovered
      after result officially announced. .6–2a/5
   – wrong information given after
      play of last hole; claim made
      after result announced 2–5/11

assisting ball lifted by opponent
   replaced on request; player's ball
   then strikes opponent's ball and
   opponent lodges claim 22/5

breach of Rule by opponent
   – discussed between player and
      opponent; penalty not applied 1–3/4

– neither player nor opponent
   aware; penalty not applied 1–3/5
– procedure for valid claim. 2–5/2

Committee error
   – disqualification penalty wrongly
      applied to winner of event;
      error discovered after two
      other competitors play off for
      first place. .34–1b/5
   – pace of play condition breached;
      referee does not penalize player
      believing he had already lost hole. .34–3/2
   – player in match plays based on
      incorrect ruling; procedure for
      player when error discovered 34–3/3
   – winner's score not posted due
      to Committee error 34–1b/6
   – wrong ball penalty not included
      in competitor's score due
      to incorrect referee ruling;
      during subsequent round error
      discovered and penalty applied
      retroactively; competitor objects .34–3/1

determination of honor at next tee
   following disputed hole. 10–1a/2

disagreement with ruling 34–2/4
   – player advised of breach of
      Rule disagrees with ruling and
      breaches same rule again prior
      to stroke 1–4/13
   – marker refuses to sign score
      card after dispute resolved in
      favor of competitor 6–6a/4
   – second ball played despite
      adverse ruling 3–3/2
   – whether player demand
      Committee consider matter if
      player disagrees with referee's
      decision 34–2/4

failure to include penalty in score
   – competitor correctly advised
      he incurred penalty by fellow-
      competitor; competitor
      disagrees and fails to include
      penalty in returned score card;
      Committee advised of incident
      after close of competition. 34–1b/1.5
   – penalty stroke omitted when
      score card returned. 34–1b/1
   – player advancing to fourth
      round in match play disqualified
      for wrong score in qualifying
      round; options for Committee. . . .34–1b/8
   – players in match unaware
      penalty incurred 1–3/5

handicap
   – extra handicap stroke taken
      by mistake in handicap match;
      status of late claim 2–5/13
   – failure to determine handicaps
      prior to start of match 6–2a/1
   – handicap stroke claimed after
      hole conceded 6–2a/4
   – handicap stroke wrongly
      claimed at hole; error
      discovered before hole completed 6–2a/3
   – wrong handicap knowingly used
      in stroke play; error discovered
      after competition closed. 6–2b/2

– wrong handicap recorded on
  score card by Committee error;
  discovered before competition
  closed. 6-2b/3.5
– wrong handicap used in match
  by mistake; error discovered
  after result officially announced. . .6-2a/5
– wrong handicap used in
  stroke play by mistake; error
  discovered after competition
  closed. 6-2b/1

invalid claim
– not disputed 2-5/5
– player concedes hole on basis of
  invalid claim. 2-4/12
– player concedes match after
  winning it when opponent
  lodges invalid claim regarding
  strokes taken 2-4/15
– player plays extra hole believing
  match all square; error
  discovered and claim made after
  player loses match on 20th hole. . .2-5/6
– player under impression match
  is over later realizes it was all
  square and makes claim. 2-3/1
– rightful winner of match agrees
  to play extra holes thinking
  match all square; after losing
  match player realizes wrong
  information was given on 18th
  hole and opponent should have
  lost that hole and match 2-5/7
– wrong information given about
  strokes made upon completion
  of last hole; error realized and
  claim made after result
  announced. 2-5/11

late claim
– after playing wrong ball, player
  wins hole with original ball;
  opponent does not lodge claim
  during hole; claim lodged next day.2-5/4
– believing match is all square
  after 18 holes, players play extra
  hole without timely claim being
  made 2-5/6
– breach of 14-club Rule
  discovered after match
  concluded; claim made before
  result officially announced 2-5/5.5
– extra stroke taken by mistake
  in handicap match; status of late
  claim. 2-5/13
– foursome side drives for
  three holes in wrong order;
  opponents make claim during
  third hole. .29-2/2
– hole won with wrong ball
  and partner picks up; error
  discovered at next hole. 30-3c/2
– hole won with wrong ball;
  error discovered at next hole;
  opponent claims previous hole . . .9-2/8
– incorrect procedure agreed to
  in error by player and opponent;
  whether valid claim can be made
  after procedure followed 2-5/8.5
– match conceded by winning
  player after opponent lodges

invalid claim regarding strokes
  taken 2-4/15
– penalty stroke omitted when
  player advises opponent of
  score for hole; error discovered
  after match conceded by
  opponent. 9-2/10
– player agreeing with opponent
  that hole halved realizes after
  match he won hole and should
  have won match; player then
  makes claim. 2-5/9
– player given wrong information
  by opponent agrees to play
  extra
  holes and loses match; after
  result posted player discovers
  he should
  have won match without playing
  extra holes and makes claim to
  Committee .2-5/7
– player unaware of penalty
  incurred wins hole and match;
  after result posted spectator
  informs opponent who makes
  claim 2-4/15
– players under impression match
  is over later realize it was all
  square 2-3/1
– rightful winner of match makes
  no claim and agrees to play
  extra holes .2-5/7
– wrong information given after
  play of last hole; claim made
  after result announced 2-5/11

match discontinued by agreement
due to rain; player subsequently
wishes to resume
– opponent refuses although
  course playable. 6-8a/5
– opponent refuses on ground
  course unplayable. 6-8a/6

player plays partner's ball; error
discovered after opponents have
played next strokes. 30-3c/4

player reaching third round of
match play disqualified for
agreeing to waive Rules in first-
round match. 34-1a/1

players in single match accompanied
by third party; one player objects . . .2/1

player's claim ball unfit for play
disputed by opponent. 5-3/8

result of hole in dispute
– ball marked and lifted by
  opponent without player's
  authority; player lifts ball-
  marker and claims hole;
  opponent disputes claim 20-1/3
– determination of honor at next
  tee following disputed hole. 10-1a/2
– hole won with wrong ball;
  error discovered at next hole;
  opponent claims previous hole . . .9-2/8
– player and opponent agree
  hole halved; after match result
  posted player realizes he won
  hole and should have won
  match; player then makes claim . . .2-5/9

– player lifts ball before holing
out; opponent then picks up his
ball claiming player loses hole 2-5/3
– players on opposite sides
exchange balls during play of
hole and their partners pick up;
error discovered at next hole 30-3c/3
– player with ball not found
concedes hole; ball then found
in hole 2-4/11

score card
– competitor correctly advised
he incurred penalty by fellow-
competitor; competitor
disagrees and fails to include
penalty in returned score card;
Committee advised of incident
after close of competition. 34-1b/1.5
– failure to sign score card
discovered after competition
closed. 34-1b/2
– marker refuses to sign
competitor's score card after
dispute resolved in favor of
competitor 6-6a/4
– penalty stroke omitted on score
card returned by player 34-1b/1
– wrong handicap recorded on
score card by Committee error;
discovered before competition
closed. 6-2b/3.5

second ball played in match play;
whether permitted 3-3/9

spectator says ball moved by
outside agency; player not
sure; procedure for player if
Committee decision not possible
in reasonable time 18-1/4

state of match misunderstood
– players leave last green under
impression match over later
realize it was all square;
whether late claim valid. 2-3/1
– players mistakenly believe match
all square after 18 holes and play
extra hole without making claim . . 2-5/6
– rightful winner of match makes
no claim and agrees to play
extra holes 2-5/7
– true state of match not
determinable. 34-3/5

when match result "officially
announced" 2-5/14

whether competitor played from
outside teeing ground disputed at
end of round. 34-3/4

wrong ruling accepted by players
from person not on Committee;
match played to conclusion based
on ruling; whether Committee
should consider late claim 2-5/8

CLEANING BALL

acts which caddie may perform;
cleaning ball 6-4/10

ball
– dropped away from obstruction
immediately after resumption
of play; whether player may lift,
clean and place ball under Rule
6–8d(ii) 6-8d/3
– lifted from putting green thrown
to caddie for cleaning comes to
rest in lake; player substitutes
another ball 15-2/1
– lifted without authority and
cleaned. 18-2a/13
– overhanging hole lifted, cleaned
and replaced; ball then falls into
hole 16-2/0.5
– rubbed on putting green for
cleaning purposes; whether
putting green tested. 16-1d/5
– thought unfit for play lifted
under another Rule and cleaned;
ball then determined unfit for play. 5-3/6

ball lifted under Rule not permitting
cleaning
– determining whether ball
embedded in own pitch-mark or
lies in hole made by reptile, bird
or burrowing animal 20-1/0.7
– half-buried ball in rough
rotated instead of lifted for
identification purposes 12-2/2
– mud adheres to ball when lifted;
whether ball may be replaced
with mud facing different
direction 21/5
– position of ball lifted for
identification not marked,
intention to lift not announced,
and ball cleaned beyond extent
necessary to identify it 21/4

caddie places ball lifted for cleaning
immediately behind player's ball-
marker on putting green so player
can assess line of putt; whether
ball in play 20-4/2

paint from course marking line
adheres to ball; whether player
may remove it 21/1

sand from another player's stroke
from bunker affects player's
lie through the green; equity
procedure entitling player to
clean ball and remove sand
deposited by stroke. 13-2/8.5

specimen Local Rule allowing
cleaning of ball in specified areas
of course other than putting
green because of significant
amounts of mud adhering to balls . . App 1-B-4b

whether action constitutes cleaning
of ball
– caddie throws ball to player 21/3
– grass adhering to ball removed . . . 21/2
– half-buried ball in rough
rotated instead of lifted for
identification purposes 12-2/2
– insect on ball removed. 23-1/5
– rubbing ball on putting green
for cleaning purposes; whether
putting green tested. 16-1d/5

CLOSE OF COMPETITION

See also COMMITTEE; CONDITIONS OF
COMPETITION; HANDICAP COMPETITION
AND HANDICAP STROKES; PENALTIES
IMPOSED, MODIFIED OR WAIVED BY
COMMITTEE; SCORES AND SCORE CARDS

Committee errors and mistakes
  – Committee determines
    player's score for hole with
    incorrect ball played under Rule
    3–3; whether error may be
    corrected if discovered after
    close of competition 34-3/3.9
  – disqualification penalty wrongly
    imposed by Committee on
    event winner; error discovered
    after completion of play-off
    between two other competitors. .34-1b/5
  – handicap incorrectly calculated
    and posted by Committee;
    wrong competitor named event
    winner 6-2b/3
  – handicap misapplied by
    Committee to qualifying score;
    incorrect match-play draw posted 33-5/3
  – miscalculation of correct net
    score or application of wrong
    handicap results in wrong
    competitor receiving prize 33-5/2
  – players wrongly advised as to
    condition regarding handicaps 33-1/12
  – winner's score not posted. 34-1b/6
  – wrong handicap applied results
    in another competitor receiving
    prize 33-5/2
  – wrong handicap mistakenly
    recorded on score card 6-2b/3.5

Committee procedures when
  player in match play disqualified
  for wrong score in qualifying round .34-1b/8

player errors and mistakes
  discovered after close of competition
  – competitor correctly advised
    he incurred penalty by fellow-
    competitor; competitor
    disagrees and fails to include
    penalty in returned score card 34-1b/1.5
  – competitor failed to sign score
    card 34-1b/2
  – marker not appointed by
    Committee signed score cards. . . .6-6b/5
  – penalty stroke omitted when
    score card returned. 34-1b/1
  – play of wrong ball in stroke play
    not rectified 34-1b/3
  – player disqualified for wrong
    score in qualifying round
    discovered during match play 34-1b/7
  – weight of club changed during
    round. 34-1b/4
  – wrong handicap in match play
    mistakenly used by player 6-2a/5
  – wrong handicap in stroke play
    knowingly used. 6-2b/2
  – wrong handicap in stroke
    play recorded by partner in
    foursome competition. 6-2b/2.5
  – wrong handicap in stroke play
    used by mistake 6-2b/1

CLUBHOUSE OR HALF-WAY HOUSE

due to inoperable motorized cart
  players discontinue play and
  return to clubhouse; whether
  reason for discontinuance
  satisfactory 6-8a/4
entering clubhouse or half-way
  house for refreshment during round 6-8a/2.7
watching television for 45 minutes
  after nine holes 6-8a/1
window of clubhouse opened and
  ball played through window 24-2b/14

CLUB(S)

See also GRIPS AND GRIPPING;
GROUNDING CLUB; STATUS OF OBJECT;
STROKE

another caddie or friend carries
  clubs while player's caddie returns
  to tee with players glove. 6-4/4.5
attachment to grip of club of player
  with artificial arm 14-3/15
ball deflected or stopped by clubs
  belonging to different side but
  carried in same bag 19-2/5
ball moved by putter dropped by
  player approaching ball to lift it 20-1/14
borrowing
  – another player's club for
    measuring purposes. 20/2
  – another player's putter during
    round to make practice stroke. . . .4-4a/13
  – fellow-competitor's putter 4-4a/12
  – partner's putter 4-4b/1
breach of 14-club Rule
  – additional clubs carried for
    player by person walking with
    group 4-4a/16
  – borrowing fellow-competitor's
    putter. 4-4a/12
  – borrowing partner's putter. 4-4b/1
  – clarification of match-play penalty .4-4a/9
  – clarification of stroke-play penalty 4-4a/10
  – discovered after match
    concluded but before result
    officially announced 2-5/5.5
  – excess club declared out of play
    before round and placed on
    floor of golf cart 4-4c/1
  – excess club discovered before
    player plays from 2nd tee but
    after opponent or fellow-
    competitor plays 4-4a/11
  – excess club put in player's golf
    bag after group's starting time
    and before player begins round;
    error discovered after player
    starts round .4-4a/6
  – fellow-competitor inadvertently
    uses and thereafter carries
    another competitor's club 4-4a/5
  – in concurrent four-ball and
    individual stroke play. 31/1
  – in concurrent four-ball and
    single match play. 30-3/1

– player discovers he has 15 clubs
at 2nd hole; opponent refuses
to apply penalty 1-3/4

breaking during swing
– club breaks during backswing;
swing completed 14/2
– club breaks during downswing;
swing completed but misses ball;
clubhead falls and moves ball 14/5
– club breaks during downswing;
swing stopped short of ball;
clubhead falls and moves ball 14/4
– clubhead separates from shaft
on downswing. 14/3

caddie hires boy to carry all of
player's clubs except putter 6-4/4

club placed beside or behind ball to
indicate line of play 8-2a/2

club used as flagstick to mark
position of hole 17-3/6

clubhead cleaned in water of water
hazard when ball lies therein 13-4/40

competitor withdraws during round
carries fellow-competitor's clubs
for remainder of round. 6-4/9

components of clubs (heads
and shafts) assembled during
stipulated round; application of
Rule 4–4 . . . . 4-4a/15

concurrent four-ball and individual
stroke play; application of
penalties when one partner
breaches Rule 4–4 . . . . 31/1

concurrent four-ball and single matches
– player makes stroke with non-
conforming club; whether
player's partner disqualified in
his single match. 30-3/1
– player starts round with 15
clubs; whether four-ball partner
incurs penalty in single match. 30-3/1

condition of competition requiring use of
– clubs conforming with groove
and punch mark specifications
effective January 1, 2010 . . . . 4-1/1
– driving club listed on current
List of Conforming Driver Heads . App I-C-1a

damaged club; whether
replacement
permitted
– club broken due to habit of
hitting head of club on ground 4-3/9
– club broken on practice ground
while play suspended 4-3/11
– club broken while used as cane 4-3/7
– club damaged in normal course
of play breaks into pieces when
repaired 4-3/3
– club rendered unfit for play by
outside agency or opponent's side 4-3/9.5
– material in head of metal wood
club broken away from shell 4-1/2
– player starting with 13 clubs
breaks club in anger and
replaces it 4-3/8

diagram illustrating player unable to
determine nearest point of relief . . . 24-2b/3.7

excess club
– club broken into pieces prior to
round discovered in player's bag
during round. 4-4a/14
– club of player put in another
player's bag by mistake during
suspension of play 4-4a/5.5
– declared out of play before
round and placed on floor of
golf cart 4-4c/1
– declared out of play during
round; whether it may replace
club damaged later in round 4-4c/2
– discovered before player
plays from 2nd tee but after
opponent or fellow-competitor
plays 4-4a/11
– lost club of another player
carried in player's bag 4-4a/8
– put in player's golf bag after
group's starting time and before
player begins round; error
discovered after player starts
round 4-4a/6

face of club
– applying chalk; whether
permitted 4-2/3
– applying saliva; whether
permitted 4-2/4
– ball adheres to face of club after
stroke. 1-4/2
– ball falls on club face after stroke
and sticks to mud thereon 14-4/1
– ball strikes pipeline and on
rebound deflects off face of club . . 14-4/2
– condition requiring clubs
conforming with groove and
punch mark specifications
effective January 1, 2010 . . . . 4-1/1

grip
– attachment to grip of club of
player with artificial arm 14-3/15
– changing clubs because of wet
grips 4-3/5
– holding ball in hand against grip
when putting. 14-3/6

"grounded"
– when club considered grounded
in grass. 18-2b/5
– when club considered grounded
in grass in water hazard. 13-4/8

indicating alignment or distance
– player aligns partner's club
before stroke 14-2/1
– placing club on ground to align feet 8-2a/1
– placing club on ground to
indicate distance for pitch-shot . . . 8-2a/3

leaning on club in hazard while
waiting to play 13-4/2

making stroke with back of clubhead . . 14-1/1

marking position of hole with club
instead of flagstick 17-3/6

meaning of
– damage sustained in "normal
course of play" 4-3/1
– "repair" 4-3/2

measuring
- borrowed club used for
  measuring purposes...........20/2
- club to be used in measuring......20/1
- club-lengths directly through
  fence, tree or wall, or across
  ditch.......................20-2b/2

nearest point of relief
- club used to determine nearest
  point not used for next stroke....24-2b/4
- determining club, address
  position, direction of play and
  swing used to identify nearest
  point of relief.................24-2b/1
- dropped ball rolls nearer
  condition than nearest point
  of relief; whether re-drop
  necessary if player changes clubs
  and condition no longer
  interferes.....................20-2c/0.7
- diagrams illustrating nearest
  point of relief.................25-1b/2
- player determines nearest point
  of relief but physically unable to
  play intended stroke............24-2b/3
- player does not follow
  recommended procedure in
  determining nearest point of
  relief.........................24-2b/2
- player takes relief from
  condition; whether re-drop
  required if condition interferes
  for stroke with club not used to
  determine nearest point of relief..20-2c/0.8

non-conforming club
- carried in four-ball match played
  with concurrent single match....30-3/1
- material applied to clubhead to
  reduce glare or for protection;
  whether permitted..............4-1/5
- referee rules non-conforming
  club conforms with Rules;
  player uses club...............34-3/1.5

partners' clubs carried in one bag....4-4a/4

player holds grip of club with one
  hand and strikes shaft with other
  hand to move ball; whether ball
  fairly struck at................14-1/6

player steadies himself with club in
  one hand and putts with other
  hand...........................14-3/9

player uses club or cane to enter or
  leave hazard when ball lies in hazard.13-4/3.5

playing characteristics of club changed
- lead tape applied to clubhead or
  shaft before start of round.......4-1/4
- lead tape applied to clubhead or
  shaft during round.............4-2/0.5
- material applied to clubhead to
  reduce glare or for protection....4-1/5
- other than in normal course
  of play; modifying penalty for
  holing short putt with such club..4-3/4
- weight of club changed during
  round; breach discovered after
  competition closed.............34-1b/4
- while play suspended; error
  discovered before play resumed .4-2/2

putting with wrong end of putter.....14-1/3

replacement of club; whether
  permitted
- because of wet grip 4-3/5
- between rounds in 36-hole match.4-4a/2
- broken on practice ground
  while play suspended...........4-3/11
- for stroke-play play-off 4-3/12
- lost during round..............4-3/10

returning to tee to retrieve
  forgotten club; whether play
  unduly delayed.................6-7/1

status of
- additional clubs being carried
  for player during round and
  whether person carrying such
  clubs considered caddie 4-4a/16
- chipper.......................4-1/3
- components of clubs (heads and
  shafts) assembled and/or carried
  during stipulated round.........4-4a/15
- individual who transports
  player's clubs on motorized golf
  cart or trolley.................6-4/2.5

stopped on downswing by agency
  other than player................14/1

striking ball with billiard-type or
  shuffleboard motion.............14-1/2

tape applied to player's hand or
  glove; whether permitted.........14-3/8

touching casual water in bunker
  with club......................13-4/7

training club or swing aid
- carrying weighted training club ..4-4a/7
- stretching device used to make
  practice swing.................14-3/10.5
- weighted headcover or
  "doughnut" on club used to
  make stroke or practice swing....14-3/10

used as plumb line.................14-3/12

using more than one club to make
  stroke at ball..................14-1/7

when club considered added........4-4a/1

when club considered grounded in
  grass in water hazard 13-4/8

COMMITTEE

See also CLAIMS AND DISPUTES; CLOSE
OF COMPETITION; CONDITIONS OF
COMPETITION; COURSE UNPLAYABLE
OR CLOSED; DISCONTINUANCE AND
RESUMPTION OF PLAY; DOUBT REGARDING
FACTS; LOCAL RULES; MARKING OR
DEFINING COURSE; OBSERVER; PENALTIES
IMPOSED, MODIFIED OR WAIVED BY
COMMITTEE; REFEREE

attachment to grip of club of player
  with artificial arm; Committee
  deems attachment gives player
  undue advantage 14-3/15

ball moved out of bounds by flow of
  water in water hazard; suggested
  preventative measure 26-1/7

canceling round in stroke play
- guidelines on whether to cancel
  round..........................33-2d/1

– incorrect information on
Rules given by Committee
to competitor(s) significantly
affects competition result........34-3/1.5

Committee decision required when
doubt exists as to questions of fact
– ball cleaned through act of
caddie throwing it to player 21/3
– ball deliberately deflected or
stopped through the green by
spectator......................19-1/4.1
– ball falls into bunker when
person walks nearby 18/10
– ball knocked away along line
of putt after player concedes
opponent's stroke 16-1d/2
– ball lifted by opponent's caddie
when ball may have been out of
bounds.........................18-3b/5
– ball moved after player takes
practice swings touching grass
behind ball.....................18-2a/30
– ball moved in water in water
hazard after stance taken 14-6/1
– ball moves after removal of
nearby loose impediment 18-2a/30.5
– ball played from putting green
touches but does not move
other ball on green 19-5/4
– ball played out of bunker, player
grounds club, ball rolls back into
bunker.........................13-4/35.5
– ball strikes hole-liner pulled out
with flagstick...................17/8
– ball visible from tee disappears
or moved by outside agency
while play suspended............6-8d/4
– balls inadvertently exchanged by
competitors at unknown place....15-1/2
– cleaning clubhead in water
hazard when ball lies in hazard....13-4/40
– dispute as to whether
competitor played outside
teeing ground 34-3/4
– guidelines for resolving
questions of fact................34-3/9
– hole at which wrong ball played
unknown.......................15-1/3
– meaning of "known or virtually
certain" in Rules 18–1, 24–3,
25–1c and 26–1 ....26-1/1
– player alters path of clubhead
to avoid striking ball; whether
player intended to make stroke ..14/1.5
– player proceeds on referee's
ruling based on available facts;
subsequent facts prove ruling
incorrect.......................34-3/7
– player proceeds on referee's
ruling based on player's version
of facts; player's version later
found incorrect.................34-3/8
– player uses half-inch backswing;
whether ball pushed or fairly
struck at.......................14-1/4
– provisional ball not
distinguishable from original ball ..27/11
– score card alleged incorrect by
spectators.....................6-6d/5

– true state of match not
determinable..................34-3/5

Committee error
– Committee determines player's
score for hole with incorrect
ball played under Rule 3–3;
error discovered after score
card returned; whether error
may be corrected...............34-3/3.9
– competitor wins competition
with incorrect handicap due
to Committee error; error
discovered several days later 6-2b/3
– incorrect ruling; correction of 34-3/1
– incorrect ruling; whether player
should be exempt from penalty
and for what duration 34-3/1.5
– incorrect ruling puts player
in stroke play at serious
disadvantage 34-3/3.3
– misapplication of handicap by
Committee affects match-play
draw; error discovered during
first-round matches.............33-5/3
– pace of play condition breached;
referee does not penalize player
believing he had already lost hole. 34-3/2
– play of wrong ball not rectified
in stroke play; Committee did
not ask if error rectified; error
discovered after competition
closed.........................34-1b/3
– play of wrong ball not rectified
on advice of referee.............33-7/5
– player in match plays based on
incorrect ruling; procedure for
player when error discovered 34-3/3
– player incorrectly advised to
continue play with provisional
ball by referee..................34-3/3.7
– referee authorises player to
infringe Rule 34-2/2
– referee incorrectly advises
player of loss of hole penalty;
both sides lift their balls; then
referee discovers error..........34-2/7
– referee incorrectly advises
player to cancel and replay stroke .34-3/1.3
– referee reverses ruling made at
last hole of match after players
leave putting green..............34-2/5
– referee reverses ruling made on
previous hole after play of next
hole begun.....................34-2/6
– winner wrongly disqualified;
error discovered after two
other competitors play off for
first place......................34-1b/5
– winner's score not posted due
to Committee error 34-1b/6
– wrong form of play (four-ball
instead of foursome) used in
match as result of Committee
error 6-1/1
– wrong handicap applied by
Committee results in player not
receiving prize 33-5/2
– wrong handicap recorded on
score card by Committee; error

discovered before competition
closed.........................6-2b/3.5
— wrong handicap used due to
Committee misinformation 33-1/12
Committee intervention
— ball assisting fellow-competitor
on putting green; procedure for
refereee if competitor does not
lift ball 22/7
— ball thought unfit for play;
Committee involvement when
opponent, marker or fellow-
competitor not readily available. . .5-3/7
— competitor correctly advised
he incurred penalty by fellow-
competitor; competitor
disagrees and fails to include
penalty in returned score card;
Committee advised of incident
after close of competition.......34-1b/1.5
— hole damaged; Committee
involvement required if referee
readily available 16-1a/6
— referee finds player's original
ball; player prefers to continue
with provisional ball............27-2/2
— referee warns player not to
infringe Rule 34-2/3
— retroactive appointment of
marker by Committee..........33-1/5
Committee options
— bunker totally under repair......25/13
— casual water covering entire
teeing ground 25-1b/4
— casual water surrounding hole 33-2d/2
— relocating hole due to severity
of location during stroke-play
round........................33-2b/1.5
— relocating hole when damaged
after ball already positioned
nearby on putting green 33-2b/2
— relocating holes and/or tee-
markers during stroke-play
round, general 33-2b/1
— tree falls onto fairway during
stipulated round...............25/9.5
competitor plays second ball
without announcing intention
to invoke Rule 3–3 and fails to
report facts to Committee 3-3/6.5
concurrently playing four-ball and
single matches 30-3/1
concurrently playing match and
stroke play
— competitor in stroke-play
event without marker joins
two players engaged in match;
whether breach of combining
match and stroke play 33-1/5
— players in single match
concurrently compete in
stroke-play event..............33-1/6
conditions of competition
— altering conditions after
competition starts..............33-1/1
— condition regarding footwear.....33-1/14
— golf cart used in competition;
whether permitted 33-1/8

— making competitors responsible
for adding scores 33-1/7
— number of holes of stroke-play
competition reduced during
competition 33-1/2
— prohibiting players from having
person(s) in addition to caddie
carry items, other than clubs,
for them......................6-4/5.3
— restriction on which partner in
foursome competition may play
from 1st tee...................33-1/3.5
— transportation condition
breached by caddie 33-1/9.5
defaulting player plays informal
match with opponent and wins 2-4/18
defining bounds, margins and
marking course
— attachment to flagstick to
indicate position of hole on green .17/1
— boundary altered by
unauthorized removal of
boundary stake................33-2a/19
— declaring area as ground under
repair during round 33-2a/2
— declaring damage due to heavy
rain and traffic ground under
repair during round 33-2a/3
— deeming area of adjoining
hole out of bounds for play of
particular hole but not for play
of other holes.................33-2a/14
— deeming area of adjoining
hole out of bounds for stroke
played from teeing ground only;
whether authorized............33-2a/14
— deeming body of water as both
water hazard and lateral water
hazard 33-2a/7
— deeming water hazard as lateral
water hazard in play from
forward tee by Local Rule.......33-2a/6
— different colored flags used to
indicate position of hole on green .17/2
— displaced boundary stake 33-2a/20
— exposed water pipe adjacent
and parallel to boundary fence
causes problems; suggested
procedure.....................33-2a/1
— half of double green serving hole
not being played 25-3/1
— map of putting green indicating
hole position displayed at tee....33/6
— marking island green 33-2a/10
— part of lateral water hazard
where impossible to drop not
nearer hole 33-2a/9
— river or other body of water
adjacent to hole but off club
property 33-2a/11
— treating ocean and beach as
through the green 33-2a/8
— where to place lines or stakes
defining margin of water hazard. . .33-2a/4
disagreement with ruling
— player advised of breach of
Rule disagrees with ruling and
breaches same rule again prior
to stroke 1-4/13

– marker refuses to sign score card after dispute resolved in favor of competitor 6-6a/4
– second ball played despite adverse ruling 3-3/2
– whether player demand Committee consider matter if player disagrees with referee's decision 34-2/4

discontinuance and resumption of play
– competitor refuses to start or picks up because of weather conditions; round subsequently canceled. 33-2d/3
– competitors playing hole when play suspended discontinue play immediately but then complete hole before Committee orders resumption of play 6-8b/1
– drop from obstruction made immediately after resumption of play; whether player may lift and clean or substitute then place ball under Rule 6–8d(ii) 6-8d/3
– explanation of "good reason to lift" when play suspended 6-8c/1
– guidelines on whether to cancel round 33-2d/1
– play suspended by Committee; competitor does not resume play at time ordered by Committee .6-8b/6
– player claiming danger from lightning, refuses to resume play when resumption ordered by Committee .6-8b/5
– player discontinues play due to physical problem 6-8a/3
– player drops ball after play suspended for dangerous situation6-8b/8
– player plays out of turn in match play after play suspended by Committee and after opponent discontinues play 6-8b/3.5
– players discontinue play due to inoperable motorized cart 6-8a/4
– players discontinue play for refreshments 6-8a/2.5
– when players must be present for resumption of play 6-8b/9

dispute as to whether competitor played from outside teeing ground . .34-3/4

flagstick; whether tapered or varying diameters permitted 17/3

footprints made in bunker by referee making ruling; whether smoothing permitted before player plays. 13-4/10

handicap
– alteration of handicap stroke table for matches beginning other than at first hole 33-4/1
– competitor disqualified from handicap event claims gross prize .33-1/13
– meaning of "handicap" for purposes of Rule 6–2. . . . . .6-2/1
– meaning of "handicap" when full handicap not used. 6-2b/0.5

– misapplication of handicap affects match-play draw 33-5/3
– wrong handicap allowance used in match. 6-2a/6
– wrong handicap applied by Committee results in player not receiving prize 33-5/2
– wrong handicap used due to Committee misinformation 33-1/12

hole at which wrong ball played unknown. 15-1/3

incorrect procedure agreed to in error by player and opponent; whether valid claim can be made after procedure followed 2-5/8.5

line of play improved or worsened by fellow-competitor while discussing with referee whether competitor entitled to free relief . . .1-2/1.5

match begun in ignorance that course closed. 33-2d/4

match-play finalists both disqualified . 33/3

mushroom growing on line of putt. . . .16-1a/15

opponent disputes player's claim that ball unfit for play 5-3/8

player lifts ball without authority due to misunderstanding referee's instructions .34-3/3.5

player proceeds under inapplicable Rule; guidelines for Committee in determining Rule to apply 34-3/6

player reaching fourth round of match play disqualified for wrong score in qualifying round; options for Committee. 34-1b/8

player reaching third round of match play disqualified for agreeing to waive Rules in first-round match. .34-1a/1

play-offs and ties
– determining winner and positions in stroke-play play-off when player disqualified or concedes 33-6/3
– effect of disqualification penalty incurred during play-off. 3/1
– groupings for stroke-play play-off .33-3/4
– players decide method of settling tie when Committee fails to do so 33-6/4
– score cards in hole-by-hole play-off. 33-5/1

postponement of final match due to injury of player. 6-3a/1

removal of casual water or loose impediments on putting green by referee 33/1

score cards
– competitor's failure to countersign score card blamed on lack of time provided by Committee .33-7/3
– competitor's returned score card has wrong or no name on it . .6-6d/4
– in hole-by-hole play-off 33-5/1
– marker disappears with competitor's score card 6-6b/6

- marker not appointed by
  Committee signs score cards.....6-6b/5
- not returned promptly due to
  Committee failure to advise
  competitors where to return
  cards...........................6-6b/4
- requirement that score be
  entered into computer 6-6b/8
- total score recorded by
  competitor incorrect 6-6d/2
- when score card considered
  returned 6-6c/1

second ball played despite adverse
ruling by referee.................3-3/2

serious breach of Rules
- guidelines for determining
  whether serious breach of Rule
  1–2 has occurred 1-2/0.5
- meaning of "serious breach of
  etiquette" 33-7/8

spectators allege competitor's
score incorrect 6-6d/5

status of
- half of double green serving hole
  not being played 25-3/1
- starting time fixed by players 33-3/1
- team captain or coach 33-1/11.5
- tree basins.....................33-2a/10.5
- two holes on each green of nine
  hole course....................16/7
- wrong ruling accepted by
  players from person not on
  Committee 2-5/8

swing aid; whether Committee may
authorise use for medical reasons
during stipulated round 14-3/15.5

teeing ground
- competitors determine spot
  from which to play from tee
  when both tee-markers missing...11-4b/3
- competitors estimate area of
  teeing ground when one tee-
  marker missing 11-4b/2
- play from wrong teeing ground
  attributed to Committee failure
  to indicate hole numbers on
  teeing ground 11-5/2

true state of match not determinable .34-3/5

time of starting
- all competitors must be present .6-3a/2
- circumstances which warrant
  waiving disqualification penalty
  for lateness 6-3a/1.5
- competitors determining own
  groupings and starting times.....33-3/3
- meaning of "time of starting" 6-3a/2.5
- player not present at time of
  starting; course closed at that
  time 33-3/2
- players start early..............6-3a/5
- starting players from 1st and
  10th tees 33-1/3
- status of starting time fixed by
  players 33-3/1
- when players must be present
  for resumption of play.........6-8b/9

waiving, modifying or imposing
disqualification penalty
- application of disqualification
  penalty in team competition in
  which not all team members'
  scores count for each round.....33/8
- authority to waive or modify
  disqualification penalty 33-7/1
- breach of anti-doping condition
  discovered after close of
  competition 34-1b/9
- circumstances which warrant
  waiving disqualification penalty
  for lateness 6-3a/1.5
- competitor, other than marker,
  fails to notify player, marker or
  Committee of player's breach of
  Rules in timely manner 33-7/9
- competitor repeatedly replaces
  ball nearer hole on green 33-7/6
- competitor seeks help from
  fellow-competitor to avoid
  penalty........................33-7/7
- competitor unaware of
  penalty returns wrong score;
  whether waiving or modifying
  disqualification penalty justified..33-7/4.5
- modifying penalty for not holing
  out in stroke play 33-7/2
- modifying penalty for returning
  wrong score 33-7/4
- player intentionally gives
  incorrect information on Rules ...9/1
- wrong form of play used in
  match; players agree losing side
  will default to winners.........33-1/4

when match result "officially
announced" 2-5/14

whether player disqualified in
match-play event entitled to prize
won prior to disqualification 33/7

wrong form of play used in match
play 6-1/1

wrong handicap
- recorded on score card by
  Committee; error discovered
  before competition closed 6-2b/3.5
- used in stroke play by mistake;
  error discovered after
  competition closed 6-2b/1

CONCESSION

See also DEFAULT; FOUR-BALL MATCH PLAY;
FOURSOMES; SINGLE MATCH; WRONG
INFORMATION

agreement that side losing after
18 holes of 36-hole match will
concede match...................1-3/7

agreement
- to concede one or more holes....2-4/22
- to concede short putts 1-3/2
- to consider hole halved during
  play of hole 2-1/1.5

ball falls into hole after concession
of next stroke...................2-4/2

ball resting against flagstick; putt
conceded and ball removed
before player can remove flagstick ..17-4/2

caddie concedes opponent's next
stroke; ball then lifted............2-4/3.5

competitor concedes fellow-
competitor's short putt and
knocks ball away 3-2/1

concurrent four-ball and
single matches; whether
concessions made under various
circumstances apply to only four-
ball or single match or both 30-3/1

conscious failure to correct
opponent's misunderstanding of
state of match; what constitutes
wrong information 9-2/12

determining winner and positions in
stroke-play play-off when player
disqualified or concedes..........33-6/3

fellow-competitor lifts competitor's
ball conceding next stroke in
stroke play 18-4/3

foursome match conceded by play
of single match..................2-4/21

implied concession of hole withdrawn.2-4/13

incorrect information given by
player corrected before opponent
plays next stroke but after
opponent concedes player's putt ...9-2/7

opponent's ball knocked away by
player after concession moves
player's ball....................18-2a/18

opponent's misreading of number
on player's ball results in
agreement that player lost hole
for playing wrong ball 9-2/11

player concedes hole
 – after which opponent
   discovered to have played
   wrong ball 2-4/9
 – after which opponent plays
   wrong ball 2-4/10
 – handicap stroke claimed after
   hole conceded 6-2a/4
 – on basis of invalid claim 2-4/12

player concedes match
 – after winning it when opponent
   lodges invalid claim regarding
   strokes taken 2-4/15
 – due to misconception as to
   opponent's score at last hole 2-4/14

player concedes opponent's next
stroke
 – and knocks or rolls ball to
   opponent....................16-1d/1
 – and knocks opponent's ball away
   along own line of putt 16-1d/2
 – and knocks opponent's ball into
   hole 2-4/1
 – then plays before opponent has
   opportunity to lift ball..........2-4/8

player lifts ball or ball-marker
 – in mistaken belief that next
   stroke conceded...............2-4/3
 – mistakenly believing he won hole..20-1/8
 – of opponent and shakes
   opponent's hand in erroneous
   belief match over 2-4/17
 – whether lifting opponent's ball-
   marker considered concession
   of next stroke.................2-4/5

 – whether picking up opponent's
   ball considered concession of
   next stroke 2-4/4

player omits penalty stroke when
advising opponent as to score
for hole; error discovered after
match conceded by opponent 9-2/10

player unable to meet match-play
schedule defaults; schedule then
changed and player requests
reinstatement 2-4/20

player with ball not found concedes
hole; ball then found in hole.......2-4/11

putting out after concession of
stroke 2-4/6

result of match when player dormie
and opponent concedes..........2-3/2

stroke concession refused by player
and withdrawn by opponent;
player then putts and misses 2-4/7

three holes played out of sequence
in match 2-1/5

valid timely claim made after
concession of match 2-4/16

winner of match wishes to default
to beaten opponent 2-4/19

CONDITIONS OF COMPETITION
See also COMMITTEE; LOCAL RULES

agreement that side losing after
18 holes of 36-hole match will
concede match...................1-3/7

altering conditions after
competition starts; whether
permitted 33-1/1

anti-doping condition breach
discovered after close of
competition 34-1b/9

borrowing balls from another player
when "One Ball" condition in effect.5-1/5

caddies; prohibiting use of caddies
or restricting who may caddie.....App I-C-3

changing partner in foursome play
after player drives from first tee 29/1

clubs, condition requiring use of
 – club conforming with groove
   and punch mark specifications
   effective January 1, 2010 ....4-1/1
 – driving club listed on current
   List of Conforming Driver Heads .App I-C-1a

competitors play two holes not
included in stipulated round.......3/2

condition
 – making competitors responsible
   for addition of hole scores on
   score cards; whether permitted .33-1/7
 – of team competition requires
   person appointed to give advice
   must be team captain or amateur .8/1
 – prohibiting players from having
   person(s) in addition to caddie
   carry items, other than clubs,
   for them......................6-4/5.3
 – prohibiting use of electronic
   devices (mobile phones, music
   players, etc)...................14-3/16

– regarding footwear 33-1/14
– requiring alterations on score
  card be initialed; whether
  permitted 6-6a/6
– requiring immediate
  discontinuance of play;
  guidelines for waiving or
  modifying disqualification
  penalty for failure to
  discontinue play immediately 6-8b/7
– requiring scores to be entered
  into computer by players;
  whether permitted 6-6b/8
– restricting which partner in
  foursome competition may play
  from 1st tee...................33-1/3.5

discontinuance of play
– for refreshment 6-8a/2.5
– guidelines for waiving or
  modifying disqualification
  penalty for failure to
  discontinue play immediately
  when immediate discontinuance
  condition in effect 6-8b/7
– partners fail to discontinue
  play immediately contrary to
  condition of competition 30-3e/1
– specimen condition requiring
  immediate suspension of play
  due to a dangerous situation ....App I-C-5

group plays from wrong teeing
  ground; whether Committee
  should waive penalties because
  Committee failed to indicate hole
  numbers on teeing ground........11-5/2

incorrect information on conditions
– given by player.................9/1
– given by referee; whether player
  should be exempt from penalty
  and for what duration 34-3/1.5

match decided by wrong form of
  play by agreement of players 33-1/4

number of holes of stroke-play
  competition reduced during
  competition; options available to
  Committee...................33-1/2

pace of play condition breached;
  referee does not penalize player
  believing he had already lost hole ...34-3/2

practice; specimen condition
  prohibiting practice or rolling ball
  on or near putting green of hole
  last played between play of holes .App I-C-6b

restrictions on balls used
– effect of state of match penalty
  for breach of "One Ball"
  condition in four-ball play 30-3/2
– "One Ball" condition;
  prohibiting changing brands
  or types of golf balls during
  stipulated round; specimen
  optional condition ....App I-C-1c
– requiring use of ball named on
  current List of Conforming
  Golf Balls; specimen optional
  condition ....App I-C-1b

– requiring use of ball on List of
  Conforming Golf Balls; penalty
  for breach 5-1/2
– requiring use of ball on List
  of Conforming Golf Balls;
  provisional ball played not on list. .5-1/3

score cards and scores
– making competitors responsible
  for addition of hole scores on
  score cards; whether permitted ..33-1/7
– requiring alterations on score
  card be initialed; whether
  permitted 6-6a/6
– requiring scores to be entered into
  computer by players; whether
  permitted 6-6b/8
– when score card considered
  returned 6-6c/1

starting players from 1st and 10th
  tees 33-1/3

status of
– starting time fixed by players 33-3/1
– team captain or coach 33-1/11.5

team competition
– condition stipulates person
  authorized to give advice must
  be team captain and/or amateur ..8/1
– no action taken to stop team
  captain giving advice without
  authority 8-1/24
– specimen condition permitting
  appointment of one person who
  may give advice...............App I-C-7
– team captain gives advice while
  playing 8/2
– whether team captain
  authorized to give advice may
  be required to keep off putting
  greens 8-2b/4

transportation
– caddie breaches transportation
  condition....................33-1/9.5
– golf cart used in competition;
  whether permitted 33-1/8
– specimen condition prohibiting
  players from riding on any
  form of transportation during
  stipulated round ....App I-C-9

umbrella carrier employed in
  addition to caddie 6-4/5

wrong form of play used
– in match play by mistake; error
  discovered after nine holes......6-1/1
– players agree losing side will
  default to winners 33-1/4
– to decide which side will
  concede match................2-4/21

wrong handicap
– allowance used in match 6-2a/6
– knowingly used in stroke
  play; error discovered after
  competition closed 6-2b/2
– used due to Committee
  misinformation................33-1/12

COURSE UNPLAYABLE OR CLOSED
See also DISCONTINUANCE AND
RESUMPTION OF PLAY

cancelling or suspending play
- casual water completely covers
  teeing ground 25-1b/4
- guidelines on whether to cancel
  round 33-2d/1
- hole surrounded by casual water . .33-2d/2

competitor refuses to start or picks
up because of weather conditions;
round subsequently canceled 33-2d/3

match begun in ignorance that
course closed....................33-2d/4

match discontinued by agreement;
one player subsequently wishes
to resume
- opponent refuses although
  course playable................6-8a/5
- opponent refuses on basis
  course unplayable..............6-8a/6

player not present at time of
starting; course closed at that time. .33-3/2

player unable to meet match-
play schedule defaults; course
unplayable on scheduled day
of match; player requests
reinstatement 2-4/20

COURSE RECORD

guidelines and recommendations ... Misc./1

DAMAGE

See also BALL UNFIT FOR PLAY; CLUB(S);
GROUND UNDER REPAIR; REPAIR

ball
- damaged internally 5-3/1
- deemed unfit for play played at
  later hole.....................5-3/2
- not unfit for play deemed unfit....5-3/3

club
- broken due to habit of hitting
  head of club on ground 4-3/9
- broken into pieces prior to
  round discovered in player's bag
  during round...................4-4a/14
- broken while used as cane.......4-3/7
- changing clubs because of wet
  grips..........................4-3/5
- damaged in normal course of
  play breaks into pieces when
  repaired.......................4-3/3
- excess club declared out of play
  during round; whether it may
  replace a club damaged later in
  round..........................4-4c/2
- lead tape applied to clubhead or
  shaft during round.............4-2/0.5
- material in head of metal wood
  club broken away from shell.....4-1/2
- meaning of damage sustained in
  "normal course of play" 4-3/1
- meaning of "repair" 4-3/2
- player starting with 13 clubs
  breaks putter in anger and
  replaces it 4-3/8
- playing characteristics of club
  changed while play suspended;
  error discovered before play
  resumed........................4-2/2

- rendered unfit for play by outside
  agency or opponent's side 4-3/9.5
- short putt holed with club
  whose playing characteristics
  changed other than in normal
  course of play; whether
  Committee should waive or
  modify disqualification penalty....4-3/4

hole
- ball damages side of hole.........16/3
- damaged; procedure for player ...16-1a/6
- relocating hole when damaged
  after ball already positioned
  nearby on putting green 33-2b/2
- repaired by player after holing
  out but before opponent,
  fellow-competitor or partner
  holes out......................1-2/3.5
- touching inside of hole to repair
  damage; whether permitted......16-1a/5

line of putt
- altered purposely by stepping
  on it by opponent or fellow-
  competitor 1-2/1
- damaged accidentally by
  opponent, fellow-competitor or
  their caddies 16-1a/13

Local Rule
- allowing free drop outside
  bunker or smoothing of sand
  in bunker damaged by play of
  children; whether authorized....33-8/9
- allowing free relief from damage
  made by insects 33-8/21
- declaring severe damage by non-
  burrowing animals as ground
  under repair 33-8/32.5
- permitting relief from extensive
  damage to course due to heavy
  rain and foot traffic 33-2a/3
- permitting repair of turf plugs
  on putting green not 4-1/4
  inches in diameter 33-8/30
- wrong putting green deemed
  to include apron to prevent
  damage thereto 33-8/33

repair of spike mark damage
- around hole...................16-1c/4
- on competitor's line of putt by
  fellow-competitor, sanctioned
  or tacitly approved by competitor.13-2/36

DANGEROUS SITUATIONS

bees interfere with play 1-4/10

condition requiring immediate
discontinuance of play; guidelines
for waiving or modifying
disqualification penalty for failure
to discontinue play immediately 6-8b/7

danger from fire ants 33-8/22

definition 1-4/11

partners fail to discontinue
play immediately contrary to
condition of competition 30-3e/1

rattlesnake interferes with play 1-4/10

DEFAULT

See also CONCESSION; HALVED HOLE

after defaulting to opponent player
unable to play match as scheduled,
matches postponed due to
unplayable course conditions;
player requests reinstatement......2-4/20

after winning
– match, player wishes to default
   to losing opponent; whether
   permitted 2-4/19
– several matches, player
   disqualified from competition
   for wrong score in stroke play
   qualifying; Committee options
   regarding defeated opponents
   and remaining matches 34-1b/8

sides agree to play match using
wrong form of play with losers
defaulting to winners 33-1/4

DEW

removing dew or frost
– from line of putt 16-1a/3
– near ball or from line of play 13-2/35

testing surface of putting green for
wetness..........................16-1d/4

DIRECTLY ATTRIBUTABLE

"directly attributable;" meaning of
in Rules 20–1 and 20–3a..........20-1/15

ball moved accidentally
– by flagstick when measuring 18-6/2
– by foot of player asked to lift
   due to interference 20-1/13
– by foot of player during removal
   of loose impediment on putting
   green 23-1/11
– during removal of movable
   obstruction....................24-1/4
– when flagstick removed as ball
   overhangs hole.................16-2/4
– when kicked while lying in long
   grass inside water hazard while
   player probes for it in water......12-1/5

ball-marker moved accidentally
– by player after moving loose
   impediments on putting green 20-1/12
– by player in process of marking
   position of ball 20-1/6
– by putter dropped by player
   approaching ball to lift it 20-1/14

holding ball in place while removing
movable obstruction; whether
permissible......................24-1/4

DIRECTION POST

See also STATUS OF OBJECT

ball deflected by direction post.......19-1/1

DISCONTINUANCE AND RESUMPTION OF PLAY

asking advice when play suspended ...8-1/20

ball in bad lie moved during
suspension of play; player fails to
estimate position sufficiently in
replacing ball 6-8d/5

casual water covering teeing
ground; whether Committee
should discontinue play...........25-1b/4

Committee guidelines on whether
to cancel round 33-2d/1

competitor refuses to start or picks
up because of weather conditions;
round subsequently canceled 33-2d/3

due to inoperable motorized cart 6-8a/4

due to physical problem.............6-8a/3

during suspension of play
– ball moved accidentally by player ..18-2a/25
– ball visible from tee prior to
   suspension disappears or
   moved by outside agency before
   play resumed..................6-8d/4
– club put in another player's bag
   by mistake....................4-4a/5.5

entering clubhouse or half-way
house for refreshment during round6-8a/2.7

guidelines for waiving or modifying
disqualification penalty for failure
to discontinue play immediately 6-8b/7

hole surrounded by casual water 33-2d/2

hole-liner not sunk deep enough;
whether discontinuance of play
permitted 16/4

lie altered
– by natural causes during
   discontinuance of play 6-8d/1
– in bunker prior to resumption of
   play...........................6-8d/2

Local Rule or condition of play
– permitting competitors to
   discontinue play by agreement
   in bad weather; whether
   authorized.....................33-8/5
– specimen condition requiring
   immediate suspension of play
   due to a dangerous situation .....App I-C-5

match discontinued by agreement
– cannot be resumed until three
   days later; one player wishes
   to play on competition course
   prior to resumption............7-2/10
– due to rain one player
   subsequently wishes to resume;
   opponent refuses although
   course playable.................6-8a/5
– due to rain one player
   subsequently wishes to resume;
   opponent refuses on ground
   course unplayable...............6-8a/6
– players may play first 12
   holes following day if match
   discontinued on 13th tee
   previous day...................7-2/11
– replaying match when play
   discontinued instead of
   resuming from where play
   stopped.......................2-1/6

meaning of "good reason to lift"
when play suspended 6-8c/1

old hole plug on line of putt not
repairable; whether players may
discontinue play to request help
from Committee 16-1c/3

play suspended by Committee
– competitor does not resume
play at time ordered by
Committee 6-8b/6
– competitor wishes to complete
hole; fellow-competitor does
not; whether competitor may
play alone and complete hole 6-8b/3
– competitors discontinue play of
hole immediately then resume
play and complete hole before
Committee orders resumption
of play........................6-8b/1
– for dangerous situation;
partners fail to discontinue
play immediately contrary to
condition of competition 30-3e/1
– options for players if one
competitor in group has played
from tee.......................6-8b/2
– player drops ball after play
suspended for dangerous
situation......................6-8b/8
– player plays out of turn in
match after play suspended by
Committee and after opponent
discontinues play 6-8b/3.5
– player wishes to practice after
scheduled resumption but
before group plays 7-2/12

player claiming danger from
lightning, refuses to resume play
when resumption ordered by
Committee......................6-8b/5

player unable to resume suspended
match at scheduled time..........6-8b/4

playing characteristics of club
changed while play suspended;
error discovered before play
resumed 4-2/2

replacement of club broken on
practice ground while play
suspended; whether permitted 4-3/11

resumption of play
– ball dropped away from
obstruction immediately after
resumption of play; whether
player may lift and clean or
substitute then place ball under
Rule 6–8d(ii) 6-8d/3
– when players must be present 6-8b/9

returning to tee to retrieve
forgotten club 6-7/1

taking shelter while waiting to play ...6-8a/2

time permitted for search for
missing ball if play suspended
during search 27/1.5

tree falls onto fairway during
stipulated round 25/9.5

watching television for 45 minutes
after nine holes 6-8a/1

DISTANCE, DISTANCE INFORMATION AND DISTANCE MARKERS

See also MEASURING

asking
– accuracy of distance marker;
whether advice 8-1/3
– distance between objects;
whether advice 8-1/2

devices used in measuring or
determining distance
– distance meter attached to golf
cart..........................14-3/1
– distance information obtained
using electronic device 4-3/0.7
– electronic device containing
distance measurements
between various points..........14-3/5.5
– pencil or score card used to
gauge distance.................14-3/2
– reflectors (non-circular) on
flagsticks aid in use of distance-
measuring devices; whether
permitted 17/3.5

illustrations of holes with distance
measurements between various points
– booklet containing 14-3/5
– electronic device containing 14-3/5.5

Local Rule
– permitting use of distance
measuring device 14-3/0.5
– specimen Local Rule for
permitting use of devices that
measure distance only ....App I-B-9

mark placed by player to indicate
distance for pitch shot 8-2a/3

vertical distance
– ball moves vertically downward;
whether ball has moved by
definition.....................18/1
– ball moves vertically downward
when addressed; will not remain
at rest when replaced 20-3d/3
– nearest point of relief; ball lying
in burrowing animal hole under
ground on course...............25-1b/23
– nearest point of relief; ball lying
in drainpipe under ground on
course 24-2b/12
– nearest point of relief; ball lying
on elevated or in underground
obstruction...................24-2b/11
– unplayable ball in tree; player
opts to drop within two club-
lengths.......................28/11
– unplayable ball at base of cliff;
player wished to drop within
two club-lengths of point above
ball at top of cliff...............28/12

DIVOT AND DIVOT HOLE

another player's divot comes to rest
near player's ball already in bunker ..13-4/18

ball in motion deflected or
stopped by divot taken by player
subsequent to making original
stroke 19-2/9

ball rolls towards hole when
dropped behind divot hole at spot
where previous stroke played 20-2c/1.5

folded over, partially attached
divot near player's ball; whether
removal or replacement permitted .13-2/5

lie of ball to be replaced altered by divot hole
– original lie known but spot
where ball originally lay through
the green not determinable 20-3b/4
– original lie not known and spot
where ball originally lay not
determinable. 20-3b/5

on line of play; whether
replacement permitted. 13-2/6

Local Rule permitting relief from
or repair of divot holes; whether
authorized 33-8/34

player makes divot hole affecting
area of intended stance of partner,
opponent or fellow-competitor 13-2/8.7

replaced or smoothed solely for
purpose of caring for the course. 1-2/0.7

replaced in area where ball to be
dropped 13-2/4.5

when divot considered replaced. 13-2/7

DOG

ball deflected or stopped by dog on
putting green
– after stroke from off green 19-1/6
– after stroke from green. 19-1/7

DOUBT AS TO PROCEDURE

See also DOUBT REGARDING FACTS;
PROVISIONAL BALL; SECOND BALL;
SERIOUS BREACH OF RULES

determining which ball counts when
two balls played under Rule 3–3
– Committee determines player's
score for hole with incorrect
ball; error discovered after
score card returned; whether
error may be corrected. 34-3/3.9
– guidelines for determining
which ball counts when player
proceeds under Rule 3–3 . . . . . . .3-3/0.5
– whether score with second
ball counts if dropped in wrong
place and played 3-3/5

explanation of "any ball he has played" 18/7

match play
– Local Rule allowing play of
second ball in match play;
whether authorized. 33-8/3
– player invokes Rule 3–3 in
match play; whether permitted . . .3-3/9
– procedure for valid claim. 2-5/2

original ball strikes second ball or
vice versa 3-3/7

player invokes Rule 3–3 (doubt as
to procedure)
– after playing original ball 3-3/6
– ball dropped in wrong place and
played; second ball dropped in
right place; both balls played out . .3-3/3

– ball dropped in wrong place but
not played; second ball dropped
in right place; both balls played out 3-3/4
– ball played under water hazard
Rule; original ball then found in
hazard and holed out as second
ball 26-1/5
– ball selected by player to count
lifted and not holed out; player
holes out with other ball; plays
from next teeing ground 3-3/8
– guidelines for determining
which ball counts when player
proceeds under Rule 3–3 . . . . . . .3-3/0.5
– in match play; whether permitted .3-3/9
– intention to play two balls
announced; competitor plays
original ball before dropping
second ball; elects not to play
second ball. 3-3/7.5
– original ball lifted and dropped
then competitor places second
ball where original ball lay and
plays it 3-3/13
– plays second ball first then plays
original ball; whether order of
play permitted 3-3/14
– provisional ball used as second
ball when not determinable
whether original ball out of
bounds. 3-3/1
– second ball played despite
adverse ruling by referee. 3-3/2
– second ball played without
announcing intention to invoke
Rule 3–3 and competitor fails to
report facts to Committee. 3-3/6.5
– single ball dropped in
accordance with two different
Rules instead of playing second
ball 3-3/11
– single ball dropped in
accordance with two different
Rules instead of playing second
ball; dropped ball rolls back into
condition from which relief taken .3-3/12
– three balls played by competitor
doubtful of rights; whether
permitted 3-3/10

spectator says ball moved by
outside agency but player not
sure; procedure for player if
Committee decision not possible
in reasonable time. 18-1/4

wrong ball played in belief it is
provisional or second ball. 15/7

DOUBT REGARDING FACTS

See also COMMITTEE; DOUBT AS TO
PROCEDURE

ball at rest
– falls into bunker when person
walks nearby. 18/10
– moves after stance taken
in water in water hazard;
presumably due to current or
cause unclear 14-6/1

– moves after player takes
practice swings touching grass
behind ball.....................18-2a/30
– moves after removal of nearby
loose impediment..............18-2a/30.5

ball considered unfit by player
disputed; condition of ball not
preserved until Committee can
examine it.......................5-3/8

ball lifted from putting green while
another ball in motion, whether
lifted ball might have influenced
movement ball in motion..........16-1b/4

ball not found
– either in casual water or high
rough of hollow not visible from
tee...........................25-1c/1
– either in water hazard or casual
water overflowing hazard........1-4/7
– meaning of "known or virtually
certain" in Rules 18–1, 24–3,
25–1c and 26–1.................26-1/1
– treated as moved by outside
agency in absence of knowledge
or virtual certainty to that effect..27-1/2.5
– visible from tee; disappears or
moved during suspension of play.6-8d/4

ball overhanging hole moves when
flagstick removed; whether
directly attributable to removal
not determinable.................16-2/4

ball(s) not identifiable
– player unable to distinguish his
ball from another ball..........27/10
– provisional ball not
distinguishable from original ball..27/11
– wrong ball played by competitor
and cannot be found; may have
been ball of fellow-competitor....15-3b/1

caddie lifts player's ball from water
hazard; whether it was reasonable
to assume from player's actions
or statements that he would make
his next stroke from outside the
hazard.........................26-1/9

clubhead cleaned with water in
water hazard after stroke from
hazard fails to extricate ball;
stroke from ball's new location
clearly impracticable.............13-4/40

during downswing player purposely
tries to stop club; swing carries
clubhead beyond ball; whether
stroke made.....................14/1.5

footprints made by referee in
bunker making ruling; while
smoothing before playing, player
unsure all footprints are referee's...13-4/10

golf bag shadow shades ball;
whether bag positioned for that
purpose........................14-2/2.5

guidelines for Committee in
resolving questions of fact........34-3/9

hole-liner pulled out with flagstick
deflects ball; not known whether
hole-liner moving or stationary.....17/8

location unknown
– ball of player lifted by
opponent's caddie claiming it
was out of bounds; whether
original position of ball in or out
of bounds not determinable......18-3b/5
– ball overshooting green
deliberately stopped or
deflected by spectator; ball
would have come to rest just
short of or in water hazard.......19-1/4.1
– ball stolen by outside agency
from unknown spot.............18-1/5
– balls inadvertently exchanged by
competitors either during play
of previous hole or between
play of two holes...............15-1/2
– fellow-competitor asserts, at
completion of stipulated round,
competitor played from outside
teeing ground on 15th hole;
competitor asserts he played
within teeing ground...........34-3/4

player proceeds on referee's ruling
– based on available facts;
subsequent facts prove ruling
incorrect......................34-3/7
– based on player's version of
facts; player's version later
found incorrect.................34-3/8

player uses half-inch backswing;
whether ball pushed or fairly
struck at.......................14-1/4

players unable to resolve rules
problem agree to consider hole
halved.........................2-1/1

shadow of spectator shades ball;
whether positioned for that
purpose........................14-2/2.5

spectators claim score for hole
higher than score returned on
score card by player.............6-6d/5

state of match at end of stipulated
round disputed; Committee
cannot determine true state of
match.........................34-3/5

timing of events unknown
– ball played from bunker to grass
bank rolls back into bunker;
player in frustration hits sand
with club; not determinable
whether ball returned to bunker
before sand struck..............13-4/35.5
– hole at which wrong ball played
unknown......................15-1/3
– player may have failed to
discontinue play immediately
as required by Appendix I-C–5
Condition......................6-8b/7

whether action causes breach of Rule
– competitor's ball played
from putting green comes to
rest touching ball of fellow-
competitor on green; whether
competitor's ball stopped
or deflected or fellow-
competitor's moved not known...19-5/4

– flagstick removed without authority by opponent or fellow-competitor while player's ball in motion after stroke; players unsure whether ball might have reached hole when flagstick removed 17-2/2
– player attempts to take stance fairly and moves growing or fixed object (i.e., branch or boundary stake); player abandons stance and object probably returns to original position; player then takes stance without moving object. . . .13-2/1.1
– player concedes opponent's next stroke and knocks ball away along own line of putt. 16-1d/2
– player unsure whether partially embedded stone considered loose impediment or fixed 23/2
– throwing ball to caddie may have cleaned it; ball lifted under Rule prohibiting cleaning 21/3

whether ball not on current List of Conforming Balls conforms to Rules 5-1/1.5

whether virtual certainty ball is in water hazard can be established without going forward to assess conditions around hazard. 26-1/1.3

wrong ball
– balls inadvertently exchanged by competitors either during play of previous hole or between play of two holes 15-1/2
– competitor plays wrong ball and it cannot be found; may have been ball of fellow-competitor. . . .15-3b/1
– hole at which wrong ball played unknown 15-1/3
– player unable to distinguish his ball from another ball 27/10
– provisional ball not distinguishable from original ball . .27/11

DRAINPIPE

ball in drainpipe under course; entrance to drainpipe out of bounds 24-2b/12

ball in underground drainpipe not reachable or identifiable. 24-3b/1

status of movable part of drainage hose. 24-2b/15.3

DROPPING ZONE

dropping and re-dropping procedures when dropping zone established by Local Rule . . . . .App I-B-8

lateral water hazard
– defined as water hazard. 26/3.5
– part of lateral water hazard where impossible to drop not nearer hole .33-2a/9
– permissible dropping area under lateral water hazard Rule so narrow player has difficulty dropping within it. 26-1/19

Local Rule
– allowing drop on green side of water hazard when ball fails to clear hazard; whether authorized .33-8/2
– allowing line-of-sight relief without penalty from protective fence near line of play 33-8/18
– providing relief from paved path in all cases to dropping zone when nearest point of relief effectively gives no relief; whether authorized. 33-8/19
– specimen Local Rule establishing dropping zone as additional option under Rules 24-2b, 24-3, 25-1b, 25-1c, 25-3, 26-1 and 28 . . . . .App I-B-8

marking island green. 33-2a/10

tree falls onto fairway during stipulated round 25/9.5

EMBEDDED BALL
See also PITCH-MARK

ascertaining whether ball embedded
– lifting ball to determine whether embedded in own pitch-mark 20-1/0.7
– lifting ball to determine whether embedded in own pitch-mark; Committee involvement when opponent, marker or fellow-competitor not readily available. . .5-3/7
– when ball considered embedded in ground. .25-2/0.5

ball bounces out of its pitch-mark and spins back into it. 25-2/1

ball embedded
– in fruit. 23/10
– in grass bank or face of bunker. . . .25-2/5
– in ground under repair in closely mown area. 25-2/4
– in hazard; lifted to determine whether unfit for play 5-3/5
– in lip of bunker 13/4
– inside circumference of hole; all of ball below lip of hole 16/2
– inside circumference of hole; all of ball not below lip of hole. 16/3
– within teeing ground 25-2/8

ball on steep bank driven straight into ground. .25-2/6

ball returns to pitch-mark from prior stroke 25-2/3

dropped ball
– embeds 25-2/2
– embeds; procedure if ball again embeds when re-dropped 25-2/2.5

Local Rule
– allowing relief through the green for ball embedded in own pitch-mark. . . . . .App I-B-4a
– permitting re-dropping or placing when dropped ball embeds in bunker; whether authorized. .33-8/28

pitch-mark of previous stroke (ball
embedded) in dropping area
repaired before ball dropped.......13-2/10

pitch-mark of previous stroke
(ball not embedded) in area of
intended swing repaired before
ball played........................13-2/21

ENVIRONMENTALLY-SENSITIVE AREA

marking environmentally-sensitive
areas; recommendations for
Committee......................33-8/41

player enters environmentally-
sensitive area to retrieve ball.......33-8/42

specimen Local Rule clarifying relief
procedures.....................App I-B-2b

status of growing things rooted
within environmentally-sensitive
area overhanging area outside ESA.33-8/44.5

stroke made from
– environmentally-sensitive area....33-8/43
– environmentally-sensitive area;
significant advantage gained......33-8/44

EQUIPMENT

See also ARTIFICIAL DEVICES, UNUSUAL
EQUIPMENT AND UNUSUAL USE OF
EQUIPMENT; CLUB(S); GOLF CART; STATUS
OF OBJECT; TROLLEY

ball deflected, stopped or moved by
– another ball accidentally
dropped by opponent or fellow-
competitor 18/7.5
– bag of competitor and then his
caddie.........................19-2/7
– bag of opponent or fellow-
competitor left ahead by shared
caddie.........................19-2/8
– cart or trolley of opponent or
fellow-competitor; thereafter
strikes cart or trolley of player
or partner.....................19-3/3
– cart pulled by opponent or
fellow-competitor 19-2/6
– cart shared by two players; ball
at rest moved 18/8
– cart shared by two players; ball
in motion deflected 19/1
– clubs belonging to different side
carried in same bag 19-2/5
– tee marking position of player's
ball 20-1/17
– towel dropped by player and
blown by wind.................18-2a/17

ball set aside after being lifted
struck by ball played from putting
green by opponent or fellow-
competitor.....................19-5/1

borrowing equipment from another
player (i.e., balls, towels, gloves,
tees, etc); whether permitted 5-1/5

cap used to remove loose
impediment from line of putt.......16-1a/8

club put in another player's bag by
mistake during suspension of play..4-4a/5.5

condition prohibiting players from
having person(s) in addition to
caddie carry items, other than
clubs, for them..................6-4/5.3

explanation of "any ball he has
played" 18/7

Local Rule clarifying status of
motorized golf carts and persons
driving them....................33-8/4

non-conforming club ruled
conforming by referee; player
uses club......................34-3/1.5

person(s) other than caddie
– carry items, other than clubs,
for player during round 6-4/5.3
– hired to carry umbrella for player .6-4/5

status of
– glove used as indicating mark 20-2a/7
– golf carts pulled by double caddie .6-4/6
– person in shared golf cart 19/2

towel
– borrowed from another player;
whether permitted 5-1/5
– covering another player's clubs
removed by player to find out
club used 8-1/11
– dropped by player; blows onto
and moves ball 18-2a/17
– placed under or wrapped
around knees to make stroke.....13-3/2
– used by referee to remove
casual water or loose
impediments on putting green....33/1
– used by player to brush aside
loose impediments on line of putt .16-1a/8
– used to mop up casual water 16-1a/1
– waved to encourage insect in
bunker to move 23-1/5.5
– wrapped round self or placed
on cactus for protection while
making stroke 1-2/10

EQUITY

advice in team competition
– no action taken to stop team
captain without authority from
giving advice 8-1/24
– player's team mate in gallery
hits ball to green to show player
whether green will hold 8-1/23

ball or ball-marker deflected, lifted
or moved
– ball in bunker moves when
obstruction removed;
whether player may press ball
into sand or take relief outside
bunker if not possible to
replace or place in bunker not
nearer hole....................20-3d/2
– ball in tree dislodged by outside
agency 18-1/9
– ball in tree dislodged by player;
replacement of ball not possible ..18-2a/29
– ball lifted and dropped away
from movable obstruction 18-2a/4
– ball moved accidentally by player
in playing wrong ball in bunker 18-2a/21

– ball moves before address;
accidentally stopped by player's
club; player removes club and
ball rolls away 19-2/1.5
– ball moved in measuring to
determine if re-drop required 18-6/1
– ball stolen by outside agency
from unknown spot 18-1/5
– ball thrown into bounds by
outside agency and played;
neither player nor caddie aware
of action of outside agency 15/10
– ball-marker moved by
opponent's caddie accidentally. . . .20-1/7
– ball-marker pressed down by
opponent; whether opponent
subject to penalty. 20-1/6.5
– caddie shared by opponents'
side in four-ball match moves
player's ball .30/2
– lifting ball to determine whether
embedded in own pitch mark or
in hole made by reptile, bird or
burrowing animal 20-1/0.7
– opponent's caddie lifts player's
ball after player claims another
ball 18-3b/4
– player lifts ball in mistaken belief
that next stroke conceded 2-4/3
– player's golf cart being pulled by
opponent or fellow-competitor
without player's knowledge
deflects ball. 19-2/6
– referee incorrectly advises
player of loss of hole penalty;
both sides lift their balls; then
referee discovers error. 34-2/7
– whether lifting opponent's ball-
marker considered concession
of next stroke 2-4/5

ball overhanging hole
– knocked away by opponent
before player determines status . .16-2/2
– moves and strikes flagstick being
removed 16-2/5
– moves when flagstick removed. . . .16-2/4

bird's nest interferes with stroke 1-4/9

bunker
– footprints made by referee
making ruling; whether
smoothing permitted before
player plays 13-4/10
– player smoothes bunker after
playing out of turn; opponent
recalls stroke; player must drop
ball in smoothed area; whether
player in breach of Rule 13–4 . . . . .13-4/39
– second player to play wishes to
restore bunker to its condition
prior to first player's stroke 13-4/19
– smoothed after player lifts ball
and states intention to proceed
under Rule 28a 13-4/35.8

cactus, player places towel on or
wraps towel around self before
taking stance .1-2/10

caddies briefly changed by player in
order to receive advice from new
caddie 8-1/26

club
– ball adheres to club face after
stroke. I-4/2
– broken into pieces prior to
round discovered in player's bag
during round 4-4a/14
– playing characteristics of club
changed while play suspended;
error discovered before play
resumed. 4-2/2
– referee rules non-conforming
club conforms with Rules;
player uses club 34-3/1.5
– rendered unfit for play by
outside agency or opponent's
side. 4-3/9.5

Committee error;
– play of wrong ball not rectified
on advice of referee 33-7/5
– player in stroke play placed
at serious disadvantage by
committee ruling; whether
ruling can be reversed 34-3/3.3
– referee incorrectly advises
player of loss of hole penalty;
both sides lift their balls; then
referee discovers error. 34-2/7
– referee rules non-conforming
club conforms with Rules;
player uses club 34-3/1.5
– whether player should be
exempt from penalty and for
incorrect ruling by referee and
for what duration 34-3/1.5

concession
– caddie concedes opponent's
next stroke; ball then lifted 2-4/3.5
– opponent's ball in position to
assist player; player concedes
opponent's next stroke and
plays before opponent has
opportunity to lift ball 2-4/8
– player lifts ball in mistaken belief
that next stroke conceded 2-4/3
– player putts out after
concession of stroke; act assists
partner 2-4/6
– whether lifting opponent's ball-
marker considered concession
of next stroke 2-4/5

dangerous situation
– danger from fire ants 33-8/22
– meaning of term 1-4/11
– rattlesnake or bees interfere
with play 1-4/10

determination of honor at next tee
following disputed hole. 10-1a/2

divot hole just made affects area of
intended stance of another player. . . .13-2/8.7

divots replaced in area in which ball
to be dropped 13-2/4.5

dropped ball embeds; procedure if
ball again embeds when re-dropped.25-2/2.5

flagstick
– ball overhanging hole moves and
strikes flagstick being removed . . .16-2/5
– ball overhanging hole moves
when flagstick removed. 16-2/4

– player's ball strikes flagstick
deliberately left in hole by
opponent or fellow-competitor
attending flagstick 17-3/2
– stuck into green some distance
from hole by practical joker 1-4/3

gate in boundary fence 27/18

hazard
– ball dropped from casual water
in bunker at point of maximum
relief rolls elsewhere 25-1b/6
– ball in bunker moves when
obstruction removed; whether
player may press ball into sand
or take relief outside bunker if
not possible to replace or place
in bunker not nearer hole 20-3d/2
– insect flying in water hazard
swatted away 13-4/16.5
– lie in bunker changed by another
player taking stance 20-3b/2
– missing ball either in water
hazard or casual water
overflowing hazard 1-4/7
– partner's, opponent's or fellow-
competitor's divot comes to
rest near player's ball in bunker . . .13-4/18

incorrect ruling; whether player
should be exempt from penalty
and for what duration 34-3/1.5

loose impediments
– affecting lie removal of
obstruction in hazard would
move loose impediment 1-4/5
– affecting lie moved when ball
lifted through the green 23-1/7
– affecting lie removed while ball
lifted through the green 23-1/8
– assisting player's play removed
by opponent or fellow-
competitor; whether player
entitled to replace 23-1/10

match discontinued by agreement
– cannot be resumed until three
days later; one player wishes
to play on competition course
prior to resumption 7-2/10
– on 13th tee cannot be resumed
until following day; players wish
to play first 12 holes prior to
resuming match 7-2/11

nearest point of relief
– from cart path in abnormal
ground condition; nearest point
of relief from abnormal ground
condition back on cart path 1-4/8
– from cart path in abnormal
ground condition; nearest point
of relief from abnormal ground
condition back on cart path;
drop into abnormal ground
condition impracticable. 1-4/8.5

player breaches Rule or Rules either
more than once or with different penalties
– advised of breach of Rule; player
breaches same Rule prior to
stroke 1-4/13

– breaches Rules more than
once prior to stroke; whether
multiple penalties applied 1-4/12
– breaches same Rule before and
after stroke .1-4/14
– breaches two Rules with
different penalties; more severe
penalty applied 1-4/15

player distracted by ball dropped
accidentally by another player
mis-hits ball 1-4/1

player entitled to lie, line of play and
stance when ball comes to rest
after stroke
– divot hole just made by another
player affects player's area of
intended stance 13-2/8.7
– footprints made in bunker on
extension of player's line of
play by opponent or fellow-
competitor 13-2/29.5
– lie changed by removal of
gallery-control stake 20-3b/3
– lie in bunker changed by another
player taking stance 20-3b/2
– lie of ball lifted from heel print
in bunker altered by another
player's stroke 20-3b/1
– lie of ball in hazard worsened
after pine cone falls from tree
and comes to rest behind ball 13-4/18.5
– lie of ball worsened by player
then restored 13-2/29
– line of putt altered purposely by
opponent or fellow-competitor
by stepping on it 1-2/1
– line of putt damaged accidentally
by opponent, fellow-competitor
or their caddies 16-1a/13
– lie or line of play affected by
pitch-mark made by another
player's ball after player's ball
came to rest 13-2/8
– loose impediments assisting
player's play removed by
opponent or fellow-competitor;
whether player entitled to replace 23-1/10
– partner's, opponent's or fellow-
competitor's divot comes to
rest near player's ball in bunker . . .13-4/18
– player's lie affected by sand
from partner's, opponent's, or
fellow-competitor's stroke from
bunker 13-2/8.5
– position of ball worsened when
obstruction removed; player
replaces obstruction 13-2/15.5
– second player to play wishes
to restore bunker to its condition
prior to first player's stroke 13-4/19

player in anger strikes ball played by
player in following group 1-4/4

player places mark to indicate
distance for pitch shot 8-2a/3

player advancing in match play
disqualified for
– agreeing to waive Rules in
earlier match; options for
Committee .34-1a/1

– wrong score in qualifying round . . .34-1b/8

provisional ball
– not distinguishable from original
   ball 27/11
– player wishing to render original
   ball lost plays next stroke with
   provisional ball out of turn 27-2b/1
– struck by original ball 19-5/5
– when provisional ball holed
   becomes ball in play 27-2b/2

putting green
– ball-marker moved by
   opponent's caddie accidentally 20-1/7
– opponent's ball in position to
   assist player; player concedes
   opponent's next stroke and
   plays before opponent has
   opportunity to lift ball 2-4/8
– player lifts ball in mistaken belief
   next stroke conceded 2-4/3
– player lifts opponent's ball-
   marker in mistaken belief he
   won hole 2-4/5
– player plays away from hole to
   assist partner 30-3f/6
– player putts out after
   concession of stroke; act assists
   partner 2-4/6
– relocating hole when damaged
   after ball already positioned
   nearby on putting green 33-2b/2

refusal to comply with Rule in
   match play 2/3

teeing ground
– ball embeds in own pitch-mark
   in teeing ground 25-2/8
– ball lies in or on movable
   obstruction within teeing ground .25-2/8
– competitors estimate area of
   teeing ground when one tee-
   marker missing 11-4b/2
– competitors determine spot
   from which to play when both
   tee-markers missing 11-4b/3
– determination of honor at next
   tee following disputed hole 10-1a/2

test drop made by player to
   determine where ball will roll if
   relief taken under a Rule 20-2a/8

time of starting; both players in
   match late 6-3a/3

tree falls onto fairway during
   stipulated round 25/9.5

wrong ball played but hole unknown . .15-1/3

ETIQUETTE

club thrown, slammed or struck on
   ground or tree 4-3/1

competitor, other than marker,
   fails to notify player, marker or
   Committee of player's breach of
   Rules in timely manner 33-7/9

competitor seeks help from fellow-
   competitor to avoid penalty 33-7/7

conscious failure to correct
   opponent's misunderstanding of
   state of match 9-2/12

Local Rule for breach of
   sportsmanship code or
   competition policy; whether
   permitted 33-8/6

player refuses to tell opponent
   number of strokes taken 9-2/3.5

practice putt made by player before
   opponent holes out 30/6

request to attend flagstick declined
   by opponent or fellow-competitor . .17-1/2

"serious breach of etiquette,"
   meaning of 33-7/8

"sole purpose of caring for the course,"
– meaning of .1-2/0.7
– footprints made by referee
   entering bunker for ruling,
   whether player may smooth
   them prior to making next stroke .3-4/10
– footprints made in retrieving
   rake smoothed prior to making
   stroke 13-4/9
– footprints made in search
   for ball, whether player may
   smooth them prior to making
   next stroke 13-4/11
– loose impediment moved in
   bunker as player smoothes
   footprints while walking to ball . . .13-4/9.5

EXCHANGING BALLS
See also SUBSTITUTED BALL

balls inadvertently exchanged
– by competitors at unknown place .15-1/2
– by partners in four-ball
   Stableford competition 32-2b/1
– by players after one ball strikes
   and moves other 15-1/2.5
– by players between holes 15-1/1
– by players on opposite sides
   during play of hole and their
   partners pick up; error
   discovered at next hole 30-3c/3
– competitor lifts his and
   fellow-competitor's ball; balls
   exchanged when replaced 15-2/4
– when recovered from water
   hazard 15-1/4

competitor plays wrong ball and it
   cannot be found; wrong ball may
   have been fellow-competitor's ball . .15-3b/1

EXERTING INFLUENCE ON BALL/
ALTERING PHYSICAL CONDITIONS
See also SERIOUS BREACH OF RULES

altering physical conditions
– act of etiquette alters physical
   conditions affecting play 1-2/0.7
– bush branch broken in area into
   which ball may roll after drop 1-2/3
– flagstick adjustment; player's
   rights 17/4
– footprints created retrieving
   rake in bunker smoothed prior
   to player's stroke 13-4/9
– line of play altered by fellow-
   competitor .1-2/1.5

– line of putt damaged accidentally
by opponent, fellow-competitor
or their caddies 16.1a/13
– pressing ball into surface of
putting green to prevent wind
or gravity from moving it. 1-2/9
-– ragged edge of hole repaired
after player holes out but before
opponent, fellow-competitor or
partner holes out 1-2/3.5
– towel placed on cactus bush by
player before stance taken 1-2/10
– turf pressed down by player as
ball rolls towards area 1-2/8

ball on putting green that might
influence movement of another
ball in motion lifted 16-1b/4

ball purposely deflected or stopped
– by fellow-competitor. 19-1/5
– by player; where next stroke
played from .1-2/5.5
– caddie stops ball before it comes
to rest after player drops and
it rolls toward or into position
where re-drop required 20-2c/4
– catching ball in hole with one
hand after putting with other
hand. 1-2/5
– through the green by spectator . . .19-1/4.1

flagstick
– adjusted to more favorable
position 17/4
– attended without player's
authority or knowledge before
stroke; attendance ceases
upon instruction of player after
stroke 17-2/1
– lying on ground prior to stroke
within reach of opponent or
fellow-competitor lifted to
prevent ball from striking it. 17-1/7
– opponent or fellow-competitor
attends flagstick for player;
deliberately fails to remove it 17-3/2
– opponent or fellow-competitor
removes flagstick without
authority while player's ball in
motion. 17-2/2

loose impediments
– assisting player's play removed
by opponent or fellow-
competitor; penalties, if any
and whether player may replace
loose impediments. 23-1/10
– brushed along line of putt rather
than to side 16-1a/10

putting green
– ball mark in position to assist
opponent repaired by player 16-1c/2
– ball putted with one hand;
caught in hole with other hand. . . .1-2/5
– ball replaced on putting green
while another ball in motion;
player re-lifts ball thinking
moving ball might strike it. 16-1b/2
– ball replaced on putting green
while another ball in motion;
replaced ball deflects moving ball. .16-1b/3

– hole repaired by player after
holing out but before opponent,
fellow-competitor or partner
holes out 1-2/3.5
– jumping close to hole when
ball overhangs it; ball falls into
hole 1-2/4
– line of putt altered purposely by
opponent or fellow-competitor
by stepping on it 1-2/1
– line of putt damaged accidentally
by opponent, fellow-competitor
or their caddies 16-1a/13
– line of putt shielded from wind
by laying golf bag nearby 1-2/2
– player knocks partner's putted
ball back to him while still in
motion after having passed hole. . .1-2/7
– spike mark damage repaired on
player's line of putt by fellow-
competitor; player sanctions or
tacitly approves repairs 13-2/36

serious breach of exerting influence
– application of Rule 1–2
disqualification penalty in team
competition in which not all
team members' scores count
for each round 33/8
– ball deliberately deflected or
stopped on putting green by
fellow-competitor 19-1/5
– guidelines for determining. 1-2/0.5
– opponent or fellow-competitor
attending flagstick for player
deliberately fails to remove it;
ball strikes flagstick 17-3/2

"sole purpose of caring for the
course," meaning of. 1-2/0.7

spinning ball when dropping 20-2a/2

tree branch moved by competitor
improving or worsening fellow-
competitor's line of play while
discussing with referee; whether
free relief available 1-2/1.5

turf pressed down after stroke as
ball rolls back toward area 1-2/8

FAILURE TO HOLE OUT
See also HOLED AND HOLING OUT

ball blown into hole by competitor
not replaced and holed out 3-2/2

ball resting against flagstick
– lifted before being holed 17-4/1
– next stroke conceded and ball
removed by opponent before
player can remove flagstick. 17-4/2

fellow-competitor knocks
competitor's ball away from hole
"conceding" next stroke; ball not
holed by competitor 3-2/1

intention to play two balls (under
Rule 3–3) announced by competitor
– after playing original ball,
competitor elects not to play
second ball. .3-3/7.5
– second ball not holed out 3-3/8

Local Rule for temporary putting green waives requirement to hole out; whether authorized 33-8/1

modifying disqualification penalty for not holing out in stroke play; whether permitted 33-7/2

player fails to hole out; marker knowingly attests wrong score 1-3/6

putting with one hand and catching ball in hole with other hand 1-2/5

stroke-play play-off
– competitors do not complete play-off hole or holes because one competitor disqualified or withdraws 33-6/3
– next stroke of competitor "conceded" and ball lifted by fellow-competitor 18-4/3

two balls in play simultaneously at different holes 1-1/1

FAIRWAY AND CLOSELY MOWN AREAS
See also EMBEDDED BALL; THROUGH THE GREEN

ball embedded
– in grass bank or face of bunker 25-2/5
– in ground under repair in closely mown area 25-2/4

ball on steep bank driven straight into ground.....................25-2/6

ball stolen by outside agency from unknown spot 18-1/5

balls of opponents on opposite sides of fairway; procedure for referee in determining ball farther from hole 10-1b/1

dropped ball embeds
– in fairway on impact.............25-2/2
– in fairway on impact; procedure if ball embeds again when re-dropped 25-2/2.5

dropping from rough to fairway in obtaining relief from immovable obstruction or abnormal ground condition; whether permitted......24-2b/8

internal boundary between holes; whether permitted 33-2a/12

lifting ball to determine whether embedded in its own pitch-mark....20-1/0.7

Local Rule
– allowing free relief for ball in water hazard within limits of fairway; whether authorized 33-8/36
– allowing line-of-sight relief from irrigation-control boxes near fairways; whether authorized.....33-8/17
– deeming stacked turf bunker faces (whether grass covered or earthen) as not closely mown 33-8/39
– deeming partially grass-covered wall of bunker to be part of bunker......................33-8/39.5
– establishing procedure for "preferred lies" or "winter rules," specimen Local Rule .....App I-B-4c

– granting relief from ground under repair in fairway of 1st hole only during play of that hole; whether authorized 33-8/23
– permitting relief for intervention by immovable obstructions in closely mown areas near putting greens ....App I-B-6
– providing relief from unsurfaced road crossing fairway for tee shot only; whether authorized....33-8/20
– providing relief in all cases on fairway side of paved path, or dropping zone, when nearest point of relief effectively gives no relief; whether authorized.....33-8/19
– wrong putting green; deemed to include apron to prohibit dropping on and play from 33-8/33

pitch-mark in fairway dropping area repaired before ball dropped.......13-2/10

player finds ball and hits it to player who lost it.....................7-2/5.5

player's ball deflected by stroke of player in another group 19-1/2

putting on fairway while waiting to play to green....................7-2/2

relief taken from obstruction for stroke towards green; same obstruction then interferes with stance for necessary sideways stroke to fairway 24-2b/9.5

status of
– aeration holes and plugs 23/12
– fallen tree attached to stump 25/9

tree falls onto fairway..............25/9.5

FENCE
See also BOUNDARY FENCE, LINE, WALL OR STAKES; WALL

boundary fence
– ball enters burrowing animal hole in bounds near boundary fence and comes to rest underground out of bounds; status of ball and procedure for player........................25-1b/24
– bowed inside boundary line interferes with lie of ball; whether player entitled to relief .24/4
– club strikes other side of boundary fence to move ball lying against it 14-1/5
– exposed water pipe parallel to boundary effectively gives free relief from boundary fence; suggested solution for Committee 33-2a/1
– gate in boundary fence; whether movable or deemed fixed 27/18
– Local Rule deeming interior boundary fence immovable obstruction; whether permitted .33-8/14
– near player's ball necessitates abnormal stroke; obstruction interferes with abnormal stroke; whether player entitled to relief 24-2b/17

– relief from immovable
obstruction incidentally results
in relief from boundary fence 24-2b/6
– swing using half-inch backswing
used to strike ball lying close to
boundary fence.................14-1/4
– whether ball lying inside
boundary fence considered out
of bounds.....................27/19
– whether boundary fence leaning
away from course must be
straightened 33-2a/20
– whether boundary fence leaning
toward or onto course may be
straightened improving position
of ball.........................13-2/18
– whether boundary line may
be established inside fence on
property line..................33-2a/15

Local Rule
– allowing line-of-sight relief
without penalty from protective
fence near line of play 33-8/18
– deeming interior boundary
fence immovable obstruction;
whether authorized............33-8/14

measuring club-length(s) through
fence; whether permitted 20-2b/2

nearest point of relief
– from fence determined for
stroke with 4-iron; when
dropped, ball rolls to position
where stroke with 4-iron still
has interference but stroke with
other club player wishes to use
does not; whether ball must be
re-dropped 20-2c/0.7
– not possible to determine by
simulating required address
position because fence
physically prevents player from
taking stance; recommended
procedure to follow.............24-2b/3.5

part of fence off course leans across
boundary and interferes with
player's swing; whether player
entitled to relief.................13-2/20

recommendations for Committee;
how to prevent access to
environmentally-sensitive areas
with fencing and warning signs.....33-8/41

status of
– angled supports or guy wires
supporting boundary fence 24/2
– concrete bases of boundary
fence posts 24/3
– stile attached to boundary fence ..24/1

FLAGSTICK
See also PUTTING GREEN

adjustment of; player's rights.........17/4

attendant removes flagstick
– holds it upright behind hole with
bottom of flagstick touching
putting green; whether breach
of Rule 8–2b 17-1/4.5
– knob then falls from top of
flagstick and deflects ball.........17/9

attendant stands behind hole 17-1/4

attended or removed by
– opponent or fellow-competitor
without authority before
stroke; attendance ceases on
instruction of player after stroke..17-2/1
– opponent or fellow-competitor
without authority while player's
ball in motion 17-2/2
– partner without express
authority; ball strikes flagstick
or partner 17-3/4
– referee, observer or marker at
player's request 17-1/3

ball
– at rest kicked away from hole by
spectator attending flagstick 18-1/10
– lodged in flag attached to flagstick .17/6
– moved by flagstick when
used for measuring or when
accidentally dropped on ball......18-6/2
– overhanging hole moves when
flagstick removed...............16-2/4

ball resting against flagstick but not holed
– lifted by opponent after
opponent concedes next stroke ..17-4/2
– lifted by player.................17-4/1
– lifted by player; opponent lifts
his ball claiming player loses hole .2-5/3
– lifted by player; others pick up
mistakenly believing player won
hole 30-3f/3
– moved when flagstick removed
by opponent or fellow-
competitor 17-4/3
– moved when flagstick removed
by player; ball not placed on lip
of hole 17-4/4

ball strikes flagstick
– flag struck by ball when flagstick
attended 17-3/5
– lying on ground.................17-3/3
– opponent or fellow-competitor
attending flagstick for player
fails to remove it; player's ball
strikes flagstick.................17-3/2
– or partner when attended
by partner without express
authority of player 17-3/4
– when ball overhanging hole
moves during flagstick removal ...16-2/5
– wrong ruling accepted by
players from person not on
Committee; match played to
conclusion based on ruling;
whether Committee should
consider late claim 2-5/8

caddie while attending flagstick
suggests player aim at foot;
whether breach of any Rule 8-2b/2

club used as flagstick to mark
position of hole 17-3/6

dimensions and attachments
– attachment indicates position
of hole on green; whether
permitted 17/1

– different colored flags to indicate position of hole on green; whether permitted 17/2
– non-circular reflectors on flagsticks aid use of distance-measuring devices; whether permitted 17/3.5
– tapered or of varying diameters; whether permitted 17/3

holding flagstick with one hand and putting with other hand; whether permitted 17-1/5

hole-liner pulled out of hole with flagstick
– ball falls into unlined hole 17/7
– ball strikes hole-liner 17/8

holing out without ball touching flagstick in hole; whether possible ..17-3/1

Local Rule
– prohibiting removal of flagstick; whether authorized 33-8/10
– waiving penalty for ball striking unattended flagstick; whether authorized 33-8/11

meaning of "stands near the hole" 17-1/1

request to attend flagstick declined by opponent or fellow-competitor..17-1/2

placed on ground prior to stroke; lifted after stroke made 17-1/7

player attending flagstick for opponent struck by ball of opponent's partner who played out of turn 30-3f/5

stuck into green some distance from hole by practical joker......1-4/3

FLOWERS

deeming small area of rare plants close to putting green environmentally-sensitive area 33-8/41

establishing boundary line inside fence on property line to protect flower bed 33-2a/15

Local Rule requiring relief under penalty from plantation or nursery; whether permitted 33-8/29

FOOT, FEET AND FOOTWEAR

ball moved accidentally by foot
– and branch broken improving area of intended swing, whether multiple penalties apply......1-4/15
– during removal of loose impediment on putting green.....23-1/11

ball stopped by player's foot; ball moves when foot removed; whether multiple penalties apply ...19-2/1

ball-marker moved when it sticks to sole of player's shoe 20-1/5.5

bunker side knocked down with foot by player in effort to create level stance......13-3/3

caddie attending flagstick advises player to aim at his foot 8-2b/2

casual water
– pressing down hard with foot causes water to appear around shoe; whether player entitled to relief from casual water......25/4
– visible around player's feet while walking beside line of putt; whether player entitled to relief from casual water......25/5

club placed on ground to align feet....8-2a/1

condition prohibiting use of metal or traditionally designed spikes.....33-1/14

dropped ball strikes player's foot, whether player may change relief option when ball redropped 20-2a/6

loose impediments in hazard moved by player's feet in approaching ball and taking stance......13-4/13.5

putter neck bent when player hits shoe with club in disgust; player then holes short putt 4-3/4

relief taken from GUR; player chooses to play next stroke with club not used to determine nearest point of relief and foot again touches GUR, whether re-drop required......20-2c/0.8

FOOTPRINT(S)
See also ABNORMAL GROUND CONDITIONS; BUNKER; DAMAGE; GROUND UNDER REPAIR; SPIKE MARK(S)

extensive damage from spectator traffic due to heavy rain and wet conditions; Committee options 33-2a/3

in bunker or water hazard
– altered by another player's stroke while player's ball lifted from heel print because of interference......20-3b/1
– altered during suspension of play by greenkeeping staff......6-8d/2
– altered during suspension of play by natural causes 6-8d/1
– created by children; whether Local Rule providing relief authorized......33-8/9
– created during search for ball, smoothed before stroke made from bunker 13-4/11
– created and then smoothed by player on line of play before stroke made outside bunker......13-2/29
– created in retrieving rake; smoothed prior to player's stroke.13-2/9
– created on line of play by player required to retrieve ball under Rule 13-2/29.3
– created on extension of line of play by opponent or fellow-competitor 13-2/29.5
– made by stance abandoned prior to stroke filled in; whether action constitutes "testing the condition of the hazard" in breach of Rule 13–4a......13-4/0.5

– player's foot stops ball; when foot removed, ball rolls into footprint 19-2/1
– referee makes footprints in bunker while making ruling; whether smoothing permitted before player plays 13-4/10
– second player to play from bunker wishes to smooth footprints made by first player 1 . 3–4/19
– smoothed after original stance taken when player decides to play different type of shot 13-4/0.5
– smoothed after stroke made from bunker and ball either lost or out of bounds and before substituted ball dropped in bunker 13-4/37
– smoothed after ball played out of bunker; ball returns to smoothed area on subsequent stroke 13-4/38
– smoothed by player after playing out of turn in match play; opponent recalls stroke and player must drop ball in smoothed area 13-4/39
– smoothed on line of play before stroke made from outside bunker . 13-2/28
– smoothed on line of play before stroke made from outside bunker; whether multiple penalties apply 1-4/12

Local Rule providing relief from damage, including footprints, in bunkers caused by children; whether authorized 33-8/9

smoothed in bunker solely for care of the course incidentally cause loose impediments to be moved 13-4/9.5

status of footprint of burrowing animal, reptile or bird 25/19.5

FOUR-BALL MATCH PLAY
See also DEFAULT; FOUR-BALL STABLEFORD COMPETITION; FOUR-BALL STROKE PLAY; WRONG INFORMATION

absent partner
– gives advice before joining match . 30-3a/2
– joins match during play of hole 30-3a/1
– joins partner in stroke play after fellow-competitor plays from teeing ground but before partner plays 31-2/1

advice
– given by absent partner before joining match 30-3a/2
– given on request; penalties in various forms of play 8-1/25

application of Rule 2–2 in four-ball match play 30-3/3

ball of player moved or lifted without authority
– by caddie shared by player and opponent in four-ball match 30/1
– by caddie of opponents in four-ball match 30/2
– by player's partner playing his ball . 30-3f/9
– by opponent in four-ball match . . . 30-3f/10

borrowing putter from partner 4-4b/1

breach of Rule by opponent
– discussed between player and opponent; penalty not applied 1-3/4
– neither players nor opponents aware; penalty not applied 1-3/5
– procedure for valid claim 2-5/2

breach of Rule in four-ball match; whether partner assisted
– absent partner joins match during play of hole 30-3a/1
– after picking up at hole, player drops ball near partner's ball and plays practice stroke 30-3f/7
– hitting sand in bunker with club after failing to extricate ball; partner's ball in same bunker 30-3f/2
– loose impediment in bunker lifted by player when his and partner's balls in bunker 30-3f/1
– player allows partner to stand on extension of line of play or putt behind ball; assists partner with similar shot 30-3f/13
– player disqualified for next hole plays that hole 30-3f/8
– playing away from hole to assist partner 30-3f/6
– request to lift ball that might assist partner not honored 30-3f/11

concurrent four-ball and single matches
– whether concessions made under various circumstances apply to only four-ball or single match or both 30-3/1
– whether partners may exchange advice on single match after result of hole or match in four-ball decided 30-3/1

determination of honor in four-ball match in which points awarded for both better-ball and aggregate scores 30/3

effect of state of match penalties in four-ball match 30-3/2

flagstick
– ball resting against flagstick lifted by player and not holed; others in match pick up mistakenly believing player won hole; error then discovered 30-3f/3
– partner attends flagstick without express authority of player; ball strikes flagstick or partner 17-3/4
– player attending flagstick for opponent struck with ball played by opponent's partner played out of turn from deep bunker 30-3f/5

handicap allowances in four-ball match if player with lowest handicap unable to compete 30-3a/3

hitting sand in bunker with club after failing to extricate ball; partner's ball in same bunker . . . . . . 30-3f/2 incorrect ruling by Committee places player in stroke play at serious disadvantage; when ruling can be reversed............34-3/3.3

loose impediment in bunker lifted by player when his and partner's balls in bunker..................30-3f/1

match-play finalists, both sides disqualified......................33/3

partners balls lie in same bunker
– after one plays from bunker other makes practice swing touching sand; whether both partners penalized.............30-3f/2.5
– sand in bunker hit with club after first ball played not extricated; whether both partners penalized.............30-3f/2

practice
– after picking up at hole, player drops ball near partner's ball and plays practice stroke.........30-3f/7
– player practice putts after he and partner have holed out but before opponents hole out......30/6
– player practice putts on previous green after partner drives from next tee 30-3f/12
– when practice between holes permitted 7-2/1

provisional ball; order of play when played other than from teeing ground..........................10/4

putting green
– player entitled to putt stands on another player's line of putt 30-3b/1
– player knocks partner's putted ball back to him while still in motion after having passed hole...1-2/7
– player walks off green under mistaken impression partner halved hole; player then returns to putt for half 30/4
– player with putt for half picks up in error at suggestion of opponent based on misunderstanding..............30/5
– putting out after concession of stroke; partner yet to complete hole 2-4/6
– ragged edge of hole repaired by player after holing out but before opponent(s) or partner holes out....................1-2/3.5
– touching putting green to point out partner's line for putting; player incidentally touches own line of putt...................30/2.5
– waiving turn to putt in four-ball match....................30-3b/2

side plays out of turn from tee; opponents require one member of side to replay but not other......30-1/1

when stipulated round begins and ends...........................2/2

wrong ball
– player plays partner's ball 30-3c/1

– player plays partner's ball; error discovered after opponents have played next strokes........30-3c/4
– player "wins" hole with wrong ball; partner picks up; error discovered at next hole..........30-3c/2
– players on opposite sides unknowingly exchange balls during hole; both their partners pick up; error discovered at next hole......................30-3c/3

wrong information given by player out of contention in four-ball match play......................30-3f/4

FOUR-BALL STABLEFORD COMPETITION
See also FOUR-BALL MATCH PLAY; FOUR-BALL STROKE PLAY

breach of Rule by both partners at same hole 32-2b/1

practice between holes; when permitted 7-2/1

score card
– different score card returned when original lost or damaged....6-6a/7
– scores of partners transposed at hole but not to side's advantage..32-2a/1
– scores of partners transposed at hole to side's advantage.........32-2a/2

FOUR-BALL STROKE PLAY
See also FOUR-BALL MATCH PLAY; FOUR-BALL STABLEFORD COMPETITION

absent player joins partner after fellow-competitor(s) play from teeing ground but before partner plays........................31-2/1

breach of 14-club Rule by partner in stroke play discovered at 8th hole; where penalty strokes applied......4-4a/10

concurrent individual and four-ball stroke-play competitions conducted; examples of rulings....31/1

effect of state of match penalties in four-ball stroke play 30-3/2

flagstick attended by partner without express authority of player; ball strikes flagstick or partner 17-3/4

loose impediment in bunker lifted by competitor when his and partner's balls in bunker..........31-8/1

meaning of "handicap"
– for purposes of Rule 6–2.........6-2/1
– when full handicap not used 6-2b/0.5

minus or zero net score; whether permitted 2-1/2

order of play between partners
– extent to which side may play in order it considers best 31-4/2
– partner waives turn to play; circumstances under which he may complete hole..............31-4/1

player allows partner to stand on extension of line of play or putt behind ball; assists partner with similar shot .30-3f/13

playing away from hole to assist partner 30-3f/6

practice
– after picking up at hole, competitor drops ball near partner's ball and plays practice stroke. 30-3f/7
– competitor practices on previous green after partner plays from next tee 30-3f/12
– when practice between holes permitted .7-2/1

ragged edge of hole repaired by player after holing out but before fellow-competitor(s) or partner holes out. 1-2/3.5

score card
– different score card returned when original lost or damaged. 6-6a/7
– gross score of partner with better net score omitted from score card .31-3/1
– lower gross score attributed to wrong partner on score card 31-7a/2
– partners' scores transposed at hole but not to side's advantage in handicap competition 32-2a/1
– score recorded for competitor for hole not completed; partner's lower score also recorded 31-7a/1

when stipulated round begins and ends. 3/3

wrong handicap used due to Committee misinformation 33-1/12

FOURSOMES

both player and partner drive at same tee in foursome play 29-1/9

breach of Rule by opponent
– discussed between player and opponent; penalty not applied 1-3/4
– neither players nor opponents aware; penalty not applied 1-3/5
– procedure for valid claim. 2-5/2

changing partners after driving from first tee; whether permitted 29/1

concession of foursome match decided by play of single match 2-4/21

condition of competition designates which foursome partner must play from 1st tee; whether permitted 33-1/3.5

disputes and claims in foursome match
– procedure for valid claim. 2-5/2
– side drives for three holes in wrong order; opponents make claim during third hole. 29-2/2

dropping ball under Rule; which partner must drop. 29/4

foursome match
– begun as four-ball match; error discovered at 9th hole. 6-1/1
– played as four-ball match by agreement of players 33-1/4

hitting sand in bunker with club after failing to extricate ball; whether side incurs penalty 29/5

meaning of "handicap"
– for purposes of Rule 6–2 . . . . .6-2/1
– when full handicap not used. 6-2b/0.5

mixed foursome in which different tees used by men and women; tee shot out of bounds 29/2

order of play between foursome partners
– if player accidentally moves ball after address. 29-1/5
– if provisional ball played. 29-1/3
– if stroke accidentally misses ball . .29-1/6
– if swing misses ball on purpose 29-1/7
– if tee shot out of bounds 29/2
– if tee shot played outside teeing ground in match recalled by opponents. 29-1/1
– if tee shot played outside teeing ground in stroke play 29-1/2
– if wrong ball played. 29-1/8
– side drives for three holes in wrong order; opponents make claim during third hole. 29-2/2

partners' clubs carried in one bag; whether permitted 4-4a/4

player misses ball
– accidentally, when making stroke. .29-1/6
– purposely, so partner would play stroke over water. 29-1/7

player practice putts on previous green after partner drives from next tee. 29/3

provisional ball in foursome competition
– order of play when played other than from teeing ground 10/4
– which partner must play provisional ball 29-1/3
– whether partner who went ahead before tee shot played may return to tee to play provisional ball 29-1/4.5
– wrong partner plays provisional ball 29-1/4

score card
– different score card returned when original lost or damaged 6-6a/7
– incorrect handicap for partner in foursome stroke-play competition discovered after competition closed 6-2b/2.5
– individual handicaps of partners not recorded on score card 6-2b/4

stroke play
– competitor plays from outside teeing ground in foursome stroke play; partner replays stroke. 29-1/2

– order of play in foursome stroke
play when wrong ball played......29-1/8
– signing of score card in
foursome stroke play...........29/6

when stipulated round begins and
ends
– in match play..................2/2
– in stroke play.................3/3

wrong partners drive for both sides
in foursome match................29-2/1

FROST

removal of frost or dew
– from line of putt...............16-1a/3
– near ball or on line of play........13-2/35

GALLERY-CONTROL STAKE, ROPE OR LINE

See also OBSTRUCTIONS; STATUS OF OBJECT

interference by line used for gallery-
control purposes................24-2b/20

Local Rule deeming lines used for
gallery-control purposes ground
under repair....................24-2b/20

paint from course marking line
adheres to ball..................21/1

removal of
– gallery-control rope by player
worsens position of ball; player
replaces rope 13-2/15.5
– gallery-control stake by marshal
worsens lie of player's ball.......20-3b/3

GATE, DOOR OR WINDOW

barn doors opened for shot played
through barn 24-2b/15

clubhouse door or window opened;
ball played through opening.......24-2b/14

gate in boundary fence; whether
movable or deemed fixed.........27/18

open door of building interferes
with player's swing; relief options
available........................24-2b/15.5

GLOVE

See also EQUIPMENT; TAPE

another caddie or friend carries
clubs while player's caddie returns
to tee with player's glove 6-4/4.5

applying adhesive tape to glove;
when permitted..................14-3/8

used as indicating mark struck by
ball when dropped under Rule;
whether glove equipment.........20-2a/7

GOLF CART

See also EQUIPMENT; STATUS OF OBJECT; TROLLEY

ball deflected or stopped by
– golf cart shared by two players....19/1
– player's golf cart being pulled by
opponent or fellow-competitor...19-2/6

ball moved by golf cart shared by
two players......................18/8

caddie
– breaches transportation
condition.......................33-1/9.5
– Local Rule clarifying status of
person(s) hired by player(s) to
drive motorized golf cart 33-8/4
– player with clubs transported
on motorized golf cart hires
individual to perform all other
functions of caddie..............6-4/3

club rendered unfit for play when
struck by golf cart of opponent,
fellow-competitor or other
outside agency....................4-3/9.5

distance meter attached to golf
cart; whether artificial device 14-3/1

excess club declared out of play
before round and placed on floor
of golf cart......................4-4c/1

inoperable motorized cart causes
players to discontinue play;
whether discontinuance permitted .6-8a/4

Local Rule or condition of competition
– clarifying status of motorized
golf carts and persons driving
them..........................33-8/4
– specimen condition prohibiting
players from riding on any
form of transportation during
stipulated round ....App I-C-9

player builds stance by positioning
golf cart beneath tree but
corrects error before making
stroke 13-3/5

status of
– carts pulled by double caddie.....6-4/6
– individual who transports
player's clubs on motorized golf
cart or trolley...................6-4/2.5
– person in shared golf cart 19/2

used in competition; whether
permitted 33-1/8

GRASS OR TURF

See also FAIRWAY AND CLOSELY MOWN AREAS; SPIKE MARK(S); TESTING

after stroke
– from bunker to grass bank
player hits sand with club; ball
then rolls back into bunker.......13-4/35.5
– player presses down raised turf
as ball rolls toward that area.....1-2/8

ball lies outside ground under
repair area; long grass within area
interferes with swing 25-1a/1

ball lying on grass-covered ground
within bunker deemed unplayable;
explanation of relief options 28/9

ball-marker when placed presses
down grass
– changing lie of ball..............20-1/15.5
– in front of ball on putting green ...20-1/19

ball moves
– after player touches grass
behind ball and takes several
practice swings near ball.........18-2a/30
– vertically downward in long grass .18/1

ball stepped on accidentally in tall
grass; original lie altered and
spot where ball originally lay not
determinable; procedure for player .20-3b/5

bunker face or bank
  – ball embedded in grass bank or
    face of bunker; whether area
    considered closely mown 25-2/5
  – Local Rule deeming stacked turf
    bunker faces (whether grass
    covered or earthen) as not
    closely mown 33-8/39
  – Local Rule deeming partially
    grass-covered wall of bunker to
    be part of the bunker. 33-8/39.5

"embedded;" when ball considered
embedded in ground 25-2/0.5

gallery-control stake removed by
marshal with or without sanction
of player; turf in front of ball raised. .20-3b/3

"grounded"
  – when club considered grounded
    in grass. 18-2b/5
  – when club considered grounded
    in grass in water hazard. 13-4/8

line of putt altered purposely by
opponent or fellow-competitor
stepping on it .1-2/1

Local Rule
  – deeming grass-covered cable
    trenches as ground under repair . .App I-B-7b
  – deeming partially grass-covered
    walls of bunkers to be part of
    bunker 33-8/39.5
  – deeming stacked turf bunker
    faces (whether grass covered or
    earthen) as not closely mown 33-8/39

pulled from rough on line of play or
a few inches behind ball, whether
lie or line of play improved 13-2/0.5

raised turf or tuft of grass
  – pressed down or stepped on 1-2/1
  – pressed down or smoothed for
    sole purpose of caring for the
    course 1-2/0.7

removal of grass adhering to ball;
whether permitted 21/2

sod seams; specimen Local Rule
allowing relief from seams of cut
turf . . . . .App I-B-4e

status of
  – grass cuttings 25/11
  – grass-covered areas in bunkers . . .13/2
  – non-growing plants, including
    grasses, within area of ground
    under repair 25/10.9
  – turf raised by underground pipe. . .24/14

stone near ball presses down grass
when rolled away by player;
whether breach of any Rule 13-2/13

teeing ground
  – breaking off grass behind ball on
    teeing ground 13-2/3
  – player misses tee shot; presses
    down turf behind ball before
    next stroke 13-2/2

testing grass to determine whether
attached or loose impediment
  – long blade of grass through the
    green moved to determine if
    attached or loose; whether
    permitted 13-2/26
  – raised tuft of grass on line of
    putt brushed to determine if
    attached or loose; whether
    permitted 16-1a/11

touching grass with club during
practice swing in hazard 13-4/4

underground pipe raises turf above
it; whether raised turf considered
part of obstruction 24/14

when club considered grounded in
grass in water hazard 13-4/8

GREENKEEPER AND HOLE MADE BY GREENKEEPER

aeration holes; status of. 25/15

bunker raked by greenkeeper when
player's ball lies therein; lie of ball
or line of play improved 13-2/4

club rendered unfit for play after
struck by greenkeeper's vehicle 4-3/9.5

fallen tree in process of being
removed by greenkeeper;
whether ground under repair 25/7

hole made by greenkeeper
  – aeration holes 25/15
  – explanation of "hole made by
    greenkeeper" in definition of
    ground under repair. 25/14
  – hole of removed stake defining
    water hazard 25/18
  – sunken hole plug 25/17
  – two holes on each green of nine
    hole course; status of hole not
    in use 16/7

maintenance vehicle deflects ball
out of bounds; substituted ball
played from spot where original
ball deflected 20-7/1

player's lie in bunker altered prior
to resumption of play by
  – greenkeeping preparations 6-8d/2
  – natural causes 6-8d/1

rut made by tractor
  – status of 25/16
  – believing Committee might
    declare rut ground under repair,
    competitor announces intention
    to play two balls; plays original
    ball before dropping second ball;
    elects not to play second ball 3-3/7.5

sunken hole plug; status of. 25/17

two holes on each green of nine
hole course; whether permitted;
status of hole not in use 16/7

GRIP AND GRIPPING
See also CLUB(S)

attachment to grip of club of player
with artificial arm 14-3/15

changing clubs because of wet grips . .4-3/5

holding ball in hand against grip
- when putting...................14-3/6
- when making practice swing or
  practice stroke.................14-3/6.5
tape applied to hand or glove to aid
in gripping.......................14-3/8

GROUND UNDER REPAIR
See also ABNORMAL GROUND
CONDITIONS; BURROWING ANIMAL,
REPTILE OR BIRD (AND HOLES MADE
BY THEM); CASUAL WATER; MARKING
OR DEFINING COURSE; TREE OR BUSH;
VIRTUALLY CERTAIN (OR KNOWN)

ball lost or not found
- ball played from area of ground
  under repair, lost in same area....25-1c/3
- ball played under Rule for ball
  lost in ground under repair
  after another ball played under
  stroke-and-distance procedure...15/8
- clarification of point where ball
  "last entered" ground under
  repair when ball lost in condition. 25-1c/1.5
- either in ground under repair or
  high rough; whether player may
  treat ball as in ground under
  repair........................25-1c/1
- Local Rule declaring
  accumulations of leaves (at
  specified holes) through the
  green as ground under repair.....33-8/31
- not found but known to be in
  tree within ground under repair .25/10
- whether provisional ball
  becomes ball in play if original
  ball lost in ground under repair ...27-2c/1.5
- without knowledge or virtual
  certainty ball in ground under
  repair, player proceeds under
  Rule 25-1c....................25-1c/2
ball played from ground under
repair then relief taken under
ground under repair Rule
- original ball abandoned..........18-2a/8.5
- original ball retrieved by player ...18-2a/8
ball thought unfit for play; lifted
under relief from ground under
repair procedure and cleaned; ball
then determined unfit for play......5-3/6
Committee options
- declaring area as ground under
  repair during competition round .33-2a/2
- extensive damage due to heavy
  rain and traffic declared ground
  under repair 33-2a/3
- referee's authority to declare
  ground under repair.............34-2/1
competitor invokes Rule 3–3 (doubt
as to procedure)
- competitor drops one ball in
  accordance with two different
  Rules instead of playing second
  ball..........................3-3/11
- competitor drops one ball in
  accordance with two different
  Rules instead of playing second

ball; dropped ball rolls back into
condition from which relief taken .3-3/12
- competitor lifts and drops
  original ball then places second
  ball where original ball lay and
  plays it 3-3/13
explanation of "hole made by
greenkeeper" in definition of
ground under repair 25/14
fallen tree
- attached to stump 25/9
- in fairway after play begun.......25/9.5
- in process of being removed......25/7
improving line of play when taking
relief from ground under repair 25-1b/3
interference by ground under repair
and some other condition
- ball embedded in ground under
  repair in closely mown area 25-2/4
- ball in casual water within
  ground under repair.............25-1b/11
- ball in casual water within
  ground under repair; whether
  player entitled to take relief
  from both conditions in single
  procedure....................25-1b/11.5
- Local Rule deeming ground
  under repair adjacent to
  artificially-surfaced cart path to
  have same status as path........33-8/25
- obstruction in ground under
  repair interferes with player's
  swing 24-2b/10
Local Rule
- allowing free relief from damage
  made by insects 33-8/21
- altering ground under repair
  relief procedure to require
  player to drop behind condition;
  whether authorized............33-8/26
- declaring accumulations of
  leaves (at specified holes)
  through the green as ground
  under repair 33-8/31
- declaring severe damage by non-
  burrowing animals as ground
  under repair 33-8/32.5
- deeming grass-covered cable
  trenches as ground under repair . App I-B-7b
- deeming ground under repair
  adjacent to artificially-surfaced
  cart path to have same status as
  path 33-8/25
- deeming hard conical ant hills as
  ground under repair............33-8/22
- granting relief from ground
  under repair in fairway of 1st
  hole only during play of that
  hole; whether authorized.......33-8/23
- permitting relief from extensive
  damage to course due to heavy
  rain and traffic................33-2a/3
- providing relief from unsurfaced
  road for tee shot only; whether
  authorized....................33-8/20
- specimen Local Rule declaring
  area of course as ground under
  repair from which play prohibited
  and relief must be taken ....App I-B-2a

marking environmentally-sensitive
area as ground under repair.......33-8/41
material piled for removal
– fallen tree in process of being
removed 25/7
– grass cuttings 25/11
– pine needles piled for removal
interfere with line of play after
ball dropped away 25-1b/17
nearest point of relief
– ball dropped from immovable
obstruction rolls nearer
obstruction than nearest point
of relief; whether re-drop
required if player changes
clubs and obstruction no
longer interferes (also applies
to similar interference from
ground under repair)...........20-2c/0.7
– club used to determine nearest
point of relief not used for next
stroke....................24-2b/4
– determining club, address
position direction of play and
swing used to identify nearest
point of relief..............24-2b/1
– diagram illustrating player
unable to determine nearest
point of relief 24-2b/3.7
– diagrams illustrating nearest
point of relief 25-1b/2
– dropped ball rolls nearer
obstruction than nearest point
of relief; whether re-drop
necessary if player changes
clubs and obstruction no longer
interferes....................20-2c/0.7
– from cart path in ground under
repair; nearest point of relief
from ground under repair back
on cart path...................1-4/8
– from cart path in ground under
repair; nearest point of relief
from ground under repair back
on cart path; drop into ground
under repair impracticable.......1-4/8.5
– measuring across ground under
repair in obtaining relief 25-1b/15
– player determines nearest point
of relief but physically unable to
play intended stroke 24-2b/3
– player does not follow
recommended procedure in
determining nearest point of
relief.......................24-2b/2
– player takes relief from area of
ground under repair; condition
interferes for stroke with club
not used to determine nearest
point of relief 20-2c/0.8
– player unable physically to
determine nearest point of
relief.......................24-2b/3.5
– two equidistant nearest points
of relief meet requirements of
ground under repair Rule 25-1b/16
order of play when two balls lie in
ground under repair and both
players take relief................10/1

play prohibited from area of ground
under repair
– ball dropped in ground
under repair from which play
prohibited after being deemed
unplayable; ball then dropped
under ground under repair Rule ..25-1b/14.5
– stroke made from
environmentally-sensitive area
marked as ground under repair ...33-8/43
– whether player may drop ball
into ground under repair from
which play prohibited 20-7/3
player enters environmentally-
sensitive area marked as ground
under repair to retrieve ball.......33-8/42
player entitled to relief from ground
under repair lifts ball
– player then replaces ball and
plays from original position.......18-2a/12
– chooses not to take relief
and wishes to proceed under
unplayable ball Rule 18-2a/12.5
status of
– aeration holes.................25/15
– aeration plugs 23/12
– ball not found but known to be
in tree within ground under
repair........................25/10
– bunker totally under repair......25/13
– cracks in earth 25/12
– fallen tree....................23/7
– fallen tree attached to stump 25/9
– fallen tree in process of being
removed 25/7
– grass cuttings 25/11
– growing thing rooted within
environmentally-sensitive GUR...33-8/44.5
– hole not in use when two holes
on each green of nine hole course .16/7
– hole of removed stake defining
water hazard...................25/18
– non-growing plants within area
of ground under repair 25/10.9
– old hole plug sunk or raised on
line of putt....................16-1c/3
– rut made by tractor 25/16
– severe damage by non-
burrowing animals 33-8/32.5
– sunken hole plug...............25/17
– tree roots outside ground under
repair growing from tree inside
ground under repair............25/10.7
– tree stump....................25/8
virtually certain (or known) missing
ball is in ground under repair;
drop made under Rule 25–1c;
original ball then found within five
minutes........................25-1c/2.5
whether player entitled to relief
under ground under repair Rule
– ball deemed unplayable and
lifted; player then discovers ball
was in ground under repair.......28/13
– ball in tree in ground under repair .25/10.5
– ball outside ground under
repair area but tree within area
interferes with swing...........25-1a/1

– impracticable to make stroke
because of bush 25-1b/19
– impracticable to make stroke
because of tree................25-1b/20
– line of putt damaged
by opponent, fellow-competitor
or their caddies 16-1a/13
– sideways stroke behind tree......25-1b/22
– tree prevents stroke towards
green 25-1b/21

whether re-drop required if ball
dropped from ground under
repair area rolls to position where
condition interferes with stance....20-2c/0.5

GROUNDING CLUB
See also ADDRESSING THE BALL

"grounded," meaning of
– when club considered grounded
in grass........................18-2b/5
– when club considered grounded
in grass in water hazard..........13-4/8

addressing ball
– clubhead grounded immediately
in front of ball; whether ball
addressed 18-2b/5.5
– when ball addressed by player
putting "side-saddle"............18-2b/5.7

ball moves after
– club rested on grass
immediately behind ball..........18-2b/5
– player addresses it and then
steps away.....................18-2b/7
– player grounds club short
distance behind ball but not
immediately behind ball..........18-2b/4
– player takes several practice
swings near ball and touches
grass behind ball................18-2a/30
– stance taken but before ball
addressed 18-2b/1

ball played from bunker onto grass
bank; player hits sand with club;
ball then rolls back into bunker.....13-4/35.5

club grounded outside water
hazard while addressing ball in
hazard..........................13-4/29

club touches
– ball in bunker or water hazard
accidentally; ball does not
move 13-4/12
– bare earth wall of bunker during
backswing 13-4/34
– bridge in water hazard in
addressing ball 13-4/30
– casual water in bunker...........13-4/7
– grass in hazard during practice
swing 13-4/4
– ground in hazard while probing
for ball believed covered by
loose impediments..............12-1/4
– ground in hazard with
practice swing causing loose
impediments to move; player
also improves area of intended
swing by bending branch........13-4/28

– ground in hazard with practice
swing; stroke made fails to
extricate ball; before next
stroke club touches ground in
hazard with another practice
stroke..........................1-4/14
– ground in hazard with several
practice swings.................13-4/3
– ground in hazard with several
practice swings; player advised
of breach then makes several
more such swings...............1-4/13
– leaves in hazard during
backswing......................13-4/33
– mound made by burrowing
animal in bunker during
backswing 13-4/5
– sand in bunker during
backswing 13-4/31
– sand in bunker when ball lies
outside bunker.................13-4/1
– sand through the green behind
ball during backswing...........13-2/9
– sand through the green when
ball addressed, pressing it down...13-2/12
– solidly embedded stone in
hazard during backswing........13-4/6

hitting sand in bunker with club
after failing to extricate ball
– in four-ball match; partner's ball
in same bunker 30-3f/2
– in foursome match; partner to
play next stroke; position of ball
not improved 29/5
– in single play..................13-4/35

leaning on club in hazard while
waiting to play 13-4/2

GROUPS AND GROUPING
See also TIME OF STARTING

competitors determine own
groupings; whether permitted.....33-3/3

groupings for stroke-play play-off;
guidelines for Committee 33-3/4

play suspended by Committee
– competitor wishes to complete
hole; fellow-competitor does
not; whether competitor may
play alone and complete hole 6-8b/3
– one competitor in group has
played from tee; options for
players in group 6-8b/2
– player wishes to practice after
scheduled resumption but
before group plays 7-2/12

team mates playing as fellow-
competitors exchange advice;
whether permitted..............8-1/22

time of starting
– player late but group unable to
play due to delay................6-3a/4
– player late but in time to play in
correct order 6-3a/2
– players start early..............6-3a/5

GUIDELINES

authority for Committee to
  establish pace of play guidelines for .App I-C-4
    − Committee in resolving
      questions of fact 34-3/9
    − Committee to determine
      applicable Rule when player
      proceeds under inapplicable Rule .34-3/6
    − determining course record . . . . . . Misc./I
    − determining whether ball not
      on List of Conforming Ball
      conforms with Rules 5-1/1.5
    − determining whether serious
      breach of Rule 1−2 has occurred . .1-2/0.5
    − determining which ball counts
      when player proceeds under
      Rule 3−3 . . . . .3-3/0.5
    − establishing groupings for
      stroke-play play-off 33-3/4
    − relocating hole due to severity
      of location during stroke-play
      round 33-2b/1.5
    − relocating hole when damaged
      after ball already positioned
      nearby on putting green 33-2b/2
    − relocating holes and/or tee-
      markers during stroke-play
      round, general 33-2b/1
    − waiving or modifying
      disqualification penalty
      for failure to discontinue
      play immediately under
      condition requiring immediate
      discontinuance 6-8b/7
on whether to cancel round 33-2d/1

HALVED HOLE

See also CONCESSION; DEFAULT

advice given by player to opponent
  putting for half 2-2/1
agreement between player and
  opponent that hole halved
    − after match result posted player
      realizes he won hole thus should
      have won match; player then
      makes claim 2-5/9
    − after second strokes on par 5 hole 2-1/1.5
    − when rules problem cannot be
      resolved 2-1/1
ball overhanging hole after
  stroke for half knocked away
  by opponent before player
  determines status 16-2/2
believing he won hole, player picks
  up opponent's ball-marker;
  opponent's putt was for half;
  whether picking up ball-marker
  considered concession 2-4/5
determination of honor at next tee
  following disputed hole 10-1a/2
four-ball competition
  − application of Rule 2−2 in four-
    ball match play 30-3/3
  − player waives turn to putt; later
    wishes to putt for half 30-3b/2

    − player with putt for half picks
      up based on misunderstanding
      of partner's score following
      statement by opponent 30/5
    − players on opposite sides
      exchange balls during play of
      hole and their partners pick up;
      error discovered at next hole 30-3c/3
incorrect information
    − causes opponent mistakenly
      to think he has putt for half;
      opponent holes putt and then
      error discovered 9-2/14
    − reported by player causes
      opponent with stroke for half to
      pick up ball .9-2/6
player walks off green under
  mistaken impression partner
  halved hole returns and putts for
  half; whether permitted 30/4
result of match when player dormie
  and opponent concedes 2-3/2
time of starting; both players in
  match late 6-3a/3

HANDICAP COMPETITION AND
HANDICAP STROKES

See also CLAIMS AND DISPUTES; CLOSE
OF COMPETITION; SCORES AND SCORE
CARDS

Committee error
    − competitor wins competition
      with wrong handicap due
      to Committee error; error
      discovered after close of
      competition 6-2b/3
    − misapplication of handicap
      affects match play draw; error
      discovered during first-round
      matches; Committee options. 33-5/3
    − player in four-ball match
      uses wrong handicap due to
      Committee misinformation 33-1/12
    − wrong handicap applied by
      Committee results in player
      not receiving prize; error
      discovered after close of
      competition 33-5/2
    − wrong handicap printed on
      score card issued by Committee
      not corrected by competitor;
      error discovered before
      competition closed 6-2b/3.5
competitor disqualified from
  handicap event for playing off
  higher handicap; whether eligible
  for gross prize in same event 33-1/13
determining honor
    − in handicap match 10-1a/1
    − in handicap stroke-play
      competition 10-2a/1
failure of players to determine
  handicaps prior to start of match
  results in one player not receiving
  handicap stroke at hole 6-2a/1

four-ball handicap competition
– gross score of partner with
better net score not recorded
by marker; error discovered
after score card returned to
Committee 31-3/1
– player in match uses wrong
handicap due to Committee
misinformation 33-1/12
– player in match with lowest
handicap unable to participate;
handicap allowances to be used . . .30-3a/3

foursome handicap competition
– competitors fail to record
individual handicaps on score
card returned to Committee 6-2b/4
– wrong handicap recorded by
competitor for partner; error
discovered after competition
closed. 6-2b/2.5

handicap stroke
– claimed after hole conceded. 6-2a/4
– given at incorrect hole in error . . .6-2a/2
– taken by player at hole by
mistake; status of late claim 2-5/13
– wrongly claimed at hole; error
discovered before hole completed 6-2a/3

handicap stroke allocation table
altered by Committee for
matches beginning other than at
first hole; whether permitted 33-4/1

meaning of "handicap"
– for purposes of Rule 6–2 . . . . .6-2/1
– when full handicap not used 6-2b/0.5

minus or zero net score; whether
permitted 2-1/2

Stableford, par or bogey handicap
competition
– lower gross score on score card
affects result of hole (Stableford
only) 32-2a/3
– lower gross score on score card
does not affect result of hole
(Stableford only). 32-2a/4
– lower gross score on score card
does not affect result of hole
(par and bogey). 32-2a/5
– partner's scores transposed at
hole but not to side's advantage . . .32-2a/1
– partners' scores transposed at
hole to side's advantage. 32-2a/2

wrong handicap
– applied by Committee results
in player not receiving prize;
error discovered after close of
competition 33-5/2
– competitor disqualified for
returning score card with
higher handicap in first round
of competition in which best
two of four scores determines
winner; whether competitor
disqualified for entire
competition 6-2b/5
– knowingly used by competitor
in stroke play; error discovered
after competition closed. 6-2b/2
– players use 3/4 of handicap
difference instead of full

handicap difference; error
discovered after match result
decided 6-2a/6
– printed on score card issued by
Committee not corrected by
competitor; error discovered
before competition closed 6-2b/3.5
– recorded by competitor for
partner in foursome stroke-play
competition; error discovered
after competition closed. 6-2b/2.5
– used by player in four-ball
match due to Committee
misinformation 33-1/12
– used by player in match by
mistake; error discovered after
result officially announced 6-2a/5
– used by player in stroke-play
competition by mistake; error
discovered after competition
closed. 6-2b/1

HOLE

See also BALL OVERHANGING HOLE;
CLAIMS AND DISPUTES; CONCESSION;
FLAGSTICK; HOLED AND HOLING OUT;
PUTTING GREEN

ball at rest kicked away from hole by
spectator attending flagstick 18-1/10

ball blown into hole by competitor
not replaced and holed out 3-2/2

ball embedded in side of hole
– all of ball below lip of hole. 16/2
– all of ball not below lip of hole 16/3

ball knocked away from lip of hole in
disgust. 18-2a/23

ball overhanging hole
– falls into hole after being
addressed 18-2b/10
– falls into hole after concession
of next stroke 2-4/2
– falls into hole after player waits
40 seconds .16-2/1
– fellow-competitor's ball
knocked from lip of hole by
competitor not replaced. 3-2/1
– knocked away by opponent
before player determines status . .16-2/2
– lifted, cleaned and replaced; ball
then falls into hole 16-2/0.5
– player jumps close to hole to
cause ball to drop; ball falls into
hole 1-2/4

ball resting against flagstick moves
away from hole when flagstick
removed by player; ball not placed
on lip of hole. .17-4/4

ball rolls into hole after being
replaced on putting green 20-3d/1

booklet providing distances to holes
from various points. 14-3/5

concession
– ball falls into hole after
concession of next stroke. 2-4/2
– player concedes opponent's
next stroke and then knocks
opponent's ball into hole. 2-4/1

– player with ball not found
concedes hole; ball then found
in hole 2-4/11

damaged hole
– ragged edge repaired by player
after holing out but before
opponent, fellow-competitor or
partner holes out 1-2/3.5
– when repair permitted and
procedure for player 16-1a/6

flagstick attendant stands behind hole.17-1/4

hole surrounded by casual water 33-2d/2

hole-liner
– ball strikes edge of hole-liner
and bounces out of hole 16/5
– not sunk deep enough; relief
available to player. 16/4
– pulled out with flagstick; ball
falls into unlined hole. 17/7
– pulled out with flagstick; hole-
liner deflects ball 17/8

marking position of hole with club
instead of flagstick. 17-3/6

meaning of "stands near the hole". . . .17-1/1

old hole plug sunk or raised on line
of putt. 16-1c/3

original ball discovered in hole after
player searches five minutes then
continues play with provisional ball .1-1/3

player holes short putt; another
player alleges ball removed from
hole before at rest. 16/5.5

player plays away from hole to assist
partner 30-3f/6

player putts with one hand and
catches ball in hole with other hand .1-2/5

position of hole on green indicated by
– attachment to flagstick 17/1
– different colored flags 17/2
– flagstick with tapered or varying
diameters 17/3
– map of putting green indicating
hole location displayed at tee. 33/6

procedure for referee in
determining ball farther from hole .10-1b/1

relocating hole during stipulated
round
– due to severity of location 33-2b/1.5
– general 33-2b/1
– when damaged after ball already
positioned nearby on putting
green 33-2b/2

removing casual water from hole. 16-1a/4

spike mark damage around hole
repaired; whether permitted. 16-1c/4

touching inside of hole. 16-1a/5

two holes on each green of nine
hole course. 16/7

HOLE PLUG

Local Rule permitting repair of turf
plugs on putting green not 4–1/4
inches in diameter. 33-8/30

old hole plug sunk or raised on line
of putt; relief available to player 16-1c/3

spike mark on line of putt pressed
down when player repairs old hole
plug; whether permitted 16-1a/16.5

status of sunken hole plug 25/17

HOLED AND HOLING OUT
See also FAILURE TO HOLE OUT; STROKE

advice given by player after holing
out to opponent with putt for half . .2-2/1

ball embedded in side of hole
– all of ball below lip of hole. 16/2
– all of ball not below lip of hole 16/3

ball overhanging hole falls into hole
– after being addressed. 18-2b/10
– as flagstick removed from hole. . . .16-2/4
– striking flagstick while being
removed from hole 16-2/5

ball played under water hazard Rule;
original ball then found in hazard
and holed out as second ball 26-1/5

ball replaced, putted from wrong
place and
– holed 20-7c/1
– lifted then putted from right place.20-7c/2

ball still moving in bottom of hole
as player removes it; whether ball
holed. 16/5.5

competitor practices putting on
18th green immediately after
holing out in first round of
stroke-play competition played
over consecutive days; whether
practice between rounds 7-2/8

damaged hole repaired after player
holes out but before opponent,
fellow-competitor or partner
holes out. 1-2/3.5

flagstick
– ball holed while flagstick in hole
after stroke from putting green;
player claims ball did not touch
flagstick 17-3/1
– ball resting against flagstick
lifted before being holed 17-4/1
– ball resting against flagstick; putt
conceded and ball removed by
opponent before player can
remove flagstick 17-4/2
– player putts with one hand and
holes ball while holding flagstick
with other hand 17-1/5

four-ball match play; player with
putt for half picks up in error at
suggestion of opponent based on
misunderstanding 30/5

Local Rule for temporary putting
green waives requirement to hole
out; whether authorized 33-8/1

modifying penalty for not holing out
in stroke play .33-7/2

original ball discovered in hole after
– five-minute search and
continuation of play with
provisional ball 1-1/3
– player concedes hole thinking
ball lost 2-4/11

– player puts another ball into play . .1-1/2
– wrong ball played 1-1/4

player lifts ball before holing out;
opponent then picks up his ball
claiming player loses hole 2-5/3

player putts with one hand and
catches ball in hole with other hand .1-2/5

practice putt made by player after
he and partner have holed out but
before opponents hole out 30/6

when provisional ball holed
becomes ball in play 27-2b/2

whether ball considered holed
  – ball blown into hole by
    competitor not replaced and
    holed out 3-2/2
  – ball removed from hole while still
    bouncing in bottom of hole-liner . .16/5.5
  – hole-liner pulled out with
    flagstick; ball falls into unlined hole 17/7
  – lifted ball replaced on putting
    green; ball then rolls into hole 20-3d/1

HONOR

See also ORDER OF PLAY; PLAYING OUT OF TURN

determination of honor
  – at next tee following disputed hole 10-1a/2
  – in four-ball match in which
    points awarded for both better-
    ball and aggregate scores. 30/3
  – in handicap match. 10-1a/1
  – in handicap stroke play 10-2a/1
  – when opponent requires player
    with honor to cancel stroke
    played from outside teeing
    ground 11-4a/1

players agree not to tee off in
prescribed order to save time 10-1a/3

IMPROVING AREA OF INTENDED STANCE OR SWING, POSITION OR LIE OF BALL, OR LINE OF PLAY OR PUTT

See also AREA OF INTENDED SWING; LIE OF BALL ALTERED; LINE OF PLAY; LINE OF PUTT; STANCE

meaning of "improve" in Rule 13-2 . . . .13-2/0.5

altering physical conditions
  – act of etiquette alters physical
    conditions affecting play 1-2/0.7
  – bush branch broken in area into
    which ball may roll after drop. 1-2/3
  – flagstick adjustment; player's
    rights 17/4
  – line of play altered by fellow-
    competitor .1-2/1.5
  – line of putt damaged accidentally
    by opponent, fellow-competitor
    or their caddies 16.1a/13
  – pressing ball into surface of
    putting green to prevent wind
    or gravity from moving it. 1-2/9
  – ragged edge of hole repaired
    after player holes out but before
    opponent, fellow-competitor or
    partner holes out. 1-2/3.5

– towel placed on cactus bush by
  player before stance taken 1-2/10
– turf pressed down by player as
  ball is rolling towards area 1-2/8

area in which ball to be dropped or
placed; whether improved by
  – removing loose impediiments. 23-1/6
  – removing sand or loose soil 13-2/11
  – repairing pitch-mark 13-2/10
  – replacing divots. 13-2/4.5
  – tree branch held back by caddie
    to prevent it from deflecting
    dropped ball 20-2a/5

area of intended swing; whether improved by
  – act that also causes ball to move
    and whether multiple penalties
    apply. 1-4/15
  – bending boundary fence 13-2/18
  – bending shrub with hand 13-4/28
  – breaking branch interfering with
    backswing on teeing ground 13-2/14
  – breaking branch on backswing;
    swing discontinued. 13-2/14.5
  – breaking branch; player then
    chooses different direction of
    play; new area of intended swing
    not affected by broken branch 13-2/24
  – moving growing or fixed object
    situated out of bounds. 13-2/19
  – moving loose impediment in
    hazard accidentally 13-4/13
  – moving loose impediments by
    walking to ball and taking stance
    in hazard 13-4/13.5
  – moving natural object to
    determine whether attached or
    loose impediment. 13-2/26
  – pushing off-course fence leaning
    across boundary to upright
    position 13-2/20
  – removing boundary stake 13-2/17
  – removing immovable obstruction .13-2/15
  – removing moss or creepers in
    tree. 13-2/37
  – repairing pitch-mark made by
    ball on previous stroke 13-2/21
  – replacing or removing
    undetached divot interfering
    with backswing. 13-2/5
  – shaking water from tree branch
    interfering with backswing 13-2/23
  – taking stance fairly 13-2/1
  – taking stance fairly then
    changing direction of play 13-2/1.7

lie or position of ball; whether
improved by
  – alteration through natural
    causes during suspension of play . .6-8d/1
  – alterations made by
    greenkeeping staff during
    suspension of play 6-8d/2
  – bending boundary fence 13-2/18
  – bending grass in removal of
    loose impediments. 13-2/13
  – breaking off grass behind ball on
    teeing ground 13-2/3
  – greenkeeping staff member
    raking bunker when player's ball
    in bunker 13-2/4
  – marking position of ball 20-1/15.5

– moving loose impediment
affecting lie when ball through
the green lifted under Rule
requiring replacement. 23-1/7
– moving loose impediment in
hazard accidentally 13-4/13
– moving loose impediments
when approaching ball in hazard . .13-4/13.5
– pressing down irregularities on
teeing ground after missed tee
shot prior to next stroke 13-2/2
– pressing down behind ball
through the green during address .13-2/12
– probing near ball for tree roots
or rocks through the green 13-2/27
– removing dew or frost. 13-2/35
– removing loose impediment
affecting after lifting ball under
Rule requiring replacement 23-1/8
– removing sand behind ball with
backswing 13-2/9
– replacing obstruction which
worsened player's lie when
removed 13-2/15.5
– replacing or removing
undetached divot interfering
with backswing. 13-2/5
– smoothing irregularities in
bunker after stroke but before
ball extricated. 13-4/36
– taking stance fairly 13-2/1
– taking stance fairly then
changing direction of play 13-2/1.7
– throwing rake into bunker 13-4/21
– touching grass with club during
practice swing in hazard 13-4/4
– using cane or club to enter or
leave bunker when ball lies in
bunker 13-4/3.5

line of play; whether improved by
– creating and then smoothing
footprints in bunker on line of play 13-2/29
– mopping up casual water. 13-2/34
– moving interfering growing
object in attempting to take
stance fairly. 13-2/1.1
– moving tree branch affecting
fellow-competitor's line of play
while discussing with referee
whether fellow-competitor
entitled to free relief 1-2/1.5
– pressing down stone in bunker
when ball lies through the green . .13-2/31
– removing casual water from hole . .16-1a/4
– removing dew or frost. 13-2/35
– removing stone from wall 13-2/32
– replacing divot in divot hole 13-2/6
– replacing divot; when divot
replaced. 13-2/7
– sanctioning repair of spike mark
by fellow-competitor. 13-2/36
– smoothing irregularities in
bunker after player lifts ball
and states intention to proceed
under Rule 28a 13-4/35.8
– smoothing irregularities in
bunker when ball lies through
the green. .13-2/28
– taking relief from abnormal
ground condition 25-1b/3

– taking stance fairly then
changing direction of play 13-2/1.7
– testing condition of bunker
before deciding whether to play
through it. .13-2/30

line of putt; whether improved by
– brushing loose impediments
along line of putt rather than to
side. 16-1a/10
– placing ball ahead of ball-marker
then rolling or sliding back to
original position 16-1a/17
– removing casual water from hole. .16-1a/4
– removing dew or frost. 13-2/35
– sanctioning repair of spike mark
by fellow-competitor. 13-2/36
– stepping on; when done
purposely by opponent or
fellow-competitor 1-2/1
– walking on; when done
accidentally or intentionally 16-1a/12

stance or area of intended stance;
whether improved by
– moving interfering growing
object in attempting to take
stance fairly. 13-2/1.1
– moving loose impediment in
hazard accidentally 13-4/13
– moving loose impediments
when approaching ball in hazard . .13-4/13.5
– placing ball-marker in front of ball .20-1/19
– replacing divot just taken by
another player 13-2/8.7
– taking stance fairly 13-2/1
– taking stance fairly in any
direction player chooses. 13-2/1.5
– taking stance fairly then
changing direction of play 13-2/1.7

INAPPLICABLE RULE OR PROCEDURE USED

ball deemed unplayable in water hazard
– original ball dropped in hazard
and played .20-7/2
– substituted ball dropped in
hazard; player realizes error
before playing 20-7/2.5

ball dropped under water hazard
Rule without knowledge or virtual
certainty ball in hazard; original
ball then found 26-1/3.7

ball lifted and dropped away from
– boundary stake under
obstruction Rule 18-2a/3
– movable obstruction 18-2a/4

ball not found presumed lost in
ground under repair without
knowledge of virtual certainty;
player drops and plays substituted
ball under procedure in Rule 25-1c .25-1c/2

casual water mistaken for water
hazard; player drops substituted
ball under water hazard Rule 25-1b/13

competitor plays out of turn, thinks
stroke must be canceled and
replayed, drops ball at spot from
which stroke made; procedure
questioned 27/17

player proceeds under inapplicable
Rule; guidelines for Committee to
determine applicable Rule 34-3/6

player unaware ball in water hazard
takes relief from interference by
burrowing animal hole 25-1b/26

second ball played in match play
when player unsure of rights or
procedure. 3-3/9

three balls played when competitor
unsure of rights or procedure 3-3/10

INCORRECT INFORMATION ON RULES
See also INFORMATION AS TO STROKES
TAKEN; WRONG INFORMATION

given by Committee
– correction of incorrect ruling
made during subsequent round
of competition; whether
permitted 34-3/1
– non-conforming club ruled
conforming; player uses club 34-3/1.5
– places player in stroke play at
serious disadvantage 34-3/3.3
– player in match proceeds based
on incorrect Committee ruling;
guidelines for Committee when
error discovered 34-3/3
– player proceeds on referee's
ruling based on available facts;
subsequent facts prove ruling
incorrect 34-3/7
– player proceeds on referee's
ruling based on player's version
of facts; player's version later
found incorrect. 34-3/8
– referee incorrectly advises
player to cancel and replay stroke . 34-3/1.3
– whether player should be
exempt from penalty and for
what duration 34-3/1.5

given by player; guidelines for
Committee when incorrect
information given in ignorance
and knowingly 9/1

match play
– incorrect information on
penalty applicable to player
given by opponent; error
discovered after match result
announced; player then makes
claim. 2-5/10
– incorrect procedure agreed to
in error by player and opponent;
whether valid claim can be made
after procedure followed 2-5/8.5
– ruling made at final hole
reversed by referee after
players have left putting green
but before result officially
announced. 34-2/5
– ruling made on previous hole
reversed by referee after play of
next hole begun 34-2/6
– wrong ruling accepted by
players from person not on
Committee; match played to

conclusion based on ruling;
whether Committee should
consider late claim 2-5/8

INDICATING LINE FOR PUTTING
See also IMPROVING AREA OF INTENDED
STANCE OR SWING, POSITION OR LIE
OF BALL, OR LINE OF PLAY OR PUTT;
INDICATING LINE OF PLAY; LINE OF PLAY;
LINE OF PUTT; PUTTING GREEN

ball-marker in position to assist
player in lining up putt. 20-1/11

caddie while attending flagstick
suggests player aim at foot;
whether breach of any Rule 8-2b/2

condition authorises team captains
to point out line for putting but
requires they keep off putting
greens 8-2b/4

line
– drawn or on ball aimed to
indicate line for putting when
ball replaced 20-3a/2
– scratched on putting green to
mark position of ball 20-1/16

putting green touched by player
in pointing out partner's line
for putting; player incidentally
touches own line of putt; whether
multiple penalties apply 30/2.5

shadow cast by caddie to indicate
line for putting 8-2b/1

INDICATING LINE OF PLAY
See also INDICATING LINE FOR PUTTING;
LINE OF PLAY; LINE OF PUTT

club placed on ground to align feet. . . 8-2a/1

line drawn or on ball aimed to
indicate line of play when ball
replaced 20-3a/2

object or mark placed
– beside or behind ball to indicate
line of play 8-2a/2
– indicating distance for pitch shot . 8-2a/3

putting green touched to indicate
line of play before player chips
from off putting green. 8-2b/3

INFORMATION AS TO STROKES TAKEN
See also WRONG INFORMATION

"as soon as practicable" in Rule 9–2;
meaning of 9-2/1

conscious failure to correct
opponent's misunderstanding of
state of match; what constitutes
wrong information 9-2/12

four-ball match; player with putt
for half picks up in error at
suggestion of opponent based on
misunderstanding 30/5

incorrect information given
– by competitor in hole-by-hole
play-off. 9-3/1
– by player's partner or caddie to
opponent. 9-2/2

− voluntarily by player to opponent .9-2/3

player concedes match after
   winning it when opponent lodges
   invalid claim regarding strokes taken 2-4/15

player tells opponent he will
   proceed under water hazard Rule;
   changes mind after opponent plays. .9-2/13

withholding information as to
   strokes
   taken
   − player refuses to tell opponent
     number of strokes taken 9-2/3.5
   − until opponent's turn to play 9-2/4

wrong score for player reported to
   opponent
   − after play of hole; error not
     corrected; when penalty
     applicable. .9-2/15
   − error discovered several holes
     later 9-2/9
   − opponent mistakenly thinks
     he has putt for half; opponent
     holes putt then error discovered. .9-2/14
   − opponent with chance for half
     picks up 9-2/6
   − penalty stroke omitted when
     opponent advised of score for
     hole; error discovered after
     match conceded by opponent 9-2/10

INSECTS
   See also BURROWING ANIMAL, REPTILE
   OR BIRD (AND HOLES MADE BY THEM);
   LOOSE IMPEDIMENTS; STATUS OF
   OBJECT

after ball addressed on putting
   green, ball moved during attempt
   to brush insect from it 23-1/12

dangerous situation
   − bees interfering with play 1-4/10
   − fire ants interfering with play 33-8/22
   − meaning of "dangerous situation" .1-4/11

discontinuing play due to bee sting. . . .6-8a/3

Local Rule
   − allowing free relief from damage
     made by insects 33-8/21
   − deeming hard conical ant hills as
     ground under repair. 33-8/22

removal of insect from ball; whether
   permitted 23-1/5

status of
   − ant hill. 23/5
   − insect flying in water hazard 13-4/16.5
   − insect on ball in bunker or water
     hazard 23-1/5.5
   − spiders (insect-like creatures)
     and spider webs 23/5.5

INTEGRAL PART OF COURSE
   See also FENCE; GATE, DOOR OR
   WINDOW; MARKING OR DEFINING
   COURSE; OBSTRUCTIONS; WALL

Committee
   − exposed water pipe adjacent
     and parallel to boundary fence;
     in most cases player would be
     entitled to drop away from

fence by taking free relief
   from water pipe; suggested
   procedure for Committee 33-2a/1
   − immovable obstruction relief
     incidentally results in relief from
     boundary fence. 24-2b/6
   − may declare artificial surfaces
     and sides of roads and paths
     integral parts of course. . . . . .App I-A-5c
   − responsibility for clarifying
     status of objects that may be
     obstructions . . . . .App I-A-5a

grounding club on construction
   deemed integral part of course in
   bunker or water hazard 13-4/30

improving line of play by removing
   stone from wall 13-2/32

incorrect procedure agreed to in
   error by player and opponent
   thinking road obstruction;
   whether valid claim can be made
   after procedure followed and
   opponent discovers road deemed
   integral part of course 2-5/8.5

status of
   − stile attached to boundary fence . .24/1
   − tree basins. 33-2a/10.5

unsure whether road obstruction
   or integral part of course
   − competitor invokes Rule 3–3;
     whether score with second ball
     counts if played from wrong place .3-3/5
   − competitor plays second ball;
     fails to announce intention to
     invoke Rule 3–3; fails to report
     facts to Committee 3-3/6.5

window of clubhouse opened and
   ball played through it 24-2b/14

LEAVES
   See also STATUS OF OBJECT; TREE
   OR BUSH

leaf or several leaves knocked
   down in area of intended swing,
   whether area of intended swing
   improved. 13-2/0.5

Local Rule
   − declaring accumulations of
     leaves (at specified holes)
     through the green as ground
     under repair 33-8/31
   − providing relief from
     accumulations of leaves in bunkers 13-4/33

removal of leaves from putting
   green by Committee, whether
   authorized 33/1

palm of hand brushed repeatedly
   on putting green to remove small
   leaves 16-1a/9

player moved leaves in hazard by
   approaching ball and taking stance . .13-4/13.5

top of ball covered by leaves in
   hazard but part of ball visible from
   another angle .12-1/3

touching
 – ground in bunker or water
  hazard with club while probing
  for ball believed covered by leaves.12-1/4
 – leaves during backswing for
  stroke in bunker or water hazard .13-4/33

LIE OF BALL ALTERED
See also IMPROVING AREA OF INTENDED
STANCE OR SWING, POSITION OR LIE OF
BALL, OR LINE OF PLAY OR PUTT

act of marking position of ball alters
 lie..............................20-1/15.5

ball stepped on accidentally by
 player; original lie altered; player
 places ball in wrong place and plays. .18-2a/21.3

divot made by stroke of partner,
 opponent or fellow-competitor
 comes to rest near player's ball in
 bunker; whether player entitled
 to relief.........................13-4/18

embedded ball in hazard lifted to
 determine whether unfit for play;
 procedure if original lie altered.....5-3/5

gallery-control stake removed with
 or without sanction of player; lie of
 ball worsened; procedure for player .20-3b/3

in bunker
 – by greenkeeper when player's
  ball lies therein................13-2/4
 – by stance taken by another player .20-3b/2
 – by stroke made by another
  player while ball lifted from
  bunker.......................20-3b/1
 – prior to resumption of play by
  greenkeeper...................6-8d/2
 – prior to resumption of play by
  natural causes.................6-8d/1

lie of ball to be replaced altered;
 procedure for player when
 – original lie known but spot
  where ball originally lay through
  the green not determinable......20-3b/4
 – original lie known but spot
  where ball originally lay in
  bunker not determinable........20-3b/6
 – original lie not known and spot
  where ball originally lay not
  determinable..................20-3b/5

lie worsened when player removed
 obstruction; player replaces
 obstruction restoring original lie;
 whether permitted..............13-2/15.5

loose impediment affecting lie
 – moved while ball lifted
  when another player makes
  nearby stroke; whether lie
  considered altered and/or loose
  impediment must be replaced 20-3b/8
 – moves when player lifts ball
  through the green under Rule 23-1/7

obstruction removed by player
 worsens lie of ball; player replaces
 obstruction restoring original lie;
 whether permitted..............13-2/15.5

on teeing ground after player
 misses tee shot and presses down
 irregularities....................13-2/2

pine cone falls from tree and comes
 to rest behind ball lying in bunker;
 whether player entitled to relief....13-4/18.5

pitch-mark made by ball of partner,
 opponent or fellow-competitor
 affects lie of player's ball..........13-2/8

prior to resumption of play by
 natural causes...................6-8d/1

sand from bunker stroke by partner,
 opponent, or fellow-competitor
 affects player's lie on apron next
 to putting green..................13-2/8.5

wind causes ball on putting green to
 oscillate; player presses ball into
 surface of putting green to stop
 oscillation........................1-2/9

whether original lie may be "nearest
 lie most similar" 20-3b/7

LIGHTNING
See also DANGEROUS SITUATIONS;
DISCONTINUANCE AND RESUMPTION OF
PLAY; WEATHER CONDITIONS

claiming danger from lightning,
 player refuses to play when
 resumption ordered by
 Committee......................6-8b/5

failure to discontinue play
 immediately; guidelines
 for waiving or modifying
 disqualification penalty when App
 I-C–5 condition in effect 6-8b/7

specimen condition requiring
 immediate suspension of play due
 to a dangerous situation..........App I-C-5

partners fail to discontinue
 play immediately contrary to
 condition of competition 30-3e/1

LINE OF PLAY
See also IMPROVING AREA OF INTENDED
STANCE OR SWING, POSITION OR LIE
OF BALL, OR LINE OF PLAY OR PUTT;
INDICATING LINE OF PLAY

ball mark partially on and partially
 off putting green on player's line
 of play; whether repair permitted...16-1c/1.5

ball outside bunker; stone in bunker
 on line of play pressed down or
 removed.........................13-2/31

barn doors opened by player to play
 shot through barn................24-2b/15

bending grass in removal of loose
 impediments.....................13-2/13

boundary post on line of play
 removed by player then replaced
 before stroke made...............13-2/25

caddie touches putting green to
 indicate line of play before player
 chips from off green 8-2b/3

casual water on putting green
 intervenes between ball off green
 and hole 25-1a/2

clubhouse window opened by
 player and ball played through
 window.........................24-2b/14

club placed on ground to align feet. . . .8-2a/1

competitor sanctions repair of
spike damage on his line of putt by
fellow-competitor 13-2/36

divot replaced in divot hole on line
of play 13-2/6

"fairly taking his stance"
– explanation of "fairly taking his
stance". 13-2/1
– player allowed to play in any
direction in "fairly taking his
stance". 13-2/1.5
– player attempts to take stance
fairly but improves line of play
by moving interfering growing
object. 13-2/1.1
– player under tree, changes
intended direction of play and
fairly takes stance second time. . . .13-2/1.7

footprints
– created and then smoothed in
bunker on line of play by player . . .13-2/29
– created and then smoothed in
bunker on line of play by player
required to enter bunker to
retrieve ball. 13-2/29.3
– made in bunker on extension of
player's line of play by opponent
or fellow-competitor. 13-2/29.5
– second player to play from
bunker wishes to smooth
footprints made by first player. . . .13-4/19

greenkeeper rakes bunker when
player's ball lies therein improving
lie of ball or line of play 13-2/4

immovable obstruction on player's
line of play removed by outside
agency 13-2/33

Local Rule allowing line-of-sight
relief from
– irrigation-control boxes near
fairways; whether authorized. 33-8/17
– protective fence near line of play
without penalty 33-8/18

mark placed by player to indicate
distance for pitch shot 8-2a/3

object placed beside or behind ball
to indicate line of play 8-2a/2

obstruction interferes with
abnormal stroke; abnormal stroke
reasonable in circumstances 24-2b/17

pine needles piled for removal
interfere with line of play after
ball dropped away 25-1b/17

pitch-mark made by partner's,
opponent's or fellow-
competitor's ball affects player's
line of play. 13-2/8

player in match play refuses to
comply with request to lift ball 2/3

probing near ball for tree roots or
rocks; whether permitted 13-2/27

relief from obstruction interfering
with swing incidentally gives relief
from intervention on line of play 24-2b/7

removal of casual water or loose
impediments
– mopping up casual water on line
of play. 13-2/34
– mopping up casual water on line
of putt 16-1a/1
– on putting green by Committee . . .33/1
– removing casual water from hole. .16-1a/4

removal of dew or frost 13-2/35

smoothing irregularities in bunker
– after playing backwards out of
bunker player smoothes bunker
on line of play for next stroke. 13-4/37.5
– second player to play wishes to
restore bunker to its condition
prior to first player's stroke 13-4/19
– situated between ball and hole;
ball lies outside bunker 13-2/28

status of moss or creepers in tree
and on ground 13-2/37

testing condition of bunker before
deciding whether to play through it .13-2/30

whether line of play improved by
– creating and then smoothing
footprints in bunker on line of
play. 13-2/29
– mopping up casual water. 13-2/34
– moving interfering growing
object in attempting to take
stance fairly. 13-2/1.1
– pressing down stone in bunker
when ball lies through the green . .13-2/31
– removing casual water from hole. .16-1a/4
– removing dew or frost. 13-2/35
– removing stone from wall 13-2/32
– replacing divot in divot hole 13-2/6
– replacing divot; when divot
replaced. 13-2/7
– sanctioning repair of spike mark
by fellow-competitor. 13-2/36
– smoothing irregularities in
bunker after player lifts ball
and states intention to proceed
under Rule 28a 13-4/35.8
– smoothing irregularities in
bunker when ball lies through
the green 13-2/28
– taking relief from abnormal
ground condition 25-1b/3
– taking stance fairly then
changing direction of play 13-2/1.7
– testing condition of bunker
before deciding whether to
play through it. 13-2/30

LINE OF PUTT

See also HOLE; IMPROVING AREA OF
INTENDED STANCE OR SWING, POSITION
OR LIE OF BALL, OR LINE OF PLAY OR PUTT;
INDICATING LINE FOR PUTTING; PUTTING
GREEN

"line of putt;" illustration and
meaning of in context of "standing
astride or on line of putt". 16-1e/1

ball mark repaired second time;
whether permitted 16-1c/1

ball-marker positioned to side or in
front of ball; whether permitted 20-1/19

ball placed in front of ball-marker
and rolled or slid back to original
position...........................16-1a/17

caddie
– attending flagstick advises player
to aim at his foot...............8-2b/2
– casts shadow to indicate line for
putting........................8-2b/1

casual water
– mopped up or brushed aside
from line of putt by player........16-1a/1
– removed from hole by player......16-1a/4
– removed from putting green by
Committee.....................33/1
– visible when player walks beside
line of putt but not visible
elsewhere.....................25/5

damaged accidentally by opponent,
fellow-competitor or their caddies..16-1a/13

depression in putting green from
removed partially embedded
acorn repaired by player...........16-1a/7

dew or frost removed from line of
putt.............................16-1a/3

flagstick attendant stands behind
instead of beside hole; whether
permitted.......................17-1/4

hole
– damaged; when repair
permitted and procedure for
player........................16-1a/6
– inside of hole touched; whether
line of putt touched.............16-1a/5
– ragged edge repaired by player
after holing out but before
opponent, fellow-competitor or
partner holes out...............1-2/3.5

line drawn or on ball aimed to
indicate line for putting when ball
replaced.......................20-3a/2

loose impediment(s)
– brushed along line of putt then
to side.......................16-1a/10
– palm of hand used to brush line
of putt about one dozen times
to remove small leaves..........16-1a/9
– removed from putting green by
Committee.....................33/1
– towel or cap used to remove
loose impediments from line of
putt..........................16-1a/8

meaning of "extension of line of putt
behind ball" in context of standing
astride or on line of putt...........16-1e/1

mushroom growing on line of putt....16-1a/15

old hole plug sunken or raised on
line of putt.....................16-1c/3

opponent's next stroke conceded;
player knocks ball away along own
line of putt.....................16-1d/2

player
– allows partner to stand on
extension of line of putt behind
ball; assists partner with similar
putt..........................30-3f/13
– entitled to putt stands on
another player's line of putt......30-3b/1

– in match play refuses to comply
with request to lift ball..........2/3
– touches putting green to point
out partner's line for putting
and incidentally touches own
line of putt; whether multiple
penalties apply.................30/2.5

shielding line of putt from wind;
whether permitted...............1-2/2

spike mark
– competitor sanctions or tacitly
approves repair of spike damage
on his line of putt by fellow-
competitor....................13-2/36
– on line of putt pressed down
when player repairs old hole plug .16-1a/16.5
– on line of putt repaired during
repair of ball mark..............16-1a/16
– player and opponent or fellow-
competitor agree to repair
spike marks on one another's
line of putt....................1-3/3
– raised tuft of grass on line
of putt brushed or tested to
determine whether loose........16-1a/11

status of worm partially
underground....................23/8

walking on line of putt
– accidentally by player...........16-1a/12
– accidentally by opponent,
fellow-competitor or their
caddies and damaged...........16-1a/13
– intentionally by player..........16-1a/12
– purposely and altered by
opponent or fellow-competitor...1-2/1

whether line of putt improved by
– removing casual water from hole..16-1a/4
– removing dew or frost...........13-2/35
– sanctioning repair of spike mark
by fellow-competitor............13-2/36
– stepping on; when done
purposely by opponent or
fellow-competitor..............1-2/1
– walking on; when done
accidentally or intentionally......16-1a/12

LOCAL RULES
See also CONDITIONS OF COMPETITION

abnormal ground conditions
– allowing free relief from damage
made by insects...............33-8/21
– allowing relief through the green
for ball embedded in own pitch-
mark; specimen Local Rule......App I-B-4a
– altering ground under repair
relief procedure to require
player to drop behind condition;
whether authorized.............33-8/26
– declaring areas of course as
ground under repair from which
play prohibited and relief must
be taken; specimen Local Rule....App I-B-2a
– declaring severe damage by non-
burrowing animals as ground
under repair...................33-8/32.5
– declaring temporary
accumulations of leaves (at
specified holes) through the
green as ground under repair.....33-8/31

– declaring temporary
accumulations of leaves in
bunkers ground under repair 13-4/33
– declaring unsurfaced road
ground under repair for tee
shot only; whether authorized 33-8/20
– deeming fire ant mounds or hills
ground under repair. 33-8/22
– deeming ground under repair
adjacent to artificially-surfaced
cart path to have same status as
path 33-8/25
– deeming hard conical ant hills as
ground under repair. 33-8/22
– deeming lines used for gallery-
control purposes ground under
repair. 24-2b/20
– deeming mushrooms growing
on line of putt as ground under
repair 16-1a/15
– granting relief from ground
under repair in fairway of 1st
hole only during play of that
hole; whether authorized 33-8/23
– "preferred lies" or "winter
rules;" specimen Local Rule . . . . .App I-B-4c
– providing relief from exposed
tree roots without penalty;
whether authorized 33-8/8
– providing relief from flooded
bunker without penalty outside
bunker 33-8/27
– providing relief from seams of
cut turf; specimen Local Rule . . . .App I-B-4e
– requiring player to take relief
under penalty from tree nursery
(or plantation) from which play
prohibited; whether authorized. . .33-8/29
– requiring relief away from
young trees to prevent damage;
specimen Local Rule . . . . .App I-B-3

aeration holes; specimen Local Rule
allowing relief . . . . .App I-B-4d

bad weather; permitting
competitors to discontinue play
by agreement; whether authorized. .33-8/5

bunker
– casual water completely fills
bunker; allowing free relief
outside bunker 33-8/27
– damaged by children; allowing
drop outside bunker or
smoothing of sand without
penalty; whether authorized 33-8/9
– deeming material similar to sand
to have same status as sand 33-8/40
– deeming partially grass-covered
walls of bunkers to be part of
bunker 33-8/39.5
– deeming stacked turf bunker
faces (whether grass covered or
earthen) as not closely mown 33-8/39
– establishing dropping zone
through the green for relief
from lateral water hazard with
bunker adjacent 33-8/37.5
– permitting re-dropping or
placing when dropped ball
embeds in bunker; whether
authorized. .33-8/28

– totally under repair; options for
Committee .25/13

cleaning ball in specified areas of
course other than putting green;
specimen Local Rule . . . . .App I-B-4b

distance-measuring devices
– permitting use. 14-3/0.5
– specimen Local Rule for
permitting use of devices that
measure distance only . . . . .App I-B-9

divot holes, permitting relief from
or repair of; whether authorized . . .33-8/34

doubt as to rights or procedure
in match play, allowing play of
second ball; whether authorized 33-8/3

dropping zone
– for island putting green 33-2a/10
– for part of lateral water hazard
where impossible to drop not
nearer hole .33-2a/9
– for relief from area containing
young trees .33-8/26
– for relief from lateral water
hazard with bunker adjacent. 33-8/37.5
– providing relief from paved
path in all cases to dropping
zone when nearest point of
relief effectively gives no relief;
whether authorized 33-8/19
– specimen Local Rule for
establishing dropping zone as
additional option under Rules
24–2b, 24–3, 25–1b, 25–1c,
25–3, 26–1 and 28 . . . . .App I-B-8
– when protective fence
intervenes on line of play 33-8/18

environmentally-sensitive areas;
specimen Local Rule clarifying
relief procedures . . . . .App I-B-2b

establishing sportsmanship code
or competition policy; whether
permitted 33-8/6

flagstick
– prohibiting removal of flagstick;
whether authorized 33-8/10
– waiving penalty for ball striking
unattended flagstick; whether
authorized. .33-8/11

free relief procedure agreed to in
error by player and opponent
thinking road obstruction;
whether valid claim can be made
after procedure followed and
opponent discovers road deemed
integral part of course by Local Rule .2-5/8.5

incorrect information about Local
Rule given by referee; whether
player should be exempt from
penalty and for what duration 34-3/1.5

motorized golf carts and persons
appointed to drive them; clarifying
status. 33-8/4

obstructions
– allowing free relief from
immovable water hazard stake
for ball lying in water hazard;
whether authorized 33-8/15

– allowing line of play relief
without penalty from
intervention by immovable
obstruction within two club-
lengths of putting green;
specimen Local Rule . . . . App I-B-6
– allowing line-of-sight relief from
irrigation-control boxes near
fairways; whether authorized. 33-8/17
– allowing line-of-sight relief
without penalty from protective
fence near line of play 33-8/18
– allowing replay of stroke
without penalty when sprinkler
head deflects ball; whether
authorized. .33-8/12
– deeming all stakes on course
(except boundary stakes)
immovable obstructions 33-8/16
– deeming boundary stakes having
no significance in play of hole
being played as immovable
obstructions. 24/5
– deeming ground under repair
adjacent to artificially-surfaced
cart path to have same status as
path 33-8/25
– deeming interior boundary
fence immovable obstruction;
whether authorized. 33-8/14
– deeming stones in bunkers
movable obstructions; specimen
Local Rule .App I-B-5
– Local Rule permitting player
at player's option to treat
temporary immovable
obstruction (TIO) either as TIO
or immovable obstruction in
taking relief 33-8/45
– providing relief from temporary
immovable obstructions;
specimen Local Rule . . . . .App I-B-7a
– providing relief from unsurfaced
road for tee shot only; whether
authorized. .33-8/20
– providing relief in all cases on
fairway side of paved path, or
dropping zone, when nearest
point of relief effectively gives
no relief; whether authorized. 33-8/19

out of bounds
– deeming area of adjoining
hole out of bounds for play of
particular hole but not for play
of other holes. 33-2a/14
– deeming area of adjoining
hole out of bounds for stroke
made from teeing ground only;
whether authorized. 33-2a/14
– deeming area surrounding
teeing ground in bounds for
tee shot and out of bounds
thereafter; whether authorized. . .33-2a/13
– deeming ball in bounds until
beyond boundary wall 33-2a/16
– deeming ball out of bounds that
crosses public road defined as
out of bounds even though it
may lie on another part of course .27/20

– deeming boundary stakes having
no significance in play of hole
being played as immovable
obstructions 24/5
– deeming interior boundary
fence immovable obstruction;
whether authorized. 33-8/14
– to prevent cutting across "dog-
leg;" deeming ball out of bounds
that crosses boundary even if it
recrosses boundary and comes
to rest on same part of course;
whether authorized. 33-8/38

power line, tower or pole deflects
ball; requiring cancellation and
replay of stroke without penalty. . . .33-8/13

"preferred lies" or "winter rules;"
specimen Local Rule . . . . .App I-B-4c

putting green
– allowing relief from edging
grooves around putting green 33-8/24
– deeming mushrooms growing on
line of putt as ground under repair .16-1a/15
– permitting repair of turf plugs
on putting green not 4–¼
inches in diameter 33-8/30
– requiring players to putt
continuously on putting green
until ball holed; whether
authorized. .33-8/7
– waiving requirement to hole out
when temporary putting green
used; whether authorized. 33-8/1

suggested language
– deeming as ground under repair
extensive damage due to heavy
rain and traffic 33-2a/3
– deeming ground under repair
adjacent to artificially-surfaced
cart path to have same status as
cart path 33-8/25
– deeming status of ball as out of
bounds which crosses public
road which divides course and is
defined as out of bounds 27/20
– for canceling and replaying
stroke when ball deflected by
power line 33-8/13
– for events in which motorized
golf carts permitted. 33-8/4
– for providing relief without
penalty from bunker filled with
casual water 33-3/27
– permitting relief from edging
grooves around putting greens. . . .33-8/24
– prohibiting dropping on apron of
putting green when taking relief
for ball on wrong putting green . . .33-8/33

temporary power lines, cables,
telephone lines and guy wires;
specimen Local Rule . . . . .App I-B-7b

water hazards
– allowing drop on green side of
water hazard when ball fails to
clear hazard; whether authorized .33-8/2
– allowing drop opposite to spot
where ball comes to rest in
lateral water hazard; whether
authorized. .26-1/20

– allowing drop within water hazard behind point where ball lies unplayable in same hazard; whether authorized 33-8/37
– allowing free relief for ball in water hazard; whether authorized 33-8/36
– allowing free relief from immovable water hazard stake for ball lying in water hazard; whether authorized 33-8/15
– deeming body of water as both water hazard and lateral water hazard 33-2a/7
– deeming body of water as water hazard from back tee and lateral water hazard from forward tee . . . 33-2a/6
– defining areas not meeting definition of lateral water hazard, such as rough and unplayable areas adjacent to fairways, as lateral water hazard; whether authorized 33-8/35
– establishing dropping zone for island putting green 33-2a/10
– establishing dropping zone for part of lateral water hazard where impossible to drop not nearer hole 33-2a/9
– establishing dropping zone through the green for relief from lateral water hazard with bunker adjacent 33-8/37.5
– specimen Local Rule allowing ball to be played provisionally under water hazard Rule . . . . App I-B-1
wrong putting green; deemed to include apron to prohibit dropping on and play from 33-8/33

LOOSE IMPEDIMENTS
See also STATUS OF OBJECT

affecting lie
– moved when ball lifted through the green 23-1/7
– removed while ball lifted through the green 23-1/8
assistance in removing large loose impediment 23-1/3
ball in motion deflected or stopped by divot taken by player subsequent to making original stroke 19-2/9
ball through the green moves after removal of nearby loose impediment 18-2a/30.5
ball touched
– accidentally in removing loose impediments 18-2a/31
– with fir cone or stick to prevent movement when loose impediments removed 18-2a/32
bending grass in removal of loose impediments 13-2/13
breaking off part of large loose impediment 23-1/4
bunker or water hazard
– accidentally moving loose impediment in hazard 13-4/13
– ball in hazard moves when loose impediment removed 13-4/15
– ball outside bunker; stone in bunker on line of play pressed down or removed 13-2/31
– bunker covered by leaves; player touches leaves during backswing . . 13-4/33
– competitor lifts loose impediment in bunker when his ball and partner's ball in bunker . . . 31-8/1
– footprints smoothed by player while walking to ball in bunker, loose impediments moved incidentally in the process 13-4/9.5
– ground in hazard touched with club while probing for ball believed covered by loose impediments 12-1/4
– grounding club, moving loose impediments and improving area of intended swing in hazard . . 13-4/28
– insect on ball in bunker 23-1/5.5
– loose impediment affecting lie of player's ball moved by another player making nearby stroke while ball lifted; whether lie considered altered 20-3b/8
– loose impediment in water hazard partially covering ball removed to identify what turns out to be wrong ball 13-4/16
– loose impediments removed from water hazard; player then decides not to play from hazard . . . 13-4/17
– pine cone falls from tree and comes to rest behind ball lying in bunker 13-4/18.5
– player accidentally kicks pine cone into bunker and picks it up . . 13-4/14
– player deems ball unplayable in bunker; lifts ball and then removes loose impediment from bunker 13-4/35.7
– player lifts loose impediment in bunker when his ball and partner's ball in bunker 30-3f/1
– player moves loose impediments when approaching ball in hazard . . 13-4/13.5
– removal of obstruction in hazard would move loose impediment 1-4/5
competitor seeks help from fellow-competitor to move loose impediment to avoid penalty 33-7/7
dislodged by
– partner's or opponent's stroke moves player's ball 18-1/8
– practice swing cause ball to move . 18-2a/20.5
intervene between embedded ball and ground (criteria for being embedded) 25-2/0.5
meaning of "solidly embedded" in definition of loose impediments 23/2
means by which loose impediments may be removed 23-1/1
natural object interfering with swing moved to determine whether loose 13-2/26

putting green
– after ball addressed on putting
green, ball moved in attempting
to brush insect from it 23-1/12
– ball moved accidentally by
foot during removal of loose
impediment on putting green 23-1/11
– ball-marker moved accidentally
by player after having moved
loose impediments. 20-1/12
– brushing loose impediments along
line of putt rather than to side 16-1a/10
– brushing loose impediments off
line of putt with palm of hand 16-1a/9
– player repairs depression on line
of putt created when partially
embedded acorn removed 16-1a/7
– raised tuft of grass on line of
putt brushed to determine
whether loose. 16-1a/11
– removal of casual water or
loose impediments on putting
green by Committee 33/1
– removing loose impediment
from line of putt with cap or
towel 16-1a/8
removing
– loose impediment lying out of
bounds 23-1/9
– loose impediments affecting
player's play by opponent or
fellow-competitor; penalties,
if any and whether player may
replace loose impediments 23-1/10
– loose impediments from area in
which ball to be dropped. 23-1/6
– loose impediments from spot on
which ball to be placed 23-1/6.5
– sand or loose soil from dropping
area 13-2/11
status of
– aeration plugs 23/12
– ant hill. 23/5
– ball embedded in fruit 23/10
– bird's nest .1-4/9
– clod of earth 23/13
– crushed shells used to fill bunkers .33-8/40
– crushed shells used to surface
road or path 23/14
– dead land crab. 23/6
– dew or frost on line of putt. 16-1a/3
– dew or frost other than on line
of putt 13-2/35
– divot partially attached and
folded over 13-2/5
– embedded acorn. 23/9
– fallen tree 23/7
– fruit skins 23/4
– grass adhering to ball 21/2
– grass cuttings 25/11
– half-eaten pear 23/3
– insect flying in water hazard 13-4/16.5
– insect on ball 23-1/5
– insect on ball in bunker 23-1/5.5
– insect-like creatures. 23/5.5
– large stone removable only with
much effort 23-1/2
– lava dust. 33-8/40
– loose soil from cast made by
bird, reptile or burrowing animal. .23/11

– moss or creepers in tree and on
ground 13-2/37
– pine needles piled for removal 25-1b/17
– saliva. 25/6
– snake, alive and dead 23/6.5
– solidly or partially embedded
stone 23/2
– spiders and spider webs. 23/5.5
– stone used to surface road or
path 23/14
– wood chips used to surface road
or path. 23/14
– worm partially underground. 23/8
when loose impediment
transformed into obstruction 23/1

LOST BALL

See also PROVISIONAL BALL; SEARCHING
FOR AND IDENTIFYING BALL; VIRTUALLY
CERTAIN (OR KNOWN)

ball dropped in area where original
ball not found; ball then played 27-1/3
ball lost
– either water hazard or casual
water overflowing hazard 1-4/7
– in tree in ground under repair 25/10
ball played from bunker either out
of bounds or lost; player tests
condition of bunker or smoothes
footprints before dropping
another ball in bunker 13-4/37
ball played from ground under
repair abandoned and relief taken
under ground under repair Rule 18-2a/8.5
ball played in ground under repair
area lost in same area 25-1c/3
ball played out of turn from tee
abandoned and another ball
played in proper order 10-2c/1
ball played under Rule for ball lost in
ground under repair after another
ball played under stroke-and-
distance procedure 15/8
ball visible from tee disappears or
moved by outside agency while
play suspended. 6-8d/4
identifying ball by brand and number
only 12-2/1
meaning of "known or virtually
certain" in Rules 18–1, 24–3,
25–1c and 26–1 . . . . .26-1/1
original ball found
– after more than five-minute
search; ball then played 27/8
– and played after another ball put
into play 15/5
– ball assumed in water hazard
found outside hazard after
another ball played under
stroke-and-distance procedure. . .26/6
– ball declared lost found before
another ball put into play 27/16
– ball in tree identified but not
retrieved 27/14
– ball played under water hazard
Rule; original ball then found
outside hazard 26-1/3

– found in burrowing animal hole
after five-minute search 27/7
– identification of ball through
testimony of spectator 27/12
– missing ball believed in bunker;
competitor drops and plays
substituted ball in bunker; then
original ball found outside bunker .20-7c/3
– original ball beyond provisional
ball; player searches briefly for
original ball, plays provisional
ball and then finds original ball 27-2b/3
– original ball played after
provisional ball played from
point nearer hole than original
ball likely to be 27-2b/5
– player abandons original ball
and walks forward to play
provisional ball; original ball
then found .27-2b/6
– player discovers original ball in
hole after searching five minutes
and then continuing play with
provisional ball 1-1/3
– player unable to distinguish his
ball from another ball. 27/10
– player wishes to ignore original
ball and continue play with
provisional ball 27-2c/2
– player with ball not found
concedes hole; ball then found
in hole 2-4/11
– provisional ball played from
beyond where original ball likely
to be but not beyond where
original ball found. 27-2b/4
– provisional ball played in
erroneous belief it is original ball . .27-2b/7
– referee finds player's original
ball; player prefers to continue
with provisional ball. 27-2/2
– substituted ball dropped and
played under Rule 25–1c in
absence of knowledge or virtual
certainty missing original ball in
ground under repair. 25-1c/2
– time permitted for search when
ball found after two minutes
then lost again. 27/3
– within five-minute search period
after substituted ball dropped
at spot of previous stroke under
stroke and distance 27-1/2
– within five-minute search period
after substituted ball dropped;
original ball played 27-1/2.3
– within five-minute search period
after substituted ball teed but
not played 27-1/1
– within five-minute search period
not identified until after period
elapses 27/5.5
– wrong ball deemed unplayable
played under stroke-and-
distance procedure; original ball
then found .28/14
player plays wrong ball and it cannot
be found; may have been fellow-
competitor's ball 15-3b/1
player unable to find his ball because
another player has played it 27/6

provisional ball
– announcement requirements 27-2a/1
– continuation of play with
provisional ball without
searching for original ball 27-2b/1
– not distinguishable from original
ball 27/11
– order of play when played other
than from teeing ground 10/4
– original ball beyond provisional
ball; player searches briefly for
original ball, plays provisional
ball and then finds original ball 27-2b/3
– original ball played after
provisional ball played from
point nearer hole than original
ball likely to be 27-2b/5
– play of provisional ball in
absence of reasonable
possibility original ball lost or
out of bounds 27-2a/3
– played from beyond where
original ball likely to be but not
beyond where original ball found . .27-2b/4
– played in erroneous belief it is
original ball .27-2b/7
– played solely in belief original
ball might be in water hazard 27-2a/2
– player abandons original ball
and walks forward to play
provisional ball; original ball
then found .27-2b/6
– player discovers original ball in
hole after searching five minutes
and then continuing play with
provisional ball 1-1/3
– player plays provisional ball
in belief original might be lost
outside water hazard; then
determines no possibility ball
lost outside water hazard 27-2a/2.5
– player wishes to ignore original
ball and continue play with
provisional ball 27-2c/2
– possibility that original ball in
water hazard may not preclude
play of provisional ball 27-2a/2.2
– possibly lost or out of bounds;
third ball played with no
announcement 27-2a/4
– referee finds player's original
ball; player prefers to continue
with provisional ball. 27-2/2
– referee incorrectly tells player
to play out hole with provisional
ball instead of original ball found
in water hazard. 34-3/3.7
– time permitted for search for
original ball and provisional ball . . .27/4
– whether provisional ball
becomes ball in play if original
ball lost in ground under repair . . .27-2c/1.5
re-drop required when proceeding
under lost ball Rule; whether
player may substitute when
re-dropping 20-6/4
searching
– after putting another ball into
play. 27/9

- electronic instrument used to
  search for ball 14-3/14
- for ball for ten minutes 6-7/2
- player directs caddie not to search
  for ball until others can assist 27/1
- player searching for ball
  mistakes his ball for opponent's
  then discovers mistake after
  five-minute search period 27/5
- smoothing footprints made in
  search for ball in bunker before
  making stroke from bunker 13-4/11
- time permitted for search after
  wrong ball played 27/2
- time permitted for search for
  original ball and provisional ball . . 27/4
- time permitted for search if play
  suspended during search 27/1.5

treating missing ball as moved by
outside agency
- in absence of knowledge or
  virtual certainty to that effect 27-1/2.5

underground drainpipe
- ball not found but known
  or virtually certain to lie
  in drainpipe under course;
  entrance to drainpipe out of
  bounds 24-2b/12
- ball not reachable or identifiable
  in underground drainpipe 24-3b/1

whether ball must be treated as
lost or virtual certainty ball is in
water hazard can be established
without going forward to assess
conditions around hazard 26-1/1.3

whether player entitled to ascertain
whereabouts of opponent's ball
that may be lost before playing 9-2/16

MARGINS OF AREAS OF THE COURSE

bunker
- ball on edge of bunker
  overhanging sand 13/3
- ball on obstruction in bunker 13/5
- sand spilling over margin of bunker 13/1
- status of tree in bunker 13/2

casual water; overflow from water
hazard 25/2

ground under repair
- ball outside ground under repair
  but tree within interferes with
  swing 25-1a/1
- status of roots outside ground
  under repair growing from tree
  inside ground under repair 25/10.7

through the green ball deemed
unplayable dropped in water
hazard; player elects not to play
ball; wishes to proceed under
water hazard Rule 28/4.5

water hazard
- ball last crossed margin where
  marked as water hazard, comes
  to rest in area marked as lateral
  water hazard 26-1/12
- ball within natural margin of
  water hazard but outside stakes
  defining margin 26/2

- clarification of "opposite
  margin" in Rule 26-1c(ii) 26-1/14
- flying insect in water hazard 13-4/16.5
- grounding club on bridge in
  water hazard 13-4/30
- grounding club outside water
  hazard when making stroke at
  ball in hazard 13-4/29
- hole of removed stake defining
  water hazard 25/18
- opposite side of lateral water
  hazard defined as water hazard . . 26-1/13
- overflow from water hazard 25/2
- status of ball that touches both
  water hazard and another area
  of the course 26/1.5
- unmarked water hazard 26/3
- when ball in water hazard 26/1
- where to place lines or stakes
  defining margin of water hazard . . 33-2a/4

MARKER
See also BALL-MARKER; SCORES AND
SCORE CARDS

appointment of marker
- lone competitor appoints own
  marker when Committee fails
  to do so 6-6a/1
- retroactive appointment of
  marker by Committee 33-1/5

competitor, other than marker,
fails to notify player, marker or
Committee of player's breach of
Rules in timely manner 33-7/9

competitor plays several holes
without marker 6-6a/2

competitor withdraws during
round; continues as fellow-
competitor's marker and caddies
for him for remainder of round;
whether permitted 6-4/9

flagstick attended by marker at
player's request; whether permitted 17-1/3

hole scores
- entered in wrong boxes; marker
  corrects error by altering hole
  numbers on score card 6-6a/3
- for first nine holes recorded in
  boxes for second nine and vice
  versa 6-6d/3

score card
- competitor corrects score after
  marker signs and leaves scoring
  area 6-6b/7
- marker disappears with
  competitor's score card 6-6b/6
- marker other than one
  appointed by Committee signs
  competitors' score cards 6-6b/5
- marker refuses to sign
  competitor's score card after
  dispute resolved in favor of
  competitor by Committee 6-6a/4
- signatures of marker and
  competitor in wrong places 6-6b/1
- when score card considered
  returned to Committee 6-6c/1

whether one player in group may complete hole after suspension of play 6-8b/3

wrong score knowingly attested by marker
– competitor aware score wrong ...1-3/6
– competitor unaware score wrong .6-6a/5

MARKING OR DEFINING COURSE

See also ABNORMAL GROUND CONDITIONS; BOUNDARY FENCE, LINE, WALL OR STAKES; COMMITTEE; FENCE; GROUND UNDER REPAIR; LOCAL RULES; OBSTRUCTIONS; OUT OF BOUNDS; TEEING GROUND AND TEE-MARKERS; WATER HAZARDS

declaring area as ground under repair during competition round. . . .33-2a/2

Local Rule
– allowing drop on green side of water hazard when ball fails to clear hazard; whether authorized .33-8/2
– allowing drop within water hazard behind point where ball lies unplayable in same hazard; whether authorized.............33-8/37
– allowing free relief for ball in water hazard within limits of fairway; whether authorized 33-8/36
– allowing free relief from immovable water hazard stake for ball lying in water hazard; whether authorized.............33-8/15
– declaring accumulations of leaves (at specified holes) through the green as ground under repair 33-8/31
– declaring extensive damage due to heavy rain and traffic as ground under repair.............33-2a/3
– declaring severe damage by non-burrowing animals as ground under repair.............33-8/32.5
– deeming area of adjoining hole out of bounds for play of particular hole but not for play of other holes 33-2a/14
– deeming area of adjoining hole out of bounds for stroke made from teeing ground only; whether authorized.............33-2a/14
– deeming area surrounding teeing ground in bounds for tee shot and out of bounds thereafter; whether authorized. . .33-2a/13
– deeming ball in bounds until beyond boundary wall...........33-2a/16
– deeming ground under repair adjacent to artificially-surfaced cart path to have same status as path 33-8/25
– deeming hard conical ant hills as ground under repair.............33-8/22
– deeming interior boundary fence immovable obstruction; whether authorized.............33-8/14
– defining given part of body of water as water hazard from back tees and by Local Rule lateral water hazard from forward tees 33-2a/6
– defining given part of body of water as water hazard in play of one hole and by Local Rule lateral water hazard in play of another hole 33-2a/7
– to prevent cutting across "dog-leg;" deeming ball out of bounds that crosses boundary even if it recrosses boundary and comes to rest on same part of course; whether authorized.............33-8/38

out of bounds objects and procedures
– angled supports or guy wires supporting....................24/2
– boundary stakes having no significance in play of hole being played........................24/5
– concrete bases of boundary fence posts 24/3
– displaced boundary stake 33-2a/20
– establishing boundary line inside fence on property line..........33-2a/15
– gate in boundary fence...........27/18
– internal boundary between holes .33-2a/12
– Local Rule deeming area of adjoining hole out of bounds for play of particular hole but not for play of other holes 33-2a/14
– Local Rule deeming area of adjoining hole out of bounds for stroke made from teeing ground only; whether authorized 33-2a/14
– Local Rule deeming area surrounding teeing ground in bounds for tee shot and out of bounds thereafter; whether authorized....................33-2a/13
– Local Rule deeming ball in bounds until beyond boundary wall..........................33-2a/16
– Local Rule deeming interior boundary fence immovable obstruction; whether authorized .33-8/14
– Local Rule to prevent cutting across "dog-leg;" deeming ball out of bounds that crosses boundary even if it recrosses boundary and comes to rest on same part of course; whether authorized....................33-8/38
– part of boundary fence within boundary line 24/4
– preventive measures when flow of water moves ball out of bounds in water hazard.........26-1/7
– procedure for treating exposed water pipe adjacent and parallel to boundary 33-2a/1
– public road defined as out of bounds divides course; status of ball crossing road 27/20
– river or other body of water adjacent to hole but off club property 33-2a/11
– stake defining out of bounds removed during competition without authority...............33-2a/19
– stile attached to boundary fence . .24/1

- unmarked water hazard with margin out of bounds...........26/3
- when ball inside boundary fence considered out of bounds........27/19
- whether internal boundary between holes allowed 33-2a/12

putting green
- attachment to flagstick to indicate position of hole on green .17/1
- different colored flags used to indicate position of hole on green .17/2
- half of double green serving hole not being played 25-3/1
- map of putting green indicating hole position displayed at tee....33/6
- marking island green 33-2a/10
- two holes on each green of nine hole course....................16/7
- whether flagstick may have tapered or of varying diameters...17/3

recommendations for marking or defining tree basins 33-2a/10.5

teeing ground
- Local Rule deeming water hazard as lateral water hazard in play from forward tee 33-2a/6
- map of putting green indicating hole position displayed at tee.....33/6
- play from wrong teeing ground attributed to Committee failure to indicate hole numbers on teeing ground 11-5/2

water hazard
- ball within natural margin of water hazard but outside stakes defining margin.................26/2
- defining part of body of water as water hazard and remainder as lateral water hazard.............33-2a/7
- defining rough and unplayable areas adjacent to fairways (areas not meeting definition of lateral water hazard) as lateral water hazard 33-8/35
- lateral water hazard defined as water hazard.................26/3.5
- Local Rule allowing drop on green side of water hazard when ball fails to clear hazard; whether authorized............33-8/2
- Local Rule allowing drop within water hazard behind point where ball lies unplayable in hazard; whether authorized.....33-8/37
- Local Rule allowing free relief for ball in water hazard within limits of fairway; whether authorized....................33-8/36
- Local Rule allowing free relief from immovable water hazard stake for ball lying in water hazard; whether authorized.....33-8/15
- Local Rule deeming given part of body of water as water hazard from back tees and lateral water hazard from forward tees........33-2a/6
- Local Rule deeming given part of body of water as water hazard in play of one hole and lateral

water hazard in play of another hole 33-2a/7
- marking and defining margins of water hazards; where to place lines and/or stakes 33-2a/4
- marking environmentally-sensitive areas; recommendations for Committee 33-8/41
- marking island green 33-2a/10
- marking ocean and beach as through the green; whether permitted 33-2a/8
- marking river or other body of water adjacent to hole but off club property 33-2a/11
- marking water hazard with bunker adjacent 33-8/37.5
- part of lateral water hazard where impossible to drop not nearer hole 33-2a/9
- permissible dropping area under lateral water hazard Rule so narrow player has difficulty dropping within it...............26-1/19
- preventive measures when flow of water moves ball out of bounds in water hazard.........26-1/7
- unmarked water hazard with margin out of bounds...........26/3

MARKING POSITION OF BALL
See also BALL-MARKER

acceptable and unacceptable methods for marking position of ball.........................20-1/16

acts which caddie may perform; including marking position of ball ...6-4/10

ball lifted by player without marking position
- and match conceded due to player's misconception as to opponent's score at hole.........2-4/14
- before holing out; opponent then picks up his ball claiming player loses hole...............2-5/3
- in mistaken belief next stroke conceded by opponent 2-4/3
- when given wrong information by fellow-competitor in stroke-play hole-by-hole playoff 9-3/1
- when lifted for identification; intention to lift not announced; ball cleaned beyond extent necessary to identify it; whether multiple penalties apply..........21/4
- when mistaken for wrong ball.....20-1/1
- without authority due to misunderstanding referee's instructions....................34-3/3.5

ball-marker
- lifted after player given incorrect information by opponent.......................9-2/5
- moved accidentally by player after having moved loose impediments 20-1/12
- placed approximately two inches behind ball...............20-1/20
- placed other than behind ball 20-1/19

– player measures clubhead-
length to side of ball and places
ball-marker 20-1/16
– pressed down by opponent;
whether opponent subject to
penalty 20-1/6.5

ball moves when
– accidentally kicked by player
asked to lift it due to interference .20-1/13
– ball-marker removed 24-1/5
– player drops putter on ball while
approaching to lift it 20-1/14

claims and disputes
– player lifts ball resting against
flagstick without marking or
holing out; after making stroke
and learning of player's actions
opponent lifts his ball and claims
hole 2-5/3
– opponent marks and lifts
player's ball without authority;
player lifts ball-marker and
claims hole; opponent disputes
claim 20-1/3

competitor invokes Rule 3–3; lifts
and drops original ball then places
second ball where the original
marked and plays it 3-3/13

fearing ball might move on putting
green, player lifts ball 16-1b/1

knocking ball aside after marking
position before lifting 20-1/22

lie of ball altered due to act of
marking. 20-1/15.5

meaning of "directly attributable
to the specific act" in the context
of marking or replacing in Rules
20–1 and 20–3a 20-1/15

method used to
– mark position of ball 20-1/16
– move ball or ball-marker to side. .20-1/16

player's ball resting against flagstick
lifted without being holed; others
in match pick up mistakenly
believing player won hole 30-3f/3

rotating ball without marking
position or lifting
– in rough for identification
purposes 12-2/2
– on putting green to align
trademark .18-2a/33

substituted ball mistakenly placed
on putting green instead of
original then lifted and original
replaced before stroke made 15-2/2

whether marking position of ball
in a hazard with a tee constitutes
"testing the condition of the
hazard" in breach of Rule 13–4a 13-4/0.5

MATERIAL PILED FOR REMOVAL
See also GREENKEEPER AND HOLE MADE BY
GREENKEEPER; GROUND UNDER REPAIR;
STATUS OF OBJECT

pine needles piled for removal
interfere with line of play after
ball dropped away 25-1b/17

status of
– fallen tree. .23/7
– fallen tree in process of being
removed 25/7
– grass cuttings 25/11
– tree stump. .25/8

MAXIMUM AVAILABLE RELIEF
See also NEAREST POINT OF RELIEF

ball dropped from casual water
in bunker at point of maximum
available relief rolls elsewhere. 25-1b/6

ball dropped in bunker under first
option of Rule 25–1b(ii) at point
of maximum available relief; player
then wishes to invoke second
option to drop outside bunker 25-1b/9

ball lifted from bunker by player
intending to drop under first
option of Rule 25–1b(ii) at point
of maximum available relief; player
then wishes to proceed under
second option to drop outside
bunker. 24-2b/5

bunker completely covered by
casual water; player's options 25-1b/8

bunker totally under repair. 25/13

explanation of "maximum available
relief" from casual water in bunker. .25-1b/5

MEASURING
See also DISTANCE, DISTANCE
INFORMATION AND DISTANCE MARKERS

across ground under repair in
obtaining relief. 25-1b/15

ball moved
– by flagstick when used to
measure or when dropped on ball.18-6/2
– while measuring to determine if
re-drop required 18-6/1

borrowing club for measuring
purposes. 20/2

club to be used in measuring 20/1

directly through fence, tree or wall
or across ditch 20-2b/2

use of distance meter attached to
golf cart; whether permitted. 14-3/1

vertical distance
– nearest point of relief; ball lying
in burrowing animal hole under
ground on course. 25-1b/23
– nearest point of relief; ball lying
in drainpipe under ground on
course 24-2b/12
– nearest point of relief; ball lying
on elevated or in underground
obstruction. 24-2b/11
– unplayable ball in tree; player
opts to drop within two club-
lengths 28/11
– unplayable ball at base of cliff;
player wishes to drop within
two club-lengths of point above
ball at top of cliff. 28/12

MEDICAL ASSISTANCE OR CONDITION

See also ARTIFICIAL DEVICES, UNUSUAL EQUIPMENT OR UNUSUAL USE OF EQUIPMENT; PHYSICAL PROBLEM

artificial limbs; whether permitted....14-3/15

bandage worn around wrist because of injury.......................14-3/7

play discontinued due to physical problem 6-8a/3

player providing medical assistance at scene of accident late for tee time 6-3a/1.5

swing aid; whether Committee may authorise use for medical reasons during stipulated round 14-3/15.5

tape applied to hand or golf glove.....14-3/8

MULTIPLE PENALTY SITUATIONS

breach of 14-club Rule at two or more holes
- clarification of match-play penalty .4-4a/9
- clarification of stroke-play penalty 4-4a/10

breaches of Rule(s) more than once prior to stroke; whether multiple penalties apply 1-4/12

ball at rest moves
- after address; ball then stopped by player's club 18-2b/12
- before address; accidentally stopped by player's club; player removes club and ball rolls away ..19-2/1.5
- in hazard when loose impediment removed 13-4/15
- when stepped on and original lie altered; player places ball in wrong place then plays it.........18-2a/21.3

ball deflected or stopped
- by competitor's golf bag and then his caddie 19-2/7
- by player's caddie standing in bounds and comes to rest out of bounds.....................19-2/2
- by player's caddie standing out of bounds and comes to rest out of bounds.....................19-2/4
- by player's foot then ball moves when foot removed 19-2/1

ball dropped in improper manner and in wrong place...............20-2a/3

ball lifted
- and changed during play of hole to aid identification 15/6.5
- and re-dropped when it should have been played as it lay; ball then lifted again and placed 18-2a/10
- and thrown into pond in anger 18-2a/13.5
- by caddie on own initiative for identification...................18-2a/14
- for identification not marked, intention to lift not announced and ball cleaned beyond extent necessary to identify it 21/4

ball played
- following procedure for ball lost in ground under repair (Rule 25-1c) after another ball played under stroke-and-distance procedure 15/8
- from ground under repair then original ball abandoned and relief taken under ground under repair Rule......................18-2a/8.5
- two wrong balls played between strokes with ball in play 15-3b/2

bunker or water hazard
- after taking firm stance in bunker, player smoothes footprints and changes club before playing 13-4/0.5
- ball in hazard moves when loose impediment removed 13-4/15
- casual water mistaken for water hazard; substituted ball played under water hazard Rule........25-1b/13
- ground in hazard touched with several practice swings 13-4/3
- ground in hazard touched with several practice swings; player advised of breach then makes several more such swings 1-4/13
- prior to stroke from hazard, practice swing touches ground in hazard and moves loose impediments; also area of intended swing improved by bending branch.................13-4/28

competitor's ball played by fellow-competitor; competitor substitutes another ball at wrong place, plays it and then abandons it and plays out original ball from right place......................20-7c/4

foursome stroke play; ball played from outside teeing ground; partner replays stroke 29-1/2

person walks with group carrying clubs for player in addition to 14 being carried by player's caddie.....4-4a/16

general principles applying to multiple breaches of Rule(s)
- breaching Rule(s) more than once prior to stroke; whether multiple penalties apply..........1-4/12
- player advised of breach of Rule prior to stroke; player breaches same Rule again prior to stroke ...1-4/13
- same Rule breached before and after stroke 1-4/14
- two Rules with different penalties breached; more severe penalty applied 1-4/15
- two wrong balls played between strokes with ball in play 15-3b/2

NEAREST LIE MOST SIMILAR

See also LIE OF BALL ALTERED

ball accidentally stepped on altering original lie; player places ball in wrong place and plays 18-2a/21.3

lie of ball changed by removal of gallery-control stake 20-3b/3

lie of embedded ball in hazard altered when lifted to determine whether unfit for play 5-3/5

whether original lie may be "nearest lie most similar" 20-3b/7

NEAREST POINT OF RELIEF
See also MAXIMUM AVAILABLE RELIEF

casual water on putting green
  – interferes with lie of ball;
    nearest point of relief off green . . .25-1b/10
  – intervenes on line of putt;
    nearest point of relief off green . . .25-1b/10.5

club used to determine nearest
  point of relief not used for next
  stroke 24-2b/4

determining nearest point of relief
  – recommended procedure. 24-2b/1
  – diagrams illustrating
    recommended procedure. 25-1b/2
  – recommended procedure
    not followed by player in
    determining nearest point of
    relief. 24-2b/2
  – nearest point of relief located
    where player not able to play
    intended stroke 24-2b/3
  – nearest point of relief at
    physically inaccessible spot;
    procedure for player 24-2b/3.5
  – diagrams illustrating examples
    of nearest point of relief at
    physically inaccessible spots 24-2b/3.7
  – two equidistant nearest points
    of relief meet requirements of
    Rule 25-1b/16
  – when relief from two conditions
    permitted in single procedure 1-4/8
  – when relief from two conditions
    permitted in single procedure
    and impracticable to drop ball in
    one condition 1-4/8.5
  – when bird's nest interferes with
    stroke. 1-4/9
  – when rattlesnake or bees
    interfere with play; relief
    procedure 1-4/10

line of play
  – relief from obstruction
    interfering with swing
    incidentally gives relief from
    intervention on line of play 24-2b/7
  – relief taken from other
    condition improves line of play. . . .25-1b/3

Local Rule
  – allowing relief from edging
    grooves around putting green 33-8/24
  – providing relief in all cases on
    fairway side of paved path, or
    dropping zone, when nearest
    point of relief effectively gives
    no relief; whether authorized. 33-8/19
  – wrong putting green deemed
    to include apron to prohibit
    dropping on and play from 33-8/33

measuring from nearest point of
  relief across ground under repair
  to determine dropping area;
  whether permitted 25-1b/15

obstruction struck by player's club
  after relief taken under Rule 24–2;
  whether player subject to penalty. . .20-2c/6

replacing or placing moved ball
  in bunker not nearer hole not
  possible; whether player may
  press ball into sand or take relief
  outside bunker. 20-3d/2

whether re-drop required if
  – ball dropped from area of
    ground under repair rolls to
    position where same area
    interferes with stance 20-2c/0.5
  – ball dropped from area of
    ground under repair then same
    area interferes for stroke with
    club not used to determine
    nearest point of relief 20-2c/0.8
  – ball dropped from immovable
    obstruction rolls nearer hole
    than nearest point of relief
    but not nearer than where it
    originally lay 20-2c/1.7
  – ball dropped from immovable
    obstruction rolls nearer
    obstruction than nearest point
    of relief but player changes clubs
    and obstructions no longer
    interferes. .20-2c/0.7
  – dropped ball required to first
    strike course within bunker
    instead strikes course outside
    bunker then rolls into it. 25-1b/7
  – dropped ball strikes course
    within prescribed dropping area
    and rolls outside that area. 20-2c/1
  – relief taken from obstruction
    for stroke toward green; same
    obstruction interferes with
    stance for necessary sideways
    stroke. 24-2b/9.5

whether relief permitted from two
  conditions in single procedure
  – ball in casual water within
    ground under repair. 25-1b/11.5
  – relief from cart path in casual
    water; relief from casual water
    back on cart path 1-4/8
  – from cart path in casual water;
    nearest point of relief from
    casual water back on cart
    path; drop into casual water
    impracticable 1-4/8.5

OBSERVER
See also COMMITTEE; REFEREE

flagstick attended by observer,
  referee or marker at player's
  request 17-1/3

OBSTRUCTIONS
See also INTEGRAL PART OF COURSE;
LOOSE IMPEDIMENTS; STATUS OF OBJECT;
VIRTUALLY CERTAIN (OR KNOWN); WOOD
AND WOOD CHIPS

after relief taken from obstruction
  second obstruction interferes. 24-2b/9

area of intended swing
  – improved by removing
    immovable obstruction. 13-2/15

– interfered with by obstruction
in ground under repair 24-2b/10

artificial object out of bounds
– interference by immovable
artificial object situated out of
bounds.......................24-2b/21
– movable artificial object lying
out of bounds 24-1/3

artificially-surfaced road or path
– competitor not sure whether
road considered obstruction or
integral part of course, invokes
Rule 3–3; whether score with
second ball counts if played
from wrong place 3-3/5
– competitor not sure whether
road considered obstruction
or integral part of course, plays
second ball; fails to announce
intention to invoke Rule 3–3
and to report facts to Committee.3-3/6.5
– free relief agreed to in error by
player and opponent thinking
road obstruction; whether valid
claim can be made after relief
taken and opponent discovers
road deemed integral part of
course 2-5/8.5
– Local Rule deeming ground
under repair adjacent to
artificially-surfaced path as part
of path 33-8/25
– Local Rule providing relief from
unsurfaced road for tee shot
only; whether authorized 33-8/20
– loose impediments (stone,
crushed shell, wood chips or
the like) used to surface road;
whether movable if player
chooses to play ball as it lies 23/14
– meaning of "artificially-surfaced" ..24/9

ball deflected
– by direction post..............19-1/1
– by sprinkler head; Local Rule
allowing replay of stroke
without penalty; whether
authorized...................33-8/12

ball dropped in obtaining relief from
obstruction
– from rough to fairway; whether
permitted 24-2b/8
– immediately after resumption of
play; whether player may lift and
clean or substitute then place
ball under Rule 6–8d(ii) 6-8d/3
– strikes course within prescribed
dropping area then rolls out of
prescribed area; whether ball
must be re-dropped............20-2c/1

ball in plastic bag moves when bag
blown to new position by wind 18-1/7

ball lifted and dropped away from
movable obstruction.............18-2a/4

ball marked before obstruction
removed; ball moves when ball-
marker removed................24-1/5

ball played from obstruction, lost in
same obstruction...............25-1c/3

ball substituted by mistake in taking
relief from cart path; correction
of error procedure 20-6/3

barn doors opened to play shot
through barn; whether permitted...24-2b/15

boundary fence
– angled supports or guy wires
supporting boundary fence......24/2
– concrete bases of boundary
fence posts 24/3
– exposed water pipe adjacent
and parallel to boundary fence
causes problems; suggested
procedure 33-2a/1
– gate in boundary fence...........27/18
– Local Rule deeming interior
boundary fence immovable
obstruction; whether authorized .33-8/14
– part of boundary fence within
boundary line 24/4
– part of fence off course (not
boundary fence) leans across
boundary and interferes with
swing 13-2/20
– relief from immovable
obstruction incidentally results
in relief from boundary fence.....24-2b/6
– relief from immovable
obstruction parallel to
boundary fence in most
cases would result in relief
from boundary fence;
recommendation for Committee .33-2a/1
– stile attached to boundary fence ..24/1

boundary stakes
– ball lifted and dropped away
from boundary stake under
obstruction Rule 18-2a/3
– displaced boundary stake 33-2a/20
– having no significance in play of
hole being played 24/5
– removal of boundary stake
interfering with swing 13-2/17

bridge
– ball lying on elevated
obstruction over deep hollow;
where to drop.................24-2b/11
– grounding club on bridge in
water hazard..................13-4/30

bunker
– ball dropped in bunker under
first option of Rule 24–2b(ii);
player then wishes to proceed
under second option to drop
outside bunker 25-1b/9
– ball lifted from bunker by player
intending to drop under first
option of Rule 24–2b(ii); player
then wishes to proceed under
second option to drop outside
bunker 24-2b/5
– ball lying on obstruction in
bunker; whether ball considered
in bunker 13/5
– rake removal causes ball in
bunker to move; whether player
may press ball into sand or take
relief outside bunker if not

possible to replace or place in
bunker not nearer hole 20-3d/2
– rakes; whether they should be
placed in or outside bunkers Misc./2
– stone serving as part of drain in
bunker; whether obstruction or
loose impediment. 24/7

club strikes obstruction after relief
taken under Rule 24–2; whether
player subject to penalty. 20-2c/6

clubhouse window opened; ball
played through it; whether
permitted 24-2b/14

door of building in open position
interferes with player's swing;
relief options available 24-2b/15.5

drainpipe
– ball in drainpipe under course;
entrance to drainpipe out of
bounds. 24-2b/12
– ball not reachable or identifiable
in underground drainpipe 24-3b/1

flagstick
– ball lodged in flag attached to
flagstick 17/6
– lying on putting green moved
by player to prevent another
player's ball from striking it. 17-1/7

holding ball in place while removing
movable obstruction. 24-1/4

line of play improved
– by removing stone from wall. 13-2/32
– in taking relief from obstruction
interfering with swing player
incidentally gains relief from
intervention on line of play 24-2b/7

Local Rule
– allowing free relief from
immovable water hazard stake
for ball lying in water hazard;
whether authorized 33-8/15
– allowing line-of-sight relief
without penalty from protective
fence near line of play 33-8/18
– allowing line-of-sight relief from
irrigation-control boxes near
fairways; whether authorized. 33-8/17
– allowing player at player's option
to treat temporary immovable
obstruction (TIO) either as TIO
or immovable obstruction in
taking relief 33-8/45
– allowing replay of stroke
without penalty when sprinkler
head deflects ball; whether
authorized. .33-8/12
– deeming all stakes on course
(except boundary stakes)
immovable obstructions 33-8/16
– deeming ground under repair
adjacent to artificially-surfaced
cart path to have same status as
path 33-8/25
– deeming interior boundary
fence immovable obstruction;
whether authorized 33-8/14

– providing relief from temporary
immovable obstructions;
specimen Local Rule . . . . .App I-B-7a
– providing relief from temporary
power line, cables, telephone
lines and guy wires . . . . .App I-B-7b
– providing relief from unsurfaced
road for tee shot only; whether
authorized. .33-8/20
– providing relief in all cases on
fairway side of paved path, or
dropping zone, when nearest
point of relief effectively gives
no relief; whether authorized. 33-8/19
– requiring cancellation and replay
of stroke without penalty when
ball deflected by power line,
tower or pole 33-8/13
– specimen Local Rule establishing
dropping zone as additional
option under Rules 24–2b and
24–3 . . . . .App I-B-8

meaning of
– "artificially-surfaced" 24/9
– "known or virtually certain" in
Rule 24–3 . . . . .26-1/1
– point where ball "last entered"
ground under repair when ball
lost in condition 25-1c/1.5

mental interference by obstruction . . .24-2a/1

movable part of immovable
obstruction interferes with
player's swing; relief options
available. 24-2b/15.5

nearest point of relief
– club used to determine nearest
point of relief not used for next
stroke. 24-2b/4
– determining club, address
position, direction of play and
swing used to identify nearest
point of relief 24-2b/1
– diagrams illustrating nearest
point of relief 25-1b/2
– diagrams illustrating player
unable to determine nearest
point of relief 24-2b/3.7
– dropped ball rolls nearer hole
than nearest point of relief
but not nearer than where it
originally lay 20-2c/1.7
– dropped ball rolls nearer
obstruction than nearest point
of relief; whether re-drop
necessary if player changes
clubs and obstruction no longer
interferes. 20-2c/0.7
– from cart path in abnormal
ground condition; nearest point
of relief from abnormal ground
condition back on cart path 1-4/8
– from cart path in abnormal
ground condition; nearest point
of relief from abnormal ground
condition back on cart path;
drop into abnormal ground
condition impracticable. 1-4/8.5
– Local Rule providing relief in all
cases on fairway side of paved

path, or dropping zone, when nearest point of relief effectively gives no relief; whether authorized.................33-8/19

– measuring across ground under repair in obtaining relief; whether permitted............25-1b/15

– player determines nearest point of relief; intended stroke from that point physically impossible...24-2b/3

– player does not follow recommended procedure in determining nearest point of relief.................24-2b/2

– player physically unable to take stance to determine or establish location of nearest point of relief.24-2b/3.5

– player takes relief properly from ground under repair; same condition interferes for stroke with club not used to determine nearest point of relief..........20-2c/0.8

– two equidistant points meet requirements of nearest point of relief from obstruction or ground under repair............25-1b/16

player entitled to relief from immovable obstruction lifts ball then

– chooses not to take relief and wishes to proceed under unplayable ball Rule.............18-2a/12.5

– replaces ball and plays it from original position.............18-2a/12

position of ball worsened when obstruction removed; player replaces obstruction.............13-2/15.5

probing near ball for presence of immovable obstruction...........13-2/27

removal of obstruction
– in hazard would move loose impediment....................1-4/5

– on player's line of play by outside agency.............13-2/33

stake supporting tree broken in attempt to remove it.............13-2/16

stance
– after relief taken from obstruction for stroke towards green, obstruction interferes with stance for necessary sideways stroke...............24-2b/9.5

– ball dropped from immovable obstruction rolls to position where it interferes with stance; whether re-drop required.......20-2c/0.5

– player physically unable to take stance to determine or establish location of nearest point of relief..24-2b/3.5

status of
– abandoned ball.................24-1/2

– angled supports or guy wires supporting boundary fence.......24/2

– artificially-surfaced road or path.24/9

– barn doors...................24-2b/15

– clubhouse window..............24-2b/14

– concrete bases of boundary fence posts....................24/3

– flagstick when ball overhangs hole.16-2/4

– gate in boundary fence..........27/18

– half-eaten pear................23/3

– line or mark on ground for gallery-control purposes consisting of lime or paint.......24-2b/20

– loose impediments (stone, crushed shell, wood chips or the like) used to surface road.......23/14

– movable part of drainage hose....24-2b/15.3

– part of boundary fence within boundary line..................24/4

– part of fence off course leaning across boundary................13-2/20

– parked car....................24/8

– tee-markers after first stroke.....11-2/1

– tree basins....................33-2a/10.5

– turf raised by underground pipe...24/14

– wooden or earthen steps.......24/12

– wooden planks.................24/11

stone
– broken away from retaining wall in water hazard.................24/6

– line of play improved by removing stone from wall........13-2/32

– serving as part of drain in bunker..24/7

teeing ground; ball lies in or on movable obstruction..............25-2/8

temporary immovable obstructions; relief procedures; specimen Local Rule............................App I-B-7a

tunnel, ball lies in tunnel or other underground obstruction; determining nearest point of relief.24-2b/11

virtually certain (or known)
– meaning of "known or virtually certain" in Rule 24–3...........26-1/1

– missing ball is in obstruction; drop made under Rule 24–3; original ball then found within five minutes...................25-1c/2.5

when loose impediment transformed into obstruction......23/1

whether player entitled to relief if
– obstruction interferes but ball unplayable due to some other condition....................24-2b/16

– obstruction interferes with abnormal stroke; abnormal stroke reasonable in circumstances..................24-2b/17

– obstruction interferes with abnormal stroke; abnormal stroke not reasonable in circumstances..................24-2b/18

– obstruction interferes with stroke but stroke at ball not practicable due to interference by casual water.................24-2b/19

OCEAN

treating ocean and beach as through the green...............33-2a/8

ORDER OF PLAY

See also HONOR; ORDER OF PLAY IN FOURSOMES AND THREESOMES; PLAYING OUT OF TURN; STROKE CANCELED OR RECALLED competitor arrives late for scheduled tee time but in time to play in correct order; whether late for tee time 6-3a/2

competitor objects to fellow-competitor putting out of turn 10-2b/1

competitors in stroke play agree to play out of turn but not for purpose of giving one of them advantage 10-2c/2

determining ball farther from hole; procedure for referee. 10-1b/1

determining honor
 – at next tee following disputed hole 10-1a/2
 – in four-ball match in which points awarded for both better-ball and aggregate scores. 30/3
 – in handicap match. 10-1a/1
 – in handicap stroke play 10-2a/1
 – when opponent requires player with honor to cancel stroke made from outside teeing ground .11-4a/1

four-ball competition
 – determination of honor in four-ball match in which points awarded for both better-ball and aggregate scores 30/3
 – extent to which partners may play in order they consider best. . .31-4/2
 – partner waives turn to play; circumstances under which he may complete hole. 31-4/1
 – player entitled to putt stands on another player's line of putt 30-3b/1
 – side plays out of turn from tee; opponents require one member of side to replay but not other 30-1/1
 – waiving turn to putt in four-ball match play 30-3b/2

holes played out of sequence
 – competitors play two holes not included in stipulated round 3/2
 – starting players from 1st and 10th tees; whether permitted 33-1/3
 – three holes played out of sequence in match 2-1/5

meaning of "immediately" when stroke to be canceled 30-1/1

playing from outside teeing ground or from wrong teeing ground in match play
 – stroke canceled by opponent; correct order of play 11-4a/1
 – stroke canceled by opponents in foursome match; which partner replays stroke. 29-1/1
 – stroke goes out of bounds; procedure if stroke not recalled by opponent 11-5/3

provisional ball; order of play when played other than from teeing ground. 10/4

provisional balls played out of turn from teeing ground 10-3/1

request for player to replay stroke withdrawn after opponent plays 10-1c/1

stroke(s) played out of turn
 – ball played out of turn from tee abandoned and another ball played in proper order 10-2c/1
 – player attending flagstick for opponent struck by ball of opponent's partner who played out of turn. .30-3f/5
 – player plays out of turn from tee in three-ball match; one opponent requests replay and other does not 30-2/1
 – player requested to lift ball due to interference plays out of turn instead 10-1c/2
 – players agree not to tee off in prescribed order to save time 10-1a/3
 – side plays out of turn from tee; opponents require one member of side to replay but not other 30-1/1

when both balls lie in
 – ground under repair and both players take relief. 10/1
 – lateral water hazard and both players take relief. 10/2
 – lateral water hazard and neither found 10/3

withholding information on strokes taken until opponent's turn to play .9-2/4

ORDER OF PLAY IN FOURSOMES AND THREESOMES

ball played from outside teeing ground
 – which partner must replay stroke .29-1/1
 – wrong partner replays stroke in stroke play. 29-1/2

both partners drive at same tee in foursome match. 29-1/9

foursome partner accidentally moves ball after address 29-1/5

foursome partner misses ball
 – accidentally, when making stroke. .29-1/6
 – purposely, so partner would play ball over water 29-1/7

provisional ball
 – played by wrong member of side . .29-1/4
 – which partner must play provisional ball 29-1/3

side drives for three holes in wrong order; opponents make claim during third hole 29-2/2

wrong ball played in foursome stroke play 29-1/8

wrong partners drive for both sides in foursome match. 29-2/1

OUT OF BOUNDS
See also BOUNDARY FENCE, LINE, WALL OR STAKES; MARKING OR DEFINING COURSE; PROVISIONAL BALL

ball comes to rest out of bounds
 – ball accidentally strikes opponent standing out of bounds and comes to rest out of bounds. 19-3/1
 – ball dropped, comes to rest and then rolls out of bounds 20-2c/3.5

– ball dropped under Rule 20–5 strikes course through the green within inches of and not nearer hole than spot in bunker where previous stroke made 20-5/2

– ball enters burrowing animal hole in bounds and comes to rest out of bounds 25-1b/24

– ball not reachable or identifiable in underground drainpipe or culvert with entrance out of bounds 24-3b/1

– ball moved accidentally by backward movement of club after stroke misses; ball comes to rest out of bounds 18-2a/22

– ball moved out of bounds by flow of water in water hazard 26-1/7

– ball moves after address and comes to rest out of bounds; player plays ball 18-2b/9

– ball played from bunker out of bounds or lost; player tests condition of bunker or smoothes footprints before dropping another ball in bunker . . . 13-4/37

– ball played from outside teeing ground goes out of bounds 11-4b/6

– ball played from water hazard to out of bounds 26-1/10

– ball played out of bounds from wrong teeing ground in match not recalled 11-5/3

– ball thrown into bounds by outside agency and played; caddie aware of action of outside agency 15/9

– ball thrown into bounds by outside agency; neither player nor caddie aware of action of outside agency 15/10

– explanation of options under Rule 26–2b if ball played from water hazard comes to rest out of bounds 26-2/1

– maintenance vehicle deflects ball out of bounds; substituted ball played from spot where original ball deflected 20-7/1

– mixed foursome in which different tees used by men and women; tee shot out of bounds . . 29/2

– opponent's caddie lifts player's ball which may or may not have been out of bounds 18-3b/5

– original ball and provisional ball found out of bounds 27-2c/4

– original ball out of bounds; ball re-teed under stroke and distance touched at address and falls off tee 11-3/3

– player strikes ball out of bounds, picks up, drops ball where partner's ball lies and plays practice stroke 30-3f/7

– player's ball strikes own caddie; ball comes to rest out of bounds . . 19-2/2

– player's ball strikes own caddie standing out of bounds and comes to rest out of bounds 19-2/4

– stray ball found out of bounds, played under stroke-and-distance procedure; original ball then found in bounds 15/12

– stroke made from environmentally-sensitive area defined as out of bounds 33-8/43

– stroke made with ball lying out of bounds 15/6

– teed ball missed then hit out of bounds 20-5/1

– wrong ball hit out of bounds; another ball played under Rule 27–1; original ball then found nearby 15/11

ball moved into bounds by flow of water in lateral water hazard 26-1/8

ball wrongly thought out of bounds lifted; competitor plays another ball from tee 18-2a/11

objects defining out of bounds

– angled supports or guy wires supporting 24/2

– ball lifted and dropped away from boundary stake under obstruction Rule 18-2a/3

– boundary stakes having no significance in play of hole being played 24/5

– concrete bases of boundary fence posts 24/3

– deeming ball in bounds until beyond boundary wall 33-2a/16

– establishing boundary line inside fence on property line 33-2a/15

– exposed water pipe adjacent and parallel to boundary fence causes problems; suggested procedure 33-2a/1

– gate in boundary fence 27/18

– identifying stake defining out of bounds removed during competition without authority . . . 33-2a/19

– improving position of ball by bending boundary fence 13-2/18

– internal boundary between holes . 33-2a/12

– marking environmentally-sensitive areas; recommendations for Committee 33-8/41

– moving ball lying against fence defining out of bounds by striking other side of fence 14-1/5

– part of boundary fence within boundary line 24/4

– relief from immovable obstruction incidentally results in relief from boundary fence 24-2b/6

– removal of boundary stake interfering with swing 13-2/17

– removal of boundary stake on line of play but replaced before stroke 13-2/25

– river or other body of water adjacent to hole but off club property 33-2a/11

– stile attached to boundary fence . 24/1

– when ball inside boundary fence considered out of bounds 27/19

objects or condition out of bounds
- burrowing animal hole out of
  bounds, ball enters it and comes
  to rest in bounds 25-1b/23
- entrance to drainpipe out of
  bounds, ball found or missing
  but known or virtually certain
  to lie in drainpipe under course ...24-2b/12
- entrance to drainpipe out of
  bounds, ball not reachable or
  identifiable in drainpipe.........24-3b/1
- growing things rooted in
  environmentally-sensitive
  area defined as out of bounds
  overhang course 33-8/44.5
- improving area of intended
  swing by moving growing or
  fixed object situated out of
  bounds......................13-2/19
- interference by immovable
  artificial object situated out of
  bounds......................24-2b/21
- movable artificial object lying
  out of bounds 24-1/3
- part of fence off course leans
  across boundary and interferes
  with swing...................13-2/20
- removal of loose impediment
  lying out of bounds...........23-1/9
- unmarked water hazard with
  left-hand margin out of bounds ...26/3

Local Rule
- boundary stakes having no
  significance in play of hole being
  played.......................24/5
- deeming area of adjoining
  hole out of bounds for play of
  particular hole but not for play
  of other holes.................33-2a/14
- deeming area of adjoining
  hole out of bounds for stroke
  made from teeing ground only;
  whether authorized............33-2a/14
- deeming area surrounding tee
  in bounds for tee shot and out
  of bounds thereafter; whether
  authorized...................33-2a/13
- deeming ball in bounds until
  beyond boundary wall..........33-2a/16
- public road defined as out of
  bounds divides course; status of
  ball crossing road.............27/20
- to prevent cutting across "dog-
  leg;" deeming ball out of bounds
  that crosses boundary even if it
  recrosses boundary and comes
  to rest on same part of course;
  whether authorized............33-8/38

player enters environmentally-
sensitive area to retrieve ball......33-8/42

player's ball strikes own caddie
standing out of bounds and comes
to rest on course.................19-2/3

provisional ball
- announcement of 27-2a/1
- determining who plays
  provisional ball in foursome 29-1/3
- lifted in erroneous belief original
  ball in bounds 27-2b/8

- not distinguishable from original
  ball 27/11
- played from point nearer hole
  than visible original ball; player
  erroneously thought original
  ball out of bounds.............27-2c/3
- played in absence of reasonable
  possibility original ball lost or
  out of bounds 27-2a/3
- played in erroneous belief it is
  original ball 27-2b/7
- possibly lost or out of bounds;
  third ball played with no
  announcement................27-2a/4
- used as second ball when not
  determinable whether original
  ball out of bounds.............3-3/1

re-drop required when proceeding
under out of bounds Rule;
whether player may substitute
when re-dropping 20-6/4

relief from immovable obstruction
incidentally results in relief from
boundary fence 24-2b/6

whether player entitled to ascertain
whereabouts of opponent's ball
that may be out of bounds before
playing.........................9-2/16

OUTSIDE AGENCY
See also BALL DEFLECTED OR STOPPED;
LOOSE IMPEDIMENTS; STATUS OF OBJECT

ball
- dislodged in tree knocked down
  by outside agency..............18-1/9
- dropped accidentally by
  opponent or fellow-competitor
  on player's moving ball on
  putting green..................19-5/1.7
- in plastic bag moves when bag
  blown to new position by wind ...18-1/7
- moved by air propelled from fan
  or blower 18-1/2
- not found treated as moved by
  outside agency in absence of
  knowledge or virtual certainty
  to that effect..................27-1/2.5
- stolen by outside agency from
  unknown spot.................18-1/5
- visible from tee disappears or
  moved by outside agency while
  play suspended 6-8d/4

ball at rest
- kicked away from hole by
  spectator attending flagstick 18-1/10
- moved by tumbleweed blown by
  wind........................18-1/6
- moved during suspension of play
  by outside agency; player fails to
  estimate position sufficiently in
  replacing ball..................6-8d/5

ball-marker lifted by outside agency ..20-1/9

borrowing balls or towel from
another player or outside agency ...5-1/5

club rendered unfit for play by
outside agency 4-3/9.5

competitor seeks help from fellow-
competitor to avoid penalty 33-7/7

P

distance information obtained
with distance-measuring device
by outside agency unilaterally
provided to player 14-3/0.7

dog picks up or deflects ball on
putting green after stroke
– from off green 19-1/6
– from green 19-1/7

flagstick removed whereupon knob
falls from it and deflects ball in
motion 17/9

footprints made by referee in
bunker making ruling; whether
smoothing permitted before
player plays 13-4/10

hole-liner pulled out with attended
flagstick deflects ball in motion
after stroke 17/8

immovable obstruction on player's
line of play removed by outside
agency 13-2/33

loose impediment dislodged by
– partner's or opponent's stroke
moves player's ball 18-1/8
– practice swing causes ball to
move 18-2a/20.5

maintenance vehicle deflects ball
out of bounds; player drops
substituted ball near spot where
vehicle deflected original ball and
plays it 20-7/1

meaning of "good reason to lift"
when play suspended, such as
possibility outside agency may
take ball 6-8c/1

movable obstruction removed
by outside agency; position of
ball worsened; player replaces
obstruction 13-2/15.5

rake held by caddie of side (or
partner) accidentally deflects or
stops player's ball 19-2/10

person(s) walking with group other
than caddie carrys
– additional clubs for player, and
status of such clubs and person(s) .4-4a/16
– items, other than clubs, for
player; status of such items and
person(s) 6-4/5.3

player plays ball moved or lifted by
outside agency from new position
– caddie aware ball moved from
out of bounds onto course;
does not inform player 15/9
– neither player nor caddie aware
ball moved from out of bounds
onto course 15/10
– neither player nor caddie aware
ball moved until next hole begun . .18-1/3
– without competitor's
knowledge, fellow-competitor
lifts competitor's ball and sets
it aside; competitor plays ball
from where set aside 15-3b/3

player's ball deflected by stroke of
player in another group 19-1/2

snake; when outside agency 23/6.5

spectator says ball moved by
outside agency but player not
sure; procedure for player if
Committee decision not possible
in reasonable time 18-1/4

sprinkler head deflects ball; Local
Rule allowing replay of stroke
without penalty; whether
authorized 33-8/12

steps on ball in tall grass; original
lie altered and spot where ball
originally lay not determinable;
procedure player must use 20-3b/5

stroke not replayed as required by
Rule 19–1 after ball played from
putting green deflected by moving
outside agency 19-1/3

team captain or coach; status of 33-1/11.5

umbrella carrier employed in
addition to caddie; whether
second caddie or outside agency . . .6-4/5

PACE OF PLAY
See also UNDUE DELAY

authority for Committee to
establish pace of play guidelines . . .App I-C-4

players agree not to tee off in
prescribed order to save time 10-1a/3

referee does not penalize player in
breach of pace of play condition
believing player had already lost hole .34-3/2

PAR COMPETITION
See also BOGEY COMPETITION;
STABLEFORD COMPETITION

competing simultaneously in par
and stroke-play competitions 32-1/1

omitting holes in par competition . . .32-1/2

recording of lower gross score does
not affect result of hole 32-2a/5

when practice between holes
permitted 7-2/1

**PENALTIES IMPOSED, MODIFIED OR
WAIVED BY COMMITTEE**
See also CLOSE OF COMPETITION;
COMMITTEE; MULTIPLE PENALTY
SITUATIONS

authority to waive or modify
disqualification penalty 33-7/1

Committee error
– disqualification penalty wrongly
applied to winner of event;
error discovered after play-off
for first conducted with two
other competitors 34-1b/5
– incorrect ruling by Committee
in first round affecting
competitor's score corrected
during second round 34-3/1
– referee incorrectly advises
player to cancel and replay stroke . 34-3/1.3

condition of competition
– anti-doping condition breach
discovered after close of
competition 34-1b/9

– requiring immediate
discontinuance of play in
dangerous situations; guidelines
for waiving or modifying
disqualification penalty for failure
to discontinue immediately 6-8b/7
– use of ball not on List of
Conforming Golf Balls
imposes penalty other than
disqualification; whether
permitted 5-1/2

etiquette
– disqualification penalty imposed
for unacceptable behavior;
whether pemitted 33-8/6
– meaning of "serious breach of
etiquette" 33-7/8

incorrect information on Rules
given to partner, opponent or
fellow-competitor 9/1

Local Rule
– allowing drop on green side of
water hazard when ball fails to
clear hazard; whether authorized .33-8/2
– providing relief without penalty
from flooded bunker 33-8/27
– requiring player to take relief
under penalty from tree nursery
(or plantation) from which play
prohibited; whether authorized . . 33-8/29
– waiving penalty for ball striking
unattended flagstick; whether
authorized 33-8/11
– waiving requirement to hole out
when temporary putting green
used; whether authorized 33-8/1

tee-markers moved by player 11-2/2

time of starting
– all competitors must be present . 6-3a/2
– circumstances which warrant
waiving disqualification penalty
for lateness 6-3a/1.5
– meaning of "time of starting" 6-3a/2.5
– players start early 6-3a/5

whether Committee may waive or
modify penalty
– competitor plays one practice
stroke on course prior to round . 7-1b/1
– competitor resumes play after
suspension not at time ordered
by Committee (early or late) 6-8b/6
– failure to countersign score card
blamed on lack of time provided
by Committee 33-7/3
– failure to hole out in stroke play . . 33-7/2
– play of wrong ball not rectified
on advice of referee 33-7/5
– players agree not to tee off in
prescribed order to save time 10-1a/3
– practice on course between
stroke-play rounds 7-1b/2
– practice on course between
stroke-play round and play-off
on same day 7-1b/3
– short putt holed using club with
playing characteristics changed
other than in normal course of play 4-3/4
– single stroke made with non-
conforming ball 5-1/1

– wrong score returned on score
card 33-7/4
– wrong score returned on score
card because player unaware of
penalty incurred 33-7/4.5

whether Committee should impose
penalty
– application of disqualification
penalty in team competition in
which not all team members'
scores count for each round 33/8
– Committee suspends play; one
player in match discontinues
immediately; other player
completes hole playing
successive strokes out of turn 6-8b/3.5
– competitor advised during
round he incurred penalty by
fellow-competitor; competitor
disagrees and fails to include
penalty in returned score card;
Committee advised of incident
after close of competition 34-1b/1.5
– consciously failing to correct
opponent's misunderstanding of
state of match 9-2/12
– knowingly giving incorrect
information on Rules 9/1
– playing away from hole to assist
partner 30-3f/6
– refusing to identify ball 27/13
– refusing to resume play
(claiming danger from lightning)
when resumption ordered by
Committee 6-8b/5
– repeatedly replacing ball nearer
hole on green 33-7/6
– seeking help of fellow-competitor
moving loose impediment to
avoid penalty should removal
causes ball to move 33-7/7

PHYSICAL PROBLEM

See also ARTIFICIAL DEVICES, UNUSUAL
EQUIPMENT OR UNUSUAL USE OF
EQUIPMENT; MEDICAL ASSISTANCE OR
CONDITION

artificial limbs 14-3/15

club broken when used as cane;
whether replacement permitted 4-3/7

discontinuing play
– due to physical problem 6-8a/3
– for refreshment 6-8a/2.5

elastic bandage used by player with
injured wrist 14-3/7

postponement of final match due to
injury of player 6-3a/1

swing aid; whether Committee
may authorise use for player with
physical problem during stipulated
round 14-3/15.5

PITCH-MARK

See also BALL MARK; EMBEDDED BALL

ball
– bounces out of its pitch-mark
then spins back into it 25-2/1

P

– lifted to determine whether
embedded in its own pitch-mark . .20-1/0.7
– returns to pitch-mark from
prior stroke. 25-2/3

casual water contained in
embedded ball's pitch-mark; relief
options available to player 25/3

made by ball of partner, opponent
or fellow-competitor affects
player's lie or line of play; whether
player entitled to free relief 13-2/8

repaired
– eliminating interference with
player's backswing; whether
permitted .13-2/21
– in area where ball to be dropped
through the green; whether
permitted .13-2/10
– on line of play repaired, whether
line of play improved 13-2/0.5

when ball considered "embedded"
in its own pitch-mark 25-2/0.5

PLAYER RESPONSIBILITIES

ball thrown into bounds by outside
agency and played; caddie aware
of action of outside agency. 15/9

caddie
– breaches transportation
condition. .33-1/9.5
– lifts ball of fellow-competitor
without authority and
subsequently substitutes
another ball which fellow-
competitor plays 20-1/5
– practices on or tests putting
green surfaces of the course
before stroke-play round 7-1b/5

Committee provides player with
incorrect information on Rules;
duration of player's entitlement to
proceed on such information. 34-3/1.5

competitor knows player has
breached Rule does not inform
player or Committee in timely
manner 33-7/9

competitor's scores recorded
on score card with fellow-
competitor's name and vice versa. . .6-6d/4

erroneous claim accepted during
match; player disputes claim after
result announced. 2-5/10

gross score of partner with better
net score omitted from score card. .31-3/1

handicap stroke
– claimed after hole conceded. 6-2a/4
– taken by mistake in handicap
match; status of late claim. 2-5/13
– wrongly claimed at hole; error
discovered before hole completed6-2a/3

handicaps not individually recorded
on score card in foursome
competition 6-2b/4

incorrect handicap
– for partner in foursome stroke-
play competition recorded on

score card; error discovered
after competition closed. 6-2b/2.5
– recorded on score card by
Committee; error discovered
before competition closed 6-2b/3.5

incorrect information on Rules. 9/1

making competitors responsible for
adding scores 33-1/7

meaning of "handicap" when full
handicap not used 6-2b/0.5

player proceeds on basis of
referee's ruling; player's version
of facts subsequently found to be
incorrect. 34-3/8

score card
– no score entered for one hole
but total correct. 6-6d/1
– total score added incorrectly;
hole-by-hole scores correct. 6-6d/2

team captain or coach; whether
Committee may adopt condition
making them part of player's side . . .33-1/11.5

wrong teeing ground use
attributable to Committee failure
to indicate hole numbers on
teeing ground 11-5/2

waiving or modifying disqualification
penalty
– circumstances which warrant
waiving penalty for being late to
tee 6-3a/1.5
– for not holing out in stroke play . .33-7/2
– for returning wrong score. 33-7/4
– whether justified if competitor
unaware of penalty returns
wrong score 33-7/4.5

PLAYING OUT OF TURN
See also HONOR; ORDER OF PLAY; ORDER
OF PLAY IN FOURSOMES AND THREESOMES

limitations on authority of partners
to play in order they consider best .31-4/2

Local Rule requiring continuous
putting on putting greens;
whether authorized 33-8/7

match play
– in four-ball match, side plays
out of turn from tee; opponents
require one member of side to
replay but not other. 30-1/1
– in three-ball match, player
plays out of turn from tee; one
opponent requests replay, other
opponent does not 30-2/1
– player asked to lift ball plays out
of turn instead 10-1c/2
– player requests opponent to
replay stroke played out of turn;
request withdrawn after player
plays and before opponent
replays; whether opponent may
replay stroke. 10-1c/1
– player smoothes bunker after
playing out of turn; opponent
recalls stroke; player must drop
ball in smoothed area; whether
player in breach of Rule 13–4 . . . . .13-4/39

– player wishing to render original ball lost plays subsequent stroke with provisional ball out of turn . . .27-2b/1

– players agree not to tee off in prescribed order to save time 10-1a/3

– provisional balls played out of turn from teeing ground 10-3/1

stroke play

– ball played out of turn from tee abandoned; competitor plays another ball in proper order. 10-2c/1

– competitor objects to fellow-competitor putting out of turn; various circumstances discussed . .10-2b/1

– competitor plays out of turn, thinks stroke must be canceled and replayed, drops ball at spot from which stroke made; procedure questioned 27/17

– competitor wishing to render original ball lost plays subsequent stroke with provisional ball out of turn 27-2b/1

– fellow-competitors agree to play out of turn to save time; whether agreement to waive Rule.10-2c/2

PLAY-OFF AND TIES

match play

– mistakenly believing match all square after 18 holes, players play extra holes and determine winner; error then discovered 2-5/6

– players agree on method of settling tie when Committee fails to do so 33-6/4

– rightful winner of match makes no claim and agrees to play extra holes .2-5/7

stroke play

– competition over 36 holes on two courses; player completes first round, practices on same course, later in play-off on that course 7-1b/4

– competitor who practices on competition course after qualifying round subsequently in play-off on same day 7-1b/3

– determining winner and positions in stroke-play play-off when player disqualified or withdraws 33-6/3

– disqualification penalty incurred by competitor in play-off; whether penalty applies to entire competition 3/1

– fellow-competitor lifts competitor's ball conceding next stroke in stroke-play play-off.18-4/3

– groupings for stroke-play play-off .33-3/4

– replacement before play-off of club broken in anger during round.4-3/12

– score cards in hole-by-hole play-off. 33-5/1

– wrong information given by competitor in hole-by-hole play-off results in fellow-competitor lifting ball 9-3/1

POWER LINE

Local Rule requiring cancellation and replay of stroke without penalty when ball deflected by power line, tower or pole 33-8/13

relief from temporary power lines, cables, telephone lines and guy wires; specimen Local Rule . . . . . . .App I-B-7b

PRACTICE

See also PRACTICE SWING

before or between rounds

– artificial device used to listen to music or broadcast while practising 14-3/17

– caddie practices on or tests putting green surfaces of course before stroke-play round 7-1b/5

– competitor practices putting on 3rd green after finishing hole during first round of 36-hole stroke-play competition 7-1b/7

– competitor practices putting on 18th green immediately after finishing first round of stroke-play competition played over consecutive days. 7-2/8

– competitor who practices on competition course after qualifying round subsequently in play-off on same day 7-1b/3

– match discontinued by agreement on 13th tee cannot be resumed until following day; players may play first twelve holes prior to resuming match 7-2/11

– one practice stroke made on course before stroke-play round. .7-1b/1

– stroke play over 36 holes on two courses; player completes first round and practices on same course; player later in play-off on that course 7-1b/4

– stroke play over 54 holes on consecutive days; second round canceled and competitor practices on course following cancellation. 7-1b/6

during round

– competitor practices putting on 3rd green of 9-hole course during 18-hole stroke-play competition 7-2/9

– completing hole in match play after result of hole decided. 7-2/1.5

– explanation of "strokes played in completing play of a hole". 7-2/1.7

– in anger player hits ball played by player in following group; whether stroke considered practice stroke 1-4/4

– in four-ball, player disqualified for next hole plays that hole; whether strokes made on that hole were practice strokes 30-3f/8

– hitting plastic ball before playing ball in play 7-2/4

– hitting practice range ball back to range 7-2/5

P

P

- player after picking up drops ball where partner's ball lies and makes practice stroke 30-3f/7
- player finds ball and hits it to player who lost it; whether stroke considered practice stroke. 7-2/5.5
- player in four-ball match practices on previous green after partner drives from next tee 30-3f/12
- player makes practice putt after he and partner have holed out but before opponents hole out . . . 30/6
- player in foursome match practices putts on previous green after partner drives from next tee 29/3
- player makes practice stroke with ball held in hand against grip of club. 14-3/6.5
- player practices putting off green while waiting to putt. 7-2/3
- player practices with another player's putter. 4-4a/13
- putting on fairway while waiting to play to green. 7-2/2
- replacement of club broken on practice ground while play suspended; whether permitted . . . 4-3/11
- specimen condition prohibiting practice or rolling ball on or near putting green of hole last played between play of holes . . . . App I-C-6b
- when practice between holes permitted 7-2/1

play discontinued by players in match by agreement on 13th hole cannot be resumed until following day; players may play first twelve holes prior to resuming match 7-2/11

play suspended by Committee; player wishes to practice after scheduled resumption but before group plays. 7-2/12

practice swing dislodges concealed ball. 7-2/7

waiving penalty for practice on course 7-1b/2

PRACTICE SWING
See also PRACTICE

area of original intended swing improved when branch broken with practice backswing; area of intended swing finally used not affected by branch. 13-2/24

ball held in hand against grip during practice swing or practice stroke; whether permitted 14-3/6.5

ball moved
- player takes several practice swings near ball in play and touches grass behind ball; thereafter ball moves. 18-2a/30
- prior to tee shot accidentally by practice swing. 18-2a/19
- when in play accidentally by practice swing. 18-2a/20

club damaged while making practice swing; whether considered damaged in "normal course of play". 4-3/1

concealed ball dislodged by practice swing. 7-2/7

four-ball match play partners balls lie in same bunker; after one plays from bunker other makes practice swing touching sand 30-3f/2.5

ground in hazard
- touched with several practice swings 13-4/3
- touched with several practice swings; player advised of breach then makes several more such swings 1-4/13
- not touched however grass touched with club during practice swing. 13-4/4

loose impediment dislodged by practice swing moves ball in play 18-2a/20.5

player breaches Rule(s) either more than once or with different penalties
- ground in hazard touched with several practice swings; player advised of breach then makes several more such swings 1-4/13
- ground in hazard touched with practice swing; stroke made fails to extricate ball; before next stroke club touches ground in hazard with another practice swing 1-4/14
- breaches two Rules with different penalties; more severe penalty applied 1-4/15

stretching device used to make practice swing 14-3/10.5

rod used to check alignment or swing plane. 14-3/10.3

touches sand in hazard (or similar hazard); whether action constitutes "testing the condition of the hazard" in breach of Rule 13–4a 13-4/0.5

training or swing aid, such as weighted headcover or "doughnut" on club, used to make practice swing; whether permitted. . 14-3/10

PRIZE

due to Committee error
- incorrectly calculated handicap for competitor posted resulting in competitor winning event; error discovered several days later 6-2b/3
- winner of event erroneously disqualified; Committee holds play-off between two other competitors; error discovered after play-off but before close of competition 34-1b/5
- winner's score not posted; Committee awards prize to another competitor; error discovered next day. 34-1b/6

– wrong handicap deducted from
competitor's score resulting
in player not receiving prize;
error discovered after close of
competition 33-5/2

player disqualified in
– match-play event; whether
eligible for prize won prior to
disqualification 33/7
– stroke play handicap event;
whether eligible for gross prize . . .33-1/13

PROVISIONAL BALL
See also LOST BALL; OUT OF BOUNDS;
SECOND BALL

announcement requirements
– before provisional ball played 27-2a/1
– when no one present to hear
announcement 27-2a/1.3

condition requiring use of ball on
List of Conforming Golf Balls;
player uses ball not on list as
provisional 5-1/3

deemed unplayable; player drops
ball; original ball then found 27-2b/6.5

divots replaced in area in which
provisional ball to be dropped 13-2/4.5

explanation of "any ball he has played" 18/7

foursome competition
– determining which partner plays
provisional ball 29-1/3
– provisional ball played by wrong
member of side 29-1/4
– whether partner who went
ahead before tee shot played
may return to tee to play
provisional ball 29-1/4.5

lifted
– in erroneous belief original ball
in bounds 27-2b/8
– subsequently becomes ball in
play; penalty and procedure for
player 27-2b/9
– subsequently becomes ball in
play; competitor then plays
from wrong place 27-2b/10

meaning of "goes forward to search" . .27-2a/1.5

moves after being addressed;
whether penalty canceled if
provisional ball never becomes
ball in play 15/7

order of play
– provisional balls played out of
turn from teeing ground 10-3/1
– when played other than from
teeing ground 10/4

original ball
– and provisional ball found out of
bounds 27-2c/4
– and provisional ball not
distinguishable from each other . . .27/11
– and provisional ball; time
permitted for search 27/4
– found by referee; player prefers
to continue with provisional ball . .27-2/2

– found in hole after five-minute
search and continuation of play
with provisional ball 1-1/3
– found; player wishes to ignore
it and continue play with
provisional ball 27-2c/2
– not searched for; player
continues play with provisional
ball 27-2b/1
– played after provisional ball
played from point nearer hole
than original ball likely to be 27-2b/5
– search abandoned; player walks
forward to play provisional ball;
original ball then found 27-2b/6
– searched for briefly; player
makes stroke with provisional
from nearer hole than where
original likely to be; original ball
then found .27-2b/3
– strikes provisional ball 19-5/5
– struck by provisional ball 18-5/2

played
– and possibly lost or out of
bounds; third ball played with no
announcement 27-2a/4
– as second ball when player not
able to determine whether
original ball in or out of bounds . . .3-3/1
– in absence of reasonable
possibility original ball lost or
out of bounds 27-2a/3
– from beyond where original
ball likely to be but not beyond
where original ball found 27-2b/4
– from point nearer hole than
visible original ball; player
erroneously thought original
ball out of bounds 27-2c/3
– from tee; player deems original
ball unplayable while still on tee
and plays third ball; claims third
ball lying three 28/2
– in belief original ball might be
in water hazard or lost outside
water hazard or out of bounds 27-2a/2.2
– in belief original ball might
only be in water hazard (no
possibility of being out of
bounds or lost outside water
hazard) 27-2a/2
– in belief original ball might be
lost outside water hazard;
thereafter player determines
no possibility ball lost outside
water hazard 27-2a/2.5
– in erroneous belief it is original
ball 27-2b/7

player wishes provisional ball to
serve as ball in play if original
unplayable or in water hazard 27-2/1

referee
– finds player's original ball;
player prefers to continue with
provisional ball 27-2/2
– incorrectly tells player to play out
hole with provisional ball instead
of original ball found in water hazard 34-3/3.7

specimen Local Rule allowing ball
to be played provisionally under
water hazard Rule . . . . .App I-B-1

time permitted for search for
original ball and provisional ball. 27/4

when holed provisional ball
becomes player's ball in play. 27-2b/2

whether provisional ball becomes
ball in play if missing original ball
known or virtually certain to be in
ground under repair 27-2c/1.5

wrong ball played in belief it is
provisional ball. 15/7

PUTTING GREEN
See also BALL OVERHANGING HOLE;
FLAGSTICK; HOLE; HOLE PLUG; IMPROVING
AREA OF INTENDED STANCE OR SWING,
POSITION OR LIE OF BALL, OR LINE OF
PLAY OR PUTT; INDICATING LINE FOR
PUTTING; LINE OF PUTT; WRONG PUTTING
GREEN

ball assisting play
– competitor requests fellow-
competitor not lift it 22/6
– fellow-competitor could lift
ball without delaying play of
competitor; procedure for
referee if ball not lifted 22/7

ball at rest moved
– player addresses ball, steps
away, lifts ball and replaces it;
ball then moves. 18-2b/8
– player knocks opponent's ball
away after concession; ball
strikes and moves player's ball 18-2a/18
– player's foot accidentally moves
ball during removal of loose
impediment on putting green 23-1/11

ball deflected or stopped on
putting green
– after stroke from off green 19-1/6
– after stroke from green 19-1/7
– by ball replaced while other ball
in motion. 16-1b/3
– by moving outside agency;
stroke not replayed 19-1/3
– player knocks partner's putted
ball back to him while still in
motion after having passed hole. . .1-2/7
– stroke made from putting green
strikes ball on green belonging
to competitor playing in another
group 19-5/2
– stroke made from putting green
touches but does not move ball
of fellow-competitor lying on
green 19-5/4

ball enters burrowing animal hole
in bunker and comes to rest
underneath putting green. 25-1b/25

ball knocked from lip of hole in
disgust. 18-2a/23

ball lifted
– because player feared ball might
move 16-1b/1
– cleaned and replaced; ball then
falls into hole. 16-2/0.5

– from putting green while
another ball in motion; lifted ball
might influence movement of
ball in motion 16-1b/4
– on putting green placed ahead of
ball-marker and then rolled or
slid back to original position 16-1a/17

ball mark
– in position to assist opponent
repaired by player 16-1c/2
– partially on and partially off
putting green on line of play 16-1c/1.5
– repaired second time. 16-1c/1
– spike mark repaired during
repair of ball mark 16-1a/16

ball-marker
– ball replaced ahead of ball-
marker then player rolls or
slides ball back to original
position 16-1a/17
– ball replaced but ball-marker
not removed; ball then moves 20-4/1
– caddie places lifted ball behind
ball-marker so player can assess
line for putting; whether ball in
play. 20-4/2
– moved accidentally by player
after having moved loose
impediments. 20-1/12
– placed other than behind ball;
whether permitted 20-1/19
– pressed down by opponent;
whether opponent subject to
penalty. 20-1/6.5
– whether lifting opponent's ball-
marker considered concession
of next stroke 2-4/5
– whether player may use object
other than ball-marker or coin
to mark position of ball 20-1/16

ball oscillating in wind pressed into
surface of putting green 1-2/9

ball overhanging hole
– ball falls into hole after
concession of next stroke. 2-4/2
– falls into hole after being
addressed 18-2b/10
– falls into hole after player waits
40 seconds 16-2/1
– fellow-competitor's ball
knocked from lip of hole by
competitor not replaced. 3-2/1
– knocked away by opponent
before player determines status . .16-2/2
– lifted, cleaned and replaced; ball
then falls into hole 16-2/0.5
– player jumps close to hole to
cause ball to drop; ball falls into
hole 1-2/4

ball putted from wrong place lifted
and putted from right place 20-7c/2

ball replaced
– at rest on putting green; rolls
and strikes another ball on green . .19-5/1.5
– at wrong place on putting green
and holed. 20-7c/1
– ball-marker not removed after
ball replaced; ball then moves. 20-4/1

– by rolling it to correct spot with putter...........................16-1d/3

– line drawn or on ball aimed to indicate line for putting when ball replaced....................20-3a/2

– while another ball in motion; replaced ball re-lifted because moving ball might strike it........16-1b/2

– while another ball in motion; replaced ball subsequently deflects moving ball..............16-1b/3

ball substituted for original ball by competitor on putting green; error discovered after stroke made from next teeing ground.....15-2/3

bottled drink used to gauge slope of putting green; whether permitted..14-3/12.5

caddie

– casts shadow to indicate line of putt..............................8-2b/1

– places lifted ball behind ball-marker so player can assess line for putting; whether ball in play..20-4/2

– practices on or tests putting green surfaces of course before stroke-play round...............7-1b/5

– roughens surface of putting green but player does not benefit.16-1d/6

– touches putting green to indicate line of play before player chips from off green......8-2b/3

casual water on putting green

– brushing aside or mopping up casual water on line of putt.......16-1a/1

– intervenes between ball off green and hole..................25-1a/2

– nearest point of relief off putting green...........................25-1b/10

– removal of casual water or loose impediments on putting green by Committee...........33/1

– visible when player walks beside line of putt but not visible elsewhere......................25/5

– whether player entitled to relief for intervention if ball on putting green and nearest point of relief off putting green.......25-1b/10.5

club used as plumb-line.............14-3/12

concession

– agreement to concede short putts 1-3/2

– ball falls into hole after concession of next stroke.......2-4/2

– lifting opponent's ball-marker; whether considered concession of next stroke..................2-4/5

– of stroke refused by player and withdrawn by opponent; player then putts and misses..........2-4/7

– opponent's ball knocked away by player after concession moves player's ball..............18-2a/18

– picking up opponent's ball; whether considered concession of next stroke..................2-4/4

– player concedes opponent's next stroke and knocks ball away along own line of putt......16-1d/2

– player concedes opponent's next stroke and plays before opponent has opportunity to lift ball............................2-4/8

– player concedes opponent's next stroke and rolls or knocks ball to opponent................16-1d/1

– player concedes opponent's next stroke and then knocks opponent's ball into hole........2-4/1

– player lifts ball in mistaken belief that next stroke conceded......2-4/3

– putting out after concession of stroke............................2-4/6

double green; whether portion serving hole not being played considered wrong putting green....25-3/1

extension of line of putt behind ball

– meaning of "extension of line of putt behind ball" in context of standing astride or on line of putt.16-1e/1

– player allows partner to stand on extension of line of putt behind ball; assists partner with similar putt....................30-3f/13

flagstick

– attended without authority before stroke; attendance ceases upon instruction of player after stroke.............17-2/1

– held upright by attendant behind hole with bottom of flagstick touching putting green; whether breach of Rule 8–2b.............17-1/4.5

– holding with one hand and putting with other hand; whether permitted.............17-1/5

– removed without authority by opponent or fellow-competitor while player's ball in motion......17-2/2

flagstick placed on ground prior to stroke within reach of opponent or fellow-competitor; lifted after stroke made..........17-1/7

four-ball match play

– partner waives turn to putt......30-3b/2

– player knocks partner's putted ball back to him while still in motion after having passed hole...1-2/7

– player with putt for half picks up in error at suggestion of opponent based on misunderstanding...............30/5

line drawn or on ball aimed to indicate line for putting when ball replaced......................20-3a/2

line of putt

– altered purposely by opponent or fellow-competitor by stepping on it.................1-2/1

– brushing aside or mopping up casual water on line of putt.......16-1a/1

– caddie casts shadow to indicate line of putt....................8-2b/1

– caddie while attending flagstick suggests player aim at foot; whether breach of any Rule.....8-2b/2

– casual water visible when player walks beside line of putt but not visible elsewhere 25/5

– damaged accidentally by opponent, fellow-competitor or their caddies 16-1a/13

– meaning of "line of putt" in context of "standing astride or on line of putt" 16-1e/1

– mushroom growing on line of putt 16-1a/15

– old hole plug sunk or raised on line of putt..................... 16-1c/3

– player entitled to putt stands on another player's line of putt 30-3b/1

– player touches putting green in pointing out line for putting for partner and incidentally touches own line of putt 30/2.5

– player walks on line of putt 16-1a/12

– removal of casual water or loose impediments on putting green by Committee 33/1

– removing dew or frost from line of putt 16-1a/3

– shielding from wind 1-2/2

Local Rule
– allowing relief from edging grooves around putting green 33-8/24

– allowing relief for intervention by immovable obstructions in closely mown areas near putting greens .... App I-B-6

– deeming material similar to sand to have same status as sand 33-8/40

– requiring players to putt continuously on putting green until ball holed; whether authorized 33-8/7

– waives requirement to hole out for temporary putting green; whether authorized 33-8/1

– wrong putting green; deemed to include apron to prohibit dropping on and play from 33-8/33

map of putting green indicating hole position displayed at tee; whether permitted 33/6

marking island green; recommendations for Committee . 33-2a/10

mud on ball touches putting green but ball itself does not touch green; whether ball considered on putting green 16/1

player putts with one hand and catches ball in hole with other hand . 1-2/5

practice putting
– off green while waiting to putt 7-2/3

– on fairway while waiting to play to green...................... 7-2/2

– on previous green player in four-ball match practices after partner drives from next tee 30-3f/12

– with another player's putter during round 4-4a/13

relocating hole
– due to severity of location during stroke-play round 33-2b/1.5

– general 33-2b/1

– when damaged after ball already positioned nearby on putting green 33-2b/2

rotating ball on putting green without marking position 18-2a/33

rubbing ball on putting green for cleaning purposes 16-1d/5

spike mark(s)
– competitor sanctions repair of spike damage on his line of putt by fellow-competitor 13-2/36

– line of putt altered purposely by opponent or fellow-competitor by stepping on it 1-2/1

– line of putt damaged accidentally by opponent, fellow-competitor or their caddies 16-1a/13

– player and opponent or fellow-competitor agree to repair spike marks on one another's line of putt..................... 1-3/3

– pressed down when player repairs old hole plug 16-1a/16.5

– repair of spike mark damage around hole.................... 16-1c/4

– repaired during repair of ball mark 16-1a/16

status of ball touching both water hazard and putting green 26/1.5

team competition
– player's team mate in gallery hits approach shot to show player whether putting green will hold . . 8-1/23

– whether team captain authorized to give advice may be required to stay off putting greens 8-2b/4

testing surface of putting green for wetness; whether permitted 16-1d/4

RAKE

See also BUNKER; IMPROVING AREA OF INTENDED STANCE OR SWING, POSITION OR LIE OF BALL, OR LINE OF PLAY OR PUTT; LINE OF PLAY; OBSTRUCTIONS; STATUS OF OBJECT

ball in bunker moves when rake removed; whether player may press ball into sand or take relief outside bunker if not possible to replace or place in bunker not nearer hole 20-3d/2

bunker entered by player to remove rake on line of play; player smoothes footprints restoring line of play before making stroke.... 13-2/29

deflects or stops ball while being held by caddie of side (or partner) . . 19-2/10

footprints made in retrieving rake smoothed prior to player's stroke . 13-2/9

handle stuck in bunker before stroke .13-4/0.5

placed in hazard before stroke 13-4/0.5

thrown into bunker before stroke 13-4/21

whether leaning on or placing a rake in a hazard constitutes "testing the condition of the hazard" in breach of Rule 13–4a 13-4/0.5

R

whether rakes should be placed in
or outside bunkers Misc./2

REFEREE
See also COMMITTEE; OBSERVER

authority to declare ground under
repair 34-2/1

authorises player to infringe Rule 34-2/2

ball thought unfit for play; referee's
involvement when opponent,
marker or fellow-competitor not
readily available 5-3/7

flagstick attended by referee
at player's request; whether
permitted or recommended 17-1/3

guidelines for referee in resolving
questions of fact 34-3/9

imposes penalty for previous hole
after play of next hole begun 2-5/12

incorrect ruling places player
in stroke play at serious
disadvantage; when ruling may be
reversed 34-3/3.3

incorrectly advises player of loss of
hole penalty; both sides lift their
balls; then referee discovers error . 34-2/7

player disagrees with referee's
decision; whether decision may be
referred to Committee 34-2/4

procedure for determining ball
farther from hole. 10-1b/1

reverses ruling
– made at last hole of match after
players leave putting green 34-2/5
– made on previous hole after play
of next hole begun 34-2/6

warns player about to infringe Rule . . 34-2/3

when match result "officially
announced" .2-5/14

REFUSAL TO COMPLY WITH RULE

competitor not given opportunity
to lift ball assisting fellow-
competitor before fellow-
competitor plays 3-4/1

fellow competitor or opponent
refuses to attend flagstick 17-1/2

player claiming danger from
lightning, refuses to play when
resumption of play ordered by
Committee. 6-8b/5

player concedes opponent's
next stroke then plays before
opponent has opportunity to
lift ball 2-4/8

player in match play refuses to lift
ball interfering with opponent's
next stroke. 2/3

player refuses to tell opponent how
many strokes he has taken 9-2/3.5

player requests opponent's ball
be lifted because it might assist
opponent's partner; opponent
does not lift ball and opponent's
partner plays 30-3f/11

when agreement made between
players becomes breach of Rule 1–3 .1-3/0.5

REPAIR
See also DAMAGE; GROUND UNDER REPAIR

ball mark on putting green
– hole damage due to ball mark;
whether player may repair 16-1a/6
– in position to assist player;
whether player may prevent
repair by opponent 16-1c/2
– partially on and partially off
putting green on player's line of
play; whether repair permitted . . .16-1c/1.5
– repair by caddie; whether
permitted 6-4/10
– repaired second time. 16-1c/1

club or clubs
– damaged in normal course of
play breaks into pieces when
repaired; whether replacement
permitted 4-3/3
– meaning of "repair" when club
damaged in normal course of play .4-3/2
– rendered unfit for play by
outside agency or opponent's
side; whether repair or
replacement permitted. 4-3/9.5

damaged hole
– inside edge of damaged hole
touched while repaired;
whether permitted 16-1a/5
– repair procedures; damage due
to ball mark; damage due to
other cause. 16-1a/6
– repaired after player holes out
but before opponent, fellow-
competitor or partner holes out. .1-2/3.5

line of putt
– agreement to repair spike marks
on one another's line of putt
made by player and opponent
or competitor and fellow-
competitor .1-3/3
– damaged accidentally by
opponent, fellow-competitor
or their caddies; whether repair
permitted 16-1a/13
– depression exposed when
partially embedded acorn
removed; whether repair
permitted 16-1a/7
– old hole plug sunk or raised
on line of putt; relief options
available to player. 16-1c/3

old hole plugs and other turf plugs
– Local Rule permitting repair of
turf plugs on putting green not
4–1/4 inches in diameter. 33-8/30
– repair by caddie; whether
permitted 6-4/10
– sunken or raised on line of putt;
relief options available to player. . .16-1c/3

pitch-mark
– area of intended swing improved
by repair of pitch-mark made by
ball on previous stroke 13-2/21
– repaired in area where ball to be
dropped. 13-2/10

spike mark
- agreement to repair spike marks on one another's line of putt made by player and opponent or competitor and fellow-competitor 1-3/3
- damage around hole; whether repair permitted................16-1c/4
- pressed down when player repairs old hole plug 16-1a/16.5
- repaired during repair of ball mark........................16-1a/16

ROADS AND PATHS
See also STATUS OF OBJECT

ball breaks into pieces as result of striking paved cart path 5-3/4

Local Rule
- deeming ground under repair adjacent to artificially-surfaced cart paths to have same status as path 33-8/25
- providing relief from unsurfaced road for tee shot only; whether authorized......................33-8/20
- providing relief in all cases on fairway side of paved path, or dropping zone, when nearest point of relief effectively gives no relief; whether authorized.....33-8/19
- specimen Local Rule establishing dropping zone as additional option under Rules 24–2b and 24–3 ....App I-B-8

meaning of "artificially-surfaced" 24/9

nearest point of relief
- from cart path in abnormal ground condition; nearest point of relief from abnormal ground condition back on cart path 1-4/8
- from cart path in abnormal ground condition; nearest point of relief from abnormal ground condition back on cart path; drop into abnormal ground condition impracticable..........1-4/8.5

public road defined as out of bounds divides course; status of ball crossing road 27/20

status of stone, crushed shell, wood chips or the like used to surface road..........................23/14

ROOTS
See also TREE OR BUSH

divot lies substantially with all of its roots downward in divot hole; whether considered replaced 13-2/7

Local Rule providing relief from tree roots; whether authorized........33-8/8

moving natural object enough to determine whether loose impediment or attached to roots; whether breach of Rule 13–2.......13-2/26

moving raised tuft of grass on line of putt to determine if attached to roots; whether breach of Rule 13–2.16-1a/11

player misses stroke at ball between tree roots then deems it unplayable; Rule 28a option discussed.......................28/7

probing for tree roots or rocks near ball; whether permitted 13-2/27

status of roots outside area of ground under repair growing from tree inside area 25/10.7

unplayable ball between tree roots; whether relief available if obstruction interferes with player's swing...................24-2b/16

ROUGH
See also THROUGH THE GREEN

ball in rough
- found after two minutes then lost again; time permitted for search 27/3
- lifted by fellow-competitor at player's request; turns out to be player's ball in play 18-2a/16
- moved accidentally and original lie altered; ball replaced in wrong place and played 18-2a/21.3
- moved accidentally; ball placed instead of dropped when original spot not determinable....18-2a/21.5
- moved after practice swings taken near ball and grass behind ball touched 18-2a/30
- moves downward when addressed; ball will not remain at rest when replaced 20-3d/3
- touched and rotated for identification purposes 12-2/2

casual water on putting green; nearest point of relief off green in rough............................25-1b/10

concealed ball in rough dislodged by
- practice swing...................7-2/7
- stroke at player's own ball in rough 15/2

dropping from rough to fairway in obtaining relief under Rule; whether permitted 24-2b/8

lie improved due to relief from condition; whether ball must be re-dropped if condition interferes for stroke with different club.......20-2c/0.8

Local Rule defining rough and unplayable areas adjacent to fairways (areas not meeting definition of lateral water hazard) as lateral water hazard; whether authorized 33-8/35

pressed down due to removal of loose impediment 13-2/13

when club grounded in grass........18-2b/5

wrong ball played from rough
- hole conceded prior to discovery .2-4/9
- into deep water hazard; procedure for fellow-competitor to whom ball probably belonged 15-3b/1

– then player wins hole with
original ball; opponent does not
lodge claim during hole; claim
lodged next day 2-5/4

SALIVA
See also CASUAL WATER; LOOSE
IMPEDIMENTS

applying saliva to face of club. 4-2/4
status of saliva 25/6

SAND
See also BUNKER

ball against rake in bunker moves
when rake removed; whether
ball may be pressed into sand if it
cannot be placed at rest anywhere
in bunker not nearer hole. 20-3d/2
ball embedded in lip of bunker 13/4
ball overhanging edge of bunker 13/3
four-ball match play partners balls
lie in same bunker; after one plays
from bunker other makes practice
swing touching sand 30-3f/2.5
from bunker other makes practice
swing touching sand 30-3f/2.5
hitting sand in bunker with club
after failing to extricate ball
– in breach of Rule 13–4 . . . . 13-4/35
– in foursome match 29/5
– partner's ball in same bunker 30-3f/2
hitting sand in bunker with club
in frustration after stroke made
from bunker onto grass bank but
before ball rolls back into bunker . . . 13-4/35.5
in bunker club touches
– casual water without touching
sand 13-4/7
– sand during backswing 13-4/31
– sand when ball lies outside bunker . 13-4/1
lie on apron of green affected by
sand from partner's, opponent's
or fellow-competitor's stroke
from bunker 13-2/8.5
lie through the green improved
when sand behind ball removed by
backswing 13-2/9
Local Rule
– permitting re-dropping or
placing when dropped ball
embeds in bunker; whether
authorized 33-8/28
– permitting relief from sand filled
divot holes; whether authorized . . 33-8/34
pressed down behind ball through
the green when addressed 13-2/12
removing sand or loose soil from
dropping area 13-2/11
smoothing sand after ball played out
of bunker; ball later returns to
smoothed area 13-4/38
spilling over margin of bunker;
whether considered part of bunker . 13/1

SCORES AND SCORE CARDS
See also INFORMATION AS TO STROKES
TAKEN; MARKER

all scores not to count
– application of disqualification
penalty in competition in which
not all team members' scores
count for each round 33/8
– competition in which
competitors' best of two of
four scores used to determine
winner; competitor returns
score card with higher handicap . . 6-2b/5
alteration to score card
– alteration of handicap stroke
table 33-4/1
– competitor's scores recorded
on score card with fellow-
competitor's name and vice
versa 6-6d/4
– hole scores entered in wrong
boxes; marker corrects error
by altering hole numbers on card . 6-6a/3
– requirement that alteration on
score card be initialed 6-6a/6
– score corrected by competitor
after marker leaves area in
which card returned 6-6b/7
– when score card considered
returned thus prohibiting
alterations 6-6c/1
Committee error
– score cards not returned
promptly due to Committee
failure to advise competitors
where to return score cards. 6-6b/4
– winner's score not posted due
to Committee error 34-1b/6
– wrong ball penalty not included
in competitor's score due to
incorrect Committee ruling;
during subsequent round error
discovered and penalty applied
retroactively; competitor objects . 34-3/1
– wrong handicap applied by
Committee results in player not
receiving prize 33-5/2
– wrong handicap recorded on
score card by Committee; error
discovered before competition
closed 6-2b/3.5
competitor, other than marker,
fails to notify player, marker or
Committee of player's breach of
Rules in timely manner 33-7/9
four-ball play
– competitor records score for
hole not completed 31-7a/1
– gross score of partner with
better net score omitted from
score card 31-3/1
– lower gross score attributed to
wrong partner 31-7a/2
– side's scores transposed at hole
but not to side's advantage in
handicap four-ball Stableford
competition 32-2a/1

S

– side's scores transposed at hole to side's advantage in handicap four-ball Stableford competition . .32-2a/2

guidelines for determining which ball counts when player proceeds under Rule 3–3 . . . . .3-3/0.5

handicap
- competition in which best two of four scores used to determine winner; competitor returns score card with higher handicap 6-2b/5
- competitor records incorrect handicap for partner in foursome stroke-play competition; error discovered after competition closed. 6-2b/2.5
- meaning of "handicap" for purposes of Rule 6–2 . . . . .6-2/1
- meaning of "handicap" when full handicap not used. 6-2b/0.5
- recording of lower gross score affects result at hole in handicap Stableford competition 32-2a/3
- recording of lower gross score does not affect result of hole in handicap Stableford competition. .32-2a/4
- recording of lower gross score does not affect result of hole in handicap bogey or par competition 32-2a/5
- side's scores transposed at hole but not to side's advantage in handicap four-ball Stableford competition 32-2a/1
- side's scores transposed at hole to side's advantage in handicap four-ball Stableford competition . .32-2a/2
- wrong handicap applied by Committee results in player not receiving prize 33-5/2
- wrong handicap recorded on score card by Committee; error discovered before competition closed. 6-2b/3.5

hole scores
- competitor's scores recorded on fellow-competitor's score card and vice versa. 6-6d/4
- entered in wrong boxes; marker corrects error by altering hole numbers on card 6-6a/3
- for first nine holes recorded in boxes for second nine and vice versa. 6-6d/3
- no score entered for one hole but total correct. 6-6d/1

making competitors responsible for adding scores; whether permitted . .33-1/7

marker
- and competitor sign score card in wrong places. 6-6b/1
- attests wrong score knowingly; competitor aware score wrong . . .1-3/6
- attests wrong score knowingly; competitor unaware score wrong. 6-6a/5
- competitor plays several holes without marker 6-6a/2

– disappears with competitor's score card .6-6b/6
– lone competitor appoints own marker. 6-6a/1
– not appointed by Committee signs score cards 6-6b/5
– refuses to sign competitor's card after dispute resolved in favor of competitor 6-6a/4
– score corrected by competitor after marker leaves area in which score card returned 6-6b/7

match play
- player and opponent agree hole halved; after match result posted player realizes he won hole and should have won match; player then makes claim . . .2-5/9
- player concedes match after winning it when opponent lodges invalid claim regarding strokes taken 2-4/15
- player concedes match due to misconception as to opponent's score at last hole 2-4/14
- player reporting wrong score causes opponent with chance for half to pick up ball 9-2/6
- player reports wrong score for hole; error discovered several holes later 9-2/9
- wrong score on score card in qualifying round discovered during match play 34-1b/7
- wrong score on score card in qualifying round discovered; player disqualified has advanced in match play; Committee options regarding opponents beaten by player 34-1b/8

minus or zero net score. 2-1/2

modifying disqualification penalty for returning wrong score 33-7/4

penalty strokes
- breach of 14-club Rule; where penalty strokes applied 4-4a/10
- competitor correctly advised he incurred penalty by fellow-competitor; competitor disagrees and fails to include penalty in returned score card; Committee advised of incident after close of competition. 34-1b/1.5
- competitor fails to include penalty in first-round score due to incorrect Committee ruling; Committee corrects error during second round 34-3/1
- competitor unaware of penalty returns wrong score; whether waiving or modifying disqualification penalty justified. .33-7/4.5
- omitted from score card returned by player 34-1b/1

requirement that score be entered into computer 6-6b/8

returning score card
- different score card returned when original lost or damaged. . . .6-6a/7

– requirement to return score
card in hole-by-hole play-off.....33-5/1
– score cards not returned
promptly due to Committee
failure to advise competitors
where to return score cards......6-6b/4
– when score card considered
returned 6-6c/1
– with name of wrong player or
no name on it 6-6d/4

score card or pencil used to gauge
distance.........................14-3/2

score may count with wrong ball in
some circumstances
– ball thrown into bounds by
outside agency and played;
neither player nor caddie aware
of action of outside agency.......15/10
– fellow-competitor lifts
competitor's ball and sets it
aside; competitor plays ball
from where set aside...........15-3b/3
– play of wrong ball in stroke play
not rectified; error discovered
after competition closed........34-1b/3
– play of wrong ball not rectified
on advice of referee...........33-7/5
– referee incorrectly advises
player to complete hole with
provisional ball 34-3/3.7

signing of score card
– competitor and marker sign
score card in wrong places 6-6b/1
– competitor's failure to
countersign score card blamed
on lack of time provided by
Committee 33-7/3
– competitor's failure to sign
first-round card discovered on
completion of last round........6-6b/3
– competitor's failure to sign
score card discovered after
competition closed 34-1b/2
– competitor records initials in
space reserved for signature......6-6b/2
– in foursome stroke play.........29/6
– marker not appointed by
Committee signs score cards.....6-6b/5
– marker refuses to sign
competitor's card after dispute
resolved in favor of competitor ...6-6a/4
– requirement that alteration on
score card be initialed 6-6a/6

spectators allege competitor's
score incorrect 6-6d/5

total score recorded by competitor
incorrect........................6-6d/2

SEARCHING FOR AND IDENTIFYING BALL

See also LOST BALL

ball accidentally stepped on during
search by opponent's caddie 18-3b/3

ball assumed in water hazard found
outside hazard after another ball
played under stroke-and-distance
procedure......................26/6

ball changed during play of hole to
aid identification 15/6.5

ball declared lost found within five
minutes and before another ball
put into play 27/16

ball dislodged from tree
– circumstances in which player
not penalized...................18-2a/27
– circumstances in which player
penalized 18-2a/28

ball in casual water difficult to
identify or retrieve without
impracticable effort 25-1/1

ball in tree
– identified but not retrieved.......27/14
– visible but not identifiable 27/15

ball accidentally kicked in long grass
while probing for it in water in
water hazard 12-1/5

caddie
– directed not to search for ball
by player until others can assist ...27/1
– on own initiative lifts ball for
identification...................18-2a/14

continuation of play with provisional
ball without searching for original
ball 27-2b/1

ground in bunker or water hazard
touched with club while probing
for ball believed covered by loose
impediments.....................12-1/4

identifying ball
– by brand and number only........12-2/1
– player lifts ball with mud
adhering for identification and
rotates it when replaced........21/5
– through testimony of spectator ...27/12

lie of ball altered when lifted from
water hazard for identification;
whether original lie is
"nearest lie most similar"..........20-3b/7

loose impediment partially covering
ball in water hazard removed to
identify ball....................13-4/16

loose impediment affecting lie
– moved when ball lifted for
identification...................23-1/7
– removed while ball lifted for
identification...................23-1/8

meaning of "goes forward to search"..27-2a/1.5

opponent's caddie lifts player's ball
– after player claims another ball....18-3b/4
– which may or may not have been
out of bounds 18-3b/5

original ball found; player wishes to
ignore it and continue play with
provisional ball..................27-2c/2

original ball found within five-
minute search period, not
identified until after period elapses..27/5.5

player breaches two Rules with
different penalties; more severe
penalty applied...................1-4/15

player searching for ball mistakes his
ball for opponent's then discovers
mistake after five-minute search
period 27/5

player unable to distinguish his ball
from another ball. 27/10

position of ball lifted for
identification not marked,
intention to lift not announced
and ball cleaned beyond extent
necessary to identify it 21/4

provisional ball
— not distinguishable from original
ball 27/11
— played solely in belief original
ball might be in water hazard 27-2a/2

refusal to identify ball 27/13

time permitted for search
— after wrong ball played. 27/2
— for original ball and provisional
ball 27/4
— if ball found after two minutes
then lost again. 27/3
— if play suspended during search . . .27/1.5

top of ball in hazard covered by
leaves but part of ball visible from
another angle .12-1/3

touching and rotating half-buried
ball in rough for identification
purposes 12-2/2

virtually certain (or known)
— missing ball is in abnormal
ground condition or
obstruction; drop made under
applicable Rule; original ball
then found within five minutes 25-1c/2.5
— missing ball is in water hazard;
drop made under water hazard
Rule; original ball then found
within five minutes 26-1/3.5
— whether virtual certainty
ball is in water hazard can be
established without going
forward to assess conditions
around hazard. 26-1/1.3

when necessary to find and identify
ball deemed unplayable. 28/1

SECOND BALL
See also DOUBT AS TO PROCEDURE;
PROVISIONAL BALL; SERIOUS BREACH
OF RULES

determining which ball counts when
two balls played
— guidelines for determining
which ball counts when player
proceeds under Rule 3–3 . . . . .3-3/0.5
— whether score with second
ball counts if dropped in wrong
place and played 3-3/5

explanation of "any ball he has
played" 18/7

match play
— Local Rule allowing play of
second ball in match play;
whether authorized 33-8/3

— player invokes Rule 3–3 in
match play; whether permitted . . .3-3/9
— player with honor plays from
outside teeing ground; order of
play if opponent requires player
to cancel stroke 11-4a/1

meaning of "penalty strokes
incurred solely by playing ball
ruled not to count" when
competitor plays second ball
under Rule 20–7c. 20-7c/5

moves after being addressed;
whether penalty canceled if
second ball never becomes ball in
play 15/7

original ball strikes second ball or
vice versa 3-3/7

player invokes Rule 3–3 (doubt as
to procedure)
— and plays second ball despite
adverse ruling by referee. 3-3/2
— ball dropped in wrong place and
played; second ball dropped in
right place; both balls played out . .3-3/3
— ball dropped in wrong place but
not played; second ball dropped
in right place; both balls played out 3-3/4
— ball played under water hazard
Rule; original ball then found in
hazard and holed out as second
ball 26-1/5
— competitor announces intention
to play two balls; plays original
ball before dropping second ball;
elects not to play second
ball 3-3/7.5
— competitor drops one ball in
accordance with two different
Rules instead of playing second
ball 3-3/11
— competitor drops one ball in
accordance with two different
Rules instead of playing second
ball; dropped ball rolls back
into condition from which
relief taken .3-3/12
— competitor invokes Rule 3–3;
second ball played first from
spot where original ball lay 3-3/14
— competitor lifts and drops
original ball then places second
ball where original ball lay and
plays it 3-3/13
— competitor picks up second ball,
completes hole with original ball
and plays from next tee 3-3/8
— competitor plays original ball
then invokes Rule 3–3 and plays
second ball. .3-3/6
— competitor plays second ball
without announcing intention
to invoke Rule 3–3 and fails to
report facts to Committee. 3-3/6.5
— competitor plays three balls
when doubtful of rights 3-3/10
— in match play; whether
permitted 3-3/9

– provisional ball used as second
ball when not determinable
whether original ball out of
bounds 3-3/1

player wishes provisional ball to
serve as ball in play if original
unplayable or in water hazard 27-2/1

spectator claims ball moved by
outside agency; player not
sure; procedure for player if
Committee decision not possible
in reasonable time 18-1/4

wrong ball played in belief it is
provisional or second ball 15/7

SERIOUS BREACH OF RULES

See also AGREEMENT TO WAIVE RULES;
ETIQUETTE

etiquette
– disqualification penalty imposed
for unacceptable behavior;
whether permitted 33-8/6
– meaning of "serious breach of
etiquette" 33-7/8

exerting influence
– application of Rule 1–2
disqualification penalty in team
competition in which not all
team members' scores count
for each round 33/8
– ball deliberately deflected or
stopped on putting green by
fellow-competitor 19-1/5
– ball purposely stopped or
deflected 1-2/5.5
– opponent or fellow-competitor
attending flagstick for player
deliberately fails to remove it;
ball strikes flagstick 17-3/2

guidelines for determining whether
serious breach of Rule 1–2 has
occurred 1-2/0.5

meaning of "serious breach of
etiquette" 33-7/8

player in match plays from wrong
place as directed by referee;
error discovered before player
begins next hole; procedure when
serious breach involved 34-3/3

player placed at serious
disadvantage in stroke play due to
incorrect Committee ruling 34-3/3.3

playing from wrong place
– ball deemed unplayable in water
hazard; dropped in hazard and
played 20-7/2
– ball dropped and played under
Rule 25–1c in absence of
knowledge or virtual certainty
original ball in abnormal ground
condition 25-1c/2
– ball dropped in area where
original ball lost; ball then
played 27-1/3
– ball dropped outside bunker
under option of unplayable ball
Rule requiring drop in bunker 28/10

– ball knocked out of bunker by
fellow-competitor's stroke at
own ball not replaced 18-4/2
– ball played from ground under
repair abandoned and relief
taken under ground under
repair Rule 18-2a/8.5
– ball played from putting green
deflected by moving outside
agency; stroke not replayed 19-1/3
– ball played from spot where
original ball deflected out of
bounds by maintenance vehicle . . . 20-7/1
– ball played under water hazard
Rule; original ball then found
outside hazard 26-1/3
– ball played under water hazard
Rule without knowledge or
virtual certainty original ball in
hazard; original ball then found
in hazard 26-1/4
– environmentally-sensitive area,
playing from 33-8/43
– environmentally-sensitive area;
significant advantage gained
when player plays stroke from . . . 33-8/44
– example of serious breach of
lateral water hazard Rule 26-1/21
– lost ball treated as moved by
outside agency in absence of
knowledge or virtual certainty
to that effect 27-1/2.5
– missing original ball believed
in bunker; competitor drops
substituted ball in bunker and
plays it; original then found
outside bunker 20-7c/3
– player invokes Rule 3–3 (doubt
as to procedure); guidelines for
determining which ball counts 3-3/0.5
– player plays second shot, deems
ball unplayable and returns to tee . 28/6
– water hazard treated as lateral
water hazard 26-1/11

wrong ball played in belief it was
second ball played under Rule 20–7c 15/7

SINGLE MATCH

advice
– sought by player then given by
opponent 8-1/25
– whether partners may exchange
advice on single match after
result of hole or match in
concurrent four-ball match
decided 30-3/1

agreement
– to concede one or more holes 2-4/22
– to concede short putts 1-3/2
– to consider hole halved during
play of hole 2-1/1.5

ball at rest moved accidentally
– by golf cart shared by player and
opponent 18/8
– player's ball knocked away by
opponent after concession hits
and moves opponent's ball 18-2a/18
– player's stroke moves
opponent's ball lying nearby 18-3b/1

concurrent four-ball and single matches

– player causes opponent's ball to move; whether penalty stroke applies to player's single match with other opponent 30-3/1
– player causes partner's ball to move; whether penalty stroke applies to player's single match. . . .30-3/1
– player makes stroke with non-conforming club; whether player's partner disqualified in his single match. 30-3/1
– player starts round with 15 clubs; whether four-ball partner incurs penalty in single match. 30-3/1
– whether concessions made under various circumstances apply to only four-ball or single match or both. 30-3/1
– whether partners may exchange advice on single match after result of hole or match in concurrent four-ball match decided 30-3/1

concurrent match and stroke play

– players in single match concurrently competes in stroke-play event 33-1/6
– players in single match joined by competitor in stroke-play event needing marker; whether breach of combining match and stroke play. 33-1/5

golf cart shared by player and opponent deflects or stops player's ball in motion 19/1

incorrect ruling by referee places player in stroke play at serious disadvantage; when ruling may be reversed 34-3/3.3

injury or physical problem

– discontinuing play due to physical problem 6-8a/3
– postponement of final match due to injury of player 6-3a/1

match-play finalists both disqualified .33/3

order of play

– for provisional ball played other than from teeing ground 10/4
– player plays out of turn in match after play suspended by Committee and after opponent discontinues play 6-8b/3.5
– player with honor plays from outside teeing ground; order of play if opponent requires player to cancel stroke 11-4a/1

player invites third person to play along with single match; opponent objects then plays match under protest 2/1

players unable to arrange foursome match agree to single match between one player from each side to decide which team will concede; whether permitted 2-4/21

referee

– referee incorrectly advises player of loss of hole penalty; both sides lift their balls; then referee discovers error 34-2/7
– reverses ruling made at last hole of match after players leave putting green. 34-2/5
– reverses ruling made on previous hole after play of next hole begun. 34-2/6

result of match when player dormie and opponent concedes 2-3/2

true state of match not determinable; recommendations to Committee 34-3/5

when

– match result "officially announced". 2-5/14
– stipulated round begins and ends. 2/2

when play of hole completed in single match so players may practice between holes 7-2/1

SNAKE

See also BURROWING ANIMAL, REPTILE OR BIRD (AND HOLES MADE BY THEM); STATUS OF OBJECT

ball near rattlesnake. 1-4/10

status of snake. 23/6.5

SPECTATOR

See also OUTSIDE AGENCY

alleges competitor's score incorrect . .6-6d/5

assistance in removing large loose impediment 23-1/3

ball at rest kicked away from hole by spectator attending flagstick 18-1/10

ball dislodged in tree knocked down by outside agency 18-1/9

ball falls into bunker when person walks nearby 18/10

deflects or stops ball through the green. 19-1/4.1

distance information obtained with distance measuring device by spectator unilaterally provided to player. 14-3/0.7

identifying ball .27/12

Local Rule declaring areas of extensive damage due to heavy rain and spectator traffic ground under repair. .33-2a/3

marker not appointed by Committee signs score cards 6-6b/5

player concedes match then spectator informs him of opponent's breach of Rule; player lodges claim .2-4/15

seeking information on whereabouts of another player's ball from spectator 8-1/5

shadow of spectator shades ball. 14-2/2.5

spectator says ball moved by outside agency but player not sure; procedure for player if Committee decision not possible in reasonable time 18-1/4

wrong information given by mistake after play of last hole; claim made after result announced 2-5/11

SPIKE MARK(S)

See also DAMAGE; IMPROVING AREA OF INTENDED STANCE OR SWING, POSITION OR LIE OF BALL, OR LINE OF PLAY OR PUTT; LINE OF PUTT; PUTTING GREEN

agreement to repair spike marks made by player and opponent or by competitor and fellow-competitor 1-3/3

competitor sanctions or tacitly approves repair of spike marks by fellow-competitor on line of putt ...13-2/36

line of putt
– accidentally damaged by opponent, fellow-competitor or their caddies 16-1a/13
– purposely damaged or improved by opponent or fellow-competitor or their caddies 1-2/1

raised tuft of grass on line of putt
– brushed to determine whether loose impediment or attached spike mark 16-1a/11
– pressed down when ball put down ahead of ball-marker and rolled back into original position to replace ball 16-1a/17
– pressed down when ball-marker positioned in front of ball on putting green 20-1/19

repaired
– around hole....................16-1c/4
– during repair of ball mark 16-1a/16
– during repair of old hole plug 16-1a/16.5
– solely for the purpose of caring for the course 1-2/0.7

STABLEFORD COMPETITION

See also BOGEY COMPETITION; FOUR-BALL STABLEFORD COMPETITION

breach of Rule by both partners at same hole in four-ball Stableford 32-2b/1

competing simultaneously in Stableford and stroke-play competitions 32-1/1

handicap and handicap competition
– recording of lower gross score affects result of hole 32-2a/3
– recording of lower gross score does not affect result of hole 32-2a/4

in four-ball Stableford competition on handicap basis
– side's scores transposed at hole but not to side's advantage 32-2a/1
– side's scores transposed at hole to side's advantage 32-2a/2

minus or zero net score............2-1/2

omitting holes in Stableford competition 32-1/2

when practice between holes permitted 7-2/1

STAKES

See also BOUNDARY FENCE, LINE, WALL OR STAKES; STATUS OF OBJECT

ball lifted and dropped away from boundary stake under obstruction Rule 18-2a/3

ball within natural margin of water hazard but outside stakes defining margin 26/2

boundary altered by unauthorized removal of boundary stake.........33-2a/19

boundary stakes having no significance in play of hole being played 24/5

competitor with interference from water hazard stake plays original ball then invokes Rule 3–3 and plays second ball 3-3/6

displaced boundary stake 33-2a/20

dropped ball comes to rest and then rolls out of bounds 20-2c/3.5

hole of removed stake defining water hazard 25/18

lie of ball changed by removal of gallery-control stake..............20-3b/3

Local Rule
– allowing free relief from immovable water hazard stake for ball lying in water hazard; whether authorized.............33-8/15
– deeming all stakes on course (except boundary stakes) immovable obstructions 33-8/16

outside agency removes immovable obstruction on player's line of play ..13-2/33

player removes boundary post on line of play but replaces it before playing 13-2/25

provisional ball played from point nearer hole than visible original ball; player erroneously thought original ball out of bounds 27-2c/3

removal of boundary stake interfering with swing.............13-2/17

status of half of double green serving hole not being played......25-3/1

supporting tree broken in attempt to remove it 13-2/16

where to place lines or stakes defining margin of water hazard 33-2a/4

STANCE

See also ADDRESSING THE BALL; IMPROVING AREA OF INTENDED STANCE OR SWING, POSITION OR LIE OF BALL, OR LINE OF PLAY OR PUTT

ball dropped from ground under repair, rolls to position where same area interferes with stance; whether re-drop required 20-2c/0.5

ball moves
 – after player addresses it, steps
   away and re-takes stance
   without grounding club 18-2b/7
 – after stance taken but before
   club grounded. 18-2b/1
 – after club rested on grass
   immediately behind the ball 18-2b/5
 – after stance taken in bunker 18-2b/3
 – in water hazard after stance
   taken; presumably due to
   current or cause unclear. 14-6/1

building stance
 – kneeling on towel or wrapping
   towel around knees while
   making stroke. 13-3/2
 – knocking down side of bunker
   to get level stance. 13-3/3
 – player builds stance then
   corrects error before making
   stroke. 13-3/5
 – standing on mat on teeing ground . 13-3/1

environmentally-sensitive area;
   stance taken or stroke made
   from; explanation of penalties and
   procedures 33-8/43

"fairly taking his stance"
 – meaning of "fairly taking his
   stance". 13-2/1
 – player allowed to play in any
   direction in "fairly taking his
   stance". 13-2/1.5
 – player attempts to take stance
   fairly; improves line of play by
   moving growing object; stance
   abandoned and object returns
   to original position; stance then
   taken fairly without moving
   object. 13-2/1.1
 – player under tree, changes
   intended direction of play and
   fairly takes stance second time. . . . 13-2/1.7

improving stance by
 – moving interfering growing
   object in attempting to take
   stance fairly 13-2/1.1
 – moving loose impediment in
   hazard accidentally 13-4/13
 – moving loose impediments
   when approaching ball in hazard . . 13-4/13.5
 – taking stance fairly 13-2/1
 – taking stance fairly; player then
   changing direction of play 13-2/1.7

in bunker or water hazard
 – ball moves after stance taken 18-2b/3
 – digging in with feet for a stroke
   or practice stroke; whether
   action constitutes "testing
   the condition of the hazard" in
   breach of Rule 13–4a. 13-4/0.5
 – kicking ground in hazard
   or water in a water hazard;
   whether action constitutes
   "testing the condition of the
   hazard" in breach of Rule 13–4a . . 13-4/0.5
 – loose impediment accidentally
   kicked by player into bunker;
   does not interfere with player's

stance or lie in bunker; player
   lifts it; whether permitted. 13-4/14
 – loose impediment accidentally
   moved by player; stance not
   improved 13-4/13
 – loose impediments touched and
   moved by player's feet when
   approaching ball in hazard. 13-4/13.5
 – player's lie changed by another
   player taking stance 20-3b/2
 – stance leveled by knocking
   down side of bunker; whether
   permitted 13-3/3
 – stance taken with club; player
   then decides to change clubs;
   whether permitted 13-4/26
 – stance taken without club;
   whether permitted 13-4/24
 – stance taken firmly; player
   then smoothes footprints after
   deciding to play different type of
   shot 13-4/0.5
 – stance taken firmly some
   distance from where ball lies to
   simulate next stroke; whether
   permitted 13-4/0.5

interference with stance by
 – artificial object lying out of
   bounds; whether movable
   without penalty 24-1/3
 – burrowing animal hole;
   impracticable to make stroke
   because of other condition 25-1b/20
 – crawfish mound 25-1b/18
 – divot hole from stroke just
   made by another player. 13-2/8.7
 – loose impediment lying out
   of bounds; whether removal
   permitted 23-1/9
 – tee-markers for first stroke
   with ball from teeing ground;
   player moves tee-markers 11-2/2

Local Rule allowing free relief from
   condition (Committee should
   deny relief if interference occurs
   only with player's stance)
 – damage made by insects 33-8/21
 – edging grooves around putting
   green 33-8/24
 – severe damage by non-
   burrowing animals 33-8/32.5

nearest point of relief
 – diagram illustrating situations
   when player must estimate
   nearest point of relief because
   simulating stance for intended
   stroke not possible 24-2b/3.7
 – player unable to take stance for
   intended stroke at nearest point
   of relief due to interference by
   something other than condition
   from which relief taken 24-2b/3
 – relief taken properly from
   obstruction for stroke towards
   green; after taking proper relief
   same obstruction interferes
   with stance for necessary
   sideways stroke 24-2b/9.5

side-saddle putting; clarification of
  when player has taken stance and
  addressed ball. 18-2b/5.7

water visible as result of undue
  effort with feet. 25/4

when ball addressed in hazard 18-2b/2

STATUS OF OBJECT

acorn embedded in ground 23/9

aeration holes 25/15

aeration plugs 23/12

air propelled from fan or blower 18-1/2

angled supports supporting
  boundary fence 24/2

ants and ant hills 23/5

ball
  – abandoned. .24-1/2
  – artificially warmed 14-3/13.5
  – broken piece of ball struck by
    player mistaking it for his ball
    lying in heavy grass. 15/3
  – completely embedded in lip of
    bunker 13/4
  – containing radio frequency id chip .14-3/14
  – crossing public road defined
    as out of bounds that divides
    course that comes to rest on
    another part of course 27/20
  – declared lost before another
    ball put into play 27/16
  – embedded in ground (criteria
    for being embedded) 25-2/0.5
  – inside but touching boundary
    fence; when out of bounds 27/19
  – intended to be provisional
    but no one present to hear
    announcement 27-2a/1.3
  – moved accidentally by player
    during suspension of play. 18-2a/25
  – not on List of Conforming Golf
    Balls 5-1/1.7
  – on edge of bunker overhanging
    sand 13/3
  – on obstruction in bunker 13/5
  – placed behind ball-marker on
    putting green by caddie so
    player can assess line of putt. 20-4/2
  – to be removed from List of
    Conforming Golf Balls. 5-1/1.5
  – touching both water hazard and
    another part of course 26/1.5
  – warming device. 14-3/13.5
  – whether holed; embedded in
    side of hole; all below lip of hole. .16/2
  – whether holed; embedded in
    side of hole; not all below lip of
    hole 16/3
  – whether on putting green 16/1

binoculars 14-3/3

bottled drink used as level. 14-3/12.5

boundary stakes having no
  significance in play of hole being
  played 24/5

bridge in water hazard 13-4/30

bunker totally under repair 25/13

calculator. 14-3/16

carts pulled by double caddie 6-4/6

chalk applied to face of club. 4-2/3

clod of earth 23/13

club(s)
  – carried for player during round by
    person walking along with group . .4-4a/16
  – chipper 4-1/3
  – declared out of play prior to
    round but carried during round . . .4-4a/1
  – pieces of broken club carried
    during round 4-4c/1
  – components of clubs (heads and
    shafts) assembled and/or carried
    during stipulated round. 4-4a/15
  – used as plumb line. 14-3/12

compass used during round. 14-3/4

concrete bases of boundary fence
  posts 24/3

crab 23/6

crushed shell used to surface road
  or path. 23/14

crawfish mound 25-1b/18

crawfish mound 23/6

dead land crab .23/6

dew or frost on line of putt 16-1a/3

dew or frost other than on line of putt .13-2/35

displaced boundary stake 33-2a/20

distance-measuring device 14-3/0.5

distance meter attached to golf cart . .14-3/1

divot undetached 13-2/5

electronic device
  – containing distance
    measurements between various
    points. 14-3/5.5
  – used during stipulated round 14-3/16

eyeglasses. 14-3/3

fence off course leaning across
  boundary 13-2/20

field glasses. 14-3/3

finely crushed shells 33-8/40

flagstick not positioned in hole
  moved to prevent another player's
  ball from striking it removed prior
  to stroke, lying on ground within
  reach of player then lifted 17-1/7

fruit
  – in which ball embeds 23/10
  – skins 23/4

gallery-control line or mark
  consisting of lime or paint 24-2b/20

gate in boundary fence or wall 27/18

gravity. 18-2b/11

glove used as indicating mark;
  whether equipment. 20-2a/7

golf ball warmer 14-3/13.5

gradient-measuring device. 14-3/0.5

grass adhering to ball 21/2

grass cuttings. 25/11

grass-covered ground within bunker . .13/2

growing things rooted within
  environmentally-sensitive area
  overhanging area outside ESA 33-8/44.5

guy wires supporting boundary fence .24/2

half of double green serving hole
   not being played.................25-3/1
hand-held computer...............14-3/16
hand warmer......................14-3/13
immovable artificial object situated
   out of bounds.................24-2b/21
insect
  – flying in water hazard..........13-4/16.5
  – on ball......................23-1/5
  – on ball in bunker...........23-1/5.5
insect-like creatures..............23/5.5
lava dust.........................33-8/40
lie changed by removal of gallery-
   control stake 20-3b/3
logo stamped on ball..............5-1/4
loose soil from cast made by bird,
   reptile or burrowing animal.......23/11
material similar to sand 33-8/40
molehill
  – loose soil or cast made by mole...23/11
  – status of 25/23
moss or creepers in tree and on
   ground..........................13-2/37
motorized golf carts...............33-8/4
movable artificial object lying out of
   bounds..........................24-1/3
movable part of drainage hose 24-2b/15.3
mushroom, growing on line of putt...16-1a/15
non-growing plants within area of
   ground under repair 25/10.9
parked car 24/8
part of boundary fence within
   boundary line..................24/4
pear, half-eaten 23/3
person
  – hired to carry umbrella for
    player, in addition to caddie 6-4/5
  – in shared golf cart...............19/2
  – or person(s) other than caddie
    carry items, other than clubs,
    for player.....................6-4/5.3
  – transporting player's clubs on
    motorized golf cart or trolley.....6-4/2.5
  – walking along with player's
    group carrying additional clubs
    for player 4-4a/16
phone, mobile whether artificial
   device 14-3/16
plumb-line
  – club used as plumb-line during
    round.........................14-3/12
  – used during round..............14-3/11
"practice" stamped on ball.........5-1/4
provisional ball played from point
   nearer hole than visible original
   ball; player erroneously thought
   original ball out of bounds 27-2c/3
radio 14-3/16
rake while being held by caddie (or
   any player) 19-2/10
"refurbished" ball.................5-1/4
saliva...........................25/6
sand spilling over margin of bunker...13/1

snake 23/6.5
spectacles........................14-3/3
spiders and spider webs...........23/5.5
starting time fixed by players 33-3/1
steps, wooden or earthen..........24/12
stile attached to boundary fence 24/1
stone
  – broken away from retaining wall
    in water hazard...............24/6
  – serving as part of drain in bunker..24/7
  – used to surface road or path.....23/14
stretching device...................14-3/10.5
swing aid used during stipulated
   round; player claims use
   necessary for medical reasons......14-3/15.5
team captain or coach 33-1/11.5
tee-markers after first stroke........11-2/1
television 14-3/16
tree
  – basins 33-2a/10.5
  – fallen........................23/7
  – fallen, attached to stump........25/9
  – fallen, in process of being
    removed 25/7
  – in bunker....................13/2
  – roots outside ground under
    repair growing from tree inside
    ground under repair............25/10.7
  – stump.......................25/8
turf raised by underground pipe.....24/14
two holes on each green of nine
   hole course.....................16/7
weighted headcover or "doughnut"
   on club.........................14-3/10
wind gauge.......................14-3/0.5
wood chips used to surface road or
   path 23/14
wooden or earthen steps 24/12
wooden planks 24/11
worm
  – casts........................23-1/1
  – partially underground 23/8
"X-out" ball......................5-1/4

STIPULATED ROUND

See also ARTIFICIAL DEVICES, UNUSUAL
EQUIPMENT AND UNUSUAL USE OF
EQUIPMENT

advice between rounds in 36-hole
   match 8-1/19
alteration of handicap stroke table....33-4/1
asking advice when play suspended ..8-1/20
ball played from teeing ground of
   hole to be played later in round
   lifted; ball replaced at spot from
   which lifted and played out when
   that hole subsequently reached.....11-5/5
ball-marker moved by wind or
   casual water during stipulated
   round.........................20-1/10.5
borrowing balls or towel from
   another player 5-1/5

clubs
- changing between rounds in
  36-hole match. 4-4a/2
- fellow-competitor inadvertently
  uses and thereafter carries
  another competitor's club 4-4a/5
- replacement of club for stroke-
  play play-off. 4-3/12

competitors play two holes not
  included in stipulated round. 3/2

discontinuance of play for
  refreshment .6-8a/2.5

hole(s) omitted in match
- by mistake .2-1/3
- purposely. .2-1/4

match discontinued by agreement
  replayed in entirety instead of
  resumed from where discontinued. .2-1/6

number of holes reduced after play
  begins; whether permitted. 33-1/2

player who has not yet played
  seeks advice from player who has
  finished round 8-1/18

players agree to shorten stipulated
  round by conceding one or more
  holes to each other 2-4/22

playing characteristics
- changed while play suspended;
  error discovered before play
  resumed. 4-2/2
- modifying penalty for holing
  short putt with club whose
  playing characteristics changed
  other than in normal course of
  play. 4-3/4

practice
- competitor practices putting
  on 3rd green after finishing hole
  during first round of 36-hole
  stroke-play competition 7-1b/7
- competitor practices putting
  on 3rd green of 9-hole course
  during 18-hole stroke-play
  competition 7-2/9

rod used to check alignment or
  swing plane 14-3/10.3

starting players from 1st and 10th
  tees 33-1/3

three holes played out of sequence
  in match 2-1/5

two balls in play simultaneously at
  different holes 1-1/1

when stipulated round begins and ends
- in match play 2/2
- in stroke play 3/3

wrong teeing ground; play from
  attributable to Committee failure
  to indicate hole numbers on
  teeing ground 11-5/2

STONE(S), ROCK(S) OR GRAVEL
See also LOOSE IMPEDIMENTS; STATUS OF
OBJECT; WALL

ball moved by stone dislodged by
- partner's or opponent's stroke . . .18-1/8
- practice swing 18-2a/20.5

ball outside bunker; stone in bunker
  on line of play pressed down or
  removed 13-2/31

bending grass in removal of loose
  impediments. 13-2/13

competitor correctly advised he
  incurred penalty for moving stone
  from water hazard by fellow-
  competitor; competitor disagrees
  and fails to include penalty in
  returned score card; Committee
  advised of incident after close of
  competition .34-1b/1.5

gravel surfaced road or path;
  whether artificially-surfaced 24/9

improving line of play by removing
  stone from wall 13-2/32

large stone movable only with much
  effort. 23-1/2

specimen Local Rule deeming
  stones in bunkers movable
  obstructions .App I-B-5

player builds stance through use
  of object such as stone, brick, or
  golf cart; corrects error before
  making stroke. 13-3/5

probing near ball for stones or tree
  roots; whether permitted 13-2/27

solidly embedded
- meaning of "solidly embedded"
  in definition of loose impediments.23/2
- stone in hazard touched with
  club during backswing 13-4/6

status of
- stone (or the like) used to
  surface road or path 23/14
- stone broken away from
  retaining wall in water hazard. 24/6
- stone serving as part of drain in
  bunker 24/7

STROKE
See also ARTIFICIAL DEVICES, UNUSUAL
EQUIPMENT AND UNUSUAL USE OF
EQUIPMENT; BALL IN MOTION STRUCK
BY CLUB; CONCESSION; HANDICAP
COMPETITION AND HANDICAP STROKES;
PRACTICE; PRACTICE SWING; STROKE
AND DISTANCE; STROKE CANCELED OR
RECALLED; WRONG BALL

ball missed with stroke
- backward movement of club
  after stroke accidentally moves
  ball 18-2a/22
- in foursome play accidentally;
  which partner plays next stroke .29-1/6
- in foursome play purposely;
  whether stroke made and which
  partner plays next stroke 29-1/7
- player then addresses ball and
  accidentally knocks it off tee 11-3/1
- player then deems it unplayable;
  explanation of stroke-and-
  distance option. 28/7
- then discovered to be wrong ball . .15/1

ball moves during backswing; struck
   while still moving 14-5/1

ball oscillating in wind; whether
   player may make a stroke at it
   without penalty 14-5/2

caddie concedes opponent's next
   stroke; ball then lifted
   . . . . .2-4/3.5

club damaged while making stroke,
   practice swing or practice stroke;
   whether "damaged in normal
   course of play" 4-3/1

club strikes several inches behind
   ball moving it without striking it;
   as swing continues club strikes
   moving ball 14-4/3

concealed ball
   – dislodged by practice swing 7-2/7
   – dislodged by player's stroke at
     own ball 15/2

flagstick held with one hand; short
   putt holed by stroke with club
   held in other hand; whether
   breach of any Rule 17-1/5

made
   – after result of hole decided 7-2/1.5
   – at plastic ball during play of hole . .7-2/4
   – at range ball during play of hole . . .7-2/5

meaning of "strokes played in
   continuing the play of a hole" 7-2/1.7

piece of broken ball lying in heavy
   rough mistaken by player as his
   ball; player makes stroke at it;
   whether stroke with wrong ball 15/3

player holds umbrella over own
   head and makes stroke; whether
   breach of Rule 14–2 . . . . .14-2/2

practice swing
   – dislodges concealed ball 7-2/7
   – moves ball accidentally prior to
     tee shot .18-2a/19
   – moves ball accidentally through
     the green 18-2a/20

referee incorrectly advises player to
   cancel and replay stroke 34-3/1.3

whether ball struck more than once
   in course of stroke if
   – ball adheres to face of club after
     stroke 1-4/2
   – ball falls on club face after stroke
     and sticks to mud thereon 14-4/1
   – ball strikes pipeline and on
     rebound deflects off face of club . .14-4/2

whether stroke made and/or ball
   fairly struck at if
   – after nearly hit by ball played
     from following group; in anger,
     player strikes ball back toward
     group 1-4/4
   – ball knocked aside after marking
     position instead of lifting 20-1/22
   – ball knocked from lip of hole in
     disgust 18-2a/23
   – ball played from outside teeing
     ground in stroke play 11-4b/6
   – ball played from wrong teeing
     ground in match play goes out of
     bounds; stroke not recalled by
     opponent 11-5/3
   – ball struck from
     environmentally-sensitive area 33-8/43
   – ball struck with back of clubhead . .14-1/1
   – ball struck with billiard-type
     motion 14-1/2
   – ball struck with grip of putter 14-1/3
   – ball struck with half-inch
     backswing 14-1/4
   – ball struck with shuffleboard
     motion 14-1/2
   – club breaks during backswing;
     swing completed 14/2
   – club breaks during downswing;
     swing completed but misses ball;
     clubhead falls and moves ball 14/5
   – club breaks during downswing;
     swing stopped short of ball;
     clubhead falls and moves ball 14/4
   – club stopped or deflected on
     downswing by tree branch 14/1
   – clubhead separates from shaft
     on downswing 14/3
   – in foursome match ball played
     from outside teeing ground 29-1/1
   – intent to strike ball ceases
     during downswing and player
     alters path of clubhead to avoid
     striking ball 14/1.5
   – lower part of branch struck at
     to dislodge ball beyond reach
     higher in branch 14/7
   – more than one club used to
     swing at ball 14-1/7
   – other side of fence struck at to
     move ball lying against fence 14-1/5
   – player hits ball back to player
     who lost it 7-2/5.5
   – practice range ball hit back to
     range by player 7-2/5
   – swing discontinued after branch
     broken on backswing 13-2/14.5
   – swing made in disgust at ball
     popped straight up after hitting
     tree root 14/6
   – when ball addressed fearing it
     will move, player holds club with
     one hand and strikes shaft with
     other hand to move ball 14-1/6

STROKE AND DISTANCE

ball deemed unplayable
   – after player made stroke at ball
     lying through the green; player
     returns to teeing ground and plays 28/6
   – after player missed stroke at ball
     lying in tree roots; player wishes
     to return to teeing ground 28/7
   – and dropped in another
     unplayable lie; ball deemed
     unplayable second time; player
     wishes to proceed under stroke
     and distance 28/6.5
   – in bunker; player lifts ball,
     announces intention to
     proceed under Rule 28a
     then smoothes irregularities;
     whether permitted 13-4/35.8

– lying through the green;
dropped in water hazard
under Rule 28b or c; player
wishes to proceed under water
hazard Rule rather than playing
dropped ball 28/4.5
– place from which previous
stroke made nearer hole;
whether player may proceed
under stroke-and-distance
option (Rule 28a) 28/8
– regression under unplayable ball
Rule; when permitted 28/5
– when ball deemed unplayable
must be found and identified 28/1

ball moved, lifted or touched
– ball in bunker moves when
rake removed; whether player
may proceed under stroke and
distance or any other option
outside bunker or press ball into
sand if not possible to replace
or place in bunker not nearer
hole 20-3d/2
– ball lifted without intention of
proceeding under stroke and
distance and without authority;
player subsequently plays under
stroke and distance 27-2b/10
– ball moved accidentally by
practice swing prior to tee shot. . .18-2a/19
– ball moved into bounds by flow
of water in lateral water hazard. . .26-1/8
– ball moved out of bounds by
flow of water in water hazard. 26-1/7
– stroke just touches ball which
falls off tee; player lifts and
re-tees it 18-2a/2
– stroke misses teed ball; player
then addresses and accidentally
knocks ball off tee 11-3/1
– stroke misses teed ball; player
then adjusts height of ball on tee . .18-2a/1
– tee shot wrongly thought out
of bounds lifted; competitor
returns to teeing ground and
plays another ball 18-2a/11

competitor plays out of turn, thinks
stroke must be canceled and
replayed, drops ball at spot from
which stroke made; procedure
questioned 27/17

original ball not found
– ball played under stroke-and-
distance procedure lifted when
original ball found within five
minutes 15/5
– missing original ball believed
in bunker; competitor drops
substituted ball in bunker and
plays it; then original ball found
outside bunker 20-7c/3
– substituted ball dropped at spot
of previous stroke under stroke
and distance; original ball then
found within five minutes 27-1/2
– substituted ball dropped at spot
of previous stroke; original ball
then found within five minutes
and played .27-1/2.3

– substituted ball dropped in area
where original ball thought to
be and played 27-1/3
– substituted ball played under
procedure for ball lost in ground
under repair (Rule 25–1c)
after another ball played under
stroke-and-distance procedure
(Rule 27–1) 15/8
– substituted ball played under
procedure for ball lost in
abnormal ground condition
(Rule 25–1c) in absence of
knowledge or virtual certainty. . . .25-1c/2
– substituted ball teed at spot of
previous stroke; original ball
then found within five minutes. . . .27-1/1
– treated as in water hazard. 26-1/3.7
– treated as moved by outside
agency in absence of knowledge
or virtual certainty to that
effect; player substitutes ball
under procedure in Rule 18–1
and plays it. .27-1/2.5
– unaware original ball holed out,
player puts another ball into play . .1-1/2

out of bounds
– ball dropped under stroke and
distance strikes course through
the green within inches of and
not nearer hole than spot in
bunker where previous stroke
made 20-5/2
– ball moved into bounds by flow
of water in lateral water hazard. . .26-1/8
– ball moved out of bounds by
flow of water in water hazard. 26-1/7
– ball played from outside teeing
ground goes out of bounds 11-4b/6
– ball played from spot where
original ball deflected out of
bounds by maintenance vehicle . . .20-7/1
– ball wrongly thought out of
bounds lifted; competitor plays
another ball from tee. 18-2a/11
– original ball out of bounds;
ball re-teed under stroke and
distance touched at address and
falls off tee 11-3/3

player intends to play provisional
ball but no one present to hear
announcement 27-2a/1.3

spot from which previous stroke
made not precisely known;
explanation of how to determine
"estimated spot" for dropping
under stroke and distance 20-2c/1.5

stray ball
– deemed unplayable played under
stroke-and-distance procedure;
original ball then found 28/14
– found out of bounds played
under stroke-and-distance
procedure; original ball then
found in bounds 15/12

stroke played out of turn from tee
abandoned; another ball played in
proper order .10-2c/1

substituted ball played
- from area where original ball
  thought to be 27-1/3
- under procedure for ball lost
  in ground under repair (Rule
  25–1c) after another ball played
  under stroke-and-distance
  procedure (Rule 27–1) 15/8
- under procedure for ball lost
  in abnormal ground condition
  (Rule 25–1c) in absence of
  knowledge or virtual certainty
  original ball is therein 25-1c/2
- under water hazard Rule (Rule
  26–1b or c); original ball then
  found outside hazard 26-1/3
- under water hazard Rule (Rule
  26–1b or c) without knowledge
  or virtual certainty original
  ball in hazard; original ball then
  found in hazard 26-1/4

water hazard
- ball assumed in water hazard;
  knowledge or virtual certainty
  not established; player proceeds
  under stroke and distance;
  original ball found outside hazard .26/6
- ball moved into bounds by flow
  of water in lateral water hazard . . .26-1/8
- ball moved out of bounds by
  flow of water in water hazard 26-1/7
- ball played from within water
  hazard comes to rest in same
  hazard after exiting hazard 26-2/2
- ball substituted and played
  under water hazard Rule (Rule
  26–1b or c); original ball then
  found outside hazard 26-1/3
- ball substituted and played
  under water hazard Rule (Rule
  26–1b or c) without knowledge
  or virtual certainty original
  ball in hazard; original ball then
  found in hazard 26-1/4

STROKE CANCELED OR RECALLED
See also BALL DEFLECTED OR STOPPED;
ORDER OF PLAY; ORDER OF PLAY IN
FOURSOMES AND THREESOMES; STROKE
AND DISTANCE; TEEING GROUND AND
TEE-MARKERS

after stroke from putting green
- ball dropped accidentally by
  opponent or fellow-competitor
  strikes player's moving ball 19-5/1.7
- ball replaced while another
  ball in motion after stroke
  from putting green; ball in
  motion strikes replaced ball;
  procedures for accidental and
  deliberate acts 16-1b/3
- ball strikes opponent's or
  fellow-competitor's ball set
  aside after being lifted 19-5/1
- dog deflects or picks up ball in
  motion 19-1/7
- fellow-competitor deliberately
  deflects or stops player's putt;
  procedure for player 19-1/5

- flagstick struck when purposely
  not removed by fellow-
  competitor asked to attend it;
  procedure for player 17-3/2
- hole-liner deflects ball when
  accidentally pulled by flagstick
  from hole 17/8
- knob falls from top of flagstick
  as attendant removes flagstick
  and deflects ball 17/9
- moving outside agency deflects
  ball; stroke not replayed as
  required by Rule 19–1b 19-1/3

ball breaks into pieces after striking
  paved cart path; procedure for
  player 5-3/4

Committee in error
- advises player to cancel and
  replay stroke 34-3/1.3
- directs player to play from
  wrong place; error discovered
  before player begins next hole;
  procedure when serious breach
  involved 34-3/3

competitor plays out of turn, thinks
  stroke must be canceled and
  replayed, drops ball at spot from
  which stroke made; procedure
  questioned 27/17

incorrect ruling by referee places
  player in stroke play at serious
  disadvantage; whether error may
  be corrected by cancelling strokes
  played 34-3/3.3

Local Rule
- providing relief from temporary
  power lines, cables, telephone
  lines and guy wires; specimen
  Local Rule .App I-B-7b
- requiring cancellation and replay
  of stroke without penalty when
  ball deflected by power line,
  tower or pole 33-8/13

player's ball strikes opponent,
  opponent's caddie or equipment
  after stroke
- opponent struck accidentally
  while standing in bounds; ball
  comes to rest out of bounds 19-3/1
- opponent's trolley deflects
  player's ball which then strikes
  player's trolley 19-3/3
- shared golf cart struck while
  opponent driving it 19/1

provisional ball(s) played out of turn
- from teeing ground; whether
  stroke may be recalled 10-3/1
- other than from teeing ground;
  when opponent may recall stroke .10/4

stroke played from outside teeing
  ground or from wrong teeing
  ground in match play
- canceled by opponent; correct
  order of play 11-4a/1
- canceled by opponents in
  foursome match; which partner
  replays stroke 29-1/1

– goes out of bounds; procedure if
stroke not recalled by opponent . .11-5/3

stroke played out of turn in match play
– after player's stroke, opponent
claims player played out of turn;
procedure for referee 10-1b/1
– bunker smoothed by player
after playing out of turn;
opponent recalls stroke
and player must drop ball in
smoothed area 13-4/39
– opponent requests player replay
in correct order; opponent
makes stroke, then withdraws
request for player to replay
stroke; procedure for player 10-1c/1
– partners both play out of turn
from tee; opponents cancel
stroke of one partner but not
other; whether permitted 30-1/1
– player putts instead of
complying with opponent's
request to lift ball due to
interference 10-1c/2
– provisional ball nearer hole
than opponent's ball tapped in
by player to end opponent's
search for player's original ball;
whether opponent may recall
stroke. 27-2b/1
– three-ball match play; player
plays out of turn; one opponent
requests replay, other opponent
does not. 30-2/1

whether cancellation and replay of
stroke allowed if
– flagstick stuck into green some
distance from hole by practical
joker. 1-4/3
– player mis-hits ball when
distracted by ball dropped by
another player 1-4/1
– sprinkler head deflects ball 33-8/12

SUBSTITUTED BALL
See also EXCHANGING BALLS
ball changed during play of hole to
aid identification 15/6.5
ball deemed unplayable in water
hazard; substituted ball dropped
in hazard without lifting original;
error discovered before stroke
made 20-7/2.5
ball dropped away from obstruction
immediately after resumption of
play; whether player may lift and
substitute for dropped ball under
Rule 6–8d(ii). 6-8d/3
ball fit for play deemed unfit during
play of hole; player substitutes and
plays another ball. 5-3/3
ball lifted and thrown into pond in
anger 18-2a/13.5
ball mistakenly substituted when
dropped; correction of error 20-6/3
ball played from ground under
repair abandoned and relief taken
under ground under repair Rule 18-2a/8.5

ball played under Rule for ball lost in
ground under repair after another
ball played under stroke-and-
distance procedure 15/8
balls inadvertently exchanged
– by competitors at unknown place .15-1/2
– by players after one ball strikes
and moves other. 15-1/2.5
– by players between holes 15-1/1
– by partners in four-ball
Stableford competition 32-2b/1
– competitor who lifts his and
fellow-competitor's balls
inadvertently exchanges them
when replaced 15-2/4
– when recovered from water
hazard 15-1/4
casual water mistaken for water
hazard; substituted ball played
under water hazard Rule 25-1b/13
competitor's ball lifted without
authority by fellow-competitor's
caddie who subsequently
substitutes another ball which
competitor plays 20-1/5
competitor's ball played by
fellow-competitor; competitor
substitutes another ball at wrong
place, plays it and then abandons
it and plays out original ball from
right place. 20-7c/4
original ball found within five-
minute search period
– after substituted ball dropped at
spot of previous stroke 27-1/2
– after substituted ball dropped
at spot of previous stroke;
dropped ball played 27-1/2.3
– after substituted ball dropped
under water hazard Rule
without knowledge or virtual
certainty original ball in hazard . . .26-1/3.7
– after substituted ball teed but
not played .27-1/1
player lifts ball on putting green;
then throws it into lake and
announces ball unfit for play. 5-3/3.5
player mistakenly substitutes
another ball on putting green
– error discovered before stroke
made 15-2/2
– error discovered after stroke
made from next teeing ground. . . .15-2/3
player substitutes another ball on
putting green because original
ball thrown to caddie for cleaning
came to rest in lake 15-2/1
players inadvertently exchange balls
recovered from water hazard 15-1/4
re-drop required under Rule
permitting substitution; whether
player may substitute when
re-dropping .20-6/4
stray ball
– dropped and played under
stroke-and-distance procedure;
original ball then found 28/14

– dropped under unplayable ball
Rule but not played 15/13
– dropped under unplayable ball
Rule within two club-lengths
and played before error
discovered. .28/15
– found out of bounds and played
under stroke-and-distance
procedure; original ball then
found in bounds 15/12
– in bunker deemed unplayable,
dropped in bunker and played;
ball then discovered to be
wrong ball 15/14
virtually certain (or known)
– missing ball is in abnormal
ground condition or
obstruction; substituted ball
dropped under applicable Rule;
original ball then found within
five minutes. 25-1c/2.5
– missing ball is in water hazard;
substituted ball dropped under
water hazard Rule; original ball
then found within five minutes. . . .26-1/3.5

TAPE

adhesive tape
– applied to clubhead to reduce
glare during round 4-1/5
– applied to hand or golf glove. 14-3/8
lead tape
– applied to clubhead or shaft
before start of round. 4-1/4
– applied to clubhead or shaft
during round. 4-2/0.5
– weight of club changed during
round; breach discovered after
competition closed 34-1b/4

TEAM COMPETITION

advice
– given by team mate in another
group in stroke play 8-1/21
– given by unauthorized team
coach or captain. 8-1/24
– team captain gives advice while
playing 8/2
– team mates playing as fellow-
competitors exchange advice. 8-1/22
– whether team captain authorized
to give advice may be required to
keep off putting greens. 8-2b/4
application of disqualification
penalty in competition in which
not all team members' scores
count for each round 33/8
conditions of team competition
– requires person appointed
to give advice must be team
captain or amateur. 8/1
– specimen condition permitting
appointment of one person who
may give advice . . . . .App I-C-7
player's team mate in gallery hits
ball to green to show player
whether green will hold 8-1/23
status of team captain or coach 33-1/11.5

TEE

See also STATUS OF OBJECT; TEEING
GROUND AND TEE-MARKERS

ball falls off tee when stroke just
touches it; player lifts, re-tees and
plays ball 18-2a/2
ball played out of bounds from
wrong teeing ground in match not
recalled. 11-5/3
marking ball in hazard using tee,
whether authorized 13-4/0.5
original ball out of bounds; ball
re-teed under stroke and distance
touched at address and falls off tee. .11-3/3
player who misses tee shot tees ball
lower before playing next stroke . . .18-2a/1
probing with tee near ball for tree
roots or rocks 13-2/27
stroke misses ball; ball then
accidentally knocked off tee. 11-3/1
tee marking position of player's ball
deflects opponent's ball 20-1/17
teed ball missed then hit out of bounds. 20-5/1

TEEING GROUND AND TEE-
MARKERS

See also MARKING OR DEFINING COURSE;
STATUS OF OBJECT; STROKE AND
DISTANCE; TEE

ball embeds in teeing ground. 25-2/8
ball in or on movable obstruction
within teeing ground. 25-2/8
ball moved, lifted or touched
– ball moved accidentally by
practice swing prior to tee shot. . .18-2a/19
– stroke just touches ball which
falls off tee; player lifts and
re-tees it 18-2a/2
– stroke misses teed ball; player
then addresses and accidentally
knocks ball off tee 11-3/1
– stroke misses teed ball; player
then adjusts height of ball on tee . .18-2a/1
– tee shot wrongly thought out
of bounds lifted; competitor
returns to teeing ground and
plays another ball 18-2a/11
ball played from outside teeing ground
– ball played from outside teeing
ground goes out of bounds. 11-4b/6
– ball played from outside teeing
ground in foursome match 29-1/1
– competitor plays from outside
teeing ground in foursome
stroke play; partner replays
stroke. 29-1/2
– dispute as to whether
competitor played from outside
teeing ground 34-3/4
– order of play when opponent
requires player with honor
to cancel stroke made from
outside teeing ground 11-4a/1
ball played out of turn from teeing
ground abandoned and another
ball played in proper order. 10-2c/1

branch interfering with backswing
on teeing ground broken by player . .13-2/14

casual water completely covers
teeing ground; Committee
options for match and stroke play. . .25-1b/4

dew and frost; whether removal
permitted 13-2/35

foursome competition
– changing partners after driving
from first teeing ground 29/1
– condition of competition
stipulates which foursome
partner must play from 1st teeing
ground; whether permitted 33-1/3.5
– player and partner both drive
from same teeing ground in
foursome play 29-1/9
– tee shot hit out of bounds in
mixed foursome (different
teeing grounds used by men and
women); which teeing ground
partner makes next stroke from . .29/2
– whether partner who went
ahead before tee shot played
may return to tee to play
provisional ball 29-1/4.5

golf bag of player positioned to
shade teed ball .14-2/2.5

grass behind ball on teeing ground
pulled out or broken off by player. . .13-2/3

Local Rule
– deeming area of adjoining
hole out of bounds for play of
particular hole but not for play
of other holes 33-2a/14
– deeming area of adjoining
hole out of bounds for stroke
made from teeing ground only;
whether authorized 33-2a/14
– deeming area surrounding tee
in bounds for tee shot and out
of bounds thereafter; whether
authorized. .33-2a/13

original ball
– found within five-minute search
period after another ball teed
but not played. 27-1/1
– out of bounds; ball re-teed
under stroke and distance
touched at address and falls off tee 11-3/3

players agree not to play from
teeing ground in prescribed order
to save time; whether agreement
to waive Rules .10-1a/3

provisional balls played out of turn
from teeing ground 10-3/1

shadow of spectator blocks sunlight
from player's teed ball 14-2/2.5

standing on mat on teeing ground 13-3/1

starting players from 1st and 10th tees .33-1/3

stroke made at ball lying through
the green
– in tree roots misses ball; player
then deems it unplayable and
wishes to return to teeing ground.28/7
– player deems ball unplayable and
returns to teeing ground. 28/6

stroke misses teed ball
– player presses down turf behind
ball before next stroke 13-2/2
– player then addresses ball and
accidentally knocks it off tee 11-3/1
– player then pushes teed ball
lower 18-2a/1
– next stroke hit out of bounds;
whether ball for subsequent
stroke may be teed anywhere
within teeing ground 20-5/1

suspension of play declared by
Committee
– one competitor in group wishes
to complete play of hole after
other competitors discontinue
play; whether permitted 6-8b/3
– options for players if one
competitor in group has played
from tee. 6-8b/2

tee-markers
– competitors determine spot
from which to play from tee
when both tee-markers missing. . .11-4b/3
– competitors estimate area of
teeing ground when one tee-
marker missing 11-4b/2
– moved and/or holes relocated
during stroke-play round 33-2b/1
– moved by player 11-2/2
– status of after first stroke 11-2/1

wrong teeing ground
– ball played from teeing ground
of hole to be played later in
round lifted; ball replaced at
spot from which lifted and
played out when that hole
subsequently reached 11-5/5
– ball played from wrong teeing
ground in stroke play; error
corrected 11-5/4
– ball played out of bounds not
recalled 11-5/3
– meaning of "next teeing ground"
after competitors have played
from wrong teeing ground 11-5/1
– play from wrong teeing ground
attributed to Committee failure
to indicate hole numbers on
teeing ground 11-5/2

TERMINOLOGY

"added," when club considered 4-4a/1

"any ball he has played" 18/7

"artificially-surfaced". 24/9

"as soon as practicable" in Rule 9–2. . .9-2/1

"behind," as applied in Rule 26–1b 26-1/1.5

chipper. 4-1/3

"dangerous situation". 1-4/11

"directly attributable" in Rules 20–1
and 20–3a 20-1/15

"elements," as applied in Rule 14–2a . .14-2/0.5

"embedded," when ball considered
embedded in ground 25-2/0.5

"estimated spot;" explanation of
how to determine 20-2c/1.5

"fairly taking his stance"
- explanation of "fairly taking his stance"..........................13-2/1
- player allowed to play in any direction in "fairly taking his stance"..........................13-2/1.5
- player attempts to take stance fairly but improves line of play by moving interfering growing object..........................13-2/1.1
- player under tree, changes intended direction of play and fairly takes stance second time....13-2/1.7

"goes forward to search"........................27-2a/1.5

"good reason to lift" when play suspended.........................6-8c/1

"grounded"
- club rested on grass immediately behind ball.........8-2b/5
- when club considered grounded in grass in water hazard.........13-4/8

"handicap"
- for purposes of Rule 6–2.........6-2/1
- when full handicap not used......6-2b/0.5

"hole made by greenkeeper" in definition of ground under repair...25/14

"immediately recoverable"..........18/11

"immediately," when player makes stroke out of order in match play and opponent wishes to immediately cancel stroke........30-1/1

"improve," as applied in Rule 13-2 ....3-2/0.5

"line of putt" in context of "standing astride or on line of putt".........16-1e/1

"marking position of ball;" permissible methods.............20-1/16

"maximum available relief" from casual water in bunker...........25-1b/5

"might have influenced the movement of the ball" as applied in Rule 17.......................17-2/2

"nearest point of relief," diagrams illustrating......................25-1b/2

"next teeing ground" after competitors have played from wrong teeing ground..............11-5/1

"normal course of play".............4-3/1

"officially announced".............2-5/14

"opposite margin" as applied in Rule 26–1c........................26-1/14

"penalty strokes incurred solely by playing ball ruled not to count" clarified for situations where competitor plays second ball under Rule 20–7c................20-7c/5

point where ball "last entered" abnormal ground condition when ball lost in condition.............25-1c/1.5

"repair"........................4-3/2

"serious breach of etiquette".......33-7/8

"separate Rules," for purpose of determining whether multiple penalties apply..................1-4/12

"sole purpose of caring for the course".........................1-2/0.7

"solidly embedded"..............23/2

"specific directions"..............6-4/1

"stands near the hole".............17-1/1

"strokes played in continuing play of a hole".........................7-2/1.7

"test the condition of the hazard" in Rule 13–4a.....................13-4/0.5

"time of starting".................6-3a/2.5

"valid claim," procedure for.........2-5/2

"virtually certain"
- ball in abnormal ground condition.25-1c/1
- ball in water hazard.............26-1/1
- ball moved by outside agency.....27-1/2.5

when stipulated round "begins" and "ends"
- in match play...................2/2
- in stroke play..................3/3

TEST OR TESTING

meaning of "test the condition of the hazard" in Rule 13–4a.........13-4/0.5

bunker or water hazard
- ball played from bunker either out of bounds or lost; player tests condition of bunker or smoothes footprints before dropping another ball in bunker...13-4/37
- condition of bunker tested before player decides whether to play through it...............13-2/30
- player in bunker takes firm stance and then smoothes footprints after deciding to play different type of shot............13-4/0.5
- player uses cane or club to enter or leave hazard when ball lies in hazard.......................13-4/3.5
- rake placed in bunker or handle stuck in bunker before stroke....13-4/0.5
- rake thrown into bunker before stroke.........................13-4/21
- smoothing irregularities in bunker after stroke but before ball extricated.................13-4/36
- stance in bunker taken without club.........................13-4/24
- taking firm stance in bunker some distance from where ball in bunker lies to simulate next stroke.........................13-4/0.5
- taking stance in bunker and then changing clubs.................13-4/26
- touching grass with club during practice swing in water hazard...13-4/4

putting green
- caddie practices on or tests putting green surfaces of course before stroke-play round.......7-1b/5
- caddie roughens surface of putting green but player does not benefit....................16-1d/6
- knocking ball aside after marking position instead of lifting.20-1/22
- loose impediments brushed off line of putt with palm of hand.....16-1a/9

– player concedes opponent's
next stroke and knocks ball
away along own line of putt......16-1d/2
– player concedes opponent's
next stroke and rolls or knocks
ball to opponent................16-1d/1
– player returns ball to spot from
which it was lifted by rolling it
with putter....................16-1d/3
– rubbing ball on putting green for
cleaning purposes..............16-1d/5
– tested for wetness of surface
behind ball...................16-1d/4

test drop made by player to
determine where ball will roll if
relief taken under a Rule 20-2a/8

THREE-BALL MATCH PLAY

player concedes hole after which
one opponent plays wrong ball 2-4/10

player plays out of turn from tee in
three-ball match; one opponent
requests replay and other does not .30-2/1

THROUGH THE GREEN
See also FAIRWAY AND CLOSELY MOWN
AREAS; ROUGH

ball deemed unplayable through the
green
– dropped in bunker or water
hazard 28/4
– dropped in water hazard; player
elects not to play ball and
wishes to proceed under water
hazard Rule....................28/4.5

ball enters burrowing animal hole
– in bounds and comes to rest out
of bounds....................25-1b/24
– in bunker and comes to rest
underneath putting green.......25-1b/25
– out of bounds and comes to rest
in bounds.....................25-1b/23

ball hit out of bounds from bunker;
player's drop under Rule 20–5
strikes course through the green
within inches of and not nearer
hole than spot in bunker where
previous stroke made............20-5/2

ball touched accidentally in
removing loose impediments.......18-2a/31

drainpipe
– ball not found but known
or virtually certain to lie in
drainpipe through the green;
entrance to drainpipe out of
bounds.......................24-2b/12
– ball not reachable or identifiable
in underground drainpipe.......24-3b/1

dropping from rough to fairway in
obtaining relief from obstruction . . .24-2b/8

embedded ball
– ball on steep bank driven
straight into ground............25-2/6
– in ground under repair in closely
mown area 25-2/4

ground under repair or casual water
through the green
– ball dropped from ground under
repair area rolls to position
where area interferes with
stance; whether re-drop
required......................20-2c/0.5
– ball embedded in ground under
repair in closely mown area 25-2/4
– ball in tree in ground under repair .25/10.5
– bunker totally under repair;
Committee options............25/13
– Local Rule declaring
accumulations of leaves (at
specified holes) through the
green as ground under repair....33-8/31
– measuring across ground under
repair in obtaining relief 25-1b/15
– player takes relief from area of
casual water and ball comes to
rest in position where another
area of casual water interferes;
whether re-drop required 20-2c/7
– two equidistant nearest points
of relief meet requirements of
ground under repair Rule 25-1b/16

Local Rule
– deeming bunker filled with
casual water to be through the
green and authorising relief
without penalty 33-8/27
– deeming partially grass-covered
walls of bunkers to be through
the green.....................33-8/39.5

loose impediments
– affecting lie removed while ball
lifted.........................23-1/8
– competitor asks fellow-
competitor to remove loose
impediment near ball to avoid
penalty.......................33-7/7
– removal of insect on ball 23-1/5
– removal of loose impediments
from area in which ball to be
dropped......................23-1/6
– removing grass adhering to ball . . .21/2

natural object interfering with
swing moved to determine
whether loose impediment or
attached 13-2/26

pitch-mark through the green
– ball returns to pitch-mark from
prior stroke...................25-2/3
– made by partner's, opponent's
or fellow-competitor's ball
affects player's lie or line of play . . .13-2/8
– repaired in dropping area before
ball dropped 13-2/10

probing near ball for tree roots or
rocks............................13-2/27

sand or loose soil through the green
– behind ball pressed down during
address 13-2/12
– behind ball removed by backswing.13-2/9
– removed from dropping area 13-2/11

spectator deliberately deflects or
stops ball through the green 19-1/4.1

status of
- ball touching both water hazard
  and area through the green......26/1.5
- growing things rooted within
  environmentally-sensitive area
  overhanging area through the
  green 33-8/44.5

treating ocean and beach as through
  the green......................33-2a/8

tree falls onto fairway during
  stipulated round; options for
  Committee.....................25/9.5

whether ball lies through the green
- ball completely embedded in lip
  of bunker.....................13/4
- ball within natural margin of
  water hazard but outside
  stakes defining margin..........26/2

TIME OF STARTING

See also COURSE UNPLAYABLE OR CLOSED;
GROUPS AND GROUPING

"time of starting," meaning of.......6-3a/2.5

absent player joins partner after
  fellow-competitor plays from
  teeing ground but before partner
  plays..........................31-2/1

all competitors must be present......6-3a/2

application of Rule 6-3a
  disqualification penalty in team
  competition in which not all team
  members' scores count for each
  round..........................33/8

both players in match late 6-3a/3

course closed
- match begun by players unaware
  course closed 33-2d/4
- player not present at time of
  starting 33-3/2

groupings and starting times
  determined by competitors;
  whether Committee may permit ...33-3/3

player unable to meet match-play
  schedule defaults; match schedule
  subsequently changed; player
  requests reinstatement 2-4/20

player(s) not present at time of
  starting
- arrives at 9:00:45 for 9:00 tee time 6-3a/2.5
- both players in match late 6-3a/3
- circumstances which warrant
  waiving disqualification penalty
  for lateness 6-3a/1.5
- course closed at that time.......33-3/2
- group unable to start due to
  delay..........................6-3a/4
- listed as third to play in group
  arrives in time to do so 6-3a/2
- time agreed to by players as
  authorized by Committee.......33-3/1

postponement of final match due to
  injury of player.................6-3a/1

starting earlier than time of starting ..6-3a/5

status of starting time fixed by
  players.........................33-3/1

when play resumed after suspension
  of play
- competitor refuses to start or
  picks up because of weather
  conditions; round subsequently
  canceled......................33-2d/3
- player unable to resume match
  at scheduled time 6-8b/4
- when players must be present 6-8b/9

TOWEL

borrowed from another player;
  whether permitted 5-1/5

covering player's clubs removed by
  another player to determine club
  used...........................8-1/11

kneeled on to make stroke 13-3/2

moves ball when dropped by player
  and blown onto ball..............18-2a/17

placed on cactus; player leans
  against towel during stroke 1-2/10

used to remove loose impediments
- by Committee.................33/1
- by player.....................16-1a/8

used to remove casual water
- by Committee.................33/1
- by player.....................16-1a/1

waved to make insect in bunker move .23-1/5.5

whether touching ground in a
  hazard or water in a water hazard
  with a towel constitutes "testing
  the condition of the hazard" in
  breach of Rule 13-4a 13-4/0.5

wrapped around
- knees and kneeled on; used to
  make stroke 13-3/2
- player to protect him from
  cactus before taking stance with
  legs against it 1-2/10

TRADEMARK

aimed to indicate line for putting
  when ball replaced 20-3a/2

rotating ball on putting green
  without marking position.........18-2a/33

TREE OR BUSH

See also LEAVES; STATUS OF OBJECT

ball dislodged from tree
- circumstances in which player
  not penalized..................18-2a/27
- circumstances in which player
  penalized 18-2a/28
- knocked down by outside agency..18-1/9
- replacement of ball not possible...18-2a/29
- when player climbs tree to make
  stroke.........................18-2a/26

ball in tree or bush
- branch struck at to move ball
  lodged beyond reach higher in
  branch 14/7
- impracticable to make stroke
  because of bush 25-1b/19
- impracticable to make stroke
  because of tree................25-1b/20

– in fork of tree moves in relation
  to ground but not in relation to
  fork. 18/3
– in ground under repair. 25/10.5
– identified but not retrieved. 27/14
– more than one club used to
  make stroke at ball in bush 14-1/7
– not found but known to be in
  tree within ground under repair . .25/10
– unplayable; player opts to drop
  within two club-lengths. 28/11
– visible but not identifiable 27/15
ball interfered with by abnormal
ground condition
– sideways stroke behind tree
  reasonable. 25-1b/22
– tree prevents stroke towards
  green 25-1b/21
– tree within area interferes with
  stroke at ball outside area. 25-1a/1
branch
– area of original intended swing
  improved by breaking branch;
  area of intended swing finally
  used not affected by branch 13-2/24
– broken by player fearing
  dropped ball would roll near
  bush or tree 1-2/3
– broken during backswing; swing
  discontinued. 13-2/14.5
– broken off part of larger branch
  fallen from tree. 23-1/4
– held back by caddie to prevent it
  from deflecting ball when
  dropped. 20-2a/5
– moved by competitor
  improving or worsening fellow-
  competitor's line of play while
  discussing with referee whether
  fellow-competitor entitled to
  free relief. .1-2/1.5
– player breaks off branch
  interfering with backswing on
  teeing ground 13-2/14
breaching two Rules with different
penalties; whether multiple
penalties apply 1-4/15
cast of burrowing animal interferes
with stroke toward green; tree
prevents such stroke. 25-1b/21
dropped ball
– never strikes ground 20-2b/1
– strikes tree branch then ground;
  whether re-drop required 20-2c/1.3
"fairly taking his stance"
– diagram illustrating player
  unable to determine nearest
  point of relief 24-2b/3.7
– explanation of "fairly taking his
  stance". 13-2/1
– player allowed to play in any
  direction in "fairly taking his
  stance". 13-2/1.5
– player attempts to take stance
  fairly but improves line of play
  by moving interfering growing
  object. 13-2/1.1

– player determines nearest point
  of relief but physically unable to
  make intended stroke 24-2b/3
– player under tree, changes
  intended direction of play and
  fairly takes stance second time. . . .13-2/1.7
fallen tree
– attached to stump lying in fairway .25/9
– in process of being removed. 25/7
– on fairway after round begun 25/9.5
– status 23/7
Local Rule
– providing relief from exposed
  tree roots; whether authorized. . .33-8/8
– requiring player to take relief
  under penalty from tree nursery
  (or plantation) from which play
  prohibited; whether authorized. . .33-8/29
– specimen Local Rule requiring
  relief away from young trees to
  prevent damage . . . . .App I-B-3
opponent's stroke disturbs bushes
causing player's ball to move 18-3b/2
pine cone falls from tree and comes
to rest behind ball lying in bunker . . .13-4/18.5
probing near ball for tree roots or
rocks. 13-2/27
provisional ball deemed unplayable
and dropped but not played;
original ball then found 27-2b/6.5
roots outside ground under repair
growing from tree inside ground
under repair 25/10.7
shaking water from tree branch
interfering with backswing. 13-2/23
stake supporting tree broken in
attempt to remove it. 13-2/16
status of
– moss or creepers in tree. 13-2/37
– non-growing plants within area
  of ground under repair 25/10.9
– tree basins. .33-2a/10.5
– tree in bunker. 13/2
– tree stump. .25/8
taking stance under tree 13-2/1

TROLLEY
See also EQUIPMENT; GOLF CART

player's ball strikes opponent's or
fellow-competitor's trolley then
strikes own trolley 19-3/3
status of
– carts pulled by double caddie 6-4/6
– individual who transports
  player's clubs on motorized golf
  cart or trolley. 6-4/2.5

TUMBLEWEED

ball at rest moved by blowing
tumbleweed. 18-1/6
interfering with swing moved
to determine whether loose
impediment or attached. 13-2/26

UMBRELLA

player holds umbrella over own
head when making stroke.........14-2/2

umbrella carrier employed in
addition to caddie 6-4/5

UNDUE DELAY
See also PACE OF PLAY

caddie swings club to show player
how to play shot 8-1/15

competitor practices putting on 3rd
green after finishing hole during
first round of 36-hole stroke-play
competition 7-1b/7

discontinuance of play for
refreshment....................6-8a/2.5

four-ball stroke play
– extent to which side may play in
order it considers best 31-4/2
– player waives turn to play;
circumstances under which he
may complete hole.............31-4/1

player walks off green under
mistaken impression partner
halved hole returns and putts for
half..........................30/4

referee does not penalize player in
breach of pace of play condition
believing player had already lost
hole..........................34-3/2

watching television for 45 minutes
after nine holes 6-8a/1

whether Rule 6–7 prohibiting undue
delay breached if
– player ascertains whereabouts
of opponent's ball before playing ..9-2/16
– player enters clubhouse or
half-way house for refreshment
during round..................6-8a/2.7
– player requests another player
to lift player's ball in absence of
reasonable possibility that ball
might interfere or assist 22/3
– player returns to tee to retrieve
forgotten club.................6-7/1
– player searches for lost ball after
putting another ball into play 27/9
– player searches ten minutes for
ball 6-7/2
– removal of large loose
impediment delays play 23-1/2
– second ball played despite
adverse ruling 3-3/2

window of clubhouse opened and
ball played through window.......24-2b/14

UNPLAYABLE BALL
See also BALL UNFIT FOR PLAY

after declaring ball unplayable and
lifting it, player discovers ball was
in ground under repair 28/13

at base of cliff, player wishes to drop
within two club-lengths of point
above ball 28/12

ball deemed unplayable
– and dropped, then deemed
unplayable second time, player
wishes to proceed under stroke
and distance 28/6.5
– high in tree, player shakes tree
to dislodge it; whether player
exempt from penalty under Rule
18–2a 18-2a/27
– in bunker; player lifts ball,
announces intention to proceed
under Rule 28a then smoothes
irregularities; whether permitted .13-4/35.8
– in bunker; player lifts ball and
then removes loose impediment
from bunker 13-4/35.7
– in water hazard; ball dropped in
hazard and played.............20-7/2
– in water hazard; substituted
ball dropped in hazard without
lifting original; error discovered
before stroke made 20-7/2.5
– may move when neared; player
subsequently considers playing
ball; ruling if ball thereafter
moves.........................18-2a/27.5
– place from which previous
stroke made nearer hole........28/8
– through the green dropped in
hazard 28/4
– through the green dropped
in water hazard; player elects
not to play ball and wishes to
proceed under water hazard Rule .28/4.5

ball dislodged from tree
– circumstances in which player
not penalized...................18-2a/27
– replacement of ball not possible...18-2a/29

ball dropped
– outside bunker under option of
unplayable ball Rule requiring
drop in bunker 28/10
– under option 28c of unplayable
ball Rule strikes player; whether
player may change relief option
when re-dropping 20-2a/6

ball in tree
– identified but not retrieved......27/14
– player opts to drop within two
club-lengths 28/11

ball lying on grass-covered ground
within bunker deemed unplayable...28/9

ball played from water hazard to
unplayable lie outside water
hazard; explanations of options
under Rule 26–2b 26-2/1

caddie on own initiative lifts ball
considering it unplayable 18-2a/15

changing relief option
– dropped ball first strikes course
outside where applicable Rule
requires; whether player may
change relief option when
re-dropping...................20-6/2
– dropped ball first strikes course
outside where applicable Rule
requires; whether player may
replace ball in original location....20-6/5

– dropped ball rolls to position
requiring re-drop; whether
player may change relief option
when re-dropping 20-2c/5
– dropped ball strikes player;
whether player may change
relief option when re-dropping . . .20-2a/6
– player drops ball in bunker
under first option of Rule
25–1b(ii); player then wishes to
proceed under second option
to drop outside bunker 25-1b/9
– player lifts ball from bunker
intending to drop under first
option of Rule 24–2b(ii); player
then wishes to proceed under
second option to drop outside
bunker 24-2b/5
– point where ball last crossed
margin of lateral water hazard
determined and ball dropped;
point then proves to be wrong
point; whether player may
change relief option when
re-dropping 26-1/16

comes to rest back in original
position or another unplayable
position 28/3

competitor drops one ball in
accordance with two different
Rules instead of playing second ball . .3-3/11

competitor drops one ball in
accordance with two different
Rules instead of playing second
ball; dropped ball rolls back into
condition from which relief taken . . .3-3/12

dropped ball comes to rest and then
rolls out of bounds 20-2c/3.5

dropped in ground under repair
from which play prohibited; ball
then dropped under ground
under repair Rule. 25-1b/14.5

dropping zone; specimen Local
Rule for establishing as additional
option under Rule 28 . . . . .App I-B-8

Local Rule allowing drop within
water hazard behind point where
ball lies unplayable in hazard;
whether authorized 33-8/37

obstruction interferes but ball
unplayable due to some other
condition 24-2b/16

player entitled to relief without
penalty from condition lifts
ball; chooses not to take relief
and wishes to proceed under
unplayable ball Rule 18-2a/12.5

player misses ball and deems it
unplayable; wishes to return to
tee under stroke and distance 28/7

player plays second shot, deems ball
unplayable and returns to tee 28/6

provisional ball
– deemed unplayable; player lifts
and drops ball; original ball then
found 27-2b/6.5

– player wishes provisional ball
to serve as ball in play if original
unplayable or in water hazard 27-2/1
– played from tee then player
deems original ball unplayable
while still at tee and plays third
ball; claims third ball lies three 28/2

re-drop required when proceeding
under unplayable ball Rule;
whether player may substitute
when re-dropping 20-6/4

regression under unplayable ball
Rule 28/5

stray ball
– dropped within two club-
lengths and played; error then
discovered .28/15
– in bunker deemed unplayable,
dropped in bunker and played;
error then discovered 15/14
– lifted and dropped under
unplayable ball Rule but not played 15/13
– played under stroke-and-
distance procedure; original ball
then found .28/14

suggesting fellow-competitor deem
ball unplayable 8-1/16

when necessary to find and identify
ball deemed unplayable 28/1

VIRTUALLY CERTAIN (OR KNOWN)

See also ABNORMAL GROUND
CONDITIONS; BURROWING ANIMAL,
REPTILE OR BIRD (AND HOLES MADE BY
THEM); CASUAL WATER; GROUND UNDER
REPAIR; LOST BALL; OBSTRUCTIONS;
OUTSIDE AGENCY; PROVISIONAL BALL;
WATER HAZARDS

ball at rest moved
– after address player steps away
from ball; ball moves some time
thereafter due to wind 18-2b/7
– competitor and fellow-
competitor unaware ball moved
by fellow-competitor's ball until
after completion of hole 18-5/3

missing ball thought to be in
abnormal ground condition
– ball dropped and played under
Rule 25–1c in absence of
knowledge or virtual certainty
original ball is in abnormal
ground condition 25-1c/2
– ball dropped with knowledge
or virtual certainty; original ball
then found within five minutes 25-1c/2.5
– ball found in burrowing animal
hole after five-minute search 27/7
– ball in casual water difficult to
retrieve 25-1/1
– Local Rule declaring
accumulations of leaves (at
specified holes) through the
green as ground under repair 33-8/31
– or nearby area of high rough;
whether player may treat ball as
in abnormal ground condition 25-1c/1

– whether provisional ball
becomes ball in play if original
ball known or virtually certain
to be in ground under repair 27-2c/1.5

missing ball thought to be in obstruction
– ball dropped with knowledge
or virtual certainty; original ball
then found within five minutes 25-1c/2.5
– underground drainpipe 24-3b/1
– underground drainpipe with
entrance out of bounds 24-2b/12

missing ball thought to be in water hazard
– ball assumed in water hazard
found outside hazard after
another ball played under
stroke-and-distance procedure ...26/6
– ball dropped with knowledge
or virtual certainty; original ball
then found within five minutes 26-1/3.5
– ball dropped without knowledge
or virtual certainty; original ball
then found within five minutes. .26-1/3.7
– ball played under water hazard
Rule; original ball then found
outside hazard 26-1/3
– ball played under water hazard
Rule without knowledge or
virtual certainty original ball in
hazard; original ball then found
in hazard 26-1/4
– meaning of "known or virtually
certain" in Rules 18–1, 24–3,
25–1c and 26–1 ....26-1/1
– player plays provisional ball
in belief original might be lost
outside water hazard; player
then discovers no possibility ball
lost outside water hazard 27-2a/2.5
– whether virtual certainty
ball is in water hazard can be
established without going
forward to assess conditions
around hazard.................26-1/1.3

missing ball thought to be moved by
outside agency
– competitor plays wrong ball
and it cannot be found; wrong
ball may have been fellow-
competitor's ball 15-3b/1
– treated as moved by outside
agency rather than lost in
absence of knowledge or virtual
certainty 27-1/2.5

identifying ball by brand and number
only 12-2/1

player unaware ball moved by
outside agency does not replace ball .18-1/3

WALL

See also BOUNDARY FENCE, LINE, WALL
OR STAKES; FENCE; INTEGRAL PART OF
COURSE; OBSTRUCTIONS; STATUS OF
OBJECT

club-length measured directly
through wall; whether permitted ...20-2b/2

deeming ball in bounds until beyond
boundary wall....................33-2a/16

diagram illustrating player unable to
determine nearest point of relief
because of boundary wall.........24-2b/3.7

earthen wall of bunker touched on
backswing; whether breach of
Rule 13–4 ....13-4/34

status of
– artificial wall encircling tree basin .33-2a/10.5
– stone broken away from
retaining wall in water hazard.....24/6

stone removed from wall; whether
line of play improved..............13-2/32

WATER HAZARDS

See also MARKING OR DEFINING COURSE;
PROVISIONAL BALL; VIRTUALLY CERTAIN
(OR KNOWN)

ball assumed in water hazard found
outside hazard after another ball
played under stroke-and-distance
procedure.........................26/6

ball at rest moves
– after stance taken...............18-2b/3
– in water in water hazard after
stance taken; presumably due to
current or cause unclear.........14-6/1
– into bounds by flow of water in
lateral water hazard.............26-1/8
– out of bounds by flow of water
in water hazard.................26-1/7
– when accidentally kicked in
long grass while probing for
it in water hazard 12-1/5
– when loose impediment
removed 13-4/15

ball deemed unplayable
– through the green dropped in
water hazard....................28/4
– through the green dropped
in water hazard; player elects
not to play ball and wishes to
proceed under water hazard Rule .28/4.5
– in water hazard; ball dropped in
hazard and played..............20-7/2
– in water hazard; substituted
ball dropped in hazard without
lifting original; error discovered
before stroke made 20-7/2.5

ball dropped in another hazard
when proceeding under water
hazard Rule......................26-1/2

ball not found either in water
hazard or casual water
overflowing hazard 1-4/7

ball not found
– assumed in water hazard; found
outside hazard after another
ball played under stroke-and-
distance procedure 26/6
– substituted ball dropped with
knowledge or virtual certainty;
original ball then found within
five minutes....................26-1/3.5
– substituted ball dropped
without knowledge or virtual
certainty in hazard; original ball
then found within five minutes 26-1/3.7

ball played after relief taken under water hazard Rule
– original ball then found in hazard and holed out as second ball......26-1/5
– original ball then found outside hazard 26-1/3
– without knowledge or virtual certainty original ball in hazard; original ball then found in hazard .26-1/4

ball played back into water hazard from putting green side of hazard ...26-1/6

balls exchanged when recovered from water hazard................15-1/4

burrowing animal hole relief taken by player unaware ball in water hazard; error discovered before ball played........................25-1b/26

caddie lifts ball in water hazard without player's authority 26-1/9

casual water mistaken for water hazard
– original ball played under water hazard Rule....................25-1b/12
– substituted ball played under water hazard Rule 25-1b/13

changing relief option
– dropped ball first strikes course outside where applicable Rule requires; whether player may change relief option when re-dropping...................20-6/2
– dropped ball first strikes course outside where applicable Rule requires; whether player may replace ball in original location....20-6/5
– dropped ball rolls to position requiring re-drop; whether player may change relief option when re-dropping 20-2c/5
– dropped ball strikes player; whether player may change relief option when re-dropping ...20-2a/6
– player drops ball in bunker under first option of Rule 25–1b(ii); player then wishes to proceed under second option to drop outside bunker.........25-1b/9
– player lifts ball from bunker intending to drop under first option of Rule 24–2b(ii); player then wishes to proceed under second option to drop outside bunker........................24-2b/5
– point where ball last crossed margin of lateral water hazard determined and ball dropped; point then proves to be wrong point; whether player may change relief option when re-dropping....................26-1/16

club accidentally touches ball in water hazard; ball does not move ...13-4/12

dropping zone; specimen Local Rule for establishing as additional option under Rule 26–1 ....App I-B-8

embedded ball in water hazard lifted to determine whether unfit for play 5-3/5

environmentally-sensitive area
– entering to retrieve ball.........33-8/42
– marking and defining; recommendations for Committee 33-8/41
– significant advantage gained when player makes stroke from environmentally-sensitive area defined as water hazard 33-8/44
– stroke made from environmentally-sensitive water hazard 33-8/43

explanation of options under Rule 26–2 (ball played within water hazard)
– ball played from water hazard comes to rest in same hazard after exiting hazard 26-2/2
– stroke made from water hazard; ball either not extracted from hazard or comes to rest out of bounds or in unplayable lie outside hazard 26-2/1

grounding club
– cane or club used to enter or leave hazard when ball lies in hazard..........................13-4/3.5
– cleaning clubhead in water hazard when ball lies in hazard....13-4/40
– leaning on club in hazard while waiting to play...................13-4/2
– moving loose impediments and improving area of intended swing in hazard...................13-4/28
– on bridge in water hazard 13-4/30
– several practice swings touch ground in water hazard..........13-4/3
– touching grass with club during practice swing in water hazard....13-4/4
– touching ground in hazard with club while probing for ball believed covered by leaves 12-1/4
– touching solidly embedded stone in hazard with club during backswing 13-4/6
– when club considered grounded in grass in water hazard..........13-4/8

insect flying in water hazard 13-4/16.5

lateral water hazard
– allowing drop opposite to spot where ball comes to rest in lateral water hazard; whether authorized....................26-1/20
– ball dropped within 2 club-lengths of hazard margin comes to rest almost 4 club-lengths from margin; whether re-drop required.......................20-2c/1
– ball moved into bounds by flow of water in lateral water hazard...26-1/8
– clarification of "opposite margin" in Rule 26–1c 26-1/14
– deeming part of body of water as water hazard and remainder as lateral water hazard 33-2a/7
– deeming water hazard as lateral water hazard in play from forward tee by Local Rule........33-2a/6
– defined as water hazard..........26/3.5

– defining rough and unplayable
  areas adjacent to fairways (areas
  not meeting definition of lateral
  water hazard) as lateral water
  hazard 33-8/35
– example of serious breach of
  lateral water hazard Rule 26-1/21
– hazard marked as water hazard
  where ball last crosses margin
  and as lateral water hazard
  where ball comes to rest; relief
  options for player..............26-1/12
– impossible to drop not nearer
  hole than point where ball last
  crossed margin of lateral water
  hazard 26-1/18
– opposite side of lateral water
  hazard defined as water hazard;
  relief options for player.........26-1/13
– part of lateral water hazard
  where impossible to drop not
  nearer hole 33-2a/9
– permissible dropping area under
  lateral water hazard Rule so
  narrow player has difficulty
  dropping within it..............26-1/19
– point where ball last crossed
  margin of lateral water hazard
  determined and ball dropped;
  point then proves to be wrong
  point...........................26-1/16
– point where ball last crossed
  margin of lateral water hazard
  determined, ball dropped and
  played; point then proves to be
  wrong point....................26-1/17
– procedures for relief from
  lateral water hazard............26-1/15
– water hazard treated as lateral
  water hazard...................26-1/11

lie of ball altered when lifted from
  water hazard for identification;
  whether original lie may be
  "nearest lie most similar".........20-3b/7

Local Rule
– allowing drop on green side of
  water hazard when ball fails to
  clear hazard; whether authorized .33-8/2
– allowing drop within water
  hazard behind point where ball
  lies unplayable in same hazard;
  whether authorized............33-8/37
– allowing free relief for ball in
  water hazard within limits of
  fairway; whether authorized 33-8/36
– allowing free relief from
  immovable water hazard stake
  for ball lying in water hazard;
  whether authorized............33-8/15
– deeming water hazard as lateral
  water hazard in play from
  forward tee....................33-2a/6
– defining rough and unplayable
  areas adjacent to fairways (areas
  not meeting definition of lateral
  water hazard) as lateral water
  hazard; whether authorized 33-8/35
– specimen Local Rule allowing
  ball to be played provisionally
  under water hazard Rule........App I-B-1

loose impediment
– accidentally moved in hazard 13-4/13
– affecting lie is moved by another
  player making nearby stroke
  while ball lifted; whether lie
  considered altered and/or loose
  impediment must be replaced 20-3b/8
– ball in hazard moves when loose
  impediment removed 13-4/15
– removal of obstruction in
  hazard would move loose
  impediment.....................1-4/5
– removed from water hazard;
  player then decides not to play
  from hazard....................13-4/17
– partially covering ball removed
  to identify ball..................13-4/16
– top of ball in hazard covered
  by leaves but part of ball visible
  from another angle..............12-1/3

marking and defining
– ball within natural margin of
  water hazard but outside stakes
  defining margin................26/2
– deeming water hazard as lateral
  water hazard in play from
  forward tee by Local Rule........33-2a/6
– defining part of body of water as
  water hazard and remainder as
  lateral water hazard............33-2a/7
– environmentally-sensitive areas;
  recommendations for Committee 33-8/41
– island green 33-2a/10
– part of lateral water hazard
  where impossible to drop not
  nearer hole 33-2a/9
– river or other body of water
  adjacent to hole but off club
  property 33-2a/11
– treating ocean and beach as
  through the green 33-2a/8
– unmarked water hazard with
  margin out of bounds...........26/3
– where to place lines or stakes
  defining margin of water hazard...33-2a/4

meaning of
– "behind" in Rule 26-1 ....26-1/1.5
– "known or virtually certain" in
  Rule 26-1 ....26-1/1
– "opposite margin" in Rule 26-1c ..26-1/14

order of play
– when both balls in lateral water
  hazard and neither found 10/3
– when two balls lie in lateral
  water hazard and both players
  take relief.....................10/2

overflow from water hazard........25/2

placing ball
– instead of dropping when
  obvious dropped ball will roll
  into water hazard requiring
  re-drop 20-2c/3
– on bank of water hazard instead
  of dropping to prevent ball
  rolling into water 26-1/10

player tells opponent he will
  proceed under water hazard Rule;
  changes mind after opponent plays. 9-2/13

provisional ball
- played solely in belief original
  ball might be in water hazard 27-2a/2
- played in belief original might
  be lost outside water hazard;
  player then discovers no
  possibility ball lost outside
  water hazard................27-2a/2.5
- possibility that original ball in
  water hazard may not preclude
  play of provisional ball 27-2a/2.2
- referee incorrectly tells player
  to play out hole with provisional
  ball instead of original ball found
  in water hazard.................34-3/3.7
- serving as ball in play if original
  unplayable or in water hazard 27-2/1

re-drop required when proceeding
under water hazard Rule; whether
player may substitute when
re-dropping 20-6/4

serious breach
- ball deemed unplayable in water
  hazard; dropped in hazard and
  played........................20-7/2
- example of serious breach of
  lateral water hazard Rule 26-1/21
- significant advantage gained
  when player makes stroke from
  environmentally-sensitive area
  defined as water hazard 33-8/44
- stroke made from
  environmentally-sensitive water
  hazard 33-8/43
- water hazard treated as lateral
  water hazard..................26-1/11

status of
- ball touching both water hazard
  and another part of course......26/1.5
- growing things rooted within
  environmentally-sensitive
  area defined as water hazard
  overhanging area outside hazard .33-8/44.5
- hole of removed stake defining
  water hazard..................25/18
- insect flying in water hazard 13-4/16.5
- movable part of drainage hose 24-2b/15.3
- stone broken away from
  retaining wall in water hazard.....24/6
- water overflowing margin of
  water hazard..................25/2

testing condition of water hazard
- meaning of "test the condition
  of the hazard" in Rule 13—4a..13-4/0.5
- player uses cane or club to enter
  or leave hazard when ball lies in
  hazard 13-4/3.5
- touching grass with club during
  practice swing in water hazard....13-4/4

when ball addressed in water hazard .18-2b/2

when ball considered in water hazard .26/1

whether player entitled to ascertain
whereabouts of opponent's ball
that may be in water hazard
before playing...................9-2/16

whether virtual certainty ball is in
water hazard can be established
without going forward to assess
conditions around hazard.........26-1/1.3

WEATHER CONDITIONS

See also COURSE UNPLAYABLE OR CLOSED; DISCONTINUANCE AND RESUMPTION OF PLAY

ball visible from tee prior to
suspension of play disappears or
moved by outside agency during
suspension 6-8d/4

competitor refuses to start or picks
up because of weather conditions;
round subsequently canceled 33-2d/3

guidelines for Committee on
whether to cancel round 33-2d/1

lightning
- condition requiring immediate
  discontinuance of play;
  guidelines for waiving or
  modifying disqualification
  penalty for failure to
  discontinue play immediately 6-8b/7
- player claiming danger from
  lightning refuses to resume play
  when resumption ordered by
  Committee 6-8b/5

Local Rule or condition of competition
- permitting competitors to
  discontinue play by agreement
  in bad weather; whether
  authorized...................33-8/5
- permitting use of wind gauge;
  whether permitted 14-3/0.5
- specimen condition requiring
  immediate suspension of play
  due to a dangerous situation ....App I-C-5

meaning of "elements" in Rule 14—2a .14-2/0.5

player not present at time of
starting; course closed at that time. 33-3/2

rain
- extensive damage due to heavy
  rain and traffic.................33-2a/3
- match discontinued by
  agreement; one player
  subsequently wishes to resume;
  opponent refuses although
  course playable................6-8a/5
- match discontinued by
  agreement; one player
  subsequently wishes to resume;
  opponent refuses on ground
  course unplayable..............6-8a/6
- number of holes reduced after
  start of competition due to rain...33-1/2
- player holds umbrella over own
  head when making stroke........14-2/2
- resuming play from where
  discontinued; lie altered by
  rainfall 6-8d/1
- taking shelter while waiting to
  play.........................6-8a/2

wind
- ball at rest moved by blowing
  tumbleweed 18-1/6

W

– ball in plastic bag moves when bag blown to new position by wind 18-1/7
– ball moved by wind replaced instead of played as lies 18-2a/7
– ball oscillating in wind pressed into surface of putting green 1-2/9
– ball oscillating in wind, whether considered moving 14-5/2
– ball replaced and at rest thereafter moved by wind 18-1/12
– ball replaced on putting green but ball-marker not removed; ball then moves 20-4/1
– ball-marker moved by wind or casual water during stipulated round 20-1/10.5
– resuming play from where discontinued; lie altered by wind . 6-8d/1
– shielding line of putt from wind ... 1-2/2
– towel dropped by player blown onto ball causing it to move 18-2a/17

WOOD AND WOOD CHIPS
See also LOOSE IMPEDIMENTS; OBSTRUCTIONS

meaning of "artificially surfaced" 24/9
status of
– stacked wood from fallen tree 25/7
– wood chips used to surface path or road 23/14
– wood planks 24/11
– wooden or earthen steps on steep banks 24/12

WORM
means by which worm casts may be removed from line of play and line of putt 23-1/1
status of worm partially underground .23/8

WRONG BALL
ball at rest moved
– accidentally by player in playing wrong ball in bunker 18-2a/21
– after address and comes to rest out of bounds; player plays ball.... 18-2b/9
ball lifted
– by player from putting green then placed by caddie behind ball-marker; whether wrong ball if played 20-4/2
– by player, set aside and played from where set aside 15/4
– competitor's ball mistaken for wrong ball picked up by fellow-competitor at competitor's request 18-2a/16
– fellow-competitor lifts competitor's ball and sets it aside; competitor plays ball from where set aside 15-3b/3
– from putting green without its position being marked in mistaken belief it is wrong ball 20-1/1
– player wins hole with wrong ball and partner picks up; error discovered at next hole.......... 30-3c/2

– players on opposite sides exchange balls during play of hole and their partners pick up; error discovered at next hole..... 30-3c/3
– provisional ball lifted subsequently becomes ball in play after wrong ball played 27-2b/9
balls inadvertently exchanged by players between holes 15-1/1
competitor plays second ball under Rule 20–7c; clarification of "penalty strokes incurred solely by playing the ball ruled not to count" 20-7c/5
continuation of play of wrong ball..... 15/11
competitor's ball played by fellow-competitor
– in bunker not replaced.......... 20-7c/6
– balls inadvertently exchanged by competitors at unknown place.... 15-1/2
– balls inadvertently exchanged by players after one ball strikes and moves other 15-1/2.5
– competitor substitutes another ball at wrong place, plays it and then abandons it and plays out original ball from right place 20-7c/4
deemed unplayable
– dropped in bunker then played; ball then discovered to be wrong ball 15/14
– dropped under unplayable ball Rule but not played 15/13
– dropped within two club-lengths and played before error discovered 28/15
– played under stroke-and-distance procedure; original ball then found 28/14
hole at which wrong ball played unknown....................... 15-1/3
in anger, player strikes ball played by player in following group 1-4/4
loose impediment partially covering ball removed in water hazard to identify what turns out to be wrong ball 13-4/16
lost ball, provisional ball or ball out of bounds
– ball found after search exceeding five minutes; ball then played........................... 27/8
– ball hit out of bounds from bunker; player's drop under Rule 20–5 strikes course through the green within inches of and not nearer hole than spot in bunker where previous stroke made; ruling if player plays dropped ball 20-5/2
– ball thrown into bounds by outside agency and played; caddie aware of action of outside agency 15/9
– ball thrown into bounds by outside agency and played; neither player nor caddie aware of action of outside agency 15/10

– competitor plays wrong ball
and it cannot be found; wrong
ball may have been fellow-
competitor's ball 15-3b/1
– original ball found and played
after another ball put into play....15/5
– original ball found within five-
minute search period after
another ball dropped; original
ball played 27-1/2.3
– original ball played after
provisional ball played from
point nearer hole than original
ball likely to be 27-2b/5
– player unable to find his ball
because another player has
played it 27/6
– provisional ball played from
point nearer hole than visible
original ball; player erroneously
thought original ball out of bounds 27-2c/3
– stray ball found out of bounds
played under stroke-and-
distance procedure; original ball
then found in bounds............15/12
– stroke made with ball lying out
of bounds.......................15/6
– time permitted for search for
original ball after wrong ball
played..........................27/2
– wrong ball hit out of bounds;
another ball played under Rule
27–1; original ball then found
nearby 15/11
– wrong ball played in belief it is
provisional or second ball 15/7
– wrong ball played; provisional
ball lifted subsequently becomes
ball in play 27-2b/9
match play
– after playing wrong ball, player
wins hole with original ball;
opponent does not lodge claim
during hole; claim lodged next
day 2-5/4
– balls inadvertently exchanged by
players after one ball strikes and
moves other 15-1/2.5
– implied concession of hole
withdrawn after player makes
stroke with wrong ball..........2-4/13
– opponent's misreading of
number on player's ball results
in agreement that player lost
hole for playing wrong ball 9-2/11
– player concedes hole after
which opponent discovered to
have played wrong ball prior to
concession....................2-4/9
– player concedes hole after
which opponent plays wrong ball..2-4/10
– player plays partner's ball in
four-ball match 30-3c/1
– player plays partner's ball; error
discovered after opponents
have made next strokes.........30-3c/4
– player unaware original
ball holed plays wrong ball;
opponent claims hole; claim not
disputed.......................2-5/5

– player wins hole with wrong
ball and partner picks up; error
discovered at next hole.........30-3c/2
– player wins hole with wrong
ball; error discovered at next
hole, opponent claims previous
hole 9-2/8
– players on opposite sides
exchange balls during play of
hole and their partners pick up;
error discovered at next hole.....30-3c/3
– second ball played in match play;
whether permitted; status of
original and second balls 3-3/9
order of play in foursome stroke
play when wrong ball played.......29-1/8
penalty for playing wrong ball not
included in competitor's score
due to incorrect Committee
ruling; during subsequent round
error discovered and penalty
applied retroactively; competitor
objects 34-3/1
play of two different wrong balls
between strokes with ball in play ...15-3b/2
play of wrong ball not rectified in
stroke play
– error discovered after
competition closed 34-1b/3
– on advice of referee 33-7/5
played from environmentally-
sensitive area....................33-8/43
player discovers own ball in hole
after playing wrong ball...........1-1/4
player makes stroke at part of
abandoned ball which had broken
into pieces 15/3
player's stroke at own ball dislodges
concealed ball...................15/2
practice swing dislodges concealed
ball............................7-2/7
score may count with wrong ball in
some circumstances
– ball thrown into bounds by
outside agency and played;
neither player nor caddie aware
of action of outside agency 15/10
– fellow-competitor lifts
competitor's ball and sets it
aside; competitor plays ball
from where set aside 15-3b/3
– play of wrong ball in stroke play
not rectified; error discovered
after competition closed.........34-1b/3
– play of wrong ball not rectified
on advice of referee 33-7/5
– referee incorrectly tells player
to play out hole with provisional
ball instead of original ball found
in water hazard.................34-3/3.7
searching for and identifying ball by
brand and number only...........12-2/1
stroke misses wrong ball 15/1

WRONG INFORMATION

See also CLAIMS AND DISPUTES;
INCORRECT INFORMATION ON THE RULES;
INFORMATION AS TO STROKES TAKEN

balls inadvertently exchanged by
  players after one ball strikes and
  move other......................15-1/2.5

breach of 14-club Rule discovered
  after match concluded but before
  result officially announced........2-5/5.5

conscious failure to correct
  opponent's misunderstanding of
  state of match 9-2/12

four-ball match play
  – player lifts ball resting against
    flagstick before being holed;
    others in match pick up
    mistakenly believing player won
    hole 30-3f/3
  – player out of contention on
    hole gives wrong information;
    whether partner also penalized ...30-3f/4
  – player plays partner's ball; error
    discovered after opponents
    have made next strokes.........30-3c/4
  – players on opposite sides
    exchange balls during play of
    hole and their partners pick up;
    error discovered at next hole....30-3c/3
  – player wins hole with wrong
    ball and partner picks up; error
    discovered at next hole..........30-3c/2

foursome side drives for three holes
  in wrong order; opponents make
  claim during third hole 29-2/2

handicap information
  – handicap stroke wrongly
    claimed at hole; error
    discovered before hole
    completed 6-2a/3
  – wrong handicap used by
    mistake; error discovered after
    result officially announced 6-2a/5
  – wrong handicap used due to
    Committee misinformation 33-1/12

incorrect information
  – causes opponent mistakenly
    to think he has putt for half;
    opponent holes putt and then
    error discovered 9-2/14
  – causes opponent to lift ball-
    marker.......................9-2/5
  – given after play of hole; when
    penalty applicable..............9-2/15
  – given by caddie or partner.......9-2/2
  – given by player; corrected after
    opponent concedes player's
    putt but before opponent plays
    next stroke 9-2/7
  – on penalty applicable to player
    given by opponent; error
    discovered after match result
    announced; player then makes
    claim........................2-5/10
  – on Rules given to player.........9/1
  – on strokes, given voluntarily by
    player to opponent 9-2/3

invalid claim not disputed 2-5/5

match conceded by player after
  winning it when opponent lodges
  invalid claim regarding strokes
  taken 2-4/15

misunderstandings
  – opponent's misreading of
    number on player's ball results
    in agreement that player lost
    hole for playing wrong ball 9-2/11
  – player and opponent agree
    hole halved; after match result
    posted player realizes he won
    hole and should have won
    match; player then makes claim ..2-5/9
  – player and opponent mistakenly
    believe match all square after
    18 holes and play extra hole
    without making claim...........2-5/6
  – players leave last green under
    impression match over later
    realize it was all square;
    whether late claim valid.........2-3/1

opponent asks player number of
  strokes taken
  – player refuses to answer 9-2/3.5
  – player withholds information
    until opponent's turn to play 9-2/4

player lifts ball before holing out;
  opponent then picks up his ball
  claiming player loses hole.........2-5/3

player tells opponent he will
  proceed under water hazard Rule;
  changes mind after opponent plays .9-2/13

player wins hole
  – with original ball after playing
    wrong ball; opponent does not
    lodge claim during hole; claim
    lodged next day 2-5/4
  – with wrong ball and partner
    picks up; error discovered at
    next hole 30-3c/2
  – with wrong ball; error
    discovered at next hole;
    opponent claims previous hole ...9-2/8

referee
  – fails to impose penalty for undue
    delay believing player lost hole;
    whether opponent makes
    wrong information claim when
    referee's failure comes to light
    several holes later 34-3/2
  – imposes penalty for previous
    hole after play of next hole
    begun; whether permitted 2-5/12

rightful winner of match makes no
  claim and agrees to play extra holes .2-5/7

stroke play
  – competitor gives fellow-
    competitor incorrect
    information in hole-by-hole
    play-off......................9-3/1
  – incorrect information on Rules
    given.........................9/1

wrong score for hole given by player
  – causes opponent with chance
    for half to pick up ball 9-2/6
  – error discovered several holes
    later 9-2/9

– penalty stroke omitted by player
when advising opponent of
score for hole; error discovered
after match conceded by
opponent 9-2/10
– upon completion of last hole;
claim made after result
announced. 2-5/11

WRONG PLACE
See also SERIOUS BREACH OF RULES
ball deemed unplayable
– ball dropped outside bunker
under option of unplayable ball . . .28/10
Rule requiring drop in bunker
– ball dropped under option 28c
of unplayable ball Rule strikes
player; whether player may
change relief option when
re-dropping. 20-2a/6
– in water hazard; ball dropped in
hazard and played. 20-7/2
– player plays second shot, deems
ball unplayable and returns to tee .28/6
ball dropped
– in improper manner and in
wrong place. 20-2a/3
– in wrong place when proceeding
under Rule permitting
substitution; whether player
may substitute when re-dropping .20-6/4
– with knowledge or virtual
certainty missing original in
abnormal ground condition or
obstruction; whether re-drop
required if finding original
demonstrates drop made in
wrong place. 25-1c/2.5
ball moved during suspension of
play by outside agency; player fails
to estimate position sufficiently in
replacing ball .6-8d/5
ball stepped on accidentally and
original lie altered; player places
ball in wrong place and plays 18-2a/21.3
borrowing club for measuring
purposes. 20/2
changing relief option
– dropped ball first strikes course
outside where applicable Rule
requires; whether player may
change relief option when
re-dropping. 20-6/2
– dropped ball first strikes course
outside where applicable Rule
requires; whether player may
replace ball in original location. . . .20-6/5
– dropped ball rolls to position
requiring re-drop; whether
player may change relief option
when re-dropping 20-2c/5
– dropped ball strikes player;
whether player may change
relief option when re-dropping . . .20-2a/6
– player drops ball in bunker under
first option of Rule 25–1b(ii);
player then wishes to proceed

under second option to drop
outside bunker 25-1b/9
– player lifts ball from bunker
intending to drop under first
option of Rule 24–2b(ii); player
then wishes to proceed under
second option to drop outside
bunker 24-2b/5
– point where ball last crossed
margin of lateral water hazard
determined and ball dropped;
point then proves to be wrong
point; whether player may
change relief option when
re-dropping. 26-1/16
competitor's ball moved by fellow-
competitor's ball; both players
unaware until after completion of
hole 18-5/3
competitor's ball played by
fellow-competitor; competitor
substitutes another ball at wrong
place, plays it and then abandons
it and plays out original ball from
right place. 20-7c/4
competitor's ball played by fellow-
competitor in bunker not replaced .20-7c/6
environmentally-sensitive area
– ball played from
environmentally-sensitive area. . .33-8/43
– significant advantage gained
when player makes stroke from
environmentally-sensitive area
defined as water hazard 33-8/44
player does not follow
recommended procedure in
determining nearest point of relief .24-2b/2
player invokes Rule 3–3 (doubt
as to procedure)
– ball dropped and played; Rule
3–3 then invoked and second
ball dropped in right place; both
balls played out. 3-3/3
– ball dropped but not played;
Rule 3–3 then invoked and
second ball dropped in right
place; both balls played out. 3-3/4
– guidelines for determining
which ball counts when player
proceeds under Rule 3–3 . . . . .3-3/0.5
– whether score with second ball
counts if ball dropped in wrong
place and played 3-3/5
player plays from wrong place as
directed by referee
– based on available facts;
subsequent facts prove ruling
incorrect. 34-3/7
– based on player's version of
facts; player's version later
found incorrect. 34-3/8
– based on incorrect ruling;
procedure for player when
error discovered 34-3/3
provisional ball lifted by competitor
subsequently becomes ball in play;
ball played from tee instead of
replaced at spot from which lifted. . .27-2b/10

putting green
- ball putted from wrong place
lifted and putted from right place . .20-7c/2
- ball replaced at wrong place on
putting green and holed. 20-7c/1
- ball resting against flagstick
moves away from hole when
flagstick removed by player; ball
not placed on lip of hole 17-4/4
- fellow-competitor lifts
competitor's ball from putting
green and sets it aside;
competitor plays ball from
where set aside. 15-3b/3
- penalty for repeatedly replacing
ball nearer hole on green 33-7/6
- valid timely claim made after
concession of match when
player determines opponent
putted from wrong place on last
hole 2-4/16

serious breach of Rule 20–7c may
be involved
- ball deemed unplayable in water
hazard; dropped in hazard and
played. 20-7/2
- ball dropped in area where
original ball lost; ball then played . .27-1/3
- ball dropped outside bunker
under option of unplayable ball
Rule requiring drop in bunker 28/10
- ball not found treated as moved
by outside agency in absence of
knowledge or virtual certainty
to that effect. 27-1/2.5
- ball played from ground under
repair abandoned and relief
taken under ground under
repair Rule. 18-2a/8.5
- ball played from spot where
original ball deflected out of
bounds by maintenance vehicle . . .20-7/1
- ball played under water hazard
Rule without knowledge or
virtual certainty original ball in
hazard; original ball then found
in hazard 26-1/4
- competitor plays second ball
under Rule 20–7c; clarification
of "penalty strokes incurred
solely by playing the ball ruled
not to count" 20-7c/5
- competitor's ball knocked out of
bunker by fellow-competitor's
stroke at own ball not replaced . . .18-4/2
- example of serious breach of
lateral water hazard Rule 26-1/21
- missing original ball believed
in bunker; competitor drops
substituted ball in bunker and
plays it; then original ball found
outside bunker 20-7c/3
- player plays second shot, deems
ball unplayable and returns to tee .28/6
- significant advantage gained
when player makes stroke from
environmentally-sensitive area
defined as water hazard 33-8/44

- substituted ball dropped and
played under Rule 25–1c in
absence of knowledge or virtual
certainty original ball lost in
ground under repair. 25-1c/2

water hazard and lateral water hazard
- ball deemed unplayable in water
hazard; dropped in hazard and
played. 20-7/2
- ball played under water hazard
Rule original ball then found
outside hazard 26-1/3
- ball played under water hazard
Rule without knowledge or
virtual certainty original ball in
hazard; original ball then found
in hazard 26-1/4
- casual water mistaken for water
hazard; original ball played
under water hazard Rule. 25-1b/12
- casual water mistaken for water
hazard; substituted ball played
under water hazard Rule. 25-1b/13
- example of serious breach of
lateral water hazard Rule 26-1/21
- player unaware ball in water
hazard takes relief from
interference by burrowing
animal hole; error discovered
before ball played 25-1b/26
- point where ball last crossed
margin of lateral water hazard
determined and ball dropped;
point then proves to be wrong
point. 26-1/16
- point where ball last crossed
margin of lateral water hazard
determined, ball dropped and
played; point then proves to be
wrong point. 26-1/17
- water hazard treated as lateral
water hazard. 26-1/11

WRONG PUTTING GREEN

ball dropped on wrong putting
green in taking relief under a Rule;
whether permitted 20-7/3

double green; status of portion
serving hole not being played. 25-3/1

Local Rule deeming wrong putting
green to include apron to prohibit
dropping on and play from 33-8/33

recommended procedure for
determining nearest point of
relief not used by player when
taking relief from wrong putting
green. 24-2b/2

WRONG TEEING GROUND

See also TEEING GROUND AND TEE-
MARKERS

match play; ball played from
wrong teeing ground goes out of
bounds; stroke not recalled by
opponent 11-5/3

stroke play
  – competitor plays from
    teeing ground of hole to be
    played later in round; when
    hole subsequently reached
    competitor replaces ball at spot
    from which original tee shot
    lifted and plays out hole..........11-5/5
  – group plays from wrong teeing
    ground; corrects error 11-5/4
  – group plays from wrong teeing
    ground; attributes Committee
    failure to indicate hole numbers
    on teeing grounds as reason;
    whether Committee should
    waive penalties................11-5/2
  – meaning of "next teeing ground"
    after competitors have played
    from wrong teeing ground 11-5/1

"X-OUT" BALL

status 5-1/4

The USGA and You

Contact us for:

The Rules of Golf:

For all of your Rules of Golf needs, including:
- Complete Rules of Golf and Decisions on the Rules of Golf online
- Frequently asked questions regarding the Rules
- Submitting your Rules questions to our experts
- Ordering Rules of Golf-related products

www.rulesofgolf.com

USGA Publications Store:

A comprehensive selection of USGA books, pamphlets, software and videos. Publications include:
- "Decisions on the Rules of Golf — 2012-13 edition"
- "The Rules of Golf — 2012-15 edition"
- Golf Rules Illustrated
- USGA Handicap Publications
- USGA Green Section Publications
- Championship Highlights VHS and DVDs

www.usga.org/PublicationsStore • 1.800.336.4446

USGA Shop

The ultimate source for clothing and memorabilia from our National Championships, including the U.S. Open and Women's Open, plus a full line of USGA Members clothing and accessories, golf gifts and books. USGA Member discounts available.

www.USGAshop.com • 1.800.755.0293

USGA Members Program

Find out more about becoming a Member of the USGA and learn how your contribution will help fund a wide range of programs committed to enhance your enjoyment of the game while ensuring its future.

www.usga.org • 1.800.223.0041